A HISTORY OF THE UNITED STATES
SINCE THE CIVIL WAR

A HISTORY

OF

THE UNITED STATES

SINCE THE CIVIL WAR

BY

ELLIS PAXSON OBERHOLTZER

IN FIVE VOLUMES

VOLUME I: 1865–68

NEGRO UNIVERSITIES PRESS

NEW YORK

Originally published in 1917-37
by The Macmillan Company, New York

Reprinted 1969 by
Negro Universities Press
A DIVISION OF GREENWOOD PUBLISHING CORP.
NEW YORK

SBN 8371-2642-8

CONTENTS

CHAPTER I

PRESIDENT JOHNSON

CHAPTER II

THE SOUTH AFTER THE WAR

v

CHAPTER III

CONGRESS IN CONTROL

CONTENTS vii

CHAPTER IV

THE TRIUMPHANT NORTH

CHAPTER V

Beyond the Mississippi

CHAPTER VI

The Indians

CHAPTER VII

WAR UPON THE PRESIDENT

CHAPTER VIII

MEXICO, IRELAND AND ALASKA

CONTENTS

A HISTORY OF THE UNITED STATES SINCE THE CIVIL WAR

CHAPTER I

PRESIDENT JOHNSON

ON Sunday morning, April 2, 1865, when Jefferson Davis, President of the Confederate States of America, sitting in a pew in St. Paul's Church in Richmond, received a message from General Lee, saying that his lines had been broken, and that the city must be evacuated, the great Civil War was rapidly nearing its end. The rest of that day and the ensuing night were occupied with the business of departure. The President, the officers of his hard-pressed government, with their records and funds, and many of the citizens, left the place used so long by the Confederacy as its capital, which so many lives and so much treasure had been expended in seeking to capture on the one side and in defending on the other. The next day, April 3, Federal troops entered to take formal possession, and on the next following day, Tuesday, April 4, President Lincoln, with Admiral Porter and a few other companions, under guard, was landed from a barge, and walked into the city, now abandoned by its inhabitants and in flames, for an inspection of the scene.

Meantime General Lee, bent upon the salvation of his gallant army, led it out of its untenable position toward Danville in the hope of effecting a junction with General Joseph E. Johnston. Grant barred the way, and Lee changed his course; he now would reach Lynchburg. But the escape of a crumbling military force from such an antagonist was not within mortal compass, and on April 9 the two opposing

1

generals met in a small house on the edge of the village of Appomattox, where the terms of surrender were agreed upon.

History was being made with great rapidity, and the North was in the midst of its jubilee, the louder and more heartfelt because the victory, so long anticipated, had been so long deferred. The surrender of Johnston to Sherman and the capture of Jefferson Davis were expected at any moment, when it would be certain at last that the war was really at an end. Thus events stood when, on the night of Good Friday, the 14th day of April, Lincoln, while sitting in a box at Ford's Theatre in Washington, witnessing a production of "Our American Cousin," was shot at and fatally wounded by an actor bearing a distinguished name, John Wilkes Booth. The President was quickly removed to a house across the street, and at twenty-two minutes past seven o'clock the next morning, April 15, his labored breathing ceased, and he was dead. The whole city, the whole nation was stunned, the more so since it appeared that the assassination was but a part of a widespread and carefully arranged plot.

An ex-Confederate soldier named Payne was assigned the task of murdering William H. Seward, the Secretary of State. Mr. Seward lately had been thrown from his carriage. His jaw had been fractured and his right arm broken. The brute, in making his way to the bed, seriously wounded the Secretary's son and assistant in the State Department, Frederick W. Seward, and several servants and attendants. The full purpose of the assassin was defeated, for Mr. Seward was not killed, though grievously hurt. Five persons were left bleeding from their wounds as Payne departed from the house.

Another villain, Atzerodt by name, was given the task of murdering the Vice-President, Andrew Johnson. Grant also is thought to have been marked for destruction, and Chief Justice Chase, Secretary Stanton and several high officers of the government were at once put under guard. It was not known what might be the extent and scope of the conspiracy.

On the 19th day of April President Lincoln's funeral ceremonies were celebrated in Washington. The body lay in state in the Capitol, whither it was conducted with pomp and solemnity, and two days later the journey to Springfield was begun by way of Baltimore, Harrisburg, Philadelphia, New York, Albany, Syracuse, Rochester, Buffalo, Cleveland, Columbus, Indianapolis, and Chicago. It was the 3d of May when the corse and its escort reached the capital of Illinois, the 4th when the lid of the coffin was closed for the last time and the body interred.

Meantime the old order was ending and the new had begun. The assassination of the President had brought to his place a singular and an ill-proportioned man. Mr. Lincoln's second term was not yet six weeks old and, therefore, nearly four years of difficult service, the most difficult which any President has known, except possibly that of the four years just spent and gone, confronted his successor.

Andrew Johnson had been born in poverty in North Carolina in 1808. He was thus, upon coming to the Presidency, nearly fifty-seven years of age. At ten he had been apprenticed to a tailor, and at eighteen had removed to a small town in eastern Tennessee, where he followed his trade. Marrying a woman who manifested an interest in his education, he early was enabled to gain a fitness for political life in his neighborhood. He was ready of speech and an inflexible people's man, which gave him many advantages in the era dominated by the standards and principles of Andrew Jackson in a part of the Union not too nice about the manners of its public characters. He was rising from the ranks of the "poor whites," and came to represent the interests and voice the opinions of white men who held not any or but few slaves, because they lacked property of all kinds, who were looked down upon by the large slave owners, and who in turn distrusted and disliked the "chivalry" of our Southland.

"Andy," as he came to be called, told every one that he was a tailor, and sought the favor of the masses with accounts of his own toil and trial. He was an alderman and the mayor of his town, a member in turn of both branches of his state legislature, and entered Congress as early as 1843, where he sat

for ten years, through the period of the Great Compromise.
Then he was elected governor of Tennessee and in 1857 was
chosen to the United States Senate, where he was serving at
the time of Lincoln's election to the Presidency, the departure
of most of the Southern Senators and Representatives in answer
to instructions from their seceding states, and the outbreak
of the war. His loyalty to the Union in a quarter where this
was unusual gave him great distinction throughout the North,
and as soon as Grant's victories on the Mississippi made a
portion of Tennessee Union ground he was appointed to be
military governor of the state. He was serving in this office
when expediency commended his nomination for the Vice-
Presidency to the political leaders in the Republican national
convention of 1864. Other names were suggested and considered. His seemed the most available for a very uncertain
and difficult campaign, both because he formerly had been a
Democrat and because of his birth and residence in the South.
That he would come to a greater office by the chance of the
President's assassination or death none supposed, and, supposing this, probably not many would have altered their view
that Andrew Johnson's name was the one which could be most
useful in connection with Lincoln's in an appeal for the suffrages
of the people.

Now the unexpected had happened. Johnson yet had been
tested very little in the Vice-President's office. It was remembered by many that on March 4, upon appearing in the Senate chamber to be sworn in, he had shown evidences of intoxication. The reporters had laughed, the foreign ministers in
the diplomatic gallery had been shocked, the Copperheads had
rejoiced, the friends of the government had averted their faces
and hung their heads in chagrin on this occasion, while he in
maudlin voice said that he was a plebeian and thanked God for
it. He stumbled over the words of the oath and was with
difficulty prevented from rising a second time to address the
assemblage.[1]

[1] New York Herald, March 6, 1865 — "A 99th rate stump speech"
which might be appropriate "at some hustings in Tennessee." He

But now in the overwhelming disaster of Lincoln's death the effort was made to forget the Vice-President's hour of mis-doing. A man who, a biographer says, "cordially hated aristocracy and had decided objections to gentlemen," who one time declared, "Sir, I do not forget that I am a mechanic (I am proud to own it); neither do I forget that Adam was a tailor and sewed fig leaves, or that our Saviour was the son of a carpenter"[1] would now be President of the United States. That Johnson often had spoken and acted in the manner of a demagogue also at the moment was generously forgiven him. He was the hope of the Republic, and he must be supported in the performance of great tasks which had been intended for hands now still.

Nearly all the members of the Cabinet were at Lincoln's bedside on the Saturday morning when he died, and they at once signed a paper addressed to the Vice-President. "The emergency of the government," said they, "demands that you should immediately qualify according to the requirements of the Constitution and enter upon the duties of President of the United States." Only Seward's name was missing. First there was Hugh McCulloch, who after Chase's resignation and Fessenden's brief incumbency of the office, had become but lately Mr. Lincoln's Secretary of the Treasury, now in the midst of great financial operations, looking to the payment of the war debt. Then followed the names of Edwin M. Stanton,

---

addressed Chief Justice Chase, Secretary Stanton, Secretary Welles, of whose name he must be reminded by the reporters, telling them, one and all, that they were "the creatures of the people," while men and women muttered "What a shame," "Has he no friends?" "Tell him to stop and save the country further disgrace." Compare Philadelphia Public Ledger of the same date, which later (March 8) said: "There have been shameful exhibitions in public before by men occupying positions and places of honor, but in no period of our political history can there be found one which so degraded the high office the people had assembled to honor." Even Schouler, Johnson's most recent advocate, attempts nothing in extenuation of his behavior on this occasion, vol. vii, p. 7.

[1] Speeches of A. Johnson by Frank Moore, p. xii; cf. C. R. Hall, Andrew Johnson, Military Governor of Tenn., p. 22.

who almost from the beginning had been Secretary of War, a bold and capable but a domineering and arbitrary man; Gideon Welles, Secretary of the Navy; William Dennison, early in the war governor of Ohio, who in 1864 had taken Montgomery Blair's place as Postmaster-General; John P. Usher of Indiana, since 1862 Secretary of the Interior, soon to give way to James Harlan; and James Speed of Kentucky, brother of a revered friend of Lincoln's youth, now for less than six months in Mr. Bates's vacated place as Attorney-General.[1]

McCulloch and Speed were sent to find Johnson at his lodgings in the Kirkwood House. Chase, whom Lincoln with much magnanimity, in view of his recent conduct, had just appointed Chief Justice of the Supreme Court, was found to administer the oath, and in the parlor of the hotel in the presence of these three men, Francis P. Blair, Sr., his son, Montgomery Blair, Senator Foot, ex-Senator Hale and a few others the ceremony was quickly concluded. Johnson repeated the words of the oath "very distinctly and impressively," kissed the 21st verse of the 11th chapter of Ezekiel in the Bible which was handed him, whereupon the Chief Justice said: "You are President. May God support, guide and bless you in your arduous duties." The others in attendance came forward to tender their "sad congratulations" and, determining not to make a speech, the new President availed himself of the Chief Justice's offer to prepare a public address to be printed in the newspapers.[2] Mr. Chase left the room for this purpose, whereupon Mr. Johnson at once uttered some remarks as to his incompetency "to perform duties so important and responsible," and his policies which, he said, would be developed gradually, appealing to his past career "as a guarantee for the future." "Toil and an honest advocacy of the great principles of free government" had been his portion in life. The country had departed from the true way. When its present

---

[1] Annual Cyclopedia for 1865, p. 800; Diary of Gideon Welles, vol. ii, pp. 288–9.

[2] This address although it was not used was preserved by Mr. Johnson. See the Johnson Papers in Library of Congress, vol. lxxxiii.

perils were at an end, he would hope for a return to "principles consonant with popular rights."[1]

At noon of this day Johnson met the Cabinet in the office of the Secretary of the Treasury, where Welles says that he "deported himself admirably," and stated that his policy would be "in all essentials . . . the same as that of the late President." The heads of the departments were desired to continue in their places and go forward with their work. Until the White House could be put at his disposal Johnson was assigned a room in the Treasury Building adjoining Secretary McCulloch's, where he remained for about six weeks.[2]

All minds were immediately intent upon the Lincoln funeral pageant as it proceeded from place to place, and the punishment of his assassins. The declarations of the new President, as delegations of persons, negro and white, from North and from South, came to pay their addresses to him, gave assurance to the radicals. The popular rage was immense, and Johnson shared it. Forgiveness, which had been on many a tongue when Lee surrendered his army to Grant, now made way for mistrust and vindictive feeling.

Stanton asked Attorney-General Speed if, under the terms accorded Lee at Appomattox Court House, Southern officers could return to their homes in Washington, or in the loyal states. If so, might they wear their gray uniforms? Speed said that there was no place for these men on loyal ground, and as for their dress — as well "bear a traitor's flag through a loyal city as to wear a traitor's garb." It would be "an act of hostility against the government."[3]

Meantime Lincoln's assassins were being closely pursued. The crime was fixed upon a half dozen persons who made their

[1] Warden's Chase, pp. 640–1; Schuckers's Chase, p. 519; cf. MS. of Chase's Diary, from which Schuckers made extracts, in Library of Hist. Soc. of Pa.

[2] Welles, vol. ii, p. 289; McCulloch, Men and Measures, p. 374. Mrs. Lincoln made herself ready to leave the Executive Mansion in the middle of May. On the 25th of that month Johnson took possession of the White House. — Phila. Press, May 26, 1865.

[3] Phila. Press, April 27, 1865.

rendezvous at the home of Mrs. Mary E. Surratt, keeper of a boarding-house in Washington. They were Confederate in their sympathies, — some of them more or less deranged of mind. Booth, who had broken a leg in leaping from the President's box to the stage, nevertheless after his diabolical deed, managed to elude arrest until, on the night of April 25, he was found in a barn on a farm near the banks of the Rappahannock in Virginia. Refusing to surrender, the building was fired, but he was shot by a cavalryman before the flames reached him and was brought out to die three hours afterward. The others concerned in the conspiracy were taken in various places and imprisoned to await early trial for their crimes.

On April 18 when a delegation of citizens from Illinois, headed by Governor Oglesby, presented themselves at the new President's office in the Treasury Building, he told them that it was not alone the assassin of Lincoln who was guilty of his murder. Others shared the responsibility for the monstrous outrage. The American people must be taught that treason was "the blackest of crimes," and that "traitors shall suffer its penalty." This fact must be "engraven on every heart." Its President had been assassinated; should the nation be assassinated also?[1] On April 24, to a number of Southern loyalists, he said that the time had come "when the people should be taught to understand the length and breadth, the depth and height of treason." When "the conscious and intelligent traitors" were found, "the penalty and the forfeit should be paid." Treason and traitors must be driven from the land.[2] It was freely said, and implicitly believed, that Jefferson Davis, the fleeing and hated President of the late ill-starred Confederacy, was somehow a party to the murderous plot. On May 2 President Johnson put a price upon his head. For Jacob Thompson, Clement C. Clay and other Confederates, who for some time had been actively operating against the government from safe retreats in Canada,

[1] Frank Moore, Johnson's Speeches, p. 470.
[2] Ibid., Appendix; Phila. Press, April 25, 1865.

rewards also were offered. The President's proclamation recited that the Bureau of Military Justice was in possession of evidence that the "atrocious murder" of Lincoln, and the "attempted assassination" of Secretary Seward had been "incited, concerted and procured by" these great culprits. $100,000 would be paid for the arrest of Jefferson Davis, and $25,000 for each or any of four other persons.

The President's action, said the Philadelphia Press, "only gives tone and shape to the rumors of the last few days, and is a complete confirmation of the public expectation and fear." A "deliberate statesman" had now branded these "flying traitors" with "the guilt of murder." Some of the accused men from their refuge in Canada at once utterly denied over their own names in the newspapers any knowledge of the conspiracy; two called the charge "a living, burning lie" and defied "all the hired perjurers of Christendom." [1]

After Lee's surrender to Grant, the end of armed resistance to the United States was not long delayed, and Davis's capture followed fast. Already on April 13, the day before Booth had fired his fatal shot at Lincoln, General Johnston proposed an armistice to General Sherman. On the 17th the two generals met, and out of this meeting came Sherman's memorandum of agreement, about which there was instantly a great pother in Washington. He had overstepped the limits laid down for a military commander. He had undertaken to deal with political questions affecting the future relations of the South with the North. When the news reached the War Department, the Cabinet was summoned in hasty conference, the whole proceeding was unanimously disapproved and it was determined that hostilities should be resumed until surrender was made on the terms which Grant had prescribed for Lee at Appomattox. Grant himself was despatched to the scene to

[1] Johnson Papers in Library of Congress; Phila. Press, May 8 and 9. The proclamation is of course attributed to Stanton by Welles, but it seems at the time to have had the approval of all the members of the Cabinet as of the people of the North generally. — Diary, vol. ii, pp. 299–300.

bring about this object, while Stanton's conduct in the matter at Washington was so abrupt and unpleasant that Sherman was done affront which he never forgot. The new terms were presented to General Johnston, and finally, on the 26th of April, all the forces under his command laid down their arms and started away for their homes.

Davis and members of the Richmond Cabinet who had been in touch with Johnston were now recommended to seek safety in rapid flight. They, and their archives, had reached Greensboro in North Carolina on the day of Lincoln's assassination. On the 18th they were in Charlotte, where they remained eight days. Starting forth again, not knowing with what end in view, the fugitives were soon obliged to separate and go off in different directions. Davis himself was overtaken by a body of cavalry, under the command of General James H. Wilson, in a camp in the pine woods of southern Georgia on May 10. Mrs. Davis accompanied her husband in his flight. When they were warned of his danger, she put upon him her waterproof coat, which looked like a woman's coarse gown, and threw over his head and shoulders a shawl, which led to the story, soon published everywhere, that he had been taken in his "wife's clothes." He was escorted to General Wilson's headquarters and then conveyed by water from Augusta to Fortress Monroe,[1] where he was placed in a stone casemate under a strong guard.[2] His bed was damp; it lay below or near the level of the bay whose plashing waters he continually heard. He could not sleep for the incessant tramp of armed sentinels in front of his grated door. A half dozen soldiers threw him to the floor and riveted irons upon his ankles. Books, except the Bible, letters, unless they first had been read by officers of the government, the visits of friends, for long were denied him. Light came to him only from a lamp. In vain did Mrs. Davis plead

[1] For an account of this trip see Recollections of A. H. Stephens, pp. 99–122; Mrs. C. C. Clay, A Belle of the Fifties, pp. 260–8.

[2] Davis, Rise and Fall, vol. ii, pp. 704–5. See General Wilson's Under the Old Flag, vol. ii, pp. 330 et seq., for his account of the capture. Cf. Official Records, series i, vol. xlix, part ii, p. 743.

with President Johnson, though the physicians in charge expressed the fear that her husband would succumb under his sufferings. Many months passed before the captive was granted greater liberties.[1]

The Confederate Postmaster-General, Reagan, who was still with Davis at the time of the capture, accompanied him as a prisoner of the United States on the journey to Hampton Roads. Alexander H. Stephens, the Vice-President of the Confederacy, "nothing but skin, bone and cartilage," so "feeble as scarcely to be able to move about," [2] who had been put under arrest at his home in Georgia on May 11, was conveyed north by the same steamer. Stephens and Reagan parted with Davis at Hampton Roads, to be taken on in the sloop-of-war, *Tuscarora*, to Fort Warren in Boston harbor. Stephens carried on a perpetual struggle with chinches in his bed, extortionate sutlers and his bodily infirmities, much increased now by the monotony and privation of his prison life. His hair turned gray.[3]

Clement C. Clay of Alabama, earlier a United States Senator, then Confederate States Senator and an agent for the Confederacy in Canada, for whose capture President Johnson had offered $25,000, "conscious of his innocence, unwilling even to seem to fly from justice," voluntarily came to General Wilson's camp at Macon and surrendered himself.[4] He, also, was a passenger on the boat with Davis and Stephens bound for the North. His fate was confinement in a wet casemate near Davis's in Fortress Monroe. He was a delicate scholar and a fine type of the Southern gentleman. Irons were not put upon him, as upon the President, but he was obliged to eat with his fingers the coarse food passed to him through the bars of his

---

[1] W. E. Dodd, Life of Davis, pp. 366–8; O. R., series ii, vol. viii, serial no. 121, pp. 563–4, 570, 577, 710, and many other letters and despatches in the same volume as well as in the Johnson Papers in Library of Congress.

[2] Phila. Ledger, May 24, 1865.

[3] Louis Pendleton, Life of Stephens, pp. 343–5; A. H. Stephens, Recollections, pp. 181, 431.

[4] O. R., series i, vol. xlix, part ii, p. 733.

little room, kept, like Davis, from all reading matter except
the Bible, from friends, and letters from friends, while the constant survey and clatter of soldiers on their beats before his
door deprived him of sleep.[1]

S. R. Mallory, Secretary of Davis's Navy, who had accompanied his chief over a part of the way on the flight, was soon
under arrest to be taken with Senator B. H. Hill of Georgia
to Fort Lafayette in New York harbor.[2]

Robert Toombs, hearing of the designs upon his liberties,
sent his war horse "Gray Alice" to an appointed place, then
fled his home, mounted the animal and started for the hills.
He moved about until November; on the 4th day of that
month he sailed from New Orleans to Havana in Cuba, afterward exiling himself in Europe until 1867.[3]

Matthew F. Maury, a scientist of wide reputation, who had
given his talents to the South, was returning from England
with a new torpedo designed to break the blockade of the
Southern coasts. Hearing of peace while at sea, he landed in
Havana, then making his way to Mexico, where he took up service under Maximilian. He was advised by his friends in
Virginia that the course he had chosen was better than hanging
or a long term in prison, which they confidently predicted would
be his fate if he should come home. He did not reappear in
the United States until 1868.[4]

John C. Breckinridge, the Confederacy's Secretary of War,
though a bench warrant was sworn out for his arrest, made his
way into Florida and passed to Cuba by the Keys. Later he
went to Europe and remained there until 1868.

Judah P. Benjamin, the Secretary of State, escaped through
Florida in a small boat to the Bahamas, which he reached on
the 10th of July. He passed to Nassau and Havana, and then

[1] Mrs. C. C. Clay, A Belle of the Fifties, pp. 294–9, 346.

[2] O. R., series ii, vol. vii, p. 577; ibid., series i, vol. xlix, part ii,
p. 923.

[3] U. B. Phillips, Life of Toombs, pp. 254–7. Toombs was diligently sought by General Wilson. — O. R., series i, vol. xlix, part ii,
p. 859.

[4] M. F. Maury Papers in Library of Congress.

to England. He never returned to the United States, but ended his career as a distinguished barrister in London.[1]

James A. Seddon, who had preceded Breckinridge as Secretary of War, and Judge John A. Campbell, Assistant Secretary of War, were arrested in Virginia and conveyed to Fort Pulaski in Georgia to answer for their treasons. R. M. T. Hunter of Virginia was reported to be quiet and submissive at his home, but he was soon aboard a gun-boat in the James River, awaiting the orders of Secretary Stanton. He also was sent to Fort Pulaski. George A. Trenholm, Secretary of the Treasury, was confined inside government masonry at the same place.[2] George Davis, Attorney-General, when he was found, was imprisoned in Fort Lafayette. Ex-Governor Letcher of Virginia, ex-Governor William ("Extra Billy") Smith of Virginia, Governor Joseph E. Brown of Georgia, Governor Vance of North Carolina, Governor Magrath of South Carolina, ex-Governor Moore of Alabama, Governor Clark of Mississippi, Governor Allison of Florida, ex-Senator David L. Yulee of Florida and other leaders were thrown into forts or incarcerated in the Old Capitol Prison in Washington.

Ex-Governor and ex-Senator Henry S. Foote of Mississippi, hero of three duels before the war, was held on his own recognizance in New York. Senator Stewart of Nevada, his son-in-law, warmly urged his release. Secretary Stanton aimed to further the object. Foote personally addressed Johnson with many expressions of esteem, saying that he had four daughters, eight grandchildren and an only sister on the Pacific coast, whither he would go. The President ordered Stanton to bid Foote leave the limits of the United States within forty-eight hours. Otherwise he would be "arrested and dealt with for treason and rebellion against the United States government." General Dix in New York was instructed to see that this order was carried out.[3]

---

[1] Pierce Butler, Life of Benjamin, pp. 363 et seq.

[2] O. R., series ii, vol. viii, serial no. 121, pp. 550, 576, 583.

[3] Ibid., pp. 526, 532, 557. Foote proceeded to Canada. He made his appearance in Nashville, Tenn., in the middle of September, where

Howell Cobb, who had become a general in the Confederate army, was at large on military parole. On that account it was pointed out that he was 'secure from harm, unless he had violated the terms of the surrender, or some great atrocity could be laid at his door. He was arrested and ordered to Fort Lafayette. But he got no farther than Nashville. The War Department thought better of its plan and he was allowed to return to his home.[1]

A United States grand jury at Norfolk, in spite of his parole, took up the task of indicting General Robert E. Lee.[2]

Raphael Semmes, the famous commander of the *Alabama,* who had laid waste American shipping on so many seas, had been paroled with Johnston's army. He was allowed to remain peaceably at home for seven months, but was arrested in December, 1865, to be kept in prison in Washington for four months awaiting trial as a "pirate."[3]

The ends and tails of the rebellion were still to be gathered up on both land and sea. While the great body of the Southern troops were included in the two armies which had been surrendered to Grant and Sherman, various detached regular and irregular commands were yet to be captured. The soldierly determination of Lee and Johnston to yield when they were assured that further resistance would be futile, instead of permitting their armies to break up into roving bands for murder and pillage, was an example for every one to emulate in spirit

he announced that he would practise law and write a history of the war. — N. Y. Tribune, Sept. 30.

[1] O. R., series i, vol. xlix, part ii, pp. 883, 889, 902, 922. Grant believed that his parole protected a soldier, and if its terms were kept, it should be respected. See, for instance, O. R., series ii, vol. viii, serial no. 121, p. 815.

[2] Even the virtues of the leading general of the Confederacy, for whom appreciation was expressed in many circles in the North, did not prevent the New York Tribune from saying on May 1, 1865: "Robert E. Lee is one of the men who deliberately determined to betray his country. While meditating treason he retained his commission. When he made the plunge he made it with his eyes open. Such a man is more guilty than any other." What Lee's conduct was at this time may be seen in Jones, Reminiscences of R. E. Lee, p. 201.

[3] Colyer Meriwether, Life of Semmes, pp. 325 et seq.

as in fact.   General Richard ("Dick") Taylor had been closely pursued by General Wilson's cavalry and already, on April 19, overtures were made to General Canby for the surrender of all the Confederate troops still under arms east of the Mississippi. The number was about 42,000.   Taylor and Canby met in the village of Citronelle in Alabama and on May 4 came the grateful news that, on terms similar to those offered Lee by Grant, the soldiers were returning to their homes.   At the same time a quantity of ships and naval material in and around Mobile was made over to the Union commanders.

No forces of importance of an organized character remained to the Confederacy except those under General E. Kirby Smith, still at large west of the Mississippi.   Here Jefferson Davis saw visions of empire; thither he would go.   Many others, for whom life at home on terms prescribed by the victorious North seemed intolerable, looked to Texas and Mexico as havens to be sought and enjoyed.   General Smith himself, encouraged by his situation, thought that he could long resist pursuit, and on April 21 called upon his troops to continue the war.   He and they together might yet be the means of "securing the final success of our cause."   But soon he was brought into another frame of mind, and on the 26th day of May surrendered his entire command, some 18,000 men, to General Canby.

At least two war-ships, of which merchantmen had fear, continued to rove the main.   President Johnson in a proclamation on May 9 took note of the Confederate cruisers "still infesting the high seas."   He urged that they be arrested and brought in, so that their officers could be punished for their crimes, and gave notice to other nations that if hospitality were extended to such vessels in their ports, they might expect none for their ships visiting ports of the United States.   Captain J. D. Bulloch, acting for the Confederacy, had ordered a ram in France.   The Emperor forbade the transaction before the ship was completed, and she was sold to Denmark, from which government she was later purchased by the "rebel" leaders.   At first christened the *Sphinx,* her name was changed to the *Stonewall*. She finally sailed from Copenhagen, on January 6, 1865, made her way to Lisbon, and then crossed the ocean safely to Havana, where she arrived on May 11.[1] Hearing there that the war was at an end, the commander surrendered his vessel to the Captain-General of Cuba, who in due time transferred her to the United States. This event gave shipping men great satisfaction and went far to restore confidence in the movements of merchantmen at sea.

The *Shenandoah* was still at large on the other side of the world. She had been fitted out by Bulloch late in 1864 and, commanded by Captain J. I. Waddell, at once proceeded to the Pacific. She had reached Australia in January, 1865, and then set out for the north to attack the New England whaling fleet. All through the early summer, even after the commander of the vessel was in possession of the news of the collapse of the Confederacy, he continued his depredations. His conduct aroused the greatest resentment in the United States. Finally, disguising his ship as a merchantman, he ran back to England and anchored in the Mersey on the 6th of November, six months after Lee's surrender, adding his doings to those of Semmes on the *Alabama* for a great international case in an arbitration court.

The trial of the conspirators in the plot to assassinate Lincoln, Seward and other officers of the government deeply stirred the vindictive passions of the people. Stanton, according to Welles, had intended that they should be executed even before the funeral at Springfield, but on that day, the 4th of May, as the war minister's unfriendly colleague, the Secretary of the Navy, noted, the trial had not been begun. A sentiment existed in the Cabinet in favor of a regular jury trial, but it was overruled, and a military commission was appointed.[2] This body was composed of ten members with the Judge Advocate General, Joseph Holt, at its head. General ("Black") David Hunter and General Lew Wallace were among the number. A room in the penitentiary buildings at the arsenal in

[1] Phila. Press, May 18, 1865.
[2] Welles, vol. ii, p. 303.

Washington, where the prisoners were confined, was fitted up
for use as a court. The jail was surrounded by a strong
military guard. All the prisoners were put in chains; to prevent their suicide padded masks covered their heads, except for
the holes opposite their mouths through which they were fed.[1]
After discussion it was determined to admit reporters, and the
details of the trial were given out to the people through the
newspapers at length day by day. The court convened for the
first time on May 10, and proceeded with the work in hand,
throughout the following seven or eight weeks. On July 5
it sent its findings and sentences to the President, who at once
approved them. Four — Herold, Payne, Atzerodt and Mrs.
Surratt — were to be hanged; three were to be imprisoned for
life and one for six years.

No time was to be lost. General Hancock and General
Hartranft on the next day, the 6th, visited the prisoners to
inform them of their fate. The executions would take place
on the following day, the 7th. A scaffold was erected in the
south yard of the penitentiary, the coffins and burial clothes
were prepared, and the end was near. Mrs. Surratt begged
for a few days' respite. Her daughter visited the White House
and, weeping, pleaded with the President's private secretary
for an audience. Even veteran soldiers who witnessed the
scene must wipe away the tears which suffused their eyes.
Five members of the Commission had recommended that instead of death the woman's punishment should be imprisonment for life.[2] Friends, relations and counsel appeared in
behalf of the other prisoners, but the efforts of none of the
intercessors availed. The President was obdurate, if he indeed knew of the demands made upon his mercy, and the hour
of execution approached. The four victims were permitted
to see their religious advisers. Under close guard they took

[1] Phila. Press, May 10.

[2] Echoes of a long and acrimonious discussion as to whether such a
recommendation ever reached the President's eyes are found in correspondence between Holt and Attorney-General Speed in North American Review for July and September, 1888. Cf. Joseph Holt Papers
in Library of Congress, vol. liii, for earlier allusions to the subject.

leave of their families and were then led out to view the scaffolds, the open graves and the rough pine coffins in which they soon would rest. Their arms were still manacled at the wrists, their legs were tied with linen bandages, that one put around Mrs. Surratt encompassing her dress, and so the four together went out of the world.[1] The men who were sentenced to imprisonment for life were taken to the barren coral keys off the coast of Florida called the Dry Tortugas.

Sentiment in the North at the time very generally commended the executions, without exception for the case of Mrs. Surratt, whose complicity in the plot had not been active. The account of how she and the other prisoners had expiated their crimes was read with approval. The newspapers found it to be a noble assertion of the national authority. Lincoln's death had now been avenged. Many letters came to the President. "God bless you, sir," said one. Christian people would now pray for him. The hanging of Mrs. Surratt would enforce the lesson that womanhood was no excuse for crime.[2]

On all sides there were loud demands for the life of Jefferson Davis. President Johnson himself had treated the hanging of the chief officer of the Confederacy almost as a matter of course. Schuyler Colfax, Speaker of the House of Representatives, who had started away on a journey to the Pacific coast on the very day of Lincoln's assassination, alluded to it with favor in his speeches in the West, and the crowds acclaimed the sentiment.[3] Women in the North wanted Davis's life.

[1] Phila. Press, July 8, 1865. John H. Surratt, Mrs. Surratt's son, escaped to Canada, else he certainly would have met his mother's fate. He wandered over Europe and was brought back to Washington in 1867 for a prolonged civil trial, sentiment meanwhile having undergone a change to his profit. The jury disagreed and he went free.

[2] Johnson Papers in Library of Congress.

[3] Colfax said at Virginia City, Nevada, on June 26: "If there is justice left in this country we will see him ["Old Jeff"] hanging between Heaven and earth as not fit for either." Cries came from the crowd — "That is what we want!" "Send him out here!" Colfax had climbed an iron ladder over a deep shaft. He thought it would be "an appropriate doom" if Davis were compelled to go up and down that ladder until he was tired and fell. "That would be the end of him." — Phila. Ledger, Aug. 9, 1865.

Senator Doolittle's mother, with a "heart true to God and man," asked her son to write to the President. "Tell him," she said, "to be sure to have Davis tried and executed."[1] The very children for months running into years had lisped — "Hang Jeff Davis on a sour apple tree" to the tune of "John Brown's Body," and it was perhaps not unreasonably concluded that Davis had done more to disrupt the government and bring its days to an end than had old Brown on an historic occasion at Harper's Ferry. That they, one and all, in the Confederate Cabinet, feared, if they did not expect, summary retribution is proven by the efforts which they made to escape the toils of the Federal cavalry after the war. "A military court," said Toombs, "could hang me much more rightfully than it could the poor woman (Mrs. Surratt I believe) who was hung in Washington, for I did try to take the life of the nation and sorely regret the failure to do it."[2] A newspaper published in so sober a community as Philadelphia, on the day the four "assassins" were hanged, editorially observed that "these wretches only struck in obedience to orders." "Had there been no Jefferson Davis there had been no Booth," this writer continued, "and, while we thirst for no man's blood, justice demands that, when the underlings of the Great Criminal are ignominiously executed, he should not be exempted from the fate he accepted for himself, even as he forced it upon them."[3] But Davis remained in his casemate.

Another subject for the gibbet was found in the person of Henry Wirz, a native of Switzerland, a physician by education, who had practised medicine in Louisiana. He had enlisted in the Confederate army and for several months at the end of the war was in charge of the horrible prison pen at Andersonville in Georgia. He was arrested in May. His trial began before a military commission, of which General Lew Wallace was the president, in Washington, on August 23, and continued for two months. In vain was it pleaded that

---

[1] Sept. 9, 1865, in Johnson Papers.
[2] Phillips, Life of Toombs, p. 225.
[3] Phila. Press, July 7, 1865.

he had been present at the surrender of Johnston's army to
Sherman and that the arrest was in violation of the terms of
the parole.   It availed nothing to say that the whole prison
system of the South necessarily entailed great hardship upon
captives, because of the blockade of the ports and the general
paralysis of agriculture and trade.   The Southern soldiers in
the last months of the war were fed and clothed only meagrely;
how then could it fare well with the prisoners? [1]   Vain was it,
too, to point to the barbarities practised upon Southern captives in Northern prisons as at Elmira, Fort Delaware and
Camp Chase; [2] vain to allege that Wirz was but the agent of
others occupying higher places, and a creature of conditions
and circumstances; vain to explain that the soldiers of the
North continued to be confined in Libby, at Belle Isle, Salis-
bury and Andersonville because the authorities at Washington
would not agree to the plans which were proposed for a general
exchange of prisoners.   Wirz was found guilty.   President
Johnson resisted various pleas for mercy and approved the
sentence.   And on November 10 the friendless man was
hanged and buried in the jail yard beside Atzerodt.   Secretary
Stanton and the Judge Advocate-General, Joseph Holt, who
was a cheerful public executioner, in finding another victim
for the vengeance of the nation seemed to answer a real public
need. [3]

[1] For a sober discussion of this question see A. H. Stephens, Recollections, pp. 233, 444–6.

[2] A young man whom the N. Y. Nation correspondent met in the
South in 1865 said that 28 of 42 men in his company taken to Elmira
died of their sufferings. — N. Y. Nation, vol. i, p. 366.

[3] O. R., series iii, vol. v, pp. 490–4; cf. ibid., pp. 321–2; O. R.,
series ii, vol. viii, pp. 784–94.   A case of horrible cruelty, prolonged,
premeditated and systematic was made out against Wirz.   He was
charged with responsibility for the death of no less than 10,000 prisoners.   On the other side, in defence of the Southern prison system,
see Dr. R. R. Stevenson, The Southern Side, or Andersonville Prison;
J. Barbiere, Scraps from the Prison Table (for Ohio prisons); Dr.
I. W. K. Handy, United States Bonds (for Fort Delaware); C. W.
Holmes, The Elmira Prison Camp.   Many accounts of personal experiences of Southern soldiers in Northern prisons are to be found in
the Southern Historical Society Papers.

President Johnson while he breathed fire and hemp was winning the general confidence of the North. "In vain would we seek for one who has rendered greater personal service to the twin cause of Union and Liberty," said the Philadelphia Press as early as on April 21, "or who has given more convincing proofs of his unalterable attachment to those great pillars of our political fabric." The New York Tribune, at the same time, said that the new President was growing "steadily in public confidence and esteem." He knew the rebellion "egg and bird."[1] Party spirit had been entirely extinguished.[2] A Tribune correspondent in Washington, after observing the President's course for a few days, reached the conclusion that he was "not only one of the nation's foremost patriots and statesmen, but that he was also a fitting type of a modest, yet self-reliant and accomplished gentleman."[3] The Philadelphia Press's Washington correspondent, a month later, asserted that he was at the time "the most popular man in America. I have never known," he said, "such an acclaim of compliment and confidence in support of a public character." The men who demanded "forcible measures" were on his side because of his record in the past; the "men of forgiveness" because he was the "trustee of Lincoln"; the "loyal Southern men" because he had been born and brought up among them; the friends of Douglas because he had "cut loose from Breckinridge"; the Buchanan men in the North for divers reasons peculiar to them, and so on.[4]

He was stubborn and honest, said others. A number of merchants and bankers in New York had made up a purse to buy him a span of horses and a fine carriage. They had invested about $6000 in the gift. It was very significant that he would not receive it, and that the animals and all the appurtenances must be sold at auction for scarcely more than a half of their cost price. He was as little to be moved "from the plain path of duty by favor as by fear."[5]

[1] N. Y. Tribune, April 22, 1865. [3] Ibid., April 21, 1865.
[2] Ibid., April 25, 1865. [4] Phila. Press, May 22, 1865.
[5] Phila. Ledger, May 25 and June 3, 1865.

So the praise was continued by mouths from which in a short time such words would sound exceeding strange. The Philadelphia Press, on June 15, declared that the new President's counsels were entitled to respect in all quarters. "He speaks and acts," it said, "from profound and accurate knowledge," gained from a life spent in the South. A little later it was his "ardent patriotism and unblemished loyalty"[1] which called for the writer's admiration. The New York Evening Post found at about the same time that Mr. Johnson, thus far, had "discharged the duties of his office with a moderation and grace, coupled with an energy and decision that augur the best results for the future."[2] To the man whom Lincoln advised with on the subject of reconstruction in Tennessee could be committed the larger undertaking, "in the confidence that the duty will be done judiciously and with the best effect good judgment can attain."[3] Even the "slip," as Lincoln called it, on the day Johnson took his oath in the Senate Chamber as Vice-President was explained away. Some had said that he was ill, as for example Hannibal Hamlin, the retiring Vice-President, who generously assumed a share of the blame, declaring that Johnson's health was such that he had asked for spirits. When the cup was put to his lips he drank too deeply from it.[4] It remained for others to suggest that on this occasion poison had been "furtively insinuated" in his liquor with a view to making an end to him. But his "powerful nature had triumphed over the infernal draught," and his "invaluable life was saved to the nation."[5] There were not a few to believe that Johnson would be more pitiless in his hostility to slavery, to treason, to attacks upon the rights of loyalists and negroes at the South than Lincoln ever would have been, if he had been spared for the tasks of this difficult day. Lincoln "would have dealt with rebels," said Senator Doolittle of Wis-

[1] Phila. Press, June 28, 1865.
[2] Cited in Phila. Press, June 28, 1865.
[3] Phila. Ledger, June 13, 1865.
[4] Johnson Papers.
[5] Wilkes' Spirit, cited in N. Y. Tribune, April 27, 1865.

consin, "as an indulgent father deals with his erring children";
Johnson would "deal with them more like a stern and incor-
ruptible judge." "Thus in a moment," continued the Senator
"has the sceptre of power passed from a hand of flesh to a hand
of iron." [1]

Jefferson Davis, when he was taken prisoner in Georgia, had
expressed to General Wilson the fear that Johnson would exhibit "a vindictive and unforgiving temper" in his conduct
toward the President of the late Confederacy, and indeed toward
all the people of the South.[2] "God help us!" exclaimed
Clement C. Clay when he heard of the assassination of Lincoln,
which there were many to assert and believe that he had aided
in bringing about. "If that be true it is the worst blow that
yet has been struck at the South."[3]

Meantime the work of adjustment was going forward along
many different lines. It was attacked in a spirit of hope by
men acting in a good deal of friendship and harmony. In the
first place the army must be disbanded, the charges of the
war reduced, the cost reckoned and the debt paid by the issue
of notes to be funded later at the convenience of the Treasury
Department. The Northern army had been brought up to
the great total of one million men.[4] These legions of marching
troops never had been seen at one place together. They had
fought hither and yon — on the Mississippi and on the Potomac; at Richmond and at Chattanooga; in the Valley of
Virginia; in Georgia and the Carolinas, with Sherman on
his immortal "march to the sea." Before they melted away
to be seen no more, except as a phantom multitude swinging down the dim vistas of history, many of the corps in
the Army of the Potomac and in Sherman's Western army,
encamped around Washington preparatory to the muster-
out, would be brought into the city for a grand review

[1] Speech at Racine, Wis., N. Y. Tribune, April 24, 1865.

[2] Wilson, Under the Old Flag, vol. ii, p. 337; cf. Rise and Fall,
vol. ii, p. 703.

[3] Mrs. Clay, A Belle of the Fifties, p. 245.

[4] O. R., series iii, vol. iv, p. 1283. On May 1, 1865, the number
was 1,052,038.

by the President and by General Grant, on the 23d and the 24th days of May.

First, on the 23d, came the Army of the Potomac, under Meade's immediate command, though its operations at the end were personally directed by Grant, who had been called from the West for this purpose. For four years this army had stood between Washington and the North and the army of Lee. For four years, under various leaders, it had sought to invest and take Richmond. At last it had worn down the enemy and gained the great object. Strong and numerous and victorious, its career was now a long memory of carnage and death for itself and for the foe, — all brought this day to the minds of reflective onlookers as the serried columns of marching veterans, the prancing horsemen, the flying banners, some of them tattered and torn in service, and the inspiriting music of the bands for a period of six hours uninterruptedly passed the reviewing stand erected in front of the White House. The beloved Lincoln was not here to witness the great spectacle. Many a commander and many a man left on five hundred fields — at Manassas, at Antietam, at Chancellorsville, at Gettysburg, in the Wilderness and before Petersburg — were absent at this proud hour.

The next day Sherman's army marched through the capital. Its commander's leaning to the side of mercy in the offer of terms to General Johnston, the exceeding of his authority as a military leader and his prescribing a personal plan for the South's return to the Union were this day forgotten. He was the inflexible soldier who had run the iron through the heart of the Confederacy, who with his Western troops, now seen in Washington for the first and last time, had swept a wide way from the Mississippi to the sea. Rugged, tawny, hard, active men, fit for any deed, they now stepped along through the crowds massed on either side to honor them, Sherman himself at their head with a wreath of flowers depending from his shoulder and another around his horse's neck. "Animated bronzes," one writer described them. "Athletic and wiry" they seemed, as they swung past the reviewing stand for six hours, as long as Meade's army had occupied the street on the previous day. It was a mighty phalanx which aroused the patriotic fervor of every beholder.[1]

What daring had been theirs, what havoc had they not wrought! After all had not they, rather than the Army of the Potomac, dealt the fatal blow to rebellion and brought the great war to an end? Pitiless, cruel, said the South, but they were proud of their doughty adventures. Here with the rest were the "bummers." Many bestrode beautiful horses which were a part of their spoil. There were droves of mules, some carrying on their backs goats, game-chickens, dogs and raccoons, all suggestive of successful pillage. Pickaninnies, gathered up on the plantations, grinned as the procession passed — mascots of the regiments. "Contrabands" marched with the white brigades. Patriotic pride, amazement at the vastness as well as the grandeur of the display, amusement because of its incidents, were mingled to produce a profound effect upon every mind.

The disbandment of the great Northern army had begun on the 29th of April, before Lincoln had yet been put in his grave, or Davis had been captured. By August 7, 641,000 troops had returned to the peaceful walks of life, ready to be absorbed in the ranks of citizenship,[2] and the work was continued rapidly afterward. To pacify the country, if further need arose, and to reëstablish the national authority, five military divisions were created: the Atlantic, commanded by General George G. Meade, with headquarters at Philadelphia; the Mississippi, by General William T. Sherman, stationed at St. Louis; the Gulf, by General Philip H. Sheridan, at New Orleans; the Tennessee, by General George H. Thomas, at Nashville; and

---

[1] "Regiments after regiments of men so closely packed that it would seem impossible for anything to pass between them passed hour after hour." Eyes were made weary and brains dizzy by the sight. So Mrs. Seward wrote. See Seward at Washington by F. W. Seward, vol. iii, p. 282.

[2] The success of this movement is the subject of laudatory remarks in a report of Grant to Stanton, Oct. 20, 1865. — O. R., series iii, vol. v, serial no. 126, p. 126.

the Pacific, by General H. W. Halleck, at San Francisco. These five divisions comprised eighteen departments, at the head of which stood such tried commanders as Hancock, Pope, Hooker, Schofield, McDowell, Stoneman, Canby, Terry and Ord.[1]

The great purchases on account of the army ceased. The horses and mules, the munitions and supplies of war were offered for sale, and the proceeds covered into the Treasury. The prisoners who had been gathered into camps and stockades in various parts of the North took the oath of allegiance and were sent to their homes. In the navy, too, retrenchment was instantly begun. Coast squadrons and river flotillas were reduced in size, or wholly dispersed. The vessels and equipment were sold and thousands of seamen were at liberty to return to the merchant service, whence they had been drawn for the national defence.

The army had cost the government over $1,000,000,000 in the fiscal year ending June 30, 1865. Two years later when there was a full return to a peace footing the total expenditures for the same use were less than $100,000,000.[2] The debt of the United States, when it was finally adjusted, reached a grand aggregate as a result of the war of about $3,000,000,000. To the task of paying this great sum the country turned cheerfully and even humorously. Jay Cooke, the Philadelphia banker and loan agent for the government, published a pamphlet entitled "Our National Debt a National Blessing." [3] This suggestion aroused general laughter. The New York Herald announced a scheme for the speedy extinguishment of the debt. It should be capitalized and divided into 150,000 shares of $20,000 each, when it could be taken up by the wealthy men of the country in return for promises of immunity from taxation. James Gordon Bennett subscribed $40,000. He urged the appointment of a committee to "wait upon" the "moneyed men" of the country.[4] Commodore

---

[1] O. R., series i, vol. xlvii, part iii, p. 667.
[2] Reports of the Secretary of the Treasury for 1865, 1866 and 1867.
[3] Oberholtzer, Life of Jay Cooke, vol. i, pp. 637 et seq.
[4] N. Y. Herald, May 23, 1865.

Vanderbilt said that he would take twenty-five shares, or a half million dollars' worth, and others allowed their names to be seen in print in connection with the splendid plan, with the understanding, as the owner of the Herald was careful to note, that no obligation would be incurred by any until the entire sum should have been underwritten.[1] Robert Bonner of the New York Ledger would subscribe $40,000; George W. Childs of the Philadelphia Ledger and his friends in the banking house of Drexel and Company, $140,000; the Singer Sewing Machine Company, $50,000, and other advertisers of newspapers and commodities eagerly added their names to what Bennett soon was pleased to call "the roll of honor."[2] The scheme was a nine days' wonder and, strangely enough, became the subject of serious paragraphs and editorials in many gazettes.[3]

But this was jest. The work of providing the money for the payment of the accumulating warrants upon the Treasury, and of sending the soldiers home with their wages in their pockets was going forward wisely and confidently. When Mr. McCulloch came to the head of the Treasury Department with the beginning of Lincoln's second term, on March 4, 1865, he found that the pecuniary wants of the government were being met by the sale of "7-30's," i.e. three-year Treasury notes bearing interest at the rate of two cents a day, or $7.30 a year on a note of $100. The contract had been made by Mr. McCulloch's predecessor in office, William P. Fessenden, with Jay Cooke, the sanguine and energetic man through whom large sales of bonds had been effected by Secretary Chase in the early years of the war. Cooke immediately established the machinery for a nation-wide appeal. As the war came to an end hope filled every heart, and in a few months $830,000,000 worth of the notes were distributed among the people. On the day Lincoln was shot the sales reached a total of about $4,000,000, and continued at nearly this rate daily after his death. In May a new impulse was given to the movement,

[1] N. Y. Herald, May 26, 1865.
[2] Ibid., May 27, 1865.
[3] Phila. Ledger, May 27, 1865; Phila. Press, May 25, 1865.

and on one day, May 13, more than $30,000,000 were received in exchange for notes at Cooke's various sales agencies.[1] The payment of the charges of the war, by the sale of paper falling due at the expiration of short terms, would call for much adjustment of the debt at later dates, but the generous subscription of money by the people for government uses in these few weeks following Mr. Johnson's coming to the Presidency was, at once, an expression of their virility at the end of a prolonged and exhausting contest, and of their patriotic faith in the future of the nation.

The feeling of confidence which the new President's first weeks in office engendered on all sides afforded him the opportunity for the development of his policies. The vacation of Congress assured him of no interference on that side. The great authority of the incumbent of the foremost office under the Constitution had been extended and increased, of necessity, during the war. Lincoln had come to exercise extraordinary powers, and they were the inheritance of Andrew Johnson.[2]

Traitors were to be punished. Jefferson Davis lay in irons in Fortress Monroe. Other forts and prisons held the Vice-President of the Confederacy, members of the Richmond Cabinet, senators, governors, leaders of the rebellion, great and small, civil and military. What disposition was to be made of this human spoil of the war? How were the masses of the Southern people, returned to their towns and cities and to their lands, to be permitted to act in reference to their local governments? How were the seceded states to be brought back into national relationship? More than all this: what should be done, if anything, by the triumphant North with reference to the nearly four million negroes in the South? They had been made free of masters by legislative measures imposed upon these masters by force of arms. What further duty had the North toward this great body of ignorant and

[1] Oberholtzer, Life of Jay Cooke, vol. i, pp. 538 et seq.
[2] W. A. Dunning has called it a "dictatorship." — Essays on the Civil War and Reconstruction, p. 14.

suddenly emancipated people whose lives up to this time had been led in the darkness of slavery?

President Johnson had said upon more than one occasion, after coming to his office, that as events occurred, and it became necessary for him to act, he would do so. He would defer any declaration of his policies until it could be written "paragraph by paragraph in the light of events as they transpired." [1] He had said also that he would follow in the path of his predecessor. The work of the restoration, the reorganization, the reconstruction of the South had begun before Lincoln's death, and, while the way was not plain, some experiments of an interesting nature already had been undertaken. As the Northern armies made their way through the South, and gained control of territory in the seceded states, it was Lincoln's wish to provide forms of civil government for the people. Thus, as early as 1862, military governors were appointed for Tennessee, Louisiana and North Carolina. In two of these states, Tennessee and Louisiana, some progress had been achieved, particularly in Tennessee, where the office had been held by him who was now President. Here Unionist and Secessionist were at each other's throats in a civil contest the noise of which sometimes drowned the sound of actual battle in other parts of the South; its echoes were heard over all the nation. Here the pugnacious disposition of Johnson found a field for play, and a government of some kind, though it was not peacefully acquiesced in, had been established. So, too, in Arkansas, in 1863, Lincoln had taken steps toward a reorganization of the state.

Conventions were held in Tennessee, Louisiana and Arkansas in 1864 and constitutions were adopted looking to the return of these states to their old places in the Union. The governments formed by the conventions operated only within the areas held by the Federal troops, and not one of the three states succeeded in seating its representatives in either branch of Congress at Washington.

[1] Speech to the Illinois delegation, April 18, 1865, in Moore's Speeches of A. Johnson, p. 473; speech in Kirkwood House when he took the oath, Annual Cyclopedia for 1865, p. 800; Welles, vol. ii, p. 289.

The framework of a loyalist government still existed in Virginia with its ostensible capital at Alexandria. Lincoln recognized the men who pretended to direct its farcical motions, since no better were at hand, and thus the matter stood at the time of his death.[1] The other seven states in the Confederacy had only "insurgent legislatures"; these bodies were to be ignored and all their doings set aside. A half dozen of their governors were now under arrest and reposed, like Jefferson Davis, inside of strong walls, awaiting the pleasure of the Federal authorities.

Johnson's first act, by way of the development of Lincoln's policies in reference to the South, was a recognition on May 9 of the Virginia government which had its seat at Alexandria, and the governor attempting to act under it, Francis H. Peirpoint. The Secretary of the Treasury was directed to appoint revenue officers, the Postmaster-General to establish post-offices, the judges to hold courts, etc. Peirpoint at the first opportunity would change his capital and reside in Richmond. A blockade runner which had been captured from the Confederates was put at his disposition. The vessel, carrying the governor, his family and his household goods, sailed down the Potomac and, in fear of the torpedoes still believed to lie unexploded in the bed of the river, picked its way up the James. The party entered the old capital of the state on May 30 amid "thunders of artillery." Only negroes and soldiers were at hand to welcome them. The ladies of the city barred their window shutters while the governor's procession passed their homes. It was a military reception which awaited him at the Executive Mansion, made ready for his use.[2]

Three weeks after President Johnson's recognition of the Peirpoint government in Virginia, on May 29, he published his Amnesty Proclamation. In this paper he merely developed the policy which had been laid down by Lincoln in similar

[1] McPherson, History of Reconstruction, p. 8.

[2] N. Y. Tribune, June 1, 1865. Peirpoint was a lawyer fifty years of age, of anti-slavery sentiments. He had been "elected" governor in 1864.

papers issued on December 8, 1863, and March 26, 1864. The proclamation was discussed at length in the Cabinet.[1] Mr. Seward now was recovering from the fall which had fractured his jaw, and the terrible subsequent attack upon him as he lay in his bed on the night of Lincoln's assassination. His progress was more rapid than his son's, who for several weeks could not be told of his father's condition, or for that matter of the President's death. Young Seward was probably, therefore, so it was observed, the last person within the boundaries of the United States to learn of the murder of the President. The head of the Secretary of State was covered with a close-fitting cap and a rigid metal frame, which entered the mouth [2] to keep the broken bone in place, so that he could articulate only with difficulty. But his mind was clear, and, early in May, the effect of his advice was seen upon the course of the administration.[3] On May 9 the President and the members of the Cabinet held a meeting in Seward's home,[4] and ten days later the Secretary made his first appearance in his office in the State Department.[5] The plans for the amnesty and pardon of those who had been engaged actively in the enterprise to subvert the government had Seward's approval and the proclamation bore his name, the first paper to do so since his injury. Each person desiring to resume his loyal relations with the United States might appear before any commissioned officer, civil, military or naval, of the United States, or of any state or territory, qualified to administer oaths, and subscribe to this statement:

"I ——— do solemnly swear (or affirm) in the presence of Almighty God that I will henceforth faithfully support, protect and defend the Constitution of the United States and the Union of the states thereunder; and that I will in like manner abide by and faithfully support all laws and proclamations which have been made during the existing

---

[1] Welles, vol. ii, pp. 303, 305.

[2] "A machine like a Spanish bit," Sumner called it. — Pierce, Memoir and Letters of Sumner, vol. iv, p. 254.

[3] Bancroft, Life of Seward, vol. ii, p. 446; Pierce, vol. iv, p. 249.

[4] Welles, vol. ii, p. 304.

[5] Ibid., p. 307; Phila. Press, May 20, 1865.

rebellion with reference to the emancipation of slaves. So help me God."

The original certificates were to be forwarded to the State Department in Washington and copies given to the takers of the oath. Fourteen classes of persons were excepted from the provisions of the proclamation, among them military officers above the rank of colonel; naval officers above the rank of lieutenant; diplomatic officers of the "pretended government"; those who had left Congress, the army, or the navy, or judicial offices in the United States to serve this "pretended government"; governors of insurgent states; all who had crossed the military lines and deserted their homes in the North to render assistance to the South; and those "rebels" owning taxable property of a value greater than $20,000. Persons included in these excepted classes might make special application to the President and clemency would be "liberally extended," as might be "consistent with the facts in the case and the peace and dignity of the United States." [1]

The exception for persons holding property valued at more than $20,000, known as the "13th exception," was new, and where in the South dismay was not complete this feature of the plan led to protest. Memorials began to come in to the President.[2] A number of Virginians visited him in July and complained of their situation. They were seeking credits in the North and West, which were not procurable while they rested under this ban of the government. The President called upon his own knowledge of the South. "It was the wealthy men who dragooned the people into secession," said he. "I know how the thing was done. You rich men used the press and bullied your little men to force the state into secession." [3] He seemed to speak as a "poor white" for the "poor whites." The visitors departed in gloom.

[1] McPherson, pp. 9–11.
[2] N. Y. Tribune, July 4, 1865; Phila. Ledger, July 3, 1865.
[3] Phila. Press, July 10, 1865. "Damn the negroes," he had said while serving as military governor of Tennessee. "I am fighting these traitorous aristocrats, their masters." — J. M. Palmer, Personal Recollections, p. 127.

On the same day that this amnesty proclamation was issued, May 29, the President announced his policy with reference to the reorganization of the states, beginning with North Carolina. He appealed to the fourth section of Article IV of the Federal Constitution, in which it is declared that the government of the United States shall guarantee to every state in the Union a "republican form of government," and found that the occasion now existed for his intervention. A rebellion of "the most violent and revolting form" had been waged against the "properly constituted authorities of the government" of the United States. The people of North Carolina had stood in its path, and for long had been deprived of "all civil government." Therefore the President would appoint a provisional governor for the state and direct him to call together a convention of delegates to alter its constitution "at the earliest practicable period." No one should be permitted to vote for such delegates unless he first had taken the oath of amnesty. The United States military authorities in North Carolina were commanded to assist the provisional governor in the execution of his task, and the Secretary of the Treasury, the Postmaster-General and other officers of the government in Washington were asked, as in the case of Virginia, to put into force the Federal laws and systems within the geographical limits of the state.

The President's course regarding North Carolina was of immediate interest to such Confederate state governors and legislatures as yet cherished the illusion that they might put themselves back into the Union in their own ways. Similar proclamations were issued in reference to Mississippi on June 13; Georgia on June 17; Texas on June 17; Alabama on June 21; South Carolina on June 30; and Florida on July 13.

President Johnson chose William W. Holden, who had been in conference with him lately in Washington, to be provisional governor of North Carolina. He was the editor of the Raleigh Standard, a newspaper of influence, established to sustain Andrew Jackson. His sympathies were strongly Southern, but he had been the defeated candidate for governor of the anti-Jefferson Davis party in August, 1864, and now at the war's end came into prominence as a "Unionist." [1]

William L. Sharkey, a lawyer nearly seventy years of age, since boyhood a resident of Mississippi and for eighteen years its chief justice, was appointed governor of that state.

James Johnson, a lawyer, who before the war had served a term in Congress, became governor of Georgia. He was declared to be a timid man, but of "strong sense and good principles." He had gone with his state when it seceded, though the movement was against his better judgment.[2]

Andrew J. Hamilton, a native of Alabama, long a resident of Texas, and for a time its attorney-general, was Johnson's choice for governor of the great commonwealth in the southwest beyond the Mississippi River. At the breaking out of the war he had been a slaveholding lawyer and planter. But he took the part of the Union and, leaving his family behind him, started by way of Mexico for the Northern states, which he reached only after many adventures. Lincoln appointed him a brigadier-general of Texas volunteers, but he had remained in the North and was now ready to return to his home.[3]

Lewis E. Parsons, a descendant of Jonathan Edwards and a native of New York, though since 1840 a resident of the state whose affairs he was now to direct, became the governor of Alabama. He was a prominent lawyer of Talladega, a Unionist in his feeling and expressions, though he had held a seat in a "rebel legislature." [4]

Benjamin Franklin Perry, who was appointed governor of South Carolina, was a native of that state. He had long contended against Calhoun and the spirit and the doctrine of se-

---

[1] N. Y. Tribune, April 28, 1865. Such a man was not in real favor on any side, as events subsequently proved. He had said that the war should be supported to "the last man and the last dollar." So, it was alleged in North Carolina, he had supported it: he was the last man to go into it and his was the last dollar to be contributed for its prosecution. — N. Y. Tribune, Aug. 2 and Aug. 14, 1865.

[2] A. H. Stephens, Recollections, p. 231.

[3] See his testimony before the Joint Committee on Reconstruction, part iv, p. 6; cf. N. Y. Tribune, June 19, 1865.

[4] N. Y. Tribune, June 23, 1865.

cession, though he at length had protestingly embraced the cause, and held judicial and other office under the Confederate government.

The governor of Florida, William Marvin, had lived in the state since 1835. At the outbreak of the war he was a judge of the District Court of the United States in Key West, to which office he had been appointed by President Polk. He was largely occupied with the trial of prize cases. With United States military support he remained at his post in the discharge of his duties until the summer of 1863, when he went North by sea, and for two years had resided in New York City.[1]

All these men were natives or else had been residents for many years of the states they were asked to assist in fitting for a return to the Union. Not one, unless it be Governor Hamilton of Texas, had actively taken the side of the North in the war, and yet not one had been deeply involved in movements hostile to the Union. If the work in hand were to be done without bitterness, it seemed likely that the end might be effected through such agencies. The appointments were generally acquiesced in [2] as wise, if they were not definitely approved as a part of the President's plan "to place in power the popular heart of the nation." [3]

The position of the negro in the system was still undeter-

[1] N. Y. Tribune, Aug. 8, 1865.

[2] The New York Tribune, speaking for itself and its body of Radical readers, demurred on the subject of Judge Sharkey, saying that some of his pro-slavery decisions had been "little less than infernal." While the paper editorially approved of the appointment of Governor Parsons (June 23), a correspondent later called attention to the fact that he was "a very bitter rebel." The President's choice had "completely amazed every strictly loyal man" in Washington (June 26). Only Hamilton's appointment aroused enthusiasm. It was said to be "wise and noble." (Editorial, June 19.) Charles Sumner found him to be a "sincerely loyal person" (Cong. Globe, 39th Cong., 1st sess., p. 95), and the newspaper correspondent, B. C. Truman, "The noblest leader in any Southern state" (Senate Ex. Doc., 39th Cong., 1st sess., no. 43, p. 6), though he was not without enemies even among the Unionists in Texas (Report of Joint Committee on Reconstruction, part iv, p. 42), and men at once complained to the President of his personal habits. (Johnson Papers.)

[3] Johnson to the South Carolinians, June 26, 1865.

mined. This, too, was one of the events about which some declaration could be made, as the President had said, when it "transpired." To his colored visitors Mr. Johnson gave good advice. He recalled, with that garrulity and egotism which habitually marked his interviews, his own experiences as the owner of slaves whom he had manumitted. No man rightly could hold property in another man. Emancipated, the negroes now must exhibit and prove their ability to enjoy their liberties. Their freedom was simply a freedom to work and to enjoy the fruit of their own toil. The President must deplore the existence of an idea among them that "they have nothing to do but fall back upon the government for support in order that they may be taken care of in idleness and debauchery." [1]

This excellent counsel was repeated by General Oliver Otis Howard, called to the head of the new Bureau of Refugees, Freedmen and Abandoned Lands, which had been created by Congress in its expiring days in March, 1865. This bureau, attached to the War Department, had not been organized before President Lincoln's death. The philanthropic duties which it was to perform, with reference to the blacks of the South, were greatly increased by the termination of the war, and the consequent enlargement of the sphere of its authority. Howard had had a creditable record in Sherman's army. Religious and charitable sentiments dominated his heart, and Lincoln had expressed to Stanton a wish concerning his appointment, which he and Johnson were now pleased to respect.[2] Howard was called to Washington, visited the Secretary of War and on May 12 was assigned to his duties as Commissioner of what soon came to be known everywhere as the Freedmen's Bureau. Stanton, carrying a great basket, heaped full of letters and papers relating to the work, a hand at each end, presented it to Howard with a "Here, General! Here's your Bureau," [3] and he was set to work at a salary of $3000 a year in the confiscated mansion of a Confederate Senator in Wash-

[1] To the colored clergymen, May 11, 1865, in Phila. Press, May 20.
[2] General Howard's Autobiography, vol. ii, p. 207.
[3] Ibid., p. 210.

ington. Reiterating what President Johnson had more than once publicly said, Howard, in announcing his assumption of the office, observed that while the negro must be made to feel that he is "really free," he must at the same time on no account, if he be able to work, gain the impression that "the government will support him in idleness." [1]

So far there were unity and happiness, but a rumbling was heard beneath the ground. The radicals, many of whom were well enough pleased that Johnson kept Davis in a dark casemate in irons, with a view to having him hanged in due time as an example to other traitors, one and all began to wonder about the President's Roman faith, when he published his plan for the reorganization of North Carolina. Had they not been visiting him, and writing to him, and counselling him to take a course at variance, at least in one particular, with the policy which he now proclaimed? There were various reasons why the negro, having come out from under the burdens of slavery, should enjoy all the rights and privileges of white men, including the franchise. To the old Abolitionists he was still "God's image in ebony." That he should vote, as well as earn his own bread, seemed to them a kind of moral necessity. To other men negro suffrage was in some manner bound up with the general idea of democracy, and the "republican form of government" described in the Constitution of the United States. Soon again, under any system of local self-government in the South, unless they were given the ballot, the negroes would return to a condition of slavery, or peonage bordering on slavery. To still others their enfranchisement commended itself on punitive grounds. It was fairly surmised that such a policy would be in the highest degree distasteful to the classes responsible for the establishment of the Confederacy, and, by advocating it, vengeance might be visited upon a part of the Union whose subjugation it would be well to render yet more complete. One consideration overlapped another until there was a mingled mass of opinion and argument which would soon descend upon the country like a scourge.

[1] Phila. Press, May 20, 1865.

The negro suffrage leaders had wrought with Lincoln without feeling certain that they had converted him to their views and, at his death, they almost instantly turned their artillery upon Johnson. Some thought that he would prove easier of conquest and they regarded the change of presidents very hopefully. They were a motley company. First among them, perhaps, was Charles Sumner, Senator from Massachusetts. He had long been a radical on every subject appertaining to the negro. In him the "New England conscience" found full and untiring expression. Proud, patrician, with a learning so abundant that it seemed often to be a burden, he was in the vanguard of those who would make the black the equal of the white man in the exercise of the franchise, as well as in all the other relationships of life.

S. P. Chase, now Chief Justice of the Supreme Court, conscious of his own rectitude and constant in the assertion of it, was well known for his advocacy of the negro's rights. In him, too, the "New England conscience," which he had brought to Washington by way of the Western Reserve, was active. "Cold as an iceberg," as one critic averred; "selfish and caring for no friendship that could not be used for his own aggrandizement," to quote another; with a "vaulting ambition" which knew "no bounds this side the fixed stars" according to a third;[1] desirous of being President and certain that the nation's affairs would not have proper direction until after he should come to hold this great office, he lost no opportunity, earlier as a Senator of the United States and as Secretary of the Treasury, and now as Chief Justice, to impose his opinions upon other men.

Thaddeus Stevens of Pennsylvania, like Andrew Johnson an "old Commoner," had contended in many a parliamentary contest for the rights of the great masses of mankind. With a club foot that made him a marked figure wherever he was seen, a profane and satirical tongue, a most unrelenting attitude toward everything that seemed to him to savor of aristocracy, and extraordinary abilities as a debater and an orator, he could be left out of no man's reckoning in the House of Representa-

[1] Johnson Papers.

tives. He would have been a Marat or a Danton in the French Revolution. He was now the voice of the unthinking Northern populace, arousing their vindictive prejudices and crying for retribution.

Senator Benjamin F. Wade, "old Ben" Wade of Ohio, was a rough, outspoken man in whom was seen the directness and impatience of the West. George W. Julian, an old Free Soiler of Indiana; Henry Winter Davis of Maryland, and others, composed a group whose members were wagging their heads about Andrew Johnson. Speed, the Attorney-General, and Stanton were their strongest coadjutors in the Cabinet which soon was employed with the discussion of the question.

It was Sumner and Chase who most concerned themselves about Johnson's principles in the few days following Lincoln's death. A week after that event, on the evening of April 22, they together visited the new President. "He said," Sumner wrote to Francis Lieber, "that colored persons are to have the right of suffrage. . . . I was charmed with his sympathy which was entirely different from his predecessor's. . . . I had looked for a bitter contest, but with the President on our side it will be carried by simple avoirdupois." [1] To another correspondent, at about the same time (May 1), Sumner wrote concerning his demand for the elective franchise for the negro: "Our late President accepted the principle, but hesitated in the application. . . . Our new President accepts the principle and the application." [2]

Chase was less confident. He went to the President with the "rough draft" of an address, which he hoped might be issued, on the subject of "the reorganization of the rebel states." In the paper he had "incorporated a distinct recognition of the loyal colored men as citizens entitled to the right of suffrage." The author read it and re-read it to Mr. Johnson, who finally said: "I agree to all you say, but I don't see how I can issue such a document now. I am new and untried and cannot venture on what I please." Chase said that, if the President would but do this, he would attract to his side "all the young brain

[1] Pierce, vol. iv, p. 243.   [2] Ibid., p. 242.

and heart of the country." The declaration would be reprinted "in every language under Heaven, civilized and uncivilized," and give him fame equal to that of the author of the Proclamation of Emancipation. At the end Chase "almost hoped that the President's reluctance was conquered." [1]

In a few days the Chief Justice started South in a revenue cutter, at the invitation of the Secretary of the Treasury, and soon he was making speeches and granting interviews in Charleston and other places in the interest of negro suffrage.[2] As he proceeded he sent back to President Johnson long letters, in which he warmly advocated the recognition of the blacks in the new state governments.[3]

Wade, like Sumner, was confident that the President's good purpose was fixed,[4] and Thaddeus Stevens, who had had scant respect for Johnson, asking a friend after he had been nominated for Vice-President in 1864 whether they could not find a candidate for the office "without going down into one of those d—d rebel provinces to pick one up," [5] called from time to time at the White House and awaited the course of events.

While Johnson was leading Sumner to believe that there was "no difference" between them,[6] and sent him and Chase away "light hearted," [7] what treatment did the question receive in meetings of the Cabinet? On May 9, when the case of North Carolina was being discussed, and negro suffrage was under consideration, Stanton, Dennison and Speed were found to favor, and Welles, McCulloch and Usher to oppose the scheme.[8] The making of rules and regulations for the exercise of the franchise always had been a state matter, said Welles. The

[1] Chase MS. Diary — insertion under date of April 29, 1865. This or a similar "Address to the People of the United States" in Chase's hand is preserved in the Johnson Papers in the Library of Congress.

[2] Warden, p. 643; cf. Reid, After the War, early chapters.

[3] Johnson Papers.

[4] Julian, Political Recollections, p. 263.

[5] A. K. McClure, Lincoln and Men of War Time, p. 260, and Old Time Notes of Pennsylvania, vol. i, p. 141.

[6] Pierce, vol. iv, p. 242.

[7] Ibid., p. 241.

[8] Welles, vol. ii, p. 301.

contention in favor of Federal interference in this field was founded on the assumption that Southern white men were "tyrants," who would so conduct themselves toward the colored race that it everywhere would be oppressed and overborne. Even in the free states, except in a rare place, negroes were not in possession of the franchise. Why, then, should the ignorant blacks, just out of the night of slavery, be invited to discharge the "highest duties of citizenship"? The first obligation was to restore peace and allay sectional differences. Could these objects be attained by this assumption of authority, by this very radical change of the public policy?[1]

That there was a possibility of Sumner having misunderstood the President, or of the President having suffered a certain change of heart, dawned upon the negrophiles before May was yet done. The proclamation recognizing the Peirpoint government in Virginia had aroused Thaddeus Stevens. "Is there no way," he inquired of Sumner, "to arrest the insane course of the President in reorganization?" From a hotel in Philadelphia on July 6 he wrote to Johnson, begging him to "hold his hand and await the action of Congress," meantime governing the South by "military rulers." He had found not one Union man in the North, he said, who approved of the President's course.[2] While he would do their will reconstruction

---

[1] Welles, vol. ii, pp. 302–3, 324. Sumner told Welles on May 10 that the President favored negro suffrage and was privy to Chase's missionary tour in the South. (Ibid., p. 304.) Welles thought that Stanton, who was earlier opposed to the negro voting, had now changed his position (Ibid., p. 303), but as late as in January, 1866, when he and Chase together attended Winter Davis's funeral in Baltimore, Stanton expressed himself "warmly and decidedly" in favor of negro suffrage only in the District of Columbia. (Chase MS. Diary, Jan. 7, 1866; cf. Pierce, vol. iv, p. 250.) Mrs. Stanton, who was present, "expressed great horror of having negroes at her table," which was one of the crucial tests applied to the Abolitionist, a full peer of the older one embodied in the famous query "Would you marry your daughter to a nigger?" For further evidence as to Stanton's attitude on this subject, cf. Chase's letter to Stanton from Fernandina, Fla., May 20, 1865, in Stanton Papers in Library of Congress, where the writer says that enfranchisement is a policy that "you and I have always advocated."

[2] July 6, 1865, in Johnson Papers; cf. Sumner's Works, vol. ix, p. 480.

by the President was well, but in the other case his exercise of
so much power must be deemed arbitrary, and the long vacation of Congress which, at first, had seemed wholly fortunate
was grievously deplored. Wade went to Washington to persuade Johnson to convene Congress in special session, but his
visit was without avail.

The appointment of the provisional governors was declared to
be a great usurpation of authority. "If something is not done,"
said Stevens to Sumner, "the President will be crowned King
before Congress meets." [1] "The great Union or Republican
party, bound hand and foot," said Wade, was being consigned
to the "tender mercies of the rebels we have so lately conquered in the field and their Copperhead allies of the North." [2]
There was now but one path, according to Sumner; he marvelled
how the President had departed from it. "Refer the whole
question to Congress where it belongs," said he. "What right,"
he asked, "has the President to reorganize states?" [3] Some
men hesitated, as they pondered all the consequences of negro
suffrage; they would educate the freedmen and prescribe a
literacy test. Not so with such as Sumner; "we need the votes
of all," said he, "and cannot afford to wait." [4]

Horace Greeley and the New York Tribune, which he sent
into Republican homes in all parts of the country, deeply influencing the thought and opinion of the people, had accepted
Johnson as a suitable successor of Lincoln in the Presidential
office, and refrained for some months from open criticism of
his course. But the editor spoke day by day for the negroes.
Disrespectful allusions to them were promptly denounced.
Outrages upon their persons in any community assumed a
national gravity. With all his well-known controversial power
Greeley wrangled with other editors who dared to speak of the
black man with disparagement. He republished speeches and
resolutions recommending negro suffrage, and found a place
for letters which told of the high state of civilization among the

[1] Sumner's Works, vol. ix, p. 480.
[2] Sumner MS. in Harvard Library, quoted in Rhodes, vol. v, p. 533.
[3] Pierce, vol. iv, p. 256.   [4] Ibid.

four millions of people so recently enslaved. "Our own conviction," said the Tribune on May 27, "that all rights should be enjoyed irrespective of color, is not disguised, and will not easily be shaken." There was disappointment in Greeley's heart, as in Sumner's, Wade's and Stevens's, when the North Carolina proclamation appeared, but it was believed, said the Tribune's Washington correspondent, that, while the President would leave the decision of the franchise question to the several states within their respective geographical limits, he would exert "his whole moral influence" in support of the cause.[1] "If we give the negro a bayonet, why can we not give him a ballot?" Greeley asked. "If he gives his life to save the country, should we not in turn give him a voice in its management? If four millions of negroes are to remain in serfdom, what guarantee have we that 'the haughty whites' will not start another 'rebellion'?" and so on.[2]

The old Abolitionists who had served so valiantly in bringing on the war, and whose principles on the subjects of philanthropy and peace prevented them from taking any but the smallest part in its active prosecution, now again came forward with their advice. Indeed the tongue of Wendell Phillips scarcely ever had been silent. The sentiments of him and his like were in general such that they must oppose what Gerrit Smith called "a rigorous and bloody policy" toward the Southern white people,[3] but they would have the negro empowered to vote against his erstwhile master. The poet John G. Whittier, while observing with deep trouble that every one spoke of the need of hanging and similar punitive measures, complained that "only here and there" a voice was raised for the "endowment of the negro with the same rights of citizenship which are to be accorded to the rank and file of disbanded rebels." He was to be left powerless in the hands of the "white trash" who hated him more bitterly than the large slaveholders.[4]

[1] N. Y. Tribune, June 1, 1865.

[2] Ibid., June 10, 1865.

[3] Ibid., May 6, 1865.

[4] Letter in The Villager of Amesbury, Mass., cited in N. Y. Tribune, May 16, 1865.

Gerrit Smith, Henry Ward Beecher and others, while they were a unit for clemency toward the leaders of the war in the South, were also at one in asking an extension to the emancipated race of "the right of self-protection by suffrage." [1] Wendell Phillips, addressing the New England Anti-Slavery Society in Boston at the end of May, denounced the North Carolina proclamation as "a practical surrender to the Confederacy," and "a practical fraud on the North." Better for Grant to have surrendered to Lee in Virginia than for President Johnson to have surrendered to North Carolina.[2]

Violent men were writing to the President to say that he had committed the "blackest crime of the ages." He was not honest. While pretending to be a democrat, and to believe in a government founded on "the consent of the governed," what did we now see? He was dead to all sense of honor: and much in a like vein.[3]

His well wishers and supporters soon were put to the trouble of coming to his defence. Even a little was gratifying to the Southern people; a little was a signal for jubilation among the conservatives in the North. Chase's going South was to these men only an excursion with a view to advertising his own opinions, and creating a division in the party which might accrue to his personal advantage as a perennial candidate for the Presidency. He was assembling delegates for the nominating convention in 1868.[4] In vain did Sumner aim to create the impression that the journey had been undertaken with Mr. Johnson's personal approval to promote negro suffrage.[5] To the conservatives what Chase and Sumner together were doing to make the negroes believe that they could have no security in freedom without the ballot was monstrous. It must lead to "a bloody social war between the races in the South." [6]

[1] N. Y. Tribune, May 8, 1865.

[2] Ibid., June 2; Phila. Press, June 1; N. Y. Herald, June 2, 1865.

[3] Johnson Papers for May and June, 1865.

[4] Ibid.

[5] Pierce, vol. iv, p. 254.

[6] N. Y. Herald, June 1, 1865.

The Copperhead "eulogy" of Johnson in the North, as in the New York World, and by "the five dollar per month fossils of the Silurian era in Virginia," and in other Southern states, made Greeley very uncomfortable. He must defend a Republican President, but this President was beginning to be viewed favorably by men whom he had taught himself, and the people of quick consciences from New England to the Mississippi, to hate as the minions of the Evil One.[1] During the war the World had never wearied of calling Johnson "the insolent brute" of Tennessee, "a vulgar, low-bred boor" and other names as unflattering to his person and his opinions. Now there were expressions of approval in the columns of this paper,[2] which deeply disturbed the editor of the Tribune. The Baltimore American asked the conservatives not to believe that the Republican party was "split." Let them note how definite the President had been in his hostility to everything which looked to a rekindling of "the embers of slavery."[3] In proof of his devotion the Philadelphia Press cited his firm course in regard to the execution of Lincoln's assassins. Had he not hanged them? He was doing his duty in spite of "persistent and pestilent malevolence."[4]

The displeasure of the radicals was increased in the summer by the tactless courses of some of Johnson's Southern governors. B. F. Perry of South Carolina had offended more openly than any. In July, in his home in Greenville, he spoke to an assemblage of his friends and neighbors in terms which at once were commented on with great disfavor in all parts of the North. He reminded the people that the Southern states had spent three thousand millions of dollars in the war; they must now give up four million slaves, which meant a pecuniary sacrifice of two thousand millions more. Their lands had been

---

[1] N. Y. Tribune, June 30, 1865.

[2] Called out by his words to the South Carolina delegation on June 24, 1865. Editorial opinions on this subject in the N. Y. World, N. Y. Express, N. Y. Herald and other newspapers reprinted in Phila. Press, June 28 and 29, 1865.

[3] Quoted in Phila. Press, June 29.

[4] Phila. Press, July 7.

desolated; their cities and towns were smouldering ruins. No man in South Carolina had done more than he to avert this fate for his state, but none could feel "more bitterly the humiliation and degradation of going back into the Union." In the death of Lincoln they had suffered no great loss; in Johnson, born in the South, of antecedents inclining him to Democratic and state rights' views they could hope to find a friend.

What treason was this? What might not be expected of Johnson's governors, Greeley inquired, if they were made of such feeble stuff?[1] Here was a man who had been chosen governor because it was believed that he was "the only genuine Unionist" in South Carolina.[2] What, it could be fairly asked, was the condition of mind of the rest of the people of the state?

But with these not very deep disturbances upon the surface of affairs the summer passed. The governors were playing their assigned parts in arranging for the election of delegates to the constitutional conventions. The President was making every effort to acquaint himself with social and economic conditions in the South and with the temper of the people. He had spoken fairly to Chase upon the eve of the Chief Justice's departure, and asked men as widely different in their habits of mind as Carl Schurz, a German-American soldier, who had risen to be a general in the Union army; Harvey M. Watterson, a Southern Unionist,[3] and Benjamin C. Truman, a correspondent of the New York Times, while travelling through the country, to render him reports of their observations. Some went out as his authorized agents, while others volunteered their advice in conversation and by correspondence.

If the course of events were not to the mind of Chase, Sumner, Stevens and Wade, it gave no grave dissatisfaction to the main body of the people of the North, no matter what their party

[1] N. Y. Tribune, July 20.
[2] Phila. Press, July 21.
[3] Whose son, Henry Watterson, had been in the Confederate army — in later years editor of the Louisville Courier Journal.

attachments, and there was belief that a policy which would lead to an early restoration of the Union had been inaugurated. Senator Dixon of Connecticut wrote in August that "the thinking, calm, honest, unselfish masses" earnestly approved the President's course. They would support it with "zeal and energy" in a manner which had never been witnessed "except, perhaps, in the case of Washington."[1] For every "Chase radical who leaves you," said Lewis D. Campbell, writing to the President from Ohio, "at least ten fair-minded Democrats will flock to your standard."[2] Although Thaddeus Stevens in July had not met one loyal person, so he alleged, who indorsed the President's policy, Senator Doolittle in September declared that two-thirds of all the members of the Republican or Union party stood ready to do so,[3] while Senator Dixon in a further statement of his opinions thought that the number would be three-fourths "at least." It was Johnson's part to make himself "the great pacificator of this bleeding and distracted country," and in the performance of his duty he would be "nobly and triumphantly sustained."[4] A few days later Dixon found that the "sentiment of approbation" for the President was growing into the "warmth of admiration." The day of "radical fanaticism" was done. Justice for the negro was desired by the people, but they were "tired of the perpetual reiteration of his claims upon their attention."[5] Doolittle denounced "the infernal policy" of Sumner and Stevens toward the South. It was a struggle for the "constitutional Union of the states against concentration of power — of republicanism against imperialism" and it must succeed.[6] Four-fifths of the people of Ohio were on Johnson's side, said Campbell when he again wrote to the President.[7] George Bancroft declared that public opinion was "all" for Johnson.[8] A poet in New Hampshire put into homely verse the hope as well as

[1] Aug. 24, 1865. — This and the following references are to letters in the Johnson Papers.
[2] Aug. 21, 1865.
[3] Sept. 26, 1865.
[4] Sept. 26, 1865.
[5] Oct. 8, 1865.
[6] Oct. 10, 1865.
[7] Jan. 19, 1866.
[8] Dec. 1, 1865.

the conviction of a preponderating number of the people as
the year 1865 drew to a close —

> "With Andy we'll weather the storm,
> He's the man who can pilot us through;
> For his heart, it is honest and warm,
> And his head, it is steady and true."

CHAPTER II

THE news of the surrender of Lee's and Johnston's armies flew quickly from hamlet to hamlet and from plantation to plantation. The final collapse of the undertaking to create a separate government at the South was not unexpected by the large planters who were in the confidence of the leaders of the Confederacy. Yet while only one result in the end was to be anticipated, always there had been a hope that the humiliation might be averted by some miracle having its source possibly in Europe or in political divisions among the people at the North. The less intelligent from the first had been kept in a good deal of darkness concerning the progress of events. The always sluggish life of the South was now the more detached and separate from the world by reason of the blockade of the coasts, interrupted communication over the railroads, partial or complete paralysis of the telegraph lines, and the only very irregular reading of ill-informed newspapers. As for the numerous bodies of poor whites in the woods, and the negroes everywhere, they knew only what they might be told, and this was so twisted in the telling and the retelling, with the help of superstition, prejudice and fear, that the truth was not to be found. The coming of Sherman's army brought the idea of war to the people's very doors and, as was intended, filled with disgust for it those who might not yet have come into a full understanding of its awful character. They need not face the disaster until it actually had overtaken them. But the hour was now at hand and nothing stood between them and their fate.

As the news of the surrender spread over the country — it

did not reach the people of Texas until the end of April or the beginning of May [1] — those who had played leading parts in the Rebellion held their breaths in fear and indulged in the wildest apprehensions.[2] Some ran from plantation to plantation; others remained at their homes too much overwhelmed by the event to seek to escape. They were in complete panic and dejection, not knowing what horrible punishments would be meted out to them by the "Yankees," whom they so long had taught themselves to hate. They talked of the "Bloody Assizes" and already felt the halter around their necks.[3] Those who were not hanged would be imprisoned or banished. Their new "masters" were "thirsting" for their blood. Their "great revolution" was now an "unsuccessful rebellion." [4] No hope was indulged by any until President Johnson in May announced his policy regarding reconstruction and amnesty. Then little by little confidence returned and the people were ready to count their losses, face their ruin, look about them for the means of filling their mouths, and of meeting the many new and unwelcome problems which were the heritage of the war.

The eleven states which had seceded from the Union had a white population in 1860 of about 5,500,000. At the same time in these same states there were about 3,500,000 slaves.[5] Some persons had fled the Confederacy at the outbreak of hostilities, going North or to Europe. On the other hand, a number had come to aid it in its impending struggle for independence. It is computed that 258,000 men were killed, or died of wounds or disease on the Southern side while the war

[1] Southern Historical Society Papers, vol. xxiv, p. 42.

[2] Schurz, Report to President Johnson, Senate Ex. Doc., 39th Cong., 1st sess., no. 2, pp. 3–4.

[3] E. F. Andrews, The War Time Journal of a Georgia Girl, pp. 197–8; cf. Mrs. C. C. Clay, A Belle of the Fifties, p. 246; B. C. Truman's report, Senate Ex. Doc., 39th Cong., 1st sess., no. 43, p. 4.

[4] M. F. Maury Papers in Library of Congress. — Letters of May 18 and other dates in May, 1865.

[5] Adding the totals for Missouri, Kentucky, Maryland, Delaware and the District of Columbia the slave population of the United States in 1860 became 3,953,580.

was in progress.[1] If the rate of increase of the white population in such a state as South Carolina between the years 1850
and 1860 had been continued in the entire South during the
war, which is improbable, the births would have been not equal
to the deaths on military fields, and there would be besides, of
course, the mortality due to natural causes. It is likely, therefore, that less than 5,000,000 white persons resided in the seceded states in 1865 and upwards of 3,500,000 blacks.[2]

In 1860 the slave had exceeded the white population in two
states, South Carolina and Mississippi. In South Carolina
there were 291,000 white men, women and children, and 402,000
slaves; in Mississippi 353,000 whites and 436,000 slaves. In
twenty of the thirty counties of South Carolina and half the
counties of Mississippi the blacks were in a numerical preponder-
ance. In Florida there were only 16,000 fewer blacks than
whites, in Louisiana 26,000 and in Alabama 90,000. There
were only two white persons to one negro in Virginia and North
Carolina; only three in Tennessee. In many neighborhoods
in the South the blacks greatly outnumbered the whites — two
to one, three to one, four to one, and in a county in Louisiana
ten to one. In a county in Mississippi there were but 587
white persons and 7244 African slaves; in another county
1212 whites and 14,467 slaves. The negroes were gathered
together in large groups for industrial uses — in Mississippi,
Louisiana, Georgia and Alabama for the planting and picking
of cotton; in the lowlands of South Carolina and Georgia for
rice culture; in Virginia and Kentucky for the growth of
tobacco.

The entire South was a land of farms and plantations. It was
without mercantile or mechanical interests except as these
were tributary to agriculture. In 1860 New Orleans was a
city of 168,000 inhabitants and enjoyed something like a met-

[1] Rhodes, vol. v, p. 187, citing confusing accounts in T. L. Liver-
more, Numbers and Losses in the Civil War.

[2] Census Reports for 1860, which, however, were incorrect in their
details because of the outbreak of the war. The reports for 1870 are
accounted untrustworthy for other reasons.

rópolitan life. But it stood alone in this position. The next largest places within the limits of the Confederacy were Charleston with 40,000, and the capital, Richmond, in Virginia, with 38,000. Mobile contained only 29,000, Savannah 22,000, Memphis 22,000 and Norfolk 15,000 people. In Georgia, Augusta was a place of 12,000, Columbus 9000, Atlanta 9000 and Macon 8000. In Mississippi the most considerable towns were Natchez and Vicksburg, one with 6000, the other with 4000 people. In all there were only six places in the state containing a population of more than 1000. In North Carolina Wilmington had 9000, Newbern something more than 5000 and the capital, Raleigh, a few hundred less than 5000. Only thirteen places in North Carolina had as many as 1000 inhabitants. In Montgomery, the first capital of the Confederacy, which ranked next to Mobile among the cities of Alabama, but 8800 persons resided. In Texas, Galveston had but 7000 people. In Virginia, places so well known as Alexandria had a population of only 12,000, Lynchburg 7000 and Fredericksburg 5000. No town in Florida had as many as 3000 inhabitants; Tallahassee, the capital, contained less than 2000.

New England, Pennsylvania and Ohio could, if they liked, point to these conditions in the South as evidences of a primitive industrial civilization. Not a Northern state that did not number its towns and cities by the hundreds for economic reasons. The Southern people were scattered over the face of the land for the same reasons. They would have been swept out of existence by starvation if they had congregated in cities. Their life was bound up with the soil, and the negro was an agency to plant and tend and glean the crops which lay at the foundation of their welfare.

The number of very prosperous and wealthy planters was not large, but each state had such men. They frequently came of old families and possessed homes of comfort and beauty. The broad halls were furnished with taste and often elegantly. Out of them, as the history of the nation bears witness, came men of reading who contributed to the American reputation for statesmanship. Their incomes from cotton planting reached $100,000 and in some instances much more in a year. In summer they were seen with their families at Saratoga, Newport and other fashionable Northern watering places. They visited Washington and New York and held enviable positions in American society. Their intelligence, their large property interests, their superior abilities entitled them to occupy leading places in the direction of affairs in their respective counties and states. They had been Whigs and Democrats before the war; in 1860 they all together were borne into opposition to the new Republican party. The economic interests of the large landowners being then in jeopardy, as they believed, they forgot their past differences and joined hands in common defence. They had used all their influences in favor of the war, had supported it to the last extremity and now together they were downcast, hopeless and poor.

Living beside and among these large planters were the farmers who owned smaller tracts of land, and but a few slaves. They occupied a social position similar to that held by farmers in the same circumstances in the Northern states. It was a useful yeomanry, not so intelligent as it might well have been, but a respected and substantial element in the population of the South.

Below this class of small farmers there was a numerous and troublesome body of "poor whites," as miserable a tribe of human beings as ever dwelt within our national limits. These were the "sand-hillers," the "clay-eaters," the "crackers," the "tackies," the "piney-woods men," the "backwoods people," or whatever their local name, who usually lived on the higher lands and in the mountains, where some of them professed loyalty to the United States. The protection of these Union mountaineers was a subject of sentimental solicitude as well as a source of great expense to the North during the progress of the war. The poor whites hated the "big nigger-holder" and preyed upon his lands and his flocks. They hated the negro, and now that he was released from his old master's care were ready to hunt him like an animal. "They are, I suppose," wrote Mrs. Fanny Kemble Butler before the war, "the most degraded race of human beings claiming an Anglo-Saxon origin that can be found on the face of the earth, — filthy, lazy, ignorant, brutal, proud, penniless savages." They squatted and stole and starved on the outskirts of society.[1]

Such a civilization was essentially patriarchal, feudal and coarse, and it had exhibited few signs of improvement at the coming on of the war. The population increased but slowly under such economic restrictions, and the white, in the older Southern states, more slowly than the black race, which was encouraged to breed by the master class because of the commercial value of its progeny. In such states as Virginia and North Carolina there had been a considerable movement of negroes southward by sale. On the large cotton, rice and sugar plantations they served a greater purpose and commanded higher prices. The number annually sent from the upper to the lower slave states can never be given with accuracy. For Virginia it has been computed to have been about 20,000. From 1850 to 1860 there was an increase of 17.06 per cent in the white population of that state, of only 3.88 per cent in the slave population. It is demonstrable then that there was an important migratory movement from this state, for the rate of increase in the slave population of the whole South in the same period was 22 per cent.[2]

General education, the device by which many societies have been reorganized, received but sparing favor. The teaching of the slaves was forbidden by law. That they should learn even so much as to be able to read and write was not desired; it meant their dissatisfaction as laborers. There was most inadequate provision for the education of the "poor whites." Their dense ignorance as a class was due to their indisposition to be taught, but also to the failure of the wealthy planter class to bring schools within their reach. In 1860 South Carolina with a population of 703,000 had only 20,000 children in public schools; Mississippi with 791,000 only 31,000 public

[1] Journal of a Residence on a Georgia Plantation, p. 146.
[2] Census Reports for 1860, pp. vi, ix.

school children; Louisiana with 708,000 only 32,000; Georgia with 1,057,000 only 56,000. In Alabama but one in 16 of the state's inhabitants attended public schools; in Virginia one in 19. Leaving the slave population out of account, usually only one in 10 or 11 persons received public instruction in the Southern states.

On the other hand, such a Northern state as Pennsylvania with 2,906,000 people had 565,000 children in the public schools; Ohio with 2,400,000, 590,000; Illinois with 1,711,000, 433,000; while in Massachusetts 1,231,000 people furnished 206,000 children to be educated at the common expense. In the North one in every five or six persons attended a public school. The little state of Rhode Island with a population of only 174,000 souls had more children in public schools than South Carolina. Connecticut and Vermont each educated at common expense only a few thousand pupils fewer than the great Southern state of Virginia.[1]

The church also, if it were to be judged by its works, had succeeded in performing no very noble part in the reformation of the society committed to its care. It stolidly reflected the morals of the people in reference to African slavery, and not a few high ecclesiastical prelates at the end of the war distinguished themselves by openly deploring its outcome.[2] The religious "howlings" of the negroes testified to the small progress of the church as a civilizing influence in their ranks; while those denominations which wrought with the souls of the "poor whites" could point to no proud achievements in the reformation of the manners of that benighted people. So rude a civilization, which appeared to be without the means of accomplishing its own regeneration, in the view of many, abundantly

[1] Census Reports, vol. on Mortality and Misc. Statistics, pp. 502 et seq. It is clear, of course, from books descriptive of plantation life before the war that children in wealthy families in the South received private instruction. But this was the case, too, in the North.

[2] Whitaker, Life of Bishop Wilmer, pp. 123, 129. Bishop Green of Mississippi in refusing to pray for the President of the United States said that to do so would be to wish "the success and continuance of a domination which even in its mildest forms is repugnant to the spirit of the people." — Phila. Ledger, Aug. 4, 1865.

needed cure, even though the remedy should assume the
dimensions of a great war.

Now wreck, ruin, starvation were on every side. The ground
over which the contending armies had fought in Virginia was
a waste. Around Petersburg farmers could not plough the
land for the iron which had been belched out here week after
week, and still lay where it had fallen from the guns. The
blood-soaked soil and the dead animals emitted sickening
vapors which only the frosts of autumn could dispel.[1] The
rich Shenandoah Valley had been stripped. Both Federals
and Confederates had swept it from end to end repeatedly,
the final hand having been Sheridan's. He and his "barn-
burners" were to render the country such a waste that "a
crow could not fly over it without carrying his rations with
him." [2] Barns, mills and other buildings were heaps of ashes.
A garden had become a desert.[3] The country lying between
Washington and Richmond was in the same condition. The
villages were represented by solitary chimneys standing over
cellars filled with the wreckage of fire. Churches were down,
timber had disappeared, farming land, untended, had returned
to pasturage.[4] Between Alexandria and Charlottesville the
condition of the country, said Alexander H. Stephens when
he passed through it in October, was "horrible to behold." [5]
Richmond was a mass of blackened ruins. Many of the plantation houses falling within the area of Federal occupation had
been prey of the torch. Arlington, the beautiful Custis home
near Washington, where General Lee had dwelt, was only a
shell. Its precious contents had been dispersed. The fine
groves had been cut down for firewood; its lawns had been
converted into a soldiers' cemetery.

Sherman's army, on its way to the sea through Georgia
and the Carolinas, had swept that part of the South so bare
that it was almost without living reminders of human civiliza-

---

[1] Mrs. Roger A. Pryor, Reminiscences of Peace and War, p. 394.
[2] Southern Historical Society Papers, vol. xxviii, p. 98.
[3] N. Y. Tribune, June 20, 1865.
[4] Ibid., July 17, 1865.
[5] Recollections of A. H. Stephens, p. 537.

tion. "You can have no idea of the desolation of this country,"
wrote a Northern visitor to South Carolina. The stores had
been closed since 1861. The roads had known no recent attention and were unfit for teams. The railways had been torn
up. The irons were twisted around trees and telegraph poles,
and the sleepers had been burned.[1] Everything edible had been
eaten, and property had been stolen or destroyed from the Mississippi River to the seaboard. It was as though Attila had
come back into the world to lead across the South an army
of his Vandals and Huns. Alexander H. Stephens pronounced
the desolation "heart sickening." [2] The entire portion of
Atlanta devoted to business, barring one block of buildings,
had been laid in ruins. Masses of bricks and mortar, discolored
by fire and smoke, charred timber, scraps of tin roofing and
rubbish of all sorts and shapes, spoke of Sherman's visit to this
place. Cannon balls and long shot lay in the streets.[3] Columbia, the capital of South Carolina, which its inhabitants before
the war were ready to declare the most beautiful city on the
continent, and which had become the place of refuge for many
of the people and much of the treasure of South Carolina,
because of its imagined security by reason of its situation, was
now "a wilderness of ruins." The heart of the town was "but
a mass of blackened chimneys and crumbling walls." For
"three-fourths of a mile on each of twelve streets" not a building had escaped the flames.[4] The fire had swept 84 blocks
of houses, consuming in all 1386 buildings.[5] The trees which
had lined the side-walks were rows of dead trunks.[6] The city
stood "like Tadmor alone in the desert." [7] No railroad entered

[1] N. Y. Tribune, Sept. 30, 1865.

[2] Recollections, p. 539.

[3] Sidney Andrews, The South Since the War, p. 339. "Hell has
laid her egg," said a Georgian, surveying the scene in Atlanta, "and
right here it hatched." — N. Y. Tribune, July 25, 1865.

[4] Sidney Andrews, p. 33.

[5] J. P. Hollis, The Early Period of Reconstruction in South Carolina,
Johns Hopkins Studies, 1905, p. 23; Return of a Refugee in Southern
Historical Society Papers, vol. xiii, p. 502.

[6] N. Y. Nation, vol. i, p. 812.

[7] Ibid., p. 106.

it, though five had formerly done so. The end of one was 32
miles away, of another 30, another 45, a fourth 50, and a fifth
29.[1] The entire railway system in this part of the South had
been broken up, and the work was so well done that the very
iron in the tracks was now not to be found.[2] On the road
between Augusta and Atlanta hundreds of cars and locomotives
had been run off on timber rails, and stood in the fields where
whites and blacks used them as dwellings.[3]

Charleston had been bombarded and burned. It was, said
a visitor from the North in September, five months after the
war had ended, "a city of ruins, of desolation, of vacant houses,
of widowed women, of rotting wharves, of deserted warehouses,
of weed-wild gardens, of miles of grass-grown streets, of acres
of pitiful and voiceless barrenness." [4] The wharves were
overgrown with a rank plant which caused them to look like
a great swamp. Army mules grazed in the streets.[5] The
proudest men and the fairest ladies of the South no longer
walked its beautiful Promenade at the waterside, or assembled
on the Race Course, which had become the site of an army
prison camp and was now filled with countless Northern soldiers' graves. The fashionable and aristocratic life of the city
which had found its centre in St. Michael's Church was no
more. The edifice had been struck six times during the various
Union bombardments. Once rich men's homes, embowered
in the bloom of rose, jessamine and myrtle, now a wilderness,
also bore the destructive marks of the siege.

The splendid country homes of South Carolina, as of Virginia, had been confiscated or burned. Such seats as Ashley
Hall, Middleton Place and the Porcher House were in ashes.[6]
On the fertile Sea Islands, whence the owners had fled before
the Union troops in the first months of the war, army officers

[1] Sidney Andrews, p. 29.
[2] Ibid., p. 31. "Miles and miles of iron," said a South Carolinian,
had entirely disappeared; it had "gone out of existence."
[3] N. Y. Tribune, July 22, 1865.
[4] Sidney Andrews, p. 1.
[5] Carl Schurz, Reminiscences, vol. iii, p. 165.
[6] N. Y. Nation, vol. i, p. 172.

had settled their wives and children in the fine old plantation houses, or had converted them into military headquarters. The libraries had been pillaged and even family portraits, adjudged fair prizes, were sent away, so the South said, to adorn the walls of the homes of vandal Northern generals. By Sherman's orders the appertaining lands had been divided among the Congo negroes whom the masters left behind them in their flight.

In material damage New Orleans had suffered less than Charleston, Richmond and the smaller cities of the Confederacy, but the spirit of the people had been broken. English, French, Spanish, Creole, the Georgian and Circassian beauties, with scarcely a distinguishable trace of their distant black ancestry — such creatures as Chief Justice Chase saw gathered together at a fair in Senator Soulé's confiscated home — quadroons, mulattoes, negroes — all were still here.[1] But the old social order had been changed. The life of the city now was dominated by Federal soldiers and Northern cotton jobbers. Always dissolute, its moral reputation had not been improved by the war. Dire want had driven many women to the streets. The St. Charles Hotel, once a gay and fashionable place of entertainment, was a shabby third-rate hotel. Pigeons perched in the capitals of the double columns which graced its portico. In its great rotunda, where the "princes of the Mississippi," the rich young planters from fine houses up the river, had been wont to assemble, deferred to by crowds of black servants as they lavishly cast about their money, were now only broken Confederate soldiers, home from the war, and United States officers on garrison duty. The French market, whither so many had come in the mornings, often as early as four o'clock, to chatter and chaffer, to sip a cup of coffee with a friend, to see and to be seen, was still a place to be visited, but its glories were gone.[2]

In Mobile the planks had been torn from the tops of the levees to be burned for firewood. The wharves were rotting in the rain and sun. Buzzards hovered over them in clouds.

[1] Whitelaw Reid, After the War, pp. 243–4.
[2] N. Y. Tribune, June 26, 1865.

Half the warehouses and shops were closed.   Torpor and decay reigned on every hand.[1]   Hundreds of "ill-looking men" infested the "narrow and dirty streets." [2]

A New York Tribune correspondent found Galveston "a city of dogs and desolation."   He thought "no other city of its prominence so utterly insignificant and God-forsaken in appearance."   Houses and stores had been sacked, and ruin was written over everything.[3]

So it was on every hand.   The serpent slipped through the brush, the owl and the bittern cried over fields in which valuable crops had once been gleaned.   "Our rich have become poor and our poor beggars," a Southerner told a company of Northern men in Richmond.   "Our soil has been desolated by contending armies till there are no crops in the ground, few houses fit to live in, no fences and no timber to make any.   In a single night our currency perished in our hands, losing even its pitiful price of five cents on the dollar.   I know families, yes, families heretofore comfortable and even rich who would thank you for a supper of corn meal." [4]

General M. C. Butler came out of the war with but one leg, and a wife and three children dependent upon him for support. His seventy slaves were emancipated.   He had debts of $15,000 and only $1.75 in his pockets.[5]

A young lady who returned home from school in a carriage, because the railways were broken up, stopped at night at the plantation houses on her way.   She found "only corn bread and sassafras tea at one place; no servants to render attention; silver gone; family portraits punctured by bayonets; furniture and mirrors broken."   Reaching home there were no servants; all but an old Mammy had gone to the city.[6]

Another Southern woman had never made ready a meal in her life.   One morning she woke to find all the negroes gone.

[1] Reid, p. 205.
[2] N. Y. Nation, vol. ii, p. 268.
[3] N. Y. Tribune, July 7, 1865.
[4] Phila. Press, May 4, 1865.
[5] M. L. Avary, Dixie after the War, p. 161.
[6] Ibid., p. 188.

One cow was left, but this she knew not how to milk. In still another home a lady now without servants set her sons to cooking. In the army they had learned an art she had never acquired.[1]

The daughter of Judge Andrews in Georgia could not have paid the postage on a letter, if it had been necessary for her to write one.[2] General Yorke of Louisiana, who had had 30,000 acres of land and 900 negroes in that state, besides plantations in Texas, found himself in Georgia without money enough to pay his way home.[3]

A man living in Georgia wrote to Horace Greeley. He did not have a cent of money in his pocket. "If there were a toll bridge between me and Atlanta," said he, "I would have to swim the river to get to town."[4] A neighbor had had 45 negroes on the morning of the 25th of May; at night he milked his own cow and his wife cooked their supper.

A lady in North Carolina owned three plantations and 300 negroes. She had given gold and silver for $200,000 worth of Confederate bonds, had three times gone up to Richmond to see President Davis to assure him of her devotion to the Southern cause and had poured out her rich store of corn and tobacco year after year to support the war. She had left now nothing but the hungry negroes, whom somehow she must employ in freedom for the raising of new crops.[5]

Everywhere the same pitiful story was heard. Carpets were in tatters, or had gone to make army blankets. Pianos, which had not been cut to pieces with axes in the hands of Sherman's "bummers," jangled; they had not been tuned in five years. Clocks had stopped; there were no clockmakers to keep them in repair. Furniture was broken and sat unsteadily on its legs. Windows were uncurtained; the stuffs had been taken down and converted into articles of clothing. Not a complete set of dishes could be seen. Pieces were miss-

[1] M. L. Avary, p. 189.
[2] E. F. Andrews, The War Time Journal of a Georgia Girl, p. 230.
[3] Ibid., p. 222.
[4] N. Y. Tribune, Sept. 1, 1865.
[5] Ibid., Sept. 4.

ing from cups and plates; others were shabbily held together by cement. Many were eating from gourds. Hair and tooth brushes long ago had worn out and the use of them had been abandoned. Pins and needles were so scarce that they were lent about and returned. Few men any longer had pocket knives. Earthen mugs made out of local clays were seen instead of water glasses. When candles ceased to be procurable, light came from cups of pigs' grease with cloth wicks in them. Prongs were broken out of forks. In the hotels there were not enough chairs for the guests. They must sit down in turn. When the glass in windows was broken, boards had been set into the open sashes to keep out the wind and rain.

The people dressed "in styles enough to drive a tailor crazy." [1] The spinning wheel had been humming in cabins all over the South throughout the war, and there were a few small weaving mills at Macon and other places. The cotton yarn had been dyed with vegetable juices and colored clays, and even the once wealthy were wearing garments rudely made of a cloth which before the war would have been accounted scarcely fit to cover a negro. To this were added ancient and discarded garments of every period taken out of old cupboards and chests.[2] The returned soldiers continued to use their gray uniforms because they had nothing else to put on. Ladies who could no longer make over their old bonnets plaited native straw and of the braid devised hats which were trimmed with rosettes of corn shucks. Their shoes were coarse and large, fashioned of roughly tanned hides by plantation cobblers, or were of cloth, knit perhaps by hands made deft by enforced practice. The crinoline which the female world in Europe and at the North wore at this period was foresworn, though sometimes a substitute for the iron hoops was found in the pliant branches of the willow tree. The new chignon, called a "waterfall," and various other vagaries of fashion, revealed to the Southern ladies at the end of the war, seemed as strange to them as though they had been for four years in prison.

[1] Sidney Andrews, p. 226.
[2] E. F. Andrews, The War Time Journal of a Georgia Girl, p. 333.

But all such deprivations could be endured; it was only the scarcity of food and the imminence of starvation which threatened really fearful consequences. In Richmond, two weeks after the occupation of the city, according to General Ord's reports to Secretary Stanton, there were thousands of paroled soldiers of Lee's army unable to proceed to their homes, and 25,000 women and children "of all colors" without money or food. He was opening shops wherein women could be employed in the Quartermaster's Department in making shirts and pantaloons for the negro troops in Texas. He was devising the means to utilize the services, or to send away other destitute persons. "We cannot afford," said he, "to feed them in idleness." A number of well-known Confederate generals and "many prominent and formerly wealthy citizens" were asking what they could do to earn their bread.[1]

To make a bad situation worse in Virginia, and throughout the South, the negroes were leaving the plantations and were flocking into the military posts. False counsellors had filled them with a belief that, being now free, something was about to happen to them to make the work which had been the curse of Ham in America no longer necessary to their lives. In South Carolina there was a general movement of the deluded people toward the seacoast, where they had been told lands would be distributed among them. Beyond the Mississippi also, in Arkansas and Texas, the negroes were moving about restlessly.[2] Indeed they were met with in crowds "like packs of gypsies" in all the roads, "some going to one place and some to another," without an idea of how they would exist when they came to their journeys' end.[3]

In North Carolina they were "occupying every hovel and shanty . . . crowding into the towns and literally swarming about every depot of supplies." Many were dying for "want of proper food and medical supplies."[4] They were rapidly

[1] O. R., series i, vol. xlvi, part iii, p. 835; cf. N. Y. Tribune, July 7.
[2] Ibid., vol. xlviii, part ii, p. 980.
[3] N. Y. Nation, vol. i, p. 426; cf. E. F. Andrews, The War Time Journal of a Georgia Girl, pp. 322, 331-2, 340.
[4] Senate Ex. Doc., 39th Cong., 1st sess., no. 27, p. 159.

becoming a tribe of vagabonds and thieves, subsisting upon berries and what they could beg or steal, a veritable menace to the whole countryside. Others believed that they had acquired with their new liberties some indefeasible right to the property of their former masters, and would visit the garrison towns to make inquiry of the officers. "Only by their sufferance" could the owner continue to live in his old home and till his acres.[1] They were "much astonished" when they were informed that freedom did not mean that they were "to live in idleness and be fed by the government."[2]

In Richmond a Relief Commission was formed with Colonel Adam Badeau as its president. So great was the need of its services in behalf of the starving that the city was divided into thirty districts. The homes of the people were visited, and, if they were in distress, ration tickets were issued. These, when they were presented, would entitle the bearer to pork, or fish and corn meal, to beef, flour, sugar and tea. From the time the Federal army entered the city up to April 21, 128,132 rations had been given out by the commissaries of Richmond.[3] General Dent wrote from the city to Grant on May 2: "There is a starving multitude here." Some had money to feed themselves, but there was no food for sale.[4] Twenty thousand negroes were in the town, "mostly idle and destitute."[5] On June 22 General Halleck said that the number had increased to 30,000 or 35,000. Hereafter they would not be permitted to come into the city, since already far more were there than could find employment.[6] General McKibbin in Petersburg, to relieve the destitution among the freedmen in the counties in his district, despatched 200 soldiers to each county town. There, at the court-house, barracks were to be built to shelter the negroes, and they would be set to work on a government farm. He asked

---

[1] O. R., series i, vol. xlvi, part iii, p. 932.
[2] Ibid., vol. xlvii, part iii, p. 461.
[3] Ibid., vol. xlvi, part iii, p. 882.
[4] Ibid., p. 1069.
[5] General Halleck to General Grant under date of May 3, ibid., p. 1073.
[6] Ibid., p. 1291; cf. ibid., p. 1295.

the War Department for ploughs, hoes, harness, spades, axes, picks, wagons, tents, camp kettles, mess-pans, potatoes, beans, peas, travelling forges.[1] Still in July one-half the people of Richmond were drawing rations from the government.[2]

Farther south the destitution of the inhabitants, both white and black, was even greater than in Virginia. Nowhere was there such pinching want as in South Carolina and Georgia. In the interior what had not been taken to support the Southern armies had fallen a prey to Sherman's scourging hosts. These were followed by the disbanded Confederate troops released from discipline, penniless and starving, and ready for plunder in places where anything yet remained for their use.[3] Then Union cavalrymen, hunting for state prisoners and on other errands, came to commit new thefts and to destroy more property.[4] The rich were eating cowpeas, earlier thought fit only for cattle; the poor in these terrible weeks were in a far worse situation.

The Confederates, upon evacuating Charleston, had left a quantity of rice, enough, it was computed, to support the people of the city for two months. But there was such an influx of whites and blacks after the surrender of the armies that Colonel Gurney, in command, thought the supply would not hold out until May 1. He appealed to the president of the New York Produce Exchange for money, food and clothing "in the name of humanity." If aid were not soon received, the "suffering and destitution" would be terrible.[5] A sister of mercy in Charleston pictured the life behind doors in the homes of families once opulent. Women, "with eyes swimming" in tears, were silently suffering the greatest miseries. Without food, without medicines, without servants, their condition called for the sympathy of the world.[6]

[1] Ibid., p. 1159.
[2] N. Y. Nation, vol. i, p. 136.
[3] For what happened in Georgia late in April and early in May see Andrews, The War Time Journal of a Georgia Girl, p. 207.
[4] Ibid., pp. 221, 226, 259, 261.
[5] O. R., series i, vol. xlvii, part iii, pp. 94–5.
[6] Phila. Ledger, Sept. 19, 1865.

It was believed that the people must depart Columbia, the ruined capital of South Carolina. "Thus plundered by man it might fairly be assumed to be abandoned of God." There in June 10,000 people daily were being fed by the government. They crowded around the ration house, clinging to its porches, waiting for the doors to open.[1]

Still worse was it in and around Atlanta. At the end of May General Winslow said that from 25,000 to 50,000 people in ten counties of the state of Georgia were in utter destitution. Women and children walked distances of ten, and even forty miles, to get enough corn and bacon to sustain life.[2] The roads by day and by night were filled with hungry refugees. For the week ending June 10, 45,000 pounds of meat, 45,000 pounds of meal and 10,000 pounds of flour were issued to the poor in Atlanta, and not one-fourth of those who needed relief could be supplied.[3] On June 21 General Winslow reported that not less than 800 bushels of corn and 30,000 pounds of meat were required daily to feed the starving in the Atlanta district.[4]

Pitiful scenes were enacted around the court-house where the rations were given out. A New York Tribune correspondent saw 1000 women literally fighting to get into the building. Five had been smothered or trampled on in the crowds. Many were poor, wild creatures from the wood, dressed in coarse, dirty, homespun cloth, pictures of wretchedness and squalor. Ladies from once comfortable homes, whose wants were not less real, looked on at the struggling mob. Men with small carts, each drawn by an ox, stood by also. One said that he had come here four times for food, but that yet he had received nothing. He and his wife had been subsisting on wheat bran for five days. "God help us," he cried, "or we shall die." Another was the owner of 300 acres of land; he had had five slaves. They, as well as the members of his family, would starve unless they could be supplied with food from the ration

[1] N. Y. Tribune, June 24, 1865, citing the Augusta Transcript, which in turn cited the Columbia Phœnix.

[2] O. R., series i, vol. xlix, part ii, pp. 939, 945, 949.

[3] Ibid., p. 1002.

[4] Ibid., p. 1020.

house.[1] Fifteen negroes, it was said, had died of starvation near Macon, Ga.[2]

A New York Tribune correspondent, on horseback fifty miles out of Raleigh, in North Carolina, met a woman who was going to that place for food for herself, her husband, a wounded soldier of the war, and their two children.[3] At Talladega, in Alabama, at the end of May, 5000 persons were being fed from the army stores.[4]

The first impulse of many of the returning Confederate soldiers, as they viewed the ruin around them, was to flee the country. The disaster seemed too great to be faced. Suicide was not unknown. A man whose wealth had been invested in negroes and Confederate bonds, neither of which were now worth a cent, walked into a store in Lynchburg and shot himself.[5] Foreign colonies were projected and arrangements were made for early departure to them. Mexico was in many men's minds, because of the formation of Maximilian's empire, while the American Civil War had been in progress, and a belief that armed intervention on the part of the United States would soon ensue. The pursuit of arms by constant exercise during four years had become something like a profession to not a few men, both North and South. The quiet of an Illinois farm or a Mississippi plantation was an unwelcome prospect to many, who so long had known the excitement of active military service.

Ex-Senator William M. Gwin of California, after he was released from a United States prison, where he had rested for two years under a charge of treason, went to France before the war was yet done, and entered into arrangements with the Emperor Louis Napoleon for a great speculative colonial enterprise in Mexico. Some said that he would return a viceroy or a duke. Senator Pierre Soulé of Louisiana and others associated their fortunes with his, and four of Mexico's richest states (Sonora, Sinaloa, Chihuahua and Durango) were to be

[1] N. Y. Tribune, July 25, 1865.
[2] Phila. Ledger, June 19, 1865.
[3] N. Y. Tribune, Aug. 2, 1865.
[4] O. R., series i, vol. xlix, part ii, p. 947.
[5] N. Y. Tribune, July 11, 1865.

set aside for colonists from the Southern states of America. The emigrants would have the protection of 10,000 veteran Confederate soldiers to be kept under arms at the risk and expense of Maximilian. But the Emperor of Mexico failed to ratify the bargain with "Duke" Gwin, and the great scheme fell to the ground.

Other plans appeared, with similar ends in view. A number of prominent Confederate leaders had taken refuge in Mexico City — Commander M. F. Maury, General John B. Magruder, ex-Governor Isham G. Harris of Tennessee, ex-Governors Polk and Reynolds of Missouri, ex-Governors Murrah and Clark of Texas, ex-Governor Allen of Louisiana, Generals J. O. Shelby and Sterling Price of Missouri, Generals Hardeman and Terry of Texas and many lesser Confederate figures, intent upon military service or residence.[1]

Maury was appointed Imperial Commissioner of Colonization and an Honorary Councillor of State. He had quit the land of his nativity "to avoid the humiliation and contamination of the infamous people" who now had their heel upon his "prostrate but noble countrymen." He would plant his posterity where it would be "free from the hand of oppression." For this irreconcilable man Virginia was only a memory. He had loved her, but she was now to him as one of his own dead. He would rescue the spirit, but the body could be put out of his sight. The spirit of Virginia resided in her people, not in her hills and streams, and they were invited to come away to the "New Virginia" which he would found in Mexico. It was a land "flowing with milk and honey." They would be received with open arms, for not since the revocation of the Edict of Nantes had such a class of people been found willing to expatriate themselves. It was "Ho for Mexico!" in many a prospectus issued with the favor of Maximilian and his Empress Carlotta, with both of whom Maury stood in the friendliest relationship.

But the response in Virginia was sparing and slow. One thought that 3000 or 4000 persons drawn from the "first fami-

[1] Senate Ex. Doc., 39th Cong., 1st sess., no. 8.

lies" would start away in a month. But most men hesitated when they did not condemn the scheme straightway. "Nobody wants to go where you are," they wrote him; "it is an uncivilized and unsettled country." The "Yankees" were coming before long to whip him and "Max" out of their boots. Maury pretended to think that the government in Mexico was not only enlightened, but also stable and strong. As for it being unsafe to live there, he said that the doors of his house were without locks. He did not even shut them before he went to bed at night. The first shock of disgust of the Virginians, following the "occupation" of the state, as they called the coming of the Yankees, gave place to calmer feelings. There was surprise, one wrote to Maury, that the people were "settling themselves down so quietly, so composedly and so contentedly." After President Johnson's policies promised to be kindly, even those who had thought that their position at home would be too unhappy to be borne soon gave up any design to emigrate which they may have entertained. The colonists were to carry their negroes with them, for the first families of Virginia were not to toil with their own hands on their new lands. The blacks were unwilling to accompany their old masters out of the country. Radicals in the North did not scruple to say that Maury's apprenticeship system was nothing but "slavery in disguise."

Even his wife and daughters begged that he seek some lucrative post in Europe "till Herod was dead," when he could return home. They were wholly indisposed to go to him in such a place though they were diligently studying Spanish and reading "The Conquest of Mexico" in the expectation that they soon must do so. But a son, Colonel Richard L. Maury, just home from the war, in which he had been severely wounded, was ready to follow his father.[1] Finally Mrs.

[1] " What I desire," said this young man, " is complete separation from the scoundrels — every one, man, woman and child, never to hear anything from them again except their downfall into anarchy and confusion." And the Colonel's wife in the same spirit of zeal prayed God to be led away to some country where her boy could be reared " to the happy consciousness of never having been under Yankee rule," and

Maury, though she at first had loathed the very name of Mexico, after a few weeks' experience with "free nigger servants," said that she would be glad to go any whither. She and her family embarked for England and Maury went to London to meet them. He had left Mexico, never to return. In his absence he received a letter from Maximilian announcing the abolition of his office. Economy required it. He was offered another position for which his unusual scientific training would have fitted him and the Grand Cross of the Order of Guadalupe. He declined both, though he would be "again without home or country," with expressions of deep concern for the success of the Emperor's most noble undertaking to give a worthy government to the Mexican people. His son's farm, which he concluded was not "worth anything anyhow," was seized by the Liberals and the folly was done.[1]

Other expatriates had no happier experiences. General Magruder, who had been chief of the Mexican Land Office; General Price, Senator Harris, Judge Perkins and General Hardeman, who were land agents, had striven as Maury, more or less unsuccessfully, to induce immigration from various parts of the South. A considerable number of those who had been persuaded to come out had settled in Chihuahua, San Luis Potosi and Jalisco, but principally at Carlotta near Cordova. That town was reborn after the arrival of the Southern exiles. In a week the place had American hotels, livery stables, hacks and factories. The valleys filled, and settlements extended outward for a distance of thirty miles, but soon it was seen that Maximilian's power was near its end. The scheme was a huge swindle. In February, 1867, the last two families left Carlotta to its fate. Only tenantless houses, weedy gardens, ploughs, axes and hoes rusting in the ground remained to tell of the colonists' unrealized hopes.[2] Everywhere the pique of the

where he might breathe an air "untainted by the presence" of the hated foe.

[1] M. F. Maury Papers in Library of Congress.

[2] Senate Ex. Doc., 40th Cong., 1st sess., no. 20, pp. 144-9; cf. Annual Cyclopedia for 1865, p. 562.

leaders wore away, and the tide of disappointed men swept back into the United States.

A party of refugees with farming utensils and enough provisions to support them for six months left Alabama for Para in Brazil, where a colony was to be established on a branch of the Amazon River.[1] Others departed to try sheep farming on the pastures of the River Plate.[2] The movement to Brazil continued with the guidance of land jobbers throughout the summer and included a number of officers who had the intention of enlisting under Dom Pedro in his war with Paraguay.[3]

The two men most generally respected and loved in the South after the war were Robert E. Lee and Wade Hampton.[4] Their counsel was sought and their example was accounted worthy to be followed. Hampton frowned upon all the Mexican and Brazilian colonization schemes.[5] The desire to leave a country which had been "reduced to so deplorable a condition" he found to be as "widespread as it was natural." But the plight in which she now was should cause the true sons of South Carolina "to cling the more closely to her." He wished his fellow citizens to "devote their whole energies to the restoration of law and order, the reëstablishment of agriculture and commerce, the promotion of education and the rebuilding of our cities and dwellings which have been laid in ashes." [6]

Lee took a similar course. For the Maurys, father and son, General C. M. Wilcox, General J. A. Early, General Longstreet and others who had gone to or who were considering the subject of departure for Mexico he had the same words. He regretted their leaving their homes, if they already had done so; he discouraged the step, if it had not been undertaken. All should remain and "share the fate of their respective states." "The thought of abandoning the country and all that must be left in it is abhorrent to my feelings,"

1 Reid, After the War, p. 374.
2 M. F. Maury Papers.
3 Phila. Ledger, Sept. 30, 1865.
4 Southern correspondence, N. Y. Nation, vol. i, p. 524.
5 Ibid., p. 195.
6 N. Y. Tribune, Aug. 8, 1865, citing the Columbia Phœnix.

he said again, "and I prefer to struggle for its restoration. . . . The South requires the aid of her sons now more than at any period of her history." [1]

Everywhere plantations were offered for sale at preposterously low prices. Not only were their owners ready in many instances to depart the country, but they were in dire straits for money, and would sacrifice much to obtain it. Northern speculators were travelling through the South in search of bargains. A hundred acres four miles from Macon were offered for fifty cents an acre, and any desired amount of land in that neighborhood could have been purchased for $2 an acre.[2] In southwestern Georgia, near Columbus, land capable, it was said, of producing a bale of cotton (now worth $250) per acre was for sale at prices ranging from $3 to $9 per acre.[3] For the "richest estates" in North Carolina the owners asked from $1 to $10 an acre. They would sell and go North.[4] Virginia lands, worth $150 an acre before the war, could now be purchased for $2.[5] But such opportunities soon passed. The rich plantations fronting the Mississippi River from Memphis down, which could have been bought at first for $7 an acre, soon were being leased for that sum, and in a little while the rental prices rose to $12 and $14 an acre.[6] In Alabama, in September, the sale price of cotton land was only $5, but in November it was nearly $10, and was still rising. The Southern newspapers were filled with the advertisements of plantations, and many were put into the hands of Northern brokers for sale or rent.[7] The rich farms of the smitten Shenandoah Valley were seeking purchasers at $25 an acre.[8]

Much of the bitter dejection of the Southern people was due

[1] M. F. Maury Papers, Library of Congress; Mrs. Corbin's Life of M. F. Maury; J. W. Jones, Reminiscences of R. E. Lee, pp. 202 et seq.

[2] N. Y. Tribune, Aug. 2, 1865.

[3] Reid, After the War, p. 344.

[4] Phila. Ledger, June 17, 1865.

[5] Ibid., June 4, 1865.

[6] Reid, p. 414. Cf. N. Y. Tribune, Dec. 26, 1865, for conditions around Vicksburg.

[7] Reid, pp. 371–2.

[8] N. Y. Tribune, June 20, 1865.

to the belief that they could not live with the negro as a free man. Their proper course now, said their advisers, was to hire him as any free laborer would be hired and to pay him wages for his services under some kind of a contract system. The black man worked and was paid for his work, like a white man, in Pennsylvania, New York and Massachusetts; let him receive the same treatment in South Carolina, Georgia and Louisiana. But the task, difficult at best, was made the more so because the duty of facing it had come of a sudden to men who had no money and not even the seed, the implements or the animals to put in the crops from which money might later be had; and by the bitterness of feeling engendered in the war between the North which was now to command and the South which was to obey, as well as between the blacks and whites themselves within the boundaries of the late Confederacy.

Every Northern traveller, wherever he turned his steps after the war, heard the same judgment passed upon the negro by the Southern people. He would not work in freedom. God had made him lazy. As a slave he had done only that which he had been compelled to do. He must be sent to his tasks with an oath or a lick, and could be held at them only by like urging. Two or three niggers must be kept to do what one should have done. Were they, the Southern white people, who always had been surrounded by the blacks, and were now confronted with the duty of continuing in residence among them, to receive lessons from men at the North who probably had never seen a nigger except Fred Douglass? To counsel the South on such a subject must be regarded as a presumptuous proceeding. The invariable response to such a counsellor was that "You do not know the nigger," and while the speech was usually resented, since it came from "traitors," "rebels" and what not else outside the pale of good men's esteem, the statement was founded in a good deal of truth. It was undeniable, said these "rebels," that a newspaper correspondent like White-law Reid, who had made a hurried tour of the South, did not know the negro; that Carl Schurz, who went from army post to army post for President Johnson and who learned no more of the real feeling of the people than if he had been "sailing in a steamer along the coast," did not know the negro;[1] that Charles Sumner and Chief Justice Chase, and Horace Greeley and Thaddeus Stevens did not know the negro. But they, for the moment, were thought to possess much wisdom, while the judgment of the Southern man, though he be as sober and sagacious as Robert E. Lee, or Wade Hampton, or Alexander H. Stephens, it was complained, was carelessly cast aside.

C. G. Memminger, who had been the Confederate Secretary of the Treasury, wrote to President Johnson. He pointed out that the negroes occupied the houses of their employers "built upon plantations widely separate," that the system of employment involved the support not only of the laborer himself but also of his family, that in case of the employer's discontent with the service of his work people they, with all their kin, must be turned out into the woods, and so on. It was assumed at the North that the laborer would be as likely to keep his contract as his employer. But this was not so. The employer, having property, could offer a guarantee for the performance of his part of the contract not to be given by the employee, even in a general case. This was a special case. Here was a laboring population "peculiarly subject to the vices of an inferior race," and "nothing short of years of education and training could bring about in them that state of moral rectitude and habitual self-constraint which would secure the regular performance of contracts." Moreover it was a naturally indolent race, and one prone now to believe that it had been "released from any obligation to labor." Memminger could see nothing for the South, under the system which the North would prescribe, but "the probable relapse of large portions of the country into its original forest condition," unless the negroes were bound as apprentices "under indentures" so that they could be "trained and directed."[2]

But such a system of apprenticeship, even among men who

---

[1] South Carolina correspondence of N. Y. Tribune, Sept. 30, 1865.

[2] Fleming, Doc. Hist. of Reconstruction, vol. i, p. 247, quoting from Johnson Papers in the Library of Congress.

called themselves conservatives in the North, seemed to be only another name for slavery. The good faith of any who dared to make such a suggestion was brought into question at once, and the difficulties in the way of a return to mutual good-will were instantly increased.

It was an important fact, generally overlooked by Northern men, that the master had been supporting sixteen people for every group of nine who performed useful service.[1] For these non-workers he had full responsibility — the old "aunties," the old "uncles," the cripples, the idiotic, the children, all were parts of his household, and he did his duty by them with better grace and more fidelity than his critics were disposed to admit. It was not possible in any body of slaves on a plantation to enforce rules which would cause them to live a purely monogamous life. The marriage vows, when taken, were not carefully observed. The young women were likely to be surrounded with offspring of uncertain paternity. Yellow children were witnesses of the loose living of many planters, planters' sons and overseers in all parts of the South. The average number of mulattoes in one hundred slaves at the South in 1860 was officially stated to be twelve or thirteen.[2] Now each negro was to disentangle his family and to work for its support, and there was much opportunity for doubt and dispute. The old master must make a contract with the head of the family, and this head must be responsible for the sustenance of that family. But such an assortment of the slaves was not immediately feasible. There were women with children but with no husbands, and aged, decrepit and useless blacks to be supported as before.

So great did all the difficulties seem to be that many seriously discussed plans for ridding themselves of the negro and putting another laborer in his place. Henry Clay and Abraham Lincoln, both Kentuckians, had advocated colonization out of the country. In his address to a delegation of negroes in May President Johnson, a Tennesseean, told them that he hoped

[1] N. Y. Nation, vol. i, p. 109.
[2] Census Reports of 1860, vol. on Population, p. x.

a time might come when they all could be gathered together in one country adapted to their condition, if it were proved, after trial, that they could not reside here in happy relations with the whites.[1] Judge Evans, a candidate for Congress in Mississippi in 1865, found it impossible that the blacks and the whites could live in equality side by side. The negroes should be sent by the government to a place where they would be "distinct and by themselves."[2] "Parson" Brownlow, Governor of Tennessee, in his message to the legislature of that state in 1865, gave expression to the same sentiments.[3]

Liberia and Hayti, in favor before the war as negro Utopias, still had their advocates. The new Republican party, animated by the spirit of Clay and Lincoln, soon after coming into power inaugurated some experiments. Laws of April 16 and July 16, 1862, had put $600,000 at Lincoln's hand to be disposed of as his judgment might direct in settling negroes recently emancipated in the District of Columbia "beyond the limits of the United States." It was the beginning, said the Secretary of the Interior, of a "great national scheme" to relieve the country of its "surplus negro population." The Secretary of State addressed various foreign governments (on September 30, 1862), saying, that as some freedmen and free blacks had expressed a desire to emigrate, that as some countries had expressed a desire to receive "such accessions to their population," he would be pleased to have a statement of their attitude toward the question. A few replied in favorable terms while others did not attempt to conceal their hostility to the project. Owners or lessees of tracts of land in the tropics came forward with schemes to dispose of it, with profit to themselves, to the government. Many were "impracticable," but Seward had a hope, he wrote to Minister Adams in England, on November 18, 1862, that a time was drawing nigh when they would discover "a feasible policy which will solve, perhaps, the most

[1] Phila. Press, May 12, 1865; cf. Recollection of A. H. Stephens, p. 537, also Johnson's address to negro soldiers in Washington, Oct. 10, 1865, in McPherson, History of Recon., p. 49.

[2] Senate Ex. Doc., 39th Cong., 1st sess., no. 2, p. 65.

[3] N. Y. Tribune, Oct. 6, 1865.

difficult political problem that has occurred in the progress of civilization on the American continent." Two or three negro preachers were employed to gather up colonists. But the principal steps to expend the $600,000 which Congress had placed in Lincoln's hands were taken in connection with projects to settle negroes in New Granada and on the Ile A'Vache, off the coast of Hayti.

Ambrose W. Thompson was at the head of an improvement company owning two million acres of land, extending from the Atlantic to the Pacific Ocean on the Chiriqui Isthmus. A contract was made with this man by the Secretary of the Interior. Twenty-five thousand dollars were given to Senator Samuel C. Pomeroy of Kansas, who volunteered his services as "friend, agent and protector" of the negroes wishing to go out to new homes in this place. He opened an office in Washington, procured a steamer in New York, purchased supplies, made payments of money to Thompson, but because of remonstrances against the plan uttered by some of the adjoining states in Central America further operations were suspended.

Unfortunately more came to pass in A'Vache. A man named Kock, who was said to be a merchant of New Orleans, for $50 a head would carry American negroes to that island, "the most beautiful, healthy and fertile," said he, "of all the islands belonging to the Republic of Hayti." It was free of reptiles. It was well timbered. Its area was one hundred square miles. In short it appeared to be so desirable a haven for our black emigrants that Lincoln, in the presence of Senator Doolittle, was on the point of making a contract with Kock to deport 5000 persons thither. But soon the man was discredited and all promises to him were withdrawn, though not before he had involved two other men in New York, so they said, Paul S. Forbes and Charles K. Tuckerman, in a pecuniary way in the undertaking. Secretary of the Interior Caleb Smith thereupon, in April, 1863, entered into an agreement with Forbes and Tuckerman to carry out 500 negroes, under proper safeguards, to A'Vache.

A British ship, the *Ocean Ranger*, was chartered for the voyage.

Four hundred and fifty-three men, women and children, collected from various parts of the South[1] were embarked at Fortress Monroe, Kock continuing at the head of the enterprise as overseer or governor of the colony, though it appeared that all his previous knowledge of the island had been pretence. He had never set foot on its soil until he landed there with the negroes. Shortly after their arrival he abandoned them. They became a charge upon the slender resources of United States Consul De Long, stationed at Aux Cayes on the mainland, who told the Secretary of the Interior of their distressing situation. No more negroes should be permitted to come to the island, unless it was the purpose of the United States "to annihilate the race." Men had not spoken the truth about the climate. The people of Hayti were "ignorant, immoral and lazy." The Interior Department, therefore, despatched a special agent named Donnohue, to inquire into the condition of the colony. Upon the strength of his report clothing was purchased for 292 persons who remained on the island and 73 who were found on the mainland (the rest had wandered off or died of disease), and a transport was sent by the War Department to bring them back to the United States. On March 20, 1864, the ship bearing this unfortunate company anchored in the Potomac opposite Alexandria, and Lincoln's blundering experiment was done.

Tuckerman and Forbes audaciously pressed the President, the State Department, the Interior Department under three successive secretaries, and Congress for the payment of claims amounting to $80,000 or $90,000, despite conclusive proof that the emigrants while on the voyage out had been compelled to buy water to allay their thirst, that after landing they were left without shelter except for the miserable huts they raised for themselves, that the money which could have been used to

[1] The law had specified that they be taken from the District of Columbia. Probably enough could not be found in and around Washington City since there was an indisposition on all sides among the negroes to assist in forwarding any of the schemes to colonize them in other lands. The names and residences of the emigrants are to be found in the archives of the Interior Department in the Library of Congress.

build them comfortable homes was expended for hand-cuffs and leg-chains and to erect stocks wherein some of the poor creatures were maimed for life, that not a single dollar had ever been paid them for their labor, that Kock, though convicted of brutality, was permitted to remain in control of the colony. It was a fearful indictment which Secretary Usher prepared against the men. They had no ground in law or equity, he said, for compensation. To admit the performance of the contract would be a "gross abuse such as would cause any just man to exclaim against it," in view of the "preponderating evidence" to the contrary which was in possession of the government.[1]

These experiences should have sufficed. But for many the hope of solving the race problem by deportation was not dead. A colony was formed in Lynchburg, Va., with Liberia as its destination [2] though the most unfavorable accounts were received of this enterprise also. On October 11, 1865, 174 persons sailed thither from Baltimore.[3] What might be their fate many seemed to care little. Let them be sent any whither — they should not stay here to plague the future of the South. If they must remain, let them be set to work to dike the Mississippi or to build the railroad projected across the plains to the Pacific Ocean.[4] Some entertained the illusion that a Southern state, possibly South Carolina, might be set aside and converted into a vast black colony.[5]

If other considerations did not forbid their removal, a reason for their remaining where they now were would be found in the indisposition of the negroes themselves, as a body, to depart the country. Preachers and clever mulattoes became their leaders in conventions which were called together in various

[1] Archives of the Interior Department in Library of Congress; Senate Ex. Doc., 39th Cong., 1st sess., no. 55; Nicolay and Hay, Abraham Lincoln, chap. xvii.

[2] N. Y. Tribune, Nov. 3, 1865.

[3] Phila. Ledger, Oct. 13, 1865.

[4] General Howard's speech in Maine, N. Y. Tribune, Aug. 22, 1865.

[5] Reid, After the War, p. 125. General Cox, candidate for governor in Ohio in 1865, advocated this policy. — Welles, vol. ii, p. 352.

places in the South.   The chairman of such a meeting in Raleigh
declared "all talk of exportation, expatriation, colonization
and the like" to be "simple nonsense."   The negro had lived
here for one hundred and fifty years, as long as the white
man, and he would continue to do so.   Another speaker said
that he had travelled 40,000 miles over the face of the earth,
including the West Indian Islands and Africa, in search of a
better home, but he had returned to live and die in his native
North Carolina.[1]

It was passing strange, said many Northern men, after the
Southern white people had clung to the negro with a tenacity
which had been permitted to affect their whole view of the nature of the government of the United States, accounting him so
indispensable that they were willing to wage a civil war for
him, that they should now regard him as the greatest obstacle
in the way to their prosperity.

Many eagerly turned to white immigration as a means of
making over the South.   An immigrant aid society was
founded in Charleston.   Shares to be paid for either in money
or land were offered to the people.   Farms and plantations
were acquired and the managers sought to find peasants from
Europe [2] willing to become settlers.   The legislature of Alabama incorporated a "German Association" which should
promote German immigration to that state by advertising
the "aptness" of the soil for white labor in "Northern and
European papers." [3]   The Germans now coming into New
York in large numbers were recommended to direct their steps
to the South.[4]   Irishmen and Italians also were sought as
colonists.   They would be paid $10 or $12 a month, live in the
cabins which the negroes had occupied and subsist upon the
same rations.[5]   Some planters in Georgia actually went North
to place orders for white field hands.   But no European white

---

[1] N. Y. Tribune, Oct. 7, 1865.

[2] N. Y. Nation, vol. i, p. 652.

[3] Acts of Alabama for 1865–6, p. 256.

[4] N. Y. Nation, vol. ii, pp. 102, 322.

[5] Reid, p. 373; Sidney Andrews, pp. 177, 208; Fleming, Doc.
Hist. of Recon., vol. i, p. 258.

man would go on such terms to a war-wrecked and impoverished land when he could settle in the "garden of the West." [1] Texas and Arkansas could make stronger appeals to the incoming colonists.[2] Already, before the war, over 54,000 Germans and 8000 Norwegians, who remained loyal to the Union, were living in western Texas, and it was confidently believed that, with the return of peace, the number would be greatly increased.[3]

The Chinese coolies who were coming in to work upon the Pacific Railroad were also in many men's minds. They ate little; they demanded small wages. Three would do the work of two negroes. Might not they be introduced to displace black men as laborers on the plantations? Experiments, therefore, were made with Chinamen.[4]

But in general it was understood by the more intelligent people of the South that the negroes would remain on the ground, and that they must be dealt with under some system as free men. While numbers of them took to the roads and started for the army posts, numbers, too, were wise enough to stay in their homes. Some during the war had guarded the ancestral halls of their absentee masters with a fidelity finely typical of the slave in the old South. Many had small hoards of money which they would generously offer to their ruined masters and mistresses.[5] Faithfulness could not be greater than theirs, and such black folk could not have been persuaded to join in the general restless movement of their people. Planters, with a correct view of their duties, when the war had ended, called their slaves around them. The colored people were told that they were now free. If they were willing, they could remain at their tasks; they would continue to be fed, clothed

---

[1] South Carolina correspondence, N. Y. Tribune, Sept. 30, 1865.

[2] For facts concerning the Arkansas Immigrant Aid Society see Report of Joint Committee on Reconstruction, part iii, pp. 95–8. — House Reports, 39th Cong., 1st sess., no. 30.

[3] Ibid., part iv, pp. 39, 40, 136.

[4] Reid, p. 397.

[5] N. Y. Nation, vol. i, p. 682; Fleming, Doc. Hist., vol. i, p. 257; M. L. Avary, pp. 150–1; E. F. Andrews, p. 286.

and lodged and would be compensated for their labor from time
to time during the season, or at the end of the year.[1]

Arrangements of many kinds were effected. Widely varying amounts of money were offered by the planters. Usually
the negroes were to continue to live in the old slave cabins with
the privilege of raising a little corn, and keeping hogs and
poultry. They would receive food and firewood. Sometimes
they still were to be clothed by the planters, and in other cases
they were to clothe themselves. In Texas negroes were being
paid from $1 to $6 a month, "none above $6." [2] In Virginia
in July the wages were $6, $7 and $8 a month for working in
the corn and tobacco fields. A planter said that he knew no
one who paid less than $6.[3] These negroes were found. Labor-
ers who fed and clothed themselves could be had for $5, $6 and
$7 in Georgia in the summer of 1865.[4] In Louisiana the prices
were $10 or $12 a month, including food and shelter, with a
few contracts calling for as much as $18.[5]

Again the blacks shared the harvests, continuing the old
arrangements in regard to bed, board, fuel and clothing. A
tenth, a seventh, a quarter, a third, even a half of the crop was
promised to the laborers.[6]

Again they were offered definite quantities of produce, —
so many bushels of corn or bales of cotton for division among
the number contributing to the success of the crop. In many
cases their keep and the support of their children and dependent
relations were considered by their old masters sufficient com-

[1] For instance see Smedes, A Southern Planter, p. 228; Mrs. V. V.
Clayton, White and Black under the Old Régime, p. 152; Halifax,
N. C. correspondence, N. Y. Tribune, Sept. 4, 1865. Slaves were told
to discontinue calling their master by this name, to which injunction
they would reply "Yes, marster," "Yes, marster." Cf. M. B. Chesnut,
A Diary from Dixie, pp. 385, 394, 395, 403; M. L. Avary, Dixie after
the War, p. 183.

[2] Houston Telegraph quoted in N. Y. Tribune, July 17, 1865.

[3] N. Y. Nation, vol. i, p. 109; cf. ibid., p. 210.

[4] Ibid., p. 425; cf. N. Y. Tribune, Aug. 14, 1865, for rates in North
Carolina.

[5] N. Y. Nation, vol. ii, pp. 305, 368.

[6] Ibid., vol. i, pp. 210, 393; N. Y. Tribune, Sept. 30 and Oct. 6,
1865.

pensation, or at any rate all that could be paid under any circumstances during this unfortunate year. When wages and produce were offered to workers, they found often in the final reckoning that the cost, of supporting useless members of their families was deducted from their accounts. The new system at first was certain to be prolific of dispute. Soon from one end of the South to the other, from both parties to the labor contracts, came allegations of broken faith.

The negro was sorely in need of advice and he had many counsellors. From Johnson's provisional governors and major generals of the army in command of Military Departments down to the provost marshals in Southern villages men were found ready to deliver homilies meant for Sambo's advantage. "In the sweat of thy face shalt thou eat bread all the days of thy life," quoted Governor Holden of North Carolina. The same Providence which has given you your freedom, he continued, tells you that "diligence in business is required of all his creatures." [1] "Nothing makes people so beautiful, whether they are black or white, as virtue," said General Andrews in Alabama. "Adorn yourselves with that and you will have the affection of the nation." [2] "The schoolhouse, the spelling book and the Bible," said Colonel Whittlesey, Assistant Commissioner of the Freedmen's Bureau in North Carolina, "will be found better preservers of peace and good order than the revolver and the bowie knife. . . . God the author of all good will be your friend. . . . It is better to suffer wrong than to do wrong." [3]

The black people were teachable, said a New York Tribune correspondent in the South, and they could be brought to understand their place in the world if "simpletons, softies and goodies" did not turn their heads. [4] But just such persons, as well as many rogues, were mischievously contriving to unfit the blacks for their tasks and duties. Those who had left their old homes had done so, for the most part, because soldiers

[1] N. Y. Tribune, June 20, 1865.
[2] O. R., series i, vol. xlix, part ii, p. 728.
[3] Senate Ex. Doc., 39th Cong., 1st sess., no. 70, p. 2.
[4] N. Y. Tribune, June 20, 1865.

and other men had told them that the government would feed
them and present them with farms. Much was said in the
North concerning confiscation. It had been a penal measure
during the war, and now, if the policy were to be continued,
the opportunity to condemn and seize was as wide as the late
Confederacy. Both the "poor whites," who would be rewarded
for their "loyalty," and the blacks hoped that the plantations
might now be taken, divided and distributed.

This idea found encouragement in what was seen in and told
about the Sea Islands. As early as in December, 1861, Com-
modore Dupont captured a strip of the fertile Carolina coast,
nothing else than a great alluvial river delta whereon long-
staple cotton and rice plantations, employing thousands of
slaves, had been conducted successfully for many years. Northern charitable societies were asked to extend their aid to the
blacks who here came within the Union lines. They responded
with teachers and preachers, and in April, 1862, Secretary
Stanton assigned General Rufus Saxton to what was to a West
Point graduate a little acceptable task, — the administration of
the affairs of the district. The "rebel" owners had fled and
it was made his duty to carry on large farming operations
with negro labor.[1]

On January 16, 1865, General Sherman issued his famous
Order No. 15, which extended Saxton's sphere of influence.
All the islands south of Charleston, the rice fields along the
rivers for thirty miles back from the ocean, and the country
bordering the St. John's River in Florida were set aside for the
use of the negroes. Each family was to be settled on a plot
of "not more than forty acres of tillable ground."[2] After the
freeholds were distributed the people were to be organized for
self-government under military supervision. General Saxton
displayed some ability in the performance of his task and soon
his negro Arcadia was the subject of eulogy on the part of those

[1] A good detailed account of his administration is to be found in
J. P. Hollis, Early Period of Reconstruction in South Carolina, Johns
Hopkins Studies, pp. 108–14. Saxton's own account may be found
in Report of Joint Committee on Reconstruction, part ii, p. 221.

[2] Fleming, Doc. Hist. of Recon., vol. i, p. 350.

at the North who were engaged in canonizing the freedmen. Hither Chase came on his Southern tour. Here were Congo savages with flat noses, blubber-lips and coal black skins, who spoke dialects that white men could not understand, in a few months made fit to enjoy the franchise. They were saying their *a b ab's*. They had $100,000 in savings accounts in a bank which was buying government bonds from Jay Cooke.[1] The glowing accounts of the prosperity of their fellows on free land on the coast was capable of highly exciting the imaginations of the blacks of the interior.[2] So, too, in the act creating the Freedmen's Bureau, there was allusion to the leasing of forty acres to "every male citizen whether refugee or freedman,"[3] and it was a task at the agencies to correct an impression, not wholly without basis, which had become widespread. General Howard, on November 11, issued a circular to all the Bureau agents asking them "to take every possible means" to undeceive the negroes.[4]

As credulous as children, which in intellect they in many ways resembled, they were generally led to believe that, if the lands were not to be had just now, at Christmas time or around the New Year the head of each family would receive forty acres and a mule to work the crops.[5] Some one having told the negroes in a county in North Carolina that they must be married before they could get government farms they hastily

[1] By Sept. 1 the sum on deposit had reached nearly $200,000. (Reid, p. 364.) On Oct. 16 the deposits were $250,734, of which $73,690 had been paid out to the depositors. (N. Y. Nation, vol. i, p. 779.)

[2] For the remarkable impression made upon Chase and his companions during this visit to the Sea Islands see Reid, After the War, pp. 94 et seq.

[3] Section 4 of Act. See also order of General Howard of Aug. 10, House Ex. Doc., 39th Cong., 1st sess., no. 70, p. 17.

[4] House Ex. Doc., 39th Cong., 1st sess., no. 70, p. 118.

[5] M. B. Chesnut, A Diary from Dixie, p. 396; M. L. Avary, Dixie after the War, p. 346; Mrs. Clay, A Belle of the Fifties, p. 221; Gov. Marvin to Secy. Seward, Senate Ex. Doc., 39th Cong., 1st sess., no. 26, p. 206; Fleming, Doc. Hist. of Recon., vol. i, pp. 353–5; Sidney Andrews, pp. 97, 209, 212; Report of General Howard, House Ex. Doc., 39th Cong., 1st sess., no. 11, p. 12.

proceeded to take unto themselves wives. The Episcopal minister in a town during two days prior to the arrival there of a New York Tribune correspondent had performed the wedding ceremony for no less than 150 young black couples.[1] In Florida thousands of land certificates were sold to the negroes. For $5 a swindler would issue a paper pretending to convey to the purchaser right absolute to a plantation in some Promised Land which no seeker after it ever was able to find.[2] Others sold painted red, white and blue pegs which, it was asserted, had come from Washington, and could be used by whomsoever was possessed of them to mark out homesteads. This fraud, in one or another form, was successfully practised upon the negroes of the South for twenty-five years.[3] It was a common experience to meet a black fellow who had come a hundred miles to get a barrel of flour sent him by the Queen of England, or a free railway ticket to Washington that he might see the President. It was a soldier's jest to start the negroes tramping away on all kinds of preposterous errands.[4]

Their barbaric love of color and show could now be gratified. They were "crazy to ride," and it was many a negro's principal ambition to get possession of an old mule and a cart that he might drive through the streets like the white man.[5] Wenches who had worked all their lives in the cotton fields were carrying parasols to keep off the sun. Not a few must have their white cotton gloves and hoop-skirts like the mulatto girls in Charleston and New Orleans. Jewish sutlers and other adventurers went through the country selling brass rings, gaudy kerchiefs and baubles at high prices. The freedman's simplicity was imposed upon at every hand.

Plainly the place for the negroes was on their old plantations,

---

[1] N. Y. Tribune, Sept. 8. This was a gratuitous service, for the applicants were without money to pay the minister's fees.

[2] J. Wallace, Carpet Bag Rule in Fla., p. 39.

[3] Fleming, Doc. Hist. of Recon., vol. i, pp. 359-60; Fleming, Civil War and Recon. in Ala., pp. 447-8; M. L. Avary, Dixie after the War, pp. 213-4.

[4] N. Y. Nation, vol. i, p. 426.

[5] Sidney Andrews, p. 187.

if they could be persuaded to remain there and their old masters would treat them fairly as free laborers. In many parts of the South the officers of the army posts used their influences to this end.[1] The commander of a district in Florida sent chaplains and other officers into the interior. They visited the freedmen on the plantations and in many places made speeches to them. The negroes were urged to remain at home and work.[2] "Neither idleness nor vagrancy will be tolerated," said General Gillmore in May at Hilton Head, "and the government will not extend pecuniary aid to any persons, whether white or black, who are unwilling to help themselves." [3] In northern Louisiana the general moving about of the negroes became so troublesome that they were required, when they went away from home, to exhibit military passes under penalty of arrest. Transports and steamboats on Red River were prohibited from carrying them unless they had permits to wander abroad.[4]

At Galveston General Granger issued a similar order. They must keep off the "public thoroughfares" unless they had "passes or permits from their employers," and must not congregate in buildings or camps at or adjacent to garrison towns.[5]

The task of setting right the negroes in reference to their duties as freedmen was to be shared by General Howard's new Bureau which he organized at once. As the troops were withdrawn, and the garrisons were reduced in strength and numbers, with a view to an early return to civil government this new agency appeared with its officers and courts. The Commissioner in Washington was provided with nine Assistant Commissioners stationed at Richmond, Raleigh, Beaufort,

[1] As for instance in Florida, O. R., series i, vol. xlvii, part iii, pp. 623–4; in Texas, N. Y. Tribune, July 17, 1865.

[2] Report of Joint Committee on Reconstruction, part iv, p. 121.

[3] O. R., series i, vol. xlvii, part iii, pp. 498–9.

[4] General Herron's orders. The negroes were "setting out *en masse* for the military posts." But the "only place they can obtain a living for themselves and their families is in the field where they have been accustomed to work." — O. R., series i, vol. xlviii, part ii, pp. 854–5.

[5] Quoted in N. Y. Tribune, July 17, 1865 — order dated June 28.

Montgomery, Nashville, St. Louis, Vicksburg, New Orleans
and Jacksonville. These officers included such men as General Wager Swayne, General Clinton B. Fisk and General Rufus
Saxton (the latter already for some time in charge of the freedmen's interests in the Sea Islands). To act under their authority, numbers of local officers were appointed in all parts of the
South, drawn for the most part from the army. In so far as
facilities were at its hand, the Bureau aimed to relieve the
military authorities of many of the tasks which they had
assumed, and to create still more efficient agencies for establishing the negro in his new place. General Howard brought
under his supervision the work of administering abandoned and
confiscated lands, of adjusting labor contracts between the
former slaves and their former masters, of taking over old and
organizing new negro schools, of feeding the destitute and of
extending medical aid to refugees and freedmen.[1] Thousands
of negroes called "contrabands" who found their way into the
Union lines, as these were advanced during the war, had been
fed by the army in camps along the Mississippi and on the seacoast. These, now, were put under the care of the Freedmen's
Bureau until they could be distributed and set to work. The
need of reducing the number of dependent persons was immediate. General Fisk was particularly active in recommending
the examination of cases, and the withdrawal of the alms of
the government from as many as possible at the earliest day.
He said, in July, that the government was being "immensely
swindled" in the distribution of rations. Support was claimed
as a right, he complained; neighborhoods should provide for
their own poor.[2] In August he had reduced the number of
mouths to be fed in Kentucky and Tennessee to 7562, and in
September, to 2984. In North Carolina 215,285 rations were
given out to negroes and loyalists in July, and only 137,350
in September. During the month of September 1,400,643
rations in all were issued through the Freedmen's Bureau,
nearly two-thirds of the dependents being located in three

[1] House Ex. Doc., 39th Cong., 1st sess., no. 11.
[2] N. Y. Tribune, Aug. 9, 1865.

districts, Missouri and Arkansas, Georgia and South Carolina, and Virginia.[1]

The "Yankee teacher" entered the South on the heels of the soldier. Whenever a foothold had been secured by the Federal army on the Mississippi, or on the seacoast the Freedmen's Aid Societies of Massachusetts or Pennsylvania, and other philanthropic organizations sent out schoolmasters. Generals set aside buildings for the use of the negro children, who were soon saying their letters, and in many places teaching their elders to spell and write out words. The enthusiasm of the old Abolition element in the North for this work was unbounded. What the natural evolution of the species would do only by gradual means they pretended to think could now be accomplished, as by a magician's wand, through the free school. An exaggeration of the magnitude and value of the service was in keeping with the character of those who put an appraisement upon it, but, to tell the truth, a useful and indispensable work was going forward in an encouraging way.

When the Freedmen's Bureau was organized, it took complete control of educational work among the negroes, and the agents found that a good beginning had been made in several places, notably by Major R. Rush Plumly in Louisiana, and General Saxton in the Carolina Sea Islands. Major Plumly, who was chairman of the Board of Education in the Department of the Gulf, after working for a year and a half under the appointment of General Banks, in the face of obstacles, as he believed, seldom if ever met with before, had opened 126 schools with 230 teachers giving instruction to 15,000 children in the day classes and 5000 adult freedmen, who were carrying on their studies at night and on Sundays.[2]

In May General Saxton was educating 12,467 negro children in his Department of the South. There were some fifteen schools on the Port Royal Islands, which since the spring of

[1] Report of General Howard, House Ex. Doc., 39th Cong., 1st sess., no. 11.

[2] N. Y. Tribune, Aug. 8, 1865. The schools were visited and described by Congressman John Covode — see Report of Joint Committee on Reconstruction, part iv, p. 117.

1862 constantly had given instruction to many hundreds of persons.[1] James Redpath of Massachusetts was the superintendent of schools in the Northern Division of the Department of the South. In Charleston he had over 4000 pupils in nine day and five night schools under 112 teachers.[2] In the whole state of South Carolina, in November, there were 48 schools attended by 6000 pupils and taught by 108 teachers, of whom 80 had been brought from the North.[3]

In Memphis at the end of the war there were 3000 pupils receiving instruction from teachers sent out by, or, at any rate, supported by charitable societies in the Northern states.[4] Several thousand negro children were in school in Vicksburg, where the work was largely sustained by the Quakers of Ohio and Indiana.[5] While the teachers were usually white (many of them being women) some colored men were soon found to assist the missionaries. Churches, stores, lofts, lodge rooms, sheds were pressed into service as schoolrooms. The pupils often sat on boards thrown across old chairs, or supported by trestles. In summer the pickaninnies perhaps would be gathered together on a green bank out of doors. Books, maps and all kinds of paraphernalia were scarce and sometimes lacked entirely. In the crudest surroundings, under all kinds of disadvantages, the alphabet, reading, writing and some arithmetic and geography were taught to the children, and to many of the older freed people.

General Howard said in August, 1865, that more than 200,000 persons in the South had learned to read in the past three years.[6] In November, 1865, there were, according to the reports of the officers of the Freedmen's Bureau, 90 schools, 195 teachers and 11,500 pupils in Virginia, 5624 pupils in North Carolina,

---

[1] These statistics are for May. Letter of J. A. Saxton to Prof. F. J. Child in N. Y. Tribune, Aug. 14, 1865. Cf. N. Y. Nation, vol. i, p. 779.

[2] Reid, p. 60; N. Y. Tribune, Aug. 14, 1865.

[3] N. Y. Nation, vol. i, p. 779.

[4] J. T. Trowbridge, The South, p. 336.

[5] Ibid., p. 378.

[6] Phila. Ledger, Aug. 10, 1865.

9500 pupils in South Carolina and Georgia, 19,000 in Louisiana, 15,000 in Kentucky and Tennessee, 2000 in Mississippi and a few hundred in Montgomery and Mobile in Alabama.[1]

The native white people, it was complained, gave no willing support to the work of bringing to the South the boon of a new educated negro race. James Redpath observed that out of 5000 or 6000 who had taken the oath of allegiance in Charleston not one person had volunteered his services as a teacher in the schools, or had offered to aid in any way in the work of negro education.[2]

The "poor whites" were as ignorant as the colored people. Their need of education was as great as the negroes'. The war had brought them to a state even worse than that in which they were at its breaking out. One who travelled among them in 1865 said that language was not fertile enough to describe "such filthy poverty, such foul ignorance, such idiotic imbecility, such bestial instincts, such grovelling desires." [3] "For dirt and for utter ignorance of all the decencies of civilized life," said another, "no people in America of any color can compare with them." [4] They were incestuous and adulterous. They quarrelled like cats.[5] The only thing they hated more than one another, possibly, was the negro. It was said that not one in a hundred could read or write.[6] They had never seen a schoolhouse and looked upon teachers with superstitious hostility.[7] They owned no land. They squatted on little patches of ground in the wood, living in rough log cabins. The interstices were only partially chinked with mud, so that the wind blew in. The rain ran under the doors, and most of the poor wretches early became marks for consumption and other

[1] Report of General Howard for 1865, House Ex. Doc., 39th Cong., 1st sess., no. 11.

[2] N. Y. Tribune, Aug. 14, 1865; cf. N. Y. Nation, vol. i, p. 779.

[3] Sidney Andrews, p. 336.

[4] Reid, p. 348. For other accounts of the poor whites see N. Y. Nation, vol. i, pp. 331, 335, 395; N. Y. Tribune, Sept. 30, 1865.

[5] N. Y. Tribune, Oct. 4, 1865. For a Southern view see M. B. Chesnut, A Diary from Dixie, p. 401.

[6] N. Y. Tribune, Aug. 2, 1865.

[7] Senate Ex. Doc., 39th Cong., 1st sess., no. 2, p. 83.

diseases.　They had repulsive-looking skins, tallow-white, suggestive of "death in life."[1]　Girls of fifteen, bent, gaunt and colorless, looked like women of fifty.　Near the cabin there were usually some rows of corn, cowpeas, coleworts and sweet potatoes, and at times a few cows and hogs that fed in the wood.[2]　The woman visited the plantation houses to beg or steal.　The man had his dog and gun, and sallied out to ravage the neighborhood.

Some of these people, if they lived within reach of a town, would take a little produce to market.　The cart would likely have wheels of hewn fells with a body of the same material of the roughest manufacture.　It would be drawn by a galled horse, a lean mule or a steer, in harness made of rope, old rags and pieces of hide.　The collar around the shoulders of the animal would be of corn shucks.　As the vehicle plunged through the deep sand roads the man would ride the animal, while a woman or a boy or a girl, or all three, sat in the cart among the chickens, eggs and vegetables, or walked behind the vehicle.　Some came a distance of forty miles, which meant a journey of two days to market and two days home again.[3]

The use of liquor and tobacco, which had been too free in the South before the war, had not diminished.　The "poor whites" in particular were unrestrained in their indulgence in both.　Whiskey had been responsible for many a shooting affray between planters, many a family feud in the mountains.　There was drunkenness everywhere among the backwoods people without distinction of sex; even boys and girls often were seen in stupor as a result of the drinking of cheap spirits.　When they went to town, it was usually with the purpose of gratifying this taste and of returning home comfortably intoxicated.　Of a Saturday afternoon it was a common sight to meet in the roads leading out of any town in Virginia processions of two-wheeled carts made of poles.　On the planks thrown down for a floor both parents would be stretched dead drunk, while

[1] Sidney Andrews, p. 182.
[2] N. Y. Tribune, Dec. 16, 1865.
[3] Ibid., July 4 and Aug. 2, 1865.

the horse or the mule jogged along at the word of a child, or perhaps travelled the way unguided.[1]

The chewing of tobacco was well-nigh universal. This repulsive habit had been widespread among the agricultural population of America both North and South before the war. Soldiers had found the quid a solace in the field and continued to revolve it in their mouths upon returning to their homes. Out of doors where his life was principally led the chewer spat upon his lands without offence to other men, and his homes and public buildings were supplied with spittoons. Brown and yellow parabolas were projected to right and left toward these receivers, but very often without the careful aim which made for cleanly living. Even the pews of fashionable churches were likely to contain these familiar conveniences.[2] The large numbers of Southern men, and these were of the better class (officers in the Confederate army and planters, worth $20,000 or more, and barred from general amnesty by the 13th exception) who presented themselves for the pardon of President Johnson, while they sat awaiting his pleasure in the ante-room at the White House, covered its floor with pools and rivulets of their spittle.[3]

An observant traveller in the South in 1865 said that in his belief seven-tenths of all persons above the age of twelve years, both male and female, used tobacco in some form.[4] Women could be seen at the doors of their cabins in their bare feet, in their dirty one-piece cotton garments, their chairs tipped back, smoking pipes made of corn cobs into which were fitted reed stems or goose quills. Boys of eight or nine years of age and half-grown girls smoked. Women and girls "dipped" in their houses, on their porches, in the public parlors of hotels and in the streets.[5]

[1] N. Y. Tribune, Oct. 4, 1865.
[2] N. Y. Nation, vol. i, p. 209.
[3] Trowbridge, The South, p. 76.
[4] Sidney Andrews, p. 182.
[5] "Barbaric life," said a Northern visitor to the South, yielded no "filthier and more disgusting custom." — Andrews, p. 183. A piece of cloth was tied to the end of a stick, the size of a penholder. It

Such poverty, ignorance and barbarism among the negroes and the lower classes of the white population multiplied the difficulties attending the work of pacification and restoration in the South. These were made less in no way by the assignment of negro troops to garrison duty in all the principal Southern towns. This policy had commended itself to the War Department on several accounts. It was desired to provide employment for the negroes who followed the army and had been gathered into the "contraband" camps.[1] The young black fellows were recruited, organized into regiments, usually under white officers, and furnished an immense amount of material for homily and sermon on the part of that class of men at the North whom the old planters knew as "nigger worshippers." Was not the negro wearing the United States uniform and fighting his country's battles? Then might he not be trusted to vote? Was he not by test a more valuable part of the nation than those who had so recently striven. in every fibre to bring its life to an end? Furthermore the white soldiers ought now to be relieved of duty and return to their homes. They had served their country long and faithfully. The unpleasant task of policing the South could be left to the blacks who were accustomed to the climate. But beyond this it were well to place negro soldiers there because they would serve as reminders to the white people that they were in a subject place. They had struggled to preserve the institution of slavery; their slaves would now be set over them to see that they kept the peace. It was not a vindictive measure, but a mere putting of the disloyal white man in his right position with reference to the loyal black man.

The government had mustered in, all told, 186,097 negro soldiers,[2] 24,000 of them in Louisiana, 20,000 in Tennessee, 23,000 in Kentucky and nearly 18,000 in Mississippi.[3] On October 20, 1865, there were still 85,024 black troops in the

was moistened in the mouth and dipped in tobacco dust, then to be rubbed thoroughly over the teeth and gums; a process which was followed by frequent spitting; cf. N. Y. Nation, vol. i, p. 335.

[1] O. R., series iii, vol. v, p. 118.

[2] Ibid., p. 132.   [3] Ibid., p. 138.

national service.[1] The most of these men were scattered over the South,[2] very proud of their places as soldiers, and a constant source of irritation to the white people,[3] who often recognized their own former slaves in the new blue uniforms, bearing bright, gleaming muskets. Citizens were jostled from the sidewalks by these black guards marching four abreast, and were halted by negro sentinels. They filled the servant class of their own color with notions of political and social equality which were demoralizing, and their misbehavior often led to serious breaches of the peace. The white country people would come to towns in which there were negro garrisons only upon the most imperative business.[4] The black soldiers were unwelcome passengers on the railways in cars occupied by the whites.[5]

On all sides crimination and recrimination were the order of the day. The returned Confederate soldiers who continued to wear their gray uniforms, usually because they had no other dress, were required by the provost marshals to procure citizens' clothing, or at any rate to remove the braid, badges of rank and brass buttons from their coats. At Norfolk they were allowed forty-eight hours in which to comply with the rule.[6] Sometimes they were halted by white or black soldiers and their buttons were sliced off with sabres. Nearly everywhere local measures were taken to rid the country of these memorials of the war, so unwelcome in the sight of the officers of the garrisons. It was comedy near to tragedy. There were no buttons; men and women had been fastening their garments with thorns. Then said the military authorities in Richmond, let the brass be covered with cloth.[7] Previous regulations not availing, in Raleigh, in July, further orders on

[1] O. R., series iii, vol. v, p. 132.
[2] In August Sheridan had 21,000 in Texas and 19,000 in Louisiana. — O. R., series i, vol. xlviii, part ii, p. 1171.
[3] Reid, p. 297; O. R., series i, vol. xlviii, part ii, p. 901.
[4] Reid, p. 422, quoting a New Orleans newspaper. It was felt to be "a deliberate, wanton, cruel act of insult and oppression."
[5] Ibid., p. 421.
[6] O. R., series i, vol. xlvi, part iii, p. 867.
[7] Avary, Dixie after the War, p. 123; cf. E. F. Andrews, The War Time Journal of a Georgia Girl, pp. 270, 276.

the subject were necessary.[1] In Memphis,[2] in Mobile,[3] in the interior of South Carolina [4] the gray coat, often with the buttons still in place, continued to be seen. The "rebels" could be called "gray-backs" by the Yankees; the latter in turn were "blue-bellies." [5]

In Florida General Vogdes ordered the people to discontinue their custom of speaking of the government at Washington as "Federal" to distinguish it from the Confederate government, which they must understand had ceased to exist.[6] General Saxton complained in South Carolina that they would call it "your government," never "our" or "the government." [7]

Southern children must be told not to sing Confederate songs; they were admonished for pelting the children of Unionists.[8] The editor of the Richmond Whig called the "13th exception" in President Johnson's amnesty proclamation "heathenish"; the policy of confiscation "mean and cowardly." General Terry suppressed the paper. Several other gazettes offended and were dealt with by the supervising military authorities. Churches in Bishop Wilmer's diocese in Alabama were closed because he refused to direct the reading of prayers for the President of the United States.[9] Guests from the North in a well-known hotel in New Orleans were informed that they were not desired since their presence would be offensive to other guests.[10]

In general the Southern men received the "Yankee" more cordially than the women. Nearly all had been in the field

[1] N. Y. Tribune, July 25, 1865.

[2] Reid, p. 292.

[3] Ibid., p. 206.

[4] Sidney Andrews, The South since the War, p. 217; also p. 40.

[5] Report of Joint Committee of Reconstruction, part iv, p. 126, in testimony covering New Orleans. General C. B. Fisk testified for Tennessee, where they spoke of the "nasal-twanged, blue-bellied, spindle-shanked Yankees"; ibid., part iii, p. 32.

[6] O. R., series i, vol. lxvii, part iii, p. 623.

[7] Report of Joint Committee, part ii, p. 217.

[8] N. Y. Tribune, Aug. 11, 1865.

[9] Whitaker, Life of Wilmer, p. 139.

[10] N. Y. Nation, vol. ii, p. 18.

in military service and knew the meaning of the surrender;
they also in many instances had the thought of selling their
plantations to Northern capitalists. For them the war had
ended, but who, asked a Northern traveller, "shall subjugate
the women"?[1] It was said, not in jest, that the war had been
prolonged a year by the proud and inflexible mothers, wives
and daughters of the South.

They had much to remember and forgive in Sherman's
"bummers," who took the last ham from the smoke-house,
lifted invalid women out of their beds to see if treasure lay
beneath, tore rings from fair fingers at the pistol point, seized
fugitives who might be carrying family heirlooms from old
homes to which the torch had been applied, to fling the prized
possessions of generations back into the fire. The women of the
South in Sherman's track were teaching their children to hate
his name unto the latest generations. It was linked with General Butler's, that "hideous, cross-eyed beast," as he was described by one of the South's most cultivated and excellent
women,[2] who in 1862 had issued his Order No. 28, when he and
his men were taunted by the spirited sisters of her race in New
Orleans.

The streets of the post towns now were filled with Union soldiers, their flags flying, their bands triumphantly playing Northern airs from morning till night. Many of the officers were
foolish enough to suppose that they would receive a welcome
in society and made advances which were repelled.

In Richmond when the Federal troops entered it, and for
weeks afterward, the women of the city would not show their
faces at their doors or windows, or in the streets. The summer
passed before the women of Charleston came out of their
homes to mingle with the population. It was as if they had
been overwhelmed by some great personal calamity.[3] In all
the large garrison towns it was complained that they sent their

[1] Reid, pp. 46, 156, 416; cf. Truman, Senate Ex. Doc., 39th Cong.,
1st sess., no. 43, p. 6.
[2] Mrs. Chesnut, A Diary from Dixie, p. 165.
[3] Sidney Andrews, p. 9.

servants for rations, receiving government aid without gratitude, and as if it were a right.   Northern men, even when not soldiers, upon addressing Southern women, would be rebuffed.[1] Ladies would make long detours to avoid passing under a United States flag.   Officers remarked that when they approached one on the sidewalk, she would gather up the folds of her dress, as if to avoid touching what she so much abhorred.[2] General Terry was hissed by some women in Richmond as he drove through the streets of the city.[3]   General Saxton and his wife seldom appeared in the streets of Charleston without being "insulted."[4]   An officer of the garrison in Liberty, Va., complained that he could find no seat at church.   If he attempted to enter a pew, the ladies already in it rose to leave. They made grimaces at his soldiers in the street and called after them insolently.[5]   In Georgia a number of young women formed a club, the members of which were pledged not to speak to the Federal soldiers on garrison duty in their midst.[6]   "I have not as yet had a word to say to the Yankees," wrote a daughter of M. F. Maury in June, 1865, "save to order them off the premises in the most peremptory manner, and I trust I may be able to say that ten years hence."   She avowed that

[1] On a railway train in South Carolina a Boston newspaper correspondent, Mr. Andrews, asked a lady seated in front of him concerning a hotel at which he might stop in a town to which they would soon come.   Her amiability was great until she suspected that he was a "Yankee."   Confirming her suspicions, she remarked, "By what right do you presume to speak to me, sir?" a rudeness for which she later apologized, explaining that she had not spoken to a Yankee since some time before the war. — Sidney Andrews, p. 14.

[2] N. Y. Nation, vol. ii, p. 141.   The case is cited of a Southern woman in Lynchburg, who called from an upper window to a little girl on the sidewalk: "Julia, come in this minute, child.   That Yankee will rub against you if you stay there."

[3] N. Y. Tribune, Aug. 11, 1865.

[4] Report of Joint Committee on Recon., part ii, p. 218.

[5] N. Y. Nation, vol. i, p. 270.   For similar cases see Report of Joint Committee on Recon., part ii, p. 2; part iii, p. 38; part iv, p. 40.

[6] This as late as November, 1865. — Sidney Andrews, p. 361.   Confirmation of all this and much more may be had from a Southern contemporary witness. — E. F. Andrews, A War Time Journal of a Georgia Girl.

she was growing to hate them "worse and worse every day." [1]
The Southern women ridiculed the "nig schools." It was
very remarkable as well as distasteful to hear one negress say
to another as they met, "When will you come to see me?"
and to hear that other reply, "I will come to-morrow after I
have done my music lesson." [2]

Everywhere the Northern teachers in the negro schools
were objects of dislike.[3] In North Carolina they must mess
together and live as they could. They would not be received
as boarders in Southern homes.[4] Only the presence of the army,
they believed, saved them from expulsion and perhaps a worse
fate in South Carolina.[5] Two young women who went from
Wilmington, N. C., to Fayetteville, in the same state, to establish a school were not permitted to make a landing from the
boat.[6]

In Tennessee a young man who had served in the Union
army asked a young woman, two of whose brothers had been
killed on the Confederate side, to dance with him. She refused, and some remarks which ensued led to a pitched battle,
wherein three men were slain and several were injured.[7]

Throughout the spring and early summer the street corners
and the barrooms were filled with idle men who had been in
the army, or who now for other reasons were thrown out of
employment as a result of the war. Armed robbers and brigands, said General Halleck, in a report to Stanton, were in
the mountains, where Union as well as Confederate deserters
had gone for rapine and plunder.[8] Ruffians, sometimes called
rangers, prowled about the country in Louisiana, Texas, Ar-

[1] M. F. Maury Papers.
[2] Ibid.
[3] N. Y. Nation, vol. ii, p. 209.
[4] N. C. correspondence, N. Y. Tribune, Dec. 26, 1865. Much evidence in confirmation of this point may be found in Report of Joint
Com. on Recon.
[5] General Saxton's testimony, Report of Joint Com. on Recon.,
part ii, p. 218.
[6] Beaufort correspondence, Phila. Ledger, Aug. 21, 1865.
[7] N. Y. Tribune, July 27, quoting Memphis Argus of July 19.
[8] O. R., series i, vol. xlvi, part iii, p. 1295.

kansas and Missouri.[1] A newspaper correspondent said there
were 5000 men in Texas, deserters from the armies and refugees
from Arkansas and Missouri, who depended upon robbery and
murder for their precarious support.[2] In that state before
the war there had been 450 murders in a year with scarcely a
half dozen legal executions.[3] There could be no strong hope for
orderly living now.

Governor Murphy of Arkansas complained on December
9, 1865, that guerrilla bands and scouting parties were pillag-
ing almost every neighborhood north of the Arkansas River.[4]
In the neighborhood of Shreveport, La., men of families noted
for their wealth and social position before the war, finding
themselves ruined by it, had turned outlaws. Some of them
were caught and hanged.[5]

Highwaymen infested the roads in Mississippi and Alabama. Cotton, horses, cattle were stolen on all sides with
"perfect impunity." Stage lines here and there were declared
unsafe.[6] Armed men were prowling within a few miles of
Atlanta, terrorizing the soldiers of the garrison as well as the
freedmen.[7] Around Mobile in September all was "anarchy
and confusion."[8] In Quitman, Ga., 200 bales of cotton were
stolen within a period of two weeks, houses were robbed and
"a perfect reign of terror inaugurated."[9]

In truth there were few parts of the South which were free
of jayhawkers, guerrillas and common vagrants, ready to
beg and steal, if not to take human life. The whole body of
the people, North as well as South, had been sensibly brutalized
in a period during which a great part of the able-bodied males
in both sections were engaged in the business of war, and those

[1] O. R., series i, vol. xlviii, part ii, pp. 970–1; N. Y. Tribune,
July 18 and Oct. 6, 1865.

[2] Truman's Rept., Senate Ex. Doc., 39th Cong., 1st sess., no. 43, p.
3; cf. Rept. of Joint Com. on Recon., part iv, p. 156.

[3] Truman's Rept., p. 11.

[4] Annual Cyclopedia for 1866, p. 29.

[5] Shreveport correspondence, N. Y. Tribune, July 24.

[6] General Schurz's Report, Senate Ex. Doc., 29th Cong., 1st sess.,
no. 2, p. 14.   [7] Ibid., p. 18.

[8] Ibid., p. 72.   [9] N. Y. Nation, vol. i, p. 425.

left at home were employed daily in reading and relating accounts of bloodshed. It is undeniably true also that the South never had been too careful about the use of knives and firearms. The duel still had its patrons and advocates. The scattered houses in an agricultural country, the preponderating number of negroes in some neighborhoods, the white rabble in the woods and in the hills made self-protection by weapons more necessary than it ever had been in Massachusetts and New York. It is no matter of amazement, under all these circumstances, that now there were attacks upon negroes by whites and upon whites by negroes, that there were clashes between soldiers and civilians, and that society everywhere, which had been "turned completely topsy turvy,"[1] was in a condition not far removed from anarchy.

At Norfolk, in June and July, shameful outrages were committed upon the negroes by the New York white soldiers stationed there. Riots continued day after day. Two negroes were found dead, hanged to trees. Cries of "nig," "nig," were heard on every hand when a black appeared in the streets, and citizens and soldiers started in pursuit of him. Many negroes were shot at; some were killed and others wounded by the mobs.[2] Around Lynchburg the provost marshals were hanging up negroes by the thumbs, and in at least one case they put a negro in a box like a coffin, exposing only his face covered with molasses to attract the flies, in which situation he was left until the soldiers willed his release from his uncomfortable position.[3] In other places, as at Washington, Ga., the white soldiers at the post were consorting with the negro women, and committing petty and often grave outrages upon the white inhabitants.[4] A negro woman in Raleigh was violated by white soldiers and then tossed in a blanket, dying two or three days later as a result of her injuries. In that part of North Carolina the beating and robbing of blacks by the Northern

[1] N. Y. Nation, vol. i, p. 425.
[2] N. Y. Tribune, June 28 and July 11, 1865.
[3] Lynchburg correspondence, N. Y. Tribune, Nov. 3, 1865.
[4] E. F. Andrews, War Time Journal, pp. 267, 352, 364.

white soldiers was of "almost daily and nightly occurrence." The colored people of Raleigh remarked that they "suffered" now from the "abuse of the Union soldiers" more than they had in any way "during the whole period of the war." [1]

In Macon Northern men who had gone South to engage in business said that they had been "grossly insulted and fired upon without provocation" by the negro troops on garrison duty in that place. Bullets "went whistling through the streets all night long." The correspondent of the Boston cotton factors, travelling in the South, declared that he would rather "face any band of guerrillas in the country than meet a body of black troops unaccompanied by United States officers." [2]

Testimony against them multiplied. [3] They fought with one another and with the citizens. Riots in which they participated occurred nearly every night in Charleston in July. [4] In May several men in Paducah, Ky., telegraphed Secretary Stanton to say that black troops there were committing "unparalleled depredations." They were outraging persons and property, breaking into court-houses and public offices, and destroying state and county records. [5] Remonstrances against the policy of policing the country with negroes came from Mississippi, Alabama and every other part of the South. The provisional governors and the conventions, called to amend the Southern state constitutions, sent their complaints and protests to Washington to impress the President's mind. [6]

[1] Fayetteville correspondence, N. Y. Tribune, Aug. 2, 1865.

[2] N. Y. Nation, vol. i, pp. 425–6; cf. ibid., p. 780, for brutalities practised upon negroes by U. S. officers in South Carolina; Fleming, Civil War and Recon., p. 450, for cases in Alabama.

[3] N. Y. Nation, vol. i, p. 393; Sidney Andrews, The South since the War, p. 206. Mr. Andrews wrote in October, 1865 : "The negro troops ought at once to be removed from the interior and put in garrison on the coast. . . . Generally the black regiments are wretchedly officered," etc.

[4] Phila. Ledger, July 17, 1865, citing Charleston Courier. Various offences committed by these soldiers in South Carolina are catalogued in J. S. Reynolds, Recon. in S. C., pp. 4–7. For Alabama, Fleming, Civil War and Recon. in Alabama, pp. 268–9.

[5] O. R., series i, vol. xlix, part ii, p. 905.

[6] Senate Ex. Doc., no. 26, loc. cit. pp. 42, 114, 116, 126, 233.

In September some one reported to Mr. Johnson the conduct of the negro troops in garrison in his own town of Greenville, Tenn. They had not scrupled, so it was said, to take the President's house and turn it into a brothel. He had thought it "bad enough," he complained to General Thomas at Nashville, when it had been seized by traitors during the war and converted into a rebel hospital, but now it had become what was "infinitely worse." The loyal people of east Tennessee above all others should be free from "the outrages of the negro soldiery," and that part of the state must be relieved of such troops as soon as practicable.[1]

General Grant, late in 1865, as a result of a visit to the South, recommended the withdrawal of the black soldiers from the garrison towns. Their camps were resorts "for the freedmen for long distances around." They were a menace to the neighborhoods in which they were stationed, and their places should be taken by white troops.[2]

It was freely alleged that plantations were pillaged, women ravished and negroes shot by ruffians who were not in the United States service, though they wore Federal uniforms, and these reports proved sometimes to be true;[3] but the soldiers, both white and black, were not without blame for many a deed which disgraced the flag they had sworn to honor and defend.

These disorders in which the soldiers participated, the Southern people were pleased to observe, were not usually "trumpetted all over Yankeedom." They were the assaults upon negroes by Southern whites, whether by bushwhackers, "redlegs" or jayhawkers, who often persecuted them only to satisfy their bloodthirsty instincts; whether by "poor white" desperadoes; or whether by the old slave masters, which filled the

[1] O. R., series i, vol. xlix, part ii, p. 1108. General Stoneman denied the truth of the report which had reached the President's ears; nevertheless General Thomas ordered the black troops in and around Greenville to Georgia and Alabama. — Ibid., pp. 1109–10.

[2] Senate Ex. Doc., 39th Cong., 1st sess., no. 2, p. 106.

[3] Many such cases are cited in Fleming, Civil War and Reconstruction in Alabama, see, e.g., pp. 267–8.

pages of Greeley's Tribune and the other Republican newspapers
of the North. The culprits were all slave drivers, all "rebels,"
all the spawn of nullification, secession and the war just come
to an end. The indictment was an awful one. The recital
of cases made the blood run cold and had the deepest political
influence. The whole policy of the North was directed by these
evidences that the war had been "closed out two years too
soon," [1] and that troops must be kept on the ground for a long
time to come. For if such things were done in the green tree,
what would be done in the dry ? [2] And there was terrible truth,
put the best possible face upon it, in the accounts of the abuse
of the negroes all over the South, especially in the Gulf states.
As freedmen they were set to their old tasks in the fields. Of
a certainty the negro was not fond of work, and he did not now
recognize the right of any one, though he was bound under a
contract for wages, to require it of him. Howell Cobb's overseer on his Hurricane Plantation in Georgia told the men to go
into the fields. They remained in their houses for two or three
days at a time, saying that they were sick or that they were
drying fruit. "Tha air," said he, "steeling the green corn verry
rapped. Som of them go when tha pleas and wher tha pleas
an pay no attention to your orders or mine . . . You had as
well Sing Sams to a ded horse as to tri to instruct a fool negrow." [3]

The exasperations which must be endured in connection
with such laborers none but those who long had lived with
them could fully comprehend. They were told to work as
they formerly had worked. They would "stand no sech treat-
men' from no white man nohow," and gave the employer insulting answers. Then likely they were whipped or hung up
by the thumbs, as in the days when they had been slaves, and
they set off to enter complaint at the nearest military post or
Freedmen's Bureau agency, while the crops were neglected in
the fields.

[1] A sentiment voiced, for instance, in Brownlow's Knoxville Whig
and Rebel Ventilator. See Reid, p. 354.

[2] N. Y. Tribune, June 23, 1865.

[3] U. B. Phillips, Toombs-Stephens-Cobb correspondence, American
Hist. Assoc. Pub., p. 665. — Letter dated July 31, 1865.

The negro might not stand, as he formerly had stood, with his hat in his hand while the white man passed by. Possibly he would not open a gate, or make way on the sidewalk, or otherwise carry himself with that deference which earlier had marked his life. And he did fifty worse things which were not compatible with his welfare, or that of his employer, who in turn was likely to go for redress to the United States officers. Every post commandant, every Freedmen's Bureau officer, had long monthly records of the complaints of ex-slaves and ex-masters, one of the other. There were "lazy and sassy niggers" to be admonished, controversies about wages, about shares of the harvest, about the support of the unproductive black children. When the crops were taken in, employers wished to be rid of their flocks of negroes. Some were driven off. The grounds for dispute were various and many.

The remedy through provost marshals and Freedmen's Bureau agents was tedious and ineffectual.[1] Many employers determined to take matters into their own hands, especially after they had convinced themselves that the Bureau was an organization whose principal business it was to collect and publish information disparaging to the Southern people. "Paddling," flogging, bucking and gagging,[2] cutting, drowning, shooting and burning of negroes, both by employers and by

---

[1] An old planter at Yazoo City wrote President Johnson that nearly all his negroes had run off to town. If twenty remained, he pledged his word that he could not get work from five. He might visit the post to complain. But others would neglect their tasks, or perhaps leave the place while he was gone. And anyhow nothing would come of his trip but a useless lecture to the offenders. — Johnson Papers, Nov. 2, 1865.

It was a cause of great exasperation to a man of property, age and social position to ride 20 miles over bad roads in midwinter to answer the complaint of a "lazy nigger" who had charged his old master with the use of "offensive language." — Why the Solid South, p. 238.

[2] This punishment consisted of placing a stick in the negro's mouth; a rope ran from each end of this stick around his neck, while the ends of the rope were carried down to be tied tightly below his knees. The feet were thus drawn up tightly against the body. Also described by Clara Barton in Report of Joint Com. on Recon., part iii, p. 104.

ruffians who caught them in the roads and elsewhere in wanton sport, increased. The New York Tribune published accounts of scores of cases of this kind which were officially recorded in South Carolina.[1] General Schurz while he was in the South collected a number of affidavits of United States officers, reciting the outrages committed in their respective districts upon negroes. Negro schoolhouses and churches were burned, as in Mobile.[2] In a day's travel in Mississippi a colonel of a colored regiment reported that five negroes had been murdered in the five preceding days in the country through which he had passed, while as many had been wounded.[3] Ears were cropped and throats cut. Men and women were stabbed, maimed, shot and hanged. Freedmen were tied to trees and burned. Others were hunted and killed by dogs.[4] In Alabama corpses dangled for months from trees [5] to poison the air and make the traveller sick with horror.

Clearly there was misrepresentation of the facts. Incidents unfavorable to the Southern whites were exaggerated on political accounts.[6] But there was much indubitable evidence, sworn to by medical and other officers of the United States at or near the places where these gross outrages were perpetrated, in support of the charges, and they awakened great resentment in the North. The intelligent Southern leaders themselves viewed the situation with deep disquietude. The provisional governors confessed it when they formed local companies of militia, which, however, were of little use, and the burden of the duty of preserving the peace rested with the garrison officers, too often very unsuitable for their responsible tasks.

[1] Dec. 2, 1865.
[2] Schurz's Report, p. 58.
[3] Ibid., p. 69.
[4] Schurz, pp. 70–1, 73–7; O. R., series i, vol. xlix, part ii, p. 954; N. Y. Tribune, June 21, 1865; N. Y. Nation, vol. i, p. 780; Sidney Andrews, pp. 28, 100, 205, 219. The testimony taken by the Joint Com. on Reconstruction early in 1866 recites countless instances in support of the disorderly state of society in the South; though much of it was of a partisan nature, much, too, is capable of corroboration.
[5] Schurz, p. 73.
[6] Fleming, Doc. Hist. of Recon., vol. i, p. 68.

Happily there were brighter scenes. Business revival was
slow, but it was going forward certainly in many directions.
The Cape Fear Bank at Wilmington, N. C., with seven branches
in different parts of the state, had a capital before the war of
$1,600,000. The advance of Sherman's army had caused the
officers on a stormy night in February to bury $110,000 in
specie in a secret place in the woods. In June they returned
under a guard of United States soldiers and exhumed the
treasure preparatory to a resumption of business.[1] So it was
throughout the South. If banks were still open, they were
stripped of their resources. If they had been subscribers to
Confederate bonds, their capital was extinguished. If they
held Confederate currency, it was worthless in their tills. Their
own notes in many cases had no more value; or were selling
at from 25 to 60 and 65 cents on the dollar.[2] In June the
Louisiana State Bank's notes were worth $57\frac{1}{2}$ cents and those
of the Bank of New Orleans 55 to 58 cents.[3] If money had
been loaned on Southern property of whatever kind, values
had shrunk and the lenders were now unsecured. Thousands
of businesses, commercial and financial, were to be liquidated
and, if they could be, by grace of Northern credits or other aid,
put upon a new footing.

The new national banks were being founded in some places
with the support of the North. At the end of October there
were 35 in eight Southern states — 16 in Virginia, seven in
Tennessee, three in Georgia, three in Alabama, two in North
Carolina, two in Louisiana, one in South Carolina, and one in
Texas, with a combined capital of $4,474,400.[4]

Telegraphic communication between Macon, Ga., and
Washington was restored early in May,[5] and later in the month
despatches were passing between New Orleans and New York.[6]
The lines on the Mississippi from Louisville to New Orleans
were rebuilt and ready for service on May 30.[7] But it was

[1] N. Y. Tribune, June 21, 1865.   [4] Phila. Ledger, Oct. 31, 1865.
[2] Sidney Andrews, p. 35.   [5] Ibid., May 9, 1865.
[3] N. Y. Tribune, June 26, 1865.   [6] Ibid., May 23.
                  [7] Ibid., May 30.

December before the seaboard telegraph line from New York
to Mobile was repaired, and still later when connections with
New Orleans by this route were reëstablished.[1]

Post-offices and postal lines also were being reopened. The
first direct mail from Mobile to New York arrived by the
steamer Rhode Island on May 21.[2] The first mail to pass
directly between Richmond and Washington in more than four
years reached Washington on the evening of July 31.[3] But
in South Carolina, where everything in regard to restoration
went forward slowly, Governor Perry was complaining in September of the "woeful condition" of the people "without newspapers or letters."[4] In November Governor Marvin of Florida
said there was still no continuous line of telegraph out of that
state, while the mails moved irregularly and only between principal points.[5]

Communication by rail could be reëstablished only gradually,
and then, when reëstablished, it must remain of a most unsatisfactory character until capital could be secured to relay the
irons and purchase new rolling stock. Such railroads as came
within the advancing lines of the Federal army during the
war had been appropriated and put under military administration. These totalled 1855 miles, of which 1078 lay in Tennessee and in adjoining states on the Mississippi River, and
434 in Virginia.[6] Disputes arose in the War Department as to
the value of the improvements which had been made in these
lines while they were under government control. Sleepers
and irons had been renewed. The attentive officers prepared
inventories of the locomotives — the Reindeer, the Bluebird,
the Tornado, the Quickstep and the Stonewall Jackson — and
the supply of coaches and cars. The lines were gradually relin-
quished in August and September, 1865, and the property
restored to the stockholders. However much they had benefited by Northern management they were in a far from

[1] Phila. Ledger, Dec. 9.   [3] Ibid., Aug. 1.
[2] Ibid., May 23.   [4] N. Y. Tribune, Sept. 2.
[5] Senate Ex. Doc., 39th Cong., 1st sess., no. 26, p. 207.
[6] O. R., series iii, vol. v, pp. 581 et seq.

praiseworthy condition, and there were roads which the
Confederates had been using to forward troops and supplies,
and roads which Sherman had torn up on his way to the sea
in a worse situation.   The entire railway mileage in the South
in 1860 was 8945,[1] and less than one-fourth of this amount
ever came under the administration of the Federal War
Department.

It was July 11 before the first passengers from Washington
were carried into Richmond.   For more than four years, since
April 18, 1861, no trains had run between these two cities.
Grass and weeds overgrew the roadbed.   The rails had rusted.
The trestles in a bridge which had been taken out by the Confederates were found some hundreds of yards distant, and were
set in their old places by the train hands as they proceeded on
their way.   Another bridge had been burned.   The Rappahannock must be crossed in a boat.   The trip of 160 miles was
begun at nine o'clock on a Tuesday morning, and ended at
five o'clock on Wednesday morning, but it was said that trains
would soon be running through from New York to Richmond
in twenty-four hours.[2]   On October 5 it was announced that
direct railway connections had been reëstablished between
Mobile and New York, — by way of Knoxville, Tenn., and
Lynchburg, Va.[3]

The railroad from Atlanta to Chattanooga had been torn
up by Sherman, who had twisted the irons around the trees
and fused them in heaps upon piles of burning sleepers.   These
were straightened and put down again, but at points they were
still so crooked it was thought to be a marvel that trains passing over them remained upon the track.   The burnt bridges
were replaced by temporary trestles.   The first train over
this road after the war reached Chattanooga early in July.[4]

A newspaper correspondent who in July attempted the
trip from Richmond to Lynchburg, a distance of 130 miles,

[1] Census Reports, Mortality and Misc. Stat., p. 331.
[2] N. Y. Tribune, July 17, 1865.
[3] Ibid., Oct. 7, 1865.
[4] Ibid., July 31, 1865.

started early in the morning and was kept out by the slow pace
of the train and the delays occasioned by burned bridges,
and the like, all day, all night and a large part of the ensuing
day. There was no time during the journey when a passenger
might not have stepped off and on again while the train was
running.[1] Whitelaw Reid made the trip from Lynchburg to the
Tennessee line, 204 miles, in 22 hours, a rate of nine miles an
hour.[2] Another traveller covered 164 miles in 16 hours in North
Carolina.[3] The speed attained upon the railroads was about
nine miles an hour in South Carolina and eleven miles in North
Carolina.[4] The best railroad service in the South was that
between Augusta and Atlanta. The distance of 171 miles at
the end of the year 1865 was traversed at the rate of fourteen
miles an hour.[5]

The fares were high, from six to eleven cents a mile. The
average was about seven and a half cents in the Carolinas.[6]
It cost $5 to go from Charleston to Orangeburg Court-house, a
distance of 77 miles. There was one train a day and the time
was seven and a half hours.[7] Everywhere the rails were crushed
and worn down to the very limit of safety. Scarcely a half
inch of surface was left for the wheels to touch on one road
in Virginia.[8] On another stones were thrown into gaps in the
rails to prevent the cars from running off the track.[9] The
new bridges often were made of green timber and gave the
traveller an impression of being built in the cheapest and flimsi-
est manner. Inevitably there were accidents; it was a miracle
that there were not more. Such locomotives and cars had
never been seen on any American railroad. The machinery
was rusty, the headlights were gone, the bells broken, the smoke-
stacks fallen down. The cars were splashed with mud. Inside
the floors were indescribably filthy. Where cushions had
been on the seats were now only patches of plush and horse-
hair. Sometimes the seats had been entirely removed, and

---

[1] N. Y. Nation, vol. i, p. 426.   [5] N. Y. Nation, vol. ii, p. 110.
[2] Reid, p. 339.   [6] Sidney Andrews, p. 201.
[3] Sidney Andrews, p. 109.   [7] Ibid., p. 11.
[4] Ibid., p. 201.   [8] Reid, p. 330.
                    [9] Ibid., p. 339.

rough board benches were set along the sides of the cars. In the windows the glass was broken, and it remained out when the holes were not filled with boards.

Trains were made up of a coach for negroes and soldiers, another for "gentlemen," and a third for ladies, with a baggage car and two or three freight cars. When for lack of passenger coaches this arrangement could not be followed, the negroes and soldiers were packed into box freight cars, and in cases, on the Georgia and Carolina roads, white men and women, soldiers, negroes and all were carried in freight cars, which were sometimes fitted up with benches and again were wholly without seats.[1] There were long stops to take on water, and while negroes cut the wood to heat the boilers of the engine. Transfers from one train to another were made in the middle of the night, with long tramps through the sand or boat rides across streams because of interruptions in the line. Passengers were set down at junction points, where there were no stations or hotels, to wait several hours for the arrival of connecting trains.

Conditions were at their worst in Georgia and South Carolina on the line of Sherman's raid. A traveller for the Boston cotton merchants soon after the war had consumed six days in going from Savannah to Augusta.[2] Sixty miles of the road between the two cities had been destroyed. In November 45 miles were still unrepaired.[3]

Meantime travellers must be conveyed from place to place in old ambulances, hacks and market wagons, which were called stages. These usually made their trips at night at a very slow pace over wretched roads behind jaded horses and mules. A traveller was thus carried 32 miles in eight hours for $9,[4] and again, 45 miles in 19 hours for $10 in South Carolina.[5] Another traveller paid $25 for a hack ride of 50 miles between railway ends in South Carolina.[6] It would cost a million dollars to

[1] Reid, pp. 339, 365, 368; Sidney Andrews, pp. 11, 109.
[2] N. Y. Nation, vol. i, p. 426.
[3] Sidney Andrews, pp. 360–1.
[4] Ibid., p. 108. For a Southern view of the subject see E. F. Andrews, The War Time Journal of a Georgia Girl, pp. 162–5.
[5] Sidney Andrews, p. 30.   [6] N. Y. Nation, vol. i, p. 426.

put the Central Georgia road in running order as a result of
Sherman's raid.[1] But more courage and ability were being
exhibited by the railway builders in Georgia than in any of the
other states in the lower South, and the roads here were the first
to be repaired.

The hotels were very slow to exhibit signs of recovery or to
offer anything beyond the meanest hospitalities to travellers
— the newspaper correspondents sent out to describe the
country, the drummers for Northern commercial houses who
came in numbers after the war in search of trade, the Northern
capitalists and their agents looking for cotton, cheap plantations and other opportunities for investment and speculation.
Many public houses which had thriven before the war had not
reopened their doors. The food was scarce, badly cooked and
carelessly served. The beds were vile and often two or more
guests were pressed into the same room.[2] For such accommodations great prices were exacted, $3 and even $4 and $5 a day.
Everywhere out of the beaten way greenbacks were accepted
only at a discount. A guest would be asked $2 in silver or $4
in paper for a night's lodging. The people who had seen their
own notes become valueless in their purses were made doubtful
of the worth of paper money of any kind.

Little capital would reach the country during the summer to
invigorate business by the sale of agricultural products. Many
planters when they returned home from the war found that
their slaves had put corn in the cotton fields. The labor attending the growth of cotton was ungrateful to the negroes.[3]
In Georgia and Alabama travellers saw fields of corn; cotton
was "almost a thing of the past." [4] "You must work cotton

[1] N. Y. Tribune, July 17, 1865.

[2] See for instance, Sidney Andrews, p. 20.

[3] A freedman told a Northern traveller in Georgia in 1865: "If
ole massa wanta grow cotton let him plant it hisself. I'se work for
him dese twenty year and done got nothin but food and clothes, and
dem mighty mean; now I'se freedman and I tell you I ain't gone work
cotton nohow." — N. Y. Nation, vol. i, p. 426.

[4] Phila. Ledger, June 16, 1865, citing Richmond Times; cf. Phila.
Ledger, June 14.

from the time you can see the stalk before sun-up in the morning till nine o'clock at night thirteen months in the year," the old planters would say as they gloomily viewed the prospect of raising it with free labor. Some pulled up the corn and put in cotton, but the season was late and a little food to support their families, their negroes and their beasts was nearly all that most men could expect from their lands in the current year.[1]

The entire cotton crop of the United States in 1865 was not above 300,000 bales, while 4,805,000 bales had been grown in 1860.

The sugar crop in Louisiana would be about 30,000 hogsheads as compared with 11,200 in 1864. The yield before the war had sometimes amounted to 444,000 hogsheads.[2] In many places under wooden cogs moved by a horse sorghum was being ground into syrup. Women boiled the juice in kettles under the trees.[3] The war had widely increased the areas devoted to this crop and it had been a principal reliance of the people as a source of their sugar supply. In North Carolina, the famous scuppernong, as well as Choctaw and Catawba grapes throve luxuriantly, and were pressed for wine.[4] In the pine woods the trees were hacked and turpentine ran down into "boxes" cut in the trunks near the ground to catch the juice. Both men and women were employed in the orchards. The business gave employment to many persons around Mobile and in other parts of the South.[5]

The necessities of the war had led to a more extensive working of the rich iron ore and coal deposits in Alabama and Tennessee, destined in a few years to become an important source

---

[1] The same accounts came from beyond the Mississippi. In Arkansas corn was planted in the cotton fields. — Shreveport correspondence, N. Y. Tribune, July 10, 1865.

[2] Phila. Ledger, July 8, 1865. Placed by another authority later in the year at 12,000 hogsheads of sugar and 140,000 barrels of molasses. — Report of J. S. Fullerton to Gen. Howard, House Ex. Doc., 39th Cong., 1st sess., no. 70, p. 402.

[3] N. Y. Nation, vol. i, p. 427.

[4] N. Y. Tribune, Aug. 2, 1865.

[5] N. Y. Nation, vol. i, p. 557, and vol. ii, p. 209.

of wealth to the South.   Ore, pronounced to be of an excellent quality, had been mined near Talladega to supply a gun foundry and machine shops in Selma which fell a prey to the Northern raiders.[1]   Now there was a veritable fever of speculation.   No less than twenty companies to take petroleum out of the ground were incorporated by the legislature of Alabama in December, 1865, and January and February, 1866.   Sixty other companies to mine coal, make iron, build railroads, cut and manufacture lumber and for various industrial purposes received charters from the state.[2]

The South Carolina cities were being rebuilt only slowly. Not so in Mobile where in a few months a vast change came over the town.   Warehouses rose.   Torpedoes having been removed from the harbor a fleet of sailing and steam vessels stood before the wharves.   The hotels were filled with guests and the streets resounded with business life.[3]

In Atlanta the progress was yet more rapid, and men predicted that it would soon be "the foremost of the interior cities" of the South.   Four thousand mechanics were at work, and as many more would have been employed but for the scarcity of building material.   About 200 stores were opened and the streets were blocked with wagons and drays.[4]   Everywhere men were mixing mortar, carpenters were pounding, and drivers were shouting.   "No drones" were seen in this "hive."[5] There was "a never-ending throng of eager, excited and enterprising men, all bent on building and trading and swift fortune-making."[6]   In November, 1865, the trade of the city, it was said, was thirty per cent greater than it had been before the war.[7]

And this progress was being achieved with little aid from Northern men, come into the South, for few of them had the intention of permanently remaining in the country.   They would show the Southern people how to use free labor, but their

[1] Reid, pp. 384–5.
[2] Acts of Alabama of 1865–6.
[3] Reid, p. 403.
[4] Ibid., pp. 355–6.
[5] Phila. Ledger, Aug. 1, 1865.
[6] Sidney Andrews, p. 340; cf. N. Y. Nation, vol. ii, pp. 110–1.
[7] Ibid., p. 341.

success was nowhere great. The Northern planters and over-seers in the Sea Islands had worked their cotton lands at a loss in 1865, though never before had cotton sold at so high a price.[1] Northern employers had scant patience with the ne-groes as workmen and denounced their indolent and irrespon-sible ways.[2] They were soon ready to corroborate the opinion of the Southern planters that the new system was bad because the employer no longer had a necessary control of his laborers.[3] It cost one Northern man managing a Sea Island plantation over a dollar a pound to raise his cotton. A negro who had tilled six or seven acres in slavery now tended but three.[4] The experience of another Northern planter was so unsatisfactory, lacking the power to compel his hands, that he sent to the Ionian Isles for 15 Greeks at an expense of $2000. He would distribute these among fifty times their number of blacks to set them an example of industry.[5] Many of the negroes themselves found that their old masters were their best friends.[6]

Everywhere there were Southern men wise enough to strive earnestly to repair their fortunes. The substantial white element in the South did whatever it "could find to do and made merry over it." [7] Officers of the Northern and Southern armies were engaged happily as partners in mercantile pursuits in many parts of the South.[8] In Missouri returned Confederate soldiers and negroes were employed side by side on farms and in the streets.[9] Whites and blacks were seen at work together

[1] N. Y. Nation, vol. i, pp. 746–7.

[2] Fleming, Doc. Hist. of Recon., vol. i, p. 85; cf. J. W. Garner, Recon. in Miss., p. 136; Senate Ex. Doc., 39th Cong., 1st sess., no. 43, p. 10.

[3] N. Y. Nation, vol. i, p. 747.

[4] House Ex. Doc., 39th Cong., 1st sess., part ii, p. 2.

[5] Ibid., p. 18.

[6] Fleming, vol. i, pp. 89–90; Truman's Report, Senate Ex. Doc., 39th Cong., 1st sess., no. 43, p. 10; Report of Joint Com. on Recon., part iv, p. 153.

[7] M. L. Avary, Dixie after the War, pp. 155 et seq.; P. A. Hague, A Blockaded Family, p. 166.

[8] Senate Ex. Doc., 39th Cong., 1st sess., no. 43, p. 7.

[9] N. Y. Tribune, Oct. 17, 1865.

repairing the railroads in Virginia.[1] A Boston correspondent, writing home from New Orleans in October, said that the "false ideas prevalent throughout the South in relation to the dignity or indignity of labor had been done away with almost entirely." Planters and planters' sons, of great wealth before the war, who may have served as Confederate generals, were now not ashamed to perform duties they once considered "degrading." They were ploughing and hoeing in the fields. They had become overseers or clerks, or were learning mechanical trades. Men who earlier had had scores of servants at their call were hewing wood and drawing water at fifty cents per diem.[2] The young cavaliers of Dixie who used to be the delight of the ballrooms at Saratoga and Newport, a Southern woman wrote to Greeley's Tribune, were now "delving in mother earth with their own hands and with strong brave hearts earning their bread with the sweat of their brows." She and her friends were "dabbling" their "soft white hands in the wash-tub or browning their fair faces over a cooking stove," while the North would "make Cuffee a gentleman."[3] "A degree of latent force and energy," was being developed among the people "quite unexpected," and it was making them more "self-supporting and self-reliant" than they ever had been before the war.[4]

Such testimony was full of encouragement and it deserved more consideration than it would receive in the North, which was sitting in judgment upon the Southern people with only the record at its hand of their missteps and failures in this critical year.

[1] Reid, p. 331.
[2] N. Y. Nation, vol. i, p. 523.
[3] N. Y. Tribune, Oct. 21, 1865. The "wash-tub" was a great trial to many Southern ladies, since it was alleged that Sherman had pronounced this curse upon them. Although he was 70 years old Thomas Dabney, rather than let his daughters do so, himself washed and dried the family linen. For two years he continued to pay this price of the war. — Smedes, A Southern Planter, p. 234; cf. Avary, Dixie after the War, p. 119.
[4] N. Y. Nation, vol. i, p. 523.

CHAPTER III

CONGRESS IN CONTROL

WHEN Congress was ready to convene in December, the President had brought the plan of reconstruction, which was his heritage from Mr. Lincoln, to such a point that its fruits could be seen and judged by every man. An amendment of the Constitution of the United States, called the Thirteenth Amendment, forever prohibiting slavery upon the soil of the republic, had been sent to the states by Congress on the last day of January, 1865. All the members of the Cabinet and Chief Justice Chase appeared upon the floor of the House while the voting was in progress. The galleries were crowded and broke out into uncontrollable applause upon the announcement of the passage of the measure. One hundred guns were fired by three batteries of artillery in Washington. A brass band played patriotic tunes in front of the home of Senator Henderson of Missouri, who so long ago as in January, 1864, had introduced the amendment into Congress. He acknowledged the compliment in a speech. The crowd then proceeded to the White House to serenade President Lincoln, who came to the window with Henry Ward Beecher.[1] The news was flashed over the country. Governor Andrew ordered a salute on Boston Common. The event was celebrated by joyful outbursts in all parts of the North.

One state legislature after another hurried to the task of ratification. Illinois was the first to respond on February 1, and Rhode Island and Michigan were the second and third on February 2, to be followed by Maryland, New York, Massachusetts, Pennsylvania and West Virginia on the 3d, while the

---

[1] National Intelligencer, Feb. 2, 1865.

guns and the bells were still proclaiming the tidings to the
people.   There were radical suggestions that the eleven states
of the Confederacy were still outside the Union, although it
had been bravely contended throughout the war that none
might secede and leave the others.   Disregarding these theories
it was concluded that three-fourths of the states which must
ratify the amendment would be twenty-seven of the entire
thirty-six.   By May, 1865, twenty-two states had approved;
the votes of but five more were necessary to its adoption and
these were not likely to be secured until the Southern states
were reorganized.

In each state lately in rebellion such electors as had taken
the amnesty oath prescribed by the President's proclamation
of May 29 [1] were to choose delegates to assemble in a convention
to alter its old constitution, or frame a new one, so that the
government might be "republican" in form within the meaning of the Constitution of the United States.[2]   The elections
rapidly followed the appointment of the provisional governors.
Mississippi voted for delegates on August 7, Alabama on
August 31, South Carolina on September 4, North Carolina on
September 21, Georgia on October 4 and Florida on October 10.
Only Texas delayed until 1866, because of the disorder of the
country, its great area and the difficulty of reaching the people
for the purpose of administering the oath.[3]   The conventions
met soon; — Mississippi's on August 14, barely two months
after Governor Sharkey's appointment; Alabama's on September 12; South Carolina's, September 13; North Carolina's,
October 2; Georgia's, October 25 and Florida's, October 25.
Contrary to Northern hopes and expectations many of the men
chosen by the people as their representatives in these conven-

[1] Called in North Carolina the "d——d nasty oath."   Testimony
of Rev. Hope Bain in Report of Joint Com. on Reconstruction, part
ii, p. 205.

[2] See proclamation of the President appointing W. W. Holden
governor of North Carolina, in McPherson's History of Reconstruction,
p. 11.

[3] Address of Governor Hamilton, N. Y. Tribune, Aug. 8 and Oct.
16, 1865.

tions had not taken the oath.   They could not do so because
they belonged to classes of the population excepted from the
general provisions of the President's proclamation.   With
magnanimity he generally pardoned them, if this course were
recommended by the provisional governors, assuming, if their
neighbors and acquaintances set so much value upon their
services in so great an emergency, that they deserved to have
their offences condoned, and the work of restoration was proceeded with.

The total number of voters attending at the polls was small.
In general the most active leaders in the formation of the Confederacy and the effort to maintain it were not chosen as delegates.   But among them were not a few men who had more or
less heartily "gone with their states."   The Southern people
could be classified politically as they had been before the war.
For example, there were in the Mississippi convention seventy
Whigs and twenty-eight Democrats.[1]   There were those who
had been Unionists until the last moment and then had followed
their states reluctantly; a few, like Governor Hamilton in
Texas, who, totally at variance with those around them, had
left their states at the hour of secession and were only now ready
to return.   The South had had what it called Tories, and what
the North was pleased to term Unionists or Loyalists, mostly
the poor, many of whom, themselves unable to leave the area
of war, were "refugeed" by the United States government.
Then, there were men like Governor Holden, who had become
dissatisfied with President Davis's leadership, and who in the
North were considered the better for this circumstance.   In
addition to these there were the "bomb-proofs" and "feather-
beds," men who had shirked their military duties and stayed
at home in safe places while others fought the battles for
Southern independence, who were not whipped, as General
"Joe" Johnston said, "because they didn't fight." [2]   And now

---

[1] Publications of the Mississippi Historical Society, vol. iii, p. 75;
for North Carolina, cf. Sidney Andrews, The South since the War, p.
136.

[2] Phila. Ledger, Dec. 28, 1865.

there were coming to be what were known as "galvanized Yankees," men who, whatever their earlier sentiments, were glad to speak favorably of the North for the sake of winning some personal advantage at the hands of the powers at Washington, forerunners of the opprobrious scalawags.[1]

The conventions of 1865 contained few men of doubtful attachment to the Southern cause, nor yet many of the "fire-eaters." The delegates for the most part were moderates who had supported the Confederacy, as practically all the people of their communities had done once the war was instituted, and they were on this account fairly representative of the surrendered, the subjugated, the contrite people now ready to ask for the terms by which, with the President's counsel and advice, they might return to their political relations in the Union. Numbered among the delegates to the South Carolina convention were James L. Orr, one time before the war Speaker of the House of Representatives at Washington, later a Senator of the Confederate States at Richmond; F. W. Pickens, the first governor of South Carolina after secession; Confederate General McGowan, Alfred Huger, James Farrow and others known for their active devotion to the unsuccessful cause. In the body indeed were twenty-five or thirty men who had been officers in the Southern army.[2] Wade Hampton was returned from the Richland district, but did not attend the sessions.

In North Carolina nine of the delegates had been members of the convention which voted the state out of the Union;[3] all were "rebel save two," said Judge Howard.[4] In Georgia twenty-one members of the secession convention of 1861 were returned as members of the convention of 1865. Ex-Governor Herschel V. Johnson, who had been a member of the Confederate Senate, was elected to preside over the body which

[1] Conversely there had been "galvanized rebels," Union turncoats who had enlisted in the Confederate service. — E. F. Andrews, The War Time Journal of a Georgia Girl, p. 208.

[2] Sidney Andrews, The South since the War, pp. 38–9.

[3] Ibid., pp. 136–7.

[4] Phila. Ledger, Oct. 24, 1865.

assembled at Milledgeville in October. Several of the Georgia delegates had sat in the Congress at Richmond, or had held other offices, civil or military, under the Davis government.[1] The Mississippi convention was made up of men who more or less actively had sustained the Confederacy,[2] and similar conditions prevailed in all the states.

There was a general desire to know how much sitting in dust and ashes would serve the needs of the case. One and all proceeded to repeal or annul their ordinances of secession. Then came the question of the negro. It was necessary that the returning states should accept the results of the war with reference to the complete and everlasting abolition of slavery. President Johnson said that he would have their constitutions amended in this regard. "All future legislatures" must be denied "the power to legislate that there is property in man." [3] To Governor Sharkey in Mississippi, the first state to hold a convention, he suggested an extension of the elective franchise to negroes who could read the Constitution of the United States and write their names, or who owned and paid taxes on real estate worth $250.[4] He would have the states ratify the Thirteenth Amendment. Every dollar of the debt created to aid the rebellion should be repudiated "finally and forever." [5]

Each of the six conventions of 1865 adopted constitutional provisions prohibiting slavery. The requirement that the debt contracted to wage war against the Union be repudiated seemed harsh, but North Carolina passed such an ordinance by a vote of 84 to 12, Georgia, after much opposition, by a vote of 135 to 117, Alabama, by a vote of 60 to 19, and

[1] Sidney Andrews, pp. 239–40.

[2] "Conservatives," representatives of the "best type" of the state's citizenship. — Publications of Miss. Hist. Soc., vol. iii, p. 75, and vol. vi, p. 145.

[3] President Johnson to Gov. Sharkey, Aug. 15, 1865. — Senate Ex. Doc., 39th Cong., 1st sess., no. 26, p. 229.

[4] Senate Ex. Doc., 39th Cong., 1st sess., no. 26, p. 229.

[5] President Johnson to Gov. Holden, Oct. 18; to Gov. Johnson, Oct. 28; Seward to Gov. Johnson, Oct. 28; Seward to Gov. Perry, Nov. 20 and Nov. 30. All these telegrams are to be found in Senate Ex. Doc., 39th Cong., 1st sess., no. 26.

Florida followed the example of the other three states under compulsion from Washington. South Carolina carried the subject into the legislature, which declared that the debts contracted for war and for the enterprises of peace were so commingled that the separation of the parts was impossible.[1] The convention in Mississippi was in session for but ten days, in Georgia thirteen days, South Carolina sixteen days, Alabama eighteen days. Before adjournment elections for governors, members of the legislatures, representatives in Congress and other officers were set for dates in November. As in the elections for delegates to the conventions no great number of votes were cast in comparison with the poll before the war. In Mississippi and North Carolina the vote was about sixty per cent of that cast in 1860; in Alabama less than fifty per cent, and in Georgia thirty per cent. Not so many as 1500 persons voted for governor in the entire city of Charleston.[2]

Taking courage gradually, a still greater number of men who had been prominent in the management of the late Confederacy were chosen to office at these elections. The legislatures continued the task of the conventions with reference to the resumption of the states' Federal relations. The President and Secretary Seward positively declared that no state could hope to resume its old place in the Union until it had ratified the Thirteenth Amendment. South Carolina objected to the last clause, wherein Congress was given power to enforce abolition by "appropriate legislation," but on November 13 approved the amendment with qualifying statements, which, however, were not looked at too narrowly at Washington, and became the twenty-fourth state on the list. Alabama and Florida followed with similar declaratory resolutions on December 2 and December 28 respectively. North Carolina ratified unqualifiedly on December 1 and Georgia on December 6. Mississippi refused her assent on the ground that the amendment was unnecessary, since she had already abolished slavery; that she would not coerce Kentucky and Delaware into emancipation;

[1] Senate Ex. Doc., 39th Cong., 1st sess., no. 26, p. 201.
[2] Phila. Ledger, Oct. 25, 1865.

that the second section gave vague and large powers to Congress, which already exercised too much authority over local matters; that the public mind ought now to be withdrawn from unpleasant questions connected with the negro race.[1]

Mississippi passed a law setting aside a part of the state's revenues to pension Confederate soldiers and soldiers' widows,[2] and to provide the maimed with artificial legs,[3] and resolved to memorialize the President for the pardon of Jacob Thompson [4] and Jefferson Davis. Enough blood had been shed —

> " whose guiltless drops
> Are every one a woe, a sore complaint,
> 'Gainst him whose wrong gives edge unto the sword,
> That makes such waste in brief mortality." [5]

The name of Jones County was changed to Davis County.[6] The South Carolina convention appointed a committee to visit and ask the President to pardon Davis, Stephens and other Confederate leaders still confined in United States forts.[7] The Georgia convention desired the release of the prisoners. Davis, said the memorialists, had been "elevated to his high position by our suffrages and in response to our wishes." He had not sought the place. "If he is guilty, so were we. . . . Let not the retribution of a mighty nation be visited upon his head while we who urged him to his destiny are suffered to escape." [8] The same convention desired the President to pardon citizens of Georgia excepted in his amnesty proclamation and now disfranchised, "many of her finest intellects and purest patriots, and involving much of her available wealth." [9] Florida, first by the convention[10] and then by the legislature, also asked for the pardon of Davis.[11] Secretary Mallory, Senator Yulee, Governor Allison, citizens of the state, still held as prisoners,

[1] Senate Ex. Doc., 39th Cong., 1st sess., no. 26, pp. 79–80.
[2] Miss. Laws of 1865, p. 149.
[3] Ibid., p. 157.   [4] Ibid., p. 278.
[5] Ibid., pp. 280–4.   [6] Ibid., p. 240.
[7] Andrews, The South since the War, p. 55.
[8] Ibid., pp. 250–2; Confederate Records of Ga., vol. iv, p. 430.
[9] Andrews, p. 422.   [10] Fla. Laws of 1865, p. 154.
[11] Ibid., p. 106.

were the subjects of memorials addressed to the President by the convention, the legislature and Governor Marvin.[1] North Carolina,[2] Florida[3] and other states urged the President to remove the negro troops. The Georgia convention, in inserting in the newly adopted constitution a provision in regard to emancipation, declared that the "acquiescence" of the state in this "war measure" of the government was not to be held to estop later claims upon Congress for compensation for the loss of the slaves,[4] and the governor-elect of South Carolina in his inaugural address in November expressed a hope that the owners who had been dispossessed might be indemnified.[5] The United States flag, it was complained, was not displayed over the buildings in which the conventions sat; many delegates appeared in their Confederate uniforms with the brass buttons still in place; ex-Confederate generals were invited to occupy seats on the floor. When the legislature of Alabama was in session, in Montgomery, General Thomas, in command of the military department, was in the city; he was ignored, while the members stood up in their places to welcome Wade Hampton, who came upon invitation to address them about the war.[6] In Georgia ex-Governor Joseph E. Brown, who still occupied the executive mansion, was said to be the strong hand behind the scenes.[7]

Much of what was done or left undone in the Southern conventions and legislatures was disquieting to large bodies of the people in the North. Although he was not a candidate for the office Wade Hampton was probably elected, in spite of every politic consideration, to the governorship of South Carolina. It was believed for weeks that he had been the popular choice. To prepare the President's mind for what had come to pass, the garrulous provisional governor, Perry, telegraphed to the White House that Hampton was "one of the most admirable men" he ever saw, "as honorable, frank and open-

[1] Laws of 1865, pp. 105–6, 113–4; Senate Ex. Doc., 39th Cong., 1st sess., no. 26, p. 215.

[2] Senate Ex. Doc., no. 26, p. 42.   [3] Laws of Fla., pp. 113–4.

[4] Art. 1, sec. 20.   [5] N. Y. Tribune, Dec. 8, 1865.

[6] Phila. Ledger, Dec. 28, 1865.

[7] Andrews, The South since the War, pp. 242–3.

hearted as can be." Perry had had a conversation with Hampton, who pledged himself to sustain the Johnson policy of reconstruction.[1] When the time came to canvass the ballots, however, enough were thrown out, so it was charged,[2] to seat ex-Speaker Orr, a less objectionable man from every Northern point of view, and it was announced that he had been elected by 9776 votes against 9109 for Hampton.

In North Carolina Provisional Governor Holden, who had taken a position in support of President Johnson's policies, including the repudiation of the state war debt, was defeated by Jonathan Worth, who was known to be the favorite of the old secessionists.[3] The legislature would have "a clear anti-administration or secession majority," Governor Holden telegraphed President Johnson.[4] In Mississippi Benjamin G. Humphreys, an ex-brigadier-general of the Confederate army, not yet pardoned by the President, or indeed assured that he would be, was chosen over Judge Fisher, a more moderate candidate, who was defeated principally because he had been charged in the campaign with an expressed indifference during the progress of the war as to its outcome.[5] Alabama had "gone wild," a correspondent in that state wrote to the President. Three-fourths of the members of the legislature had been either officers or privates in the Confederate army. Candidates with other records were denounced as "traitors to the South," and were "premeditatedly and overwhelmingly defeated." [6]

The tender question was the negro, and the action of the

[1] Senate Ex. Doc., 39th Cong., 1st sess., no. 26, p. 253.

[2] General Saxton's testimony before the Joint Committee on Reconstruction, part ii, p. 217.

[3] Holden's paper, the Raleigh Standard, during the campaign, kept this line at the head of its columns — "Holden and go into the Union, or Worth and stay out." — Report of Joint Committee, part ii, p. 212.

[4] Senate Ex. Doc., 39th Cong., 1st sess., no. 26, p. 228.

[5] Garner, Reconstruction in Miss., p. 95; cf. N. Y. Nation, March 15, 1866; Phila. Ledger, Oct. 5, 1865. A little while since a correspondent wrote to Johnson, Humphreys would have "hung you to the first tree as he would a dog." — Letter dated Oct. 7, 1865, in Johnson Papers.

[6] Joseph C. Bradley to the President, Nov. 15, 1865, in Johnson Papers.

Southern legislatures concerning him was awaited in the confident belief that at the first possible moment he would be led back into slavery. At once there was much evidence which was held to support such a view. Humphreys in his message to the legislature of Mississippi in November said, with strange disregard of his position at the head of a state which was suing for a return to a place in the Union, that slavery had been abolished "under the pressure of Federal bayonets urged on by the misdirected sympathies of the world in behalf of the enslaved African." The four years of war, "conducted on principles of vandalism, disgraceful to the civilization of the age," were not worse for Mississippi than the "black incubus" of free negroes directed by the Freedmen's Bureau. It was a "hideous curse," and the only remedy was in laws to protect the white as well as the black man.[1]

Most of the conventions had appointed commissions to report to the legislatures measures giving a legal position to the freedmen, and such laws were passed one after another to arouse the most virulent criticism in Abolitionist, and, as the South called them, "Black Republican" circles in the North. In the first place it was contended that the negro should be able to testify in the courts. There was palpable injustice in withholding this right from him if he were to be a human being at all, yet the opposition to bringing him forward as a witness was strong. It was said that the negro did not know the truth; that he could not understand the meaning of an oath.[2] If a man's life and property were to be sworn away by his slaves, existence in the South would be tolerable no longer.

In the election in Mississippi the admission of negro testimony in the courts was the leading issue before the people, and the party opposed to it secured a majority of the members of the legislature. Next thing, said the Jackson News, it will be proposed that the negro shall be a juryman and that he shall

---

[1] Fleming, Doc. Hist. of Reconstruction, vol. i, pp. 251–3.

[2] The moral nature of the negro was discussed at length by a committee of the North Carolina legislature. — Senate Ex. Doc., 39th Cong., 1st sess., no. 26, pp. 52–5.

vote.[1] But Governor Humphreys, in spite of the temper of
his legislature, in his message to it, advocated the receiving of
negro evidence. It would be an "insult to the intelligence and
virtue" of the courts to say that they could not or would not
protect innocent persons against the perjury of black witnesses.[2]
Governor Marvin of Florida said that to receive the testimony
of the negro must be regarded, not as a privilege granted to
him, but as "the right of the state" in the interest of even-
handed justice.[3] "It would be as much for the protection of
the white man as the colored," President Johnson telegraphed
Governor Sharkey of Mississippi.[4] The Southern people might
shrug their shoulders, he said another time, but the negro's
testimony was to be taken for what it was worth by those who
examined him and the jury who heard him.[5]

No convention or legislature had touched upon this subject
until Florida on November 6 resolved that while jurors should
be white men, no person should be incompetent to testify as
a witness on account of his color in any case affecting the
rights or liberties of a negro. This was a granting of the privilege with an important qualification. Other states followed
Florida's example — the colored man could testify only when
a member of his race was a party to the suit under trial and it
must be in open court, which meant that his evidence might
not be taken by deposition in writing or in answer to written in-
terrogatories. He must come in person before the court or jury,
which should have the opportunity to judge from his appearance
and by his manner of speech as to his credibility as a witness.[6]

[1] Garner, Reconstruction in Miss., p. 94.

[2] Fleming, Doc. Hist. of Reconstruction, vol. i, p. 252.

[3] Senate Ex. Doc., 39th Cong., 1st sess., no. 26, p. 210.

[4] Ibid., p. 234.

[5] Pres. Johnson to a South Carolina delegation, N. Y. Tribune,
Oct. 14, 1865.

[6] McPherson, History of Reconstruction, p. 24; Miss. Laws of
1865, p. 83; Alabama Laws of 1865-6, p. 98; cf. Georgia Public
Laws of 1865-6, p. 239, where a somewhat different practice was instituted, though the negro was effectually barred from testifying
against the white man in disputes not directly involving the person or
property of a negro.

However disturbing such a disposition regarding negro testimony may have been to the Northern Abolitionists it was nothing to compare with their rage when they read about the so-called "Black Codes." The legislatures must make some adequate legal provision for the future government of the relations of the people with the hundreds of thousands of emancipated slaves, infesting the whole South in idleness and unrest in expectation that lands, wagons and mules would be distributed to them by some power they had heard of at Washington. Mississippi led the way with her "Black Laws." Negroes were to become lessees of lands or tenements nowhere in that state except in towns and cities. They must make annual contracts for their labor in writing; if they should run away from their tasks, they forfeited their wages for the year. Whenever it was required of them they must present licenses (in a town from the mayor; elsewhere from a member of the board of police of the beat) citing their places of residence and authorizing them to work. Fugitives from labor were to be arrested and carried back to their employers. Five dollars a head and mileage would be allowed such negro catchers. It was made a misdemeanor, punishable with fine or imprisonment, to persuade a freedman to leave his employer, or to feed the runaway. Minors were to be apprenticed, if males until they were twenty-one, if females until eighteen years of age. Such corporal punishment as a father would administer to a child might be inflicted upon apprentices by their masters.[1] Vagrants were to be fined heavily, and if they could not pay the sum, they were to be hired out to service until the claim was satisfied.[2] Negroes might not carry knives or firearms unless they were licensed so to do.[3] It was an offence, to be punished by a fine of $50 and imprisonment for thirty days, to give or sell intoxicating liquors to a negro.[4] When negroes could not pay the fines and costs after legal proceedings, they

[1] Miss. Laws of 1865, pp. 82–7.
[2] Ibid., p. 90.   [3] Ibid., p. 165.
[4] Ibid., p. 166; cf. McCarthy, Lincoln's Plan of Reconstruction, pp. 475 et seq.

were to be hired at public outcry by the sheriff to the lowest bidder.[1]

The legislature in South Carolina also provided for an apprentice system. Persons of color contracting for service were to be known as "servants," and those with whom they contracted, as "masters." On farms the hours of labor would be from sunrise to sunset daily, except on Sunday. The negroes were to get out of bed at dawn. Time lost would be deducted from their wages, as would be the cost of food, nursing, etc., during absence from sickness. Absentees on Sunday must return to the plantation by sunset. House servants were to be at call at all hours of the day and night on all days of the week. They must be "especially civil and polite to their masters, their masters' families and guests," and they in return would receive "gentle and kind treatment." Corporal and other punishment was to be administered only upon order of the district judge or other civil magistrate. A vagrant law of some severity was enacted to keep the negroes from roaming the roads and living the lives of beggars and thieves.[2]

In some states the negro was not specially named, and set out as a being different from the white man, as he had been in Mississippi and South Carolina. Not so boldly was the black man denied what they were coming in the North to call his "civil rights." But in all the states, by one device or another, protective measures against his ignorance and his childishness were taken, and he was to be put, at least for a time, under such guardianship as intimate acquaintance with him on the part of the Southern people seemed to require. Georgia would adjudge to be vagrants "all persons strolling about in idleness who are able to work and who have no property to support them"; [3] Alabama, "a stubborn or refractory servant" and "a laborer or servant who loiters away his time or refuses to comply with any contract for a term of service without just cause." [4] If

---

[1] Miss. Laws of 1865, p. 200.
[2] Statutes at Large of South Carolina, vol. xiii, p. 269.
[3] Ga. Public Laws of 1865-6, p. 234.
[4] Ala. Laws of 1865-6, p. 119.

persons so put under arrest were unable to pay their fines, they could be bound out to service for from six months to a year. Marriage between the races was interdicted under heavy penalties. Negroes, except in the case of maids accompanying their mistresses, were barred from railway cars occupied by whites in Mississippi.[1] Florida, with an appearance of impartiality to impress the sensitive public mind in the North, provided that if a negro "intruded" into a white man's railway car or church, or a white man forced his presence upon the negro in the same way in the same places, he might be made to stand in the pillory for an hour, or receive thirty-nine stripes upon his back.[2]

The system of pains and penalties in the South had remained barbarous, as measured by the improving standards of the North, and they were not to be changed immediately either for the white man or the negro. The laws prescribed hanging for grand larceny, burglary, arson and an inciting of "any portion or class" of the people to insurrection. In at least one state — Georgia — a man could be hanged for stealing a horse or a mule.[3] But as a rule equal consideration was granted the races in the general criminal codes of the Southern states except in the case of rape. In more than one state this crime against a white woman by the black man was punishable with death, while if a white man committed the same crime, the penalty was a term in prison; or it was made a capital crime, should it be committed upon the person of a white woman, without naming a penalty if the attack were directed against a black woman. The whipping post, the pillory, stocks, treadmills, work in chain gangs were words often seen in the Southern codes, and they aroused a great revulsion of feeling in the North, which nearly everywhere had passed away from these stages of penology.

Nor were the conditions in the four states in which the people had presumably resumed the conduct of their civil affairs at an earlier date at a better pass. In Louisiana the governor was J. Madison Wells, a Red River planter, who had brought

---

[1] Laws of Miss. of 1865, p. 231.
[2] Laws of Fla. of 1865, p. 25.
[3] Public Laws of Ga. of 1865–6, p. 232.

himself and his slaves within the Federal lines at the time of the occupation of the country by the Union armies. A new constitution had been adopted in 1864 while General Banks was in command of the Department of the Gulf. Under its terms slavery had been abolished. Michael Hahn had been elected governor, and Wells, who was the lieutenant-governor, had succeeded to the first place upon Hahn's resignation to accept a seat in the United States Senate, which he was not allowed to occupy. The radicals loudly complained of Wells, for it was said that he gave commissions for judges, mayors and other local officers to men in Confederate uniforms scarcely five days home from service in the "rebel army." [1] Indeed he was turning loyal men out of office in order that "rebels" could be appointed in their stead.[2] He was nothing less than "a traitor to the Union cause." [3]

Nevertheless in November, 1865, he was confirmed in his place by an election of the people, his opponent in the canvass being the late Confederate Governor Allen, who had been conducting a rival political establishment at Shreveport. Wells received some 22,000 votes and Allen only 5000 in a poll which was about one-half what it had been in 1860. The legislature which was chosen at this election was overwhelmingly Democratic, and at once began to enact "Black Laws" for the freedmen. The negro was "downtrodden" in Louisiana, his watchful friend, Horace Greeley, complained in the New York Tribune; Wells was "pandering to the worst rebel feelings." [4]

The new free state government of Tennessee had been put upon its feet in February, 1865, by the election to the governorship of "Parson" Brownlow, a Methodist circuit preacher and journalist, who early in the war had been arrested, and finally expelled from Knoxville by the Confederates. He was a voluble

[1] Report of Joint Com. on Reconstruction, part iv, p. 81; Letters to Carl Schurz on Sept. 5, 6 and 7, 1865, in Johnson Papers.

[2] Report of Joint Com., part iv, p. 115.

[3] R. King Cutler, Hahn's associate as a claimant for a seat in the United States Senate from Louisiana, to Carl Schurz Sept. 5, 1865, in Johnson Papers.

[4] N. Y. Tribune, Nov. 15, 1865; cf. ibid., Nov. 30 and Dec. 29, 1865.

and obstreperous man who was totally unfitted to have a part
in any work of pacification. He had been in favor of slavery
before the war. Like most of the East Tennessee Unionists
he was without any very friendly regard for the freedman.
He had declared in his annual message in October, 1865,
that whites and blacks could not live together politically
or socially as equals.[1] He opposed the enfranchisement of
the negroes and gladly would have seen them all banished to
Liberia.

In Virginia Governor Peirpoint called an extra session of the
legislature in the summer of 1865. Nineteen-twentieths of
the people were disfranchised because they could not take an
oath which was now to be modified along the lines laid down
in the President's amnesty proclamation. It rested with the
legislature to make this change to the advantage of those who
had been disloyal during the war. That body acted promptly
and submitted to the electorate, thus enlarged, the question of
amending the constitution to permit those who had held
office under the Confederacy to do so in the reorganized state.[2]
At the same time a new legislature was elected, made up largely
of men who had taken more or less active parts in the rebellion,[3]
and who, when they convened, sought to regain possession of
West Virginia, memorialized the President on the subject of
Jefferson Davis's release and passed various laws to regulate
the conduct of the negro.

In Arkansas a new constitution containing a provision
abolishing slavery had been adopted in 1864. Isaac Murphy
was the governor of the state. Both he and his legislature
reflected the general sense of the South in regard to the negro,
and had become thoroughly reactionary. Affairs were again

[1] Phila. Ledger, Oct. 4, 1865.

[2] A committee of "loyal Virginians," addressing the New York
Tribune, said that this legislature was "an organization not at all less
disloyal than the legislature which sat at Richmond under the auspices
of William Smith." — Issue of July 10, 1865.

[3] These movements in Virginia are described in testimony included
in the Report of the Joint Com. on Reconstruction, part ii, pp. 83,
145.

in the hands of those who had actually abetted or were in open sympathy with secession.[1]

Virginia and Louisiana had ratified the Thirteenth Amendment in February, and Arkansas and Tennessee followed in April, 1865.

Reconstruction was going forward, but would Congress admit the senators and representatives sent to Washington by the Southern states at the invitation of the President? Under present arrangements they must take the "iron-clad" test oath of July 2, 1862. They must swear not only that they would support and defend the Constitution of the United States in the future, but also that they had "never voluntarily borne arms against the United States," had "voluntarily" given "no aid, countenance, counsel or encouragement" to persons in rebellion and had exercised or attempted to exercise the functions of no office under the Confederacy.[2]

The provision had equal application to revenue officers and other agents of the Treasury Department, postmasters, United States marshals, district attorneys and judges, and unless the terms of the oath should be modified few capable or respected persons in the South would be available for Federal office in the reorganized states. The legislatures of the states quite generally adopted resolutions urging the repeal of the law. President Johnson, when he was applied to, said that he was without any kind of knowledge of what Congress would be pleased to do in the premises. He repeatedly urged the Southern people to elect as their representatives and the legislatures to choose as senators only such men as could take the oath. Some "graybacks" and "butternuts," fearful of the consequences, withdrew their names as candidates for Congress,[3] but in general there seemed to be faith that a way would be found to seat those who were sent forward to represent the restored states at Washington.

[1] Powell Clayton, The Aftermath of the Civil War in Arkansas, pp. 17–32.

[2] U. S. Statutes at Large, vol. xii, p. 502.

[3] It was so in Virginia. — N. Y. Tribune, Oct. 2, 1865.

The most notable member of the Southern delegations was
Alexander H. Stephens, Vice-President of the Confederacy, who,
although barely out of Fort Warren on parole after serving a
long term as a state prisoner, had been elected senator of the
United States from Georgia. His colleague was Herschel V.
Johnson, by reason of his course during the war as little able
to take the oath. Four of the provisional governors, Lewis
E. Parsons of Alabama, William Marvin of Florida, William
L. Sharkey of Mississippi and B. F. Perry of South Carolina,
had been chosen by their respective state legislatures as United
States senators. Not one, unless it be Judge Marvin, could
honestly swear that he had not given aid and countenance to
the rebellion. William A. Graham, an ex-member of the Confederate Congress, was almost unanimously elected a United
States senator from North Carolina. J. L. Alcorn, Sharkey's
colleague from Mississippi, had been a brigadier-general of
Confederate militia, and would have enjoyed higher military
honors but for the personal hostility of Jefferson Davis. John
L. Manning, Perry's colleague from South Carolina, was closely
identified by marriage with the old Hampton family and had
been on Beauregard's staff during the war.

So much for the Senate. How fared it with members elected
to the House? When the delegations were complete there
were 58 representatives to be seated from the Southern states,
all of them described as Democrats except three in Tennessee
and one in Virginia.[1] Governor Johnson of Georgia telegraphed
the President on November 21 that not one of the representa-
tives-elect of that state could take the oath.[2] Four out of seven
of them had been in the Confederate army and two of the three
remaining members had held civil offices under the "rebel"
government.[3] All the men chosen in North Carolina, it was
said, had been "rebels"; not one could qualify.[4] At least four
Confederate generals, four or five colonels and a half dozen

[1] N. Y. Tribune Almanac for 1866 and 1867.
[2] Senate Ex. Doc.,＄39th Cong., 1st sess., no. 26, p. 239.
[3] Report of Joint Com. on Reconstruction, part iii, p. 171.
[4] N. Y. Tribune, Nov. 8 and Nov. 20, 1865.

men who had sat in the Richmond Congress were included in the various delegations.[1] The issue was made doubtful indeed.

To add to the general suspicion of the North a number of the Southern states were organizing bodies of militia. Governor Sharkey of Mississippi, while in Washington, had asked President Johnson if he might at need form local companies of troops for the suppression of crime. In August stage wagons were being attacked and robbed, and other outrages perpetrated upon the people, and he issued a call for volunteers.[2] General Slocum, in command of the United States troops stationed in Mississippi, interfered to prevent Sharkey from going forward with his design. General Schurz, who was in the South at the time, serving as the President's personal representative, supported General Slocum, as did radical public sentiment everywhere in the North. What might not be looked for if the disbanded Confederate soldiers were now to be reorganized and put into the field in the Southern states? The dispute lasted for two or three weeks when Slocum was compelled to rescind his order, and the governor continued the work of forming his military organization.[3] Governor Perry on September 18 issued a proclamation authorizing the enlistment of military companies in South Carolina [4] and most of the conventions and legislatures, when they met, specifically provided for the organization of bodies of state troops for police duty.[5]

It is very plain that the Southern leaders of 1865 were little acquainted with the temper of the North at the end of a long

[1] McPherson's Hist. of Reconstruction, p. 109.

[2] Schurz's Report, Senate Ex. Doc., 39th Cong., 1st sess., no. 2, pp. 102–4.

[3] Senate Ex. Doc., 39th Cong., 1st sess., no. 26, pp. 231–2; Garner, Reconstruction in Miss., pp. 100–3; N. Y. Tribune, Sept. 11, 12, 21, 1865. For Sharkey's account of the dispute, see Report of Joint Com. on Reconstruction, part iii, p. 136.

[4] N. Y. Tribune, Sept. 29, 1865.

[5] For Florida see Senate Ex. Doc., no. 26, p. 216, and Laws of 1865, p. 2; Georgia — Senate Ex. Doc., no. 26, pp. 91, 92, 238; Alabama — ibid., p. 108; North Carolina — ibid., p. 31; Mississippi — Laws of 1865, p. 2.

and triumphant war, or else were regardless of it. Prohibiting the negro from leasing land outside of towns and cities in Mississippi, the leader in the offending, since her convention and legislature met first and set the standards for the other states; confining negro testimony to cases in which the black man was a defendant; requiring him to show a license to work, if he were not to be arrested for vagrancy; establishing long sunrise to sunset hours, as in South Carolina, were unwise regulations. Moreover, they were advertisements of unwisdom, since they were put into writing under the eyes of the whole country. The men who had brought this reproach upon Mississippi, said one newspaper, the Columbus (Miss.) Sentinel, were "as complete a set of political Goths as were ever turned loose to work destruction upon a state. The fortunes of the whole South have been injured by their folly."[1] Looking back at the course of Mississippi's leaders during this period a Southern writer says that he is amazed at their "stupidity." They acted as though they had been asleep during the war. Upon waking they had begun to legislate for the negroes at the point "just where the Code of 1857 had left off."[2]

The friends of the negro at the North were profoundly impressed by what was every day revealed to them in the columns of such a paper as the New York Tribune. It was of no avail to say that the Northern states had vagrant laws, and laws for "masters" and apprentices almost as severe as those enacted in the South.[3] These were the "slave codes" revived for the freedmen. The good men of the North would "convert the state of Mississippi into a frog pond," said the Chicago Tribune, before they would permit such laws to "disgrace one foot of

[1] Quoted in Garner, p. 116.
[2] Publications of Miss. Hist. Society, vii, pp. 156–8. Article by J. H. Jones, a lawyer and once lieutenant-governor of his state, who had been a colonel in the Confederate army. W. L. Fleming would explain the mistakes of this year in the South by the fact that the conventions and legislatures were made up mainly of non-slaveholders who had been Unionists or lukewarm Confederates during the war. — Documentary Hist. of Reconstruction, vol. i, p. 245.
[3] Garner, p. 119; Herbert, Why the Solid South, pp. 32–5, 240.

soil in which the bones of our soldiers sleep and over which the flag of freedom waves." [1] The only test which the people of Mississippi required of a candidate for office, said the New York Tribune, was this — "Is he a thorough rebel? Is he still as rebellious as he can be and pass muster? Will he be as hard on the negroes as possible?" [2] The "rebel soldiers and rebel magnates" meant to show the North that they were returning to the Union "because they must, not because they would." [3] What one state, it was asked, had "come back frankly and accepted all the issues of the war, even the issues of the President?" Not one had done so. "The moment we remove the iron hand from the rebels' throats," said Greeley, whose utterances are important because he spoke for the whole radical Republican element from the Atlantic Ocean to the outermost lines of settlement in the West, "they will rise and attempt the mastery." The mistake made by President Johnson was that, instead of waiting till the prodigal had come home, he had sent the fatted calf to him. The first fruits of reconstruction promised "a most deplorable harvest, and the sooner we gather the tares, plough the ground again and sow new seed the better." [4] The denial of the right of the negro to testify in court was "an outrage against civilization." The only place a negro could occupy in a court-room in Alabama was at the prisoner's dock. The South was pursuing a policy which would not "stop short of the extermination of the black race." [5] To exclude or restrict the negro in the giving of testimony in court was "not more insulting and degrading to the blacks than injurious and perilous to the whites." [6]

Governor Parsons of Alabama was regarded as one of the most acceptable of Johnson's governors, but in a message to the legislature he spoke of certain "rebel flags" as "sacred souvenirs of the courage and endurance of those who went forth to battle under their folds." [7] The Southern legislatures were

---

[1] Dec. 1, 1865 — quoted in Garner, p. 115.
[2] Oct. 14, 1865.
[3] N. Y. Tribune, Nov. 13, 1865.
[4] Ibid., Nov. 15, 1865.
[5] Ibid., Oct. 3, 1865.
[6] Ibid., Dec. 23, 1865.
[7] Ibid., Dec. 13, 1865.

only repealing, not annulling, their ordinances of secession. In Tennessee one hundred "rebels" and negroes had been butchered since June 1, 1865, in and around Knoxville, under the administration of "a reverend blackguard" who was "styled governor." The state was yet "no more fit for self-government than Dahomey." [1]   It would be "as easy to extract milk from flint" as "practical mercy" from a vagrant law in Alabama. [2]

So day after day Greeley and his editors fulminated; so their words went out over the country to increase suspicion and distrust in the North, and to irritate the South.

The elections in the North in 1865 had been of no great importance, but in so far as there was any meaning in them they betokened little disposition to temporize with the Southern question. The Republican party platforms in the main contained indorsements of the President's policy. But Pennsylvania had declared that his "mild and generous method" had not been "accepted in the spirit of honest loyalty and gratitude" by the Southern people, rather "with such evidence of defiance and hostility as to impel us to the conviction that they cannot safely be intrusted with the political rights which they forfeited by their treason." The states should be "held in subjugation," and the laws which were to govern them should be "referred to the law-making power of the nation to which it legitimately belongs." The Massachusetts convention, meeting a little later, reiterated these sentiments. [3]

The New England states all elected Republican governors by majorities which were entirely satisfying to the leaders of the party. Pennsylvania chose a Republican auditor-general, the principal officer on the ticket, by a somewhat larger majority than Lincoln had received in the state in the preceding year. But the greatest significance was attached by the Republicans to the result in New York and New Jersey. In New York, where only minor offices were to be filled, a warm canvass

---

[1] N. Y. Tribune, Dec. 8, 1865.   [2] Ibid., Dec. 26, 1865.
[3] N. Y. Tribune Almanac for 1866, pp. 43–4.

was conducted and a Union majority of from 27,000 to 30,000 was secured, while Lincoln's majority in 1864 had been less than 7000. New Jersey, which had been carried by McClellan in 1864, and had refused to ratify the Thirteenth Amendment, the only Northern state to take such a course, now elected a Republican governor by a majority of 3000.[1] "New Jersey Redeemed," said the New York Tribune in the lines over its news from the polling places in that state. "She is admitted into the Union with all the honors — Let men and angels rejoice — Let the eagle scream — The place that knew the Copperhead shall know him no more forever," etc.[2]

Plainly with social conditions in the South in such disturbance that the governors must form and call out companies of militia, though the United States army still occupied the country — with Southern conventions and legislatures doing all things reluctantly, except asking for the pardon of Jefferson Davis and other "arch traitors," and reënacting their old "slave codes," the times demanded one important measure, viz., the enfranchisement of the negro. Sumner, Stevens, all who were nursing this precious idea a few months before, had not yielded one jot or tittle of their faith, and the hour was near at hand when, in obedience to a provision of the Constitution of the United States, the Congress would convene, and they, and the men who thought as they, would make themselves heard and felt in the land.

The President had said little, but he was not unmindful of the rising tide of radical opinion on this critical question. To no Southern state convention had he offered counsel on the subject except Mississippi's semi-privately by way of Governor Sharkey, in a message transmitted in cipher on August 15. In this course he was closely following the example of President Lincoln, who a year before had given similar advice to Governor Hahn of Louisiana. Johnson recommended the extension of the franchise "to all persons of color who can read the Constitution of the United States in English and write their names,

[1] N. Y. Tribune Almanac for 1866, pp. 53 et seq.
[2] N. Y. Tribune, Nov. 8, 1865.

and to all persons of color who own real estate valued at not less than $250 and pay taxes thereon." This would "completely disarm the adversary." Thereby the radicals who were "wild upon negro franchise" would be "completely foiled in their attempt to keep the Southern states from renewing their relations to the Union by not accepting their senators and representatives." [1] It is true that the President here spoke of the radicals as "adversaries," and that he said they were "wild" on the subject of negro suffrage. He suggested the granting of voting privileges to the blacks on grounds of political expediency only, not as a moral right. But a different course would have betokened an inconceivable lack of knowledge of the negro and the whole spirit of the masses of the people, North as well as South, for not anywhere, except in five New England states, could the black vote as the white man, and four Northern states, Connecticut, Colorado (a candidate for early admission to the Union), Wisconsin and Minnesota, had just now in September, October and November, 1865, rejected the proposal to let him do so by impressive popular majorities. [2]

Not one Southern convention gave the suggestion which President Johnson had made to Judge Sharkey the least consideration. A few of the governors alluded to the possibility of endowing the negro with a vote. Governor Marvin of Florida said that the subject would "necessarily" come before the convention of that state for review. In his own judgment the freedmen did not desire the privilege of suffrage. Nor would the public good be promoted by such a step. "Neither the white people nor the colored people are prepared for so radical a change in their social relations." [3] Governor Holden spoke of the "superior intelligence of the white race." It was not to be expected, said he, that the negro could "comprehend and appreciate . . . the wise provisions and limitations of con-

[1] Senate Ex. Doc., 39th Cong., 1st sess., no. 26, p. 229.

[2] The various state laws bearing upon this question are summarized in N. Y. Tribune Almanac for 1866, pp. 46–8. The majority against negro suffrage in Wisconsin was 9000; in Connecticut 6000; in Minnesota 2600 and in Colorado 3700.

[3] Senate Ex. Doc., 39th Cong., 1st sess., no. 26, p. 210.

stitutions and laws," or that he could now have "that knowledge of public affairs" necessary to qualify him "to discharge all the duties of the citizen."[1] Governor Perry of South Carolina went much farther. The extension of the suffrage to the freedmen "in their present ignorant and degraded condition would be little less than folly and madness." The radicals in the North forget that "this is a white man's government and intended for white men only." The convention will settle the "grave question," he said, "as the interest and honor of the state demands."[2] Brownlow told his legislature in Tennessee that he thought it would be "bad policy as well as wrong in principle to open the ballot-box to the uninformed and exceedingly stupid slaves of the Southern cotton, rice and sugar fields." The people of Tennessee would extend the franchise to the negro when they thought he was "worthy of it, and not before."[3]

General J. M. Schofield at Raleigh, soon after the end of the war, spoke to General Grant of the "absolute unfitness of the negroes as a class" to exercise the ballot. They could not read or write; they had "no knowledge whatever of law or government." It was so generally recognized that they ought to be educated before they were enfranchised that argument was "superfluous." Not a single Union man in North Carolina would willingly submit to being placed on a political equality with the black man.[4] General Sherman told Chase in Beaufort Harbor in May, while the Chief Justice was travelling in the South, in the interest of negro suffrage: "I say honestly that the assertion openly of your ideas as a fixed policy of our government to be backed by physical power will produce new war, and one which from its desultory character will be more bloody and destructive than the last."[5]

Nevertheless the campaign in the North proceeded, and gained in ardor and strength. The negroes themselves were

[1] N. Y. Tribune, June 20, 1865.
[2] Senate Ex. Doc., 39th Cong., 1st sess., no. 26, p. 124.
[3] Annual Cyclopedia for 1865, p. 781.
[4] O. R., series i, vol. xlvii, part iii, pp. 461-3.
[5] Ibid., p. 410.

induced to hold conventions in which they passed resolutions asking for the franchise. A meeting of this kind was convened in Alexandria, Va., early in August, 1865,[1] and another was held a few days later in Nashville, Tenn.[2] Two or three score negroes purporting to represent their race in North Carolina met in a church in Raleigh in October, just prior to the assembling of the constitutional convention.[3] A similar meeting was held in Charleston in November.[4] The delegates declared themselves in favor of suffrage and their statements were published widely in the North in support of the race's wish for and title to political privileges. The South Carolina convention forwarded a memorial to Congress.[5] Petitions of colored men numerously signed were sent to the President.[6]

In October, in an interview with George L. Stearns of Boston, Johnson made the most important declaration he had yet publicly uttered upon the subject of negro suffrage. He observed that in the North seven years ago, even the possibility of it might not have been broached. Many changes had taken place since then. Still more rapid had been the movement of events in the South, and the people there must have the time to "digest" what had so suddenly come to them. The regulation of the suffrage was a matter for the states individually. For the general government to assume power over it would be to create "a central despotism." As for his own state, Tennessee, he averred that he would favor the introduction of negro suffrage gradually by the enfranchisement of literate black men and those holding property. But the step was fraught with grave danger; for the negroes, were they to vote, would support their old masters, not the poor or non-slaveholding white men whom they had long looked down upon and had taught themselves to hate. Universal suffrage now, he concluded, would breed a war of races.[7]

[1] Phila. Ledger, Aug. 3, 1865.
[2] Nashville corr., N. Y. Tribune, Aug. 19, 1865.
[3] N. Y. Tribune, Oct. 7, 1865; Sidney Andrews, The South since the War, pp. 119–31.   [4] N. Y. Tribune, Nov. 29, 1865.
[5] Ibid.   [6] Johnson Papers.
[7] McPherson, History of Reconstruction, p. 49, and the news-

Whoever will follow the record of the events of the summer and autumn of 1865 cannot fail to form the opinion that the President throughout this time labored with industry, tact and patriotism to heal the great sectional wound, and cure the body of the state. He received visitors of all classes from every part of the Union, and patiently heard them utter their views and register their various complaints. His health broke down under the strain of exacting public service. For a month after moving into the White House he did not once go outside its doors. He was threatened with apoplexy.[1] The members of his Cabinet were profoundly concerned about his condition, and discussed plans to relieve him of some of the burdens which so hardly bore upon him.

His telegrams to the provisional governors breathed a sincere desire to restore peace and good feeling. He reasoned with them and commanded them by turns. He praised them and congratulated them when they did well. They must ratify the Thirteenth Amendment, repudiate the Confederate war debts and make provision for the legal protection of the freedmen. He addressed them all in a circular telegram in August in regard to the assertion of the radicals that "rebels" were being preferred over "true Union men" for appointment to office. Instead of this they should use in the work of reorganization those who had "never faltered in their allegiance to the government."[2] "God grant that the Southern people will see their true interests and the welfare of the whole country and act accordingly," he said to Governor Holden.[3] "I do hope the Southern people will see the position they now occupy, and avail themselves of the favorable opportunity of once more resuming all their former relations to the government," he telegraphed to Governor Sharkey in November.[4] "If I know

papers, e.g. the N. Y. Tribune, Oct. 23, and Phila. Ledger, Oct. 26, 1865.

[1] Welles, vol. ii, pp. 324–5, 327, 329, 340, 342, 347, 354, and Johnson Papers.

[2] Senate Ex. Doc., 39th Cong., 1st sess., no. 26, p. 221, for North Carolina. Similar telegrams were forwarded to the other governors.

[3] Ibid., p. 222.   [4] Ibid., p. 234.

my own heart and every passion which enters it," he said to Governor Perry, "my earnest desire is to restore the blessings of the Union, and tie up and heal every bleeding wound which has been caused by this fratricidal war." [1]   He told a delegation of South Carolinians in October: "If I could be instrumental in restoring the government to its former relations, and see the people once more united I should feel that I had more than filled the measure of my ambition. If I could feel that I had contributed to this in any degree my heart would be more than gratified, and my ambition full." [2]

The moderates still commended him for his generous sentiments. For example the Philadelphia Ledger in September said that "an ounce of kindness now will be worth any quantity of it years hence." If the President shall err on any side "it is much better it should be on that designed to restore fraternal feeling." [3]   The same gazette just before the Christmas holidays pronounced him "a strong, firm, vigorous thinker, an unimpeachable patriot." [4]   If he were supported by his party he would "hand his name down to posterity, a second Washington." [5]   Did his "assailants expect to carry the country on the Massachusetts idea of negro suffrage, female suffrage, confiscation and hanging?" Let them attempt it; they would drive all moderate men out of the party. [6]   His chart, Johnson said one day, was the Constitution. He would not deviate from it a "hair's breadth," if he could help it. [7]   He was certain, he said again, that the Southern people would "come up and rally around the Union and the Constitution." [8]

The President strove manfully to keep his administration free of the influences of extremists and to find some middle

---

[1] Senate Ex. Doc., 39th Cong., 1st sess., no. 26, p. 254.
[2] N. Y. Tribune, Oct. 14, 1865.
[3] Sept. 25, 1865.   [4] Dec. 21, 1865.
[5] Washington corr., Phila. Ledger, Sept. 14, 1865.
[6] Dr. C. H. Ray to Senator Trumbull. — Horace White, Life of Trumbull, p. 243.
[7] Washington corr., Phila. Ledger, Sept. 14, 1865.
[8] Ibid., Sept. 12, 1865.

ground, but he was thanked on neither side. Sumner, Chase and Stevens alleged that he had fallen completely under the influence of the Blairs and their border state morals on the negro question.[1] Whitelaw Reid complained that the ante-rooms of the White House were crowded with Southerners. They "filled all avenues of approach." Unionists finding the city "rife with the old rebel talk became disgusted and hurried back to the North."[2] On the other hand, the Jackson (Miss.) News said that the South would not sacrifice her rights inch by inch to secure representation in Congress. Of what use to her would be her representation if her rights were gone?[3] The Mobile Register said that there must be a "limit to the Northern demands on the South."[4]

The President's faith was being shaken. He was sincerely disappointed. The more the Southern states were given the more they seemed to require. He had made conditions which were "indispensable," and asked that they be fully and squarely met. Compliance was reluctant and slow.[5] The people tele-graphed and wrote and visited him about confiscation, par-dons, the test oath, the Freedmen's Bureau, the removal of the black troops, the dishonest cotton agents. He reminded a North Carolina delegation that their legislature had not yet ratified the Thirteenth Amendment abolishing slavery.[6] The people of the state had done it much mischief; by choosing disloyal men to office, they had damaged its prospects of an early return to the Union.[7] Several of the governors elected under the new constitutions, among them the Confederate

---

[1] Pierce, Memoir of Sumner, iv, p. 254. "With impetuous alac-rity they [the Blairs] seize the White House and hold possession of it until shaken off by the overpowering force of public indignation." — Thaddeus Stevens in a speech at Lancaster, Pa., printed in N. Y. Trib-une, Sept. 11, 1865.

[2] After the War, p. 304.

[3] Jackson News, Oct. 4, 1865, quoted in N. Y. Tribune, Oct. 14, 1865.

[4] Quoted in Phila. Ledger, Nov. 13, 1865.

[5] Washington corr., Phila. Ledger, Nov. 13, 1865.

[6] Phila. Ledger, Nov. 11, 1865.

[7] Pres. Johnson to Gov. Holden, Nov. 27, in Senate Ex. Doc., loc. cit., no. 26, pp. 227–8.

General Humphreys of Mississippi, were inaugurated, and had proceeded to perform their duties. The President suspended their functions, and bade the provisional governors continue in office until his directions had been obeyed.

Although the Southern states had fallen far short of what the President's hopes had been for them, on the eve of the meeting of Congress, under date of December 4, 1865, Secretary Seward addressed the provisional governors of North Carolina, South Carolina, Georgia, Alabama, Mississippi and Florida to tell them that they were relieved of their duties. A time had come when "the care and conduct of the proper affairs of the state" might be "remitted to the constitutional authorities chosen by the people thereof." The new governors were tendered "the coöperation of the government of the United States wherever it may be found necessary in effecting the early restoration and the permanent prosperity and welfare" of their states.[1] For local reasons the despatch of the letters was in some cases delayed for a few days, but before the end of the year all the new governors were in their places, and the regular political course in the South, except in Texas, had been resumed.

Governor Parsons telegraphed Secretary Seward on December 2 announcing the ratification of the Thirteenth Amendment by the legislature of Alabama, and seeking the honor of a place as the twenty-seventh state.[2] Georgia followed on December 6.[3] The Secretary of State was not notified at once in an official way of the action of the various legislatures,[4] but on December 18, with certificates from twenty-seven states in hand, he issued a proclamation declaring the amendment a part of the Constitution of the Union.[5] The work of abolition was now complete and the black man became free in Kentucky and Delaware, where slavery had persisted up to this day.[6]

[1] Senate Ex. Doc., loc. cit., no. 26, pp. 47–8.
[2] Ibid., pp. 109, 110.
[3] Ibid., p. 240.
[4] Washington corr., N. Y. Tribune, Dec. 11, 1865.
[5] McPherson, History of Reconstruction, p. 6.
[6] Slavery had been abolished in Maryland by a new constitution in 1864, and in Missouri in like manner in January, 1865.

"Praise be to God," said the New York Tribune. "We live at last in a country where no human creature can be held as a slave." [1]

On the first day of December, 1865, the President restored the privilege of the writ of habeas corpus in all parts of the United States except the eleven states which had been in insurrection, in Kentucky, in the District of Columbia and in the territories of New Mexico and Arizona.[2] The day of arbitrary arrests of suspects, of trial, sentence and execution by military commission was declared to be at an end over the greater part of the Union. At the same time the censorship of the telegraph ceased, the Old Capitol Prison at Washington, where many had been incarcerated upon the mere suspicion of irresponsible men, was closed, and the early disbandment of Baker's body of detectives, who had made so many arrests for political crimes, was near at hand. It was a "red letter day," said the Philadelphia Ledger. These acts had been too long delayed. The President would have "the warm approval of the great body of his countrymen to whose American feelings such things were very distasteful." [3] The New York Tribune welcomed "most heartily the restoration of one of those great safeguards of personal liberty most precious to every free people." [4]

As rapidly as the owners of Southern property were pardoned by the President, if this property had fallen into the hands of the Freedmen's Bureau, it was returned to them. This policy on the part of Mr. Johnson caused the greatest distress and confusion in the Sea Islands, where homesteads had been distributed by General Saxton to the freedmen under an impression that they were to remain in possession of the land. In October, General Howard, by direction of the President, proceeded to the South Carolina, Georgia and Florida coasts to adjust these differences. His tasks were difficult. Finally, after

---

[1] N. Y. Tribune, Dec. 19, 1865.
[2] McPherson, Hist. of Reconstruction, **p. 15.**
[3] Phila. Ledger, Dec. 2, 1865.
[4] N. Y. Tribune, Dec. 1, 1865.

he had addressed the disturbed blacks at several places, boards of supervisors, composed of representatives of the government, of the planters in interest, and of the freedmen were appointed to execute leases, or contracts for wages which would afford the negroes the necessary protection. This work was going forward as rapidly as possible.[1] William Henry Trescott was appointed by the reorganized South Carolina government to be an agent of the state to treat with the United States on this subject. He visited the President and urged the removal of General Saxton. Now a negro had been placed on one of General Howard's arbitration boards and Trescott, supported by Governor Perry and Governor-elect Orr, telegraphed to Washington asking that the request for Saxton's removal should receive the President's attention at once.[2]

Arrangements were being made for a further reduction of the number of men in garrison in the South. At the end of the year 1865 there were 123,356 volunteer troops (65,766 colored and 57,590 white) still in the service — nearly 30,000 in Texas and about 10,000 in Missouri, Mississippi, Alabama, Tennessee and Louisiana respectively. Before February 15, 1866, it was promised that 41,744 more men would be mustered out (18,654 white and 23,090 colored), including all the negro troops in Tennessee, and 16,000 negroes in the Department of the Gulf.[3]

President Johnson now had set forth his policy in regard to the Southern states. He could go no farther on his way prior to the meeting of Congress. His success had not been so great as he could have hoped for, or as he desired it to be. But he had formulated his course carefully, with a full regard for the various conflicting interests. He had tried to put him-

[1] House Ex. Doc., 39th Cong., 1st sess., no. 11, pp. 6–11. How these changes were made is revealed in some degree in General C. H. Howard's testimony in the Report of the Joint Com. on Reconstruction, part iii, pp. 35–6.

[2] Senate Ex. Doc., 39th Cong., 1st sess., no. 26, p. 257. Some of the difficulties experienced by the planters in repossessing themselves of their lands which had come into the hands of the angry negroes are described in Avary, Dixie after the War, chap. xxix.

[3] Senate Ex. Doc., 39th Cong., 1st sess., no. 71.

self in his place as the President of the whole country, suppressed his own sentiments in matters upon which his convictions were strong, and stood ready to receive the judgment of Congress and of the people. Well might he have prayed to be delivered from his friends. The South better could have crossed his way, if they had sincerely wished to make it the easier for him. Instead they gave him assurances of their favor which they often mingled with adulation and flattery. In April, May and June he had been the "drunken tailor," the "bloody-minded tailor," the "vulgar renegade."[1] Now the Jackson (Miss.) News nominated him as the South's candidate for the Presidency in 1868.[2] General Beauregard said that he had thought of seeking refuge from the Northern fanatics in Brazil, but the "generous sentiments" expressed by Mr. Johnson had persuaded him to remain in Louisiana.[3] The constitutional convention of North Carolina found the President's administration to be "eminently national and conservative." He was "entitled to the gratitude" of the people of the state.[4] The convention of South Carolina commended the President's "wise measures" and his "mode of pacification."[5] The Florida convention bore grateful testimony to his "liberality and magnanimity."[6] He was deserving of the support of the members in Congress from Mississippi, said Judge Evans, a candidate for one of the seats, in a speech at Vicksburg, for he was trying "to stay the tide of fanaticism at the North," which promised to overwhelm the Southern people.[7] The committee of the South Carolina convention, which visited the President in October to present its memorials asking for the pardon of

---

[1] These are names bestowed upon the President by two Southern gentlewomen — Mrs. Chesnut, who occupied a distinguished place in Southern society, in A Diary of Dixie, p. 398, and Miss E. F. Andrews, in The War Time Journal of a Georgia Girl, p. 173. Southern men designated him in still more uncomplimentary terms.

[2] Jackson correspondence, N. Y. Tribune, Sept. 11, 1865.

[3] N. Y. Tribune, Dec. 14, 1865.

[4] Senate Ex. Doc., 39th Cong., 1st sess., no. 26, p. 44.

[5] Ibid., p. 155.

[6] Ibid., p. 208.

[7] Ibid., no. 2, p. 65.

Jefferson Davis and other prisoners, told him that he was the
one man standing between them and the harsh use of power
by the government. All South Carolina reposed confidence in
him.[1] Governor Orr in his inaugural address said that the
President's clemency in pardoning participants in the "late
revolution" did honor to his "statesmanship and his sense of
justice." His policy would attach the South to the Union by
cords "stronger than triple steel." [2]

But now the thunder rolled and the floods descended; it was
the doom of reconstruction by the President's method. The
day for the meeting of the 39th Congress, Monday, December
4, approached. Whittier, speaking for the Abolitionists,
apostrophized the members in verse:

> "O people-chosen! Are ye not?
> Likewise the chosen of the Lord,
> To do His will and speak His word;
>
> "Say to the pardon seekers: Keep
> Your manhood; bend no suppliant knees,
> Nor palter with unworthy pleas;
>
> "Make all men peers before the law,
> Take hands from off the negro's throat,
> Give black and white an equal vote." [3]

A considerable number of the Southern senators and representatives had come to Washington to claim their seats on the
opening day of the session. Some delegates from Virginia,
representing the loyal Peirpoint government, and from Tennessee had sat in Congress during the war. Louisiana delegates
were granted the privileges of the floor in the second session of
the 38th Congress.[4] Would the Southern claimants now be
extended like courtesies pending a discussion of their cases?
A Republican caucus had been held,[5] Thaddeus Stevens direct-

---

[1] N. Y. Tribune, Oct. 14, 1865.

[2] Ibid., Dec. 8, 1865.

[3] Ibid., Dec. 14, 1865.

[4] Cong. Globe, 38th Cong., 2d sess., p. 2; cf. ibid., 39th Cong.,
1st sess., p. 4.

[5] Welles, vol. ii, p. 387; C. R. Williams, Life of R. B. Hayes, vol. i,
p. 278.

ing its course, and Edward McPherson, the clerk of the House, whose duty it was to call the body to order and preside until a speaker should be chosen, was instructed in the premises. The floor, the galleries, the ante-rooms were packed with people who had come to witness the scene. The hour of twelve o'clock arrived, and the "middle-sized, smooth-faced young man with blue eyes, high forehead and light sunny hair "[1] rapped for order. He called the roll. Kentucky finished he proceeded to Indiana; Tennessee with its eight members, at least five of them firmly loyal men,[2] had been passed over, and the time was at hand for Horace Maynard of the second district in that state, armed with a certificate of election from "Parson" Brownlow, to rise and address the clerk. This "black snake of the mountains,"[3] who like President Johnson had fought tooth and nail for the Union in East Tennessee, and remained in the House until 1863 as a member from Knoxville, though he was in exile, and his state was in rebellion, was known to all men. He was called to order. "Does the clerk decline to hear me?" The clerk did decline, though Maynard rose thrice. One hundred and seventy-six representatives were present; it was a quorum for the transaction of business without calling one Southern member's name, and the majority desired to proceed at once to the election of Schuyler Colfax to the speakership.

But first James Brooks of New York, the minority leader, gained the floor. "If Tennessee is not in the Union," said he, "and has not been in the Union, and is not a loyal state, and the people of Tennessee are aliens and foreigners to this Union, by what right does the President of the United States usurp his place in the White House?" He asked that Mr. Maynard be allowed to be heard, but Thaddeus Stevens and others effectually interposed, and the House was soon listening to Schuyler Colfax's periods in an address of thanks about "a

[1] Washington corr., N. Y. Tribune, Dec. 5, 1865.
[2] N. Y. Tribune, Aug. 19, 1865.
[3] A "long black-haired, black-faced, Indian-looking" man. — Reid, After the War, p. 432.

republican form of government," "the men who had died that
the republic might live," "the fires of civil war" which had
"melted every fetter in the land and proved the funerál.pyre
of slavery," and the "stars on our banner that paled when the
states they represented arrayed themselves in arms against
the nation." [1] "The door had been shut in the rebel faces;
it was still to be bolted" [2] In a few minutes Thaddeus Stevens,
his old wig awry, reared his venerable frame and moved the
appointment of a joint committee of fifteen, nine members from
the House and six from the Senate, to "inquire into the condition of the states which formed the so-called Confederate
States of America and report whether they or any of them are
entitled to be represented in either house of Congress." He
had driven this scheme through the caucus on Saturday night,[3]
and the resolution was passed by a vote of 129 to 35.[4]

Meantime proceedings in similar disregard of the President's
work throughout the six or seven months just past signalized
the Senate's first day. Immediately upon his arrival in Washington Sumner had visited the White House. He remained
two and a half hours in Mr. Johnson's company, but without
reclaiming him to radicalism. The senator from Massachusetts
found him, who had once been trusted so confidently, "harsh,
petulant and unreasonable," his "whole soul set as a flint against
the good cause." [5] This visit ended the social relations of the
two men. Sumner went into the Senate on the opening day of
the session with a series of ten bills and resolutions expressive
of his views on the Southern question. On the following day,
the 5th, the first credentials of the representatives of a Southern
state to appear in the Senate were read, those of Governor
Sharkey and General Alcorn of Mississippi. They were laid

---

[1] Cong. Globe, 39th Cong., 1st sess., pp. 3–5.
[2] Reid, After the War, p. 437.
[3] C. R. Williams, Life of R. B. Hayes, vol. i, p. 278.
[4] Cong. Globe, 39th Cong., 1st sess., p. 6.
[5] Pierce, Memoir of Charles Sumner, vol. iv, p. 268. Another time
Sumner spoke of the President's "prejudice, ignorance and perver-
sity" on this occasion. — Ibid., p. 269; cf. Schurz, Reminiscences, vol.
iii, p. 212.

upon the table to await future action at the wish of Senator Cowan of Pennsylvania who had presented them.[1]

Now came the President's message. This state paper had been the object of secret planning between Mr. Johnson and George Bancroft, and the historian, at this time in easy literary retirement in New York, is proven to have been the principal if not its sole author. Every essential portion of it in Bancroft's hand reposes among the Johnson Papers in the Library of Congress at Washington. Already on the 9th of November he had written to the President that his task would be completed on the morrow. But no one knew what he was about, and, as he was perforce his own secretary, he asked for a day or two more. He had spared no pains to express the President's ideas with "exactness." [2]

The House listened to the message attentively.[3] Its smooth, flowing style, its sober, logical form, its admirable temper caused it to be praised on all sides.[4] Bancroft himself was captivated by its tone, and he predicted that "in less than twenty days the extreme radical opposition would be over." [5] The New York Nation found Johnson as a writer to be "not an unworthy successor of Mr. Lincoln." Indeed his style had even greater clarity. The message was one which "any democrat as well as any American" could read "with pride." [6] Foreign papers, extracts from which Bancroft forwarded to the President from time to time, expressed a similar view. The message treated the affairs of the day, said the Journal des Débats of Paris, with a clearness and precision seldom to be found in similar documents emanating from European govern-

[1] Cong. Globe, 39th Cong., 1st sess., p. 7.

[2] Johnson Papers; W. A. Dunning, Proceedings of Mass. Hist. Society, Nov., 1905; Fleming, Doc. Hist. of Reconstruction, vol. i, p. 186. Welles was in complete ignorance of the authorship of the message. He seems to have thought it the President's own work with some aid from Seward, Diary, vol. ii, p. 392.

[3] C. R. Williams, Life of R. B. Hayes, vol. i, p. 279.

[4] Dunning has brought together much newspaper opinion on the subject, op. cit.

[5] Dec. 6, in Johnson Papers.

[6] N. Y. Nation, vol. i, p. 742.

ments. The confidence inspired by it in Europe, Bancroft thought, had raised the debt of the United States ninety millions of dollars in value.[1] Men wrote Johnson to say that they were reading it and re-reading it. It was able, dignified and statesmanlike. It was one of the noblest political documents ever given to the world. Andrew Jackson could not have written a better one, said an old Democrat, who knew not how to frame words of warmer praise.[2]

Mr. Bancroft had reviewed, and Mr. Johnson had ratified the argument by making it his own, the recent course of affairs in connection with the restoration of the Southern states. They were, he said, in a condition of suspended vitality; they had refused for a time to perform their offices. He had sought to restore their old and rightful energy to them. But first they must assist in the amendment of the Constitution, the amendment which would remove slavery, "the element which has so long perplexed and divided the country," and which would "make us once more a united people, renewed and strengthened, bound more than ever to mutual affection and support." When this should be done they might send their delegates to Congress, though the President did not urge that these delegates be received. It would be "for you, fellow citizens of the Senate, and for you, fellow citizens of the House of Representatives, to judge, each of you for yourselves, of the elections, returns and qualifications of your own members." As for the enfranchisement of the negroes, he conclusively argued, with all historical theory and practice on his side, that if this step were to be taken, it must be by and through the separate states. For him to have extended the suffrage to the freedmen would have been "an assumption of power . . . which nothing in the Constitution or laws of the United States could have warranted." When the "tumult of emotions" had subsided, it might be that they would receive "the kindest usage from some of those" on whom they had heretofore "most closely depended."[3]

[1] Feb. 8, 1866, in Johnson Papers.   [2] Johnson Papers.
[3] Richardson, Messages and Papers, vol. vi, pp. 353–71.

But, however much admiration might be spent upon the message, it all would be without any power to compose the perturbed spirits who were gathered together under the dome of the Capitol. Sumner called upon Welles on December 8. He said that the President's method of reorganizing the South was "the greatest and most criminal error ever committed by any government." He, Welles, a New England man, and Seward were "foully, fatally culpable" in giving their support to the President's policies.[1] Already there were hints of the impeachment of the President.[2]

Near his home at Lancaster in September Thaddeus Stevens had insisted that "the property of the chief rebels should be seized and appropriated to the payment of the national debt," and for the indemnification of "freedmen and loyal sufferers."[3] On December 18 he made his first extended speech in the House. Speaking for the system of restoration by Congress and in defence of the views he held on the subject of "conquered provinces," he denounced the men who had been sitting "without legal authority" in conventions and legislatures in the capitals of the "late rebel states" as an "aggregation of white-washed rebels." The old Southern states to-day had no more existence "than the revolted cities of Latium, two-thirds of whose people were colonized and their property confiscated."[4] He knew of no arrangement so proper for the people of the South as territorial governments. There they could "learn the principles of freedom and eat the fruit of foul rebellion." Their states ought never to be counted as valid until their constitutions should be so amended as "to secure perpetual ascendency to the party of the Union."[5]

Sumner, fortified by his "state suicide" theory, first essayed

[1] Diary, vol. ii, p. 395.
[2] Washington corr., Phila. Ledger, Sept. 8, 1865; Welles, vol. ii, p. 395, under date of Dec. 11, 1865.
[3] N. Y. Tribune, Sept. 11, 1865. For Greeley's view of this speech see the editorial in the Tribune of the following day, Sept. 12.
[4] "Defunct states," Stevens called them on Feb. 13, 1866. — Cong. Globe, 39th Cong., 1st sess., p. 12.
[5] Ibid., p. 74.

vituperative speech on the following day, the 19th. When
Carl Schurz had returned home from his trip through the
South, he wrote out a long report which he was determined to
spread upon the records of Congress, and to have published
in the radical newspapers. During the summer and autumn
of 1865 Mr. Johnson, as has been seen, had asked a number of
men to apprise him of the state of feeling in the South. They
wrote him from time to time reporting their observations.
Schurz took his commission very seriously. Because of his
active personal sympathies he awakened many antipathies, as
he passed on his way, especially in Mississippi and Louisiana.
It was complained that he consorted only with the radical
soldiers, politicians and Freedmen's Bureau agents in the places
he visited, imbibed their views and made public biassed conclusions. He was a foreigner with "New England fancies."
His reports to Mr. Johnson of social disorder and of complete
unrepentance on the part of the people, which were lengthy
and frequent, soon were set down at the White House as
partisan, and worthy to receive but scant respect.[1] To give
direction to his zeal, if possible, when his credentials were
called for in Mississippi in August, the President had said
that the "main object" of his journey was "to aid, as far as
practicable, in carrying out the policy adopted by the government for restoring the states to their former relations with
the Federal government."[2]

Upon his return to Washington Schurz alleged that he was
not warmly received by the power which had accredited him
as a commissioner,[3] though he had accepted his appointment
contrary to his own desires at inadequate compensation, in view
of his obligations to his family and the increased premiums
exacted by the life insurance companies because of the perilous
character of his journey. Repeatedly he had asked the President, without success, for permission to publish a report which
he had prepared summarizing what he earlier had said in his

[1] Johnson Papers.
[2] Senate Ex. Doc., 39th Cong., 1st sess., no. 26, p. 232.
[3] Schurz, Reminiscences, vol. iii, p. 202.

letters.[1] That it was entirely unfavorable to the Johnson policy was a fact familiar to the radicals with whom he was on terms of intimacy, and on December 12 Sumner called for the paper.[2] On the 18th the President forwarded it, together with a brief statement from General Grant in which conclusions different from Schurz's were arrived at, and a still briefer statement of his own.

In this connection the President said that in North Carolina, South Carolina, Georgia, Alabama, Mississippi, Louisiana, Arkansas and Tennessee the governments had been reorganized "with more willingness and greater promptitude than, under the circumstances, could reasonably have been anticipated." The Thirteenth Amendment had been adopted by all except Mississippi. In Florida and Texas the work was still in progress, and would be completed without doubt at an early period. Disorder was local in character. "Sectional animosity" was surely and rapidly merging itself into "a spirit of nationality." "Representation" with a proper system of taxation would result in "a harmonious restoration of the relations of the states to the national Union."

On the day after the Schurz report appeared in the Senate, December 19, Sumner insisted, against objection, that it be read. He declared that President Johnson's message accompanying it was like "the white-washing message of Franklin Pierce with regard to the enormities in Kansas." The reading was proceeded with until Senator Sherman grew tired of it and rose in protest. Then Senators Doolittle of Wisconsin, Dixon of Connecticut and Reverdy Johnson of Maryland took Sumner to task for his insult of the President, and the discussion for the present came to an end.[3]

---

[1] Johnson Papers.

[2] Cong. Globe, 39th Cong., 1st sess., p. 30. John Covode, a radical Republican member of Congress from Pennsylvania, had gone South for the War Department. He also made a report to the President which Sumner wished to secure, but as his relations were with Secretary Stanton, Mr. Johnson had asked its author to render the account of his trip to that officer. — Report of Joint Com. on Reconstruction, part iv, p. 113.   [3] Cong. Globe, 39th Cong., 1st sess., p. 79.

On the following day, December 20, Sumner, supporting
Schurz's position, brought into the Senate a mass of letters
and other testimony from Northern travellers in the South,
extracts from the proceedings of the Southern conventions, etc.,
and in an impassioned speech for an hour or two proceeded
with an indictment of the "rebels." "In the name of God,"
he said, "let us protect them [the negroes]. . . . An avenging
God cannot sleep while such things find countenance." Alluding to a speech of President Johnson's, when in Nashville he
had promised to be a Moses of the black race, Sumner continued — "If you are not ready to be the Moses of an oppressed
people, do not become its Pharaoh." [1]

On the 19th of April, 1866, the Senate called for any additional reports which President Johnson might have received
concerning the condition of the late Confederate states, and
on May 7 he transmitted a summary which the newspaper
correspondent, Benjamin C. Truman, had prepared covering
the results of his recent trip through the South. His reports,
like Harvey Watterson's, came to hand almost as frequently
as Schurz's, and, like Watterson's also, gave the President an
entirely different view of the mental attitude of the people as
well as the state of their society. Truman explained that he
was not writing for the public or for Congress, "à la Schurz,"
but for the President's private self, which he had been asked
to do. When he returned, after seven months, it was to say
that he had visited, by railway, boat and stage wagon, all parts
of seven of the seceded states, that he had met nearly all the
leading Southern politicians, editors and "rebel" generals, as
well as many of the Northern officers stationed there.[2] His
conclusions supported the President's policies. He found that
disorder was diminishing everywhere, save in Texas, that the
spirit of the people was improving, except, possibly, in Mississippi, and made out a case for the return of the Southern states
to their old places in the Union under their reconstructed
governments.[3] Sumner moved that the report be laid upon

[1] Cong. Globe, 39th Cong., 1st sess., p. 95.   [2] Johnson Papers.
[3] Senate Ex. Doc., 39th Cong., 1st sess., no. 43.

the table and be printed.[1] As wide as Mr. Truman's observations had been, as temperate as was the language he had used in describing them, his findings were not to the mind of the radicals. Anyhow, his report was brought forward too late to exert the slightest influence upon the troubled course of affairs.

Outside of Congress Wendell Phillips raised his voice from time to time in characteristic tones. He had prepared and was delivering a lecture which he called "The South Victorious." In it he mercilessly assailed the President's Southern policy. The Republican party had ceased to exist. There was a spectre walking over the country in its shroud.[2] Friends asked him to repeat the lecture in New York, but he refused, saying that he was sickened by the complicity of men of that city with the schemes at Washington for "reëstablishing slavery," and he would "rather not breathe the same atmosphere with them."[3] In Brooklyn in February, 1866, he declared that the President meant "to crush Massachusetts." She accepted the war. "If he succeeds," said Phillips, "he shall write his name higher than that of Burr or Arnold."[4]

Meantime the Southern Congressmen were not yet in their seats. Horace Maynard, when he was asked what he thought of the prospect of the admission of Tennessee's delegation, said that "Thad Stevens had the whole Southern Confederacy in his breeches pocket and meant to keep it there for a good while to come."[5] Convinced that their mission would prove not immediately fruitful a number of the Southern Congressmen-elect held a caucus on the evening of December 20 and determined to go back to their homes. The holidays which they wished to spend with their families drew near; they would return to Washington on March 4 next.[6]

[1] Cong. Globe, p. 2443.

[2] Phila. Ledger, Oct. 19, 1865.

[3] Ibid., Oct. 24. He did come in a few days and spoke in Cooper Institute on the evening of Oct. 25. — N. Y. Tribune, Oct. 26.

[4] Phila. Ledger, Feb. 15, 1866.

[5] Wash. corr., Phila. Ledger, Dec. 16, 1865.

[6] Ibid., Dec. 22, 1865.

On December 14 Stevens's Committee of Fifteen was constituted by the following appointments on the part of the House: Thaddeus Stevens of Pennsylvania; Elihu B. Washburne of Illinois; Justin S. Morrill of Vermont; Henry Grider of Kentucky; John A. Bingham of Ohio; Roscoe Conkling of New York; George S. Boutwell of Massachusetts; Henry T. Blow of Missouri and Andrew J. Rogers of New Jersey. On December 21 the Senate named its six members: William Pitt Fessenden of Maine; James W. Grimes of Iowa; Ira Harris of New York; Jacob M. Howard of Michigan; Reverdy Johnson of Maryland and George H. Williams of Oregon. All but Senator Johnson and Representatives Grider and Rogers were members of the Union Republican party. To this committee every bill or resolution in either House relating to reconstruction in the next following months was immediately referred, and there it rested as in a tomb,[1] until the controlling spirits were willing to bring forth the measures which would be expressive of their policy in regard to the Southern states.

The first bill to be presented in the Senate on the opening day was Wade's to enfranchise the negro in the District of Columbia. Over this ground within the unquestioned control of Congress the battle for Abolition had long been waged. It was designed now to make the District the exemplar for the nation on the subject of negro suffrage. A bill similar to Wade's appeared in the House, where it was passed on January 18 by a vote of 116 to 54, only fourteen Republicans arraying themselves against it.[2] The President made it sufficiently plain that when it should come to him, he must disapprove it. He told Senator Dixon on January 28 that the proposal to enfranchise the blacks in the District of Columbia was "a mere entering wedge." The question now would be agitated throughout the states. It was in his view "ill timed, uncalled for and calculated to do great harm."[3]

[1] "The tomb of the Capulets," it was called by Brooks, the minority leader in the House. — Cong. Globe, 39th Cong., 1st sess., p. 714.

[2] Cong. Globe, 39th Cong., 1st sess., p. 311; cf. McPherson, Hist. of Reconstruction, p. 115.

[3] McPherson, Hist. of Reconstruction, p. 52.

The vote in the House sensibly raised the hopes of the negro leaders, and Fred Douglass and some other colored men visited the President on February 27. He received them in kindness, and repeated that he would be their Moses, but he could not favor a policy which in the end must lead to "a contest between the races," and which, if persisted in, must certainly result "in the extermination of one or the other." God knew that he had no desire "but the good of the whole human race." The driving of this matter of suffrage upon the country would work injury to both the blacks and the whites. Douglass and his negro friends departed, saying that they would "go to the people"[1] to whom so much else was soon to be referred.

The Freedmen's Bureau had been established to continue during the war, and "for one year thereafter," by act of Congress on March 3d, 1865. Many of its officers and agents were undeniably incompetent, corrupt and fanatical persons. All of them were Northern by birth or in their sympathies. No man could occupy an office under the Bureau unless he had first taken the "iron-clad" test oath. Many had been officers in the Union army. General Fullerton, who became the assistant commissioner in Louisiana in 1865, said that in his opinion there were agents who went to the South "to foster disunion rather than to cure and heal." They listened to the black man. His word was accepted while the white man's was cast aside.[2] Much testimony of the same character was given by persons whose friendliness for the Union was above any kind of question.[3] General Grant himself, as a result of his trip through the South in 1865, made free to criticise the operations of the Bureau, and complained, as others had, of the conflict of authority in many places between the garrison

---

[1] McPherson, pp. 52–6.

[2] House Ex. Doc., 39th Cong., 1st sess., no. 70, p. 394.

[3] Truman's Report, Senate Ex. Doc., 39th Cong., 1st sess., no. 43; Statement of Stephen Powers, a Cincinnati journalist, before Joint Com. on Reconstruction, part iv, p. 148; John Minor Botts's statement, ibid., part ii, p. 123; General Tarbell's statement, ibid., part ii, p. 156.

officers and the Bureau agents.[1]   In addition to its incompetent and dishonest employees, ignorant of local conditions, and its unfair discrimination in favor of the negro as against the white man, it was accounted a source of political disturbance. Practically it was a system of espionage which the people daily resented.[2] It began by exerting an influence unfriendly to the President's policies on the subject of restoration,[3] and later, as the difference between him and Congress increased, often took an active part in shaping political opinion and in controlling elections.

Immediately after the Christmas holidays Senator Trumbull of Illinois introduced a bill to enlarge the powers and extend the term of life of the Bureau,[4] and it was referred to the Judiciary Committee of which he was the chairman.   Seven days later, on January 12, discussion of it began in the Senate.   The bill specified that the Bureau should continue to exist "until otherwise provided by law"; that its benefits should be extended to refugees and freedmen, not only in the late Confederate states but in other states, if the President "by and with the advice and consent of the Senate," should so determine; that the number of districts and sub-districts, and agents should be increased; that three million acres of public land in Florida, Mississippi, Alabama, Louisiana and Arkansas should be set aside for allotment to freedmen and loyal refugees in parcels not exceeding forty acres each for such periods of time, and at such rental prices as should be agreed upon by the Bureau, with the privilege of purchase at the expiration of the designated period; that the Sea Island negroes should be confirmed in the possession of their titles for three years against ouster unless they should be willing to be transferred to other lands; that asylums and schools should be built for the freedmen and white loyalists; that military protection should be accorded by the President to negroes when they were anywhere denied

---

[1] Senate Ex. Doc., 39th Cong., 1st sess., no. 2, p. 117.
[2] Fleming, Doc. Hist. of Reconstruction, vol. i, p. 270.
[3] Ibid., p. 315.
[4] Cong. Globe, 39th Cong., 1st sess., p. 129.

civil rights equal to those enjoyed by white men by any state
or local law.[1]

The Democratic opposition attacked the measure from many
sides. As for Senator Hendricks of Indiana he said that since
the session had begun he had not heard of any negro who had
done a wrong in this country in very many years, or of a white
man coming in contact with a black man who had done right
in years.   If he were to take sides in such a matter, which he
would not do of choice, his sympathies would be with men of
his own color.[2]   It was a scheme to make into a permanent
organization a bureau which plainly had been created to
serve a temporary purpose.   Senator Saulsbury of Delaware
said that the bill would involve the United States government
in an expense of probably 250 millions of dollars; McDougall
of California said that in giving lands to and building houses
for negroes the government was doing that for an African which
no man, or company of men, or government had ever done
for him, or for any of his fellow senators in Congress.[3]
Garrett Davis of Kentucky called it an "enormous, outrageous
and monstrous measure."[4]   It was a device to grind the
Southern white men in the dust.[5]   It was the majority's design
to establish "a great system of lazzaroni, a great system of
poor houses for the support of lazy negroes all over the Southern
states."[6]   But on January 25 the bill passed the Senate by
a party vote of 37 to 10, whereupon Senator Davis rose and
fruitlessly, and as he thought humorously, moved to amend
the title to read: "A bill to appropriate a portion of the
public land in some of the Southern states, and to
authorize the United States government to purchase lands
to supply farms and build houses upon them for the freed
negroes; to promote strife and conflict between the white
and black races; and to invest the Freedmen's Bureau with
unconstitutional powers," etc.[7]   The House on February 6

---

[1] McPherson, Hist. of Reconstruction, pp. 73–4.
[2] Cong. Globe, 39th Cong., 1st sess., p. 319.
[3] Ibid., p. 401.   [4] Ibid., p. 417.   [5] Ibid., p. 419.
[6] Ibid., p. 396.   [7] Ibid., p. 421.

passed the measure by a party vote of 137 to 33, and it went
to the President.

In the Cabinet, as elsewhere, Stevens and Sumner were
actively at work trying to promote schism. McCulloch and
Welles warmly supported the President. When Sumner made
his "usual weekly visit" to the Secretary of the Navy early in
February he was asked if he really thought Massachusetts
could govern Georgia better than Georgia could govern herself.
Sumner said that this was Massachusetts' mission.[1] Both
Stanton and Seward seemed to be on the point of joining the
radicals against the President,[2] who was led to understand that
Thaddeus Stevens, and the men on his Reconstruction Committee of Fifteen would take the government into their own
hands — already they nearly had done so — and get rid of
him by declaring Tennessee out of the Union, if he did not
ratify their imperious will. The committee was likened to
the French Directory.[3] It was a "revolutionary cabal," said
the National Intelligencer in Washington, which espoused
President Johnson's cause, and spoke with so much authority as
to be regarded generally as his organ. The "Rump Congress"
was the name the New York World placed at the head of its
report of the proceedings day by day. Thaddeus Stevens in
debate with Henry J. Raymond, the editor of the New York
Times, who was Johnson's principal representative in the
House, had said in his most brutal manner on January 31,
alluding to a recently published interview with Senator Dixon,
that the President's utterance "centuries ago, had it been made
to Parliament by a British king, would have cost him his head."[4]

Day by day relationships were becoming more strained. The
bill was discussed with the members of the Cabinet individually
and collectively. Delegates appeared to say that if the President would sign it the House would admit the senators and
representatives of Tennessee. But the President could not

---

[1] Welles, vol. ii, pp. 430–1.
[2] Ibid., vol. ii, pp. 424–5.
[3] Ibid., p. 432.
[4] Cong. Globe, 39th Cong., 1st sess., p. 536.

be influenced "to do wrong in order to secure right," said his friend Welles. His veto of the bill was resolved upon. In Cabinet meeting Seward, Welles, McCulloch and Dennison supported him, while Stanton, Harlan and Speed, though not openly dissenting, expressed their disappointment and were apprehensive of the result.[1]

The veto message was received and read in the Senate on February 19. It was a temperate argument. No legislation on the subject was at this time necessary, as the law of 1865 had not yet expired.[2] While he shared with Congress the strongest desire to favor the freedmen, this bill, the President said, was not warranted by the Constitution, nor was it well designed to serve the ends in view. It proposed to extend military jurisdiction over every part of the United States containing refugees or freedmen. In the President's view there was peace in the land; he would not advertise it to the world that the nation was still in a condition of civil strife. Here was a plan to make a Bureau, established for an emergency, "a permanent branch of the public administration with its powers greatly enlarged." The Congress of the United States under the Constitution had never yet felt itself at liberty to establish schools and asylums for the white people, or to expend money, that they might have farms and homes. When the slave was assisted to his liberty the idea was entertained that upon becoming free he would be a self-sustaining person. Now with such legislation he would be filled with restlessness and uncertain expectation, while the white people among whom he lived would be kept constantly in a state of apprehension. Agents for all the counties would create an expensive patronage,

[1] Welles, vol. ii, pp. 434–5.

[2] Senator Trumbull said that the war had ended when the last "rebels" laid down their arms in Texas in May, 1865. — Cong. Globe, 39th Cong., 1st sess., p. 937. Therefore the Bureau law of 1865 would expire by limitation in May, 1866. The President, on the other hand, let it be understood that he would soon issue a proclamation officially declaring the war at an end. The law then would have a year to run after that date. Johnson expressed this view to General Howard and he so apprised the agents of the Bureau. — Wash. corr., N. Y. Tribune, Feb. 24, 1866.

and one which the Executive could use, if he chose, for his own political ends. Moreover, the bill had been passed by a Congress in which eleven states were without representation. To exclude them longer was a course which must be "attended by a spirit of disquiet and complaint." [1]

The reading of the message was accompanied by applause and hissing in the galleries, which caused the major portions of them to be cleared,[2] and on the following day, the 20th, after a long speech by Senator Trumbull in defence of the bill, it was put upon its passage a second time, notwithstanding the President's objections. Thirty votes were cast in its favor and eighteen against it. Senators Cowan of Pennsylvania, Dixon of Connecticut, Doolittle of Wisconsin, Morgan of New York, Stewart of Nevada and Van Winkle and Willey of West Virginia, all accounted Republicans, came to the President's support. There were two absentees. Two-thirds of the senators present not having voted for the bill, it failed. The disturbance in the galleries was resumed, and they were again cleared.[3]

The House at this time was in a still louder uproar. Stevens's reply to the President's message was a resolution from the Committee of Fifteen declaring that in order "to close disturbing agitation no senator or representative from any of the eleven insurgent states should be admitted to either branch of Congress" until Congress had "declared such state entitled to such representation." The filibustering of the minority was futile, and the vote in favor of the resolution was 109 to 40, 34 members not voting. Eight Republicans, led by Mr. Raymond, opposed the measure.[4] On March 2 the Senate passed the resolution by a vote of 29 to 18, the President holding the support of Cowan, Dixon, Doolittle, Morgan, Stewart and Van Winkle, and receiving, in addition, the votes of Norton of Minnesota and Lane of Kansas.[5]

The veto was the signal for a demonstration of party feeling

[1] Richardson, Messages and Papers of the Presidents, vol. vi, pp. 398–405.

[2] Cong. Globe, 39th Cong., 1st sess., p. 917.

[3] Ibid., p. 943.   [4] Ibid., p. 950.

[5] Ibid., p. 1147.

in all portions of the country. A mob of perhaps 2000 persons assembled at Willard's Hotel in Washington on the evening of February 19, where several Congressmen were called out for speeches. Then the crowd proceeded to the White House with a band of music to serenade the President. He was acclaimed with rounds of cheers, but he declined to appear.

He would have done better had he followed the same course on Washington's Birthday, when after a meeting organized in support of his policies at Grover's Theatre, addressed by Montgomery Blair, Green Clay Smith of Kentucky, Senator Hendricks, S. S. ("Sunset") Cox and others he was again visited and asked to speak. He was recommended by his friends to respond but briefly, if he were tempted to do so at all,[1] but his combative nature was now thoroughly aroused. In the Cabinet he was uttering spirited denunciations of the radical intrigues against his administration.[2] He forgot for the time that he was not on the hustings in East Tennessee, and he was led into a wild, incoherent harangue of more than an hour in length. As he proceeded his choler rose, he gnashed his teeth, his voice grew loud and boisterous, and at times, when he was interrupted by cries of "Give it to them, Andy," "Hit them again," etc., and rowdies asked him questions, he seemed to be entirely beside himself. His words were reported differently by different persons, but in all the forms they were so little in keeping with the dignity of the Presidential office that, after they were "put upon the wires" for the newspapers, some censor forbade their going out. It was late at night before the prohibitory order was revoked and the transmission of the speech was resumed.[3]

In the course of the harangue the President expressed his disapproval of "the Davises, the Toombses and the Slidells," but there were men on the other side, said he, as much opposed to the Union as they had ever been, and, after being urged to

[1] Doolittle urged silence upon him. — Welles, vol. ii, p. 647. He had promised McCulloch to speak only briefly if he spoke at all. — Men and Measures, p. 393.

[2] Welles, vol. ii, p. 435.

[3] N. Y. Tribune, Feb. 24 and Feb. 27, 1866.

it by the crowd, he named Thaddeus Stevens, Charles Sumner and Wendell Phillips. "How about Forney?" some one cried, alluding to Colonel John W. Forney, the secretary of the Senate, and editor of the Washington Chronicle and the Philadelphia Press, "both daily," who until a very recent time had warmly supported the President.[1] "I do not waste my fire on dead ducks," Johnson replied amid laughter. He passed then to the charges of his usurpation of power, to Thaddeus Stevens's wish to take off his head like Charles the First's, to a fear of assassination by the radicals, even as Lincoln had been assassinated, to his skill as a tailor, to his simple and unaffected life in the White House, to his career in Tennessee and elsewhere as a people's man, and to many other inappropriate subjects.[2]

On the same day a great meeting was held in Cooper Institute in New York to sustain the President. Here Secretary Seward was the principal speaker. Postmaster-General Dennison and Henry J. Raymond also addressed the audience, while the resolutions were presented by David Dudley Field.

The board of aldermen of New York indorsed the President's "conservative, liberal, enlightened and Christian policy."[3] The Senate of New Jersey passed a resolution approving the veto. The Democratic members of the Ohio legislature, assembled in caucus, did the same.[4] In Nashville, St. Louis, San Francisco — from Maine to the Rio Grande and from ocean to ocean — those whose sympathies were with the President came together to adopt preambles and resolutions. Town meetings, village assemblies, library companies and private associations voted their confidence and admiration, printed their fulsome words in the local newspapers and forwarded

[1] As recently as on Jan. 18, 1866, the Press had said that "no better person could have been found for the difficult work of restoration." Johnson's experience in Tennessee and his conduct since had "fully endeared him to the hearts of the people of both sections. . . . Andrew Johnson must be sustained."

[2] From the report of the speech in President Johnson's Washington organ, the National Intelligencer.

[3] N. Y. Herald, Feb. 24, 1866.　　　　[4] Ibid., Feb. 22, 1866.

copies to the White House. One hundred guns were fired on
February 21 by employees of the sheriff's office and one hundred more on the 22d by order of the board of aldermen at
the City Hall in New York; a great cheer followed each discharge.[1] One hundred shots were heard at Syracuse, at Manchester, N. H., at Dayton, O., at Keokuk, Iowa, at Wheeling,
W. Va. A salute of thirty-six guns in honor of the thirty-six
states was given at Hudson, N. Y., at New Haven, Conn., and
at other places.[2]

There was a veritable outpouring of epistolary praise in the
President's mail. The Jacksonians were in a kind of seventh
heaven. Men, both prominent and obscure, North and South,
East and West, wrote to tell him of their admiration and faith.
Earlier named with Jackson he was now greater than "Old
Hickory." He stood upon the "highest pinnacle of the mount
of fame." Only Washington had a place at his side. "From
every city, village and hamlet in the nation," said an enthusiastic friend, "ascends one universal song of thanksgiving to
God." A Kentuckian invoked ten thousand benedictions upon
the President's head. His feet were planted upon the Constitution of his country. "There was rock; all else was turbid
sea." With the "heroic and holy patriotism" of Washington,
he united the "dauntless determination and devotion" of Jackson. One man thanked God that they had now in the national
capital what had not been seen there since Jackson's day —
"backbone." Another found him to be " a modern edition (un-
abridged) of Andrew Jackson bound in calf." Letters came to
"the President of (all) the United States." He had made the
issue with these Dantons, Marats and Robespierres of this age
and of this land, said one who could not spell their names; he
would save the nation from "anarchy and blood." More than
any question of constitutional liberty or right in the average
mind was the hatred and fear of negro suffrage. "The ma-

---

[1] N. Y. Tribune, Feb. 23, 1866.

[2] More powder was burned in honor of the veto by the Copperheads, said the Springfield (Ill.) State Journal, than they had consumed during the four years of war for the Union. — Quoted in N. Y.
Tribune, March 3, 1866.

jority of the people of this state," wrote a fellow from Conkey Store in Vermilion County, Ill., "is opposed to negro equality." "By god," he swore, "I will di before a negro shal put a ballet in the box on mine" — and this was a fact "beyond de Spute." "Go on and preserve the Union," said another correspondent of the President. He would succeed. The people would stand by him while he stood by the Constitution. "Man may rule the worst by ever daring to be first."

Preachers quoted the Scriptures and prayed for him; women asked him to suffer all things as Christ did. Parents christened their "beautiful boys" with his "immortal name," which would ever be "near and dear to the great masses of the American people." He was besought for autographs and photographs, and was elected an honorary member of literary societies and baseball clubs. The Butchers' Hide and Melting Association of New York forwarded him a piece of a fat ox, the largest of which they had any account in their records. The animal had weighed after dressing nearly twenty-five hundred pounds.[1]

Unfortunately for Mr. Johnson, most of the enthusiasm evoked by his course came from the South, and from the Democrats and Copperheads of the North, which it was pleasing and effective for his enemies to bring to public notice. Vallandigham, the chief of Confederate advocates in the North during the war, made a speech at Dayton, O., in which he said that while the Democrats had not elected Mr. Johnson it was now their duty to sustain his policies.[2] Lesser Copperheads everywhere were openly exultant. Their gazettes spoke of "the noble act of President Johnson," his "sublime moral courage."[3] "The stone which the builders rejected," said the Norfolk (Va.) Post, "has become the head of the corner, and Andrew Johnson is now enshrined in every Southern heart."[4] The

[1] Johnson Papers for the period.

[2] Phila. Press, Feb. 24, commented on by Senator Sherman in his speech of Feb. 26, 1866. — Appendix of Cong. Globe, 39th Cong., 1st sess., p. 132.

[3] See excerpts from various papers reprinted in N. Y. Tribune, Feb. 27, 1866.

[4] Quoted by N. Y. Tribune, March 2, 1866.

Daily News of New York, incessant in uttering disloyal sentiments throughout the war, had not before been so much gratified
by any act of the President.[1] "The name of Andrew Johnson,"
it said, "is upon the lips of the people in accents of delight and
admiration." [2]   The Chicago Times urged the arrest of Stevens,
Sumner and Phillips for "the crime of treason."   The "Northern rebellion" could be quelled and public quiet restored in no
other way.   It was the President's opportunity to become a
Cromwell and dissolve the "Rump Congress" which sat at
Washington.[3]

On the other hand, many meetings were called to indorse
the policy of Congress.   The legislatures of a half dozen states
passed resolutions unfriendly to the President.   The Republican press had little but condemnation and censure for him.
The veto, said the Boston Transcript, would be read "with
profound regret and dissatisfaction by a vast majority" of the
members of the Union Party.[4]   "It fell," said the Washington
Chronicle, "like the cold hand of death upon the warm impulses of the American people." [5]   The Chicago Tribune
averred that "the masses of the loyal people must rise against
this veto of a measure, intended as a bulwark against slavery
and treason, as they rose in their might when the flag of the
Union was first hauled down from Fort Sumter." [6]   There
was "a feeling of indignation in every loyal heart," said the
Cleveland Leader.[7]   "Mr. Johnson has made a grave mistake,"
said the New York Tribune.   "Hereafter whatever wrongs
may be inflicted upon or indignities suffered by the Southern
blacks will be charged to the President, who has left them naked
to their enemies." [8]   There was "not one rebel from Canada
to Brazil inclusive," but would "bless" him for uttering
this veto.[9]

[1] Quoted by N. Y. Tribune, Feb. 21, 1866.
[2] Ibid., Feb. 26, 1866.
[3] Ibid., March 2, 1866.   [4] Ibid., March 3, 1866.
[5] Quoted in Phila. Ledger, Feb. 20, 1866.
[6] Quoted in N. Y. Tribune, March 3, 1866.   [7] Ibid.
[8] N. Y. Tribune, Feb. 20, 1866.
[9] Ibid., Feb. 21, 1866.

As for the maundering speech to the crowd on Washington's Birthday, it, too, was condemned or defended according to the political sympathies of him who judged it. The New York Times most untruthfully remarked that it would "arrest the attention and command the assent of the great body of the American people." Its language was "strong, direct, manly," etc.[1] The New York Herald found the speech to be "bold, manly and outspoken" — "suited to the man and to the times."[2] Seward gave it the seal of his approval. "It is all right and safe," he telegraphed from New York. "The Union is restored and the country saved. The President's speech is triumphant."[3] It was a "glorious speech," Thurlow Weed wrote to the President. "It vindicates and saves our government and our Union. . . . Traitors will seek hiding places."[4] Welles was of opinion that it was "earnest, honest and strong," though he regretted that Mr. Johnson had allowed himself to be drawn into answering questions promiscuously.[5] The "Dead Duck" Forney in his two papers openly attributed the outburst to the President's inebriated condition. It was an "appalling picture." It would suffuse "every honest brow with shame."[6] "The nation held its nose ez one man," wrote Petroleum V. Nasby; "the Ablishnists who had previously sworn that he wuzn't drunk when he was inoggerated, admitted that they might hev bin, and ondoubtedly wuz, mistaken."[7] The New York Tribune, when it was denied that the President had been in his cups, was filled with regret that "the best excuse which could be offered for it could no longer be pleaded in palliation."[8] Others, in apology, pointed to the fact that the President had grown hysterical in fear of assassination,[9] and again that he was overwrought by the burdens of his office. He should be

[1] Feb. 24, 1866.   [2] Feb. 24, 1866.
[3] N. Y. Herald, Feb. 28, 1866.
[4] Johnson Papers, letter under date of Feb. 23, 1866.
[5] Welles, vol. ii, p. 439.
[6] Phila. Press, Feb. 24, 1866; Welles, vol. ii, p. 439.
[7] Andy's Trip to the West, Together with a Life of its Hero, p. 29.
[8] Feb. 24, 1866.
[9] Washington corr., N. Y. Tribune, Feb. 24, 1866.

spared the trouble of addressing intruding crowds, which so frequently broke in upon his hours of rest.[1]

But the President's course was adopted in no transient fit of hysteria or anger. It was due to a vital difference of temper and belief which was a full reflection of the division in the public mind. On the one, side were the visionary but pertinacious philanthropists, such as Sumner and Greeley, assisted by the politicians who wished to hold present power and assure themselves and their party of future advantages, through appeals to the vindictive prejudices of the Northern people. This group became a host as soon as it was understood that in order to win an election it was but necessary to brand a political opponent as a "rebel" or a "copperhead."

On the other side were those, like the President, who sincerely wished to unite the dissevered parts of the country by kindly courses, hindered, not aided, by the too eager and too exultant Democratic party in the North, and practically the whole body of the white people in the South.

From the first day of the session Congress had exasperated the President by requests for information. If he had papers in his possession they must be surrendered, so that it could judge whether the policies based upon them which he had formulated were warranted by the facts. If there were delay in meeting a request it was ascribed to unpatriotic motives. If the President made a recommendation, on the other hand, no note was taken of it by Congress. He was under suspicion of doubtful purposes before his word was heard. Throughout the summer and autumn of 1865 there had been unpleasant radical criticism of his exercise of the pardoning power. It was charged that he was appointing to office in the South those who had not taken, because they could not take, the "ironclad test" oath. Congress would know about these grave matters. To what oaths had the provisional governors, the Treasury agents officiating in the South and the postmasters subscribed?[2]

[1] Phila. Ledger, Feb. 24, 1866.
[2] Senate Ex. Doc., 39th Cong., 1st sess., nos. 1, 3, and 26.

Believing that Congress at an early day would amend the law bearing upon the subject, many had been permitted under necessity to modify the form of the declaration. Secretary McCulloch pleaded that men suitable to administer the affairs of the Treasury Department, who had not taken part in the rebellion could not be found in the South, and he presumed that it would not be the wish of Congress to humiliate the people by sending Northern men thither as tax gatherers. He was greatly embarrassed in the work of reorganizing his department in the late Confederate states. Postmaster-General Dennison could re-open only a fourth part of the Southern post-offices,[1] and some of these were in the hands of postmasters who had not taken the oath. It was suggested that he appoint women but they had been more devoted to the Confederacy than the men.[2] Of the 2258 mail routes in operation in the seceded states at the outbreak of the war the service of only 757 had been restored in March, 1866; for 8902 post-offices in these states only 2042 appointments of postmasters had been made, and of this number but 1177 had been able to qualify for their duties, 757 of these being males and 420 females.[3] To overcome his difficulties the Postmaster-General appealed to Congress for permission to designate "receivers and venders of stamps," and such a bill passed the Senate in February.[4] Radicals in the House asked why postal facilities should be provided for communities in which not one person could be found to take a loyal man's oath, but only about thirty members of the House, including Thaddeus Stevens, subscribed to the opinion that the Southern people were deserving of the further punishment of a prolonged existence without the means of sending away and receiving mail.[5] Nevertheless the bill did not become

[1] Cong. Globe, 39th Cong., 1st sess., pp. 593, 839.

[2] Testifying in regard to Texas before the Committee of Fifteen a witness said it had been "extremely difficult" to open the post-offices; "only women and children could be found to perform the functions and very rarely the women." — Report of Committee on Reconstruction, part iv, p. 129.

[3] House Ex. Doc., 39th Cong., 1st sess., no. 81, p. 5.

[4] Cong. Globe, 39th Cong., 1st sess., pp. 594, 838.

[5] Ibid., pp. 839, 855.

a law. McCulloch and Dennison appealed to the President and he forwarded their letters to Congress, earnestly recommending a modification of the oath.[1]

Again Congress called for information about the return of forfeited property to "the enemies of the government who claimed to be its original owners," and the number of pardons granted to Southerners excepted by the thirteenth provision of the Amnesty Proclamation. In April, 1866, General Howard, Commissioner of the Freedmen's Bureau, said that up to that date he had restored 430,000 acres of land to its former owners, and Attorney-General Speed reported favorable recommendations concerning the cases of 7197 persons who had applied for special pardons. Over 2000 of these were citizens of Virginia, 1300 of Alabama, 1200 of Georgia, 700 of Mississippi and 600 of South Carolina.[2]

The protection of the negro, in the midst of such local conditions as were described by Carl Schurz, by the writers of letters to Charles Sumner and in the newspapers, seemed to many of the Republican leaders an imperative national duty. Extracts from the "Black Codes" were called for and printed by Congress to intensify the feeling against the legislatures which had enacted them.[3] General Terry, in January, issued a military order setting aside the vagrant laws in Virginia.[4] General Sickles declared null and void the provisions in the laws of South Carolina discriminating against the negro.[5]

While Senator Trumbull's Freedmen's Bureau bill was still pending he brought forward from his Judiciary Committee a Civil Rights bill and pressed its passage in the Senate. By its terms negroes were declared to be citizens of the United States. Everywhere within the limits of the country they were to have rights equal to white men to make and enforce contracts; to sue and be sued and to give evidence; to buy, sell and hold property. They were to be subject to equal pains

---

[1] House Ex. Doc., 39th Cong., 1st sess., no. 81.
[2] Ibid., no. 99.   [3] Ibid., no. 118.
[4] McPherson, History of Reconstruction, pp. 41–2.
[5] Ibid., pp. 36–8.

and penalties and none other, local or state laws to the contrary notwithstanding. Large powers were conferred upon United States marshals, district attorneys and judges to secure the enforcement of the law, and, in case of resistance, the President might use such part of the land and naval forces of the United States and the militia as should be necessary to gain the ends in view. The measure passed the Senate on February 2, only three Republican votes being cast against it, and the House on March 11.

The opportunity was at hand for the President's second veto which was received on March 27. He argued that citizens of the United States should become so through citizenship in the separate states. While eleven of the thirty-six states were still unrepresented in Congress it was not "sound policy" to confer these new rights on 4,000,000 persons just emerged from slavery residing in these unrepresented states. "Can it be reasonably supposed that they possess the requisite qualifications to entitle them to all the privileges and immunities of citizens of the United States?" Discriminations were made against intelligent and worthy foreigners in favor of the negro,[1] "to whom after long years of bondage the avenues to freedom and intelligence have just now been suddenly opened." Hitherto all the various matters which Congress wished to regulate from Washington had been left to the individual states. The measure indicated "another step or rather stride towards centralization and the concentration of all legislative power in the national government." Its tendency would be "to resuscitate the spirit of the rebellion, and to arrest the progress of those influences which are more closely drawing around the states the bonds of union and peace."[2]

The message was ably conceived and carefully phrased from the point of view of a state rights' man, but this was a view not respected by the majority in Congress, or by any large

---

[1] A rather unfortunate allusion since the disqualification of foreigners for a time is due to other quite good and sufficient causes. — N. Y. Nation, vol. ii, p. 417.

[2] Richardson, Messages and Papers, vol. vi, pp. 405–13.

portion of the party which in 1864 had elected the ticket bearing Andrew Johnson's name upon it. Its publication was the signal for a fresh outburst of praise from the letter writers. Many of these on obvious accounts addressed the President privately and in confidence. Ben and Fernando Wood in New York gave unmistakable evidences of pleasure. General George B. McClellan wrote from Dresden, before he yet knew of the second veto. "Whether you succeed or fail," he said, "you have earned the everlasting gratitude of those who love their country."[1] Alexander H. Stephens grew warmer and warmer in the expression of his admiration.[2] Ex-President Franklin Pierce, spending his last years at his home in New Hampshire, thanked Johnson for his "brave devotion to the Constitution and the Union and for the unanswered and unanswerable arguments," with which he had "confounded the enemies of both."[3] Old Amos Kendall, friend and associate of Andrew Jackson, with quivering pen, and many others whose names were not liked by Republicans, wrote to the President to commend his course.

When the bill was put upon its passage over the veto, every influence was brought to bear upon the moderates in the Senate who had voted to sustain the President in February on the subject of the Freedmen's Bureau. John P. Stockton, a Democratic senator from New Jersey, because of an alleged irregular election by the legislature of that state, had been unseated and he was out of the way.[4] Senator Morgan of New York was the centre of fire from both parties.[5] He was closely affiliated with Secretary Seward and Thurlow Weed, who were supposed to be supporting the President, but it became clear a day or two before the vote was taken that he now would go with the majority. Senator Dixon of Connecticut, who was ill, would have been brought into the Senate for the occasion, if Morgan had

[1] March 20, 1866, in Johnson Papers.

[2] See, e.g., letter of April 17, in Johnson Papers.

[3] Letter of April 13, in Johnson Papers.

[4] For an account of this proceeding see Horace White, Life of Trumbull, pp. 262–3.

[5] Welles, vol. ii, pp. 475, 476.

stood his ground.[1] But it was now useless. The galleries
were crowded, many negroes occupying places there, as was
regularly their custom.[2] Senator Morgan's loud "aye" was
greeted with applause, and when the result was announced,
all upon the floor and in the galleries rose and joined in "a
tumultuous outburst of cheering such as was never heard within
those walls before."[3] Thirty-three senators had voted for
and only fifteen against the bill. Three who had supported
the President in his veto of the scheme to continue the Freedmen's Bureau — Morgan of New York, Stewart of Nevada
and Willey of West Virginia — were now on the other side, and
the measure secured the necessary two-thirds vote. The House
on April 9 approved it a second time, whereupon the Speaker
declared it to be a law.

Again the radicals were painfully impressed by the President's want of consideration and sympathy for the negro
There was nothing for the blacks now, said the New York
Tribune, but suffrage, as all men could see, if they were not to
remain "Pariahs in the land of their birth."[4] The whole
message, said the New York Nation, could have been summed
up in one sentence — "If I know myself I have no prejudices,
but I do hate a nigger."[5]

The President under criticism in no manner mended his
ways. He was still the rough, violent frontier demagogue
when he assayed *ex tempore* speech. On April 18, in response
to serenaders at the White House, he returned to the maudlin
manner of February 22. "The foul whelp of sin has been turned
loose against me," he said. While he had been exposed personally and publicly and in every way during the war, his
"present traducers and calumniators" were far removed from

[1] Welles, vol. ii, pp. 478–9.

[2] This fact led to many remarks from such senators as Garrett Davis
concerning their idleness: "The vagabond negroes that are hovering
over this Capitol like a dark cloud"—"The lazy, indolent negroes"
who should be sent out "from this Capitol" to work instead of asking
government alms for their race, etc. — Cong. Globe, 39th Cong., 1st
sess., p. 397.   [3] N. Y. Nation, vol. ii, p. 451.

[4] March 28, 1866.   [5] Vol. ii, p. 449.

the foe and enjoying ease and comfort at home. "Tray,
Blanche and Sweetheart, little dogs and all, come along snapping
and snarling at my heels, but I heed them not." He would
"live long enough to live down" the whole pack of his "traducers and slanderers," and so on at great length.[1]

The President told a foreign correspondent in the middle of
April that "these men," meaning Sumner, Stevens and the
other radicals, knew nothing of the "real state of the South"
which was his home. They had raised "the cry of mad dog"
about his ears, though he had been brought up under the very
shadow of slavery. The South would treat the negro more
kindly than "these men," if her people were let alone and were
not exasperated by ignorant critics and persecutors.[2] Again
and again the President most unwisely and most distastefully
would tell how he had "perilled his all" for the Union, how he
had been born in one of the "humblest cabins" of the land, how
he had risen from the position of an alderman to the highest
office in the republic.

It is at this point that many who have passed judgment upon
President Johnson's career, and who have been able to follow
it with favor in its earlier stages, part company with him. It
is here, they believe, that he made a grave tactical mistake.
This opinion was held by not a few men at the time. By a conciliatory course now, said Rutherford B. Hayes, he could have
avoided a "complete rupture" with Congress.[3] If he would
but sign the Civil Rights bill, a correspondent wrote to Senator
Trumbull, "Andy Johnson would be cock of the walk." On
such a platform he could have appealed successfully to the
moderate feeling of the country against the negro suffragists.[4]
Henry Ward Beecher wrote to urge this policy upon the President. By approving the bill he would gain popular strength.
This action would at once weaken the influence of his enemies,

[1] Phila. Ledger and N. Y. Herald, April 19, 1866.

[2] N. Y. Tribune, May 14, 1866.

[3] C. R. Williams, Life of R. B. Hayes, vol. i, p. 286.

[4] Horace White, Life of Trumbull, p. 261; cf. Rhodes, vol. v, pp.
581, 587; Schouler, vol. vii, p. 56; Schurz, Reminiscences, vol. iii,
p. 229.

and prove how wrong they had been in making him appear to be unfriendly to the negro race.[1]

Six weeks after his veto of the Civil Rights bill the President disapproved a bill to admit the state of Colorado into the Union. This territory of the Rocky Mountains, which had recently made rapid strides forward because of the development of its silver mines, in accordance with the terms of an enabling act of Congress of 1864, had adopted a constitution in September, 1865, and elected senators and a representative, who now, like the delegations from the Southern states, awaited the course of events in Washington. On May 15 the Colorado bill was returned to the Senate with the President's objections. He said that the population of the territory at most was not above 40,000 persons, all of them recent and migratory settlers. The admission of such a state was, in the President's opinion, "incompatible with the public interests of the country." Moreover, he reiterated, eleven states remained without representation in Congress, therefore no new state should be "prematurely and unnecessarily admitted to a participation in the political power which the Federal government wields."[2] Much discussion ensued in the Senate, but as the majority was not a unit on this subject the bill was not pressed to passage a second time.

A bill to admit Nebraska, which also had adopted a constitution, in answer to an earlier invitation of Congress, was passed shortly before the adjournment of the session on July 27, 1866. It was the subject of a pocket veto.[3]

Meanwhile the Congressional leaders were busily giving form to a second Freedmen's Bureau bill. The President, on April 2, 1866, officially declared the rebellion at an end in all the Southern states except Texas,[4] where the work of establishing a civil government was proceeding. A convention to change the constitution of the state had met in March. A Confederate

[1] Letter dated Mar. 17, 1866, in Johnson Papers.

[2] Richardson, Messages and Papers, vol. vi, pp. 413–6.

[3] Cong. Globe, 39th Cong., 1st sess., p. 4276. Pres. Johnson's message of Jan. 29, 1867, Richardson, vol. vi, p. 489.

[4] McPherson, Hist. of Recon., p. 15.

brigadier-general, J. W. Throckmorton, presided. The secretary pro tem. wore a Confederate gray uniform, which was the dress of many of the members of the body. The constitution which they framed was submitted to and adopted by the people in June. State officers and a legislature could now be elected. The people proved to be no wiser than Alabama's, for they chose General Throckmorton to be their governor over E. M. Pease, a man who had had a better political career.[1]

The bill which the House and Senate now passed and presented to the President for his signature, known as the Second Freedmen's Bureau bill, provided that the Bureau be continued for two years instead of indefinitely, as in the case of the measure which he had disapproved in February. Some increase in the number of officers to be employed was made, though it was limited. Certain lands in the Sea Islands, bid in by the United States government at public tax sales, were to be distributed to the negroes on convenient terms. No lands in this district now being cultivated by freedmen should be restored to the owners until after the crops of the present year were gleaned.[2]

The veto came on July 16. The President's objections in effect were the same as those which he had offered to the first bill. The Bureau was assured of existence under the law which had created it for yet several months (for one year after the date of his proclamation declaring the war at an end), at the expiration of which time he thought that the freedmen would no longer require the benefit of its provisions.

The President in March had commissioned General James B. Steedman and General J. H. Fullerton to visit the South and render a report or reports concerning the operations of the Bureau.[3] It was a "spy mission," said the negrophile radicals. Steedman, like Johnson, was persuaded beforehand that the Bureau was a "nuisance."[4] As for Fullerton he had

---

[1] For Pease's platform see his printed address to the people of Texas preserved in Joseph Holt Papers in Library of Congress.

[2] McPherson, Hist. of Recon., p. 149.

[3] N. Y. Tribune, April 23, 1866.   [4] Ibid., June 13, 1866.

replaced Conway, as assistant commissioner for Louisiana, and to such a degree did he possess the regard of the "New Orleans rebels" that he had been "offered a dinner on his departure."[1] "Come curse me, Israel" was Johnson's command to Steedman and Fullerton as it had been Balak's of old.[2] The "combined generals travelling in the interests of the President"[3] went first to Virginia, and thence to the Sea Islands and into the Gulf states. They heard testimony and rendered three reports to the Secretary of War covering separate parts of the South, the last for Georgia, Alabama, Mississippi, Louisiana and Texas under date of July 20. Steedman wrote Johnson privately that the Bureau officers, with a very few exceptions, constituted "a radical close corporation," devoted to the defeat of the policy of his administration.[4] The commissioners found many instances of incompetent men, even of corrupt management, and as a result of their observations several officers were ordered under arrest by the President.[5] In their belief the Bureau demoralized the negroes as laborers and promoted bitterness between the races. The necessity for such an organization had now come to an end.[6]

The President in his veto message, basing his words upon these reports and other opinions which reached him, asserted that "in numerous instances" the Bureau is "used by its agents as a means of promoting their individual advantage, and that the freedmen are employed for the advancement of the personal ends of the officers instead of their own improvement and welfare."[7]

On the same day the message vetoing this bill was received by Congress it was repassed by both houses — in the Senate by

[1] N. Y. Tribune, May 14, 1866.

[2] Ibid., Aug. 11, 1866.   [3] Ibid., May 30, 1866.

[4] June 26, 1866, in Johnson Papers.

[5] N. Y. Tribune, May 30, 1866; House Ex. Doc., 39th Cong., 1st sess., no. 120, p. 2.

[6] See N. Y. Tribune, May 18, May 30, May 31, June 13, Aug. 10, Aug. 11, 1866, and House Ex. Doc., no. 120 and no. 123, for statements and counter statements called out by the Steedman-Fullerton investigation.

[7] McPherson, History of Reconstruction, p. 148.

a vote of 33 to 12, Doolittle, Norton and Van Winkle alone ally-
ing themselves with the Democrats in support of the President.

The Joint Committee of Fifteen had determined at the earliest
day to put a number of its policies into permanent form, and
offer to the legislatures of the states several amendments to
the Constitution of the United States. The provision which
gave to the Southern white people representation in Congress
for three-fifths of their slaves engaged general attention. Thaddeus Stevens, on January 22, reported an amendment providing that there should be representation for the whole number
of persons, whenever the elective franchise should cease to be
denied to these persons on account of race or color. The
measure passed the House on January 31, but in March was
rejected by the Senate, where the vote was 25 ayes and 22 noes,
a two-thirds majority being necessary. On February 13 another amendment was reported to the House by Mr. Bingham
on behalf of the Committee of Fifteen. It conferred upon
Congress the power to make "all laws which shall be necessary
and proper to secure to the citizens of each state all privileges
and immunities of citizens in the several states, and to all
persons in the several states equal protection in the rights of
life, liberty and property." James F. Wilson reported from
the House Judiciary Committee an amendment forbidding
the payment by the United States, or by any state, of any
"rebel debt." It was passed in the House on December 19,
1865, by the aid of many Democrats. Only eleven representatives voted in the negative.[1] These three proposals of Mr.
Stevens, Mr. Bingham and Mr. Wilson were gradually fused,
and on April 30 the Joint Committee reported what at length
came to be the Fourteenth Amendment.[2] It provided:

(1) That the negroes shall be citizens of the United States
and the state in which they reside, and that no state shall make
or enforce any law in abridgment of the privileges of citizens
of the United States, or deny to any person within its jurisdiction the equal protection of the laws.

[1] McPherson, pp. 104–5.
[2] Cong. Globe, 39th Cong., 1st sess., p. 2286.

(2) That in the apportionment of representatives among the states the whole number of persons shall be counted, excluding Indians not taxed, but when the right to vote is denied "to any of the male inhabitants of, such state being twenty-one years of age and citizens of the United States" the basis of representation shall be proportionally reduced.

(3) That no person shall hold any office under the United States, or any state of the United States, who may have violated an oath previously taken to support the Constitution of the United States by engaging in rebellion against it, except by a vote of two-thirds of each house of Congress.

(4) That the rebel debt shall not be assumed or paid by the United States or by any state, and shall be invalid.[1]

Two bills accompanied the amendment when it came from the Joint Committee on April 30 — one promising the state which should ratify it (after a sufficient number of states of the Union should have taken the same course and it should have become a part of the Constitution of the United States) the readmission of its members to Congress, if they could qualify by taking the required oaths of office — another barring from any office under the government of the United States all the principal civil and military officers of the late Confederacy.[2]

Neither of these measures passed; they were mere empty proposals to which in truth many of the leaders of Congress, bent upon more radical action, had no wish to give effect. The Fourteenth Amendment was approved by the Senate on June 8 by a vote of 33 to 11 and by the House on June 13, where the vote was 138 to 38.

President Johnson had told Senator Dixon on January 28 that he doubted the propriety of further amendment of the Constitution. Proposals to this end were "as numerous as preambles and resolutions at town meetings." If anything more of this character were to be attempted Congress, he thought, should content itself with a simple statement that representa-

---

[1] McPherson's History of Reconstruction, p. 102.

[2] Cong. Globe, 39th Cong., 1st sess., pp. 2286-7; McPherson, pp. 103-4.

tives should be apportioned among the several states "according to the number of qualified voters in each state." [1] But now he was called upon to act. On the 16th of June the enrolled resolution of Congress was delivered to Secretary Seward who, after consultation with the President, not to obstruct the course of political procedure, on the same day forwarded attested copies to the governors of the various states including those in the South. The President on June 22 addressed a message to Congress reporting the action of the Secretary of State, which he would wish to have regarded as "purely ministerial" and in no way in approval on the part of the Executive of the amendment. The resolution, he observed, had not been submitted to him for his favor. "The interests of national order, harmony and union," he repeated, made it very doubtful whether such proposals should be addressed to the states, while eleven of them were still denied representation in Congress. Nor should a proposal which had not been before the "sovereign people" be taken up by state legislatures elected "without reference to such an issue." [2]

On June 8 [3] the Committee of Fifteen was ready to make its report concerning conditions in the South. Through four sub-committees, sitting for four geographical areas, it had heard a large number of witnesses, including Alexander H. Stephens, John Covode, General Robert E. Lee, General George H. Thomas, General Rufus Saxton, [4] General Edward Hatch, United States Senator-elect Snow of Arkansas, Provisional Governor and Senator-elect W. L. Sharkey of Mississippi, Provisional Governor and Senator-elect William Marvin of Florida, Provisional Governor James Johnson of Georgia, General C. H. Howard, brother of General O. O. Howard; General Clinton B. Fisk, General Wager Swayne, General John W. Turner, in command in Richmond; John Minor Botts, the Virginia Unionist; Brigadier-General Corse, Miss Clara Barton, Gen-

[1] McPherson, p. 51.   [2] Ibid., p. 83.
[3] Cong. Globe, 39th Cong., 1st sess., p. 3051.
[4] Relieved of his duties in South Carolina on Jan. 15, 1866, as a result of the agitation conducted against him in that state. — Report of Joint Committee on Reconstruction, part ii, p. 216.

eral George A. Custer, and Sidney Andrews, Stephen Powers
and Benjamin C. Truman, newspaper correspondents.

A mass of information both for and against the President's
course was obtained. It covered subjects as far afield as
Lincoln's last hour effort to keep Virginia in the Union, the
prison cruelties at Belle Isle and Andersonville, the cotton
frauds during the war, the sugar crop in Louisiana, the bravery
of the black troops in battle and the popularity of Jefferson
Davis. Though the most of the witnesses were United States
army officers or Freedmen's Bureau agents, ready to furnish
very unfavorable accounts of conditions at the South, Confederates as prominent as Alexander H. Stephens and Robert
E. Lee gave variety to the testimony. Not one South Carolina
witness was a citizen of the state [1] about which he offered
evidence, and this was as true of the men who told of the conditions existing in North Carolina and other states. A considerable number of Virginia Unionists were brought over the
river from Alexandria, and such politicians and army officers
as happened to be in the city were called upon for their opinions
concerning the Southern situation.

The fact that the committees did not in any case visit the
ground but heard all the testimony in Washington prepared
the public mind for just such a report as it was now to receive.
The statement was certain to make an eloquent appeal to anti-
Southern prejudices in all parts of the North in preparation
for the coming elections. The political caldron would soon
be made to seethe and the committee-men were not unmindful
of what they might do to increase the ardor of the rising flames.
The President was accused of attempting to usurp powers
which were constitutionally vested in Congress. There was no
peace in the South, else he could restore the writ of habeas
corpus. The negroes were without protection. Northern
men visiting or residing in the South were subjected to insult
and physical abuse. The "rebels" everywhere were unrepent-
ant. It was no matter whether the states had ever been out

[1] J. P. Hollis, The Early Period of Reconstruction in South Carolina, p. 54, Johns Hopkins Studies, 1905.

of the Union; they must not be allowed to resume their old relations to the Federal government until they could prove that they were still not its treasonable enemies. They must ratify the Fourteenth Amendment before they could expect to win the favor of Congress. Ten members signed the report.

Senator Reverdy Johnson of Maryland, and Representatives Rogers of New Jersey and Grider of Kentucky, the Democratic members, submitted another report in which they reached opposite conclusions from the same testimony. They pointed out that President Johnson's policy had been President Lincoln's. "The sole object of each was to effect a complete and early union of all the states." Mr. Johnson's career during the rebellion might be studied by every friend of the Constitution with full satisfaction. Whoever should venture to "impeach his patriotism" sinned against light. To charge him now with disloyalty was "either a folly or a slander, folly in the fool who believes it; slander in the man of sense, if any such there be, who utters it." [1]

Finally when Congress was about to adjourn it reached the cases of the senators and representatives from Tennessee. Under Brownlow's scourge of scorpions the legislature of that state had promptly ratified the new Fourteenth Amendment amid some of the most violent and irregular scenes in the history of parliamentary government in America. He proclaimed his victory over Johnson, whom he called "the dead dog of the White House," [2] to Congress and the country. Congress carefully declared in the preamble to the Tennessee resolution that state governments could "only be restored" to their former relationships "by the consent of the law-making power of the United States," to which sentiment the President responded in a message of less good nature than any he had yet issued. [3] It was read in the House on July 24 amid much ironical laughter. [4]

---

[1] Report of the Joint Committee on Reconstruction, in House Reports, 39th Cong., 1st sess., no. 30; also McPherson, History of Reconstruction, pp. 84–101.

[2] To John W. Forney, Secretary of the United States Senate.

[3] McPherson, pp. 152–4.

[4] Cong. Globe, 39th Cong., 1st sess., p. 4103.

On the same day Horace Maynard and two of his associates appeared to take the oath of office.[1] Joseph S. Fowler was seated in the Senate on July 25.[2] But David T. Patterson, the other senator, President Johnson's son-in-law, was subjected to a variety of indignities before he was received. He had acted as a circuit judge in East Tennessee during the war under the "rebel authorities." Therefore, senators said that he was unfitted to sit among them and they referred his case to a committee, to which he offered satisfactory explanations of his action. Failing here, the radicals made him the subject of a joint resolution which passed the Senate, but was defeated in the House.[3] Finally on July 28, on the last day of the session, an hour or two before the adjournment, he, too, was allowed to take his seat.[4]

The President's own state, for which he had a sincere affection, was again in its old position in the Union. The issue between him and Congress was submitted to the people for months of turbulent dispute.

[1] Cong. Globe, 39th Cong., 1st sess., p. 4106.
[2] Ibid., p. 4113.
[3] Ibid., pp. 4162–9, 4213–6, 4243–5, 4267–73.
[4] Ibid., p. 4293.

CHAPTER IV

THE TRIUMPHANT NORTH

THE end of the war found the North in the midst of a period of great speculative activity. The currency had been expanded by large issues of paper money. To meet the country's extraordinary needs Congress, in February, 1862, authorized the emission of $150,000,000 worth of paper to which it gave the quality of legal tender, and in the July following $150,000,000 of the same bills, or "greenbacks," were added to the circulation. In March, 1863, there was still another issue of $150,-000,000.[1] On the 31st day of October, 1865, the total amount of these bills outstanding was $428,160,569, together with about $26,000,000 of fractional currency; $185,000,000 of the notes of the new national banks, now numbering more than 1500 in 28 states, two territories and the District of Columbia,[2] and $65,000,000 of state bank notes, a total paper circulation of $704,000,000.[3]

The effect of such an inflation of the circulating medium was immediately seen. Specie disappeared. Prices being measured by the paper money standard rose, as in the South, under a similar system of financial management. Gold came to have a separate value and was dealt in as a commodity on "Gold Boards" in New York and elsewhere, the price in terms

[1] House Ex. Doc., 38th Cong., 2d sess., no. 3 — Report of the Secretary of the Treasury for 1864, p. 3.

[2] On the first Monday of January, 1865, there were 643 national banks; up to the first Monday of October of that year 1572 had been organized under the national banking law. — Report of Comptroller of the Currency for 1865, House Ex. Doc., 39th Cong., 1st sess., no. 4, pp. 130, 142.

[3] House Ex. Doc., 39th Cong., 1st sess., no. 3 — Report of the Secretary of the Treasury for 1865, pp. 9, 17.

of "greenbacks" rising and falling as the credit of the government fluctuated by reason of the progress or defeat of the Union armies, and on other accounts. In the summer of 1864, in the fear of an unfavorable outcome of the presidential election, the price rose above 200. On July 17 the high mark, 285, was reached and the price did not fall below 200 until February, 1865. It was 146 on the day Lincoln was assassinated, and hovered between 130 and 150 for the rest of the year. To say that gold was worth 200 was to say simply that the "greenback" dollar, which had become the measure of price, was worth only 50 cents. If gold had risen to 300, the paper dollar would have been worth but 33⅓ cents. It was equivalent to declaring that the "greenbacks" were circulating at two to one, or three to one; that two or three paper dollars were worth but one dollar in the money of Europe and of California (which was so isolated that it could continue specie payments), where they frankly quoted "greenbacks" and United States government bonds at 40, 50 or 60 cents, according as the markets changed, in response to influences which were the same as those controlling the price of gold in New York.

The prices of all commodities rose because of the cheapening of the standard of value; of many, too, because of the increased demand for or the reduced supplies of these commodities by reason of the general derangements of the time. A careful examination and comparison of the wholesale prices of various articles, of wages and of rents before and after the war was made by David A. Wells, who by an act of Congress in 1866 [1] was appointed Special Revenue Commissioner of the Government. Brown sheetings, which in July, 1860, were quoted at 6 to 10 cents a yard in gold, had advanced in October, 1866, to 19 to 24 cents in currency. The price of calico prints in the same time had increased from 8 to 11 cents to 18½ to 22 cents; of ginghams from 10 to 12½ cents to 17 to 26 cents; of canton flannels from 8½ to 14 cents to 26 to 40 cents.[2] The changes in the prices of a number of articles in the wholesale markets, tak-

[1] Act of July 13, 1866, 66th section.
[2] Senate Ex. Doc., 39th Cong., 2d sess., no. 2, p. 11.

ing their mean prices of four years, 1859–62, and the prices of October, 1866, for the comparison, were found by Mr. Wells to have been as follows:[1]

	MEAN PRICE IN FOUR YEARS, 1859–62	PRICES IN OCTOBER, 1866	INCREASE OR DECREASE PER CENT	
	Gold	Currency	Nominal	In Gold
Wheat flour, barrel	$5.87½	$11.55	97 inc.	31 inc.
Rye flour, barrel	3.58	7.15	100 inc.	33 inc.
Wheat, Genesee, bushel . .	1.44	3.07½	114 inc.	43 inc.
Oats, Northern, bushel . .	.43	.56½	31 inc.	12½ inc.
Corn, Northern, bushel . .	.71	.98	38 inc.	8 dec.
Coal, anthracite, ton . . .	5.43	9.00	66 inc.	11 inc.
Coffee, Brazil, lb.	.15	.18½	23 inc.	18 dec.
Coffee, Java, lb.	.18½	.26	41 inc.	16 dec.
Cotton, middling, lb. . . .	.11	.40¾	270 inc.	147 inc.
Iron, English pig, cwt. . . .	24.26	52.00	114 inc.	43 inc.
Iron, common English bar cwt.	47.65	101.00	131 inc.	54 inc.
Pork, mess, bbl.	15.64	32.15	106 inc.	37 inc.
Beef, mess, bbl.	6.32	15.50	145 inc.	63 inc.
Pickled hams, lb.	.07½	.18	140 inc.	60 inc.
Lard, lb.	.10	.17¾	77½ inc.	18 inc.
Butter, lb.	.17½	.37	111 inc.	41 inc.
Cheese, lb.	.08¼	.13¾	67 inc.	11 inc.
Rice, ordinary, cwt. . . .	5.00	10.00	100 inc.	33 inc.
Salt, Liverpool, sack . . .	.89¼	1.92½	115 inc.	43 inc.
Sugar, muscovado, lb. . . .	.06¼	.11	76 inc.	17 inc.
Tea, young hyson, lb. . . .	.38	.97½	157 inc.	71 inc.
Wool, common, lb.	.39¼	.50	27 inc.	15 dec.

The nominal or apparent increase of price of eighty leading articles averaged nearly 90 per cent. In the same period Mr. Wells found that rents had grown higher at about the same rate, and that wages had advanced about 60 per cent.[2]

The housewife in New York in October, 1865, must pay 60 cents a pound for her table butter, and 35 cents a pound for a sirloin steak or a fowl. The wheat flour for her bread or pastry cost her $11.50 to $14.50 a barrel. The cheapest oysters in the market were to be had at $1.25 a hundred; the best at

[1] Senate Ex. Doc., 39th Cong., 2d sess., No. 2, p. 188. [2] Ibid., p. 14.

$5. Eggs were 50 cents a dozen. The best coffee was sold for 55 cents and tea, according to quality, from 90 cents to $2.25 a pound. Brown sugar was 18 cents and the powdered kind 22 cents a pound. The retail price of molasses ranged from 75 cents to $1.40 a gallon, while 80 cents must be paid for a broom, $13 for a ton of coal and $1 for a gallon of kerosene for the lamp.[1]

Immediately after the conclusion of peace some reduction was noted in the cost of living, and there was hope among the people that they had seen the end of "war prices."[2] But it was a vain expectation. Prices, "already enormously high," Secretary of the Treasury McCulloch said in December, 1865, were "steadily advancing." The expansion of the currency had gone so far that conditions had become "oppressive to a large portion of the people."[3]

But daring had come with military training, hope and some arrogance and heedlessness with success. We emerged from the war with a public debt which at its highest point, on August 31, 1865, amounted to $2,846,021,742.04. Revenue Commissioner Wells found that it was $74.28 for each inhabitant of the republic and the taxes in 1865–6 amounted to $11.46 per capita in gold, a levy in excess of that made in any other country in the world.[4] But, said he, the nation was infected with "a spirit of enterprise" which seemed "to redouble its energy with every additional burden placed upon it." The discovery, in western Pennsylvania, of petroleum, which was

[1] N. Y. Tribune, Oct. 14, 1865.

[2] For instance, butter was 25 cents a pound cheaper in Philadelphia (Phila. Ledger, May 22, 1865). Coal in Cleveland fell from $12 to $7; in Philadelphia anthracite coal underwent a reduction in price of $3 a ton (ibid., May 8, 1865). Horses became cheaper when the government ceased to buy for cavalry, artillery and transport uses (ibid., June 13, 1865). Butchers' meats must continue to be dear, said the president of the Pennsylvania Agricultural Society, because of the slaughter of the flocks and herds during the war, while no attention was given, at the same time, to the breeding of food animals. The pastures of many of the border states which had been overrun by the armies were entirely withdrawn from use (ibid., July 1, 1865).

[3] House Ex. Doc., 39th Cong., 1st sess., no. 3, pp. 8, 9.

[4] Senate Ex. Doc., 39th Cong., 2d sess., no. 2, p. 27.

exported in large quantities to create credit balances abroad, and the mighty development of the new agricultural regions in the Mississippi Valley and of the mines of the Rocky Mountains and California were powerful influences for prosperity. In the months following the war more coal was mined and sent to market than in any previous year, more oil and lumber were produced and sold. New cotton factories were built and the employment of labor in them was full. The iron furnaces were busy. Six thousand patents in 1865 at the Patent Office testified to the eagerness and ingenuity of the American mind in the field of invention; nearly 10,000 were granted to applicants in 1866.[1] An increasing postal business reflected the commercial activity of the people.[2] The foreign trade instantly gained a new impulse. The imports, which had reached a value of $234,000,000 in the year ending June 30, 1865, were $437,000,000 in 1866. The value of the exports of American merchandise in the same time increased from $306,000,000 to $550,000,000.[3] The telegraph, the railroad, the shipping lines were being extended to answer the growing demands of trade.

In a few years the entire national territory had been netted with wires. The mileage was about 50,000 in 1859; experts said that the total had been increased during the war to such an extent that in 1866 it was 150,000.[4] The Western plains had been crossed until "the Atlantic and the Pacific heard the dash of each other's waters." [5] Congress had subsidized the line. In 1862 the first despatches passed over it from New York to San Francisco and it had been in service continuously during the war, except when hostile Indians removed the poles

[1] Senate Ex. Doc., 39th Cong., 2d sess., no. 2, p. 10.

[2] House Ex. Doc., 39th Cong., 2d sess., vol. iv — Report of the Postmaster-General for 1866.

[3] Commerce and Navigation Reports for the fiscal years 1865 and 1866.

[4] G. B. Prescott to Postmaster-General Dennison, Senate Ex. Doc., 39th Cong., 1st sess., no. 49, p. 4. Probably an overstatement of the case as the Western Union officers at the same time said that the mileage of their allied lines was 90,000. — Ibid., p. 27.

[5] Ibid., p. 17.

and carried away the wire. At first in the hands of many small competing companies the business rapidly came under the direction of two principal companies, the Western Union, the result of a series of combinations in the West,[1] and the American. These two corporations while seeming to be separate had a harmonious working alliance, the same capitalists owning "into each to such an extent as to make them virtually one."[2] It was an "oppressive monopoly" which must be broken, and Congress in 1864 authorized another group of capitalists under the name of the United States Telegraph Company to build a line to the Pacific coast.[3] Difficulties were put in their way by the "monopoly." When they reached the boundaries of Nevada, an injunction was served upon them and work perforce was stopped.[4] In a little while the stockholders were ready to enter the "combination" and on April 1, 1866, the new company with $6,000,000 worth of shares was absorbed by the Western Union, which by this time had come to control a capital of about $40,000,000.[5]

Senator B. Gratz Brown of Missouri, in February, 1866, moved that inquiry be begun to establish the propriety of operating government telegraphs in connection with the post-office. The business was "sealed against" private enterprise "as much as Brigham Young's heaven against a rebellious wife." The Western Union Company "had it all its own way." It practised "extortion" upon the public.[6] Rivals were no sooner created than they were bought out. A land case had been decided in the Supreme Court, but the transmission of an account of it to California had been delayed until capitalists in the Western Union Company could carry out a great specula-

[1] "A mass of weak and perishing organizations culminated in the Western Union Telegraph Company." — Senate Ex. Doc., 39th Cong., 1st sess., no. 49, p. 17.

[2] Senator B. Gratz Brown in the United States Senate, Feb. 23, 1866.

[3] Laws of 1864, chap. ccxx.

[4] Remarks of Senator Nye, Cong. Globe, 39th Cong., 1st sess., p. 3481.

[5] Senate Ex. Doc., 39th Cong., 1st sess., no. 49, p. 21; cf. Philadelphia Public Ledger, April 6, 1865.

[6] Cong. Globe, 39th Cong., 1st sess., pp. 979–80.

tion on the Pacific coast.[1] The Postmaster-General to whom
the Senate inquiry was referred disapproved of the scheme to
conduct a telegraph business under the patronage of the government and Congress gave its attention to the work of subsidizing
another private competing company to be called the National
Telegraph Company. The undertaking was denounced as
but another effort to secure a franchise which could be offered
for sale to the "monopoly," and it at length took the form of a
law inviting any company of men to a tourney with the "monster," and bestowing favors upon them all with an equal hand.[2]

Meantime the lines were being rebuilt and the service was
being improved. The poles became larger and of a more endur-
ing wood, such as cedar, black locust or chestnut. The wires,
earlier of light iron, were now heavy and coated with zinc.[3]
Eighteen Western Union lines ran into New York from the west;
the American company controlled 28 wires reaching New York
from the south and 33 from the east. There were 74 telegraph
offices in New York, 35 in Philadelphia, 24 in Boston, 19 in
Baltimore and 16 in Washington. Yet the service still was
slow. There were various relay stations on the line to California. A message from San Francisco to New York was
seldom received the day it was sent.[4] A despatch from San
Francisco on October 26, 1865, did not reach Philadelphia until
the night of October 31. It had been nearly six days on the
way.[5] It was a feat to be remarked when a man in Washington
in April, 1866, sent a telegram to Salt Lake City at 10.30 A.M.
and received a reply at 5.30 P.M.[6]

In other countries, too, lines of telegraph were extended and
multiplied. London was in communication with all parts of
Europe — with Cairo, Algiers and Tripoli in Africa, and in
Asia with Teheran, Bagdad, Nineveh and Jerusalem, with
Calcutta, Bombay and the other cities of India. Russia had

[1] Cong. Globe, 39th Cong., 1st sess., p. 3481.
[2] Chap. ccxxx, Act of July 24, 1866.
[3] Senate Ex. Doc., 39th Cong., 1st sess., no. 49, p. 5.
[4] Philadelphia Ledger, July 20, 1865.
[5] Ibid., Nov. 4, 1865.
[6] Ibid., April 11, 1866.

built a line northward to Archangel and eastward over half
of Siberia to Irkutsk, the capital of her great Asiatic province.
How could the lines of the Old World be brought into connection with those of the new? Two men nursed two projects
tenaciously; one, Cyrus West Field, would go east by cable
under the Atlantic Ocean, and the other, Perry McDonough
Collins, would go west by way of Behring Strait to meet the
wires in Asia.

Field was one of seven brothers, sons of a Massachusetts
clergyman.[1] In 1835, when he was sixteen years old, he
went to New York to embark in business. In his first venture
he failed, but by 1852 he was ready to retire with a fortune.
Some short cables connecting England with the Continent
had been laid successfully, and Field interested himself in
the project, which dreamers had now and then discussed,
of joining Europe and America in this manner. He wrote
to Professor Morse to ascertain if telegraphy over so great a
distance were feasible, and to the Navy Department at Washington, which had been making surveys of the "Atlantic plateau." Was there such a plateau? He was assured of its
existence. Then he invited his brother, David Dudley Field,
Peter Cooper, Marshall O. Roberts, Moses Taylor and Chandler
White to his home in Gramercy Park in New York City. Together on several successive evenings they discussed the scheme,
and after due consideration resolved to lay a cable to connect
the shore of Valentia Bay on the west coast of Ireland and
the shore of Trinity Bay in Newfoundland, over the shortest
distance which anywhere separated the two continents.

Mr. Field at once proceeded to Newfoundland, where the
government granted him a charter for the New York, Newfoundland and London Telegraph Company, and some terminal and other concessions. Returning home, the company
was organized with Peter Cooper as president, and the line over

[1] Several attained distinction, — David Dudley Field in the law in
New York, Stephen J. Field in the law in California, later as a Justice
of the Supreme Court of the United States, Henry M. Field as a
preacher, writer and editor, and Cyrus as the promoter of the Atlantic
telegraph.

land and by cable, across the Gulf of St. Lawrence, to bring the
fishing villages on Trinity Bay in telegraphic communication
with New York, had been completed in 1856. A million dollars were expended by the company in carrying the telegraph
from the United States hither to this farthest point of the
American coast, Cyrus Field, Peter Cooper, Moses Taylor
and Marshall Roberts having each contributed about $200,000
in money to realize the project.[1] The government made new
soundings and further confirmed the existence of a plateau
on which the cable might rest. The ocean's greatest depth
over this course was about two and a half miles and the bottom
was comparatively level except at one point, some 200 miles
west of the Irish coast, where in a space of twelve miles a plunge
of 7200 feet was made from hard rock into the slime of the
sea. The British government despatched the steamer *Cyclops*
for still further surveys of the route without altering the conclusions of the American engineers.

Meantime Mr. Field was interesting British capitalists in
the enterprise. He soon organized the Atlantic Telegraph
Company which was to continue the existing line between New
York and Newfoundland, to England by way of a deep-sea
cable. There were 350 shares of £1000 each, 100 of which
were taken in London, 86 in Liverpool, 37 in Glasgow and
28 in Manchester. Mr. Field himself reserved 100 shares for
sale in America upon his return.[2]

Both the British and American governments proffered the
company the use of men-of-war to lay the cable. One granted
it an annual subsidy of £14,000 and the other $70,000 in return
for the transmission of official despatches over the line. The
work of manufacturing the cable proceeded apace. In the
summer of 1857 it was ready to be put in its place at the bottom
of the sea. No ship was large enough to bear it away, so half
the length was loaded upon a United States frigate, the *Niagara*,
the other half upon a British man-of-war, the *Agamemnon*.
The centre of the cord consisted of a strand of seven copper

---

[1] H. M. Field, Story of the Atlantic Telegraph, p. 49.
[2] Ibid., p. 85.

wires which were surrounded with gutta percha, tarred hemp and a heavy outer armor of twisted wire. The work of submersion would be begun on the Irish coast. When one ship had paid out its half of the cable, the ends would be spliced and the other ship would finish the service. Each vessel had its tenders and consorts, together forming an imposing squadron. The western shore end was landed at the harbor of Valentia. The Lord Lieutenant of Ireland spoke of the event as the "betrothal of England and America." In twenty days he would hope to see the "marriage consummated." [1] But six days out from the coast, when 334 miles of the cable had been paid out, the stress upon it was too great and it parted.[2] The fleet perforce returned to England. More cable must be manufactured and the renewal of the effort to span the ocean would be postponed until the following year.

The summer of 1858 found the *Niagara* and the *Agamemnon* ready to repeat the service which they had undertaken in 1857. They were supplied with new paying out machinery. The cable was coiled differently. This time the submersion would be begun in mid-ocean, and when the ends were spliced and put down into the sea one vessel would steam away to Ireland and the other to Newfoundland. After various trials and experiments in the Bay of Biscay the squadron headed for the appointed rendezvous in the North Atlantic Ocean. But on the way the *Agamemnon* encountered a fearful gale, the coils of the cable were so stored on board that she became unmanageable and she nearly foundered before she reached her destination. When three miles of the wire and rubber strand were under water, it caught in the machinery and broke. It was respliced and again sunk. Each ship paid out about forty miles when another accident occurred. The "continuity" was interrupted; the electrical current ceased to flow between the ships. They were brought together again, the ends were rejoined and the operation was resumed. In two or three days, after more than 200 miles had been successfully laid,

[1] The Laying of the Atlantic Cable, by John Mullaly, p. 131.
[2] Ibid., p. 151.

the current again ceased, and the cable ships returned to
Queenstown.

The directors of the company despaired. The shares of
£1000 which had been quoted in London at £600 were offered
at £200.[1] But Mr. Field was indomitable. The company
had lost but 300 miles of cable, the ships were riding at anchor
at his service and after recoaling they once more proceeded
to mid-ocean. It was the end of July when they again were
paying out the wire, and the signals passed over it with very
slight and temporary interruptions until the *Niagara* on August
5 anchored in Trinity Bay and the *Agamemnon* finished her
journey in the harbor of Valentia. The two ships had submerged 2050 geographical miles of cable, and the celebration
of the success of an event, in doubt so long that men on both
continents had come to look upon the possibility of its achievement with the greatest incredulity, was begun. Mr. Field
at once notified the Associated Press of the completion of the
work and the news was spread over the country. Everywhere
men left their places of business and ran into the streets. Children let out of school cried, "The cable is laid! The cable is
laid!"[2] Bells were rung, guns were fired, flags were flung to
the breeze. Towns and cities were illuminated. Mr. Field
found his name linked with the names of Franklin and Columbus.
Congratulatory messages, addresses expressive of public appreciation, from individuals and organizations, poured in upon him.

Preachers turned to the Psalms and found a text — "Their
line is gone out through all the earth and their words to the end
of the world," and then to the Book of Job where they found
another — "Canst thou send forth the lightnings that they
may go and say unto thee, Here we are?" The mayor headed
a great torch-light procession in St. John's in Newfoundland.
Many American cities arranged similar jubilees. In New
York there was a procession several miles in length in which
Lord Napier, the British minister, participated, a firemen's

[1] Field, op. cit., p. 163; Briggs and Maverick, The Story of the
Telegraph, p. 172.

[2] Mullaly, op. cit., p. 284.

parade at night, at which time the City Hall was set on fire, a public dinner, services in Trinity Church, the delivery of an address to Mr. Field and a presentation of medals. Queen Victoria

> "Flashed o'er the wires below the tossing waves,
> Training the floors of ocean's sunless caves," [1]

a message to President Buchanan expressive of a hope that the cable would prove to be "an additional link between the nations" whose friendship was "founded upon their common interest and reciprocal esteem." Poets burst out into song,[2] but in less than a month, after flaring up at times with promise of full energy, the signals ceased to pass over the wires, and the cable was dead. The revulsion of public feeling was complete. The scheme had been a great moon hoax. The plateau was a myth. The cable had hung over jagged Alpine peaks and had been cut. From the beginning Mr. Field had been engineering a suspicious stock speculation. He had sold his shares while he could and escaped the wreck, leaving others to suffer the consequences of the collapse of his visionary undertaking. Even he shared a little in the public despondency, and, the war between the North and the South coming on, new attempts to execute his plans must be deferred.

Meantime Perry McDonough Collins was doggedly pushing forward his project for a line to Europe across Behring

[1] W. C. Richards, Electron, p. 82.
[2]
> "Bold Cyrus Field, he said, says he,
> I have a pretty notion
> That I can run a telegraph
> Across the Atlantic Ocean."

But the people laughed at his foolish plan —
> "He might as well go hang himself
> With his Atlantic cable."

Now at last it had been laid —
> "Loud ring the bells — for flashing through
> Six hundred leagues of water
> Old Mother England's benison
> Salutes her eldest daughter."

— The Money King and Other Poems, by J. G. Saxe, pp. 71–3.

Strait. He was a citizen of California interested in the development of a trade with Asia by way of the Pacific Ocean. At his own request he was appointed Commercial Agent of the United States for the great Amoor River valley in Siberia, which he soon would visit.[1] In 1856 he set out for St. Petersburg, and by horse in Chinese caravans, by boat and the various other conveyances of the country proceeded on his way. He was, it was said, the first American to traverse the whole breadth of Asiatic Russia eastwardly. He returned home via the Sandwich Islands, having travelled over 30,000 miles in his absence which had covered two years.

While on this mission Mr. Collins conceived the idea that it would be feasible to build an intercontinental telegraph line. At this time Russia still had no telegraphs east of Moscow; the United States none west of St. Louis, but he opened an active campaign in behalf of the enterprise, writing, speaking, travelling in its behalf at his own expense. Though the war occupied the attention of Congress, Collins in 1862 asked for a government survey of the route. "We hold the ball of the earth in our hand," said the Senate Committee on Military Affairs in reporting a bill, "and wind upon it a net-work of living and thinking wire till the whole is held together and bound with the same wishes, projects and interests." [2] But Congress moved slowly and Collins went to Russia, where he was commended to Simon Cameron, the American Minister, by Secretary Seward.[3] His negotiations were successful. In 1863 the government at St. Petersburg gave him the right of way over its territory in Asia north from the mouth of the Amoor River, to which point it agreed to extend its Siberian lines, and in America. In the following year England granted him similar privileges in British Columbia.[4]

But Congress still delayed. He renewed his appeals.[5] The members of the New York Chamber of Commerce indorsed

---

[1] House Ex. Doc., 35th Cong., 2d sess., no. 53.
[2] Ibid., 37th Cong., 2d sess., no. 13.   [3] Ibid., 3d sess., no. 10.
[4] Senate Mis. Doc., 38th Cong., 1st sess., no. 126.
[5] Ibid., no. 98.

the project; it would redound, said they, to the benefit of the "whole family of man."[1] Secretary Seward, who had warmly espoused the scheme, declared that "it would be as easy now to dispense with the use of the steam engine on land or on sea in the business of commerce, in social intercourse or in political affairs, as it would be to forego the telegraph." Mr. Collins was "an enlightened, assiduous and faithful man who had worked abroad with the favor of the State Department, gaining favors which should not be withheld from him at home."[2] Senator Zachariah Chandler defended the cause as though it were his own. Senator Lot Morrill, testifying to Mr. Collins's public spirit and devotion to a "great end," predicted that "among the great things of the last half century" none would "stand higher in history" than the telegraph over Behring Strait.[3] The plan to award Mr. Collins a subsidy, similar to that which had been voted to the projectors of the Pacific telegraph line to California, failed after a bitter contest in the Senate,[4] but in 1864 he was given lands, the right to erect stations and poles and the use of a war-ship.[5]

With his Russian, British and American concessions in hand he immediately assigned them to the Western Union Company, which had formed a separate Western Union Extension Company with a capital of $10,000,000 to forward the work of construction.[6] The line could and would be built, said Colonel Bulkley, who headed an expedition to Behring Strait to sound its waters, explore the shores for ground on which to set the poles and to feel the temper of the Indian tribes.[7] No engineering difficulty seemed to intervene. The obstacles standing in the way were not so great as many had supposed. It had been proven that messages could be transmitted electrically

[1] Senate Mis. Doc., 38th Cong., 1st sess., no. 116.

[2] Ibid., no. 123.

[3] Cong. Globe, 38th Cong., 1st sess., p. 3119.

[4] Ibid., p. 3126.

[5] Chap. cxcix, Laws of United States of 1864.

[6] Appleton's Annual Cyclopedia for 1864, p. 760; ibid., for 1866, p. 723; Cong. Globe, 38th Cong., 1st sess., p. 3118.

[7] San Francisco despatch to Philadelphia Ledger, Nov. 1, 1865.

amid the snow and ice of northern latitudes. The poles would stand in the frozen earth as if "mortised in rock." Trees there were not at hand to fall upon the wires; sleet would not weight them to the earth. They would stretch away unmolested "over the frozen desolation." [1] The distance to be traversed was not less than 5400 miles — 600 miles in British America; 1900 miles in Russian America; 400 miles of cable under the waters of the strait; 2500 miles in Asiatic Russia south to the mouth of the Amoor. The whole distance from New York to Paris by this route would be near 14,000 miles. It was observed that, at the rate at which messages then were forwarded between New York and San Francisco, the time occupied in telegraphing over the proposed new line backwards around the world might be expected to be not less than five days.[2]

The work proceeded. The first pole of the "Collins Overland Line" was set in place at New Westminster, the capital of British Columbia, on February 24, 1865,[3] and the wires were soon stretching north along the valley of the Fraser River. Operations were begun simultaneously at several points in America and Asia. A Russian corvette and a United States naval vessel were sailing hither and thither in the service of the telegraph builders, and it was firmly believed that London and Paris would be reached through California and Siberia before the doubtful task of putting a cable under the Atlantic Ocean could be accomplished.[4]

Meanwhile Mr. Field was not idle. He found that the cable of 1858 had been imperfectly constructed. It had been coiled out of doors and left in the sun until the gutta percha had melted. Then it had been twisted and injured on the *Agamemnon* during the storm. The British government was asked for a guaranty of interest on stock which, when sold, would enable the projectors to make and sink a new cable. But in

[1] Philadelphia Ledger, Jan. 30, 1866.

[2] Ibid., July 20, 1865.

[3] Harper's Weekly, Aug. 12, 1865.

[4] "The Progress of the Electric Telegraph," in Atlantic Monthly, November, 1865.

1859 a cable 3500 miles in length had been laid from the Red Sea to India. It, like the line to Newfoundland, carried the signals for a little while and then ceased to work, with the result that public confidence in all submarine telegraphs was shaken. The government did appoint a committee to investigate and report upon the general subject of cables, ordered new soundings to be taken in the North Atlantic and increased its subsidy from £14,000 to £20,000 a year with a guaranty of eight per cent on £600,000 for 25 years subject to the still doubtful condition that the cable should work.   Mr. Field again visited capitalists in England and America, and at length, through the assistance of the manufacturers of cable and cable material, the necessary sum was subscribed so that the enterprise could be started forward once more.

Much was being learned as a result of various experiments persistently conducted under other waters. France and Algiers had been connected by a cable 520 miles in length in 1860.   In the following year messages were despatched from the island of Malta in the Mediterranean, which enjoyed earlier connection with Sicily and Italy, to Alexandria in Egypt, a distance of 1535 miles.   The East Indian disaster was repaired to such a degree that a submarine line 1450 miles in length was laid in 1864 from the head of the Persian Gulf to Gwadur in Baluchistan.   In all the world there were in operation in 1865 55 submarine telegraph cables varying in length from two to 1535 miles.[1]

In the first place important changes were made in the composition of the strand which was to be sunk under the Atlantic. The seven copper wires in the centre of the cord now weighed 300 instead of 107 pounds to the mile.   The protecting gutta percha was heavier and thicker.   The cover was of ten wires wrapped with tarred hemp, which made it stronger and more flexible.   The new cable would weigh 35¾ cwt. per mile, while the old weighed but 20 cwt.   Two ships earlier were required to carry the load; there was now fortunately a monster of the sea able to bear the entire cargo.   This was the *Great Eastern*,

[1] Atlantic Monthly, November, 1865.

an eighth of a mile long, built at a cost of more than three millions of dollars. When she came into New York in 1860, crowds paid to go aboard her to view her wonders,[1] which were generally admired. But she had served no commercial purpose and lay in port useless to her owners. She was purchased and the drums of wire, set in salt water, through which an electrical current constantly passed in a search for defects, provided her with a cargo, including her machinery, of a weight of 21,000 tons.

Mr. Field's triumph now seemed near at hand. He had toiled since 1858, for seven years, as long as Jacob served for Rachel [2] and in July, 1865, the *Great Eastern* bore the cable to the Irish coast in Foilhommerun Bay, a half dozen miles from Valentia, the terminus of the cable of 1858. The shore end, of greater thickness, to protect it from ships' anchors, was landed and carried out to a buoy, where it was spliced to the thinner sea line, and the work of submersion began. Day after day the paying out continued until 1200 miles had been laid, when a defect was discovered, and it was necessary to use the "picking up" machinery to pull on board again a portion of the line which had been sunk. The ship swung around, chafed the cable, which broke, and the end plunged like a plummet to the bottom of the sea. The grapnels were brought out and thrown over to be dragged up and down in the hope of catching it. The outstretched flukes seized the cord after a few hours' search and it was hauled up. But the wire holding the grapnels broke, and the prize must be fished for again. Misfortune attended a second, a third and finally a fourth effort to bring the cable on board with such machinery as the *Great Eastern* was provided with, so the ship returned to England.[3]

In America the response to the news of failure was apathy. It had been predicted that the undertaking would not succeed; it had not succeeded. The line to Europe overland by way

[1] N. Y. Tribune, April 10, 1867.

[2] H. M. Field, The Story of the Atlantic Telegraph, p. 258.

[3] The trip was described with interesting illustrations by W. H. Russell in The Atlantic Telegraph, Mr. Russell having accompanied the expedition as a newspaper correspondent.

of Behring Strait soon would give the United States all it needed in the way of an intercontinental telegraph. There the subject might rest.[1] Like the captain's tea-kettle which the Irish sailor had dropped overboard, the cable was not lost because any fool knew where to find it. The rubbing and the chafing of the rocks at either end would break such a strand at any rate. Some living thing in the sea would eat the gutta percha. An iron ship foundering would sink upon the wire and destroy the insulation. Cod hooks on the Grand Banks would tear it. An enemy would grapple for it, cut it, reel it up and carry it off as a spoil of war. Anyhow it would be something like a bridge, — more than a bridge between England and her colonies in America and who could wish her so much good fortune? Certainly not Irishmen, of whom there were so many spreading their propaganda in the fertile field which the United States had come to be in view of the great unfriendliness for England developed in the Northern states in the course of the Civil War.[2] A bill made its appearance in the Senate of the United States — to incorporate an International Telegraph Company to build a line to the Bermudas which might be extended to Europe by way of the Azores. It could be brought into operation sooner than the "immensely long cable" from the coast of Ireland to Newfoundland.[3]

If there were no great surprise in New York, disappointment was felt in the little fishing village of Heart's Content set on a quiet inlet of Trinity Bay, twenty miles from that point chosen for the western landing in 1858, now selected as a better terminus for the line. Newspaper correspondents and other visitors huddled in fishermen's huts to await the coming of the *Big Eastern*. Spruce beer was sold for fifty cents in specie by the glass, said one wag, who uncomfortably tarried here,[4] and crackers were carried about in place of coin. All must go back to their homes after a schooner arrived with word of the failure of the expedition.

---

[1] Philadelphia Public Ledger, Aug. 21, 1865.
[2] Ibid., Aug. 30, 1865.   [3] Ibid., Dec. 8, 1865.
[4] N. Y. Tribune, Aug. 8, 1865.

But the return of Mr. Field and his associates to England was in hope, not in the despair which was felt in 1858. More stock was sold and the manufacturers set to work to manufacture a new cable. The mechanical equipment of the *Great Eastern* was improved and in June, 1866, the huge ship with her consorts once more left the Irish coast, paying out wire as she proceeded toward the west. Though in mid-ocean, the cable party was daily in receipt of the quotations on the London Stock Exchange, of news of the debates in Parliament and of the European war. Finally after fourteen days, on July 27, the great ship steamed into Trinity Bay with the end of the cable which still was signalling constantly to Ireland ready to make the connection with Mr. Field's old line to New York. But now he found this line in disuse. The cable under the Gulf of St. Lawrence was broken. Until it could be repaired a steamer must be brought into service to carry the European despatches to Cape Breton. It was, therefore, Sunday, though the cable had been landed in Newfoundland on Friday, three days after London was apprised of the fact, before the people of the United States were brought to know of the successful completion of the work.

The cable of 1858 had flashed up and down and had given out its news reluctantly. Not so now. In less than a week the New York Tribune said that it would print every morning the European news of the day before. It was "impossible to realize at once a fact of such tremendous significance." "Another grand step in the onward march of civilization" had been taken. The completion of the work marked "an epoch in the world's history." [1] All the movements of men were quickened. Methods of diplomacy and government, the systems of trade and commerce were soon to be altered so greatly that it would bring on something near a social revolution.

Mr. Field and his associates were congratulated. Messages were exchanged between President Johnson and the Queen. From San Francisco, from Alexandria in Egypt and other distant, as well as nearer, places the wires brought greetings to the

[1] N. Y. Tribune, July 30, 1866.

men who after long striving at last had laid this vital cord beneath the sea.

Mr. Field had staked his entire fortune on the result. America and England to complete the work had sunk $12,-000,000 before success had come, and nearly all of this sum of money had been contributed in response to his personal endeavors.[1] More than forty times he had crossed the ocean in behalf of the object which now had been gained. The "Columbus of our time," said his friend, John Bright, he, at length, by his cable, had "moored the new world close alongside the old." [2]

The muses of newspaper poets again grew active, and much verse was written in commemoration of the event. Quip and jest filled the press. Puck had promised to "put a girdle round about the earth in forty minutes." Mr. Field had actually done so.[3]

But the exultation of the people was not so high as in 1858. The news was received in New York and Philadelphia quietly.[4] The enthusiasm had been spent. The New York Tribune had said in 1865 that it would not be worth the while of the councilmen to set the City Hall afire in another cable jubilee organized with borrowed or stolen money. With the former experience in mind there was a suspicion that the current under the sea might be broken at any moment. There must be "repeaters" over so long a line. The messages must be relayed on land; the "dullest reader" could understand that it must be so too, at sea. It was "manifestly ridiculous" to suppose that men could telegraph from Europe to America. Again the

[1] His speech to the New York Chamber of Commerce, N. Y. Tribune, Nov. 16, 1866.

[2] H. M. Field, Story of the Atlantic Telegraph, p. 386.

[3] "During the voyage of the *Great Eastern*," said one, "an indignation meeting" had been held. The cable was "played out." The sailors shouted "Down with the cable." "Who was the greatest wire puller of modern times? Cyrus W. Field." "Why was a happy husband like the Atlantic Cable? Because he was spliced to his Heart's Content," etc., etc. — Phila. Press, Aug. 1, 1866, citing the New York Post.

[4] N. Y. Herald, July 31 and Phila. Ledger, July 31, 1866.

fear was expressed that the cable would wear itself out on sharp rocks. The great pressure of the water upon it soon would render it of no use.[1] The public would do well to be cautious. Already it was rumored that quotations of prices in London were being withheld to promote the interests of speculators. How much better it had been when reports of these things came into the country by ship.[2] Many pretended not to believe that the cable yet did work.[3] Anyhow it must be admitted that it was a great money-making scheme.

Meanwhile the gazettes were offering their readers the news of Europe "By the Atlantic Cable." By the liberal use of leads and the introduction of large headlines the editors made it fill more than a column of space. Succinct, condensed, a mere announcement of facts it was, but with accounts of the movements of armies, the proceedings of Parliaments and the proclamations of kings came the prices of Consols and of Five-Twenties in London and of cotton and pork in Liverpool, and tidings about the arrival and departure of ships. On August 2 Mr. Field was able to telegraph from Heart's Content that the cable was transmitting despatches at the rate of $12\frac{1}{2}$ words a minute.[4] In a little while the broken cable under the Gulf of St. Lawrence was raised and repaired, the land lines to New York were put in better order and every town and city in the United States, provided with a telegraphic instrument, was in direct communication with Europe, Asia and Africa.

The *Great Eastern* took on new supplies of coal, despatched in colliers to her from Wales. Encouraged by the success which had just been achieved, the cable fleet was now ready to return to mid-ocean to grapple for the strand which had been broken in 1865. A rope of 49 wires, each wrapped with manila, the whole being six and a half inches round, was to be put down two and a half miles to the bottom of the sea.[5] One of the boats in the squadron had nearly caught the prize

[1] Washington corr., Phila. Ledger, Aug. 2, 1866.
[2] Phila. Ledger, July 31 and Aug. 2, 1866.
[3] N. Y. Herald, Aug. 4, 1866.
[4] N. Y. Tribune, Aug. 3, 1866.
[5] Lardner's Electric Telegraph, revised by E. B. Bright, p. 129.

before the *Great Eastern* arrived, but again it escaped. Finally on August 17 it was brought above the water, white with the ooze in which it had been resting for more than a year, but it broke just as it was about to be taken on board. Much fishing for it followed, and it was only when the grapnels had been thrown over for the thirtieth time, on the last day of August, that the cable was secured. The electricians were given the task of discovering if the great wire were "alive or dead." [1] It immediately responded to the tests and in an instant the ship was in communication with the coast of Ireland. The line was spliced and the fleet once more turned toward Heart's Content. Soon Europe and America were joined by two cables. The gutta percha, it was said, had been improved by lying for a year under the sea [2] and the old line actually gave the company better service than the new.

Now the work was done, doubly done. It was time for the New York Chamber of Commerce to honor Mr. Field with a testimonial dinner which was attended by many distinguished men. [3] Congress tendered him a vote of thanks, and presented him with a gold medal. [4] The Queen would have knighted him except for the fact that he was a citizen of the United States. [5] As it was, many pleasant attentions were to be shown him when next he visited England, among the number a dinner in his honor in London presided over by the Duke of Argyll. [6]

A very high tariff of charges marred the achievement in some men's minds. For twenty words or less, including the names and addresses of the sender and receiver between any place in the United States and any place in Great Britain the price was fixed at £20 in gold. Every additional word of not more than five letters would be transmitted for 20 shillings. From any place in America to any place on the continent of Europe the rate was £21, and 21 shillings for each additional word of

---

[1] H. M. Field, op. cit., p. 366.

[2] Lardner's Electric Telegraph, p. 135; Field before the N. Y. Chamber of Commerce, in N. Y. Tribune, Nov. 16, 1866.

[3] N. Y. Tribune, Nov. 16, 1866.

[4] Act of March 2, 1867.

[5] H. M. Field, op. cit., pp. 376 and 389.　　　　　[6] Ibid., p. 390.

five letters. To Asia or Africa the rate was £25, and 25 shillings for each additional word. The letters in words in excess of twenty would be counted and divided by five. Messages in cipher must pay double rates.[1] The longest despatch sent over the line in the first few days the cable was in operation was that received on August 8, giving the speech of King William upon the opening of the Prussian chambers in Berlin. It contained 1158 words, which cost the Associated Press $5790 in gold or more than $8500 in currency.[2] The Emperor of France was enabled now to communicate constantly with Maximilian in Mexico — from Paris, to London, to New York, to Galveston whence a fast steamer bore his messages to Vera Cruz.[3] In October Maximilian cabled 478 words to the Empress Carlotta at a cost of $4780.[4] But the most expensive adventure with the new line was Secretary Seward's despatch of 5000 words to our minister in Paris, in November, demanding that the French withdraw their troops from Mexico. This is said to have cost the government of the United States $25,000 in gold.[5]

On November 1 the cable rates were reduced fifty per cent. Instead of $100 for twenty words to Great Britain the price would be $50,[6] and Mr. Field announced a further reduction in the price of the service to take effect at an early date.[7] The lines were not worked at one-half of their capacity.[8] When an iceberg off the coast of Newfoundland damaged the cable of 1866 it was stated that the service of the company would not be disturbed. The old cable which many had thought not worth grappling for was more than able to meet the requirements of the business.[9] On March 1, 1867, Mr. Field's promise was made good. The price again was halved and became $1.25 a word.[10]

With these changes the cable enjoyed wider use and the

[1] N. Y. Tribune, Aug. 1, 1866.

[2] Phila. Ledger, Aug. 13, 1866; see also Harper's Magazine, vol. xxxiv, p. 517.   [3] Phila. Ledger, Aug. 18, 1866.

[4] Ibid., Oct. 18, 1866.   [5] Ibid., Nov. 28, 1866.

[6] Ibid., Oct. 26 and Nov. 17, 1866.

[7] N. Y. Tribune, Nov. 15, 1866.   [9] Ibid., May 20, 1867.

[8] Phila. Ledger, Feb. 16, 1867.   [10] Ibid., Feb. 16, 1867.

trade increased. The company's income when the rate was
$100 for 20 words had been about $2600 a day, in gold. At
the much lower prices, in May, 1867, the receipts averaged
$3810 daily.[1] They were, in April, 1867, $178,700, on 1410
messages westward and 1142 coming east. Since the opening
of the line at the end of July, 1866, until May 1, 1867, the
income had been $1,221,646;[2] for the first year it was
$1,660,000.[3]

A service so well paid for did not escape criticism. Some
complained of the confused character of the cable news.[4] It
related to matters for which no one in America cared "a jot,"
said the New York Tribune,[5] and similar dissatisfaction was
expressed concerning American despatches forwarded to England.[6] To Matthew Arnold the cable was "that great rope
with a Philistine at each end of it talking inutilities." At first
it had seemed very wonderful to bankers and brokers to be
put in possession, upon their arrival at their places of business
in the morning, of the opening quotations for stocks in London.
Now they would have the closing quotations at this time instead of at three and sometimes a later hour in the afternoon.[7]
It required two days and five hours and cost $500 for a mer-
chant in Newburyport, Mass., to communicate by telegraph
with Calcutta.[8]

But the service was being improved constantly. In December, 1866, it was said that five minutes sufficed to send a message from New York to Ireland.[9] In the winter of 1868 the
California-New York line, the New York-Heart's Content
line and the cable were connected, and a message was conveyed
from San Francisco to Valentia and answered inside of two minutes.[10] Even China and Japan were not far away. In April,
1866, a man in Boston received news from the Orient by ship
to San Francisco and then by telegraph east in twenty-six days,

[1] Phila. Ledger, Aug. 9, 1867.   [5] N. Y. Tribune, Nov. 2, 1866.
[2] Ibid., June 5, 1867.   [6] London Spectator, Oct. 20, 1866.
[3] Ibid., Sept. 3, 1867.   [7] Phila. Ledger, March 1, 1867.
[4] Ibid., Jan. 29, 1867.   [8] Ibid., May 10, 1867.
                [9] Ibid., Dec. 19, 1866.
        [10] Ibid., Feb. 4, 1868, citing Journal of the Telegraph.

which was said to be the "quickest time" on record.[1] By various adjustments of rates the prices were so much reduced that on September 1, 1868, the patrons of the cable were paying $16.85 in gold for a message of ten words (five additional words to cover address and signature being forwarded free) from New York to any point in Great Britain or Ireland. Words above ten in number must be paid for at the rate of $1.67 each.[2]

So much success by way of the Atlantic Ocean spelled the doom of the Collins line over Behring Strait to Siberia. It was believed that it might be made ready for use by the end of the year 1868. Now the work was brought to a stop abruptly. In March, 1867, the Secretary of State at Washington was apprised by the Western Union Company that it had indefinitely suspended operations upon the line after having carried the wires to a point about 850 miles north of Vancouver, with progress of various kinds at other places along the route.[3]

There broke out now what the New York Herald called a "cable fever."[4] The feasibility of submarine telegraphy was established; great profits awaited men ready to invest their money in the lines. Many companies were organized; many routes were surveyed. A party of capitalists projected a cable from Cape Charles to Bermuda, to run thence to the Azores and to Lisbon,[5] and work upon it was in progress in 1867.[6] French financiers planned to stretch a line from Brest to the island of St. Pierre at the mouth of the Gulf of St. Lawrence, whence it would proceed to New York by way of Duxbury, Mass. Another company interested itself in Cuba, Porto Rico, Brazil and Panama and proposed a cable running southward from the capes of Florida.[7] The International Ocean Telegraph Company obtained grants from the United States [8]

---

[1] Phila. Ledger, April 11, 1866.

[2] Ibid., July 23 and Aug. 27, 1868.

[3] Appleton's Cyclopedia for 1866, p. 727.

[4] N. Y. Herald, Sept. 7, 1867.

[5] N. Y. Tribune, Aug. 30, 1866.

[6] N. Y. Herald, Sept. 7, 1867.

[7] Phila. Ledger, Aug. 10, 1865, citing N. Y. Journal of Commerce.

[8] Chapter lxxiv of Laws of 1866. The president of this company was the Union General W. F. ("Baldy") Smith.

and from Spain, and in September, 1867, finished laying 191 miles of cable to Havana. Greetings were exchanged between Havana and Washington, and Havana and Madrid. The price for a telegram of twenty words from New York or Philadelphia to Cuba was $10, with a fifty cent rate for each additional word.[1] Soon the journals were publishing news "via the Cuban cable," and the business attained such a volume that in the summer of 1868 a second cable was ordered in England and was laid down on this line.[2]

The American ship, except the coasting vessel which was protected by law, had been swept from the ocean, during the war. Freight, passengers and the mails had gone to neutral bottoms. Some of the ships which had borne the American flag to Europe and into farther seas had been destroyed by the Confederate privateers; others sought safety in foreign registry. Few new vessels were added to the mercantile fleet. No voyage could be planned with a reasonable expectation of profit to the undertakers. One hundred and ninety-one ships had been engaged in the trade to Brazil and to other countries in South America in 1861. Now, in 1866, said David A. Wells, in a report to Congress, only 62 remained. In the same period foreign vessels engaged in this commerce had increased in number threefold. Our shipyards were idle. Before the war they were filled with keels laid down for owners in all parts of the world. This business had gone to Europe or the British provinces of America. Wages and the cost of materials were so high that ships which could be built in New Brunswick or Nova Scotia for $40 in gold per ton would cost in the United States not less than $100 in currency.[3]

In 1853 the American tonnage was 15 per cent greater than Great Britain's. It was about as great as England's up to the outbreak of the war. At the end of the war it was little more than a third as large.[4] The fleet of the United States had sunk to the fourth place among the merchant navies of the world.[5]

[1] Phila. Ledger, Sept. 12, 1867.   [2] Ibid., June 2, 1868.
[3] Senate Ex. Doc., 39th Cong., 2d sess., no. 2, pp. 17–18.
[4] Ibid., p. 201.   [5] Phila. Ledger, Dec. 15, 1865.

In 1860 $262,000,000 worth of goods had been exported from the United States in American vessels and only $110,000,000 worth in ships of foreign nationality.[1] American vessels carried $228,000,000 worth of our imports, while but $134,000,000 came in foreign bottoms.[2] In 1865, on the other hand, $75,000,-000 represented the value of the cargoes exported under the American flag; foreign ships bore away merchandise valued at $230,000,000.[3] Imports valued at $66,000,000 came in American vessels and $168,000,000 in foreign vessels.[4] In 1860 two-thirds of our imports and more than two-thirds of our exports were carried in American bottoms; in 1866 nearly three-fourths of our imports and over three-fifths of our exports, in foreign bottoms.[5]

The American ship on the high seas, when it was met with at all, was a sailing vessel.[6] No citizen of the country at the war's close could go to Europe under his own flag,[7] though later in the year two vessels the *Arago* and the *Fulton* began monthly sailings between New York and Havre. Eight foreign lines plied the North Atlantic with passenger steamers. Their combined fleet numbered 58 ships. Fifteen more were in course of construction and soon would be ready for the service. The Inman Line had 14 vessels, the Cunard 11, the Anchor 4, the French 3, the German companies — the North German Lloyd and the Hamburg — each 5.[8]

The Cunard Line which had been in existence for 25 years was established by Sir Samuel Cunard of Halifax. He owned a number of "tubs" which ran to Liverpool, after several of them had gone to the bottom, widely known as "coffins." Extending his line to Boston, he increased the speed and size of his ships. He was granted a subsidy by the British government in return for the carriage of the American mails and

[1] Commerce and Navigation Report for 1860, p. 50.
[2] Ibid., p. 290.
[3] Commerce and Navigation Report for 1865, p. 53.
[4] Ibid., p. 523.
[5] Senate Ex. Doc., 39th Cong., 2d sess., no. 2, pp. 17–18.
[6] N. Y. Tribune, Dec. 13, 1866.
[7] Phila. Ledger, May 8, 1865.　　　　　　　　　[8] Ibid., June 8, 1865.

an agreement to convert his vessels into troop ships in time of war. Still later the line ran to New York. In the summer of 1865 there were weekly departures from New York and Boston alternately. The Cunard boats were preferred by most Americans bound to and from Europe. The sailings became more frequent. The importance of the New York trade increased, and on January 1, 1868, the service to Boston was discontinued.[1] Many of the old mail steamers were sold and in 1867 the fleet was made to consist of twenty good modern steam vessels.

The type of the day was a ship of a capacity of little more than 3000 tons, and there was a turning now from the side wheel boats to boats which were propelled by screws in the stern. Much surprise was expressed at first that these could go as fast as the old paddle wheel boats.[2] The size — a length of 350 or 400 feet and a width of about 40 feet — caused passengers to remark the "thumping and bumping" of the machinery. Sails were set to aid the engines when the wind was fair,[3] and often a high speed was attained. The *Scotia*, a paddle wheel boat of the Cunard Line,[4] completed the trip from Queenstown to New York in November, 1866, in a few hours more than eight days, while the *Pereire*, a new ship on the French Line, arrived in New York in nine days from Havre.[5]

The new and better ships of the Inman Line, bearing the names of the cities, also gained a reputation for fast passages. In a race with the *Cuba* of the Cunard Line in April, 1868, from New York to Queenstown, the *City of Paris* won in 8 days 14 hours and 30 minutes.[6] An Inman Line boat on a voyage in May, 1867, covered 390 miles in one day.[7] A Bremen steamer reached New York from Southampton in January, 1867, in 9 days and 14 hours which was nearly equal to the time made by the best English and French boats.[8]

---

[1] Phila. Ledger, Jan. 1, 1868.
[2] Ibid., Nov. 30, 1866, citing Boston Journal.
[3] Ibid., June 24, 1866.   [4] Ibid., Jan. 30, 1868.
[5] Ibid., Nov. 29, 1866, and June 19, 1867.
[6] Ibid., April 21, 1868.   [7] Ibid., May 29, 1867.
[8] Ibid., Jan. 28, 1867. The price of tickets to Europe in 1865 was

The *Arago* and the *Fulton*, advertised as "the only American line to England and France," [1] consumed twelve days on the voyage. In December, 1866, after having reduced their rates, without increasing their patronage, the two ships were put up at auction in New York and were sold for $150,000 each. Thus ended for the present the attempt of American ship owners to regain control of the North Atlantic trade. To this pass had our merchant navy come, though in the fifties it had been the pride of the country and "the admiration of the whole maritime world." [2]

Many would have the government hold out a helping hand to the shipping industry. What a service would be performed if the old plan of connecting the Atlantic and Pacific oceans by an artificial strait somewhere upon the isthmus, joining the North and South American continents, could now be realized! The work upon the Suez Canal under the direction of Ferdinand de Lesseps was in progress. A fresh-water channel through which small boats might pass from the Red Sea to the Mediterranean was opened for trade on August 15, 1865. [3] In a few years it would be ready for the use of ships of deep draught. The Isthmus of Panama was "the only obstacle to the complete circumnavigation of the globe by the most direct and shortest route." [4]

The increasing trade to California over this neck of land kept it in the public mind. The railroad there, 47 miles in length, was built under the greatest difficulties. Every lignum vitæ sleeper, it was said, represented a dead man's body. In the eleven years during which it had been in operation, from 1856 to 1867, it had carried nearly 400,000 passengers, 614,535 tons of freight and $675,000,000 in treasure from the gold and silver

$132.50 in gold on the Cunard Line, $135 on the French Line, $90 on the Inman Line.

[1] N. Y. Tribune, Oct. 4, 1865.

[2] Ibid., Dec. 24 and 25, 1866.

[3] Goods were transshipped on flatboats. The fresh-water channel had a depth of two metres. — Report of Secretary of the Interior for 1867, pp. 145-7.

[4] N. Y. Tribune, Aug. 31, 1865.

mines. The company's income in 1856 had been $136,741; it had increased in 1866 to $2,423,977.[1]

The trade became so large that in the summer of 1866 a company instituted a monthly service from New York to California by way of the Nicaragua route which had been in use before the war, offering passage for travellers and freight at rates much lower than by the Panama line.[2] From the Isthmus lines of steamers served the east and west coasts of South America. A line was established to run by way of Panama, between England and New Zealand, whence there would be an intercolonial service to Australia. The time from New Zealand to Panama was 25 days and from New Zealand to Southampton 45 days.[3] Eight days more brought passengers or freight to or from Melbourne and Sydney.[4] In 1867 nine steamer lines converged at the Isthmus, all except one sailing their ships under foreign flags.[5]

This American line was the Pacific Mail Steamship Company, which had been formed with a capital of $400,000 in 1847 to open a service between Panama and Oregon. In 1865 its capital was $10,000,000, which was increased to $20,000,000 in 1866.[6] The Atlantic Mail Steamship Company, the "Vanderbilt Line," which ran between New York and Aspinwall, was much complained of by travellers,[7] and it was purchased by the Pacific Mail in September, 1865, for $4,500,000.[8] Now good steamships were despatched from New York to Aspinwall three times a month.[9] The trains were met at Panama on the west side with fast boats bound for San Francisco. One of this company's vessels had run from Aspinwall to New York in seven days and two hours, and the passage through from New

---

[1] Phila. Ledger, May 29 and Oct. 23, 1867.
[2] N. Y. Tribune, Nov. 18, 1865.
[3] Phila. Ledger, July 13, 1865, citing N. Y. Journal of Commerce.
[4] Advertisement in N. Y. Tribune, Aug. 3, 1866.
[5] Phila. Ledger, Sept. 12, 1867.
[6] N. Y. Tribune, July 10, 1867.
[7] Ibid., June 14, 1865, and May 4, 1866; Samuel Bowles, Across the Continent, p. 386.
[8] N. Y. Nation, Sept. 28, 1865.
[9] Beginning Nov. 1, 1865.

York to San Francisco could be accomplished in less than 21 days.[1]

The Pacific Mail was paid to carry to California the heavy mails which could not be conveyed by the overland stage route, and was soon to be in receipt of $500,000 a year for maintaining a postal steamer service to Japan and China. Congress voted the money, if the company would agree to make twelve round trips annually. The ships must touch at Honolulu which, however, was declared to be impracticable, and the Sandwich Islands must be served separately.[2] Four fine vessels were being built at New York for the new line, — the *Great Republic*,—which was launched in November, 1866, and would be ready for service in May, 1867,—the *America*, the *Celestial Empire* and the *Nippon*.[3] In December, 1866, New York heard the cry of "All aboard for San Francisco, Japan and China." The *Henry Chauncey* sailed away for the Isthmus with through passengers for Yokohama and Hong Kong. At Panama they would board the *Golden City*, and on January 1, 1867, sail from San Francisco for Asia on the *Colorado*, which had been detached from the fleet for the service until the new ships were ready for use.[4] The fare from San Francisco to Yokohama in the first-class saloons was $250, and to Hong Kong $300.[5] It was believed that this new line of trans-Pacific steamers would beat the Asia-Europe mails via Marseilles.

[1] Phila. Ledger, Dec. 19, 1867.

[2] Appendix Cong. Globe, 38th Cong., 2d sess., p. 116; ibid., 39th Cong., 1st sess., p. 323; ibid., 39th Cong., 2d sess., p. 186; Report of Postmaster-General for 1866.

[3] N. Y. Tribune, Dec. 10. 1866; Report of Postmaster-General for 1866.

[4] San Francisco corr., N. Y. Tribune, Feb. 1, 1867.

[5] The through rates from New York to San Francisco were $350 first class, $250 second class and $125 steerage in currency, while all baggage above 100 pounds in weight must be paid for at the rate of ten cents a pound (advertisement of the line in N. Y. Tribune, Oct. 19, 1865). The passenger fare on the railroad across the Isthmus was $25. Cattle were paid for on steamer trains at the rate of $25 a head, horses $40, coal $5 a ton and gold one quarter of one per cent of its value (Phila. Ledger, May 30, 1867).

Sometimes seventy days separated Japan from New York over this route.[1]

There was no communication with Brazil except by way of Great Britain and France, and Congress in 1864 agreed to coöperate with the Brazilian government in the establishment of an American line of mail steamers to run from New York to Rio de Janeiro. The United States would pay $150,000 a year to support this service [2] and after some negotiation it was undertaken by the United States and Brazil Mail Steamship Company which agreed to despatch a good steamer southward once a month.[3]

Why might not a canal be cut through the American isthmus as well as at Suez? Senator Conness of California brought up the subject in Congress, and Rear Admiral C. H. Davis, Superintendent of the Naval Observatory, was assigned the task of preparing a report. He made out a list of the various books and pamphlets bearing upon the topic in hand, brought to light old charts, profiles and maps and estimated in tables the saving of distance to ships travelling between principal points, and the amount of commerce which might pass over such a line. He found that no less than 26 routes, 19 for canals and 7 for wagon roads, over the American isthmus had been proposed and in some degree explored. He briefly considered six courses which might be followed in the construction of a canal. He started at Tehuantepec in Mexico in the north, where a railroad had been begun,[4] and going south considered the claims of Honduras, Nicaragua, by way of the navigable San Juan River and Nicaragua Lake, Chiriqui, Panama and Atrato. He quickly dismissed all but the Panama routes. These he

[1] Phila. Ledger, Dec. 11 and 12, 1866.

[2] Chap. xcviii, Laws of 1864; chap. lxxxv, Laws of 1866.

[3] House Ex. Doc., 38th Cong., 2d sess., vol. v, p. 791, Report of Postmaster-General for 1864; House Ex. Doc., 39th Cong., 2d sess., vol. iv, Report of Postmaster-General for 1866, p. 7; ibid., pp. 63–7, for the article of contract.

[4] A Tehuantepec colonization company with a capital of a million dollars was formed in New York in 1867 to take up lands on this isthmus for the production of mahogany, indigo, rubber, tile, tea, coffee, cotton, sugar, etc. — Advertisement in N. Y. Tribune, Nov. 27, 1867.

thought might be three, all lying south of that line taken by the Panama Railroad, which had been examined but was not highly regarded though later chosen by de Lesseps. There were, according to Admiral Davis, the San Blas route, which called for a tunnel through the mountains, seven miles in length, similar to the Mt. Cenis and St. Gothard tunnels then being cut in the Alps; the old "Darien route" from the Gulf of San Miguel to Caledonia Bay; and the route from the Gulf of San Miguel by way of the Tuyra River to the valley of the Atrato, and thence to the Gulf of Darien, now being surveyed at the personal expense of Senator Sprague, the wealthy young manufacturer of calico prints in Providence.[1] Admiral Davis said that it might be premature to advocate the construction of the canal; the time had come, however, for engineers to go thoroughly over the ground.[2]

The Senate ordered the report to be printed, and Congress on July 28, 1866, appropriated $40,000 for exploration of the routes under the direction of the War Department.[3] The enterprise might cost $100,000,000, said the New York Tribune, but it would be worth $5,000,000 a year to the United States. Upon the completion of the canal the "great Pacific" would be thrilled "as by an electric shock."[4]

On June 30, 1865, there were 20,550 post-offices in the United States. The number was increased in a year to 23,826, the gain being chiefly in the South where the service was being reorganized. In 1866, 46 cities enjoyed free carrier service.[5] During the year over 13,000,000 letters in New York City and 7,000,000 letters in Philadelphia were delivered in this way.[6] The sorting of mails on the trains had been begun during the war. In 1864 mail cars were added to trains between New York and Washington, and upon routes running out of

[1] N. Y. Tribune, Jan. 30, 1867.

[2] Senate Ex. Doc., 39th Cong., 1st sess., no. 62.

[3] Appendix to Cong. Globe, 39th Cong., 1st sess., p. 413.

[4] N. Y. Tribune, Jan. 30, 1867.

[5] House Ex. Doc., 39th Cong., 2d sess., vol. iv, p. 10. This service was authorized by a law of March 3, 1863.

[6] Ibid., p. 17.

Chicago into Iowa. These experiments were soon followed by others on railroads east and west from Cleveland.[1] On postal cars put into service in 1868 cranes were installed to catch up the mail sacks at stations at which the trains did not stop.[2] The registry system had been in use for a number of years, but the sending of money by post to and by the soldiers during the war was followed by much loss,[3] and in 1864 a money order system was established. In the fiscal year 1865–6 orders of a value of nearly $4,000,000 were issued. The number of money order offices in operation at the end of 1866 was 766, and they were rapidly increasing.[4]

In the year following the war, from July 1, 1865, to June 30, 1866, Congress voted $7,800,000 to transport the inland mails, $3,175,000 to compensate the postmasters, $1,330,000 for clerks and $400,000 for letter carriers.[5] In the next year, ending June 30, 1867, $9,550,000 were expended for inland mail transportation and $4,250,000 for postmasters' salaries. The government paid $750,000 a year to the contractors on the overland route to California, $160,000 more for the supplementary service by way of the Isthmus,[6] and $225,000 [7] for the stage service between Sacramento and Portland, Ore.[8]

More than a million dollars were expended, Postmaster-General Dennison complained, in a territory which yielded the government in postal revenues only $60,000 [9] though his successor in office, Mr. Randall, said that the service was not established on the principle that it should pay its own way. He begrudged

[1] House Ex. Doc., 38th Cong., 2d sess., vol. v, p. 786, in Report of Postmaster-General for 1864.

[2] Phila. Ledger, July 20, 1868.

[3] House Ex. Doc., 38th Cong., 1st sess., vol. v, Report of Postmaster-General, p. 18.

[4] Ibid., 39th Cong., 2d sess., vol. iv, Report of Postmaster-General, p. 11.

[5] Chap. xxiii, Laws of 1865.

[6] Law of March 25, 1864.

[7] For the fiscal year 1866.

[8] Report of Postmaster-General for 1865.

[9] House Ex. Doc., 39th Cong., 1st sess., no. 1, Annual Report of 1865, p. 14.

no such outlays, for the post-office had done more to enlighten and Christianize the people than anything else "except the spelling book and the Bible."[1] Postal facilities beyond the frontier invited settlement and gave encouragement to enterprise. The return was incalculable and many fold.

Letters were transmitted anywhere within the United States, including the Pacific slope, at the rate of three cents for each half ounce. By law of March 3, 1863, the postage need not be prepaid at the time of mailing; it might be collected from the addressee at a double rate. By law of March 3, 1865, this privilege was withdrawn. Unstamped letters were sent at once to the Dead Letter Office.[2] "Drop letters" in cities were received and delivered by the carriers for two cents a half ounce. Books up to sixteen ounces in weight were forwarded at the rate of four cents for four ounces; circulars, three for two cents; other printed matter, photographs, seeds and roots, two cents for four ounces. Postage on newspapers and magazines was payable by the quarter or year in advance — daily papers at the rate of 35 cents for three months; weekly papers, five cents; monthly magazines, if not over four ounces in weight, six cents. Weekly papers were carried free to bona fide subscribers within the county in which they were published. "Exchange" copies of newspapers and periodicals were forwarded everywhere without cost. Printed matter for California, except single copies of newspapers addressed to subscribers, must pass over the slower route via the Isthmus, unless the sender were willing to pay letter rates.

Foreign postal charges were in the most confused condition and were very dear. For a half ounce it cost 10 cents to Canada and Cuba; 24 cents to Great Britain and Ireland; 30 cents to France; 30 cents to the German states, except by way of Bremen and Hamburg, when the rate was 15 cents; 42 cents to the Sardinian states in Italy by one route and 23 by another;

[1] House Ex. Doc., 39th Cong., 2d sess., Report of Postmaster-General, p. 15.

[2] Many remained ignorant of the change and for a time unpaid letters reached the Dead Letter Office at the rate of 15,000 a week. — Washington corr., Phila. Ledger, June 12, 1865; cf. ibid., Aug. 1, 1865.

37 cents to Russia by one route, 29 by another and 60 cents by
a third; 45 to 72 cents to China according to the route preferred; 30 to 60 cents to Egypt; 33 cents to $1.02 to Australia;
45 cents to the Argentine Republic; 33 cents to Jerusalem by
way of England and 60 cents by way of France. In certain
cases there was a half rate for a letter weighing a fourth of
an ounce. Sometimes the postage must be prepaid; again it
need not be.[1] Such a system confounded even the postmasters.
The rate to England was declared to be outrageously high.
A letter which could be sent from Land's End to John O'Groat's
for a penny, and from Passamaquoddy Bay to the Golden Gate
for three cents, if it crossed the sea, though it lay still in a mail
sack was subject to a charge of 24 cents. The price was four
times what it ought to be;[2] but international conventions
were being arranged and order would be put into a system now
in a hopeless state.

Beyond the Allegheny Mountains west to the Mississippi
the rich loamy prairies had been converted into grain fields.
The settler pressed farther and farther into this land —

> "Stretching in airy undulations far away,
> As if the ocean in his gentlest swell
> Stood still with all his rounded billows
> Fixed and motionless forever."

Taking his plough and cattle with him to break the ground,
he erected his cabin and his barn. His low buildings were
hidden behind the bountiful growth of his crops. To enclose
his acres, and as shields against the wind on this great treeless
space he planted osage orange hedges of which now, after the
war, there had come to be thousands of miles in Illinois and
the other prairie states.[3] The Mississippi had been crossed.

[1] Postage Directory, by J. A. Campbell, 1865.

[2] Phila. Ledger, Oct. 13, 1866.

[3] Professor Turner of Illinois College is credited with having introduced the osage orange plant. He sent two men with a team to
Texas where they extracted a load of seed from the "oranges" with a
machine which they had taken with them. At first the farmers in
Illinois would not buy, but soon the demand exceeded the supply and
the "oranges" were selling for $3 a bushel, the seed for $250 a bushel,
the plants for $10 a thousand. — N. Y. Tribune, Aug. 4, 1865.

On its farther bank in Iowa, already in 1860 there were 675,-
000 people.   A vast storehouse of agricultural wealth, its eastern
counties were filled and the frontiers of settlement were being
advanced to the Missouri.

Wisconsin had a similarly rapid growth.   Bates county in
that state in 1865 had had not 500 inhabitants.   It was without schools and churches.   Two years later it had 45 schools
and contained over 3000 persons under the age of twenty-one
years.[1]

Minnesota, the land of ten thousand lakes, with its rich prairies, upon which forty bushels of wheat could be grown on an
acre in a short season, and its great pineries had become the
dwelling-place before 1860 of 172,000 people.   During the war
it had forged ahead swiftly.   Horace Greeley visited the region
in October, 1865.   He found St. Paul already a place of 13,000,
while Minneapolis had 8000 inhabitants.   They were involved
in a rivalry which he considered absurd, since always one would
be supreme at the head of steamboat navigation on the Mississippi, the other supreme in the possession of water power unex-
ampled except at Niagara.   Wheat filled wagons, barges and
warehouses.   Small towns boasted of their half million bushel
crops.   The rivers were jammed with logs and rafts of manufactured lumber.   There were saw-mills, the machinery of which
was propelled by their own sawdust.   Consumptives came
hither; the climate healed their lungs.   Greeley liked the tem-
perature of 40 degrees below zero no more than the Equator,
but the residents of the state told him of the clear, dry, sunny
winters; they would not live elsewhere.[2]

Three cities had preëminence in this great land of grain, —
Cincinnati, the metropolis of the Ohio Valley, with 161,000
inhabitants in 1860, St. Louis on the Mississippi with 160,000
and the new city of Chicago on Lake Michigan with 109,000.
There were as yet in the West no other places of considerable
size except Cleveland, Detroit and Milwaukee, each of which
had come to have a population of from 40,000 to 45,000.   In-

[1] Phila. Ledger, Dec. 31, 1867.
[2] N. Y. Tribune, Oct. 6 and 7, 1865.

dianapolis had but 18,000 inhabitants; the principal towns in Iowa, Dubuque and Davenport, 13,000 and 11,000 respectively.

The day of the steamboat was coming to an end, but the disorganization of the railways in the southwest, by reason of the war, made the traffic upon the Mississippi and its navigable tributaries for a time as great as it had ever been. The steamers plying the Ohio alone, if they were brought together, so it was said, would form a floating city in which 100,000 persons could dwell in comfort.[1] At the levee in Cincinnati for a distance of five or six miles they were tied up one against another taking on and discharging freights. They came, perhaps through Pittsburgh, from the petroleum wells on the upper waters of the Allegheny River in Pennsylvania, or from the coal mines on the Youghiogheny in West Virginia; from St. Paul at the head of navigation on the Mississippi, from New Orleans at its foot; from little towns and trading posts up the Missouri or the Red River of Arkansas. They moved over 16,000 miles of inland water. Smaller boats could ascend to higher points along shallower channels. Many were laden with pedler's wares to be hawked from village to village. Menageries, circuses and theatrical troupes in house-boats made long voyages up this stream and that, calling the country people to the water side with the sound of a calliope. They departed in the spring and returned only at the end of the season.[2]

St. Louis was an even busier place. In 1866, 2922 steamboats arrived in that city; in the following year 3080 of 947,647 tons burden.[3] Tied up at the levee in close order, their bows thrust into the sand of the shore and their sterns, swept by the swift current, pointing down the stream, they were the centre of the town's trade. Over the steep levee merchandise was borne to and from the boats. The captains, the pilots, the stokers and the stevedores overran the water front, filling the saloons, the variety theatres and the other places established for their entertainment. Hither came nearly the entire popu-

[1] Phila. Ledger, July 27, 1867.
[2] Article on Cincinnati in Atlantic Monthly, August, 1867.
[3] Phila. Ledger, Jan. 14, 1868.

lation when the ice began to move in a mass in the spring. The
fire bells were rung, but in spite of every effort to save the fleet
some boats would be crushed by the weight of the frozen river.[1]
But this was far from an entirely satisfactory system of transportation for passengers and freight. The period of enforced
inactivity in winter because of the ice was often long. Its
violent movement in the spring was full of danger. The channels were shifting and uncertain at all times. The most
careful pilots lost their vessels. The Mississippi, flowing
through the soft prairie, said James Parton, rolled about in its
bed "like a sick hippopotamus." [2] One year it would flood a
town, and taking houses and streets sweep them into the Gulf of
Mexico; the next year it would leave the same town far inland.
Of the river's great western branch, the Missouri, this might
be said with even greater truth. Flowing into the main channel
twenty miles above St. Louis, crossing the state of Missouri
and turning north its course could be followed 3000 miles into
the Rocky Mountains. Senator Benton once had said that it
was too thick to swim in and not quite thick enough to walk
on. It was a "swift tide of liquid yellow mud," said Bayard
Taylor; it was "the ugliest of all rivers." [3] If a glass were
filled with the water an eighth of an inch of mud sank to the bottom. It was the prairie in solution taken at will by the river
as it flowed along its way. A cottonwood tree on the bank
was undermined and swept on until it lodged in the bed of the
stream. Sometimes the roots would protrude above the surface of the water when it would catch other trees and drift,
perhaps at length to form an island. At other times the tree
was submerged to snag the steamers. So sharp were the roots
and branches in some cases that they would impale the light
wooden boats as a needle would a fly. The wrecks themselves
became obstructions in the channel. Accidents from many
causes were frequent. Collisions, fires, bursting boilers led to
the loss of hundreds of lives annually. The dangers of navi-

[1] Article on St. Louis in Atlantic Monthly, June, 1867.
[2] Ibid., p. 668.
[3] N. Y. Tribune, June 30, 1866.

gation were increased when two boats sighted each other and their reckless captains and pilots, encouraged perhaps by excited passengers who may have laid wagers on the result, started away on a race. Then in went the tar, down went the safety valve, on went the *Prairie Belle* and the *Ocean Wave*, as their names may have been, and up went the passengers. Many of the boats were large and were likely to be garishly ornamented. If the owners would give more care to their engines, said a cavilling observer, commenting upon a disaster in 1865, and less to the "gingerbread blue and gold decorations" of the saloons and cabins, travel on American rivers would be more safe.[1]

Within a few days in the winter of 1866 the boilers of three western steamboats exploded. In the case of the *Miami* on the Ohio the passengers were gathered in the evening around the stoves in the saloon. Suddenly the floor burst open and they all were precipitated into a fiery crater.[2] In a collision in 1868 petroleum in barrels on board one of the vessels caught fire and took a toll of one hundred lives.[3]

In the Ohio River in 1866 the government engineer, W. Milnor Roberts, found after an inspection between Pittsburgh and Cairo, a distance of 1015 miles, 90 snags, 66 logs, 46 wrecks and 83 sunken boats.[4] Between Cairo and St. Louis on the Mississippi there were 8 wrecks, 63 "breaks," or submerged snags, and 137 dry snags. When the river should fall six feet the number of obstructions would be doubled.[5] By the use of "snag boats" and dynamite the course was being cleared and improved. A large force of workmen were enlarging the canal around the Falls of the Ohio near Louisville. In 1866 it was announced that $1,800,000 had been expended upon this undertaking which it would require $365,000 more in money and two more years of time to complete.[6]

[1] Phila. Ledger, Oct. 30, 1865.
[2] Ibid., Feb. 1 and 6, 1866.
[3] Ibid., Dec. 7 and 11, 1868.
[4] Report of Secretary of War for 1867, vol. ii, p. 403.
[5] Ibid., pp. 385–7.
[6] Phila. Ledger, July 20, 1866.

The melting of the ice and snow in the spring in this great watershed, extending in the north to the Canadian border, in the east to the Allegheny Mountains and in the west to the Rockies, brought into the Mississippi, after it had received the contributions of its various branches, a flood of waters, which seemed almost to defy human control. The Ohio at Cincinnati was forty feet deeper when in flood than at low water. It had a maximum recorded rise at this place of 74 feet.[1] The dangers of overflow to towns and plantations behind the levees, raised to keep the river in its bed, recurred annually. Alluvium was deposited to fill the channel and force the water over the bank. Protection which each individual gave his own lands often was rendered useless, no matter what its local value, because of the neglect of a neighbor in whose weaker parapets a crevasse would be formed to flood the entire back country. It was said that there were 16 millions of acres subject to overflow in the states of Missouri, Arkansas, Mississippi and Louisiana.[2] The planters of the flooded Yazoo Valley appealed to Congress for aid in rebuilding the levees which had been neglected during the war, and were now in ruins.[3] The New York Tribune approved. Congress could well develop a comprehensive system of river protection, it said,[4] though the planters who would reap the benefits included some of the principal "rebels" of the war.[5] General Humphreys made a survey for the War Department. The area to be protected from overflow, he said, would cover 31,700 square miles. It would cost $26,000,000 to insure this great alluvial region against inundation; if such levees as were in place could be utilized and raised to a proper height the expense might be reduced to $17,000,000.[6]

Thaws and rain storms together were responsible for a great flood in the spring of 1867 and directed attention anew to the

---

[1] Article on Cincinnati in Atlantic Monthly, August, 1867.

[2] N. Y. Tribune, May 26, 1866.

[3] Ibid., June 14, 1866.

[4] Ibid., Oct. 9, 1865; May 26, 1866; April 11, 1867.

[5] Ibid., July 6, 1868.

[6] Senate Ex. Doc., 40th Cong., 1st sess., no. 8; N. Y. Tribune, May 26, 1866.

subject of levees.[1] Another plan appeared calling for the expenditure of no less than $104,000,000, $52,000 a mile on each bank of the Mississippi from the mouth of the Ohio to the Gulf.[2]

The commercial importance of Cincinnati and St. Louis was derived in large part from their positions upon this great Western river system. They became large outfitting and distributing centres. Cincinnati smoked and cured pork and beef. It was the seat of a variety of manufacturing industries, founded to supply the wants of the Mississippi Valley. In the hills above the cloud of "soft" coal smoke, from the factory chimneys and the steamboat funnels, which hung over the valleys, were handsome homes of men who had prospered in trade. Nicholas Longworth had brought the Catawba grape to Ohio. His wine cellars were objects of interest to every visitor to the city. The hills were covered with sheep and the state's large clip of wool found its way to market here. Cincinnati had had the first place in population and in the volume of its commerce among the cities beyond the Allegheny Mountains, and it guarded its preëminence in reference to St. Louis as jealously as both viewed the rapid rise of the rival on the Great Lakes.

History bore St. Louis back to a time preceding the Louisiana Purchase when the city had been a French frontier post. Now it had 280 miles of streets which were underlaid with 80 miles of water and 86 miles of gas pipes. Its street car lines were 36 miles in length.[3] It looked north as well as south; it stood on the way to a great new West, and by many was regarded as the city which in no long while must become "the natural capital of the United States" — "the centre of politics, of business and of distribution."[4] Indeed it was proposed that the rest of the nation should accord the place this recognition by making it the seat of Federal government, and the movement

[1] Senate Mis. Doc., 41st Cong., 1st sess., no. 8.
[2] N. Y. Tribune, July 6, 1868.
[3] Phila. Ledger, Aug. 15, 1867.
[4] Article on St. Louis in Atlantic Monthly, June, 1867.

to have the President and Congress abandon Washington and to establish their homes for the future in St. Louis became a favorite topic of discussion.[1]

But such prophecies of St. Louis's future position as the capital of American empire fell upon grateful ears only in some parts of the West. Cincinnati and St. Louis traded over the rivers. Chicago was a city of the lakes. Up and down this great inland waterway ships of larger size than any which could use the Ohio and the Mississippi proceeded in safety and ease to the new metropolis of Illinois. When Goldwin Smith came to America his friend, Richard Cobden, bade him see two things — the Niagara cataract and Chicago. In 1831 there were but twelve white families settled on this spot. It had been a military post at which a few soldiers were stationed, a meeting point for fur traders and Indians. An inlet of Lake Michigan, which was cut into the miry prairie, would shelter ships. It came to be called the Chicago River. But little was at hand to suggest a great future for the place. The site of the city was barely six feet above the level of the lake. The wind washed the water over it; rain converted the soft earth into deep mud. At this place, in Nature's despite, there were 30,000 people in 1850. Ten years later the population was nearly four times as great, and at the end of the war it was supposed to have increased to 180,000.[2] The grade was raised until the entire city was set twelve feet above the level of the surrounding prairie, though the result could be accomplished only gradually. For a time the sidewalks must pass up and down stairways until all could be brought to the common new height. The new Nicholson pavement gave the people good streets.[3] Dwellings, stores, hotels were rising on all sides. During the single year of 1867 no less than 7000 buildings were erected at a cost of $8,000,000. There were "business blocks" of brick and stone. The assessed valuation of real and

[1] N. Y. Tribune, July 22, 1869; N. Y. Nation, Sept. 2, 1869.

[2] Article on Chicago in Atlantic Monthly, March, 1867.

[3] The task of the people of Chicago was to build "the metropolis of an empire upon the floor of a dismal marsh and to finish it within a single generation." — Chicago corr., N. Y. Tribune, June 20, 1866.

personal property within the city had increased from $37,000,-
000 in 1860 to $192,000,000 in 1868.[1] The demand for homes
still exceeded the supply and little towns sprang up in the sub-
urbs. In 1867 Chicago had come to have a population of 220,-
000 or 230,000 souls.[2] It extended beside the lake for a distance
of eight miles and ran back over the prairie for two. It was
growing, said the New York Tribune, "like a cornfield in July." [3]
If St. Louis were "the serene and comfortable Philadelphia,"
Chicago was the New York of the West.[4] Its men were young,
active and able; they made money rapidly in real estate and
every kind of trade. Its streets roared with traffic. At seventeen drawbridges crowds of people on foot and in wagons waited
while fleets of merchant ships passed up or down the "river"
until tunnels could be built beneath it. The sewage flowed
into this sluggish channel, but a canal was being built to clear
it; the offending waters would be swept into the Illinois River
and on to the Mississippi. The Erie Canal had a capacity of
80 large railway trains of goods daily. Now it was proposed
by an enlargement of the locks to increase this limit to 200
trains.[5] Prophets had visions of ship canals to the Mississippi
and the Atlantic seaboard. A tunnel was run out under Lake
Michigan a distance of two miles to secure a supply of pure
water which in March, 1867, began to flow beneath the streets
of the city and into the houses of the people. A procession
was formed and other exercises were arranged in honor of the
achievement.[6]

The life of the city was found in its trade, and its trade was
in wheat, corn, oats, beef, cattle, hogs and lumber. In 1866
904 vessels, employing 10,000 sailors, plied between Chicago

[1] N. Y. Tribune, Jan. 4 and 28, 1868.
[2] Ibid., Jan. 4, 1868; Article on Chicago in Atlantic Monthly,
March, 1867.
[3] N. Y. Tribune, Sept. 8, 1865.
[4] Atlantic Monthly for June, 1867, p. 655.
[5] Phila. Ledger, Jan. 24, 1867.
[6] Ibid., March 26, 1867. The tunnel is described in Phila. Ledger,
Nov. 30, 1866, citing Chicago Tribune; N. Y. Tribune, Nov. 27 and
Dec. 7, 1866.

and the other lake ports. The Illinois Central was the first of the Western railroads to be laid down over unsettled lands in return for grants from the public domain. The 2,500,000 acres given to Illinois by Congress for the erection of this road had been put under the plough. The United States had sold practically all of its lands within the state before the end of the war.[1] A state which had had only 95 miles of railways in 1852 had come to have 3000 in 1860; in the meantime it had doubled its population. It was said that no farmer in Illinois resided more than fifty miles from a railroad, and probably the average distance which he must go to reach a station was not above seven miles.[2] Lines stretched out their arms into Iowa, Wisconsin, Minnesota and Missouri. Chicago had become a railroad city as well as a lake city. It was a centre for 8000 miles of track; not less than 200 trains came into or left the place in a day and a night. In 1854 the receipts of lines connecting Chicago and the Mississippi River had been only $1,200,000; in 1866 they had increased to more than $30,000,000.[3]

The lumber to build the towns and the farm-houses on the bare prairies arrived by water from the tree-covered shores of the upper lakes. In 1866, 15,000,000 feet reached Chicago in a single fleet.[4] During that year 614,000,000 feet were received to be used in or forwarded from the city.[5] The grain from the prairies was stored in warehouses called "elevators." The outward trade began with 78 bushels in 1838; it was more than 50,000,000 bushels in 1866. However the wheat or corn came to the city, whether by water or rail, it was inspected, graded for quality and pumped into great bins from which it could be poured out again. Nothing but a slip of paper certifying to the existence of the grain ever came before the eyes of the merchants, who met together in an exchange called a Board of Trade. These elevator certificates were the basis for a large

[1] Speech of Senator Yates, Appendix of Cong. Globe, 29th Cong., 1st sess., p. 282.

[2] Article on Chicago in Atlantic Monthly, March, 1867.

[3] Phila. Ledger, Aug. 2, 1867.

[4] N. Y. Tribune, June 20, 1866.

[5] Atlantic Monthly, March, 1867, p. 333.

legitimate and speculative business carried on amid much excitement and noise. The old building was too small; in September, 1865, a new hall, erected at a cost of $400,000, was opened with ceremonies.[1] Here prices were fixed and, before long, bold and cunning men sought to "corner" the markets. Many would "sell short," *i.e.* sell grain which they did not possess for delivery at some future time, as in May if the month were September, or in September if the month were May. The most successful "corner" in wheat which yet had been arranged collapsed on September 18, 1865, when the price fell twenty cents a bushel in a day.[2] A victim held these operations to be on a plane with the gambler's, within the meaning of the law, and swore out warrants in August, 1867, for the arrest of eight prominent members of the Board of Trade, including B. P. Hutchinson, afterward famous for the fortunes he made and lost in Chicago "corners," generally known in later years as "Old Hutch." The sheriff of Cook county entered the exchange and haled the men before a justice, where they severally gave bail for their future appearance in court.[3]

Many flour mills were built that the wheat might be ground and shipped away, with a saving in freight, in its finished form. But this economy was small in comparison with that which was practised as soon as the West learned how to pack fifteen bushels of corn into a pig, and then to pack that pig into a barrel.[4] Soon an industry was founded on new and mammoth lines. Three hundred thousand head of cattle, 1,500,000 hogs, sheep and calves were brought to Chicago by rail or water in a year and placed in the stock-yards which covered nearly a square mile of land. Pens and sheds received the food animals which were collected in the prairie states from Texas

[1] N. Y. Tribune, Sept. 7, 1865.

[2] Chicago Tribune, Sept. 19, 1865; also Phila. Ledger, Sept. 25, 1865.

[3] Chicago Post, Aug. 10, 1867; Phila. Ledger, Aug. 14, 1867.

[4] Article on Cincinnati in Atlantic Monthly, August, 1867. "The hog eats the corn and Europe eats the hog. Corn thus becomes incarnate, for what is a hog but fifteen or twenty bushels of corn on four legs?" — S. B. Ruggles, quoted in Atlantic Monthly, March, 1867, p. 331.

north to Minnesota and held them until they were sent to the local slaughter-houses, or were shipped to other destinations.[1]

The pork-packing house appeared first in Cincinnati; it was perfected in Chicago. In one of these establishments a hog was knocked on the head by a hammer, stuck, scalded, disembowelled, dismembered and delivered to the men at the barrels in exactly twenty seconds of time. Three animals were packed in each minute of a working day.[2] In one year during the war, 1863, 300,000,000 pounds of American pork were sent to Europe, equal, it was said, to 1,500,000 hogs marching across the ocean. The swine which were killed in one year in Chicago, if formed in a single line, would reach from that city to New York.[3] So, too, were cattle received, killed, salted and packed in this city near the lands on which they were fed, and sent away to consumers in the East and in Europe.

But the agricultural riches of the Mississippi Valley were founded not alone on crops of wheat and corn and oats. The beet was being grown for sugar manufacture in Illinois,[4] grapes for wine on the banks of the Ohio and on the islands and shores of Lake Erie.[5] It was predicted that they would thrive also in Missouri and other states. Hogs were fed from the cornfields and cattle on the wild grass of the prairies, but sheep and the wool shorn from their backs also became important products, especially in Ohio and Michigan. In 1866 Ohio supported on her pastures no less than 7,000,000 head with a clip of 20,000,000 pounds; Michigan, in 1867, 2,371,000 head with a clip of 9,000,000 pounds.[6] The country's flocks already numbered 30,000,000 sheep; they should be doubled in size, said Greeley in the New York Tribune, so that American manufacturers need turn no longer to South America and Australia

---

[1] Atlantic Monthly, March, 1867, p. 332.
[2] Ibid., August, 1867, p. 241.
[3] Ibid., March, 1867, p. 332.
[4] N. Y. Tribune, May 5, 1865.
[5] Ibid., Aug. 25, 1865.   [6] Phila. Ledger, Aug. 27, 1867.

for wool,[1] and he spared no effort to encourage farmers to undertake sheep raising.[2]

The mineral wealth of the country was of unknown extent. There were iron mountains in Missouri, — enough ore, it was said, to supply a million tons of manufactured iron per annum for 200 years to come.[3] Furnaces were at work in this district, but so little had been achieved that in building a railroad over beds of solid iron ore the owners had laid English rails.[4] The iron mined on the southern shores of Lake Superior and in Michigan and Wisconsin was brought by water through the Great Lakes. Although ten years before a piece of Lake Superior ore was a curiosity, with the completion of the Sault Ste. Marie Canal it came into the market in considerable quantities, and now, in 1865, the mines in Marquette county furnished the ore for one-eighth of all the iron smelted in the United States.[5] Reports of valuable deposits near the head of the lake in Minnesota heralded the great mines to be opened there at a later day.[6] There was coal in Illinois, Indiana and Missouri, lead in Illinois and Iowa, copper in Michigan, while petroleum and gold and silver were reckoned among the possibilities in most men's minds in all parts of the country. Tin was discovered in Missouri in 1867, and farms which could have been bought for $10 an acre were being sold a week later to crazy men for $300 an acre.[7]

There had been 31,185 miles of railway in the United States in 1860. Largely because of the continued development of the West, in spite of the war, this total had been increased in 1865

[1] N. Y. Tribune, June 2, 1865.

[2] Facts about the clip of the United States at this time were submitted to the first annual convention of the woollen manufacturers of America which met in Philadelphia in September, 1865. — N. Y. Tribune, Sept. 8, 1865.

[3] Sir Morton Peto, Resources and Prospects of America, p. 167.

[4] R. H. Lamborn, in N. Y. Tribune, Sept. 30, 1865.

[5] Ibid., June 26, 1865; Report of Sec. of War for 1867, vol. ii, p. 66.

[6] House Ex. Doc., 40th Cong., 2d sess., no. 1, p. 301, Report of Surveyor General of Minnesota.

[7] Phila. Ledger, Aug. 5, 1867, citing Ironton Register.

to about 34,000 miles.[1]   Attention was directed to this development in a prominent way in the autumn of 1865 when a party
of British capitalists visited the United States.   They had
come under the escort of James McHenry, a Philadelphian
residing in England, upon whose representations the British
people had invested $50,000,000 during the progress of the war
in the Atlantic and Great Western Railroad, projected to run
between Cincinnati and New York.[2]   The most distinguished
member of the party was Sir Morton Peto, who had built a
railway for the use of the English army during the Crimean
War to convey their guns and ammunition from Balaclava up
to the heights around Sebastopol.   He had subscribed a
quarter of a million dollars to the London Exhibition of 1851
when the enterprise might have failed but for his support, and
was building a system of underground railroads in London.
He proceeded through the country as far west as St. Louis.
He promised Chicago and St. Louis four instead of two express
trains daily to New York, and to carry freight in five days at
a lower rate than they now paid for the service.   Everywhere
he was dined and wined by chambers of commerce and boards
of trade.   Statesmen and financiers competed with one another
to honor him.   Before he departed the country he tendered
his principal friends a banquet in New York, the like of which
none who attended it had ever seen,[3] and afterward wrote a
book founded upon the observations he had made during his
trip.[4]

Peto criticised the construction of the American railroads
of the day, as well as the system by which their owners operated them.   They were hastily and cheaply made of light
rails on road-beds not drained or ballasted.   The stations for
passengers and freight were usually mere wooden sheds.   The

[1] Phila. Ledger, Jan. 13, 1865.

[2] N. Y. Herald, Sept. 23, 1865.

[3] N. Y. Tribune, Oct. 31, 1865.

[4] Peto and his firms fell with a crash in 1867.   Claims against him
for many millions of dollars were filed and public feeling underwent
a complete revulsion concerning him. — Phila. Ledger, July 27 and
Aug. 8, 1867.

lines were "single track"; the trains, which were run infre-
quently, passed each other at designated points. Under the
most various managements and built for the most part in short
lengths there was no convenient system of travel.[1] Passengers
must wait long at junctions. The hours of arrival and departure of trains set down in the time-tables were little regarded.[2]
The coaches, except such as were reserved for ladies, were dirty.
The seats were narrow and hard. The aisles, it was complained,
were often filled with standing passengers because of the owners' refusal to provide sufficient rolling stock for their lines.
Little or no care was given to the ventilation of the coaches.
Boys passed through the trains yelling and loading the laps of
travellers with novels, periodicals and sweetmeats for their
examination with a view to later purchase.[3] The speed attained by the locomotives did not exceed thirty miles an hour.[4]
Stops were made for meals at railway restaurants, at which the
food was both unpalatable and dear. Light came from candles
or the new petroleum lamps, and heat from stoves set at the
ends of the cars, their red coals falling out in case of accident to
cause many a dreadful fire. For wrecks of greater or less gravity were frequent. The buffers or platforms were seldom well
made. The cars were joined together with pins or bolts passing through links. When the train was started or stopped, the
slack in these links led to a jerking and jolting which ran from
the first to the last car. Passengers were injured on the platforms, employees in coupling the cars and at the brakes. The
light wooden coaches "oscillated" and were sometimes thrown
from the rough tracks; again they were "telescoped," one
crushing through another with terrible loss of life.[5] A traveller
met with six accidents on one journey between New York and
Cincinnati.[6] The telegraph, in a day, in 1865, brought news of

[1] Peto, Resources and Prospects of America, pp. 273–7.
[2] Bayard Taylor, in the Atlantic Monthly, April, 1867.
[3] Passengers were "dumped into a small room, dirty as a cattle pen,
close as an oven, and with as little provision for comfort as a police
station." — New York Nation, March 22, 1856.
[4] Peto, op. cit., p. 290.   [5] Phila. Ledger, Dec. 2, 1868.
[6] Bayard Taylor, Atlantic Monthly, April, 1867.

five railway accidents, several of them attended with great fatality.[1]

Not only land, when it was available, but public credit, rights of way and terminal facilities were freely bestowed upon the powers in charge of the railway business of the country, Bayard Taylor complained, and they were regarded as the benefactors rather than the servants of the people.[2] Yet their profits in many cases were large. The traffic between the East and West was constantly growing because of the remarkable agricultural development of the Mississippi Valley. Running into the West there were the northern roads,—the New York Central, the Erie and the Atlantic and Great Western, in process of building, — and farther south, the Pennsylvania Central from Philadelphia to Pittsburgh, and the Baltimore and Ohio, passing out of Baltimore through the Maryland and Virginia mountains. In 1865, 300 of the leading railway companies had made 30 per cent gross profits upon the money invested in building them. They had earned $11\frac{1}{2}$ per cent net in profits. Thirteen of them had paid the stockholders 10 per cent, two 12 per cent, one 15 per cent, one 31 per cent and two 35 per cent.[3]

Improvements came with the extension of the lines. In 1867 a second track was laid beside the old one on the Hudson River Railroad between New York and Albany,[4] and on the Pennsylvania Railroad from Philadelphia to Pittsburgh.[5] An act of legislature in New York state required railway companies to dress their conductors and other train employees in uniforms so that they might be more easily distinguished by the passengers.[6] The coaches on the through lines came to be "elegantly" ornamented and "luxuriously" furnished, though nickel, velvet and frosted glass of themselves added little to the comfort or safety of travel.

A new type of sleeping car, in which the awkward partitions did not appear, the berths being separated by draperies, was

[1] Phila. Ledger, Aug. 30, 1865.   [2] Bayard Taylor, loc. cit.
[3] Phila. Ledger, July 25, 1866.   [4] Ibid., Dec. 19, 1867.
[5] Ibid., Nov. 6, 1867.
[6] Ibid., July 25 and Sept. 27, 1867.

devised by James Woodruff. It was converted from a sleeping car into a day coach and back again with ease.[1] A similar car made its appearance in the West. It was manufactured by George M. Pullman, "an old quartz miner from the Rocky Mountains." In 1866 his business had advanced to such a degree, on lines running out of Chicago, that it was yielding him $40,000 a month. Pullman's sleeping cars cost from $25,000 to $40,000 each. They ran "like a pair of skates on even ice," said A. D. Richardson. The charge per night was but $2 for a double bed.[2]

Elsewhere railway managers were testing the "silver palace cars." Several of them made up into a train conveyed two or three hundred invited guests from New York to Chicago. They contained private state-rooms, sofas and easy-chairs to sit upon, tables at which the passengers could play whist or chess. A restaurant served food and liquors as the train proceeded on its way.[3]

The largest locomotive works in the country, Baldwin's, in Philadelphia, employed 1200 men. In 1867 they were making railway engines at the rate of twelve in a month, of a weight varying from 25 to 38 tons each.[4] Many of these had great power in drawing freight up grades; others were built for the attainment of speed in the passenger service.

Steel rails were being put down to replace the old iron rails. Their greater endurance and the increased safety of travel over them more than compensated for their higher cost.[5]

A series of awful railway disasters in 1867 and 1868 led to a recommendation that the companies introduce heat into the cars through a pipe running back from the locomotive. The stove which had set fire to so many wrecks must be abolished. Indeed it was suggested that the managers of railways should construct iron cars which would be not "a hundredth part as liable" as the light wooden cars to be crushed in accidents,

[1] N. Y. Tribune, March 19, 1866; Peto, op. cit., p. 289.
[2] N. Y. Tribune, Oct. 6, 1866.
[3] Phila. Ledger, July 25 and 29, 1867.
[4] Ibid., July 31, 1867.   [5] Ibid., March 30, 1868.

due to collisions between trains, to open drawbridges, to broken
rails and misplaced switches. To avoid "telescoping," said
one ingenious man, the ends might be pointed so that one car
would glance off another when they were dashed together.[1]

Fine new bridges were being thrown across the rivers. The
Philadelphia and Baltimore Railroad had ferried its trains
over the Susquehanna at Havre de Grace. In November,
1866, a bridge which had cost a million and a half dollars was
opened for use at this place.[2] A suspension bridge set high
above the river to allow the passage of boats under it was swung
over the Ohio at Cincinnati. It was completed in 1866, when
3000 people stood upon it without causing a perceptible vibra-
tion, though one of its spans was 1057 feet in length.[3] It
weighed but 600 tons, yet it would sustain a burden of 16,000
tons; it cost nearly $2,000,000.[4] Work was begun soon upon
another suspension bridge farther down the river at Louisville.
The entire length of this structure would be 5220 feet, or nearly
a mile.[5] A bridge of the same type was projected at Niagara
Falls.[6] An "ice bridge" in the following winter facilitated the
placing of the cables.[7]

The building of horse railroads in cities had been begun even
before the outbreak of the war, and the taking of stock in the
companies often had assumed the character of a wild speculation.[8] The cars gliding smoothly on their iron tracks were
held to be very superior to the old omnibuses which, propelled
by horses with raw shoulders and crippled limbs, rattled over
the rough streets. So far had the change gone in New York
before November, 1867, that at that time there remained still
in that city but eight omnibus lines, using 275 vehicles.[9] The
number of passengers carried on the street railroads of New

[1] Phila. Ledger, Dec. 30, 1867, and April 22, 1868.
[2] Ibid., Nov. 27, 1866.
[3] Ibid., July 20, 1865, and Dec. 1 and 4, 1866.
[4] Article on Cincinnati in Atlantic Monthly, August, 1867.
[5] Phila. Ledger, Aug. 8, 1867.
[6] Ibid.   [7] Ibid., Feb. 27, 1868.
[8] As in Philadelphia. See Oberholtzer, History of Phila., vol. ii,
pp. 327–8.   [9] Phila. Ledger, Nov. 8, 1867.

York increased from 32,000,000 in 1859 to more than 60,000,000 in 1864.[1]

In Washington and New Orleans there were one-horse cars. In these the conductor was done away with. The fare box in front of the car was in the care of the driver.[2] From America the horse street-car passed to Europe; it soon appeared in Paris.[3] Indeed, the American manufacturers were "leading the world," exporting their cars to England, India, South America and other countries.[4]

The first elevated railroad in New York was built in Greenwich Street. A half mile of the line at the lower end of the city was in successful operation in 1868, and it was to be extended to Harlem. A passenger would be taken from the Battery to 30th Street in fifteen minutes.[5]

A mysterious chemical agent known as nitroglycerine made its appearance immediately after the war. Its name, which had been unknown before 1865, except to a few scientists, was advertised far and wide through a series of explosions. The inventor was Alfred Nobel, a Swedish engineer. His brother had been killed and he himself had been injured while conducting their experiments with blasting compounds. Nitroglycerine was declared to possess fifteen times the power of gunpowder. It had blown to atoms an anvil weighing 400 pounds in a test in Hamburg. It would explode under water. A little of it would do the work of a large quantity of gunpowder, so that the expense of drilling into rock was reduced and other advantages were cited in favor of its employment in quarries and mines.[6]

In November, 1865, a box which had been shifted about in the baggage room of a hotel in New York, used sometimes as a seat for a guest and sometimes as a footstool for a bootblack, was discovered to be on fire. Hurriedly it was set out into the street, whereupon it exploded with a terrible detonation, hurling the paving stones through windows and injuring more than

---

[1] Phila. Ledger, Jan. 13, 1865, citing the Railroad Journal.
[2] Ibid., Oct. 11, 1867.   [3] Ibid., Feb. 4, 1868.
[4] Ibid., Jan. 16, 1867.   [5] Ibid., Oct. 27, 1868.   [6] Ibid., Nov. 8, 1865.

twenty persons. No one knew the contents of the box except, it was said, that they were chemical oils, brought from Germany by a boarder who had departed the hotel, leaving this behind him to be called for at a later date. The man was found and arrested. He said that the box had been intrusted to his care by another. He had rested his head upon it during the voyage over the sea and so on. It was concluded, quite fairly, that the substance which had caused the explosion was nitroglycerine.[1]

Mr. Nobel and his associates, who had commercialized the discovery, opened a factory in Hamburg and aimed to sell the explosive in the mining districts of America. Shipments were made to New York, reshipments were made to the Pacific coast by way of the Isthmus of Panama, all without particular designation of the contents of the cases. A small quantity stored at the freight offices of Wells, Fargo and Company in San Francisco in April, 1866, exploded, shaking the ground like an earthquake, ruining a block of buildings and blowing a number of men and several horses to atoms.[2] A few days later a ton or more of the same "demoniac compound," as the New York Herald described it (though it was urged by Mr. Nobel afterward that the material in this case was gun cotton), carried as cargo in an iron ship, exploded while it was being unloaded at Aspinwall. The vessel and the docks were destroyed and upwards of fifty men were killed.[3] There was great excitement on all sides. The New York Herald said that the importation of the murderous stuff should be made by Congress into a crime "punishable with the utmost severity." Perhaps it might be not too wild a hope that this body would now finally act in behalf of the common welfare, since, as they had been told, a negro was included among the victims of the disaster in San Francisco.[4] The Public Ledger in Philadelphia remarked the "reckless wickedness" of men who would ship such explo-

[1] N. Y. Tribune, Nov. 6 and 7, 1865; Phila. Ledger, Nov. 7 and 8, 1865.

[2] N. Y. Herald, April 17 and 18, 1866.

[3] Phila. Ledger, April 23, 1866.

[4] N. Y. Herald, April 18, 1866.

sive material on vessels which were crowded with passengers. "The severest punishment." it said, would be "too light for such a crime." [1]

The board of supervisors in San Francisco ordered all nitroglycerine found in that city to be seized and destroyed,[2] while in other cities, as in Philadelphia and New York, search for it was instituted by the fire marshals and the police. In the midst of the excitement Nobel himself arrived in the country. He was put under arrest and brought before the mayor in New York. He declared that his blasting oil was harmless except under conditions which were not present at usual times, and he published a "card" in the newspapers, asking for a suspension of public judgment concerning himself and his compound until he could be heard. Meantime he would say that it was "less dangerous" than gunpowder.[3] A series of experiments were carried on in Central Park.[4] Meantime some of the oil was found and seized. In May, 1866, a bark, containing several cases of it, which lay at the docks was ordered out into the river. Finally Mr. Nobel gained permission to convey it by water to a point opposite a certain shanty on 83d Street, and then to carry it up the river bank to that building wherein he would store his property.[5]

Bills and resolutions appeared in Congress and the legislatures of the states. Congress on July 3 passed a law prohibiting the traffic in nitroglycerine between foreign countries and the United States, or between states of the United States, in wagons, cars or ships carrying passengers, under penalty of a fine of from $1000 to $10,000. When it was forwarded in freight as distinguished from passenger cars or ships, it must be packed in metallic vessels protected by plaster of paris, with the words "Nitroglycerine — Dangerous" marked upon the package. If, after these precautions were observed, death came to any one from the material, while it was in transit,

---

[1] Phila. Ledger, April 19, 1866.
[2] San Francisco corr., N. Y. Herald, April 19, 1866.
[3] N. Y. Tribune, April 21 and 26, 1866.
[4] Ibid., May 7, 1866.   [5] Ibid., June 12, 1866.

the shipper and his agents separately and together would be deemed guilty of manslaughter.[1]

The invention of the sewing machine by Elias Howe, and the industry of an adventurer named Singer in manufacturing and selling it, were noted before the war. The trade afterward assumed huge proportions abroad as well as at home. Twenty firms were engaged in the business in 1866 and the country boasted several "sewing machine kings." In a French diligence drawn by five horses Singer was a man of mark in Central Park. He amazed Paris by his equipages and the singular splendor of his life. Howe rose from dire poverty until he enjoyed an income of $200,000 a year.[2] Selling agencies were established over all the world. Up to the end of the year 1866 about 750,000 sewing machines had been manufactured in America. The rate of production in that year was computed to be 1000 a day at an average cost to the purchaser of $60 each.[3] At least one-half of the output found its way to foreign countries. One company, which had sent abroad 7000 in 1861, five years later, in 1866, was exporting its machines at the rate of 25,000 a year.[4] Not alone did they serve to save the fingers of housewives; they revolutionized many manufacturing industries. Machines were now used in making coats, trousers and shirts, hats, gloves and underwear, harness, whips and horse blankets, valises, suspenders, trusses and corsets, boots, shoes and pocket-books.

The rapid extension of the farming areas in the West led to marked advances in the business of making mowing and reaping machines. The scythe and the grain cradle were cast aside except where the farms were small and there was great poverty. The machine drawn by horses in the fields reduced the labor of the harvest and it had become a "necessity." [5] McCormick, one of the principal manufacturers, was the richest man in

[1] Laws of the United States, Appendix Cong. Globe, 39th Cong., 1st sess., p. 334.

[2] James Parton, History of the Sewing Machine, Atlantic Monthly, May, 1867.

[3] Ibid.   [4] N. Y. Tribune, Sept. 24, 1866.

[5] Senate Ex. Doc., 39th Cong., 2d sess., no. 2, p. 23.

Chicago and one of the wealthiest in America.[1] Statisticians declared that a quarter of a million reaping machines were in use in the United States in 1866, each of them capable of cutting ten acres of grain in a day.[2] When eleven mowing machines of different makes were to be given a test on the grass meadows of the Bronx River, thousands of persons from New York went out to view the sight. Horses of various colors, flags and ribbons on the animals and the machines, and gayly dressed women, made the field a festal scene.[3]

The farms were large and labor was scarce. Inventors set their heads to work to devise steam ploughs, rotary ploughs, sulky ploughs, new and better threshing machines, "separators," "cultivators," binders, machines to sow seed, corn cutters, hay rakes, potato diggers, fans, corn shellers. Every implement from the hoe to the machine for reaping wheat was being simplified and improved.

The manufacture of paper from wood-pulp was begun in mills, covering ten acres of ground, at Manayunk in Philadelphia in 1866. Publishers of books and newspapers from all parts of the country were invited to witness the conversion, in five hours' time, of a poplar tree taken from the hillside into sheets ready for the printing-press. More than a million dollars were said to be invested in the plant. The price of paper which hitherto had been made of rags almost immediately fell three cents a pound.[4]

Immigration, which had shown a marked falling off during the war, increased as soon as news of the peace reached Europe. To encourage the coming of colonists for the West, and now for the South, was taken to be a public duty. Some proposed that Congress offer money bounties to immigrants, or that it pay their steamship fares.[5] But these suggestions bore no fruit. The New York state government maintained an immigration bureau in New York City, and in 1864 Congress established a

[1] His income in 1867 was over $230,000. — Phila. Ledger, April 20, 1868.

[2] Peto, op. cit., p. 111.

[3] N. Y. Tribune, July 28, 1865; Harper's Weekly, Aug. 12, 1865.

[4] N. Y. Tribune, April 13 and 16, 1866; Phila. Ledger, April 13, 1866.

[5] Senate Ex. Doc., 38th Cong., 1st sess., no. 15.

United States Emigrant Office there. It was put in charge of a superintendent, who would receive, protect, secure employment for, when possible, and send on to their destinations settlers arriving at the port from European countries.[1]

Now, as before the war, immigration was chiefly from Ireland and Germany. On Wednesday, May 17, 1865, it was announced that nearly 6000 persons had come to New York from Europe since the preceding Saturday night.[2] For the week ending June 19, 1865, the arrivals reached a total of 8000.[3] The packet ship *Helvetia* from Liverpool bore 1317 persons, the largest cargo of human beings, it was said, ever brought in upon the decks of a single steamer.[4] In the calendar year 1864, 193,418 immigrants had been received in the United States; in 1865 the arrivals numbered 248,120, and in 1866, 318,568, more than in any year since 1854.[5] Included in the quarter of a million immigrants of 1865 were 83,000 Germans and 112,000 British (largely Irish). In 1866, 116,000 were German, while 131,000 were Irish and English.[6] More than three-fourths of the immigrants of all nationalities came from Germany or the British Islands. While there were complaints about the emigrant ships, — as of the *Villa Franca*, which arrived in September, 1865, sixty-three days out of Liverpool, the captain being arrested on charges of gross cruelty to the passengers,[7] — methods of transportation were improving. For one thing steamships were coming to supersede sailing vessels, thus quickening the trip. In 1863 less than half the immigrants had arrived in steamships; 73 per cent did so in 1865 and 81 per cent in 1866.[8] Still, however, avaricious ship-owners overcrowded their vessels. Cases of this kind, brought to the attention of Secretary McCulloch in 1867, led him to issue instructions on the point to the revenue officers stationed in New York.[9]

[1] Chapter ccxlvi, Laws of 1864.   [2] Phila. Ledger, May 17, 1865.
[3] Ibid., June 20, 1865.   [4] Ibid., June 5, 1865.
[5] Arrivals of Alien Passengers and Immigrants in the United States from 1820 to 1892, Treasury Dept. publication, 1893.
[6] Ibid.
[7] N. Y. Herald, Sept. 19, 1865.   [8] Phila. Ledger, Aug. 3, 1867.
[9] Ibid., July 25, 1867, citing N. Y. Sun.

An old fort called Castle Clinton, on the lower end of Manhattan Island, had been converted into a concert hall to be known afterward as Castle Garden. Here fairs were held, bands played, singers from Europe, including Jenny Lind, were heard. Now it was fitted up as an immigrant station. To this point came the passengers with their children and their packs and boxes, to be inspected and sent out on their various ways. Railway tickets were sold in the building. Men who had no work in view were helped to secure it through an employment bureau. Aid was extended to the destitute.[1]

Scandinavians were beginning to arrive to go on to the rich farming lands northwest of Chicago. A Swedish newspaper had been started in the new city of St. Paul.[2] Many of the Germans went West: to Missouri, where they had made important settlements; to Milwaukee, to Cincinnati, as well as to Chicago and other places. Some were willing to work upon the farms, but the Irish preferred life in the large Eastern cities. In New York, in 1866, it was computed that there were more than 200,000 persons of Irish birth,[3] though the whole city, by the state census, had a population of but 800,000.[4] Forty-nine per cent of the population was foreign in New York, 36 per cent in Boston, 34 per cent in Baltimore and 31 per cent in Philadelphia.[5] With this concentration of population within small areas in cities, squalor and poverty developed. Two houses in one street in New York, each but 18 feet in width and 5 stories in height, contained 900 souls.[6] Fire frequently swept through the foreign rookeries. They became the nursing grounds of vice and crime. The moral feeling of many classes of the people was stirred and the old antipathy for "foreigners" again awoke. Hideous outrages by aliens reminded the people of the peril which attended this increased inpouring from Europe.

[1] N. Y. Tribune, June 19, 1865.
[2] Phila. Ledger, Aug. 24, 1866. Enough of the people remained in the East to support four churches in New York. — Ibid., July 4, 1867.
[3] Ibid., Aug. 9, 1866, citing N. Y. Times.
[4] Ibid., Aug. 22, 1865.
[5] Ibid., Aug. 9, 1866, citing N. Y. Times.
[6] Ibid., Jan. 24, 1865.

One or more of the assassins of President Lincoln had foreign names. The hated Wirz of Andersonville was a foreigner. A German named Probst in Philadelphia killed eight persons with an axe, under circumstances that appalled the nation. Throughout the land aliens out of Europe were connected with brutal crimes. They had been drawn here in many instances by the war. The country's preoccupation and the general disorder of the time prevented their earlier apprehension and punishment. It was complained, too, that men from the emigrant ships were overfilling the labor markets to the disadvantage of native wage-earners.[1]

Nearly magical seemed the gushing of oil out of the earth in the northeastern part of Pennsylvania. No such excitement had been seen before outside of the gold and silver camps of California, Colorado and Nevada. That there was a strange and inflammable liquid in the ground near Pittsburgh and farther up the Allegheny River in the neighborhood of Meadville and Franklin was very well known. It appeared on the surface of pools and streams. When men went into this greasy country to till its infertile fields, their friends, condoling with them, would say that if they could not raise wheat and corn, they might at least find a "soap mine."[2] Wild turkeys, hung in natural pits which occurred frequently hereabouts, were corrupted by a gas escaping from the earth. The Indians for long had known of the oil. Hither they came to bathe their sore joints and with wild incantations they at times put a flame to the surface of the water in some spirit of fire worship, which had attracted the attention of divers travellers. These being the Seneca Indians the oil was called Seneca oil, and under this name, or as rock oil, or American oil, or Indian oil, it was sold rather widely for medicinal purposes. About 1849 a man named Kier, who owned certain salt wells at Tarentum on the Allegheny River, twenty miles above Pittsburgh, having found oil with his brine, conceived the idea of making it into a panacea for the ills of man. The discovery of this great enemy

---

[1] N. Y. corr., Phila. Ledger, May 15, 1865.
[2] Derrick and Drill, p. 185.

of disease was heralded as "a new era in medicine." Rheumatism, gout and neuralgia were cured. The blind were made to see again. Crowds of witnesses would testify that petroleum had done for them what no medicine could ever do before. Physicians were recommending its use, for its "ingredients, from the beds of substances" which it passed over in its "secret channel," were "blended together in such a form as to defy all human competition." [1] The filling of half-pint bottles and their sale at a half dollar each, out of gilded chariots, which Mr. Kier sent about the country, accounted for a considerable part of the product of his wells, but a surplus remained and he began experiments in distillation. After a while he was enabled to rid the oil of much of its smoke when it was burned, perfected a lamp and made a market for it as an illuminating fluid.[2] But his business, as well as the trade in coal oils, which were being introduced for lighting uses, was doomed as soon as wells began to be sunk in Venango county.

This county was formed in the year 1800. Its capital was the little town of Franklin on the Allegheny River. The people who tilled the barren soil eked out a living by trips into the wood with their rifles. At certain seasons of the year they cut timber. The logs were made into rafts which on the spring freshets were floated down to Pittsburgh. Oil Creek had long borne this name. It ran north from the Allegheny across Venango county to the little village of Titusville in Crawford county. The Pennsylvania Rock Oil Company, incorporated in New York in 1854 with a capital of $250,000, acquired a farm on the bank of the creek and the stock was offered for sale. In 1857 E. L. Drake, a New England railway conductor, was employed to go out to Venango county to direct the company's affairs. He developed a plan for sinking an artesian well.

[1] "The healthful balm from Nature's secret spring,
    The bloom of health and life to man will bring;
    As from her depths the magic liquid flows
    To calm our sufferings and assuage our woes."
Verses on the wrappers of the bottles. — J. T. Henry, History of Petroleum, pp. 56–7.
[2] Ibid., pp. 58–9.

After reaching a depth of 69½ feet the workmen on a Saturday afternoon lost their drill in a crevice. They withdrew their tools from the hole and went home. The next day, Sunday, some one, looking into the tube, saw oil rising within eight or ten feet of the top. A pump was installed and production began at the rate of about 25 barrels daily.

The news of Mr. Drake's success spread like wild fire — to Titusville, and then over the state and throughout the country. Crowds came for miles around to see the well. Other men began to buy and lease lands in the neighborhood.[1] At one stride the whole narrow valley of Oil Creek, from Titusville down through a new town called Petroleum Centre, to another new town on the Allegheny River which was named Oil City, a distance of 16 miles, was occupied by eager men looking for fortunes in "grease." Many wells were sunk with varying but always moderate success, until in June, 1861, prospectors at work on farms near Petroleum Centre bored to a greater depth, about 500 feet, to the third and even the fourth "sand." The Fountain well on the Funk farm began to flow at the rate of 300 barrels a day and continued its yield for fifteen months. The Phillips well on the Tarr farm gave forth a stream of 3000 barrels, at one time nearly 4000 barrels a day,[2] and the Empire well, near the older Fountain well, 3000 barrels daily. The excitement was redoubled, and throughout the war, in spite of the absorption of the people in the progress and retreat of its fortunes, the furore continued. Immense prices were paid for land which was sold in a few hours or days for much higher prices. Thousands of companies were formed, and oil stock was offered for sale up and down the country. Cooks and cham-

---

[1] Mr. Drake himself had not this foresight. In possession of a few thousand dollars he removed to New York during the war and lost his all in stock speculations. Reduced by poverty and illness to dire straits, more successful men in the oil regions made up a purse for him, and at length the legislature of Pennsylvania voted him and his wife a pension for life of $1500 per annum in recognition of his services during the early years of the development of the petroleum industry. — Laws of Pa. for 1873, p. 557.

[2] The Oil Regions of Pennsylvania, by Wm. Wright, p. 136.

bermaids heard of the fabulous wealth of the "oil princes" and put their wages in shares; laboring men took their savings from banks that they might not miss the opportunity of gaining great riches. Children begged their guardians for permission to join in the general speculation. The stock of a company capitalized at a million dollars could be sold in three days.[1] Soon there was scarcely a farm within thirty miles of Oil City, not only on Oil Creek but also on Cherry Run, French Creek, Sugar Creek, the Big Sandy, the East Sandy and other streams which had not been leased or sold. Derricks were as thick as masts in the North River.

Warning voices were heard on many sides. Petroleum would go the way of the *morus multicaulis*, the merino sheep and the tulip manias of other years.[2] The companies consisted principally of "a few decoy ducks and many geese."[3] A governor, a congressman or a Union general of the war, who had bargained away his reputation for a block of the stock, at the importunate desire of the promoter, led many an innocent to his death. Again and again it seemed that "the limit of public gullibility" had been reached. The market was "glutted with oil stocks" which "predatory guerrillas" offered for sale. The public was a mouse in the claws of a cat.[4] Men who had honest and regular employment were "throwing up safe and useful occupations" and going to the oil regions, or, worse still, watched at home the rise and fall of petroleum company share prices "as madly as ever gambler watched the turning up of the dice."[5]

Not more than one well out of twenty properly sunk and well managed, and all men knew how many were outside this class, would produce ten barrels, the minimum yield for profitable operation.[6] The sales of printed certificates, at prices doubling at every turn on telegrams and letters from the wells or mere verbal rumors contrived for speculative purposes, had beggared

[1] N. Y. Tribune, June 27, 1865.

[2] Phila. Ledger, June 29, 1865.   [3] Ibid., July 27, 1865.

[4] Phila. Press, Dec. 19, 1864.   [5] Phila. Ledger, Feb. 17, 1865.

[6] N. Y. Tribune, June 27, 1865. Another thought that not more than one well in fifty would pay the cost of working it. — Phila. Ledger, Feb. 8, 1866.

many honest people. Millions upon millions of dollars represented by paper shares had been swept from existence and never would be heard of again.[1]

In Philadelphia, where the oil excitement had begun, it broke out anew early in the year 1865.[2] Men who never before had speculated in anything borrowed money to buy shares. They would not purchase a house and lot on their own street without a rigid examination of its title deeds, but they had a few thousands to invest in the shares of the Inexhaustible Moonshine Petroleum Company with a capital of a million dollars whose assets were a bottle of oil in its office window and a dozen seductive maps.[3]

Companies issued full-paid stock of a par value of $1 and $2 for twenty-five or fifty cents. A company in Pittsburgh offered its shares at six cents each.[4] Promoters promised investors 20 or 30 per cent annually in dividends with monthly payments, which often would be continued until the stock was sold when, like the rogues that they were, they would move off to prepare some new trap to catch the people's money. A stock bought at $1, perhaps, could be sold within a few days for $10. The announcement that a well yielding 1500 barrels a day had been drilled on a company's land instantly increased the price of its stock from $18 to $45. When a 400-barrel well began to flow on another farm, the shares of the controlling company, which had been selling at $3.50, went up to $6.50.[5] Such flurries brought new capital into the vortex and increased the fury of the speculation.

In January, 1865, it was computed that the capital of oil companies of which there was public knowledge amounted to $326,000,000 ($163,000,000 in Philadelphia and $134,000,000 in New York), and there were many private and semi-private enterprises.[6] New companies early in the year 1865 were formed at an unprecedented rate. On March 1 nine new companies

---

[1] Phila. Ledger, June 29, 1865.   [2] Derrick and Drill, p. 270.
[3] Ibid., p. 260, citing Meadville Republican.
[4] Phila. Press, March 11, 1865.
[5] Derrick and Drill, p. 273.   [6] Ibid., p. 258.

came forward in Philadelphia with stock for sale of a par value of $3,500,000; [1] a week later 26 with a capital of $12,000,000; [2] the next week 20 with a capital of $12,500,000; [3] and in the week ending March 20 no less than 51 companies capitalized at $20,000,000.[4] In July, 1865, a statistician in the New York Tribune estimated that the total capital of public petroleum companies was not less than $500,000,000.[5] The people had "oil fever"; they had "oil on the brain." [6]

The sudden bursting forth from the ground of geysers of this dark green, viscous, greasy fluid taxed all the facilities at hand for storing, shipping and selling it. The cooper shops could not make enough barrels to hold it. It overflowed the storage vats to soak the ground and swell the currents of the streams. The price of oil fell precipitately. It was not worth the cooper's price for barrels and the charge of carrying it to market. Before the flowing wells were opened in February, 1861, the production of the entire Venango county district was only about 150 barrels daily. This total was increased to 3000 barrels daily in September, and 6000 barrels in December. The price fell as low as ten cents a barrel. No large or important uses had yet been found for petroleum. But with new and better refining processes, improved lamps, which gave it universal value as an illuminating agent, the discovery of its worth as a lubricant and in the arts, the market was extended. The export trade absorbed great quantities of it, and in 1864 the price rose to $13.50 a

---

[1] Phila. Press, March 1, 1865.
[2] Ibid., March 6, 1865.   [3] Ibid., March 14, 1865.
[4] Ibid., March 20.   [5] N. Y. Tribune, July 12, 1875.
[6] The refrain of a popular song:

"The Yankees boast that they make clocks
    Which just beat all creation,
But they never made one could keep time
    With our great speculation.
Our stocks, like clocks, go with a spring,
    Wind up, run down again,
But all our strikes are sure to cause
    Oil on the Brain.
Stocks par, stocks up, then on the wane,
Everybody troubled with, Oil on the Brain."

barrel at the wells.[1]   In that year the yield was about 2,116,000
barrels.[2]   More than a third part of this large output was sent
away to foreign countries, chiefly through the ports of Philadelphia and New York — to Europe, Asia, Africa, Australia,
South America and the West Indies.   The demand for it, indeed, was as wide as the world.[3]

Men grew poetic in contemplating its wonders.   The new
light, one said, had woven a "golden web" over all America.
It shone across the sea from the summits of cliffs and the bin-
nacles of ships, a beacon blest by mariners in storms.   Its soft
rays fell from chandeliers upon the dinner tables of Englishr-
men; the Swiss cottager smoked his pipe beside his petroleum
lamp.   Pennsylvania oil was shedding its picturesque gleam
along the streets of Italian cities.   It illuminated the revelries
of Paris and made bright the dark ways of Jerusalem and Peking.
It had "crept round the globe in place of the moon." [4]   One
well at Titusville produced more oil than 800 whale ships of
New Bedford had been able to collect at sea in a year.[5]   Many
of the fishermen, it was said, had laid aside the harpoon and
had emigrated to Venango county, where the fat of no one knew
how many prehistoric whales, as some pretended to think, lay
under the ground at the beck and call of the human family.

The production became so large that petroleum was chosen
by the government as an object of taxation.   As early as in
1862 Congress levied a tax of 10 cents per gallon upon refined
petroleum sold for domestic use.   In 1864 the tax was increased
to 20 cents, and in 1865 a duty of $1 a barrel was laid upon crude
oil.[6]

By this time a district twenty miles square was well covered
with derricks.   The skeletons with their walking beams were
seen on the hillsides, in forests, perhaps in a garden or on the
sidewalk of a new town.   The superstitious would send out
wizards with forked sticks of hazel or peachwood, as men had

---

[1] Henry, op. cit., pp. 277–8.   [2] Ibid., p. 306.
[3] House Ex. Doc., 39th Cong., 1st sess., no. 51, p. 18.
[4] Derrick and Drill, p. 29.   [5] Ibid., p. 50.
[6] House Ex. Doc., 39th Cong., 1st sess., no. 51, pp. 1–2.

formerly looked for likely places for water wells. If oil lay underneath the ground, the handle of the fork would fall and at that spot the boring might begin. Many of the early wells had been drilled by hand with a spring pole consisting of a green sapling. But this method of "jigging it down" and a kindred method of "knocking it down" were very laborious. Again horses and water power were utilized to operate the boring implements, but steam had so many advantages that an engine came to be an indispensable part of every oil man's "rig." He must spend probably $7000, without counting the cost of his land, before he could discover whether he was on the "grease" or in "dry territory." Thousands of derricks standing idle, many more over wells which must be pumped to yield a few barrels a day, and the very few of abundant flow attested to the great uncertainty of fortune in "Petrolia."

Meadville, some twenty-five miles west of Oil Creek, was the point from which men usually entered the fields. At once its population was increased. Titusville, before the war a little village of 150 persons, had gained a population in 1865 of 5000. Franklin, the Venango county-town, had come to have 3000 inhabitants. Corry, a junction town, at which Sir Morton Peto's new road from Cincinnati to New York, the Atlantic and Great Western, connected with the Philadelphia and Erie Railroad, had had no existence before the discovery of petroleum. Now it was a place of 4000 people.

New cities were brought into being in a week. The town called Oil City rose at the point at which Oil Creek joins the Allegheny River. On one long street crowded with shops, boarding-houses and saloons wedged between the rocky cliffs and the river were thousands of excited fortune seekers gathered from near and far places.[1] From Oil City along Oil Creek up to Titusville were towns which men prophesied soon would form one continuous city with a central street to rival Broadway in New York.[2] A farm of 200 or 300 acres on the banks of this

[1] Derrick and Drill, pp. 23–5.
[2] Ibid., p. 54.

creek which it had been hard to sell a few years since for $2000 would now bring its owner $600,000 or $1,000,000.[1]

Yet more wonderful was Pithole City on Pithole Creek, a small and rapid stream which flowed into the Allegheny River a few miles east of Oil Creek. The United States Petroleum Company sank its first well on the Thomas Holmden farm in Cornplanter township, the so-called Frazier well, which began to flow on January 8, 1865, at the rate of 250 barrels a day, a yield soon increased to 900 barrels. Other wells, the Pool, the Twins, the Grant and the Forty-seven, were drilled on the same farm. From a few acres of barren land oil worth two millions of dollars in gold was taken in a year.[2] In October, 1865, the production in this neighborhood was 5000 barrels and by some for a time it was assumed to have reached 8500 barrels a day.[3]

The tribe of fortune hunters which had been wandering over "Oil Dorado" now rushed to Pithole. Soldiers released for civil pursuits at the end of the war, adventurers from the gold and silver camps in the West, city men tired of their humdrum lives flocked in. There were only three wooden buildings in this part of the county before the discovery of oil. In six weeks Pithole City had a population of 10,000 persons, and a little later it was reckoned to contain 15,000, with several smaller towns of 1000 and 2000 inhabitants on its outskirts. Tents and shanties rose on every hand. Soon there were large hotels, one of them four stories in height, built at a cost of $100,000, and three others the erection of each of which involved an outlay of more than $40,000. The city came in a little while to have fifty hotels and hundreds of boarding-houses and restaurants. Theatres, churches, saloons, casinos, concert halls, brothels, groceries, land offices, agencies for the sale of engines, blowers, drills and other paraphernalia used in boring for oil were open for business. Newspapers were started. The excitement reached its height when some tubing broke beneath the ground and oil began to appear in the springs and water wells. Women

---

[1] Derrick and Drill, p. 99.   [2] C. C. Leonard, History of Pithole, p. 10.
[3] N. Y. Tribune, Oct. 24, 1865.

and children were now dipping up oil. A washerwoman who had a water well 16 feet deep was offered $5000 for it.[1] A man named Hill who could fill a barrel with oil in five minutes by pressing his pump handle refused $7000 for the hole which led him to the underground store of wealth.[2] The surface soils were so saturated with petroleum that water became scarce. It was sold in wagons in the streets. Sometimes it would fetch as much as ten cents a tincupful, or $1 a pail.

Speculation was rampant, not only in oil lands but in city lots. Pithole itself was soon an old story. New towns were laid out in the forests and quagmires roundabout. The whole world which had aught to do with Cornplanter township was on the point of becoming immensely rich.

To send the oil to market was very difficult and expensive. It had been so on Oil Creek before the railroad was built. The petroleum flowed from the ground more rapidly than it could be barrelled and stored. Thousands of teams drew it to the Allegheny River for shipment to Pittsburgh, but the roads were deep. The rains, the leaking oil and the incessant passing back and forth of heavy wagons made them at some seasons of the year nearly bottomless. At high water barrels, joined together in rafts, were navigated down Oil Creek to the Allegheny ; again they would be loaded upon "flats" or the oil perhaps would be poured in bulk into tank boats which could be taken without reloading to Pittsburgh. At low water arrangements would be made with the owners of mill dams to release the water which they had impounded and "pond freshets" were formed to float the navy of "Petrolia." From time to time the rafts and boats would collide with loss of their cargoes.[3] The empty "flats" were drawn up the stream by horses wading in its bed, at times, humane visitors observed, amid ice which cruelly struck their legs, while the cold water incrusted their flanks and tails.

[1] Leonard, History of Pithole City, p. 28.

[2] "Yesterday I wasn't worth a cint and bejabers to-day I'm worth me thousands upon thousands," said an Irishman who had caught the spirit of the hour.

[3] J. H. A. Bone, Petroleum and Petroleum Wells, pp. 28-9.

Pithole City and the wells in its vicinity were even less well situated, for Pithole Creek was a very shallow stream. All the oil must be hauled in wagons, south to the Allegheny or north eleven miles to Titusville, or possibly to Miller Farm, a station on the Oil Creek Railroad. A continuous line of teams took the oil away; a continuous line returned the vehicles empty or laden with machinery and merchandise. Many a wheel was broken, many a wagon mired and many a horse injured or killed when 2000 teams which at times could not transport more than two barrels of oil each because of the condition of the roads, served Pithole City. In a few months plank roads were built to Titusville and Miller Farm. A pipe six inches in diameter, which followed the course of Pithole Creek and crossed it 21 times, was laid between Pithole City and Oleopolis, a new oil town on the Allegheny River. Over a distance of seven miles petroleum flowed by gravity from the tanks beside the wells at Pithole into the boats bound for Pittsburgh. The cost of transportation, which by wagon had been from $2.50 to $3, was now reduced to fifty cents or a dollar a barrel.[1]

Meantime work was begun upon a railroad. The first train of cars passed down the Pithole Valley from Pithole City to Oleopolis in December, 1865. The connection between Oleopolis and Oil City in the valley of the Allegheny was completed in March, 1866. The ground was levelled and the trestles set in place for a second railway into Pithole, but disaster came to its projectors as well as to the city itself and it was never built.

The life in this region was as wild as any led in a Western mining camp. Like the miners in the Rocky Mountains the adventurers who went into "Oildom" spoke of the rest of the country as "the states." They had crossed the boundaries of civilized society and gone out of the world. On all sides were men on foot, in long cowhide boots, on horses, in buggies and, in winter time, in hack sleighs, looking for land upon which to

[1] Phila. Ledger, Nov. 8, 1865. Pipes, through which the oil must be pumped, were laid also in the other direction to the railroad lines at Miller Farm and Titusville.

sink wells. A million dollars would change hands in a few minutes. The streets and barrooms in the towns swarmed with teamsters, commercial drummers and land jobbers; intermingled with them were the thieves and cutthroats of two continents. Engines and drills would be stolen at night unless the owners guarded them with firearms. Men were waylaid, garroted and robbed, and vigilance committees were formed to shoot and hang the outlaws.[1] Visitors looking for anything like beauty and good order left in disgust. Houses, wagons, horses and men were bespattered with mud. Oil City was declared to be the "filthiest of cities"; it was a "sewer of cities." Its people resembled a "lower class of scarecrows under the influence of a powerful galvanic battery."[2]

Now and again the country was swept by fire. A pall of flame and smoke would hang over the hills and rivers. Derricks, barrels, boats, vats, villages were left a blackened mass. The very water, which was full of oil, instead of serving to extinguish the flames often made them glow the brighter. In March, 1866, two great fires ran over the farms near Petroleum Centre. The oil released from the vats rolled, a burning stream, into Oil Creek, destroying everything in its path.[3] In April Titusville was gutted by a great fire,[4] in May a million dollars' worth of property was destroyed in Oil City,[5] and in August the vats, sheds and "rigs" of twenty-seven wells near Pithole City were burned.[6]

Several of the new towns, such as Titusville, Corry and Oil City, survived their fires, the failure of particular wells and the shifting of oil-producing areas. Others greatly declined in importance and some in a little while entirely ceased to exist. Pithole's fall was nearly as rapid as its rise. From a yield of 5000 barrels daily this district's output had diminished to 500 barrels before the end of the year 1868.[7] At one time more mail matter had passed through its post-office than was sent

[1] Phila. Ledger, Oct. 10, 1865.   [2] N. Y. Nation, Sept. 21, 1865.
[3] N. Y. Herald, March 23, 1866, and Phila. Ledger, April 2, 1866.
[4] N. Y. Herald, April 19, 1866.   [5] Phila. Ledger, May 28, 1866.
[6] N. Y. Herald, Aug. 3, 1866; History of Pithole, p. 54.
[7] Phila. Ledger, Feb. 18, 1868.

or received through any other in Pennsylvania, save Philadelphia and Pittsburgh. In the October election in 1867 only
92 votes were cast in the place.[1] What remained of it was
swept away in a fire which was started by the explosion of a
petroleum lamp in a dwelling-house in February, 1868.[2] To-
day the very fact of its existence is nearly forgotten, even in
the neighborhood in which it one time led its flourishing life.

As towns rose and fell so did the fortunes of individuals.
Farmers, teamsters, poor men who had earlier made a living
cutting timber in the wood, adventurers — suddenly became rich in the oil fields. Gamblers who had never seen a
derrick made money in New York or Philadelphia buying and
selling oil stocks. The lucky fellow who had "struck ile"[3]
became a well-known figure in our social life. Such an "oil
prince" was "Johnny" Steel, who once had an income of
$2000 a day. For a few months he literally threw around his
money. He would enter a hotel and hire the entire building
with its staff of servants for his own use. With his great bills
for liquors and cigars, for jewelry and horses, carriages and harness, and his antics of many kinds he amazed the Eastern cities
for a brief day. But in the winter of 1868 he was a bankrupt
with proven debts in Pittsburgh of more than $100,000, and
soon he was once more driving an oil team.[4]

The bubble of a better reputation burst when Charles Vernon
Culver's failure came. He was a young man who had entered
the oil regions from Ohio. He reorganized a bank at Meadville and opened a series of branch offices of discount and deposit,
which increased their business so rapidly that they soon were
made into independent banks. Two of these, — the Venango
Bank of Franklin and the Petroleum Bank of Titusville, — together had a capital of $1,300,000 in 1865.[5] From state banks
he passed to national banks, organizing and owning in large

[1] Phila. Ledger, Nov. 11, 1867.   [2] Ibid., Feb. 28, 1868.
[3] This phrase seems to have originated in a story about a pioneer's
pretty daughter who had a suitor. She had favored him. He came
again to plead his cause but was refused, for, said she, "Dad's struck ile."
[4] Phila. Ledger, Feb. 19, 1868, citing Pittsburgh Commercial.
[5] Ibid., Jan. 20, 1865.

part institutions of this character in Oil City, Corry, Titusville, Erie, Pittsburgh and New York. At the same time he formed private banking firms in Philadelphia and New York, and at 34 years of age was reckoned to be the wealthiest man in Pennsylvania.[1] Before August, 1865, he had given $100,000 to Meadville College, and had a reputation as one of the country's leading philanthropists.[2] The oil counties in Pennsylvania elected him to Congress. With his banking business he combined speculations in petroleum lands, railroads, storehouses and docks. A party of congressmen, capitalists and journalists were taken through the oil district at his expense,[3] when he was organizing his new Reno Oil and Land Company with a capital of $10,000,000. Ex-Speaker of the House of Representatives, Galusha A. Grow, was its president, Mr. Culver, its vice-president. A distinguished company of men were numbered among the directors. Three hundred oil wells would be sunk on 1200 acres of land at a place situated on the Allegheny River below Oil City. It would be called Reno and was destined to become the "great central commercial town of the oil regions" — the metropolis of petroleum as Chicago was the metropolis of grain, San Francisco of gold and New Orleans of sugar and cotton.[4] But in a few months Culver's banking houses failed.[5] Throughout the oil regions, with all who held the notes of his banks which were now worthless, from the rich men who had struck oil down to the greasy teamsters, the feeling was intense.[6] One of his creditors caused his arrest on a charge of conspiracy,[7] and he went to prison, where he remained until December, 1866, when his jailer delivered him to the sergeant-at-arms of the House of Representatives, and he was taken back to serve out his term in Congress.[8] Three months later he was acquitted of the charges lodged against him,[9] but he had had his day and his career was done.

[1] Derrick and Drill, pp. 104–5.   [2] Phila. Ledger, Aug. 10, 1865.
[3] N. Y. Tribune, Oct. 24, 1865.   [4] Ibid., March 14, 1866.
[5] N. Y. Herald, March 29 and 30, 1866.
[6] Phila. Ledger, April 5, 1866, citing Rochester Union.
[7] N. Y. Tribune, July 10, 1866.
[8] Ibid., Dec. 19, 1866.   [9] Ibid., Feb. 7, 1867.

Other territory which it was suspected might contain oil was not neglected by the speculators. The Clarion River, paralleling the Allegheny at a distance varying from 18 to 30 miles, was explored. Many wells were sunk in Clarion and Butler counties, a district not of importance at once, but since proven to be of great value. It was the beginning of the development of what have since come to be known as "the lower oil fields" of Pennsylvania.

The fever spread to other states — West Virginia, Ohio, Indiana, Kentucky and California. The barest traces of oil led to great excitement. Speculators came in to buy the farmers' lands, derricks were built and boring began. West Virginia gave the fairest promise of rivalling Pennsylvania, and a number of productive wells were opened just before and in the first years of the war, though the operations of bands of guerrillas in this region made the conduct of the business so unsafe that most of the owners retired until the reëstablishment of peace. Parkersburg, a straggling town at the junction of the Ohio and the Kanawha rivers, and the terminus of the Baltimore and Ohio Railroad, became the entrepôt for the West Virginia oil men. Many of the wells were on Burning Spring Creek, which had long borne this name because the gas and the greasy water expelled from the earth here, when ignited, by chance, produced a flame. To this creek from Parkersburg was a distance of more than thirty miles. The oil when it was caught in vats either could be hauled in barrels to that place over bad roads for $3.50 a barrel or carried down the Kanawha River in flatboats at high water. Productive wells were found also on Hughes River and Bull Creek. Indeed, the exploration covered nine counties, with the excitement rising and falling with the fortunes of the drill.[1]

As Oil City and Parkersburg were the capitals of the petroleum regions in Pennsylvania and West Virginia, so Marietta in the valley of the Muskingum became the centre of a district in Ohio in which many Pittsburgh and Cincinnati men made

[1] J. R. Young, in Derrick and Drill, chap. v; Phila. Ledger, May 4, 1865.

investments. Catlettsburg in Kentucky was filled with strangers busily talking about oil and moving toward the banks of the various creeks flowing into the Big Sandy River.[1] An oily stone was used in a building which was going up in Chicago. Speculators began to bore for petroleum in the neighborhood of the quarry. Seven thousand acres of land in Perry county, Indiana, were leased by an oil company. Prospectors were buying and leasing land in other counties of the state. In Michigan they had "struck ile," and there were "surface indications" in the vicinity of Chattanooga, Tenn. In a town in Yates county, N. Y., three companies were sinking wells. The price of land was rising at leaps and bounds.[2] The first shipment of petroleum to San Francisco, 120 barrels, went forward from Humboldt county in June, 1865.[3]

The petroleum found outside of Pennsylvania was heavy, designed, it was believed, for use only as a lubricant, and the yield was small in comparison with what came from the wells in the Oil Creek district. The New York Journal of Commerce in October, 1865, estimated that the daily production in the United States was 9000 barrels, of which 7000 barrels came from Pennsylvania, 1140 from West Virginia, 520 from Ohio, 320 from Kentucky and 20 from California.[4]

Wells dried up, "oil princes" lost their fortunes, towns fell, but the business all the while enjoyed a stable growth. The earth would continue its yield, said Galusha A. Grow, because Providence never gave to mankind anything so useful which was afterward withdrawn.[5] Despite the industry's ups and downs in neighborhoods the country's total output which was 2,500,000 barrels in 1865 rose to 3,600,000 barrels in 1866 and to more than 4,000,000 barrels in 1869.[6]

With what was heralded as a blessing of Heaven had come untold perils which caused old people to wag their heads and to descant upon the advantages of whale oil for use in lamps.

---

[1] Derrick and Drill, p. 206.   [2] Ibid., pp. 214–5.
[3] San Francisco corr., Phila. Ledger, June 20, 1865.
[4] Phila. Ledger, Oct. 12, 1865.
[5] N. Y. Tribune, Oct. 28, 1865.   [6] Henry, op. cit., p. 306.

Not alone at the wells and in the petroleum fields was there danger of fire. The oil was refined, separated into naphtha, kerosene, paraffine and other products, at the refineries, some of which were set up near the points of production, many more near the points of consumption and on the seaboard. But the processes were still imperfect and crude. Kerosene cost at retail in Philadelphia or New York from 75 cents to $1 a gallon. Often it was thick, greasy and yellow; it yielded a sediment upon standing in the can which the careful housewife was likely to set outside her door. It smoked and sputtered in the lamp when it was burned, and it often "exploded." Many a fearful accident came from this source. Towns were burned, steamboats destroyed,[1] lives lost in fires which were started by the "explosion" of lamps. Servants poured kerosene upon wood in laggard stoves with dire results. There were fires among the barrels on railway trains and in the iron tank cars, which soon came into use, in the refineries, in oil warehouses and on oil ships. All New York was shaken by an explosion which took place on an oil dock in Jersey City in the summer of 1866.[2] Six lives were lost and 51 buildings were destroyed in Philadelphia in February, 1865, when fire broke out in a storehouse in that city. Petroleum in its nature was "worse than gunpowder," said the judge in making a presentment to the grand jury. It should be stored in large cities, if kept there at all, only on vacant lots.[3] The councils of cities and legislatures of states passed ordinances and laws for the regulation of the shipment, housing and use of the dangerous stuff.

Despite these unmistakable signs of advancement and prosperity Revenue Commissioner Wells observed that the country was in "an abnormal and unsatisfactory condition."[4] The inflation of the currency by the issue of "greenbacks" was a measure "necessary in the great emergency in which it was adopted," said Secretary of the Treasury McCulloch in 1865,

[1] N. Y. Herald, April 14, 1866.
[2] Ibid., Aug. 20, 1866.
[3] Phila. Ledger, Feb. 9 and 11, 1865.
[4] Senate Ex. Doc., 39th Cong., 2d sess., no. 2, p. 11.

in reviewing the financial management of the war, though it
was unconstitutional (a statement finding confirmation later
in a decision of the Supreme Court) and one fraught with the
greatest peril, if it were to be continued in time of peace.[1]
He, too, found that the business of the country was in "an unhealthy condition." The "circulating medium" was "altogether larger" than was needed for "legitimate business and the
excess was used in speculation." The inflation was exerting
an evil influence upon the morals of the people by encouraging
"waste and extravagance." Men gambled to get rich instead
of working for their gains. An irredeemable paper currency
could not fail to be "a calamity to any people." [2]

It is not too much to say that while the South pinched and
starved, eating their cowpeas, pinning together their rags with
thorns, writing the complaints of their hearts upon paper
stripped from the walls in ink pressed from the berries of the
fields, the North rioted in great luxury. To Southern eyes
which viewed the sight after the long imprisonment behind
the blockade such prosperity was mistaken for Babylon's.
The dress of the women who at Hampton Roads boarded the
boat, bearing Jefferson Davis and Clement C. Clay to their
casemates in the North, to strip and search the rebel leaders'
wives, was merely typical of the day, but to Mrs. Clay,
with their flaring hoop skirts,[3] their high-heeled shoes, their

[1] Report of the Secretary of the Treasury in House Ex. Doc., 39th
Cong., 1st sess., no. 3.

[2] McCulloch's speech at Fort Wayne, Ind., reported in Phila.
Ledger, Oct. 16, 1865.

[3] The "street displays" made by women wearing the "tilters,"
said an outraged writer in the New York Nation, gave undoubted encouragement to vice. (N. Y. Nation, vol. iv, p. 220.) On the other
hand to Leland, the humorist, the "hoop" seemed to be a "war hoop."

> "He walked the lady round and round,
> She seemed intrenched upon a mound,
> Securely spanned and fortified
> As if all lovers she defied."

What could be done with the iron cages when they had served the
wearer and she was done with them? They burdened the tops of ash
barrels or went to the attic. One writer recommended hanging them

gayly colored petticoats, their frizzed hair and powdered faces and their great chignons or "waterfalls," the false hair adornments universally worn at the back of the head,[1] they had the appearance of holding scarcely reputable places in society.

To the Confederate General, "Dick" Taylor, the city of Washington, upon his first visit there after the war, in 1865, seemed to be in "high carnival." Women "resplendent in jewels" swarmed the inns, the Capitol and the ante-chambers of the White House itself. They all were mistaken for courtesans.[2] The bales and barrels of goods on the wharves in New York, the lavish expenditure of money in the theatres, hotels and restaurants, the fruit shops, the stores filled with precious stones, silks, the rich stuffs of the world so long unseen by the Southern people, awakened their amazement.[3] The truth is that the North was in the midst of a period of plenty, pleasure and speculation which was deplored by all thoughtful and prudent men.

The free and excited sale of "seven-thirty" Treasury notes in the spring and summer of 1865 through the government bond-agent in Philadelphia, Jay Cooke, was but an evidence of the cheapness of money and the desire to make large profits.

on poles as trellises for morning glories. Another would resmelt the metal to make nails and cannon. (N. Y. Tribune, May 6, 1865.) It could be said chivalrously at this period in the history of female dress that the virtues of the ladies exceeded the magnitude of their skirts, while their faults were as small as their bonnets. (Phila. Ledger, Dec. 28, 1866.)

> [1] "What is that clumsy bunch of hair
> On the back of the head of the lady fair,
> A bundle as large as a loaf of bread
> Hung from the back of that elegant head?
> That clumsy bundle is what they call
> By the singular name of a waterfall. . . .
>
> "How do they manage to grow so much hair
> On the back of the head of the lady fair?
> Where the whole of the waterfall grows
> Is a matter that nobody certainly knows;
> But it's said that the principal part of the crop
> Was bought for cash at a barber's shop."
> Phila. Ledger, Sept. 9, 1865.

[2] Richard Taylor, Destruction and Reconstruction, p. 241.
[3] For example see Mrs. Clay, A Belle of the Fifties, p. 304.

The various issues of government securities were sold and resold upon the exchanges of the country. Gold was still dealt in on the Gold Boards. Clever merchants from the South, driven to New York by the war — traders of Louisiana, planters from Georgia, clergymen from the Carolinas — a varied assortment of men with Southern sympathies [1] were gathered in the Gold Room in that city to speculate on their own account or as brokers for others. Often they would "corner" the market to the disturbance of the credit of the government and the embarrassment of the operations of business men. They were denounced as "copperheads" and "rebels," as "the left wing of General Lee's army," [2] but the buying and selling continued day after day. Many were enriched, while many more were reduced to beggary. Until specie payments should be resumed the business would continue and the fluctuations, if not so wide as during the war, were still large enough to prove an inviting field to the gambler. The premium was 24 in March, 1866. For no reason except that a "corner" had been formed, it was 48 in August, 1866. Men who needed gold for legitimate uses must pay the price set upon it by the speculators.[3]

The petroleum companies had added their large issues of stock to the general mass of shares upon the security markets of the large cities. The granting of land by Congress to companies projected to build railroads hither and yonder in the West increased the material at hand. The Milwaukee and Prairie du Chien Railroad Company had but 29,000 shares of stock; in the fall of 1865 some "bears" in New York sold 60,000 shares, whereupon a rival party of gamblers appeared in Wall Street, bought the entire issue and raised its price in one day from $110 to $230, compelling the original clique to buy at a loss of about $10,000,000 or go into bankruptcy.[4]

The day was not long enough for speculation in New York. An evening exchange was opened. Gamblers passed from one board to another until midnight "like a pack of howling der-

[1] N. Y. Nation, vol. iii, p. 173.   [2] Jay Cooke, vol. ii, p. 141.
[3] N. Y. Nation, loc. cit.   [4] Phila. Ledger, Nov. 9, 1865.

vishes." It was "not business; it was frenzy." [1] The transactions of brokers in Wall Street for the year ending June 30, 1865, reached a total of six billions of dollars. Each of nine firms carried on a business in excess of $100,000,000.[2] "The tales of the petroleum princes" had "set people crazy," said the New York Herald. The contractors of the war and the men made rich by oil, said the Philadelphia Ledger, were indulging in so ostentatious a display of their wealth that it tended to unsettle all the usual ideas about money won by industry, and to weaken the principles of integrity. A "spirit of gambling" was "rife in the land." [3] The man to be emulated measured his money by millions; the woman to be admired was overdressed, fond of her own amusement and seen much in public places. An entirely new system of morals was uppermost; it had overturned an older and a better order of society.

From all parts of the country the rich began a movement toward New York, the centre of speculation and of fashionable life. The glitter of jewelry at the opera created amazement. One lady, an observer said, bore $50,000 worth of gems upon her head; another displayed enough precious stones to furnish out a jeweller's window in Broadway.[4] The streets on opera nights were blocked with carriages. Eight hundred dollars a month were asked for a small furnished house on Fifth Avenue as far out as Central Park. So great was the demand for handsome and expensive places of residence that entire rows of houses were being planned in fashionable neighborhoods for completion in the spring of 1866.[5] A block of land bounded by Madison and Fifth Avenues between 45th and 46th Streets was sold for $315,000; another lying between Fourth and Fifth Avenues and 59th and 60th Streets, for $500,000.[6] Eight building lots on Fifth Avenue near 50th Street, each of them 25 feet wide by 100 feet deep, brought the "enormous" price of $160,000.[7] In March, 1866, it was computed that Fifth

[1] N. Y. Herald, Aug. 18, 1865.   [2] N. Y. Tribune, Oct. 14, 1865.
[3] Phila. Ledger, Aug. 17, 1865.
[4] Ibid., Feb. 4 and Oct. 16, 1865.
[5] N. Y. corr., Phila. Ledger, Oct. 16, 1865.
[6] Ibid., Oct. 3, 1865.   [7] Ibid., Oct. 4, 1865.

Avenue contained 341 dwellings, not one of which had cost less than $30,000. The lowest rental price was $6000 a year. A. T. Stewart, the dry goods merchant, whose income for 1866 was reputed to be $4,000,000, was building [1] a marble mansion to cost $1,000,000.[2] Jay Cooke, who had sold the war loans, was erecting "Ogontz," a great home a few miles from Philadelphia, upon which he would expend a like sum of money. The Spragues, calico manufacturers at Providence, were paying taxes on property thought to have a value of $25,000,000.[3]

The returns of the Internal Revenue Department indicated that $7,000,000 were expended in New York in a year in the theatres and kindred places of amusement.[4] In that city in two years, in 1864 and 1865, it was stated that $1,000,000 had been paid out for the work of foreign and native artists.[5] Even the poor aimed to make an appearance of wealth, and the business of selling dry goods to women, newly come to the glass of fashion, fine equipages, precious stones and jewelry and of keeping open restaurants, bars, theatres and concert halls yielded large profits. The Northern cities, with New York leading the number, became the centres for the display of a kind of barbaric splendor not seen in them before.

Many boarded ocean steamships and betook themselves to Europe. They carried great letters of credit, and dazzled the eyes of England, France, Switzerland and Italy with the evidences of their material prosperity. In the summer months they flocked to the springs or the seaside resorts — to Saratoga, Newport, Lake George, Lake Champlain, Long Branch, Cape May and Atlantic City. Invalids had been taken to spas and to the beaches; now the rich and those who would seem rich closed their city homes for two or three months and went thither in a body, hiring cottages or living at hotels to enjoy their pleasure. Washington, Baltimore and Philadelphia

---

[1] Harper's Magazine, vol. xxxiv, p. 523; cf. N. Y. Herald, July 11, 1865, for earlier years.

[2] Phila. Ledger, March 24, 1866.

[3] Providence corr. of Hartford Courant, cited in Phila. Ledger, Aug. 8, 1867.   [4] Phila. Ledger, July 25, 1865.

[5] Ibid., April 18, 1866, citing N. Y. Post.

people had long frequented Cape May on the southern New Jersey coast. After the war it came to have a summer population of about 15,000 persons. Its broad, hard strand, upon which carriages could be driven at low tide and upon which the crowd sat or walked to watch the bathers "frolic in the breakers," caused many to regard it as "one of the most beautiful and satisfactory watering places" in America.[1] Atlantic City was new. It was the "excursion train" resort. The poor arrived there packed in cars like cattle till they were "purple in the face." The city was "all sand" and as yet unfashionable.[2]

In New York the clerk or shopkeeper who wished a day's recreation might go down to Coney Island by boat or by one or the other of two railroads, hire a bathing dress in a shed erected upon the beach and, after an hour in the surf, enjoy a dinner of "roast clams."[3]

The rich thronged Long Branch, Newport and Saratoga. Long Branch could be approached earlier only by boat at high water on the Shrewsbury River. Now a railroad brought it within two and a half hours of New York. There were a dozen or more hotels in the place, some of them large in size. Pavilions sat upon the bluffs and overlooked the sea. Stairways led down the bank, which was crumbling before the tides, to the steep and narrow beach. A bell in every room to summon the servants, gas, introduced in a large hotel like the United States in 1866 for the first time, and the assurance that a guest would be lodged without a strange bedfellow were advantages to be enjoyed for about $5 a day.[4]

Newport, "cool yet with an Italian warmth and dreaminess in the atmosphere," quiet and respectable in its age, was the summer seat of a more solid aristocracy. But its cottages were for hire to those who were ready to pay for their use, and its hotels were filled with pleasure-loving people drawn from all ranks of moneyed society.[5]

[1] N. Y. Tribune, June 25, 1866; Phila. Ledger, Aug. 21, 1865.
[2] N. Y. Tribune, June 25, 1866.   [3] Ibid., July 11, 1865.
[4] Ibid., June 25 and 29, 1866.
[5] Ibid., July 4, 1865, and June 25, 1866.

It was at Saratoga Springs that visitors found the "wealthiest men, the handsomest women, the finest horses, the most costly equipages, the grandest dresses and the best living." [1] The village was old; its streets were wide; its houses were shaded by venerable elms. Mineral waters gushed from the earth. The Congress Spring was sold in 1865 for $310,000. [2] Several great rambling caravansaries of wood, the United States, the Union, Congress Hall, and the Clarendon, were found here. The Union would accommodate 1400 guests and it was declared to be the largest hotel in the country. All had broad piazzas and enormous dining-rooms and ball-rooms. One rich man went there with his family; others followed him until the place became the capital for the entire shoddy aristocracy of America. They sipped the waters,[3] played croquet on the lawns and billiards in the hotels, bowled, rode, drove their spanking teams, ate, drank, dressed, looked at one another with critical eyes and danced. The dinner from two to five a visitor found to be a mere "exhibition" of loud-voiced men and their over-adorned wives and daughters. The "hop" after tea at night, which gave place once or twice a week to a "grand ball," called for new sartorial displays. Women had frocks for every hour of the day. Their immodest tilting cages of hoops, their tightly laced waists, their powdered and painted faces led to much homily to the disadvantage of the age. While the races were in progress jockeys, pickpockets and gaming men joined the throng. Pools were sold and much money was laid upon the fleetness of horses' feet. It was New York "transplanted and intensified," one said, "because the frivolity and silliness that fill a year in New York are crowded into two months at Saratoga." [4]

[1] Saratoga corr., N. Y. Tribune, Aug. 11, 1865.

[2] Phila. Ledger, Aug. 21, 1865.

[3] John G. Saxe described the difference between Newport and Saratoga —

> "— 'Tis the easiest matter
> At once to distinguish the two.
> At one you go into the water;
> At t'other it goes into you."

[4] N. Y. Tribune, June 13, 1865, June 25, Aug. 6, 11 and 20, 1866.

Such methods of life, such moral views had for their fruit fraud, forgery and defalcation. The poor who would grow rich suddenly were tempted and fell. Oil companies came into the courts. Several of the many swindling schemes of assembling capital for drilling petroleum wells were exposed. A man named Windsor stole $300,000 from the Mercantile Bank in New York, built himself a palace on Staten Island and fled to Europe.[1] An assistant cashier robbed a bank in New Haven, Conn., of $100,000. He was apprehended in Liverpool and brought home for punishment.[2] An internal revenue collector in Ohio, who earlier had been the treasurer of the state, speculated, lost public moneys which he had misappropriated and committed suicide.[3] Mumford, a New York gold operator, paid his debts in checks on funds which he did not possess, failed and underwent arrest.[4] Jenkins, a sober-sided paying teller in the Phœnix Bank in New York, abstracted money for a period of two years before the discovery of his crime. About $300,000 had disappeared. At first he gave his filchings to a man named Earle for use in stock speculations, then he lavished it upon "pretty waiter girls" and other Cyprians of the underworld. Earle killed himself with a penknife in a police station and Jenkins went to Sing Sing.[5]

But the crowning iniquity in this series of crimes in 1865 was the theft and dissipation of about $4,000,000 by Edward Ketchum, the 25-year-old son of Morris Ketchum, a wealthy banker of New York. He had abstracted securities belonging to his father's firms and to customers dealing with those firms, and forged "gold checks" or clearing-house certificates. Prices of stocks fell from five to eight points. Speculators enjoying their ease at Saratoga hurried back to town on calls from their brokers for "margin" money.[6] Ketchum was pursued by the police who in a fortnight found him in New York; he had never

[1] N. Y. Herald, Aug. 12, 1865.
[2] Ibid., Aug. 16, 1865.
[3] Phila. Ledger, Aug. 16, 1865, citing Cincinnati Commercial.
[4] N. Y. Herald, Aug. 15 and 17, 1865.
[5] Ibid., for Aug. 11, 1865, and succeeding days.
[6] Phila. Ledger, Aug. 18, 1865; N. Y. Herald, Aug. 17, 1865.

left the city. His father was obliged to sell his fine house on Fifth Avenue to pay the reprobate's debts,[1] and the young man after trial upon one count of his several indictments was sentenced to four years and a half in prison. He was taken to Sing Sing and set to work making shoes.[2]

Four men went into an old man's office in New York in broad daylight. While he was engaged in conversation they took bonds valued at $1,500,000 out of a safe, and, when pursued, demanded $100,000 and immunity from punishment for returning them.[3] A month later the Merchants' National Bank in Washington failed. One of the directors, a stock speculator in Baltimore, had withdrawn about $800,000 for his own use.[4] A man named Ross in New York, by borrowing money on fraudulent stock certificates and forging checks, mulcted several firms of about a half million dollars and made his escape to Aspinwall.[5]

Within a few days, in March, 1867, bank defalcations by trusted employees were announced in Baltimore, Boston, Newton, Mass., Pittsburgh and Hudson, N. Y.[6]

So it was from month to month and year after year. In the spring of 1866 at the time of the fall of Culver's banks in the oil regions there were several failures and suspensions in New York. A banking firm in Rochester, N. Y., closed its doors; a "run" was started on all the banks in that city.[7] "Croakers" believed this to be "the beginning of the end." [8] Secretary McCulloch had said that "a brief period of seductive prosperity" would be followed by "widespread bankruptcy and disaster." [9] But the end was yet as far away as 1873.

---

[1] Phila. Ledger, Nov. 9, 1865.
[2] N. Y. Tribune, Jan. 1, 1866; Phila. Ledger, Jan. 2, 1866.
[3] Phila. Ledger, April 5, 1866.   [4] Ibid., May 7, 1866.
[5] Ibid., May 3 and 4, 1866.   [6] Ibid., March 5, 1867.
[7] Ibid., April 9, 1866.   [8] Ibid., April 6, 1866.

[9] Speech at Fort Wayne, Ind., reported in Phila. Ledger, Oct. 16, 1865. Cf. his report for 1865, House Ex. Doc., 39th Cong., 1st sess., no. 3, pp. 6, 8, 9.

CHAPTER V

BEYOND THE MISSISSIPPI

FROM sea to sea, and from Canada in the North to the borders of Mexico, the United States comprised 3,025,000 square miles of territory, of which 2,265,625 square miles, or upwards of 1,450,000,000 acres, more than two-thirds of the national area, had been included in the public domain. Up to the year 1860, 441,000,000 acres in this great landed estate had been surveyed and 394,000,000 acres had been sold or granted away by the government; 1,056,000,000 acres, therefore, remained, subject to later sale and distribution.[1] Here stretching away to the Rocky Mountains, over their crest, down into the Salt Lake valley and across the Sierra Nevada range to the Pacific Ocean lay an empire three times as large as the entire country had been when it gained its independence from Great Britain.[2]

In charge of the work of making this empire ready for settlement, in 1865, were nine surveyor-generals stationed in the various "land states and territories" — at St. Paul, Dubuque, Leavenworth, Yankton, Denver, Santa Fé, San Francisco, Eugene City, Oregon, and Olympia in Washington Territory.

The duty of these officers was to precede, or at any rate keep abreast of the advancing columns of emigration. First, the Indian titles were to be extinguished. The making of treaties with the tribes, their removal to reservations out of the path of progress, their conciliation by the distribution of presents and annuities, a work which now and again was interrupted by earnest warfare, taxing the military power of the government,

---

[1] Senate Ex. Doc., 36th Cong., 2d sess., vol. i, Report of Commr. of General Land Office for 1860, p. 65; cf. his report for 1866, p. 367.

[2] Report of Commr. of General Land Office for 1860, p. 49.

were the order of the day. Then the men with axes, compasses and chains were sent out to plat the country into townships (six miles square), sections (containing one square mile of 640 acres), half sections and quarter sections. Monuments were erected to mark the lines. The work was begun in Ohio; it had continued until the surveyors before the outbreak of the war were well beyond the Mississippi. In Ohio, Indiana, Illinois and Michigan it had been entirely, in Iowa and Wisconsin practically completed, and now, at the war's end, was proceeding along the northwestern lines of settlement into Minnesota, and along the central lines into the eastern parts of Nebraska and Kansas. Farther west, except upon the Pacific coast, the surveyors had established their meridians and platted the lands only at a few isolated points.[1]

Some 132,000,000 acres, already made ready for settlement by the government, remained undisposed of in September, 1865.[2] About 815,000,000 acres were yet to be surveyed. Altogether a billion acres, approximately one-half the entire area of the republic, awaited distribution and use, a territory large enough to form forty states of the size of Ohio. If this great wilderness were populated as densely as England it would furnish homes for 539,000,000 men, women and children.[3] Millions of acres in Wisconsin and Michigan, much of it covered with valuable timber, the rich wheat lands of the valley of the Red River of the North in Minnesota, and no less than 4,500,000 acres of deep, black prairie in Iowa were still among the treasures held by the government to be transferred, almost for the asking, to industrious men willing to use the axe and the plough.

After they had been surveyed it was the custom of the President of the United States to issue a proclamation offering the lands at public sale. Those which could not be distributed

[1] Map of the Public Land States and Territories accompanying Report of Commr. of General Land Office, House Ex. Doc., 39th Cong., 1st sess., no. 1.

[2] Ibid., p. 5.

[3] Report of Commr. of General Land Office for 1866–7, p. 397.

in this manner were then subject to private entry at the land offices at an established minimum price of $1.25 an acre, unless they fell within the limits of railway or similar grants, when the price was $2.50 an acre. Furthermore a settler might preempt a farm of 160 acres, *i.e.* a quarter section, in any part of the public domain not set aside for town sites or as saline or mineral lands, whether it yet had or had not been surveyed, if he were a citizen of the United States, twenty-one years of age, or had filed a notice of his intention to become a citizen, and would swear that he did not own 320 acres elsewhere, on the condition that he would build a house upon it and live there in person. At the end of a year he might pay for his farm at the minimum rate and take title to the property.[1]

But even this policy, as liberal as it seemed to be, put unnecessary obstacles in the way of the settler in the view of many men. Uncle Sam was "rich enough" to give every one a farm,[2] and to encourage the movement into the West, he should do so. The Homestead bill came forward in many Congresses, to encounter the opposition of the South, since it would be an influence to extend the area of "free" territory, and destroy the balance of power between the sections. At last, in 1860, the measure passed both Houses, to meet the veto of President Buchanan. As soon as possible after the Republican party gained control of the national government, in 1862, the bill was brought up again and made into law. It provided that any person above twenty-one years of age, a citizen of the United States, or one who had declared his intention of ac-

---

[1] Act of Sept. 4, 1841; system described in Report of Commr. of General Land Office for 1868, p. 93.

[2] The words of a popular song which began:

"Of all the mighty nations in the East or in the West
This glorious Yankee nation is the greatest and the best;
We have room for all creation and our banner is unfurled,
Here's a general invitation to the people of the world.

Come along, come along, make no delay,
Come from every nation, come from every way;
Our lands are broad enough, don't be alarmed,
For Uncle Sam is rich enough to give us all a farm."

quiring citizenship, might occupy and use a piece of surveyed land not exceeding 160 acres, and at the completion of five years' residence upon it, by the payment of $10 to meet the cost of entry, become its owner.[1] The policy was new, and the law was an invitation to migration from the East and from Europe on a large scale. Horace Greeley, in the New York Tribune, was untiring in behalf of the West. He had urged its settlement at the earliest day. His "Go West, young man!" started many a clerk, mechanic, shopkeeper and small farmer into the Mississippi Valley, where, finding sea room for the first time, they were coming to be a vital power in the population. Now the Tribune urged soldiers returned from the war to take up Western homesteads.[2] Greeley warmly defended every policy calculated in his belief to upbuild and forward the interests of this section of the country. Men said that he was "wild" about the West, but its growth bore out his most extravagant prophecies. In the year ending June 30, 1865, 1,160,000 acres were entered under the homestead laws;[3] in 1866, 1,892,000 acres, with cash sales of only 388,000 acres;[4] in 1867, 1,788,000 acres;[5] and in 1868, 2,328,923 acres.[6]

In addition to the preëmption and other sales and the homestead entries there were swamp lands to be distributed to the states for drainage and reclamation; and the grants in benefit of railroads, wagon roads, ship canals and internal improvements, for the new agricultural and mechanic colleges endowed from the public domain during the war,[7] for old soldiers as bounties for service, for the public schools (two sections in each township) when the territories became states, for government buildings, for the Indians, for public parks, as, for example, the Yosemite and Big Tree reservations in California in 1864.

---

[1] Act of May 20, 1862, chap. lxxv.

[2] N. Y. Tribune, July 13, 1865.

[3] Report of Sec. of Interior, House Ex. Doc., 39th Cong., 1st sess., no. 1, p. 5.

[4] Ibid., 39th Cong., 2d sess., no. 1, p. 375.

[5] Ibid., 40th Cong., 2d sess., no. 1, p. 31.

[6] Ibid., 40th Cong., 3d sess., no. 1, p. 3.

[7] Act of July 2, 1862.

In the years immediately following the war the public lands were being sold and granted away at the rate of from 5,000,000 to 7,000,000 acres annually.

The management of this enormous domain became one of the most important branches of national administration. Already there were plans for irrigating the inarable tracts, for conserving and replanting the forests, for protecting the timber from incendiaries and thieves.

Beyond the farming frontier, which extended, roughly, from Minnesota through Iowa and the eastern portions of Nebraska and Kansas down into Texas, were cattle grazing on the public lands, herds of buffaloes which when running made the earth tremble, antelope bounding about with agile limb, deer, elk, prairie dogs in their burrows, — which every traveller said that they shared with the rattlesnake and the owl, — flocks of prairie chickens, killed indiscriminately and destined soon to become extinct,[1] the Indians who made this their hunting-ground and now and again attacked the westwardly moving van of white settlement, the soldiers at the various military posts, the miners for gold and silver in the Rocky Mountains, the Mormons farther west around the Great Salt Lake, miners again in the Sierra Nevada range, and the fringe of civilization upon the coast of the Pacific Ocean. Into this land railroads were pointing their heads; through it telegrams sped over the transcontinental wires, fast stage-coaches conveyed passengers and the mails, and freight and emigrant trains proceeded at the ox's pace.

The "Great American Desert," a dry sandy Sahara which for long had marked the map of the United States, was being pressed into constantly narrowing bounds. Yet still at a point about 150 miles west of the Missouri, so it was believed, the good land came to an end. General Pope, in command here after the war, said that a belt never less than 500 miles in width, running to the base of the Rocky Mountains and extending from Canada

---

[1] For sale sometimes within forty miles of Chicago at 37½ cents a dozen and so abundant at times in New York that tons of them rotted in the hands of the dealers. — N. Y. Tribune, June 26, 1865.

to the Mexican border, was "beyond the reach of agriculture." It was a region of high, timberless plains. The few streams were usually dry. Nothing but buffalo grass, sage-brush, cactus and the prickly pear would grow in such a soil. The country was "utterly unproductive and uninhabitable by civilized man." It must "always remain a great uninhabited desert." [1] General Sherman said, too, after passing over these plains, that they would "never be filled with inhabitants capable of self-government and self-defence"; at best the country could be but "a vast pasture field, open and free to all for the rearing of herds of horses, mules, cattle and sheep." [2]

Separated from the East by this desert belt were the rapidly rising mining settlements in the Rocky Mountains. The gold excitement at Pike's Peak in western Kansas had reached its height just before the Civil War. Many gulches were explored, and wherever ore was found camps were established by the prospectors. Denver became an entrepôt for the settlements. After the Southern members had departed from Congress to form their separate Confederacy the long and bitter dispute about Kansas was brought to an end, and that territory of disturbed history was admitted as the thirty-fourth state. [3] The western portion was joined with parts of Utah and Nebraska to form a new territory, which was called Colorado. [4] At the same time the great territory of Nebraska was broken up. What lay north of the 43d parallel, extending from the Red River of the North to the Rocky Mountains, was organized as a new territory under the name of Dakota. [5]

Emigrants continued to arrive in Colorado from "the states." The census-takers of 1860 found its population to be 34,000, and the people, though it so lately had become a territory, began to covet the dignity of statehood. But a fire swept through Denver in 1863. In the following year the dry creek,

---

[1] General Pope in House Ex. Doc., 39th Cong., 1st sess., no. 76, p. 2; cf. General Dodge in O. R., series i, vol. xlviii, part i, p. 341, — "These plains are not susceptible of cultivation or settlement."

[2] Report of Secretary of War for 1866, p. 20.

[3] Act of Jan. 29, 1861.

[4] Act of Feb. 28, 1861.   [5] Act of March 2, 1861.

in and near which many had built their cabins, suddenly became a torrent and much property was destroyed. Grasshoppers, a pest of the prairie states, extended their ravages to the fertile and green parts of the Western territories.[1] At one place they obscured the sun.[2] General Sully, in the Indian service on the Upper Missouri, with somewhat more feeling than truth, said that they were eating his tents and wagon covers, and even attacked his soldiers while asleep.[3] They swept through Colorado, leaving a path of destruction behind them. The mining industry collapsed. Speculators in New York had financed it. Of eighty mines in one district only fifteen, in 1866, were in operation.[4] Fine mills stood guard over holes in the ground which contained no workable ore.[5] Millions of dollars had been sunk, and Colorado was discredited before the world. Indian risings made communication with the East unsafe. It was said that the population of the territory had actually declined during the war, though soon again it was advancing rapidly.

When Greeley had visited Denver in 1859, it was yet only a place of Indian lodges and a couple of hundred log cabins with mud roofs and earth floors.[6] There were not a half dozen glass windows or ten white women in the town. But in 1865, in spite of fire, flood and other misfortunes, it was thought to have a population of 4000. If every fifth house were a whiskey saloon, and every tenth house a brothel, or gambling hell, or both in one, as the English visitor, W. Hepworth Dixon, declared,[7] it was also true that the town had banks, schools, two daily newspapers, pleasantly furnished homes, stores well stocked with merchandise and a branch United States mint.

[1] They fell upon gardens, fields and trees in Kansas, Colorado, Utah, Texas, Iowa, in the valleys of Montana, in Dakota and Oregon. — O. R., series i, vol. xlviii, part ii. p. 1124; Phila. Ledger, July 19, 1865, Aug. 6, Sept. 16 and Nov. 4, 1867.

[2] Phila. Ledger, Aug. 22, 1868.

[3] O. R., series i, vol. xlviii, part ii, p. 897.

[4] Report of Secretary of Interior for 1866, p. 465.

[5] It was a "colossal tomb of buried hopes." — A. K. McClure in N. Y. Tribune, May 31, 1867; cf. ibid., Dec. 6, 1866.

[6] A. D. Richardson, Beyond the Mississippi, p. 186.

[7] New America, p. 96.

A building lot on a desirable corner had been sold for $12,000. A "glorious Alpine view" was one of the chief possessions of the place, said Bayard Taylor, who visited it in 1866. Even women, in spite of the loneliness and privation of the life which they must lead, felt the wild charm of the country no less than the men, and were resolved to remain here rather than return to their old homes in the East.[1]

Up to the end of June, 1864, the Colorado mines had sent nearly $10,000,000 of gold to the United States mints.[2] Silver, too, had been found, and the deposits of coal and iron in the southern part of the territory gave promise of a rich industrial development. Ten thousand people were settled in Central City, Black Hawk and other mining towns in the Clear Creek Canyon. Here were two more daily newspapers; stage and telegraph lines ran down to Denver.[3]

Although General Pope and other military commanders of the United States, assigned to service in this country, had said that the people who were crowding into the mining districts of the Rocky Mountains must always draw their food supply from the Mississippi and Missouri valleys,[4] Colorado soon gave convincing proof that she could support herself. In the mountains were bowls of rich meadow land called parks. Cattle and sheep, said Governor Evans, would thrive here the year through. General Babcock, while on his tour of inspection of military posts in 1866, found grains growing luxuriantly in these fertile depressions among the mountains.[5] General Sherman, after his visit in connection with the performance of his military duties, was brought to appreciate the arable value even of the plains. Near Denver he saw farmers irrigating their lands with the clear, cold water from the mountains; they were raising wheat, corn, oats, vegetables equal to any of the East, to be sold at prices far below what they would have

[1] N. Y. Tribune, July 30, 1866.

[2] Much higher estimates of the whole production of the territory were given. — Bowles, Across the Continent, p. 39.

[3] A. D. Richardson, in N. Y. Tribune, June 26, 1865.

[4] House Ex. Doc., 39th Cong., 1st sess., no. 76, p. 2.

[5] Ibid., 2d sess., no. 20, p. 4.

been if hauled by oxen over the roads from the Missouri River.[1]
He found settlements at the foot of the mountains all the
way down to Pueblo on the Arkansas River. The entire valley
of this river, he said, could be ditched and watered.[2] It could
be made as productive as India, Egypt and Mexico.

In Colorado, in the years 1865 and 1866, 400,000 acres were
taken up by settlers for agricultural uses.[3] In the summer of
1866 the new territory was producing its own butter at fifty
cents, cheese at forty cents, potatoes, wheat, corn and oats at
five cents, beef and other meats at ten to twenty cents a
pound. These prices had been twice as high in 1865.[4] A
large agricultural fair at Denver in 1866 impressively directed
attention to the fertility of the soil.[5] Though yet no fruit
had been produced this fact was due only to ignorance of the
methods which should be used in watering the trees.[6] In 1867
it was believed that the production of breadstuffs was equal to
their consumption in the territory.

During the war some Colorado miners, while travelling toward the Deer Lodge valley, lost their way. They found gold
at a place which they called Bannack, the name of an Indian
tribe living in the vicinity. Soon 2000 persons — prospectors
from the exhausted gulches in other parts of the West, border
desperadoes and Southern guerrillas — were settled here in log
cabins on a crooked street in a narrow chasm formed by Grass-
hopper Creek, an affluent of the Missouri. But the discovery
of richer diggings east of this point started a stampede thither.
At first called Varina, in honor of Mrs. Jefferson Davis, and in
a little while Virginia City, this town grew so fast that in 1866
it had come to have a population of 10,000 souls. It was said
then that in the three years past upwards of $16,000,000 in
gold had been taken from Alder Gulch.[7] The log huts set in a

[1] House Ex. Doc., 39th Cong., 2d sess., no. 23, p. 13.
[2] Ibid., p. 17.   [3] Ibid., no. 92, p. 5.
[4] Report of Surveyor-General in Report of Secretary of Interior
for 1866, p. 465.
[5] S. Seymour, Incidents of a Trip, p. 28.
[6] Report of Surveyor-General for 1865, p. 104.
[7] Montana corr., N. Y. Tribune, March 17, 1866.

ravine and running up the hillsides gave place to granite buildings. Men sent home for their wives and children. Two
churches were built.

In 1861, when Dakota was formed, these mountains and
valleys were included in that great territory, and on March 3,
1863, they were swept into a still newer territory called Idaho,
which was made to extend from Oregon east to the meridian
now marking the western boundary of North Dakota,
South Dakota and Nebraska. But the mining development
was so rapid that a year later the district was separately organized as Montana,[1] and Virginia City became its capital.
Emigrants moved west from Minnesota. Already in June,
1862, Captain James L. Fisk had led a northern overland
expedition out of St. Paul and had succeeded in making a wagon
road to Montana. Two more parties of settlers under his escort followed this one, and in the summer of 1865 he was in
New York organizing a fourth emigrant train. He said that
he had more than 2000 persons ready to accompany him from
St. Cloud.[2]

Some of these pioneers from Minnesota founded the town of
Helena, set amid majestic mountain scenery, 125 miles north
of Virginia City. Not a single cabin had stood upon this spot
in 1864; a year later it contained several hundred houses. The
miners who were as fluid as quicksilver had hurried to this new
place. In the year 1865 it was stated that, at a low estimate,
gold worth $16,000,000 had been taken out of Montana.[3] It
was thought that the production in 1867 would be $20,000,000;
only California would have a greater yield.[4] The territory,
said A. K. McClure, who visited it, was "one vast field of
bewildering wealth." [5]

The beautiful valleys of the Gallatin, the Jefferson and the
Madison, which united their waters here in the mountains to

[1] Act of May 26, 1864.
[2] N. Y. Tribune, June 15, 1865; see the pamphlet he issued in this
year for distribution to intending emigrants; also N. P. Langford,
Vigilante Days and Ways, vol. i, p. 230.
[3] N. Y. Tribune, March 17, 1866.
[4] Ibid., Aug. 3, 1867.   [5] Ibid., Aug. 26, 1867.

form the Missouri, were soon occupied by industrious graziers and husbandmen. The lands were planted with wheat. Sheep and cattle fed over ground which a year or two earlier had been trod only by the foot of the savage. Better beef and mutton, travellers from the East said, they had never eaten. The streams were filled with fish; wild game abounded. There was timber for building purposes and coal was at hand for fuel.[1] It was supposed already in 1867 that the people were self-supporting, and that, like the pioneers in Colorado, they had become independent of the East in the matter of a food supply.[2] In the summer of 1865 it was said that the territory, though but three years had elapsed since the first white settlements were made within its borders, contained 50,000 inhabitants.[3]

Behind the mountains in an arid, alkaline plain lay the settlements formed by the Latter Day Saints. Their colony was a semi-socialistic and proprietary, ecclesiastical commonwealth. Driven beyond the mountains, this body of religious fanatics had established their homes beside the Great Salt Lake. Here they indulged their polygamous practices and still, more or less openly, defied the government of the United States. There had been 40,000 people in Utah in 1860; now, after the war, the leaders of the church boasted 100,000 inhabitants. A few Gentiles made their homes among the Mormons, and the actual number of persons in 166 settlements ruled by the bishops and elders was probably, in fact, about 75,000. The spread of the teachings of the church was attempted by missionaries sent into the East and to Europe, and the population was increasing at a steady pace. Brigham Young held this curious community in the "hollow of his hand." He sent a son to Liverpool to direct the movements of his agents in England and on the Continent. Many poor and credulous people, numbering perhaps from 3000 to 5000 in a year, were put aboard ships and sent to America to strengthen the colonies in Utah. Often their passage money was advanced to them to rest as a lien

[1] House Ex. Doc., 39th Cong., 2d sess., no. 23, p. 53.
[2] N. Y. Tribune, Aug. 3 and 26, 1867.
[3] Ibid., June 15 and Oct. 28, 1865.

against their services as laborers after they should arrive in their new homes. These recruits came principally from England, Germany and Scandinavia, but many other lands were represented in Young's theocratic state. He told visitors who halted on the overland journey to hear him preach, in 1865, that he could call up fifty men in the audience seated before him to deliver sermons in as many different tongues.[1]

Salt Lake City itself was built on spacious lines and presented an attractive appearance to the transcontinental traveller. It was the most considerable place between the Missouri River and San Francisco. Possibly 20,000 people dwelt here. The town was laid out into squares of ten acres, and these were subdivided into lots containing one and a quarter acres each, except in the business district. Water flowed through the streets. The adobe houses, with vine-covered trellises, were surrounded by waving orchards. One entire square of ground was occupied by Young's seraglios, the schools for his children, his business offices, etc.; while another, near by, contained the Tabernacle, about to be replaced by a new building, in which Young and the other heads of the church preached to the people; the Bowery, a huge arbor thatched with green boughs for use as an assembly room in summer time; and the foundations of an uncompleted stone temple.

Young, the supreme temporal as well as spiritual head of this community, had amassed a large fortune. His police maintained good order in the town. No whiskey was sold, no gambling was allowed and when the miners came in to spend the winter, they were compelled to lead circumspect lives. He taught the people to work early and late, to live simply and to save their money. He discouraged mining for the precious metals; for every dollar gained by this means, he said, four dollars were expended. When the Mormons came upon this dry plain, Jim Bridger, the old Wahsatch trapper and scout, who lived inside a stockade on the western side of the mountains (later the site of Fort Bridger), declared that he would pay $1000 to any man who could raise an ear of corn down yonder in that

[1] N. Y. Tribune, July 14, 1865.

salt valley. But the Mormons irrigated the sand, and their
crops were large. Grains, fruits, vegetables grew prolifically.
The desert rejoiced and blossomed as the rose. The emigrants
stopped on their way to the Pacific coast to buy food at high
prices. There were a hundred flouring mills in Utah.[1] The
miners in Colorado and Montana, before they were able to
produce their own, found here a valuable source of supplies.
In 1866 Montana paid more than a million dollars to the
Mormons for flour alone.[2] They had a surplus of butter, bacon
and dried peaches. Their women spun yarn and knitted socks;
curriers tanned hides and cobblers made boots and shoes.

Young had built a theatre in which plays were given by young
men and women drawn from the Mormon population. The
edifice would seat 1800 persons. Not west of New York, it
was said, was there a building so large, barring the opera-houses
in Cincinnati and Chicago, as this one rising here hundreds of
miles from a steamboat or a railroad. Except for the system
of concubinage, which he aimed to justify by revelation and
appeals to Holy Writ, Young's experiments as a politician and
business manager could be viewed with a certain amount of
approval. The president of the church himself had, it was
supposed, some thirty wives and fifty or more children.[3] Perhaps not one in four Mormons was a polygamist, but plural
marriage was openly defended, as it had been from the beginning, by the leaders of the strange sect.

The anti-polygamy law which Congress had passed in 1862 [4]
Young declared to be unconstitutional. It remained unen-
forceable because the witnesses were Mormons and the cases
must be tried before Mormon juries.[5] Such territorial officers
as were elective were Mormons, though the people generally

[1] Bowles, Across the Continent, p. 94.
[2] House Ex. Doc., 39th Cong., 2d sess., no. 23, p. 52.
[3] Salt Lake City, where "nearly all the pretty Mormon women
marry Young," said Artemus Ward; where "all the Saints are sin-
ners and all the Jews are Gentiles," said another wag.
[4] Act of July 1, 1862.
[5] A. D. Richardson, in N. Y. Tribune, July 31, 1865; House Ex.
Doc., 39th Cong., 2d sess., no. 20, p. 7.

refused to become citizens of the United States and could not vote. A body of soldiers stationed at Camp Douglas, three miles from Salt Lake City, established by Colonel (afterward General) Connor, early in the war, to subdue the sympathies of the people for the Southern Confederacy, quietly observed the course of events.[1] The day for anything like active resistance to the authority of the government had passed. Congress contented itself, as the opportunity came, with plans for reducing the size of Utah Territory, in order to bring Mormonism within a narrower sphere.

As a beginning a corner was taken to form the territory of Colorado, and a few days later, by act of March 2, 1861, the entire western portion was cut off, to be given a separate organization and called Nevada. The discovery of enormously rich veins of silver on the Comstock Ledge had drawn thousands of miners into western Utah. Immediately after the war it was computed that already upwards of $60,000,000 of silver bullion had been taken out of Nevada, and the yield was at the rate of $20,000,000 annually. Virginia City in this rich district was five years old. The great Gould and Curry mine had a mill of 80 stamps costing the owners nearly a million dollars. In 1865 it had paid its stockholders $4,000,000 in dividends.[2] Virginia City, including Gold Hill and Silver City near by, contained not less than 18,000 people. It had theatres, churches, three daily newspapers, four daily stages and three telegraph wires to the Pacific coast, one daily stage and one wire to the East. A new silver-mining camp in the Reese River country, called Austin, had gained in two years 3000 or 4000 inhabitants. Productive farms and good grazing grounds were found in the Humboldt, Carson, Washoe, Truckee and other valleys.

Much was said as to the future prospects of the territory. The need of loyal states which would ratify the Thirteenth Amendment to the Constitution of the United States and permit Congress to carry out its policies with reference to the

---

[1] W. A. Linn, The Story of the Mormons, p. 543; H. H. Bancroft, History of Utah, pp. 611-2.

[2] Bowles, Across the Continent, p. 148.

South [1] led in 1864 to the passage of enabling acts for Nevada, Colorado and Nebraska.[2] Nevada adopted a constitution and was promptly made into a state. Further to reduce the sphere of Mormon influence its size was increased in 1866 by the annexation of a strip of territory on its eastern border, covering one degree of longitude earlier included in Utah,[3] and in the next year it was ready, though its population was probably not above 30,000, to absorb all of Utah, if Congress would agree to merge the Mormon territory in the Gentile state.[4]

To the north lay Idaho, another new territory, formed in 1863 to include the eastern part of Washington and the western part of Dakota.[5] When Montana was organized in the following year, that quadrilateral belt lying south, later to become Wyoming, was returned to Dakota, and Idaho assumed practically its present boundaries. A gold miners' stampede in 1861 brought many people into the mountains along the course of the Snake River, and Lewiston in the north, accessible from the Columbia in small steamboats, a new town filled with prospectors with whom were mingled many gamblers and thieves, became the seat of government. The mining excitement had spread to a district in which was located a new army post called Fort Boisé, on the Boisé River, and Boisé City was founded near by. To this trading town on a treeless plain the capital was soon taken. Seventy miles south in the southwestern part of the territory lay the rich Owyhee mining district. Here were Boonville, Ruby City and Silver City set upon metalliferous ground. The country was beset with hostile Indians, and it was one of the most inaccessible portions of the United States to which men yet had determined to carry quartz mills.

South of Nevada the territory of New Mexico had been

---

[1] Cf. C. A. Dana, Recollections of the Civil War, pp. 174–5.

[2] The acts for Nevada and Colorado were passed on March 21, 1864, and for Nebraska on April 19, 1864.

[3] Act of May 5, 1866.

[4] N. Y. Nation, March 14, 1867.

[5] Act of March 3, 1863.

divided; in 1863 the western part, bordering upon California, was separately organized as Arizona.[1] Here were the marks of an ancient Indian civilization, and of the Spanish tide which at a later time had swept up from the south. Some of the tribes still were skilful potters; of native fibres they wove baskets which were impervious to water, and bright rugs. But, the Apaches, whose daily life was war, ran almost at will over the entire country to terrorize the settlements and to check their growth. For purposes of government the territory was divided into four counties which had come to contain several gold, silver and copper mining camps. Mexicans, speaking Spanish, mingled with prospectors from "the states." Arizona was distant ninety days by train from the Missouri by way of the Santa Fé trail, the overland route used before the war. From San Francisco it was approached through the ports near Los Angeles, or perhaps through Guaymas or some other harbor on the west coast of Mexico, where goods could be transferred to wagons for long journeys over the sand behind oxen. Again they were conveyed up the Gulf of California and into the Colorado River, which was found to be navigable for hundreds of miles. Steamers had been brought around from San Francisco; in 1867 eight were navigating this stream as far north as the dry plains south of Salt Lake.[2]

More than a half million people were settled beyond the Sierra Nevada Mountains on the Pacific coast. In 1860 California's population was nearly 400,000. It was still the land of gold miners. The yield of this metal was steadily large, but wealth was coming from many other sources. Climate and soil fitted the state to be one of the gardens of the world. Now that California had been found, said A. D. Richardson, "Jonah's gourd" had ceased to be "the symbol of miraculous growth."[3] In the northern counties the vegetation appertained to the temperate zone. Wheat literally sprang from the

[1] Act of Feb. 23, 1863.

[2] Adams's Report in N. Y. Tribune, April 5, 1867; cf. Laws of Arizona for 1864, p. 79; ibid. for 1865, p. 77; ibid. for 1866, p. 61.

[3] N. Y. Tribune, May 4, 1866.

earth. General Bidwell owned 900 acres in the Sacramento valley from which he gleaned 36,000 bushels, an average yield of forty b ishels for an acre.[1] In March, 1868, 89 vessels were on the sea bound from San Francisco to New York laden with this grain. The cargoes would attain a grand total of five million bushels.[2]

The grape was planted and a large export trade in wine was begun. Hock, claret, port and sherry, as well as brandy and champagne, were sent to New York and other cities. The Spanish fathers had planted vines around the missions on irrigated ground in the eighteenth century. After the gold excitement had spent itself in some degree, and when men of other interests had come to California, the culture was begun at several centres, particularly in Sonoma county. Rhenish vine dressers were brought from Europe to establish the industry on successful lines.[3] The yield in 1866 was 2,000,000 gallons, and in 1867, 3,500,000 gallons. The Alta California said that the state's vintage, within the lifetime of young men, would reach a total of 100,000,000 gallons annually.[4] The New York Tribune exhibited in its office in New York in 1866 a sugar beet, 55 pounds in weight, which had been grown in California. The mulberry was being planted for the production of silk. Louis Prevost in San José was gathering cocoons and making fine displays of native silk dress goods in the shop windows of San Francisco. The legislature was extending encouragement to the industry.[5] Other men sought to acclimate the tea plant of China.

In the southern part of the state oranges, lemons, limes, apricots, figs, pomegranates, English walnuts and almonds were growing in sub-tropical luxuriance. The olive tree was being planted. The crop would bring California "as much wealth," said the New York Tribune, "as all her mines of precious metals."[6]

[1] Bowles, Across the Continent, p. 170.
[2] Phila. Ledger, March 19, 1868.   [3] N. Y. Tribune, June 19, 1866.
[4] Phila. Ledger, Jan. 31 and Aug. 14, 1867.
[5] N. Y. Tribune, Aug. 23, 1867.   [6] Ibid., July 30, 1868.

San Francisco, which had had a population of 56,000 in 1860, had grown in size and importance during the war. It contained fine blocks of buildings of brick and stone. It had markets, churches, gaslights and street railroads, and four hotels which, travellers said, would have done credit to any city in the world. The harbor was full of ships. On the streets were seen faces from every part of the habitable globe. Riches suddenly acquired were freely spent, and the life of the place was noted for its ostentation and extravagance. A corn exchange was opened here in 1867. The city contained several foundries and shops for making engines, stamps, crushers and other machinery for the mines, thus saving the charges of transportation from the East. Ships of considerable tonnage were built in California yards. Wool from the sheep ranches was being made into blankets and various fabrics, for sale in the tributary mining camps. Now, in 1866, a cotton factory was in operation in Oakland, weaving brown sheetings for shipment to Honolulu and other places.[1] The chief financial institution, the Bank of California, had a capital of $2,000,000. Many large business houses were located in the city.

The California Steam Navigation Company plied the inland waters with its boats, and railroads ran from Sacramento, 150 miles from San Francisco by the Sacramento River, up toward the mountains, to Folsom and Placerville, where they met the stage-coaches from Nevada and the East. The Pacific Mail Steamship Company traded with Panama, and now, having secured a government subsidy, with Asia. In 1861 this line had had in its service but eleven comparatively small steamers; in 1868 its fleet consisted of thirty-three ships of large size, while four more were on the ways and would soon be completed. It was a memorable event when several hundred merchants sat down to dinner at the Occidental Hotel, under the chairmanship of Governor Low, on the last day of the year 1866, to speed the *Colorado*, the first ship of this line, sailing the next day with the American mails for China and Japan. Crowds filled the piers and beaches, as she

[1] N. Y. Tribune, March 31, 1866.

made her way, amid the salutes of other ships and of the forts, out of the Golden Gate.[1] In 27¼ days she reached Shanghai; returning from Yokohama, three weeks out, with a cargo of teas, silks and other Asiatic merchandise. The first five voyages upon this line netted the company, so it was said, $30,000 each.[2]

For several years there had been a line of fast sailing packets to Honolulu. They made the trip in 12 or 15 days, bringing in sugar, molasses, coffee and whale oil, and taking back assorted merchandise. On September 5, 1867, the first ship on a new monthly steamer line to the Sandwich Islands sailed out of San Francisco harbor. Other ships ran up the coast to Portland and Vancouver; down the coast to Santa Barbara, to San Diego, and to San Pedro and Wilmington, the ports for Los Angeles, — through which passed much of the Arizona trade, and, in the winter months, when the mountain roads east of San Francisco were impassable for trains, large quantities of goods bound for Salt Lake, and even for Montana and Idaho by way of the Cayon Pass.[3]

But more wonderful to many was the great commercial organization built up by Wells, Fargo and Company, — "the ready companion of civilization," as Samuel Bowles called it, "the omnipresent, universal business agent of all the region from the Rocky Mountains to the Pacific coast." [4] The name upon a shingle raised over a cabin door was seen in every mining town. The company was at once banker, express and insurance agent, postman and messenger. It served a wild community in a dozen needful ways. Its armed men escorted treasure wagons to the coast. Its coaches carried passengers hither and thither over difficult roads.

Farther north, in Oregon, there were from 60,000 to 75,000 people, one-half or two-thirds of them settled on the rich, deep bottoms of the Willamette Valley. The wheat which was

---

[1] N. Y. Herald, Jan. 7, 1867.
[2] Report of Secretary of Interior for 1868, p. 166.
[3] N. Y. Tribune, March 31, 1866.
[4] Bowles, Across the Continent, p. 294.

grown here supplied many flour mills. Already a quarter of a
million dollars' worth of apples in a year were shipped out of
the state.[1] Timber was · abundant. Straight pieces, a yard
square and a hundred feet long, could be taken from the great
trees in the forests. Iron ore was found, and the first pig iron
to be manufactured in Oregon was exhibited in San Francisco
in 1867.[2] Sheep throve in the pastures. There was so much
wool in Oregon in 1865 that the growers held a convention and
resolved not to sell their product for less than 25 cents a pound.[3]
Woollen mills here, as in California, made cloth of a good
quality. Fish, especially the salmon, which twice a year
stemmed the powerful current of the Columbia River for more
than a thousand miles, were scooped up and cured for commerce. Not without its gold diggings, in the Rogue River
valley and elsewhere, yet the state clearly had resources of
more importance than its mines.

The principal city, Portland, on the Willamette, a few miles
from the point at which this river flows into the Columbia, was
already the home of 5000 people. At its wharves lay sailing
vessels from Hawaii, ships from San Francisco and river steamers. Thus by water Oregon could be approached from California, but there was a stage route in regular use from Sacramento (which had river communication with San Francisco)
a distance of 642 miles, traversed by the coaches in summer
time in less than a week.

The Oregon Steam Navigation Company was formed in 1861.
In 1865 it had come to own a fleet of twenty steamers. They
had carried 100,000 passengers, so it was said, and 60,000 tons
of goods during the four years of the war. This enterprising
corporation was opening the country to settlement as far as
the mountains. The boats ran on amid beautiful river scenery
to a series of rapids, or a cataract, where a railroad was found
to carry passengers and merchandise around the obstruction,
when the journey by water could be resumed. For a time
the head of navigation was Umatilla, then Wallula, and still

[1] N. Y. Tribune, Sept. 30, 1865.   [2] Ibid., Sept. 2, 1867.
[3] Phila. Ledger, July 29, 1865.

later White Bluffs. Here, after a wagon portage, which cut off a wide angle in the river, smooth water was met with again and boats could proceed as far as the Cariboo gold region in British Columbia, as well as out toward Montana.

Thus were the eastern parts of Washington Territory brought into communication with the world. In 1865 it was said that 2000 persons were settled in the Walla Walla valley. The farmers in this remote place in that year were importing flour for bread. Two years later they were shipping it down the Columbia to San Francisco. Although the population of Washington was sparse and scattered, settlements of size and promise were situated on the sinuous shores of Puget Sound. In 1865 Olympia, the capital, contained only 600 people. But in the forests of great trees, the sawmills, the lumber trade were prophecies of an early and rapid development of wealth. Vast fields of coal were found near the waters of the Sound, and here one day, it was said, the government would find the fuel for its Pacific fleet.[1]

Labor upon the Pacific coast was scarce and wages were high. Early in the history of California large bodies of coolies had been brought across the sea from China. Some 60,000 were now living in California, Nevada, Oregon, Idaho and Montana, by far the greater part, nearly 50,000, in California. They were adaptable, imitative, frugal and industrious. They were employed as house servants and laundrymen; in San Francisco, indeed, some mothers used them as child nurses. They worked in the woollen mills and in the vineyards. They cultivated vegetables and found their way into the mines, where they patiently gleaned gold in placers which had been abandoned by the white man. The "China boys" stood under the supervision of the Six Companies, who imported rice and other food for them to eat, and sent home the bodies of the dead. But the white workingmen already viewed with alarm the presence of so many clever and thrifty competitors settled in their midst. It was the politicians' opportunity, and it was eagerly embraced. Votes could be made at the expense of a people who were not

[1] Report of Secretary of Interior for 1865, p. 161.

enfranchised. Stump speeches to "greasers" and Irishmen and party platforms might ring with denunciations of the yellow hordes who, coming here, injured and degraded free American labor. One hostile law followed another in the California legislature. In the first place a Chinaman mining for gold must pay $4 a month for a license.[1] If he wished to fish for abalone, an industry in which this people were largely engaged, there was a tax of $4 a month by a law of 1860. In 1862 a head tax called a "police tax" of $2½ a month was laid on Chinese not paying other taxes to the state. The legislature had gone so far in 1858 as to prohibit any Chinaman from landing on California soil; the immigration was to be brought to an end at once. Sooner or later all these laws were found to be unconstitutional,[2] though, in the case of the miners' license law, not before it had largely benefited the treasury of the state. In twenty years, from 1850 to 1870, the government received $5,000,000 from the anti-Chinese taxes, one-half of its income from all sources during this period.[3]

So, too, was it elsewhere on the Pacific coast. In Oregon the Chinese miner's tax was $4 a quarter;[4] in Idaho $4 a month in 1864,[5] raised to $5 in 1866.[6] Washington Territory, following California, laid a "police tax" on Chinese of $6 per quarter per capita[7] which it reduced in 1866 to $16 a year.[8]

Many of the little yellow men were mobbed and driven away from the placers; scores of them were killed in the mountains by white ruffians and by the Indians.[9]

The rapid settlement of the Pacific coast, with the development in a few years of towns and cities, industries and civilized institutions, was largely attributable to the fact that the people were in communication by water with the rest of the world.

---

[1] Statutes of Cal. for 1853, p. 62.
[2] M. R. Coolidge, Chinese Immigration, p. 80.
[3] Ibid., pp. 36, 70.
[4] Laws of Oregon for 1866, p. 41.
[5] Laws of Idaho for 1864, p. 406.
[6] Ibid., for 1866, p. 174.
[7] Laws of Washington for 1863-4, p. 56.
[8] Ibid., for 1866, p. 115.   [9] N. Y. Tribune, April 27, 1866.

The way to the East by Panama was roundabout, long and expensive. It cost a passenger $350 to make the trip to New York and occupied nearly a month. The steamer service on the Atlantic side, until the "Vanderbilt Line" was taken over by the Pacific Mail in the autumn of 1865, was justly a subject of complaint. The trip by Nicaragua, if not quite so costly, was about as long and was made with still less comfort. Rates of carriage for merchandise were high. Nevertheless the advantages which were enjoyed by San Francisco, and the towns and farms within reach of that city, because of its water lines, as compared with the country lying between the Missouri and the Sierra Nevada range of mountains, were obvious to all men. For in this great space, beyond what aid could be obtained from the Missouri in the Montana trade, and from the Columbia and its tributaries by the Oregon Navigation Company's steamers, the people were wholly at the mercy of the stage-coaches and the bull and mule trains which patiently toiled along the roads.

Thus were the government supplies conveyed to the Indian agencies for distribution to the tribes, thus were the military posts provisioned, thus did the miners obtain food to eat and their tools and machinery. The principal route across the plains followed the course of the Platte River through Nebraska. It could be entered from any one of a dozen rising little towns on the Missouri, such as Kansas City, Leavenworth, which Bayard Taylor found to be "the liveliest and most thriving place" on the river;[1] Atchison, St. Joseph, Nebraska City in the southwestern corner of Nebraska Territory; Plattsmouth and Omaha.

The first railroad to reach the Missouri was the Hannibal and St. Joseph in 1859. "St. Joe," therefore, became the principal terminus for the stage-coaches and wagon trains until railway connections were established with Atchison. Then that town was the usual starting-point for travel into the West. When the census of 1860 was taken, not one of the Missouri River towns had a population of 10,000. All the roads from

[1] Ibid., June 30, 1866.

the east converged near Fort Kearney on the Platte River, and back and forth, past this post, proceeded perhaps ninety per cent of the overland trade with Colorado, Montana, Utah and California.[1]

The Platte Valley was followed to the forks of the river. At Julesburg, a village of dug-outs near a military post called Fort Sedgwick, in the northeastern corner of Colorado, the road divided again, the northern branch following the North Platte by Fort Laramie and the South Pass to Fort Bridger. This was the route taken by the telegraph line. The southern branch from Julesburg, on the other hand, ran along the valley of Lodge Pole Creek, through Cheyenne and Bridger's Passes, over the old "Cherokee Trail," joining the North Platte road beyond the mountains at Fort Bridger, in what was then Utah but is now Wyoming, from which place travel proceeded over a common route to Salt Lake.

From Julesburg a third road followed the South Platte to Denver, or before reaching that town turned up the valley of the Cache la Poudre, to the "Cherokee Trail," and passed on by Bridger's Pass to Salt Lake. The overland mail, after 1862, took one or the other of the southern routes.[2] Grass for the cattle in the trains, water for man and beast, wood for fuel were to be found on this line. It was "by far the best natural road from the Missouri River to the Pacific coast."[3]

The old Santa Fé trail in the south was little used as a route to the coast, although it was an essential highway to New Mexico, old Mexico and Texas. Two lines from the Missouri were joined at Fort Larned on the Arkansas River to pursue the valley of that stream to Fort Dodge, where again there was a division ; a shorter, called the Cimarron or "Dry" route, crossed and left the river, while a longer, by a hundred miles, but a

[1] General Sherman in Senate Ex. Doc., 40th Cong., 1st sess., no. 2, p. 2.

[2] General Pope's report, House Ex. Doc., 39th Cong., 1st sess., no. 76, pp. 5–6.

[3] O. R., series i, vol. xlviii, part i, pp. 341–2.

safer route ran by way of the Raton Pass. The two roads again came together in New Mexico.[1]

New routes were being sought ; Congress appropriated money to survey them and sent out soldiers to guard them. Freight carriers and emigrants tested them. To shorten the road to Denver, which was the destination of so many emigrants and so much merchandise, a line over which there had been some travel before the war was opened in Kansas. After running beside the Kansas River to Fort Riley it followed, beyond that post, the main Santa Fé road, as far as Fort Ellsworth. At this point it struck out along the Smoky Hill fork, crossed to the Big Sandy and reached Denver by a course which placed that active young mining camp only 600 miles from the Missouri. This was a saving of one hundred miles, as compared with the Platte route, for towns on the river south of St. Joseph.

The new road passed through a dry country. But springs had been found and elsewhere wells had been sunk so that water was now to be had at points not above fifteen and sometimes only eight miles apart.[2] The advocates of this line said that the alkali water on the Platte route killed the cattle going that way, that grass grew earlier in Kansas than farther north, wherefore freighters and emigrants could find here a longer season for travel.[3] On the other hand it was remarked that there was no military post on the Smoky Hill route west of Fort Ellsworth for a distance of 200 miles. The new road penetrated the Indian hunting grounds. Buffaloes and other wild animals were seen on every hand. The danger of attack was much greater than on the older and more frequented road.

At Denver the traveller going farther west must use the road which carried him north to the Platte route, or, when it should be ready, a new road, surveyed in the summer of 1865, by way of Middle Park, White River and the Uintah Valley over a well-wooded, well-watered grazing country inhabited by the

[1] House Ex. Doc., 39th Cong., 1st sess., no. 76, p. 6; O. R., series i, vol. xlvii, part i, p. 342; O. R., series iii, vol. v, p. 442.

[2] O. R., series i, vol. xlviii, part i, p. 342.

[3] N. Y. Tribune, Sept. 7, 1865.

Utes. The distance between Denver and Salt Lake by this way would be 200 miles less than over the Platte route.[1]

To reach Montana there was a road from St. Paul, and the towns on the Mississippi River, across Dakota under the protection of a northern line of forts to the Missouri, and up the valley of that river to the mountains; a road, too, farther south, by way of Sioux Falls, to Fort Pierre and, by the valley of the Big Cheyenne, north of the Black Hills to the Powder River — neither one nor the other safe for general use.[2]

To find a new road to Montana a party of government engineers, in charge of Colonel Sawyer, was sent out under military escort in 1865. The point of departure was Sioux City, which, some men supposed, would soon be a rival of St. Louis.[3] The expedition would proceed up the valley of the Niobrara in northern Nebraska. Skirting the Black Hills on the south side, the pathfinders would reach Virginia City by way of the Powder River and the Big Horn Mountains. Without good guides and insufficiently guarded, they lost their way in the Bad Lands. They fell in with a train of emigrant wagons and, to save it and themselves from the Indians, abandoned the purpose for which they had set out.[4] The route was declared to be impracticable for use.[5]

A better one was the Bozeman "cut-off," called so because it was used by an old pioneer named Bozeman,[6] who lived in one of a half dozen cabins in a place known as Bozeman City. The road would leave the Platte route at Fort Laramie, and reach Virginia City by the Powder River and the Big Horn Mountains, over the course, on the upper part of the way, fol-

---

[1] O. R., series i, vol. xlviii, part i, pp. 340, 342; House Ex. Doc., 39th Cong., 1st sess., no. 76, p. 6.

[2] General Pope in House Ex. Doc., 39th Cong., 1st sess., no. 76, pp. 4–5.

[3] N. Y. Tribune, June 26, 1866.

[4] O. R., series i, vol. xlviii, part i, pp. 340–1, 388; Report of the expedition in House Ex. Doc., 39th Cong., 1st sess., no. 58.

[5] O. R., series i, vol. xlviii, part ii, pp. 1123–4; House Ex. Doc., 39th Cong., 2d sess., no. 32, pp. 21–2.

[6] Article on Montana in Atlantic Monthly for August, 1866.

lowed by Colonel Sawyer. It would bring Fort Laramie
within 450 miles of the Three Forks of the Missouri.[1] If it
could be opened, it would be 350 miles shorter than the old
road, by way of the South Pass, which up to this time had been
in general use.[2]

The aid of the Missouri River was sought on the one side, and
of the Columbia on the other. The Missouri was a thread which
had connected the old Louisiana with the French settlements
of Canada, through the storied land of fur traders, voyageurs
and priestly missionaries to the Indians. Daring men with a
cordelle or towing line toiled with mackinaw boats a distance
of 3000 miles — all the way from the Mississippi up to Fort
Benton, an old post of Astor's American Fur Company in the
heart of the wilderness, among the Blackfeet Indians, within
a few miles of the Great Falls of the Missouri. Then came
the steamboat. Annually it left St. Louis filled with Indian
traders with their freights. The levee was crowded when it
departed. Indians and "mountaineers" awaited its coming
at the forts on the river side. In 1864 the Montana trade began, and Fort Benton was no longer a trading post surrounded
by camps of the Blackfeet; it was a place of warehouses,
stores and freight wagons, which were being laden with goods
to be carried over the roads to Helena, Virginia City and other
mining towns.[3]

The start from St. Louis must be made in March, as soon as
the river became free of ice. In the best seasons the rapids
above the mouth of the Musselshell were impassable after
August 1. Only light draft and powerful steamers could be
employed successfully.[4] The bluffs on the river banks crum-
bled, bearing cottonwood trees into the channel, to endanger
navigation. Travel at night was impossible. It was officially
stated that the loss to steamboat owners on the Missouri south

[1] O. R., series i, vol. xlviii, part i, pp. 340–1.

[2] Ibid., p. 341; ibid., part ii, p. 1229.

[3] H. A. Boller, Among the Indians, pp. 17–21, 415.

[4] Report of Captain Howell, House Ex. Doc., 40th Cong., 2d sess.,
no. 136.

of Sioux City, due to snags alone, was a half million dollars annually. As travel increased the government made an effort to improve the channel. It was recommended that a ploughing machine be attached to the bow of each boat, so that a way could be cut through sand-bars to obviate delays due to grounding. Wood to heat the boilers at some points was scarcely to be had, even at high prices. The crew must disembark from time to time to obtain driftwood on the shore. Thus it was that 60 or 65 days were consumed on the voyage up, while 15 or 20 days were required for the return trip.[1] Progress was so slow that a passenger bound for Montana could leave New York a week after the boat had made its departure from St. Louis, and board it at Sioux City, though this place was three days by rail and stage wagon from Chicago.[2]

In seasons when the water was low, or when the steamers arrived up the river too late, the cargoes must be landed at Fort Union, another old fur company post, six miles above the mouth of the Yellowstone, or even lower down, at the mouth of the Musselshell, to escape the rocky rapids near this point over which the boats must be warped or cordelled laboriously. Then the goods must be hauled to Benton by wagon, or else be conveyed directly to Helena and Virginia City, to which places roads were being built.[3] In 1865, 24 steamers started to Benton, but only two arrived at that place. Four thousand tons of freight were set upon the shore at Fort Union, and 250 wagons were carrying it into the interior.[4] In 1866 some 30 boats left St. Louis on the spring rise, and, as the water was high, nearly all arrived at Fort Benton.[5] In 1867 the "mountain fleet" comprised 43 boats. One made two round trips, two essayed the feat but failed. These steamers were of a lighter draft than craft which had been used in earlier years. They carried

---

[1] Report of Captain Howell, House Ex. Doc., 40th Cong., 2d sess., no. 136.

[2] N. Y. Tribune, June 26, 1865.

[3] House Ex. Doc., 39th Cong., 2d sess., no. 23, p. 47.

[4] Report of Commr. of Indian Affairs for 1865, p. 699.

[5] House Ex. Doc., 39th Cong., 2d sess., no. 23, p. 48.

10,000 passengers and 8000 tons of mining machinery and other supplies, bringing back hides, horns, furs and gold and silver.[1] It would be better, it was said, if the boats should start from Sioux City, instead of St. Louis, so that they might get away at an earlier day. Then if they should unburden at the Musselshell, instead of trying to reach the mountains, they might make four or even five round trips in a season. Despite the difficulties attending the navigation of the Missouri the price of a passage up the river was $150 or $200, of freight carriage eight or ten cents per pound, approximately but a third of the coaching fares and ox train charges overland.

On the other side of the mountains the enterprising men directing the affairs of the Oregon Steam Navigation Company, not content with their water and portage service into eastern Washington, placed steamers on Lake Pend d'Oreille, and the rivers running up toward Montana,[2] until the navigation of the Columbia and the Missouri had come to be separated by but 280 miles of wagon roads.[3] A section of the Snake River, a branch of the Columbia, was found to be navigable, and boats, taken apart, hauled to and reërected in the wilderness, could ascend this channel into southern Idaho to a point not more than 200 miles from Salt Lake.[4] The Columbia River afforded the best route to Boisé and the Owyhee mines.

But the ox, the mule and the horse must remain the principal freight carriers over the great central expanses of the continent until railroads could be stretched across it. At the end of the war there was a veritable outpouring of people into the West. They came in "incredible numbers," said General Pope.[5] Never before had there been such a crowding of the roads as in the summer of 1865. This movement was due in

[1] Report of Commr. of Indian Affairs for 1867; cf. St. Louis despatch in Phila. Ledger, June 10, 1867.

[2] House Ex. Doc., 39th Cong., 2d sess., no. 23, pp. 54–5.

[3] Report of Secretary of War for 1867, vol. ii, p. 510.

[4] Bowles, Across the Continent, pp. 194–5; J. F. Rusling, Across America, p. 230; H. H. Bancroft, History of Washington, Idaho and Montana, p. 438.

[5] House Ex. Doc., 39th Cong., 1st sess., no. 76, p. 3.

part to accounts of new discoveries of gold and silver in the mountains, but in still greater degree to the revival of hope and assurance in the people with the return of peace, and the release of the soldiers for civil employment. The tide ran from the South as well as from the North. Thousands of families of Southern sympathies in Missouri, Arkansas, Kentucky and states farther east left their homes for the West.[1] General Dodge said in 1865 that the trade into the Rocky Mountains and beyond was doubling annually. He estimated that in that year the number of teams crossing the plains was not less than 5000 a month.[2] From the first day of March to August 10, 1865, 9386 teams and 11,885 persons in stage-coaches, in ox and mule trains, and in other parties, had passed Fort Kearney in Nebraska on the Platte route.[3] Travellers from Denver to Fort Leavenworth (a few miles outside the town of Leavenworth) in Kansas, a distance of 683 miles, in July, 1865, said that they were never out of sight of emigrant and freight trains.[4] A man coming east from Denver on a stage-coach counted in three days 3384 teams bound west.[5] The movement continued through the winter of 1865–6. The officers in command of military posts reported that their hospitals were filled with frost-bitten teamsters and emigrants, whose mules had frozen to death and whose trains, stalled on the plains, were now buried in snow.[6]

The usual type of freight wagon was the large canvas-covered prairie schooner drawn by eight, ten or twelve oxen, which were allowed to graze by the way. In winter, when there was no grass, mules were used. With an average load of 5000 or 6000 pounds the shaggy drivers, tawny as Indians, covered from twelve to twenty miles in a day. In wet weather progress was yet slower. Then a train would rest, as plunging through the deep mire was full of danger for the wagons as well as the animals. They were corralled for the night. The

---

[1] O. R., series i, vol. xlviii, part ii, p. 1150.
[2] Ibid., p. 1158.   [3] Ibid., part i, p. 342.
[4] Ibid., series iii, vol. v, p. 245.   [5] J. P. Whitney, Colorado, p. 33.
[6] House Ex. Doc., 39th Cong., 1st sess., no. 76, p. 3.

teamsters passed between Fort Leavenworth and Denver in
from 45 to 74 days.[1] Some completed two round trips between
the Missouri and the mountains in a season; usually they
went out and back again but once. At Atchison alone twenty-
seven individuals or firms were engaged in the overland freight
trade in 1865. In that year these undertakers had carried to
and from the Missouri 21,500,000 pounds, over half of this
amount having passed between the river and Colorado. Six
million dollars were invested at Atchison in the business which
employed upwards of 5000 men, 5000 wagons, 7000 mules
and horses and 28,000 oxen. The traffic in 1865 was seven times
what it had been in 1861, four times as great as in 1863.[2] It
was computed that in 1865 the shipments into Colorado had
aggregated 104,000,000 pounds of goods.[3]

Much of this business was for the account of the government
of the United States, which had no means of conveying supplies to its Indian agencies and garrisoned posts except by contract with private freighting lines. The cost to the Interior
and War Departments was enormous. The charges were dependent, in the first place, upon the distance to be traversed;
then, also, upon the amount of freight offered for carriage,
the time of year it was presented for shipment, the number of
wagons equipped for the service, and the state of the roads
with reference to the Indians. In 1865 the government was
paying $15\frac{1}{2}$ cents for carrying a pound of corn to Denver, $27\frac{3}{4}$
cents for carrying it to Salt Lake, making the price of a bushel
of this grain at the one place $10.05, and at the other $17.[4]
Transportation charges into Colorado in the winter of 1864–5
rose to 25 cents a pound,[5] but the average in three years
was about ten cents.[6] Twenty cents a pound were paid to

[1] O. R., series iii, vol. v, p. 245.

[2] N. Y. Tribune, Jan. 4, 1866, citing Daily Champion of Atchison,
Kan.

[3] Report of Secretary of Interior for 1866, p. 467; N. Y. Tribune,
June 30, 1866.

[4] O. R., series ii, vol. v, p. 244.

[5] Report of Secretary of the Interior for 1865, p. 106.

[6] Ibid. for 1866, p. 467; cf. N. Y. Tribune, June 30, 1866.

wagoners for carrying Indian supplies from Atchison to Santa Fé in 1865.[1] Teamsters, at one time, received as much as 65 cents a pound for hauling freight from San Francisco into the Owyhee mining district in southern Idaho.[2]

The government's contract price for transportation upon the plains in 1865 was $2.26 per hundred pounds per hundred miles;[3] in 1866 it ranged from $1.45 to $1.79, according to the roads to be traversed.[4]

The shipments to the forts and Indian agencies, west from the Missouri, on the overland routes in 1866 reached a total of no less than 81,000,000 pounds, for which $3,314,495 were paid in freights. If, as was supposed, the government trade made up one-ninth part of the whole, the entire sum paid to the teamsters moving west from the Missouri River in 1866 was about $31,000,000. It was said that they received $13,000,000 as early as in 1863 on merchandise sent out of San Francisco, east to Nevada and the mining camps on the Pacific slope.[5]

Such a system of transportation was a heavy tax upon the pioneers. There were trading houses in Denver, Salt Lake and Virginia City, Mont., which were paying more than $100,000 each in a year for freights. These charges were added to the prices of all kinds of merchandise. In Central City, Col., in the winter of 1865–6, flour was sold at $26 for a hundred pounds, potatoes at 30 cents a pound.[6] At Julesburg, and Fort Sedgwick near by, on the Platte road, in 1865, wood brought $111 a cord; the next year the price was $46, while hay sold for $34 a ton.[7] In Montana, during the winter of 1865–6, the current prices were $20 to $30 for a sack of flour, 35 to 50 cents per pound for onions, 10 to 18 cents per pound for potatoes, $5 each for axe

[1] Report of Commr. of Indian Affairs for 1865, p. 549.

[2] A. D. Richardson, Our New States and Territories, p. 79.

[3] O. R., series i, vol. xlviii, part i, p. 344.

[4] Report of Secretary of War for 1866, p. 158.

[5] Ibid.; House Ex. Doc., 39th Cong., 2d sess., no. 92, p. 27.

[6] N. Y. Tribune, Jan. 3, 1866.

[7] House Ex. Doc., 39th Cong., 2d sess., no. 20, p. 2; ibid., no. 23, p. 7.

helves, 50 to 75 cents a box for matches. A farmer must pay at least $500 for the seed to plant 40 acres of ground.[1]

Often dealers would monopolize the stock of supplies. In the winter of 1864-5 the range on the Salt Lake road lay under fifteen feet of snow and famine threatened Virginia City. Flour was selling for $1 and $1.25 a pound in gold dust. Mobs attacked the merchants' stores. The poor, forced to live upon beef alone, grew sick; there was great suffering among the people.[2] Machinery, by reason of the freights, was made to cost at the mines many times its price at the place of manufacture.

Passengers, the mails and express matter found faster carriage by the stage wagons. The chief coach line was Ben Holladay's. A native of Kentucky, while yet a boy, he emigrated to Missouri, where at Weston, a centre for the Missouri River trade, he kept a tavern and a store. Then he founded a western freighting business. He drove his own ox-teams. He was one of the first Gentiles to trade successfully with the Mormons. He got some profitable contracts for the transportation of government stores over the plains, and was ready, when the war broke out, for new feats of enterprise.

The California overland mails were being carried twice a week west and twice a week east under a contract made by the Post-Office Department in 1858 with John Butterfield and several other men identified, for the most part, with the firm of Wells, Fargo and Company. For the sum of $600,000 per annum, for a term of six years, they were to run four-horse passenger stages or "spring wagons" from St. Louis and Memphis, by way of El Paso, to Fort Yuma and thence "through the best passes and along the best valleys," to San Francisco. But when the war came, the route was impracticable, since it covered Confederate ground, and the line must be taken north. One of the first acts of Lincoln's Postmaster-General, Montgomery Blair, was to establish a daily service on the

[1] N. Y. Tribune, June 19, 1866.
[2] Article on Montana in Atlantic Monthly for August, 1866; cf. N. Y. Tribune, June 19, 1866.

Platte route. The contractors had organized themselves into the Overland Mail Company, under the presidency of W. B. Dinsmore of New York, and for $1,000,000 annually, they agreed to carry the mails to and from California six times in the week — letters in 20 days during eight months, in 23 days during the other four months of the year, newspapers and other mail in 35 days, with the privilege of sending postal matter of the last-named class around to California by sea. The route was from St. Joseph in Missouri, or Atchison in Kansas, to Placerville in California, and the contract, which would become operative on July 1, 1861, would expire on July 1, 1864.[1]

The stage line to Salt Lake at the outbreak of the war was owned by William H. Russell and his partners in a large plains freighting business.[2] It bore the name of the Central Overland California and Pike's Peak Express. The line was unprofitable. Mr. Holladay had lent money to the owners; he foreclosed, and was soon in possession of the property, which now became the Overland Stage Line. He bought new coaches and fine stock, built new stations and increased the number of his employees. He said that his business represented an investment of $2,000,000.[3] He controlled the passenger, mail and express trade over the Platte route as far west as Salt Lake, where connection was made with Wells, Fargo and Company's line to California.

Daily over this route, from Atchison to Placerville, one coach went west and one came east, except in winter, when the roads were so blocked with snow that even sledges could not pass, or when communication was interrupted by forays of the Indians. A line ran down to Denver, another from that city up to Black Hawk and Central City in the Colorado mountains. At Bear River, 90 miles west of Salt Lake, coaches proceeded tri-weekly past Fort Hall on the Snake River. There, or near that old post the road forked, one coach going to Montana,

[1] Cong. Record, 46th Cong., 3d sess., pp. 520–1.

[2] Russell, Majors and Waddell, at one time owners of 75,000 head of oxen, engaged in the forwarding business on the plains. — F. A. Root, The Overland Stage to California, p. 308.

[3] Senate Mis. Doc., 46th Cong., 2d sess., no. 19, p. 61.

another to Boisé City in Idaho, and farther on to connect with the steam navigation of the Columbia. Holladay's lines had a combined length of 2760 miles. He owned 6000 horses and mules, 260 coaches, scores of stage stations and other buildings, together with fuel, hay, grain and property of various kinds set out here and there along the roads.[1]

The Missouri River boats to Montana, and the emigrant and freight trains on the plains rested at night. The overland stage-coach travelled during all the 24 hours of the day. From Atchison west to Denver and from California east to Austin in Nevada this vehicle was of the old-fashioned type, with an oval wooden top and a high box seat, made in Concord, N. H. On the central route, between these points, and on the roads up to Montana and Idaho a hack covered with canvas, less likely to be overturned, also made in Concord, was in use.[2] Nine persons could be carried inside, and two or three more, at need, upon the box, while the mail sacks, passengers' luggage and express matter were stowed in the "boot" behind, or in space not filled by the passengers. The fares in 1865 were $175 to Denver, $350 to Salt Lake, and $500 to Nevada, California, Montana or Idaho.[3]

It was an event in the history of the "Overland," in the summer of 1865, when Schuyler Colfax of Indiana, the young Speaker of the House of Representatives, passed over it to San Francisco. He was a well-known and a popular member of the Order of Odd Fellows, which had aided in putting him forward in public life, spoke with ease and amiability on every conceivable subject, and was as acceptable a figure in Congress as he had been earlier upon the stump during electoral campaigns in the West. Recently he had conferred with President Lincoln concerning the trip, which thus was given a semi-official character. He bore some messages to the people, settled in the mountains and upon the plains, which were delivered with the more effect now since the President was dead.

[1] Bowles, Across the Continent, p. 52.
[2] N. Y. Tribune, Jan. 25, 1866.
[3] Bowles, Across the Continent, p. 53.

Accompanying the Speaker were William Bross, a Republican editor and stump orator of Illinois, at the time lieutenant-governor of the state; A. D. Richardson, a newspaper correspondent, escaped lately from a "rebel" prison and an old traveller on the plains, representing the New York Tribune; and Samuel Bowles of the Springfield Republican. At the Missouri River Holladay put his best horses and stages at the disposition of the party. Cavalrymen rode beside the coach as a guard against the Indians. The Associated Press despatches were taken off the overland wires for the enjoyment of Colfax as he rode along the way.

The horses galloped up the Platte Valley, over the course of the prairie schooners, cutting in and out among "the snowy sails of these great land fleets" moving into the West.[1] "A more dreary waste," said General Sherman, when he passed over the line in the following year, it would be impossible to find. Not a tree or bush was to be seen — "nothing but the long dusty road with its occasional ox-team and the everlasting line of telegraph poles."[2] Here and there was a "ranch," a sod-and-earth cabin, set in a patch of ground planted with corn, or perhaps merely a trading post with some bacon, flour and whiskey for sale to passing emigrants. After a run of ten, fifteen or twenty miles the stage would reach a station, located with reference to a supply of water. Here in a trice the jaded horses were taken out, and fresh ones were put in their places. This was called a "swing station." A group of huts, where drivers were changed and where a meal might be eaten, formed a "home station." At each one of these stopping places Holladay supported from two to six men to care for his stock. Revolvers were slung at their belts, rifles hung upon the walls of the cabins, which sometimes were built half underground with loopholes, after the manner of forts. At a military post, or a larger settlement, there would be mail and telegraph offices.

On went the coach, past villages of prairie dogs, which

[1] N. Y. Tribune, July 23, 1865.
[2] House Ex. Doc., 39th Cong., 2d sess., no. 23, p. 7.

barked "comically," as one traveller remarked, and then with a wag of their little tails darted into their underground habitations; the wallows in which the buffaloes had rolled while shedding their fur and which pitted the plains; across the broad, deep trails they had followed to grass, or water, or salt, though the animals themselves had been made so shy that now, on the Platte route, they were seldom seen, except at a distance; among the nimble antelopes and wild sheep whose succulent meat was eaten at the stage stations in the mountains. The coach coming east met the party daily with a "What news from the states?" and a "Give us some papers," while they inquired in return "Did you meet any Indians?" Then with an "All set! Go on, driver" the black-snakes were curled over the horses' flanks and the journey was continued.

The party frequently travelled at the rate of ten miles an hour. They covered the distance from Atchison to Denver in four days and twenty-two hours, the usual time between these places being five days and four hours.[1] After reaching Salt Lake City, where they met the coaches of Wells, Fargo and Company, they were shown attentions as pleasant as those which had been enjoyed on Holladay's line. Though they had spent eight days in coming to that city from Denver, a distance of 600 miles, because of hostile Indians,[2] they were carried over the 400 miles separating Salt Lake and Austin in 51 hours, and entered Virginia City, Nev., 597 miles, in 72 hours out of Salt Lake.[3] From this point, over the Sierras, there were two well-travelled toll roads, daily sprinkled and rolled to keep down the dust, and Mr. Colfax and his companions were soon looking out upon the wonders of California.

Without breaking the journey travellers could span the continent by the "Overland" in about three weeks. Holladay made spectacular trips in less time. Once, in reckless disregard of the fate of his stages and cattle, he passed from Folsom in California to Atchison, 2030 miles, in 12 days and two hours. He was driven between two stations, a distance of 14 miles, in

---

[1] Richardson, in N. Y. Tribune, June 23, 1865.
[2] Ibid., July 8, 1865.   [3] Ibid., Aug. 23, 1865.

45 minutes. But Mr. Colfax's party, stopping en route, were seven weeks on the way. They were filled with admiration for the mail contractors and the transcontinental passenger line. Richardson enjoyed soothing sleep as the coaches rolled along; Bowles praised the meals at the stations and pronounced it "the best stage road in the world."

But if Colfax and his companions were well served by the line while on their western excursion, and Holladay himself flew over it behind Arabian steeds in a private coach with mattresses which he might lie down upon at night,[1] others found the journey much less pleasant. At times the clouds would burst, and wind and rain descended upon man and beast with the fury of the cyclone. The coaches rocked and reeled. Driver and passengers must hold the wheels to the ground while the horses cried piteously or broke away in suffering and fright. Teamsters were blown into rivers or dragged long distances by their animals, bull trains were broken up, emigrants were killed. On a government expedition in western Dakota in 1865, 414 animals perished in a storm,[2] and few travellers' diaries or explorers' reports were free of accounts of the tornadoes on this broad, treeless space.

The dry grass, where there was vegetation, would burn like tinder. An emigrant who stopped upon his way to collect wood, if it could be found, or the "buffalo chips" (the dried excrement of the buffalo) while they lasted, over which to cook his bacon and warm his coffee-pot; a spark from a locomotive after the railroads came; an Indian, or some white ruffian by design, started a fire which, spreading, wrought terrible devastation — encompassing settlers' cabins, ranch cattle, trains of prairie schooners, herds of buffaloes. Every animate thing fled before the rolling mass of flame and smoke.

Here and there was seen the new-made grave of an emigrant, who, with no doctors near, died, to be buried by the way; or of some victim of the Indians. Wolves howled round every wagon camp at night and followed a train, as sharks do a ship

---

[1] S. Seymour, Incidents of a Trip, p. 49.
[2] O. R., series i, vol. xlviii, part i, p. 376.

at sea, until by powder, shot and strychnine the pioneers put an end to this pest of the plains.[1] They shared with carrion birds the feast at the cadavers of mules and oxen left by the roadside. As far as eye could see were whitening skeletons of animals lost from emigrant trains, and of buffaloes, ruthlessly slaughtered, or starved and frozen during hard winters,[2] until the railroads were built and the bones could be gathered up to be sent east to the guano mills.

Often at night, though the air was so cold that greatcoats and blankets must be used, the mosquitoes settled upon the stages like swarms of bees.[3] Passengers were obliged to throw gauze cages over their heads. The roads led at times through water up to the floor of the coach. Bayard Taylor told of breathing the thick, acrid dust of the plains under a burning sun, and the discomfort which travellers suffered in the coaches. Once he was "flung backward and forward, right and left, pummelled, pounded and bruised," all night long.[4] A. K. McClure was jolted, wedged, bruised and blistered on his western trip.[5] The overland stage, said W. Hepworth Dixon, the English traveller, was "designed by some infernal genius as a place of torture." In it a man could not sit or stand or lie down.[6] When passengers slept at all on the way across the continent, it was in sheer exhaustion, and they arrived at their journey's end begrimed, unshaven, in the clothing in which they had left their homes, and sore of flesh and bone.

The timid shuddered as they were driven at high speed along the narrow mountain roads, beside steep precipices, where awkwardness by a driver or accident to an animal would overturn the occupants of the coach to certain death. Though stage driving in such places had become a fine art, mishaps were not unknown.

---

[1] W. E. Webb, Buffalo Land, p. 293.
[2] J. H. Beadle, The Undeveloped West, pp. 436–67; J. F. Meline, Two Thousand Miles on Horseback, pp. 6, 32; J. F. Rusling, Across America, p. 151; S. Seymour, Incidents of a Trip, p. 47.
[3] N. Y. Tribune, Aug. 3, 1863. [4] Ibid., July 17, 1866.
[5] A. K. McClure, Three Thousand Miles through the Rocky Mountains, p. 77. [6] New America, p. 44.

But of all the offences and perils to be met with on the overland road the most fearful were the hostile Indians who stood ready to strip off the traveller's scalp, and the desperate highwaymen who would stop the coach to rifle his pockets and pillage the mail sacks and express boxes.

Holladay himself had enemies on every hand. That he and his business associates received a large sum from the government, and that the service which they rendered was not always good, stirred their critics to activity. Holladay's fast trips over the line, they said, were made but to influence Congress, so that it would continue his mail contract, or for his own accommodation. As he passed he left at the stations broken-down stock, scarcely fit to drag the regular coach over the next stage. If passengers or express packages filled the vehicle, the mail must wait until the next trip. If these packages were numerous, the passengers would be asked to get out and walk up the mountain roads.[1] Tons of mail sacks were stacked or scattered along the way. They would be thrown out at need to fill mud-holes, that the coach might pass. A Boisé City correspondent of the New York Tribune said that he was receiving his eastern papers four, five and six months after the date of issue; scarcely one in ten ever reached him at all. Some of May 26 and July 26 came to hand on the same day late in August.[2] A correspondent of the Tribune in Silver City, Idaho, received his February and March copies of that paper in September.[3]

A. K. McClure, in Montana, found the privilege enjoyed by Wells, Fargo and Company of conducting a post-office on their own account to be the cause of the bad service. They held back the government mails, said he, in order to build up their private business.[4] In the first place the company was favored improperly by the provision in the postal law of March 25, 1864, requiring senders of newspapers, except one copy to one address to a regular subscriber, and all other mailable matter going west to points beyond the western boundary of Kansas

---

[1] N. Y. Tribune, Dec. 27, 1867.
[3] Ibid., Oct. 11, 1867.
[2] Ibid., Sept. 9, 1867.
[4] Ibid., Aug. 3, 1867.

and coming east beyond the eastern boundary of California to pay letter rates. Thus protected they could secure much of the newspaper mail as express matter. Furthermore in 1863 they had bought from the government over 2,000,000 three-cent stamped envelopes and many of higher denominations; in 1864 over 2,500,000.[1] Upon these they placed their own frank and for 12½ cents each carried merchants' and other letters over all the West. Government mail agents threatened to bring the business to an end, but the company was adjudged to be within its rights and the people were glad to pay the additional fee for a service which was certain and prompt.[2] The contractors put the blame for the irregularity of the mails upon the Indians, but the papers and letters expressed in the care of Wells, Fargo and Company were carried from place to place without delay. Then, men asked, why were not the mails also?[3] There were no hostile Indians in the West, said a senator in Congress, except some that Ben Holladay brought out from time to time as an excuse for the execrable service which he gave the people on the "Overland."

But the difficulties to be overcome in establishing and maintaining such a line were enormous. The officers of the army in command on the plains gave their protection to the stage company when it came in their way to do so. General Grant himself told General Pope that it was not a military duty.[4] Drivers and the passengers, both male and female, were armed for their own defence. The number of employees at the stage stations must be increased for the protection of the horses and mules, and the grain brought for their use at great expense from the Missouri River. When stock was stolen it must be replaced. When stations were burned they must be rebuilt. If roads and bridges were damaged by floods they must be repaired; if ferry boats were sunk Holladay must buy new ones. When the routes were changed the stations must be relocated.

---

[1] Bowles, Across the Continent, pp. 295–7.
[2] A. D. Richardson, in N. Y. Tribune, May 4, 1866.
[3] N. Y. Tribune, July 10 and Aug. 3, 1867.
[4] O. R., series i, vol. xlviii, part ii, p. 1244.

First, in 1862, when the Indians made the Fort Laramie and South Pass line unsafe for travel, the stables and other buildings were brought down from 100 to 300 miles to the "Cherokee Trail" over Bridger's Pass. For a while the coaches went up the Lodge Pole Creek from Julesburg, and then, as Denver grew, in 1863, they followed the South Platte and the Cache la Poudre. In 1864, in answer to military orders, they were compelled to use the so-called Denver "cut-off" which left the South Platte road east of the Cache la Poudre. Communication between the East and California, as well as with the settlements on the way, must not be interrupted, said Lincoln to Holladay, when the President was told during the war of the difficulties which attended the operation of the line. The Mormons, if left to themselves, would use this opportunity, and men knew not what Southern ruffians were settled in the mining gulches. The whole Southwest was on the point of being seized for the Confederacy when the Californians and "Pike's Peakers" moved against the Texas Rangers who had swept into New Mexico.[1] That the North should not be separated from its loyal friends in the great empire lying beyond the Missouri River the "Overland" service proceeded, though the preoccupation of the army in the South left few troops to guard the line.[2]

In 1864, on the desert west of Salt Lake, the mail company must pay the Mormons 25 cents a pound for oats and barley to feed its mules until it laid out and irrigated a farm of its own, thus effecting a saving of $50,000 annually.[3] Once when travel was interfered with for several weeks, because of Indian depredations, one of the owners paid assessments of $24,000 on his stock in the company that the line might continue to be run in fulfilment of its contracts with the government.[4]

Another trader on the plains was D. A. Butterfield. For several years he had lived in Denver. Then he returned east

[1] H. H. Bancroft, History of Arizona and New Mexico, pp. 680–700.
[2] Senate Mis. Doc., 46th Cong., 2d sess., no. 19, pp. 57–61.
[3] H. H. Bancroft, History of Nevada, Colorado and Wyoming, p. 229.
[4] A. D. Richardson, Our New States and Territories, p. 42.

and engaged in a commission business at Atchison. In 1865 he was induced to establish an overland despatch company to rival Holladay's as a passenger line, and to engage, too, in a general freighting trade. He would use the Smoky Hill route to Denver and go on to Salt Lake over the new road by Middle Park and the White River.[1] Half of Denver came out on the plains to welcome him when his first stage approached the town on September 23, 1865. He was taken to the leading hotel for a banquet. The mayor and other men made complimentary speeches. But it was a wild, rough, unsafe road, as Bayard Taylor and Hepworth Dixon learned when they passed over it in 1866. The Indians killed Butterfield's drivers and horses, and attacked his freight trains. Though he had carried 25,000 tons of goods in 1865,[2] he was soon ready to sell his line to Holladay.

This man was now at the height of his reputation. He called his consolidated company the Overland Mail and Express Company. He had two routes to Denver in addition to his Salt Lake, and Montana and Idaho lines. His coaches covered 3300 miles of roads; he reduced the fare from the Missouri to Denver to $125, to Salt Lake to $250. He promised to carry his passengers to Denver in 5, to Salt Lake in $9\frac{1}{2}$, to Boisé in $12\frac{1}{2}$, to Virginia City in Montana in 13, and to San Francisco in 16 days.[3] From 1862 to 1868 inclusive Holladay received nearly $2,000,000 from the government as a postal contractor, without taking account of the payments made to him as a sub-contractor (as upon the Platte route prior to 1864), and as a stockholder of Wells, Fargo and Company and other forwarding lines.[4] For a fleet of steamships which he owned on the Pacific coast, running north to Oregon and south to ports on the western coast of Mexico, he was seeking mail subsidies from the Congress of the United States

[1] F. A. Root, The Overland Stage to California, p. 397.

[2] N. Y. Tribune, Sept. 7, 1865.

[3] Advertisement in N. Y. Tribune, Sept. 7, 1866. Passengers now proceeded over the Pacific Railroad to Fort Kearney, which had become the eastern terminus for the stage line.

[4] Senate Ex. Doc., 46th Cong., 2d sess., no. 211.

.and from Emperor Maximilian. He had one mansion on Fifth Avenue, another in Washington where he resided for a part of each year to guard his political interests. He was building a "castle" up the Hudson River near White Plains which he called "Ophir Farm."[1] His two daughters married European noblemen, and he was reckoned to be one of the rich men of the age.

But the Indians still raided his stations and the advance into the West of the Pacific railroads proceeded, so he sold his lines late in 1866 to his associates in the firm of Wells, Fargo and Company, who continued to run coaches over them in connection with the service west of Salt Lake.[2]

[1] Afterward long the residence of Mr. Whitelaw Reid.

[2] To cover the value of property taken from him by commanders on the plains, the losses he had sustained by reason of the inadequate protection afforded him by the troops, and the expense to which he had been put because of the changing of his routes by direction of the military authorities he filed a claim upon the government. A bill to refer the case to the Court of Claims passed Congress in 1866, but the Houses disagreed as to the terms of the measure, and it fell in conference. (Cong. Globe, 39th Cong., 1st sess., pp. 4170, 4190.) The Senate Committee on Claims reported a bill again proposing to send the case to the Court of Claims, but the Senate itself in 1878 voted to refer the subject back to the committee. (Cong. Record, 45th Cong., 2d sess., pp. 1553–60, 1631–43, 1689.) Holladay had adventured unsuccessfully in railroads in Oregon (H. H. Bancroft, History of Oregon, vol. ii, pp. 700–4), and made other speculations which failed. His homes were sold perforce, and his fortune was scattered. As he saw his property being swept away he pressed his case against the government. He reminded Congress of President Lincoln's promises and recited his services to the country, while it was in the throes of its Civil War. The Senate Committee in 1880, after hearing much testimony, recommended that he be paid the sum of $526,000. But while some said that for what he had done he should be loaded with honors (in England they would have made him a baronet) others found that he already had been overpaid, and, therefore, merited no more at the hands of the government. The Senate on January 18, 1881, resolved to give him $100,000 in settlement of the account. This sum he said that he would not accept, but even so much was not at his disposal, for the bill did not pass the House and Holladay died in comparative poverty as well as obscurity in Portland, Ore., on July 8, 1887, before there had been any adjustment of the case. (Cong. Record, 46th Cong., 2d sess., pp. 2945–51, 2969–72; ibid., 46th Cong., 3d sess., pp. 373–82, 482–9, 515–26,

It was believed in 1866 and 1867 that one million people were settled west of the Missouri River. Men everywhere greatly predominated, but women were to be found in the loneliest ranch houses and in the farthest mining towns. Well meant but little successful movements were begun to start female emigration. Colorado needed women as wives for its miners, said the Rocky Mountain News. They would be welcomed in Nevada. Instead of striving to earn a living by needlework and adding by their competition to the misery of seamstresses, said the Public Ledger of Philadelphia, they should be married to the enterprising men who were taking gold and silver from the earth in the West.[1] Men in Arizona wrote to Governor Andrew of Massachusetts urging him to send them some of the spinsters of that state.[2] But it remained for Washington to accredit an emigration agent to the East. In 1864 A. S. Mercer, a member of the legislature of that territory, had carried with him to the West a number of women whose fares he had paid with the understanding that the sum advanced to them should be returned out of their wages after they arrived at their new homes. Thirty members of his party disembarked at San Francisco and twelve continued on the way to Seattle. The next year, with his credentials as an officer of the territory, he visited Washington city and asked the Secretary of the Navy for a ship to carry the women around the Horn to Puget Sound. About a thousand, mostly from New England, together with some shoemakers, machinists and other mechanics of whom the territory stood in need, were brought to New York ready for their voyage to the northwest. But the government ship failed to arrive. The newspapers rang with humorous accounts of Mercer's hunt for "wives for the wifeless," the enterprise won the eloquent enmity of Anna Dickinson, the well-known lyceum orator, and his plans bade fair to be frustrated altogether. Many who came to New York

671–82, 714–24. Also Senate Mis. Doc., 46th Cong., 2d sess., no. 19; Senate Reports, 46th Cong., 2d sess., no. 216; Senate Ex. Doc., 46th Cong., 2d sess., no. 211.)

[1] Phila. Ledger, July 3, 1865.
[2] Ibid., Aug. 9, 1865, quoting Boston Transcript.

to embark wearied of long waiting. At this juncture Ben Holladay bought a ship, the *Continental*, for his new Pacific coast line, and on January 16, 1866 with but 125 persons on board, she left her pier in the North River on her far journey.[1]

All who knew aught about the West agreed that its greatest need was a transcontinental railway. The project had been discussed for a generation. Some said that the road should follow one line and some another. The Missouri River could not be bridged. The Rocky Mountains could not be crossed. The snows in the Sierras would block the trains, even if the engineers should succeed in finding a course for the rails. On the plains there was no water to fill the boilers of the locomotives and no wood to put under them to make steam. If it were built, there would be no business to support the line. General Sherman in the month of August in the year 1865 said that he would not buy a ticket on the Pacific Railroad for his youngest grandchild.[2]

But the Republican party espoused this with other undertakings for the advantage of the West, the development of which had been held back so long while the North and the South wrangled over the question of negro slavery. Congress passed the act and the President signed it on the first day of July, 1862. One hundred and sixty persons, residing in 24 states and territories, to serve with five men appointed by the Secretary of the Interior, to represent the government, were named as the incorporators or commissioners of the Union Pacific Railroad Company, which would take charge of the work on the eastern end of the line. The road should run westwardly, the law said, "from a point on the western boundary of the state of Iowa" by a course lying between the south margin of the valley of the Solomon and the north margin of the valley of the Platte River to the western boundary of Nevada. The Central Pacific Railroad Company, which had

[1] Phila. Ledger, July 27 and Sept. 29, 1865; N. Y. Tribune, Oct. 6, 1865, and Jan. 18, 1866.

[2] The Westward March of Emigration, Lancaster, Pa., March, 1874, p. 12.

been formed in California, was to build such part of the line as lay within that state, with the privilege of continuing it in an eastwardly direction until it should meet the western end of the Union Pacific.

That Chicago, St. Louis and, indeed, all sections and interests, both North and South, should be equally served by the railroad, Congress arranged for the construction of branches. The Leavenworth, Pawnee and Western Railroad Company of Kansas was authorized to build a line from the point at which the Kansas River flowed into the Missouri (connecting there with the new Missouri Pacific Railroad which was crossing that state), to run west and intersect the Union Pacific on the 100th meridian. The Hannibal and St. Joseph Railroad should construct a link to connect St. Joseph and Atchison with the Kansas road. Another branch should be built from Sioux City down to the main western line. The government offered the companies the usual land subsidies comprising the odd-numbered sections for ten miles on each side of the track, and $16,000 worth of six per cent bonds per mile of completed road. The Kansas and the Sioux City branches were to receive bonds only as far west as the 100th meridian; the Hannibal and St. Joseph for a distance not exceeding 100 miles. The Union Pacific and Central Pacific each would receive thrice the usual bond subsidy, or $48,000, for 150 miles of road in the Rocky Mountains and 150 miles in the Sierra Nevadas, and twice the amount, or $32,000, for crossing the desert which lay between the two ranges. The Union Pacific and the Kansas companies were to complete 100 miles of their respective roads within two years, and go forward then at the rate of at least 100 miles annually; while the Central Pacific Company was allowed two years in which to finish 50 miles and was to proceed thereafter at the rate of at least 50 miles per annum.

The commissioners met in Chicago on September 2, 1862, and elected William B. Ogden president. Congress had fixed the amount of stock at $100,000,000, and the shares were now offered for sale. Directors were chosen, two of them on the

part of the government of the United States. To this board
the interests of the company passed. General John A. Dix
was elected president, Thomas C. Durant, vice-president,
and J. J. Cisco, treasurer. Under Peter A. Dey several parties
of engineers were organized and put into the field to determine
the lines to be taken by the road. President Lincoln, in
conformity with the provisions of the law, fixed the principal
Missouri River terminus at Omaha, a place which in 1860
had contained but 1800 people, but which now had visions of
metropolitan grandeur. On the opposite shore of the Missouri
lay high ground which the Indians had been wont to use for
conferences with the agents of the government, whence its
name, Council Bluffs. This place was the home of about 2000
people. The mayors of the two towns, and Governor Saun-
ders of Nebraska, met at Omaha on December 2, 1863, and
amid the "roar of artillery," ground was broken for the construction of the railroad. In the evening the houses were
illuminated and officers of the company and their guests were
dined at the leading hotel.[1]

But progress promised to be slow and expensive. Other
towns said that Omaha had gained the prize by underhand
means, and the land jobbers who had placed their money here
sprang to its defence. Six railroads were projected, or in course
of construction across the state of Iowa from the Mississippi
River, but not one had yet reached the Missouri.[2] The nearest
rail end was 150 miles from Council Bluffs.[3] No bridge connected Omaha with the Iowa shore; the crossing was made by
ferry, and it was uncertain because of the current and the
shifting bottom of the river. The material for the new road
must be conveyed by coasting vessels to the Gulf and up the
Mississippi and Missouri, or else down the Ohio from Pittsburgh and then up those rivers.[4] Some cottonwood and a
little oak for sleepers for use on the first section of 100 miles

[1] N. Y. Tribune, Dec. 3, 1863.
[2] Senate Ex. Doc., 40th Cong., special session, no. 2, p. 8.
[3] Report of Lieut.-Col. James H. Simpson to Secretary Harlan,
Nov. 23, 1865, p. 82.
[4] Article on Pacific Railroads in Atlantic Monthly, December, 1867.

could be procured on the banks of the Missouri to be floated down to Omaha. But all the rails, locomotives, cars, machinery and tools must come from the East. Laborers were scarce and demanded high wages. The interferences of the war were many, both with reference to financing the road and carrying on the practical work of construction. Congress on March 3, 1863, had fixed the gauge at four feet, eight and a half inches, which was the width of most of the tracks in the country, though the Missouri Pacific had a gauge of five and a half feet, and the Erie and the Atlantic and Great Western drew trains to St. Louis from the East over an unbroken line of six feet.[1]

On July 2, 1864 the government granted new privileges to the road. The land grant was doubled and made to include the odd-numbered sections for 20 instead of 10 miles on each side of the way; the United States bonds were made a second lien upon the property to facilitate the public sale of the company's securities. The par value of the shares was reduced from $1000 to $100. The number of government directors was increased to five. As each section of 20 miles should be completed it became the duty of commissioners representing the United States government to examine the work of construction, and if it were found to be satisfactory, then the appertaining bonds and lands would be delivered to the company.

These larger grants, together with the improved conditions of business and finance at the close of the war, promoted the sale of the stock and bonds. General Dix had been busily employed with his military duties, for which reason much responsibility was taken by the vice-president, Thomas C. Durant. It was in August and September, 1864, that Durant arranged a contract with a man named Hoxie to build the first 100 miles of the road at the rate of $50,000 a mile, extended later to the 100th meridian. Hoxie had been a Missouri River ferryman; obviously he would be unable to carry out such an agreement, and it was assigned to Durant, who sought to form a construction company. He procured subscriptions amounting to $1,600,000, and 25 per cent of the

[1] N. Y. Tribune, Jan. 18, 1867.

sum was paid in. Then the subscribers took fright and, to relieve them from individual responsibility, cover was sought in the charter of a company called the Pennsylvania Fiscal Agency.[1] At the time there was a successful Crédit Mobilier of France carrying on railway and other financial operations. Under the influence of the florid imagination and fluent tongue of George Francis Train, Durant was persuaded to adopt the strange name. The Pennsylvania Fiscal Agency by act of the legislature of Pennsylvania in 1864 became the Crédit Mobilier of America. Durant caused himself to be elected president while still serving as the vice-president, if not the actual president of the Union Pacific Company. Oakes Ames, a member of Congress from Massachusetts and his brother Oliver, rich, able, confident, full of energy, and Rowland G. and Isaac P. Hazard, manufacturers of Rhode Island, now appeared on the list of subscribers, and by September 21, 1865, the capital of the company was increased to $2,500,000 fully paid in. The Hoxie contract to the 100th meridian was taken over and the work proceeded.[2]

Track laying began near Omaha on July 10, 1865, and on November 4 President Dix reported to Secretary Harlan that trains were running west for a distance of 20 miles. The grading on the first section of 100 miles was practically finished; it had been begun on the second section of 100 miles.[3] Rails from Pennsylvania were delivered at Omaha by steamboat for $135 a ton; their cost after the railroads had crossed Iowa to Council Bluffs was still $97.50.[4] Machine shops were being built at Omaha. The surveyors were at work in the mountains seeking the most available passes over them into the Salt Lake basin. There was lamentation in Denver when it was declared impracticable to lay down the road through that city, and to proceed west by the Berthoud or Boulder Pass. A spur must be swung southward into Colorado. In western Dakota, soon

[1] J. B. Crawford, The Crédit Mobilier of America, p. 17.
[2] R. Hazard, The Crédit Mobilier of America, pp. 16–19.
[3] Simpson, loc. cit., p. 86.
[4] Senate Ex. Doc., 47th Cong., 1st sess., no. 69, p. 54.

to be called Wyoming, the range was broken into three ranges. To go over the first of these it would be necessary to mount to a height of 8245 feet. Then the road would descend into the so-called Laramie Plains, a mountainous, grazing country of a high altitude, cross the Medicine Bow Mountains at a level of 7050 feet and proceed at length through the old Bridger's Pass in the Wahsatch Mountains, to come finally into the valley of the Great Salt Lake. For a distance of more than 500 miles the track would be laid at an elevation exceeding one mile above sea level.[1]

The managers of the Crédit Mobilier, after the road was completed as far as the 100th meridian, became involved in disputes. The brothers Ames and their New England friends accused Durant of taking profits improperly, and he, on his side, determined that no more contracts should be awarded to the construction company. Finally his authority was materially curtailed. Sidney Dillon was elected to the presidency of the Crédit Mobilier and Oliver Ames to the presidency of the Union Pacific, though Durant continued to be vice-president, and a factor of power in the management of the railroad company. The work must proceed, if the whole investment were not to be lost, and the Crédit Mobilier went forward without contracts. After a while Durant and his party agreed that they could be issued in the name of Oakes Ames, who, on August 16, 1867, undertook to build 667 miles of the road at prices varying from $42,000 to $96,000 per mile, according to the nature of the country to be traversed.[2] By legal instruments Ames now assigned his contract, which involved him personally to the extent of nearly $50,000,000, to trustees. These men represented the stockholders of the Crédit Mobilier, who thus were brought to share the profits as before.[3]

Not all of these facts were of public knowledge until Congress instituted an investigation into the methods by which

---

[1] Report of Secretary of Interior for 1867, p. 11.

[2] Crawford, loc. cit., p. 38; Senate Ex. Doc., 47th Cong., 1st sess., no. 69, p. 39.

[3] Hazard, pp. 19–23.

the railroad had been built. What was known was that the work after it had been fairly begun proceeded at an unexpected pace. Though no railroad entered Council Bluffs, and the material still must be conveyed by boat up the Missouri River, when the Secretary of the Interior made his report in November, 1866, the railhead was 270 miles west of Omaha. On October 5 it had crossed the 100th meridian and Durant organized a party of congressmen (with Senator Wade at their head), railroad men and journalists to accompany him to the end of the track. No expense was spared upon the guests. In "palace cars" they were borne to St. Joseph. For two days they were well fed on two Missouri steamboats set aside for their use, and landed at Omaha, where they were tendered a ball. Here they found awaiting them a train of nine cars bearing mottoes and flags and they proceeded out over the line. At night they stopped at camps of tents set up on the plains. Pawnee Indians danced and fought sham battles for the amusement of the guests; at Durant's direction at night a prairie fire was lighted that they should miss no Western experience. Parties were organized to hunt buffaloes and other wild game; the train halted that the excursionists might inspect a prairie dog " city." A daily paper containing telegraphic news was issued on a hand press; two bands of music played popular airs.[1]

On July 1, 1867, the track layers reached Julesburg, 377 miles from Omaha; and the end of the year, officers of the company said, would bring the railhead 537 miles from the Missouri, or twenty miles beyond a new town called Cheyenne, at the foot of the most eastern of the three ranges of mountains which were to be crossed by the road. No less than 3500 men were engaged in levelling the way and 500 in laying the rails, which were being put down at a rate averaging 50 miles in a month. Sometimes in the summer three or four miles were laid in a single day. Not less than $27,000,000 had been expended in bringing the road to the mountains through a country which was still the hunting ground of the Indian.

[1] S. Seymour, Incidents of a Trip, pp. 72 et seq.

Of the Leavenworth, Pawnee and Western Railroad General
John C. Frémont was the president in 1863, but he became involved in a quarrel with a border character named Sam Hal-
lett. United States cavalrymen were used before peace could
be restored and a new group of capitalists obtained control of
the property.[1] The name was changed to the Union Pacific
Railway Company, Eastern Division, pursuant to a law of
the state of Kansas, and it took up the work of constructing
the Kansas branch, from Wyandotte at the mouth of the
Kansas River, opposite Kansas City, the proposed terminus of
the new Missouri Pacific, fifteen years in building, but finally
in September, 1865, complete. St. Louis could exult. She
was in possession of advantages which were out of the reach of
Chicago,[2] for by this time she had railway connections far into
the West. The Kansas road had entered Lawrence, and had
passed Topeka on its way up the valley of the Kaw.[3]   In
November, 1866, the line had been advanced to Fort Riley,
135 miles west of Wyandotte, affording railway and telegraphic
service 418 miles west of St. Louis.   A branch road, as Congress
required, had been built from Leavenworth to Lawrence, thus
giving the line another terminal town on the Missouri River.[4]

Already in 1865 surveyors had gone up the Smoky Hill
along the way which had been taken by Butterfield's stages
and wagon trains. Congress on July 3, 1866, changed the terms
of the grant, enabling the company to join its line with the
Union Pacific on or near the meridian of Denver, instead of
on the 100th meridian, and the opportunity was at hand for
the construction of a short direct road to that city. Before
winter had set in, in 1867, the rails of this south branch
of the Pacific Railroad extended more than 300 miles from
Kansas City, and had reached a point in western Kansas near
Fort Wallace. The company had earned over $1,200,000
from the traffic on its lines in ten months.[5]

[1] N. Y. Tribune, Aug. 25, 1865; Article on Pacific Railroads, Atlantic Monthly for December, 1867.
[2] N. Y. Nation, Sept. 28, 1865.   [3] N. Y. Tribune, Sept. 7, 1865.
[4] Report of Secretary of Interior for 1866, p. 11.
[5] Ibid. for 1867, p. 17.

So, too, was there progress on the other branches of the Pacific railway system. The Hannibal and St. Joseph company had accepted the provisions of the law in reference to a connecting road from St. Joseph by way of Atchison. It used the Kansas charter of the Atchison and Pike's Peak Railroad, and the line afterward was called the Central Branch of the Union Pacific Railroad. Its president was Senator S. C. Pomeroy of Kansas. The first section of twenty miles was completed before the end of the year 1865.[1] In 1868 the company had finished the 100 miles of the road for which it could receive government bonds; the track ended in the valley of the Little Blue River in northern Kansas.[2]

The north branch from Sioux City was being constructed by the Sioux City and Pacific Railroad Company.[3] It would join the main road at Fremont, a place less than fifty miles west of Omaha. The Secretary of the Interior announced that 100 miles of the road had been laid down and were ready for use in 1868.[4]

If the railway builders in the East found their work hampered because of the want of connections at Omaha, and must use the uncertain channels of the Missouri River to convey their rails, sleepers, cars, locomotives and machinery to the scene, still greater difficulties were encountered by the men who had undertaken to construct the line in California. Two railroads to run beside the two toll roads for wagons were started from Sacramento, the head of river navigation, up the Sierra slope, on the way over the mountains to Virginia City to care for the valuable Nevada trade. One followed the Dutch Flat and Donner Lake route, the other, by Placerville, the line used by Wells, Fargo and Company's stages. An engineer, Theodore D. Judah, surveyed the Dutch Flat road, and satisfied Congress that the mountains could be crossed over his line, the con-

---

[1] Simpson, pp. 110–1; Report of Secretary of Interior for 1865, p. xiii; cf. Senate Ex. Doc., 47th Cong., 1st sess., no. 69, p. 27.

[2] Reports of Secretary of Interior for 1867, p. 16, and for 1868, p. xiv.

[3] Simpson, p. 111.

[4] Report of Secretary of Interior for 1868, p. xv.

struction of which had been undertaken by the Central Pacific
Railroad Company, incorporated by the legislature of California in 1861. Its president was ex-Governor Leland Stanford;
its vice-president, Collis P. Huntington; its secretary, Mark
Hopkins. Most of the wealthy and enterprising pioneers were
members of the board of directors.[1] They promptly accepted
the terms of the Pacific Railroad act,[2] formed a small company,
the Western Pacific Company, to put down rails around the
bay and serve the territory lying between San Francisco and
Sacramento, and a construction company, not unlike the
Crédit Mobilier, called the Contract and Finance Company.[3]
Soon they were pressing into the mountains to join their end of
the line at the first possible day to the railhead moving west
from Omaha.

Every pound of iron used in the work must be carried by sea
from the Atlantic coast states, said President Stanford, "running the gauntlet of the rebel pirates." It must be insured
against capture, thus increasing its cost. Ten months would
elapse after it was shipped from Philadelphia or New York
before it came to hand in Sacramento. Only gold and silver
were in use as money in California; not enough could be had
in San Francisco to serve the purposes of the company. To
obtain specie in the East the enormous premium of the New
York Gold Room must be paid. The ruling rate of interest
in California was two per cent a month. Only a few Irish
could be secured for the work of construction. White men
preferred agricultural labor and the excitement and chance of
mining, so the Six Companies were asked to furnish Chinese
coolies. President Stanford carefully explained to the Secretary of the Interior that no system similar to peonage or slavery
prevailed among these laborers. Without them it would be
impossible to complete the work, so they were employed.[4]
Grading began in February, 1863; the first iron was received
in October of that year; and in June, 1864, before a single rail

[1] Atlantic Monthly for December, 1867; Bowles, Across the Continent, pp. 267–9.   [2] Simpson, p. 112.
[3] Crawford, The Crédit Mobilier, p. 77.   [4] Simpson, p. 120.

had yet been put down at Omaha, the line was ready for use for a distance of 31 miles. Fifty-five miles were finished before September, 1865, and three trains were running daily each way between Sacramento and Colfax, a place named in honor of the speaker of the House of Representatives.[1] In 1865 the company had 5000 men, nearly all Chinese, out on the line, and the Secretary of the Interior found that it was manifesting "the greatest vigor and activity in carrying on its operations." [2] The number of coolies was increased in 1866 to more than 10,000.[3]

The road mounted to a height of more than 7000 feet in order to effect a crossing of the summit of the range. Between the 77th and 137th mileposts there were fifteen tunnels. Snow galleries, sheds thrown over the track, similar to those in use on railroads in Switzerland, were built. Six miles of these were in service in the Sierras in the severe winter of 1866–7.[4] With such protection to the line traffic was interrupted for but a short time, not longer, it was said, than on the Eastern roads. The company had laid down 390 miles of irons when the Secretary of the Interior made his report in 1868, and the workmen were moving eastwardly through Nevada toward the Great Salt Lake.[5]

The engineering difficulties in the mountains, the hostility of the Indians, the crossing of great spaces of country without wood or water under the escort of the military, the arming of the workmen engaged in levelling the bed and laying the track, their aversion to labor under such conditions except for very high wages, the cost of hauling materials for hundreds and thousands of miles to the rail-ends could not quench the spirit of enterprise in the West in the years following the war. The completion of one road had not yet been accomplished, but the impatient desires of the people called for activity in other belts of settlement. A dozen companies which were extend-

---

[1] Simpson, pp. 118–20.

[2] Report of Secretary of Interior for 1865, p. xiv.

[3] Ibid. for 1866, p. 12.

[4] N. Y. Tribune, Dec. 13, 1867, citing San Francisco Alta.

[5] Report of the Secretary for that year, p. xiii.

ing their rails toward the frontiers of civilization had visions of a destination on the Pacific coast. Many were making surveys of the country with a view to asking Congress for grants; some received them and set about the work of laying track.

Not a few there had been to proclaim the northern route the better one for the government to select for its favor in 1862, in spite of the claims of Denver, Salt Lake City, the Nevada silver mining towns, and San Francisco standing on the central line. On July 2, 1864, Congress incorporated the Northern Pacific Railroad Company to construct a railway from Lake Superior to Puget Sound, with a branch to Portland, Ore. The provisions of the bill followed those adopted in reference to the other Pacific road, except that no bonds were offered to the company. The land grants were more liberal, for the Puget Sound line was to receive the alternate sections in a belt 80 miles in width, 40 miles upon each side of the track, from the western boundary of Minnesota to the Pacific Ocean. In Minnesota, and in Oregon, for the branch line, the gift would• include the alternate sections in a strip 40 miles wide, as in the case of the Union Pacific. Josiah Perham, who had been a merchant in Maine, and now lived in Massachusetts, was the president of the company. He believed that he could build the road without a mortgage. The Northern Pacific would be a great "People's Railroad." To its support men would gravitate for sentimental reasons. Such a railway would quicken Canada's desire for annexation, said the New York Tribune. It would bring the commerce of the Hudson Bay Company to New York. In five years after the line should be completed that city would possess itself of the trade of all British North America.[1]

Perham's board of directors met, accepted the terms of the act and "served notice" upon Mr. Lincoln, as the President said, in forwarding the paper to Mr. Usher, who told Perham hereafter to address his communications to the Secretary of the Interior.[2] Some stock was sold, but the revenues from this source soon failed, whereupon the charter was offered for sale

[1] N. Y. Tribune, Aug. 19, 1865.　　　　[2] Simpson, p. 122.

in Wall Street and other banking centres. It was about to be transferred to the Grand Trunk Railroad of Canada, when Perham, just before his death, succeeded in disposing of it to a group of railway managers in Vermont.[1] A certain number of miles must be completed in a specified period of time; the limits were extended by act of Congress. Jay Cooke, who had sold the war loans, was besought to come to the aid of the company and undertake to finance its operations. He had just finished selling the bonds of the Lake Superior and Mississippi Railroad, to extend from St. Paul, the head of navigation on the Mississippi, to the new town of Duluth at the western end of Lake Superior, which was to serve as the starting-point for the railroad, across the prairies of Minnesota and Dakota, to Montana and the Pacific coast. But he still demurred, and the officers of the company year by year had nothing to report to the Secretary of the Interior except that they had surveyors in the field seeking out the most feasible route.[2]

The St. Paul and Pacific Railroad was being built to St. Cloud following the Mississippi Valley. It was expected to reach the settlements in the valley of the Saskatchewan and go west over British territory.[3]

Various lines to the coast were projected in the south. The Union Pacific Railway, Eastern Division, bound for Denver, soon to be called the Kansas Pacific, was surveying a line to California, and was appealing for the favor of Congress.[4]

The Southwest Pacific, directed by John C. Frémont, was a road which left the Missouri Pacific line some miles west of St. Louis and extended its irons for 310 miles in a southwesterly direction to Springfield. It was reorganized as the Atlantic and Pacific Railroad, to be continued to California on the 35th parallel. From Springfield to San Francisco was a distance of 1800 miles by a direct and easy way, said Frémont; for the

---

[1] Oberholtzer, Jay Cooke, vol. ii, pp. 97, 99–100.

[2] Article on Pacific Railroads in Atlantic Monthly for March, 1866.

[3] Jay Cooke, vol. ii, p. 342.

[4] Report of Secretary of Interior for 1867, p. 15; ibid. for 1868, pp. 162, 370; Wm. A. Bell, in New Tracks in North America, gives an account of the surveys for this line.

most part in the valleys of streams.[1] The road was incorporated by act of Congress of July 27, 1866, and was endowed with one-half the public lands in a belt 80 miles wide in the territories, and 40 miles wide in the states through which it should pass, as in the case of the Northern Pacific Company, computed to amount in all to 46,000,000 acres. Another company, called the Southern Pacific, would carry the line from the eastern boundary of California to San Francisco.

In the South, too, there were the Central Pacific of Arkansas to run from Memphis and Little Rock to Fort Smith; the South Pacific, projected from Shreveport, La., through Texas to meet the South Pacific of California at San Diego; the Memphis, El Paso and Pacific to pass through Arkansas and Texas to the coast; the Gulf and Pacific to follow a line from Matagorda Bay to San Diego.[2]

Up to 1867 it was computed that Congress in different acts had pledged 184,000,000 acres of the public lands to railroads, and that 21,000,000 acres had actually been patented to the companies. The Union Pacific was receiving 12,800 acres for each mile of finished road; the Northern Pacific and the Atlantic and Pacific were promised 25,600. The empire thus granted away exceeded the area of the six New England states, New York, New Jersey, Pennsylvania, Ohio, Delaware, Maryland and Virginia.[3] The Northern Pacific land grant alone, said the promoters of that railroad, comprised 50,000,000 acres, a domain larger in extent than all New England and Maryland besides.[4]

Still more roads were seeking lands, and some of those which had these grants were lobbying actively at Washington for bond subsidies, such as had been given to the Union Pacific and its connecting railroads. But the government had pledged its credit for a sum which it was estimated would reach a total of $60,000,000, and a sentiment arose very unfavorable to fur-

---

[1] N. Y. Tribune, Oct. 18, 1866.
[2] Senate Ex. Doc., 47th Cong., 1st sess., no. 69, p. 27.
[3] Report of Secretary of the Interior for 1867, p. 141.
[4] Oberholtzer, Jay Cooke, vol. ii, p. 313.

ther direct money grants of this kind by Congress to any corporation.[1]

Of law in this vast western wilderness there was practically none. Even after the territories were organized local government failed. Mingled with industrious and well-meaning people were ruffians and cut-throats, gathered from every part of the world. How were they to be controlled? — where would they find punishment for their crimes? Gold and silver, the treasure of the mountains, was the coveted booty of thieves. Miners who had gained it by hard labor and bore it away were shot. Stage-coaches which carried express packages containing gold-dust were waylaid and the drivers and passengers were killed. These desperadoes in Idaho and Montana came to be called "road agents."

The discovery of gold in the mountains along the Snake River on the eastern boundaries of Oregon drew to this region in the first years of the war a miscellaneous rabble of adventurers and villains who were sometimes in Wallula, sometimes at Walla Walla, and again at Lewiston, which became the capital of the new territory, when it was formed in 1863. Robbery and murder were almost daily events. Into Lewiston, when the wickedness of that mining emporium was at its height, came an intelligent and affable young man of a good family in Connecticut, Henry Plummer. He soon put himself at the head of a band of outlaws who struck terror into every town in the northern mountains.[2] In the stampede to the Boisé district these men moved down to Boisé City and Idaho City; then later in the Montana excitement over to Bannack and Virginia City.[3]

Plummer by his likeable qualities succeeded in causing himself to be elected sheriff. In this office he shielded his confederates, in all some 50 desperate men, and 100 more who acted as stool-pigeons and spies. Every placer was watched,

---

[1] Cf. Report of Government Director Taylor, Jan. 30, 1867, Senate Ex. Doc., 47th Cong., 1st sess., no. 69, pp. 26 et seq.

[2] N. P. Langford, Vigilante Days and Ways, vol. i, pp. 78-9.

[3] Ibid., vol. ii, pp. 169-70.

and when the treasure started out by coach, or whatever conveyance, it was overtaken and stolen. The situation became intolerable long before any way was found to better it. There had been vigilantes in Lewiston and some of the Idaho towns, as earlier in California, but to cope with such a band as Plummer's an unusual organization was required. Several dauntless and determined men, among them John X. Beidler from Chambersburg, Pa., known to every one as "X," led the movement. The vigilantes of Montana came to number 3000. Plummer was caught while he was washing his face in his cabin at Bannack, and was hanged from a gallows tree from which the bodies of two of his confederates already dangled in the air. One winter night the members of his gang in Virginia City found all the roads leading out of the place picketed. The entire town was surrounded by armed men and five of the reprobates were taken, to be hanged together the next day at high noon in the sight of thousands of people.[1] Before the vigilantes were done there were executed by legal methods or by lynch law in Montana upwards of a hundred men, while other offenders returned to Idaho, or took refuge in Canada.[2]

Such additions to the lawless population of Idaho caused men to say that it would be well if there were some union of the citizens of that territory to punish desperadoes; there were "scores and scores of murders," but no man was ever tried and hanged for his crimes.[3] The people took matters into their own hands with salutary effect. From 1861 to 1866, in Idaho and Montana together, at least 200 outlaws came to the end of their wicked days through vigilance committees.[4]

So, too, was it in Denver, which to W. Hepworth Dixon, the English traveller, seemed "a city of demons." Men were shot

[1] Article on Montana, Atlantic Monthly for August, 1866.

[2] N. Y. Tribune, Aug. 21, 1867; Boller, Among the Indians, pp. 388–93.

[3] Boisé City corr., N. Y. Tribune, March 7, 1866.

[4] H. H. Bancroft, History of Washington, Idaho and Montana, p. 462.

in front of his window. Nightly there were fatal brawls in the saloons and gambling dens. Murder was committed with impunity in the principal streets until a vigilance committee was formed to hang the worst of the ruffians from telegraph poles and cottonwood trees. This committee, said a New York Tribune correspondent, was better "than all the courts and all the civil officers in the land." [1] In the space of a few days, in the summer of 1865, fifteen horse and cattle thieves were lynched in and around Wallula on the northeastern frontier of Oregon.[2] Along the roads and in the mountain towns of this yet wild West no man need be surprised, if he should see dead bodies dangling from pieces of timber put out of the upper windows of cabins, or from the boughs of trees, a warning to their like who still went about unpunished for their frightful sins.

As the railroad advanced across Nebraska, gamblers, brothel keepers and blacklegs of every type gathered in the town at its head. Hither the workmen came to squander their wages, here the stage drivers and the mule and bull whackers congregated instead of at Atchison and the towns on the Missouri, where they earlier had found their passengers and freight. This town was aptly named a "hell on wheels." The harpies and sutlers with their whiskey saloons, hurdy-gurdy houses and faro dens set them up first in North Platte, then at Julesburg, Cheyenne, Laramie and Benton City in turn. Julesburg, which had been a place of six huts on the stage road along the Platte, became in six weeks a city covering ten acres, with 900 saloons and a population of several thousand. Revolvers rang and bowie knives flashed night and day until the tide of sin moved on. The gamblers elected one of their number mayor, when General Augur stepped in, proclaimed martial law and detailed soldiers to patrol the streets.[3]

Beyond Nebraska lay a tract of country which now for several years had been a part of the territory of Dakota. The town of Cheyenne was platted on July 4, 1867. It was the

---

[1] N. Y. Tribune, Feb. 24, 1866.
[2] Ibid., July 11, 1865.   [3] Ibid., Aug. 9 and 28, 1867.

site of railroad shops, and it soon gained a population of 5000, but it was 600 miles by the nearest route from Yankton, the territorial capital.[1] Other towns on the Union Pacific Railroad were still farther away from the seat of government. It was proposed, therefore, to take this western end of Dakota, south of Montana and north of Colorado, together with a strip of Utah — again desirably limiting the jurisdiction of the Mormons — and a corner of Idaho to form a new territory. But the plan met with opposition in Congress. It was a scheme, so it was said, of a few speculators engaged in building "paper cities" and of men desirous of holding political office. Such movements were contagious. Citizens in the southern part of New Mexico were petitioning Congress for a new territory to be called Montezuma; others in Montana, Idaho and Washington, near the British line, found inconvenience in their situation and would have a separate territory of Columbia.[2]

When a territory was formed, it was but a short way to statehood. Here were Oregon and Nevada, both states of the Union, but neither of them had sufficient population for one Congressional district. This proposed new territory in western Dakota was large enough for separate political organization; so much indeed was true. It was "almost as boundless as the desert of Sahara," said a representative in Congress, and it was "for the most part as worthless." [3]

But if it were to be organized, what should its name be? The House proposed Wyoming, but the Senate suggested Lincoln instead. There was a territory of Washington; why not honor the Civil War President, a nation's martyr, in the same way? One senator regretted that a territory had ever been called after Washington; he would not depart from the custom of using Indian names. Very well; but why, it was asked, this particular Indian name for a territory lying out among the Rocky Mountains? Wyoming was borrowed from Pennsylvania, a fact which led Senator Cameron of that state to thank

[1] Laws of Dakota for 1867–8, p. 286.
[2] Laws of Idaho for 1866, p. 293; ibid. for 1867, p. 196.
[3] Cong. Globe, 40th Cong., 2d sess., pp. 4344–5.

his colleagues for their compliment. The name should be of local origin and application. Let it be Shoshone, which it was complained was too difficult to spell. Or Cheyenne? But this word was French, said one. It was merely *chien*, said another. It might be prairie dog as a third, or female dog as a fourth averred, for which reason a fifth would *cur*-tail it. But, even if it were the name of an animal, why might it not be chosen? Chicago bore a respectable reputation and that word was Indian for skunk. To still another Cheyenne was suggestive of cayenne, a substance very offensive to him. It made the world sneeze. Senator Sherman sent to Mr. Spofford, in the Library of Congress, who consulted Schoolcraft and Hayden. But after men had spoken for Platte and Arapahoe it was determined, as Wyoming was a word of pleasant syllables, as it was liked by the inhabitants of the country, as it meant, so it was alleged, "big plains," as no two men could agree upon a better one, that this should be the name of the new territory.[1]

[1] Cong. Globe, 40th Cong., 2d sess., pp. 2792–4.

CHAPTER VI

THE INDIANS

THE opening and use of new wagon roads, such as those along the Smoky Hill to Denver and over the Bozeman route to Montana, the endless caravans upon the plains, the digging up of the earth and the sound of crushers and stamps in the mountains, the steamboats on the upper Missouri and on the head waters of the Columbia, and now, lately, the laying down of sleepers and irons for railways in Nebraska and Kansas disturbed the Indians. They had been little in the popular mind in the midst of the great events of the war. Their outrages upon the frontiersmen were overlooked while great battles were waged on the Mississippi and in Virginia. But at least two occurrences during this period had directed attention to the red man. One of these was a terrible massacre of white settlers in Minnesota in 1862, and the other a not much less terrible retribution for a long series of outrages upon the pioneers of Colorado, visited upon the Indians in that territory, by Colonel J. M. Chivington and some volunteer troops at Sand Creek in 1864.

Prior to the year 1862 various sub-tribes of the Sioux still occupied the western part of Minnesota. The frontier line of settlement was pressing forward rapidly, German and Norwegian families being prominent in the movement. A drunken band, under a chief called Little Crow, began the reign of butchery in August, 1862, and hundreds of the savages were soon on the war-path, scalping men, violating and killing women, beating out the brains of infants and committing all the hideous cruelties peculiar to Indian warfare. From outrages upon isolated farm-houses they passed to attacks upon towns which were

339

beleaguered and burned. Agency buildings were destroyed; government posts were besieged. Militiamen were sent out against the savages, and late in September General Pope arrived to command a body of regulars. Not less than 50,000 persons, abandoning their farms, fled to St. Paul, Minneapolis and the towns on the Mississippi River, where they became charges upon charity. Some have estimated that 1000 settlers lost their lives, many of them under the most atrocious circumstances, in this series of massacres. About 2000 Indians were captured or surrendered themselves to the soldiery. Hundreds of these were tried by court martial, convicted and sentenced to death. President Lincoln, after reviewing the proceedings, remitted the penalties imposed upon many of the prisoners, but caused 39 to be hanged. The others were put under guard at Davenport, Iowa, and were sent finally to a reservation in Dakota.[1] Military expeditions against the Sioux who had escaped in 1862 were organized in 1863 and 1864 under Generals Sully and Sibley, and practically all the Indians in Minnesota, in answer to the demands of the frightened people, either were driven by force or were removed peacefully to lands outside the state.[2]

While the Minnesota outrages were a count in the long indictment against the Indians, the Sand Creek affair, two years later, brought dishonor to the white man. This barbarity was the culmination of a movement to avenge fearful atrocities committed by the Cheyennes and Arapahoes. Property and life were nowhere secure. Cattle and horses were run off by the savages, emigrants were ambushed and killed, ranch houses were attacked, prisoners were tortured, the bodies of the slain were mutilated, women and children were carried away to an awful captivity. For weeks, in the summer of 1864, no stages could pass out or in upon the overland road. Such outrages, the

[1] The legislature of Dakota called them "hell hounds," and protested against their coming into the territory. — Laws of Dakota for 1866–7, p. 123; cf. Report of Secretary of Interior for 1866, pp. 229–31.

[2] O. R., series i, vol. xlviii, part ii, p. 565; Report of Commr. of Indian Affairs for 1867, p. 19.

Colorado people said, were not longer to be borne, and, if they could not have the protection of the military forces of the United States, they would take matters into their own hands, meet the foe with his own warfare and deliver him a blow that he might not soon forget. John Evans, of Pennsylvania-Quaker ancestry, for some years a prominent citizen of Chicago, was appointed by President Lincoln governor of the territory. In August, 1864, he issued a proclamation directing such friendly Indians as were scattered over the plains to come into the forts; others, he said, would be "pursued and destroyed." All the citizens of Colorado, acting either individually or in parties, were authorized to kill, as enemies of the country, Indians wherever they might be found remaining outside the places of rendezvous. Property captured should belong to the captors. "All good citizens" were urged "to do their duty for the defence of their homes and families." [1]

A body of Cheyennes with some Arapahoes, under White Antelope, Black Kettle and other chiefs, were gathered together at Fort Lyon in Colorado and had been assured, it was said, of the protection of the troops. This for a time they enjoyed, but the post passed to the command of another officer and the Indians were told to go out upon the plains. They formed a camp at the Bend of the Big Sandy, or Sand Creek, about forty miles north of the fort, where they were surprised at sunrise on November 29, 1864, by Colonel Chivington advancing at the head of a force of Colorado volunteers. He was a native of Ohio and had been a man of peace. Indeed he had been a presiding elder of the Methodist church and a missionary to the Indians.[2] But, enlisting with the territorial militia, he led a body of "Pike's Peakers," who had fought like demons against the Texas Rangers in New Mexico in 1862. For these exploits he had been thanked by the legislature, and by this time had become a true son of Mars.[3] Whatever his earlier

[1] Report of Joint Committee on the Conduct of the War, vol. iii, Massacre of Cheyenne Indians, p. 47.

[2] H. H. Bancroft, History of Nevada, Colorado and Wyoming, p. 422.

[3] H. H. Bancroft, History of Arizona and New Mexico, p. 697.

sympathies, he was moved no longer by any sentimental considerations in reference to the aboriginal inhabitants of America. He called them "red scoundrels." He "damned" any man who dared to wish them well,[1] and had been heard to say in a public speech that it was a duty "to kill and scalp all, big and little, for nits made lice." [2] Various accounts of the event have been given, but the truth seems to be that Chivington knew that the Indians at Sand Creek had expressed a desire for peace and that from one-half to two-thirds of them were women and children. It is said that some 1200 were in the camp at the time of the attack, which was conducted by about 750 men, armed with muskets and carbines, some of them mounted. The troops were supported by four 12-pound mountain howitzers. One of the chiefs ran up an American flag, but indiscriminate slaughter continued until the middle of the afternoon. Witnesses appeared to say that Chivington forbade the taking of prisoners, that even sucking babes were not spared, that men and women alike were scalped, that the corpses were otherwise mutilated. Chivington himself boasted that his troops had killed 500 or 600 Indians (though others declared his estimate much too high) for a loss of 7 men slain and 47 wounded. It was "one of the most bloody Indian battles ever fought on these plains," he continued.[3] He had nearly annihilated the entire tribe.[4] Six hundred horses, mules and ponies were captured, together with many buffalo skins and other property. Chivington warmly complimented his men. "All did nobly," said he in his official report of the event to General Curtis at Fort Leavenworth.[5] In a similar spirit the second in command of the expedition, Colonel Shoup, said that it was "the severest chastisement ever given to Indians in battle on the American continent." [6] The historian would "search in vain for braver deeds than were committed on that field of battle." [7]

[1] Senate Reports, 39th Cong., 2d sess., no. 156, p. 74.
[2] Ibid., p. 71.   [3] Ibid., p. 92.
[4] Report of Joint Committee on the Conduct of the War, loc. cit., p. 48.
[5] Senate Reports, 39th Cong., 2d sess., no. 156, p. 91.
[6] Ibid., p. 92.   [7] Report of Joint Committee, loc. cit., p. 51.

In Colorado, the soldiers returning from the bloody scene received enthusiastic praise. They had "covered themselves with glory," said the Rocky Mountain News of Denver. The engagement would stand among the most brilliant feats of arms in Indian warfare.[1] ꞏ Chivington believed that he would be made a brigadier-general as a reward for his gallantry.[2]

But men who lived with their wives and children in safe places in the East, and who knew only the Indians of the Leatherstocking Tales and the Metamora of Edwin Forrest, saw what had taken place through other eyes. They were filled with indignation. The subject appeared in Congress. It was referred to the Joint Committee on the Conduct of the War, of which Senator B. F. Wade was the chairman. He and his colleagues found it "difficult to believe that beings in the form of men" could commit or countenance "the commission of such acts of barbarity." As for Chivington himself, though he wore the uniform of a United States soldier, he had "deliberately planned and executed a foul and dastardly massacre which would have disgraced the veriest savage among those who were the victims of his cruelty," and so on. He and such others as might be responsible for this crime against civilization should suffer appropriate punishment.[3]

A military commission was appointed and sat for seventy-six days at Fort Lyon and in Denver, taking the testimony of witnesses of the massacre.[4] It was labor in vain. The sympathy of the Colorado pioneers for Chivington was general. He had espoused their cause. For long it had been a dangerous thing in Denver, in Central City, or along the line of any of the over-

[1] Report of Joint Committee, loc. cit., pp. 56–7.
[2] Senate Reports, 39th Cong., 2d sess., no. 156, p. 74.
[3] Joint Committee Report, loc. cit., pp. iv–vi.
[4] This is published in Senate Ex. Doc., 39th Cong., 2d sess., no. 26. Much testimony is incorporated, too, in the Report of the Joint Committee on the Conduct of the War, loc. cit., and in the Report of Senator Doolittle's Joint Special Committee, 39th Cong., 2d sess., Senate Reports, no. 156. In this report Governor Evans makes a statement in his own vindication in reply to the censure of Wade's committee. Cf., for comment, Grinnell, The Fighting Cheyennes, chap. xiv.

land roads, travellers observed, to say aught that was favorable of the Indian. He would not scruple to break the finger joints of his prisoners, to kindle fires under their bare feet, to rack and mutilate their bodies in a thousand fiendish ways. If squaws had been killed at Sand Creek, let it be so. The Indian women no less than the men were torturers of white captives. They had fought furiously beside the "braves" on the bloody ground on the banks of the Big Sandy.[1] Chivington had struck the savages with their own weapons in their own way; now there might be safety and peace.

Possibly the lesson so barbarously administered might have been salutary but for the knowledge, soon spread among the Indians, that the act was disavowed by the government and condemned by opinion generally in the East. The relations between the "Great Father" at Washington and the various tribes were controlled by a commissioner at the head of a bureau, attached to the Department of the Interior. The whole country, for administrative purposes, was divided into four-teen superintendencies. Immediately west of the frontiers of settlement in the Mississippi Valley were the Northern Superin-tendency, with headquarters earlier at St. Paul but now removed to Omaha; the Central, with offices at Atchison; and the South-ern, covering the Indian country south of Kansas, inhabited by the Cherokees, Creeks, Seminoles, Choctaws, Chickasaws and some other tribes. Farther west there were superintendencies for each state and territory — in Dakota, Montana, Colorado, New Mexico, Arizona, Idaho, Utah, Nevada, California, Oregon and Washington. Serving under each superintendent were a number of agents who were supposed to live upon the reservations in proximity to the Indians assigned to their care, when these Indians were settled upon reservations. Some of the agents were at the same time traders, licensed by the govern-ment to traffic in goods with the savages. A few were mission-aries and teachers. In the north, near the Canadian line, French priests were aiming to bring the tribes to Christianity.

[1] Dixon, New America, p. 68; A. K. McClure, Three Thousand Miles through the Rocky Mountains, p. 51.

Father Chirouse had labored with the greatest devotion for many years among the Tulalips in Washington Territory.[1] The Society of Friends and other religious denominations still strove to uplift and civilize the American aborigine, a work which had been uninterrupted almost from the day white men had first established settlements upon the continent. The tribes had been set here and there on reservations, and were to be taught to farm, as the wards of a charitable state. Connected with some of the agencies were agricultural and industrial schools; flour and saw mills were built. The government bought seeds and implements, paid the wages of teachers, plough-makers, farriers, gunsmiths, millers, sawyers, farmers, carpenters, physicians and other men who were to raise the red people out of savagery, and make them fit in due time to take their places as American citizens.

In all it was computed that there were 300,000 Indians in the United States — about 26,000 in California, 34,000 in Arizona, 20,000 in Utah, 20,000 in New Mexico, 24,000 in Dakota, 18,000 in the Northern, 13,000 in the Central and 54,000 in the Southern Superintendencies.[2] It was commonly said, and as commonly believed, that the whole number of them in the country was diminishing. They soon would be extinct, but for the intercessions of philanthropists. The Abolitionist sentiment which had triumphed in the war, and had made the black man the equal of his white brother, would demand not less for these remnants of the red race scattered over the West. The influence of the Indian Bureau, from the commissioner at Washington down to the agent on a reservation, was on the side of the aborigine. His wrongs had been many and his burdens were heavy to bear. Likewise the traders were his apologists. By pretending to friendship they drove many a good bargain. So it was that the Indians, cozened and cajoled as they long had been, were told again by the traders, the half-breeds and other intermediaries around the agencies that there would be atonement for the day of blood at Sand Creek.

[1] Report of Commr. of Indian Affairs for 1865, p. 243.
[2] Senate Ex. Doc., 40th Cong., special sess., no. 4, pp. 28–30.

The entire frontier was ablaze in the winter and spring following the Chivington massacre. The Platte route was raided
from Living Springs, fifty miles east of Denver, almost to the
Missouri. Telegraph lines were down as in 1864. For six
weeks no mails passed east or west.[1] Trains were captured,
stages attacked, cattle run off, men, women and children
butchered in cold blood.[2] Scarcely a station or ranch escaped,
barring Godfrey's sod house, on the road beyond Julesburg.
For many hours, with little aid, he stood off more than 150
Indians, who, at length, after trying vainly to burn him out,
gave up the siege. For this feat he was known thereafter as
"Old Wicked," and his house as "Fort Wicked."[3]

On the Santa Fé trail similar conditions prevailed. The
legislature of New Mexico memorialized Congress on the subject of the depredations. The secretary of the territory was in
possession of proof that the Indians had killed 123 persons,
wounded 32, made captives of 21 and that they had stolen 3500
horses and mules, 13,000 head of cattle and 294,000 sheep and
goats — all together valued at not less than $1,377,000.[4] The
people asked for reimbursement under the provisions of the
Treaty of Guadalupe Hidalgo.[5]

If the Indians had been allowed to do as they would to the
advancing columns of white settlement while the war was in
progress, it must not be so now. Expeditions should be sent
against them; they should be made to feel the power of the
government in one grand campaign. St. Louis was the centre
for the organization of the military operations in the Southwest. General Pope, who had gained a valuable knowledge of
Indian affairs in Minnesota, was now in command of the so-
called Division of the Missouri. General Grenville M. Dodge
served under him as the commander of the Department of the
Missouri, and proved to be a vigorous officer. He sent troops

[1] N. Y. Tribune, Nov. 21, 1867.

[2] Julesburg corr., N. Y. Tribune, Oct. 21, 1865.

[3] A. K. McClure, Three Thousand Miles through the Rocky Mountains, pp. 63, 70–1.

[4] Report of Commr. of Indian Affairs for 1866, p. 153.

[5] Ibid. for 1867, p. 196.

over the roads to reopen overland mail and telegraph lines, but peace was still far away, for in June, 1865, he wrote the new Secretary of the Interior, who, the Western settlers were assured, would pursue a more energetic policy,[1] that every Indian tribe capable of mischief from the British possessions in the north to the Red River of Arkansas was on the war-path. Not an emigrant train or a coach could pass over the plains without military guard.[2] A new stage road running into the Owyhee mines in Idaho must be abandoned. Indians attacked the stations and stole the stock. Dastardly outrages were perpetrated upon emigrants. One hundred and sixty-three persons appealed for protection to the governor of the territory of Idaho.[3] Indians had murdered a settler's family in Minnesota, and, frightened by the recollection of what had occurred in 1862, a stampede ensued.[4]

The campaign began. General Sully was sent with a force of cavalry to operate against the Sioux around Devil's Lake in Dakota to reassure the people of Minnesota. General Dodge stationed troops upon the more than 3000 miles of overland roads lying within his department and equipped seven expeditions, numbering about 22,000 men, to penetrate the Indian country in as many directions. General Connor, in command of the District of the Plains (Nebraska, Colorado and Utah), a redoubtable Irishman with much experience in Indian warfare, was despatched into the Black Hills and to the Powder River country, north of Fort Laramie, along the line of the Bozeman road to Montana. Practised Indian fighters were assigned to western Kansas to operate against the savages which were raiding the Smoky Hill route and to the country lying north and south of the Santa Fé trail, and there was promise of a successful campaign.

At this point a Congressional committee, appointed by resolution of March 3, 1865, to inquire into the present condition of

[1] St. Louis corr. of N. Y. Tribune, Sept. 18, 1865.
[2] O. R., series i, vol. xlviii, part ii, p. 971; also ibid., part i, pp. 329 et seq. and 335 et seq.   [3] Ibid., vol. l, part ii, p. 1279.
[4] Ibid., vol. xlviii, part ii, pp. 565, 764.

the Indian tribes, and the manner in which they were being treated by the civil and military authorities, until $15,000 appropriated for its use should be expended, appeared upon the scene. It was headed by President Johnson's friend, Senator Doolittle of Wisconsin. Some of its members had started to the Northwest, others to the plains, and still others to the Pacific coast for a thorough examination of the Indian question. Doolittle himself visited Kansas and Colorado with the olive branch in his hand, though "the most fiendish outrages and vilest depredations" were committed upon the frontier within a few days after he had passed on his mission of peace.[1] He found that the war had been induced by Chivington's "treacherous, brutal, cowardly butchery" of the Cheyennes. "A fiend would blush to record" such deeds as were committed on that day in November, 1864, on Sand Creek. This campaign of 1865 had been organized by some general acting "on his own hook." Millions of money would be spent without avail. In the end government and chiefs must sign treaties, which could be signed as well before as after a military operation. Doolittle halted the plans for an expedition against the Comanches and Kiowas by an appeal to General Pope.[2] He wrote to Secretary Harlan and telegraphed to the President. Indian Commissioner Dole spoke for peace, but said that his efforts to obtain it were "constantly thwarted" by the military commanders stationed in the West. The correspondence was forwarded to Secretary Stanton,[3] and the newspapers began an agitation in behalf of the mistreated Indian. He had a "charm" similar to that of the Highlander of Scotland, said the New York Tribune. We had done justice to the negro, now let us address ourselves to the needs of the Indian. Ours was the "freebooter's" doctrine, that might made right. Our missionaries had been our sutlers and dragoons; our Bibles, rum and smallpox.[4]

[1] Fort Riley corr., N. Y. Tribune, June 26, 1865.
[2] Senate Reports, 39th Cong., 2d sess., no. 156, p. 9; O. R., series i, vol. xlviii, part i, pp. 338, 361.
[3] O. R., series i, vol. xlviii, part ii, pp. 868–70.
[4] N. Y. Tribune, Sept. 13, 1865.

Stanton was moved in July to the extent of telegraphing to
Grant to complain of the cost of the "war." The transportation expenses alone were $2,000,000 a month at Fort Leaven-
worth. Secretary of the Treasury McCulloch could not meet so
large and unexpected a demand for funds. President Johnson
would know what were the object and design of the campaign.
Who had planned it?[1] The Secretary of War said that he
had not authorized such operations. Grant, in turn, disclaimed
knowledge of them; he would telegraph to Sherman,[2] in command of the new military Division of the Mississippi. But
Sherman had only lately come to his place. He had been
marching through Georgia when this Indian campaign was
begun by Pope and Dodge.[3] Grant, in response to popular
clamor, instructed Sherman to "stop all unnecessary expeditions and reduce all necessary ones to actual requirements."[4]
Pope received the orders in August and transmitted them to
Dodge,[5] who reluctantly prepared to comply.

Arrayed against his forces were no less than 15,000 red
warriors in the north and 10,000 in the south.[6] What might
be done? The expeditions were "launched beyond recall,"
Quartermaster-General Meigs told Secretary Stanton. Supplies worth $10,000,000, exclusive of the "outfits" taken by
the troops in their own trains, had gone to the depots on the
plains.[7] Of telegraphs and railroads into the country which
the expeditions were penetrating there were none. The campaign must proceed, and it was waged vigorously.

Settlers living around Mankato, in Minnesota, asked General
Curtis for permission to hunt the skulking redskins in that
neighborhood with bloodhounds, but he said that this system
of warfare had been tried in Florida during Van Buren's ad-

---

[1] O. R., series i, vol. xlviii, part ii, p. 1178.

[2] Ibid., pp. 1127-8.

[3] General Dodge's reply to Doolittle's and Dole's charges that he had
begun the war is to be found in ibid., p. 971.

[4] Ibid., pp. 1128, 1199.

[5] Ibid., pp. 1149, 1154; part i of same volume, pp. 350 et seq.

[6] Ibid., part ii, pp. 1156-8.

[7] Ibid., p. 1167.

ministration, where it had ended in failure and disgrace. Anyhow Indians were not afraid of dogs; they ate them.[1] The legislature of Dakota made a similar request of the Secretary of War. This "reliable auxiliary force" should be at hand at each military post.[2] General Sully at Sioux City sought authority of General Pope to take friendly Indians into his service and to pay them $50 each for scalps, as he had done in 1864.[3] Connor on the Powder River told his men to take no prisoners, but to kill every male Indian over twelve years of age,[4] an order which Pope, when it came to his attention, called "atrocious"; it would cost Connor his commission and must be countermanded at once.[5]

But the campaign continued. Connor's operations were as decisive as any of the year. He established a post, named Fort Connor, in the very heart of the Indian country, and, although much interfered with by the slowness of his transport and the reduction of his forces, in conformity to orders from Washington, he chastised one tribe "in a manner seldom equalled and never excelled," while he "severely punished" two other tribes. General Dodge recommended his promotion for his "energy, capacity and fidelity to duty." [6] But his reward was only reproof from Washington and his transfer to Salt Lake City.[7]

The course of events was very disquieting to the Indian agents and the humane people in the East, who had befriended the aboriginal race. "A bale of blankets or a sack of flour," said the superintendent in Utah, in establishing good relations with the Indians, would be worth much more than its weight in gold expended for war.[8] Let there be more treaties, — more kindness, more gifts.

---

[1] O. R., series i, vol. xlviii, part ii, p. 801.
[2] Laws of Dakota for 1865-6, p. 545.
[3] O. R., series i, vol. xlviii, part ii, p. 852.
[4] Ibid., p. 1131.   [5] Ibid., part i, p. 356.
[6] Ibid., pp. 335 et seq.
[7] Ibid., part ii, pp. 1201, 1209; cf. Grinnell, The Fighting Cheyennes, chap. xvi.
[8] Report of Commr. of Indian Affairs for 1866, p. 126.

The President appointed a commission of seven members, including General J. B. Sanborn, General W. S. Harney, Kit Carson and the Indian agent Leavenworth to make treaties with the southwestern Indians, and they held their first council on the upper Arkansas River in October, 1865. At the same time a commission composed of General Curtis, N. G. Taylor, Governor Edmunds of Dakota, General Sibley and others proceeded to the upper Missouri to treat with the Sioux.[1]

Many now pretended to see the signs of a better day for the Indian. He had been driven from pillar to post. Some of the tribes had been sent out of their homes on the Atlantic seaboard. They had betaken themselves to new lands beyond the Allegheny Mountains, whence they had passed to the plains at the foot of the Rocky Mountains. They had nowhere to lay their heads, the white man pressing them farther and farther into the wilderness and out upon the desert.[2] If they had rich lands or valuable mines which the white man coveted, they were dispossessed in spite of the most solemn treaties between their chiefs and the government of the United States. They were no sooner at home on one reservation than they were driven to another. They depended upon the buffalo for their food, the skins of this animal to cover them in winter and to make their tents. But the country in which the herds had roamed was now penetrated by railroads. The prairies were planted with wheat and corn. Beyond, on the plains, whither the animals had gone, emigrant trains passed over the roads, ranchmen everywhere grazed their cattle upon the sparse growth of grass, ruthless hunters pursued the wild game in mere love of the chase. The Indian, as General Sherman vividly declared, was "wriggling against his doom."

Although, at times, as in the last days of August, 1867, the Platte Valley in Nebraska was covered with buffaloes, spread out like "a vast surging black sea," [3] they now, for some years, seldom came near this well-travelled highway. Not so on the

---

[1] Report of Commr. of Indian Affairs for 1865, pp. 699 et seq.
[2] Ibid. for 1866, p. 172.
[3] Omaha corr., N. Y. Tribune, Sept. 5, 1867.

Smoky Hill road to Denver and the Powder River road to Montana. These roads crossed the principal ranges remaining to the animals. For forty hours on the Smoky Hill, said the English traveller Dixon in 1866, buffaloes were always in sight of the Denver stage, "thousands on thousands, tens of thousands after tens of thousands." [1]

The Indians themselves, now that they often had guns instead of only bows and arrows, decimated the herds. Although they numbered but 670 souls the Kaws secured 3000 buffaloes on their hunt in 1865, and sold $21,000 worth of hides.[2] The meat of the bull, except the tongue, especially if he were an old animal, was tough and rank, and the hair, except upon his neck, was little longer than a horse's. The cow, on the other hand, had a fine fur and a tender "hump" and loin, and she was usually preferred for slaughter with disadvantage to the herds. Captain Raynolds, when he was sent out to explore Montana, upon mounting the bluffs and looking down into the Yellowstone Valley, beheld fifty square miles covered with buffaloes, but he thought that not more than one in ten was a female.[3]

Men shot at the herds from car windows when the railways invaded the plains. Caravans of wagons loaded with hides came in over the Platte and Santa Fé roads to the railway stations, where sheds were filled with them awaiting shipment to the East. General Sully, during a northwestern campaign, overtook more than 1500 carts in a corral, where Canadian half-breeds, with their women and children, and a priest, were drying buffalo meat. They had killed 600 animals in a day.[4]

There was scarce a family in America which did not possess one or more "robes," and many were exported annually. The

---

[1] W. H. Dixon, New America, p. 42; cf. O. R., series i, vol. xlviii, part i, p. 342; Field Notes Crossing the Prairies and Plains from Atchison to Denver, J. B. Chandler, Phila., p. 4.

[2] Report of Commr. of Indian Affairs for 1866, p. 53.

[3] Senate Ex. Doc., 40th Cong., 2d sess., no. 77, p. 11.

[4] Report of Commr. of Indian Affairs for 1865, p. 390. See R. I. Dodge, The Plains of the Great West, pp. 119 et seq., for facts about the destruction of the buffalo, though most of this information is for a somewhat later date; also W. E. Webb, Buffalo Land.

American Union Cattle Association was formed in the summer of 1865 to surround 10,000 head of the brutes, and drive them to the Mississippi River to be put upon railway trains and steamboats for transport to the slaughter-houses of the East.[1] Whether the Indian, or the animal which sheltered and fed him, would be exterminated first, men did not know. The trade in skins, some said, should be prohibited; war should be waged upon the wolves which destroyed the young; the half-breeds who came over the border into Dakota and Montana and killed thousands in a year should be sent about their business.[2]

It was plain to be seen, said their advocates, that all Indians were no more alike than all white men. Yet, if one stole a government mule, ran off a ranchman's stock or killed a colonist, a whole tribe and, indeed, the entire race was made to answer for it. The act of one excited band led to a war upon fifty innocent tribes. The old chiefs who made the treaties could not govern the younger men eager for adventure. An Indian made hungry would not starve. Of course he would steal and, if need be, kill to save his life. He had been deprived of the means of support; he must be fed by the government for the rest of his days, for had not he owned, in fee simple, the whole continent to which the white man had come, and over which that white man now ruled in a sense of complete proprietorship? Much was heard of the outrages of Indians upon the miners and settlers of the West; very little of the outrages perpetrated by the settlers on every side upon the Indians. It was but human nature to retaliate, if rights were infringed and wrongs must be suffered.

The superintendent of Indian affairs in Utah said that in all his experience he knew of but one outrage by the Indians which was not due to the misconduct of representatives of the white race.[3] In eight cases out of ten, said the superintendent in Washington Territory, the white man was the aggressor. The

[1] N. Y. Tribune, July 17, 1865.
[2] Report of Commr. of Indian Affairs for 1865, p. 395.
[3] Ibid., p. 315.

Indian was plundered and cheated; he was made drunk that he might be the more easily robbed.[1]

To sell him whiskey for money or for goods by way of barter, or to put it into his hands as a gift, was forbidden, but the rule was violated secretly if not openly, nearly everywhere. Nine-tenths, if not ninety nine-one hundredths of all the troubles with the savages were ascribable to the contraband liquor traffic.[2] Not a depredation was committed in Montana, said an agent in that territory, which could not be traced to the "whiskey traders," who thus far had been able to escape the clutches of the law.[3] Every mining camp had wretches who found in this nefarious business their only means of support.[4]

The Indian's worst foes were "corrupt white men." [5] The "nations" in the Indian Territory had taken sides for or against the Union during the war with the South. More than one-half of the Cherokees remained loyal. The Creeks, too, were divided in their sympathies, while most of the Chickasaws and Choctaws had cast their lot with the Confederacy. Tribe made war upon tribe, lands were raided and valuable property was destroyed. The Cherokees had attained some degree of civilization, but now their country was "one vast scene of desolation." Stupendous frauds were reported in that quarter at the end of the war. Not less than 300,000 head of cattle had been driven out of the Indian country, so it was charged, taken to Kansas and sold. Both civil and military officers of the United States seemed to be involved in this great robbery. For long it was impossible to break up the infamous system.[6] In New Mexico traders crossed the border with asses, laden with whiskey, powder, shot and other merchandise for illicit trade with the Comanches. The superintendent of Indian affairs at Santa Fé met a train of 60 or 70 donkeys. One man had got 100 head of Texas cattle for $150 worth of goods.[7] On the northern border the same con-

---

[1] Report of Commr. of Indian Affairs for 1867, p. 35.
[2] Ibid. for 1865, pp. 240, 253.   [3] Ibid., p. 698.
[4] Ibid., p. 421.   [5] Ibid., p. 235.
[6] Ibid., pp. 436 et seq.
[7] Report of Commr. of Indian Affairs for 1866, p. 151.

ditions prevailed. French Canadian half-breeds came into Dakota to sell the Indians guns, ammunition and rum.[1]

The truth is that the Indian was the victim of every dishonest man at home as well as beyond the national borders. The annuities sent him by the government often arrived late, and on that account bad feeling was engendered in his breast. The delay caused the tribe to remain at home when they should have been away on the chase procuring a supply of meat for the winter. Thus they were left to suffer during the cold weather. The blankets given to them were likely to be of shoddy. The upper Missouri commission of 1865 said that goods intended for the Indians were never received. Some would be made over to them by the agents; the rest were sold. The vouchers bearing the marks of the recipients were insufficient in number; often they were forged. It was the opinion of Father de Smet, a Jesuit missionary in service in this region, that no more than 25 per cent of what the government purchased for the Dakota and Montana Indians in the years following the war ever reached them.[2] The goods were sometimes loaded in "worthless boats," and were lost in transit on the Missouri River.[3] Food and other supplies were not properly stored. Thieves entered the warehouses; perishable merchandise was allowed to decay.[4]

Although there was in San Francisco a good market in which the wants of the California Indians could have been supplied great freight charges were paid on cheap and useless material sent thither from the East.[5] In bales of blankets coming into Montana 113 pairs were missing; they had been stolen en route. Twenty cents a pound, twice an equitable rate of freight, had been paid for the conveyance of these blankets from Fort Benton to the Flathead agency.[6] Mining tools of traders were

[1] Governor Edmunds to Commr. Dole, May 15, 1865, in Report of Commr. of Indian Affairs for 1865, p. 379; Laws of Dakota for 1866–7, p. 122.

[2] N. Y. Tribune, Dec. 17, 1868.

[3] Laws of Dakota for 1867–8, p. 278.

[4] Report of Commr. of Indian Affairs for 1866, p. 174.

[5] Ibid. for 1867, p. 107.

[6] Ibid. for 1868, p. 678.

transported by the government as Indian goods.[1] Cattle were bought for the Indians and put to private use. Fat kine were exchanged for poor animals which then were fed to the wards of the government. The traders would give three or four cups of sugar, or a butcher knife and a little red paint, or again a few plugs of tobacco for a buffalo robe, worth $10 or $12. They would demand three robes for fifty pounds of flour.[2]

It was said and believed that the Red River half-breeds who crossed the border into the Sioux country, the Mormons in Utah, the Southern men of Confederate sympathies who had settled in the West during and after the war, fomented Indian troubles. Then there were the teamsters and freight contractors who labored to the same end that they might profit in hauling the supplies for the troops. Money was "never so plenty," said men in the Western territories to General Babcock in 1866, as during an Indian war.[3] Speculators wanted war in Colorado, said General Sherman, to make a market for the grain and the cattle which they then could sell to the government at "famine prices."[4] Thus it was that unprincipled persons would persuade the Indians to think that their food was poisoned, or that their blankets were infected with disease; thus, too, it was that, in a time of peace, an Indian would be shot down in cold blood in the hope that widespread strife might ensue.

That the Indian had been wronged in a thousand ways ever since the white race had come to America, and that he was being incited to evil courses by false and designing men was very true. It was true, too, on the other hand, that he was by nature stealthy, treacherous and vengeful. His history was "a record of nameless outrage and cruelty."[5] The tribes had

[1] House Ex. Doc., 39th Cong., 2d sess., no. 20, p. 13.

[2] Report of Doolittle Committee, Senate Reports, 39th Cong., 2d sess., no. 156, p. 412, for evidence attesting to the dishonest treatment of the Indians by traders, agents, military officers and others brought into relation with them. For irregularities at the Yankton agency see Report of Commr. of Indian Affairs for 1866, pp. 181 et seq.

[3] House Ex. Doc., 39th Cong., 2d sess., no. 20, p. 4; cf. Report of Commr. of Indian Affairs for 1866, p. 16.

[4] House Ex. Doc., 39th Cong., 2d sess., no. 23, p. 15.

[5] N. Y. Tribune, Dec. 29, 1866.

been at war with one another from time immemorial. They had
a thousand and one hideous and repulsive customs which they
would not put off. It could be remembered that the Indian
had starved before the white people of Europe came to America, that the food which he had procured for himself was not
the best in the world. If millions of dollars of money had been
expended in fighting him, millions, too, had been paid out of
public and private coffers to improve his social condition and
make his character compatible with the new system of civilization which was being spread across the continent.

But he came in contact with the white race only to acquire
its vices. The groups gathered around the government posts
and agencies were lazy, improvident, immoral and drunken.
They were asked to settle on farming land and till it. Some chose
a fixed place of residence, but they yet had made no marked
progress in the arts of husbandry. If placed on reservations,
they would rather be fed by the government than live by the
sweat of their bodies. Many could not be persuaded to reside at
any definite spot. These "blanket Indians" would roam, as
their natural instincts inclined them, chasing wild game, stealing
up to take the buffaloes which other bands had killed, plundering
and murdering in other tribes' lodges. It was not far to go to
rob and kill a white man, and the Western settlers, who felt that
they knew the Indian by close observation and sore experience,
would laugh at, when they were not enraged by, the love and
pity which the Abolitionist element in New England expended
upon such an object. Ninety nine out of one hundred men beyond the Mississippi favored in their hearts, if they were not
ready openly to assist in, the extermination of the race, and
the proverb that the only good Indian was a dead one was subscribed to in every ranch house, military post, overland stage
station and mining gulch in the Western states and territories.

But the horror with which the East generally drew back from
the thought of the extinction of this original American people
was immense. The War Department at Washington was
believed to be at one with the Western settlers in a wish to
execute this repellant design at the earliest day.

The campaign of 1865 came in for much denunciation after the event, as well as while it was in progress. It had cost the government $40,000,000, N. G. Taylor, now commissioner of Indian Affairs, said in 1867.[1] Each regiment in the Indian service, said the Secretary of the Interior, meant an expenditure of $2,000,000 annually.[2] The last three campaigns against the Sioux, Governor Edmunds of Dakota alleged in 1865, had cost the government $40,000,000.[3] And with what result? If the object in view were the extermination of the race, the Indian Bureau officers declared in their exchange of amenities with the War Department, it would not soon be effected by the army of the United States. The price of slaying an Indian, said Commissioner Taylor, as he advanced for the combat, was about $1,000,000 and the lives of 25 soldiers. If the 300,000 Indians still living within the boundaries of the United States were to be extirpated, at the present rate of destruction, which with all the effort put forth by the army, barring the method adopted at Sand Creek, was about one in a month, the task would be prolonged for 25,000 years; the cost of the work would be 300 billions of dollars and the lives of seven and a half millions of troops![4]

So the dispute waxed in warmth with the advantage seeming to be now on one side and now on the other. The hour had come to test the efficacy of the treaty system, so much recommended in the East. The southwestern commission under the presidency of General Sanborn had concluded treaties in 1865 with the Arapahoes and Cheyennes, offering them annuities, pensions and lands at a very generous rate to atone for their sufferings at the hands of Chivington and the Colorado men. The Apaches, Kiowas and Comanches also made pledges of peace. The northwestern commission under Governor Edmunds concluded negotiations with nine different bands of the Sioux in Dakota. This commission was divided into two parts and reconstituted in 1866 to continue its labors

---

[1] Senate Ex. Doc., 40th Cong., 1st sess., no. 13, p. 2.
[2] Report for 1865, p. viii.   [3] Ibid., p. 379.
[4] Report of Commr. of Indian Affairs for 1868, p. 470.

with tribes north of Fort Laramie and in Montana. As a result of their labors treaties were arranged with the Arickarees, Gros Ventres, Mandans, Assinaboines, the Ogallala and Brulé Sioux and the northern Cheyennes.

Many of the Indians would see "where all the white people came from,"[1] and scores of chiefs were brought on to Washington at the expense of the government to state their grievances to the "Great Father." For months the halls of the Interior Department building were filled with these visitors. In their feathers and beads and other barbaric finery they stalked into the houses of Congress and the chambers of the Supreme Court.[2] These conferences at Washington also ended in treaties and the Interior Department officials insisted that the year 1866, as a result of all this conciliatory activity on their part, was one of quiet on the frontier.[3] General Sherman who travelled the central route over the plains, both by the North and the South Platte branches of the road, and went down through Colorado as far as the Arkansas River, on many parts of the journey without escort, found all the tribes at peace.[4]

Yet, it must be admitted that the Blackfeet, the Sioux in the Black Hills, the Apaches in Arizona and some of the Arapahoes and Cheyennes were still committing depredations.[5] The Snakes were troublesome in Oregon.[6] Black Hawk, with a band of warriors, continued his forays and butcheries in Utah.[7] Piutes and Shoshones had killed 100 Chinamen and many white men, and had driven off stock in southwestern Idaho.[8] Precautions were needed in reference to emigrant trains. General Pope acted promptly and decisively. On the routes from Minnesota to Montana parties should rendezvous at Forts Ridgley and Abercrombie; on the Platte route at Fort Kearney; on the Smoky Hill to Denver at Fort Riley; on the Santa Fé route at Fort Larned. At these posts emigrants must be held

[1] Report of Commr. of Indian Affairs for 1866, p. 79.   [2] Ibid., p. 2.
[3] See, e.g., Report of Secretary of the Interior for 1866, p. 7; Report of Commr. of Indian Affairs for the same year, p. 15.
[4] House Ex. Doc., 39th Cong., 2d sess., no. 23, p. 17.
[5] Report of Commr. of Indian Affairs for 1866, p. 16.
[6] Ibid., p. 79.   [7] Ibid., pp. 124, 128, 129.   [8] Ibid., p. 190.

until at least twenty wagons and thirty men were at hand.
Then each man should be armed and put under the command
of a captain, elected by the units in the party, before it were
allowed to proceed.   Military officers as far west as Washington
and Arizona territories were directed to arrest all persons
travelling on the plains who did not conform to these rules.[1]

The skill of the treaty makers was put to a severe test when
they were brought face to face with the problem of obtaining
concessions from the tribes north of the Platte with reference
to the Powder River road to Montana.   General Connor, as
we have seen, penetrated the country lying north of Fort
Laramie in the summer of 1865, and established a post to which
he gave his own name.   The men of peace said that they would
obtain the consent of the Indians touching the use of this so-
called Bozeman route, and the chiefs were invited to meet
with the commissioners.   The negotiations were carried on with
some friendly leaders, principally drawn from a band which lived
in and around Fort Laramie, known as the "Laramie Loafers."
They, for presents and promises of annuities, gave the government the desired privilege.   Such an agreement, however, could
be in no way binding upon Red Cloud, The Man Afraid of His
Horses, Iron Shell and other chieftains, who either had refused
to attend the council, or had left it before it had broken up
without expressing their approval of what had been done.[2]

In disregard of the manner in which the treaty had been
negotiated, or deceived, perhaps, by the signs of friendship
displayed by unauthorized agents of the tribes, the government
proceeded to open the road.   Colonel Carrington, in the summer
of 1866, went up and garrisoned three posts, — the first at
Fort Connor, rechristened Fort Reno, 157 miles from Laramie,
another, 66 miles farther north, called Fort Phil Kearny, and
the third, 70 miles still farther north, which was given the name
of Fort C. F. Smith,[3] for the protection of the Montana emigrants who should pass this way.   Then the trouble began.

---

[1] Senate Ex. Doc., 40th Cong., 1st sess., no. ii, pp. 2–4.

[2] Ibid., no. 13, p. 57.

[3] House Ex. Doc., 39th Cong., 2d sess., no. 23, p. 10.

Carrington could scarcely protect himself, much less travellers going from Fort Laramie up to the mines.[1] Men descending the Missouri in mackinaw boats were fired on from the banks of the river. Steamboats carried howitzers. Why had Sherman told Grant, after passing over the roads, that all was peace? The Indians were in arms on every side. From New Mexico and Colorado came accounts of raids and butcheries. The savages were buying guns and ammunition, and accumulating them for a war on the white settlements.[2] The oncoming winter promised to be bloody, and Carrington, at Fort Phil Kearny, was calling frantically upon General Cooke at Omaha for reënforcements. Twenty-four soldiers and about twenty citizens were killed on the Powder River road before cold weather had set in.[3] No one was safe except in the largest trains. The Indians were on the war-path "in good earnest," said the Helena Republican, and Sherman in forwarding his reassuring despatches to Washington had been "criminally negligent of duty." The very arms given to the Indians in the treaty council at Fort Laramie were now turned against the whites.[4] It was nonsense, said A. K. McClure, who made himself the spokesman of the people of Montana in letters to thé New York Tribune, and whose sentiments Greeley editorially disavowed, to speak of friendly Indians upon the plains; there were none.[5]

At Fort Phil Kearny Carrington had 411 men. Parties of hostile savages in the fall and early winter had appeared before it no less than 51 times and had picked off a number of his troops. On the morning of December 21 a wagon train started out for timber for use in the saw mill. Shots were heard and Captain Fetterman was despatched to the scene. He seems to have disobeyed orders and to have acted without discretion. The entire party, consisting, after reënforcement, of 81 men, was ambushed by a band of 1500 or 2000 Sioux aided by some Cheyennes and Arapahoes led, it is believed, though this

[1] Leavenworth Times, cited in N. Y. Tribune, Oct. 17, 1866.
[2] N. Y. Tribune, Oct. 11, 17, 20, 1866.
[3] Sherman to Rawlins, Report of Secretary of War for 1866, p. 21.
[4] N. Y. Tribune, Oct. 11, 1866.
[5] See, e.g., N. Y. Tribune, Nov. 21, 1867.

point is in dispute, by Red Cloud together with some less well-known chiefs.[1] Not one white man escaped. When another body of troops came out of the fort they found the corpses of their comrades shot, scalped, gashed, and filled with arrows lying in tangled heaps upon the field.[2]

Sherman demanded vengeance for this shameless slaughter of his troops. "We must act in vindictive earnestness against the Sioux," said he to Grant, even to the point of their extermination — men, women and children.[3] Some recommended the abandonment of the road, but this was not to be thought of, said General Augur; the government then would lose all it had expended upon the route. Moreover, such a movement would inspire the Indians to new attacks upon the white settlements.[4] Bozeman, who had given his name to the road, while travelling with a companion, had been approached by a party of Blackfeet, pretending to friendship, and was treacherously slain.[5] The people of Montana loudly demanded retribution. What was Sherman about — secure in his headquarters at St. Louis? Was he so soon become a senile old man?[6] For a commander in an Indian war, said men on the plains, "give us Chivington or Connor."[7] After the massacre at Kearny the three forts for the rest of the winter were virtually in a state of siege.[8] General Augur reported that the troops must fight almost daily to get wood for their fires and hay to feed their animals.[9]

[1] Grinnell, The Fighting Cheyennes, p. 225.

[2] General Sherman in Report of Secretary of War for 1867, vol. i, p. 32; Reports in Senate Ex. Doc., 39th Cong., 2d sess., nos. 15 and 16; Senate Ex. Doc., 49th Cong., 2d sess., no. 97; Senate Ex. Doc., 50th Cong., 1st sess., no. 33; account of the massacre by a soldier at the fort sent home to the Janesville, Wis., Gazette, quoted in Phila. Ledger, Feb. 6, 1867.

[3] Senate Ex. Doc., 40th Cong., 1st sess., no. 13, p. 27.

[4] Report of Secretary of War for 1867, vol. i, p. 58.

[5] Fort Sedgwick corr., N. Y. Tribune, June 10, 1867.

[6] Cheyenne corr., N. Y. Tribune, Nov. 5, 1868, and the various McClure letters in the same newspaper.

[7] Denver corr., N. Y. Tribune, May 25, 1867.

[8] House Ex. Doc., 39th Cong., 2d sess., no. 71, p. 9.

[9] Report of Secretary of War for 1867, vol. i, p. 58.

Carrington was transferred to another post; the service in the district was overhauled; a new fort named for the ill-fated Fetterman was located on the Montana road where it crossed the North Platte.[1] The Indian Bureau, in its usual manner, began to undermine the influence of the army at Washington. This bureau was now in charge of a man named Bogy. The Indians, he declared, had come to the fort on a friendly visit to ask that General St. George Cooke's order against their purchase of guns should be rescinded, so that they might go out on their winter hunt. To deny them firearms, in the opinion of Mr. Bogy, was an "injudicious military interference."[2] Freighters were found to say that they would not use the Montana road anyhow. Those who had travelled over it would not do so again, if it were as free of Indians as Paradise. It was "one of the most complete and expensive humbugs of the day."[3]

So the President appointed another commission, with General Sully at its head. He and his colleagues visited Fort Phil Kearny to ascertain the facts, and, if possible, devise a plan of action to avert a general Indian war. Again presents and rations were to be distributed to the savages,[4] and the way was prepared for a retirement from the Powder River road upon which the government had expended $20,000,000,[5] without the punishment of any Indian concerned in the butchery.

Whatever wisdom there may have been in the adoption of such a course it is a fact that Indian outrages in the spring of 1867 were reported on every hand. Terry was fighting the savages along the exposed route from Minnesota to Montana; Crook, beyond the mountains in Idaho and Oregon;[6] Augur, who had succeeded Cooke in command of the Department of

---

[1] Report of Secretary of War for 1867, vol. i, p. 61.

[2] House Ex. Doc., 39th Cong., 2d sess., no. 71, pp. 3, 12, 14.

[3] Superintendent Head of Utah in Report of Commr. of Indian Affairs for 1866, p. 187.

[4] Senate Ex. Doc., 40th Cong., 1st sess., no. 13, pp. 55 et seq.

[5] John B. Sanborn to Secretary Browning, Senate Ex. Doc., 40th Cong., 1st sess., no. 13, p. 74.

[6] Report of Commr. of Indian Affairs for 1867, pp. 95–103.

the Platte, in Nebraska; Hancock, who had taken Pope's place in the Department of the Missouri, aided by Custer, down in Kansas, where the Cheyennes and other tribes still were resisting the passage of trains over the Smoky Hill route to Denver.

To avenge depredations on this line of travel Hancock in April, 1867, marched up to a village containing 300 Cheyenne and Sioux lodges, 35 miles west of Fort Larned. After a council with the chiefs, in which he satisfied himself that their temper was ill, he entered the village, stacked their huts, representing the skins of 3000 buffaloes, and other possessions, and built a fire which, spreading to the dry grass, lighted up the plains for a distance of sixty miles.[1] The rage of the agents, Wynkoop and Leavenworth, who had been heard from after the Sand Creek affair, was again aroused. They made the country ring with their denunciations. These Indians were not hostile.[2] The New York Tribune spoke of "the ineffable wickedness" of the government's Indian policy.[3] The system was but "a sheath to rub the rust from an idle army."[4] Hancock came in for nearly as much criticism as had been the portion of Chivington,[5] and the commissioner of Indian affairs asked for an appropriation of $100,000 to reimburse the savages for the destruction of the buffalo robes, knives, stew pans, lariats, rubbing horns, sacks of feathers and what not else which were the subject of careful inventories.[6] Four months later Commissioner Taylor computed and proved to his own satisfaction that General Hancock's act in burning this Cheyenne village already had cost the United States more than $5,000,000 and at least 100 human lives.[7]

The war proceeded. Militiamen were in the field in several

[1] Kansas corr., N. Y. Tribune, May 4, 1867; cf. T. R. Davis, A Summer on the Plains, February, 1868.
[2] Report of Commr. of Indian Affairs for 1867, p. 4. For an opinion of Leavenworth as an Indian agent see S. J. Crawford, Kansas in the Sixties, p. 272.
[3] N. Y. Tribune, May 21, 1867.
[4] Ibid., May 14, 1867.
[5] Report of Commr. of Indian Affairs for 1867, pp. 310–4.
[6] Senate Ex. Doc., 40th Cong., 1st sess., no. 13, pp. 6, 91, 111–3.
[7] Ibid., p. 4.

territories giving the settlements protection which was not afforded them by the troops at the posts. The black flag was unfurled in the streets of Denver, a signal for a war of extermination; men in mining towns subscribed money to a fund, and offered rewards for "scalps with the ears on."[1] Governor Hunt, together with the superintendent of the mint, the chief justice, the postmaster of Denver, the surveyor and other officers of the Federal government in Colorado, appealed to President Johnson. Lines of communication with the East were cut, they said, mails were captured, stage stations destroyed, passengers in coaches murdered and trains plundered. Every branch of industry was paralyzed. The lives of such savages should be considered worthless in comparison with those of American citizens. "In the name of God and humanity," they asked that the "too long continued temporizing policy toward these merciless devils" should cease.[2]

Governor Crawford of Kansas said in October, 1867, that during the three years past thousands of people in the West had been murdered and scalped, hundreds of women captured and violated and millions of dollars' worth of property destroyed or stolen by the "red-handed fiends." The atrocities upon citizens of Kansas which he recorded in detail were heartrending in their brutality.[3]

In the last two years, said Governor Throckmorton of Texas, the Indians on the borders of that state had murdered 155 persons, wounded 24 and made captives of 43.[4] At Plum Creek, on the uncompleted Union Pacific Railroad, 32 miles west of Fort Kearney, in Nebraska, they cut the telegraph wires and piled sleepers on the track. One freight train was wrecked; another barely escaped the same fate. Then the savages set fire to the splintered cars and threw the corpses of seven men, whom they had killed and scalped, into the flames.[5] One outrage followed another with but little effective activity on the part of the troops.

[1] N. Y. Tribune, June 25, 1867.   [2] Ibid., June 17, 1867.
[3] S. J. Crawford, Kansas in the Sixties, p. 266.
[4] Phila. Ledger, Aug. 29, 1867.   [5] N. Y. Tribune, Aug. 13, 1867.

Sentiment in the East still favored the making of treaties, and Congress created a new commission to devise plans "to end forever" the nation's troubles with the Indians.[1] It was given considerable sums of money for its use. It was empowered to select a district or districts not on the lines of the proposed northern, central or southern railroads to the Pacific coast for the Indians to occupy. Then, finally, if this policy should fail, the Secretary of War would be authorized to accept the services of mounted volunteers in the Western states and territories for the purpose of bringing hostilities to an end by force.[2]

N. G. Taylor, commissioner of Indian affairs, became the president of the commission, while associated with him upon it were J. B. Henderson, chairman of the committee on Indian affairs in the Senate; John B. Sanborn, S. F. Tappan and three army officers, General Sherman,[3] General W. S. Harney and General Alfred H. Terry. Later General C. C. Augur, to represent Sherman in his absence, was added to the board.

By these commissioners and others specially appointed for particular tasks, in 1867 and 1868, treaties, in pursuit of the policy of kindness and peace, were negotiated with more than a score of tribes in all parts of the West.[4] But the irregular warfare of the Indians upon the settlements, the coaches and the emigrant trains continued.

With Sherman in a determined spirit, goaded as he had been by charges of the Indians' partisans against the army,[5] and Sheridan, who upon leaving New Orleans had taken Hancock's

[1] Phila. Ledger, July 31, 1867.　　　[2] Act of July 20, 1867.

[3] Although he had said that he would have nothing to do with "Indian agencies, Indian traders or making Indian treaties," since the business might become "as corrupting and mischievous" to the military as to the civil agents of the government. — Report of Secretary of War for 1867, vol. i, p. 67.

[4] Report of Secretary of the Interior for 1868, pp. 464-6.

[5] "To accuse us," he said, "of inaugurating or wishing such a war [a war of extermination] is to accuse us of a want of common sense, and of that regard for order and peace which has ever characterized our regular army." — Senate Ex. Doc., 40th Cong., 3d sess., no. 18, p. 5.

place, in command of the Department of the Missouri, a vigorous movement against the Cheyennes and the other tribes in Kansas was begun in the fall and winter of 1868. Having brought about the abandonment of the Powder River road, they sought, by the same means, to force the whites from the Smoky Hill. So they attacked every party of emigrants using this route.[1] For months the outrages committed upon the settlers of Kansas and Colorado, Sheridan said in ordering the Indians to their reservations under penalty of immediate chastisement, had been "too atrocious to mention in detail."[2] They had raided the settlements along the Smoky Hill and Saline Rivers, and, leaving a trail of blood behind them, appeared for further massacres in the valleys of the Solomon and Republican. Governor Crawford of Kansas had appealed to President Johnson, demanding in the most vigorous terms government protection from the "savage devils."[3] The agents, as usual, found that the blame rested with the government which had not performed its part in supplying the tribes with subsistence and arms. They were starving. They were nursing memories of the butcher Chivington and the firebrand Hancock.

But the excuses did not avail. Too many settlers had been killed, too many of their wives and children carried off into cruel captivity. Sheridan set his troops in motion to administer punishment, although until the snow fell he complained that he found it "much like chasing the *Alabama*." Early in September fifty men left Fort Wallace in pursuit of a troublesome band of Cheyennes. They were ambushed on Arickaree Creek and were nearly annihilated before help came from the fort.[4] The war was now on in earnest. Early in December Custer swooped down on Black Kettle's village and several other camps of Cheyennes, Arapahoes, Kiowas and Comanches on the Washita River. Charging, while the band played "Garry

[1] Phila. Ledger, Nov. 24, 1868.

[2] Ibid., Aug. 25, 1868; cf. despatches in issues of that paper of Aug. 24, 27 and 29 and Sept. 12, 1868.

[3] S. J. Crawford, Kansas in the Sixties, pp. 290–2; Personal Memoirs of P. H. Sheridan, vol. ii, pp. 281 et seq.

[4] S. J. Crawford, op. cit., pp. 293–5.

Owen," a few hours of desperate fighting ensued.   About 300 Indians were included in the list of killed, wounded and prisoners.   Custer on his side lost 21 men killed and 14 wounded. He pursued his advantage and was able to announce on January 1, 1869, the breaking of "the backbone of the Indian rebellion." Agent Wynkoop resigned, declaring Washita River worse than Sand Creek and Custer the peer of Chivington.   Commissioner Tappan, Bishop Whipple and other men in the East entered their emphatic protests against such barbarities.[1]   Black Kettle, who had been killed, was a saint in a red skin, and so on.   But Sherman and Sheridan so well supported Custer with indubitable proof that blood was on the hands of these Indians that the Congressional inquiries came to naught.[2]

The issue between the Indian Bureau and the agency system on the one side and the division, department and post commanders on the other was now clearly drawn.   It was tacitly agreed that the bureau should not continue its relations with a tribe with which the army was at war.[3]   But a war with such savages admitted of little discrimination.'   An Indian of one tribe, when he descended upon a stage station or a settler's cabin, was not easily distinguishable from an Indian of some other band.   It was agreed, too, that they should be placed upon reservations out of the reach of the white man.   But where were such places to be found, and how were such a people to be kept within chosen bounds?   They were as difficult to confine, said Sherman, as the wild buffaloes.   Gifts and annuities must never be distributed to them in the form of money, which immediately fell into the hands of the traders.   Payments in bright calicoes, tobacco, butcher knives, vermilion and trinkets ought to be brought to an end.   In a case cited by Commissioner Sanborn the government's gifts had taken the form of mosquito netting, umbrellas and children's shawls.[4]

[1] N. Y. Tribune, Dec. 14 and 17, 1868.

[2] Senate Ex. Doc., 40th Cong., 3d sess., nos. 13, 18, 40; a soldier's account of the fight is in the N. Y. Tribune, Dec. 29, 1868.

[3] Report of the Secretary of the Interior for 1865, p. ix.

[4] Senate Ex. Doc., 40th Cong., 1st sess., no. 13, p. 72.

But others found that our aboriginal Americans must have firearms and ammunition to kill game that they might not starve; they must have knives to skin and cut it into steaks and roasting pieces. Everywhere the antelope was so wild that it could be taken no longer with the bow and arrow, and without horses, which they were trading at the Missouri and elsewhere for whiskey, they could not make the "approach" and the "surround," and capture the buffalo with their old weapons. Thus it was that men on the plains found many Indians armed by the agents of one branch of the Federal service to destroy the agents of another branch of the service, a truly intolerable condition of affairs.

General Hancock in Kansas in 1867 said that the Indians there were supplied with arms in such quantities that some of them had three revolvers each. For guns, powder and lead they would give Butterfield and other traders skins and horses of twenty times the value.[1] General Sherman told Hancock to disregard the permits granted by the agents to such traders. It was an "absurdity," said he, when the army was made responsible for the peace of the frontier, for another department of the government to legalize such a traffic.[2] Grant supported Sherman, and asked Secretary Stanton to cause the President to stop the arming of the Indians by the agents.[3]

But Mr. Bogy, the head of the Indian Bureau, had declared the enforcement of such a policy "cruel and calculated to produce the very worst effect."[4] And he correctly sensed the opinion of other men in the Indian civil service and in the country at large. Always the fault lay with the army. Who violated solemn treaties? The officers of the army! Who shed innocent Indian blood? The army! The half-breeds gathered around every government post upon the plains attested to the kind of civilization which the soldiers had brought into the West. Even men as high in the popular estimation as Sherman,

---

[1] Senate Ex. Doc., 40th Cong., 1st sess., no. 13, pp. 52–3, 106 et seq.
[2] House Ex. Doc., 39th Cong., 2d sess., no. 71, p. 18.
[3] Senate Ex. Doc., 40th Cong., 1st sess., no. 13, p. 41.
[4] House Ex. Doc., 39th Cong., 2d sess., no. 71, p. 2; see also pp. 16, 17.

Hancock and Pope were told that they did not "understand the Indian character." The agents and traders established newspapers on the frontier and conducted press campaigns to blast the reputations of military men, who were giving the country self-sacrificing service. The best-laid plans of distinguished generals could be defeated by some obscure employee of the Interior Department. The forces, when expeditions were undertaken, were never large enough, the supplies were always inadequate, and the commanders, after a successful campaign, denounced as barbarians, lost their commissions or were transferred to minor posts.

Service on the frontier for good and sufficient reasons was distasteful to every soldier. Not only did it ruin many a reputation earned honestly and well in civilized warfare; it was also accompanied by daily suffering of the body and the spirit of man. The troops were sheltered in caves, in sod houses roofed with cottonwood boughs over which turf was thrown, in adobe and log huts, and in the best case, in walls of stone, where this was to be had, laid in mud. Fort Dodge, Kansas, consisted of "a few huts made of poles set endwise in the ground and covered with dirt and tents, enclosed by a ditch and a dirt embankment." [1] Always the ceilings were low. Seldom were the floors of wood. Light, ventilation, sleeping quarters — all the living accommodations were unworthy of the army of the United States. Rats ran through the store-rooms to destroy the supplies obtained with so much difficulty and expense. If the planters of the South had put negroes in such hovels, said Sherman, when he first saw them, samples of the buildings would have been conveyed to Boston in proof of the cruelty of the slave masters.[2] At Fort Sully an inspector found that the only structure which had the least value was the flagstaff, and that was but "a tolerable one."[3]

The men were cut off from every social relationship. The telegraph reached few of the forts, the mails were received most irregularly, usually by special couriers. The principal employ-

---

[1] O. R., series iii, vol. v, p. 443.
[2] House Ex. Doc., 39th Cong., 2d sess., no. 23, p. 6.   [3] Ibid., p. 33.

ments, such as hauling water and wood, grazing mules and cutting grass for hay were unsoldier-like. Inspectors who went out among the posts found that drill and discipline nearly everywhere had been abandoned. With long hair and bushy beards the men came to look like the trappers, scouts and half-breeds among whom they dwelt.[1]

Placed in such a situation, the army, when it was assailed by the officers of the Interior Department, was not slow in retort. An Indian agency was greatly sought after; it was as profitable as the consulship to Liverpool.[2] Bishop Whipple of Minnesota said that though they received salaries of but $1500 each, many an agent retired from office at the end of four years worth $50,000.[3] By trading, by withholding annuities, by appropriating and using government land, from contracts with freighters and other men these officers made large fortunes. Some were honest, said General Pope, but that most of them were "true only to their personal and pecuniary interests" none familiar with the subject would dispute.[4] They came from distant places, said the legislature of Dakota. The safety of their families and property was not at stake. They were rarely at their posts. Their first sight of an Indian was gained upon their arrival at the agency house.[5] Their dishonesty was susceptible of proof. In their own midst the Leavenworth Times called them "peculators, plunderers of the Indians and breeders of war";[6] McClure in Montana, "the white vampires of the plains" — "the great curse of the West."[7]

Each Congress brought forward a long appropriation bill with items for the benefit of this, that and the other tribe on account of some treaty. Herein lay the patronage of the agents.

[1] See, e.g., Report of Col. Sackett to General Sherman, House Ex. Doc., 39th Cong., 2d sess., no. 23, pp. 24 et seq.

[2] Report of Commr. of Indian Affairs for 1867, p. 36.

[3] Phila. Ledger, Dec. 20, 1866.

[4] Senate Ex. Doc., 40th Cong., 1st sess., no. 13, p. 51.

[5] Laws of Dakota for 1865-6, p. 551; ibid. for 1867-8, p. 277.

[6] Cited in Phila. Ledger, Dec. 19, 1866.

[7] N. Y. Tribune, Nov. 21, 1867; cf. S. J. Crawford, Kansas in the Sixties, p. 263.

For the year ending June 30, 1864, the Indian Bureau's expenditures were $2,538,297 ; in the next year, $3,802,393, and in 1867, $4,586,393.[1]

The entire system was denounced ; it was demoralizing and it should be abandoned at once. It was a proverb in the West that as soon as the supplies furnished to the tribes were used up they would go down to the Platte road and scalp a few emigrants. Then the government would send out a commission to make a new treaty and they would live in plenty again.[2] For years the Indians in Montana had not received their supplies, said Colonel Sackett, after an inspection of the posts in that region. If they had misbehaved, their claims would have had prompt and early consideration.[3] Whatever might be done, urged General Dodge, let the government not "pay them for the outrages they have committed or hire them to keep the peace."[4]

As for the treaties of the Interior Department they were a farce, said General Halleck, in command on the Pacific coast ; [5] they were not worth the paper they were written on, said General Pope.[6] The only treaty which could have any value would be one binding the Indians to amity, with an understanding that when they violated it, the military forces of the United States would march into their country to punish them. They would be quiet when they feared the consequence of their depredations, not when, as now, it was to their advantage to engage in war.[7]

In answer to the humane requirements of the service General Carleton had corralled 8000 Navajoes in New Mexico, and was feeding them as prisoners of war. General Sherman, who

[1] Reports of Secretary of the Treasury for these years, pp. 37, 47 and xlvii.

[2] O. R., series i, vol. xlviii, part ii, pp. 764, 880 ; cf. S. J. Crawford, Kansas in the Sixties, p. 271 ; R. I. Dodge, The Plains of the Great West, pp. 350–1.

[3] House Ex. Doc., 39th Cong., 2d sess., no. 23, p. 50.

[4] O. R., series i, vol. xlviii, part ii, p. 973 ; cf. Report of Commr. of Indian Affairs for 1866, p. 138.

[5] Report of Secretary of War for 1867, vol. i, p. 74.

[6] Ibid., for 1866, p. 30.

[7] O. R., series i, vol. xlviii, part ii, pp. 880–1.

added the only touch of humor to the dismal history of our Indian relations during these years, told Grant that they might better be taken to New York to be boarded at the Fifth Avenue Hotel. They could be carried thither and fed there at less expense to the government than where they then were in New Mexico.[1] After expending $1,500,000 to subsist them in 1866, in answer to the demand of the Indian Bureau they were transferred early in 1867 to its care.

But it was easy enough for the commanders on the plains to criticise the Indian policy. What did they propose in its stead? In the first place they advocated restricted grounds and the establishment of large new reservations. Sully thought that the Indians might be permitted to roam north of the Cheyenne, if they would not molest passing boats on the Missouri, or the government posts, since "no sane white man would ever want to go into that country."[2] Inspector-General Sackett shared Sully's views; he would donate every foot of Dakota to the Indians, and then pay them to live in the country, — of so little use, in his opinion, would it ever be to the white man.[3] The principal herds of buffaloes remaining on the continent grazed upon these northern lands, said Captain Fisk, and here the Indians might be left to their own devices for all time.[4]

General Sherman, on his side, would limit the Sioux to a region north of the Platte, west and east of the Powder River road; the southern tribes to a space south of the Arkansas, so that they would not interfere with the lines of transportation across the continent. Indians found outside their allotted districts without military passes should be dealt with summarily by the troops.[5] The plan was approved by General Grant and Secretary Stanton, who asked the Interior Department if it would conflict with treaty stipulations. They were told that

---

[1] House Ex. Doc., 39th Cong., 2d sess., no. 23, p. 15.

[2] O. R., series i, vol. xlviii, part ii, p. 800.

[3] House Ex. Doc., 39th Cong., 1st sess., no. 23, p. 46.

[4] Report of Secretary of Interior for 1865, p. 415.

[5] Report of Secretary of War for 1866, p. 21; also Report for 1867, vol. i, p. 67; House Ex. Doc., 39th Cong., 2d sess., no. 23, p. 16.

it would do so.[1] Anyhow the savages, said Sherman, must be removed from the region lying between the Arkansas and the Platte, and he was ready to say to Stanton in June, 1867, that it made "little difference whether they be coaxed out by Indian commissioners or killed."[2]

General Pope's plan differed from that of some other men in that he recognized the continuing need of feeding the Indians. Therefore he would assemble the tribes on reserved areas near the Mississippi and Missouri rivers, so that it would not be so costly for the government to communicate with them and to satisfy their wants.[3]

Finally all the army men were agreed that the administration of Indian affairs should be returned to the War Department, where it earlier had been for seventeen years.[4] The confusion which existed and made every policy ineffective must be brought to an end and sooner or later Grant,[5] Sherman, Pope[6] and practically all the other officers in the service came to advocate a consolidation and centralization of authority in the hands of a disciplined body of men, such as were to be found nowhere but in the regular army of the United States. There must be one head and one policy from this time on. The military officers were necessary to protect property and life, the civil were not, said Pope. Therefore it was clear which should give way to the other. To get rid of the "formidable army of Indian superintendents, agents, sub-agents, special agents, jobbers, contractors and hangers-on" who now infested the frontier states and territories was the pressing problem of the hour.[7] The annuities must be distributed only under military supervision. The generals in command must have the power to punish breaches of the peace, and enforce

[1] House Ex. Doc., 39th Cong., 2d sess., no. 71, pp. 11–14.
[2] Senate Ex. Doc., 40th Cong., 1st sess., no. 13, p. 121.
[3] Report of War Department for 1866, pp. 27–8.
[4] Report of Commr. of Indian Affairs for 1868, p. 474.
[5] Senate Ex. Doc., 40th Cong., 1st sess., no. 13, pp. 40–1.
[6] O. R., series i, vol. xlviii, part ii, p. 881; Senate Ex. Doc., 40th Cong., 1st sess., no. 13, pp. 49–52.
[7] Senate Ex. Doc., 40th Cong., 1st sess., no. 13, p. 51.

rules and regulations concerning the areas to be occupied by
the tribes.

The New York Nation favored the transfer back to the War
Department. This was "the primal remedy for our evils," it
said.[1] But Greeley, in the New York Tribune, cried " a plague
on both your houses." The army was bad, the Indian agents
were worse.[2] The whole system was "a tissue of rascality,
'conceived in sin and brought forth in iniquity.'" The Indian
Bureau was "a paddock into which lean political stock" was
turned to be fattened. We gave the Indians "a few perishing
blankets for the acres of patrimony" which were taken from
them forever. "Nothing could exceed the botchwork and
corruption" of the government's management of this subject.[3]

Dozens of reasons were found — in the Indian Bureau itself
by its officers, in Congress, in the educational and religious
societies, in the press — why the War Department should have
no new and greater power over the fading aboriginal race. The
generals and their troops wished this power only that they might
hurry it to extinction. And so it was that no progress was
achieved.

Doolittle's Congressional committee made the amazing discovery that the antagonism between the two departments of
the government was beneficial to the service, since one always
would check and restrain the other. These investigators of
the subject would have the Indian country divided into five
districts, each under the control of a board of inspection composed of three persons — an officer of the Interior Department,
to be called an assistant Indian commissioner, an army officer
and a representative of the religious and philanthropic societies.[4]
After prolonged discussion one house of Congress passed the
bill while the other failed to do so, so this plan came to naught.

The peace commissioners of 1867 also met, talked and
adopted resolutions. They would have the frontier settler
take the Indian by the hand and regard him as a friend. They

---

[1] N. Y. Nation, Jan. 17, 1867.
[2] N. Y. Tribune, Dec. 29, 1866.   [3] Ibid., Feb. 5, 1867.
[4] Senate Reports, 39th Cong., 2d sess., no. 156, p. 8.

would give the Indian muskets, powder and lead to conciliate him; abandon the forts on the Powder River road to Montana; cease fighting him with state and territorial militia; continue the distribution of presents, — not money, but domestic animals, agricultural implements, clothing and provisions, — until he could be taught to support himself in civilized life; create a new and separate department of government unconnected with either the Interior or War Departments to administer Indian affairs. Furthermore the commission recommended the establishment of two great reservations, one in the northwest — running north of Nebraska to the Canadian line; [1] the other in the southwest — south of Kansas, to include the already existing Indian Territory, the Staked Plains of Texas and parts of New Mexico, and in addition one or perhaps more reservations on the Pacific coast. [2]

But the only result of all this beating of the air by many men was the endless making of treaties and the endless violation of them, while the depredations of the Indians and the punitive expeditions of the troops continued as before.

[1] Sully's commission to investigate the Fort Phil Kearny massacre had recommended the laying out of a northern reservation. — Senate Ex. Doc., 40th Cong., 1st sess., no. 13, p. 60.

[2] The Report of this Commission is to be found in House Ex. Doc., 40th Cong., 2d sess., no. 97; also in Report of Commr. of Indian Affairs for 1868, pp. 486 et seq. See also Senate Ex. Doc., 40th Cong., 1st sess., no. 13, pp. 5–6; Report of Commr. of Indian Affairs for 1868, pp. 505–6, 835.

CHAPTER VII

THE President, completing the work which had been begun by his predecessor, Mr. Lincoln, had returned the eleven states of the late Southern Confederacy into the hands of their own constitutionally chosen magistrates. He announced that they had been duly restored to their old places in the Federal Union, and their senators and representatives stood at the doors of Congress. But the members of only one of these various Southern delegations, Tennessee's, had been admitted to their seats and they not until the closing hours of the long session of the 39th Congress in July, 1866. Here the President rested his case and he would appeal to the people for an indorsement of his course.

Congress on its side had passed the Fourteenth Amendment and had announced through its powerful Committee on Reconstruction that no state could hope to have its representatives seated until it had ratified the measure. The President had presented his objections to the amendment in a characteristic manner; he had performed only a ministerial duty in sending it out to the various governors. To what lengths he might proceed in the use of his influence to prevent its adoption by the Southern legislatures no Radical knew. Connecticut responded favorably on June 29, 1866, a fortnight after Congress had passed the resolution to submit the measure to the states; New Hampshire on July 6 and Tennessee on July 19.[1]

Notwithstanding the signs of courage and industry of the Southern people many persons still were idle and starving.

---

[1] McPherson, History of Reconstruction, p. 194; Fertig, Secession and Reconstruction in Tennessee, pp. 77 et seq.

Not a few complaints of young men who were indisposed to put their hands to any useful task were heard. They were riding labor, said the Southwestern newspaper, like the old man of the sea.[1] They would practise law or medicine, lecture or manage a plantation; all of them would be gentlemen. Thus it was that in every community there were young fellows from the better classes of society, as well as from the rabble, ready to bait the negroes, embezzle funds, steal horses, make forays for adventure, robbery or revenge, murder men, ravish women, start fires and riots.[2] One day guerrillas stole a steamboat on the Mississippi, another day they waylaid a sheriff or a judge. Black men in some neighborhoods were hunted like rabbits. A Vicksburg correspondent of the New York Tribune said in July, 1866, that he knew of 153 negroes who had been killed in Mississippi and Arkansas since the beginning of the year.[3] General George A. Custer testified that five hundred men had been indicted for murder in Texas, but that conviction had followed in not a single case.[4] Crime went unpunished from Washington city to the Gulf. Each day's news from the states lately in rebellion belied the President's declarations that peace was at hand, and that the people, if left to themselves, would pursue orderly ways. Such reading, mornings and evenings, improved the humor of no man in the North, though he might persuade himself that the accounts at times were exaggerated to serve political ends. Constantly there was systematic misrepresentation in partisan sheets to the gross disadvantage of the South.[5] At a time when property and life were not too secure and punishment for crime was neither certain nor prompt in the North it would have bordered upon the miraculous, if the states at the end of four years of war, in the throes of a change from slave to free labor conditions, were to fulfil every captious requirement of them who

---

[1] Cited in Phila. Ledger, Oct. 17, 1866.

[2] Lynchburg Virginian, quoted in Phila. Ledger, July 16, 1866; Atlanta (Ga.) Era, quoted in Phila. Ledger, Oct. 17, 1866.

[3] N. Y. Tribune, Aug. 3, 1866.

[4] Cong. Globe, 39th Cong., 2d sess., pp. 1567–8.

[5] Cf. Dunning, Essays, p. 139.

had been so recently an enemy in arms. The "Black Codes" which had been passed by the Southern state legislatures of 1865, and had seemed so harsh, were being modified by the same legislatures in 1866, either in answer to Northern criticism, or as the result of a sober conviction that the problem of dealing with the freedmen might be better met by milder measures.[1]

Some social and economic adjustments there may have been, but the occupation of making the Radicals at the North perceive the wrong of heaping outrage upon outrage at the doors of the late "rebels" to prove that the President had erred when he declared that the Southern states were again fit to govern themselves, was interrupted by two grievous occurrences — the riots in Memphis in May and in New Orleans in August. The Third United States Colored Artillery had been stationed in Memphis. Many of the men were disorderly and had repeatedly come into conflict in the streets with the police of the city, who for the most part were Irishmen. On the afternoon of April 30 four of these Irish officers of the peace jostled as many negro soldiers on the sidewalk. The next day another collision occurred, and the police, joined by a white mob, began an indiscriminate attack upon the black population. The riots continued until midnight and were resumed when the sun rose on May 2, at which time General Stoneman, in command of the Federal forces in the district, succeeded in re-establishing order.[2] Meanwhile no less than 46 negroes, young and old, and of both sexes, had been killed outright, many in the most brutal ways. More than 80 had been injured by guns, knives and clubs. Negresses were violated and their shanties burned. Four churches and twelve schoolhouses of negroes fell a prey to incendiary flames.

The outbreak awakened a feeling of pronounced revulsion in the North. Brownlow's Tennessee legislature passed a law putting the police of Memphis under the direction of state commissioners.[3] General Stoneman appointed a military

[1] Fleming, Documentary History of Reconstruction, vol. i, p. 244.
[2] House Ex. Doc., 39th Cong., 1st sess., no. 122.
[3] N. Y. Nation, May 24, 1866.

board to conduct an investigation. The officers of the Freedmen's Bureau took a like course, heard witnesses and recorded testimony. The House of Representatives sent to the scene a special committee of three, with Elihu B. Washburne as chairman. No less than 170 persons, white and black, came before the congressmen to give their versions of the affair. The mob, said the report when it was ready, had been "actuated by feelings of the most deadly hatred to the colored race." The deeds of barbarity which it had perpetrated were almost without a parallel in the history of nations, and must inspire "the most profound emotions of horror" among all civilized men.[1] The Democratic member dissented. Without attempting to condone the riot he found that it had been begun by the negro troops, that it was ascribable in large degree to the policy of Congress in disfranchising the "better classes of society" in the South, *i.e.* those who had taken part in the rebellion, and that if a repetition of such an occurrence were to be averted political rights must be restored to them at once.[2]

But the Memphis mob's savageries seemed to few in the North to teach any such lesson. This outrage was but one of many horrors which might be expected to ensue in all parts of the late Confederate states if the Federal troops were withdrawn as the people of the South desired. Memphis was not faithful to the Union; it was growing more disloyal day by day. In that city the flag of the United States was never seen. "Yankee Doodle" and "Hail Columbia" were never heard; only "rebel airs" were played in the theatres. Pictures of "rebel" generals were displayed in the windows of the shops. The newspapers daily voiced the people's unregeneracy. Had not the Memphis Avalanche said, a day or two after the riots were at an end, that they had convinced all men of one thing? — it was now plain that the South would not be ruled by the negro. "We congratulate the country," said the editor of this newspaper. "We congratulate our

[1] House Reports, 39th Cong., 1st sess., no. 101.
[2] Ibid., pp. 42, 44.

readers. Soon we shall have no more black troops among us. Thank Heaven the white race are once more rulers of Memphis." [1]

Still more did the riots in New Orleans inflame the Northern mind. Everywhere popular feeling grew tense as the date of the elections which were to determine the merits of the issue between the President and the Congress approached. If there had been no reason except general race prejudice for what had occurred in Memphis there was in New Orleans a definite political proposal which could be referred to as the cause of the outbreak. The state convention which in 1864 had adopted a constitution for Louisiana was to be reconvoked and an attempt would be made to extend the suffrage to the negroes. It was an unusual, many said a grossly irregular, proceeding, to reassemble a convention which had adjourned, and which, it was supposed, had finished its work. A battle raged over this question. But it was enough to know that the Northern Radical plan to enfranchise the ex-slaves of the Southern people, especially when so many whites were deprived of the ballot, was the end to be attained by the leaders of the movement. President Johnson by letter and telegram employed all his energies to prevent the delegates from coming together again. Governor Wells had pursued a vacillating course and avoided taking sides in the dispute. The lieutenant-governor and other officers of the state were frankly hostile to the Radical plan. General Sheridan, who was in command of the troops in this district, had gone to Texas. The mayor of the city, a man named Monroe, was determined to use every agency at his hand to break up the meeting. He issued a proclamation in which he called it an "extinct convention" under the control of the "enemies of the reconstruction policy of President Johnson." It was, he said, an unlawful assembly and he assumed that General Sheridan would intervene to disperse it.[2]

[1] Issue of May 5, 1866, quoted in House Reports, 39th Cong., 1st sess., no. 101, p. 334.

[2] House Ex. Doc., 39th Cong., 2d sess., no. 68, p. 26.

The delegates would meet on Monday, July 30, 1866. On the night of the preceding Friday, July 27, a procession of negroes passed through the streets and crowds were addressed by a number of speakers in front of the City Hall and at other places. Accounts of what had been said at this time differed widely. Some declared that the negroes were told to come "in their might." The very stones of the streets, an impassioned orator said (so it was alleged) were "crying out for the blood of rebels." Whether these words were used or not it was agreed that one or more of the speakers had urged the blacks to strike, if need be, in their own defence.[1]

The attack upon the Mechanics' Institute where the convention was held, on the next Monday about midday, when it met for organization, was deliberately planned. All signs pointed to this fact. As during the war, when it was desired to announce to the population that the Yankees were coming, the bells of the city were rung. Immediately work ceased in saw mills and shops, and Mayor Monroe's police, the firemen with their iron wrenches, bands of ex-Confederate soldiers and the rabble generally, ran into the streets and rushed pell mell for the convention hall. Whites and blacks inside and outside the building were stabbed, clubbed and shot. The wounded, pleading for mercy, were cruelly beaten with brickbats. The disorder spread to far parts of the city. Negroes fell in a general massacre, their dwellings were burned to the ground. Sheridan hurried back from Texas,[2] but before he came 45 or 50 persons had been killed and 150 more had been wounded. It was not a riot, he telegraphed to Grant, but "an absolute massacre by the police which was not excelled in its murderous cruelty by that of Fort Pillow."[3] The inevitable commissions of inquiry which followed, both military and Congressional,

[1] Certainly the speech of Dr. Dostie, a white dentist, leader of the negrophiles, killed in the riots to become a martyr of the Northern Radicals, was inflammatory, if it were reported at all correctly in the New Orleans Times. — Appleton's Cyclopedia for 1866, p. 454.

[2] Sheridan's Personal Memoirs, vol. ii, p. 335.

[3] House Ex. Doc., 39th Cong., 2d sess., no. 68, p. 11; cf. House Reports, 39th Cong., 2d sess., no. 16, p. 351 of Testimony.

heard witnesses as in Memphis and attempted to fix the responsibility. The committee of the House said that there had been no massacre so inhuman and fiendlike in the national history;[1] the military board, that the work of murder had been pursued with "a cowardly ferocity unsurpassed in the annals of crime."[2]

Sheridan, having denounced the occurrence in an unqualified way, was himself denounced for his partisan Northern sympathies. His outspoken statements were displeasing to the people of New Orleans and to President Johnson alike. On his side he charged that his despatches had been garbled by agents of the administration at Washington before they were given to the press.[3] Johnson had telegraphed to the governor, to the lieutenant-governor, to the attorney-general of Louisiana, expressing his disapproval of the convention. Usurpations by this body, he had said on the very day of the riot, were not to be tolerated.[4] He even urged that the Federal troops should be used to support the courts in a plan to arrest the members of the revolutionary body.[5] He asked many questions of General Sheridan concerning the "illegal and extinct convention" and the "inflammatory and insurrectionary speeches" made to the mob, placing himself squarely upon the ground which he soon publicly occupied. The riot was due to the agitation for negro suffrage; it had been instigated directly by the Radicals in the North.[6] The President's friend, Welles, believed it to be a "deliberate conspiracy," originating among his enemies in Congress. It was but one of "a series of bloody affrays" soon to follow. The country was to be "involved in civil war, if necessary, to secure negro suffrage in the states and Radical ascendency in the general government." Only Stanton in the Cabinet openly expressed a different view. It was, the Secretary of War dared to say

---

[1] House Reports, 39th Cong., 2d sess., no. 16, p. 1.
[2] House Ex. Doc., 39th Cong., 2d sess., no. 68, p. 40.
[3] Ibid., pp. 2–3; Sheridan's Memoirs, vol. ii, p. 236.
[4] House Ex. Doc., 39th Cong., 2d sess., no. 68, p. 5.
[5] Ibid., p. 8.   [6] Ibid., p. 12.

to the President, the pardoned rebels, the attorney-general of Louisiana, Andrew J. Herron, and Mayor Monroe who were the guilty instigators of the affair.[1] The Radicals outside the Cabinet went farther. They did not hesitate to put the responsibility directly at the door of the President. The New York Tribune, voicing the sentiments of this party, said: "The hands of the rebels are again red with loyal blood. Rebel armies have once more begun the work of massacre."[2] The President had engendered the spirit which broke forth in riot, which murdered Unionists and which again unfurled the "rebel" flag. Here in New Orleans notice was served upon the North that henceforward every loyal convention which dared to meet upon Southern soil would be violently dispersed.[3]

The campaign for the election of a new Congress which would support Johnson's policies with respect to the rebel states, or would continue to oppose him as the old one had done, advanced rapidly. Two leading movements were planned by the Johnson men — a great non-partisan convention conceived in the spirit of brotherhood and peace to meet in Philadelphia on August 14, and a "swing around the circle" by the President supported by Seward, Grant, Farragut and a retinue of political spellbinders and war heroes for the making of speeches and the shaking of hands on the way to and from exercises attending the dedication of a monument to Stephen A. Douglas in Chicago in September.

The Philadelphia convention assumed mammoth proportions. The President's Cabinet could not be held together in a time of so many bitter differences. For months Johnson had been urgently recommended to reorganize this body. Its reconstruction should have been his first step, said Lewis D. Campbell of Ohio. "Put the rascals out," a correspondent counselled him. "Be surrounded by your friends or you are forever gone." Seward should be dismissed, said Montgomery Blair; many desired to see General Steedman established in Stanton's place.[4] But while rumor spoke repeatedly of the resig-

<hr>

[1] Welles, vol. ii, pp. 569–70.   [2] N. Y. Tribune, July 31, 1866.
[3] Ibid., Aug. 2, 1866.   [4] Johnson Papers.

nation of the Secretary of War it was not received. On July 11, a few days before the adjournment of the Congress, William Dennison of Ohio, once the governor of that state, since October, 1864, the postmaster-general, retired from that position. He had presided over the convention in Baltimore which nominated Lincoln and Johnson in 1864, and he could go no farther with the President. A few days later James Speed of Kentucky, brother of the friend of Lincoln's youth, Attorney-General since December, 1864, announced his desire to retire, and the resignation soon followed of James Harlan of Iowa, a United States senator for that state during the war, who had been appointed Secretary of the Interior by Lincoln just before his assassination. Thus three Cabinet members had made their departure before the 1st day of August. All issued statements, Dennison, one of length, giving the reasons for his course in a good political style which warmly commended him to the Radical press.[1] None of these men could join such members of the Cabinet as Seward, Welles and McCulloch in forwarding the arrangements for the President's campaign and in a manly way they withdrew.

Johnson adherents to take their places were found in the persons of A. W. Randall of Wisconsin, earlier a governor of that state and for a short time our minister to Italy, more lately Mr. Dennison's assistant in the direction of the affairs of the post-office department, now advanced to become Postmaster-General; Judge Henry Stanbery of Ohio to succeed Speed as Attorney-General, and Orville H. Browning of Kentucky to succeed Harlan as Secretary of the Interior. These men, with Senator Doolittle and the Blairs, formed a kind of managing committee to prepare the way for the Philadelphia convention.

Delegates were chosen in all parts of the country, both North and South, without regard to party. Whether Republicans or Democrats hitherto, they were now to come to the "City of Brotherly Love" to save the Union from what the New York Herald denounced every day as the "Jacobins." Montgomery

[1] N. Y. Tribune, Aug. 11, 1866; cf. ibid., Aug. 14, 1866.

Blair and other members of the Johnson party thought that they saw impending a new civil war.[1] The action of Congress in refusing to admit to their seats the representatives of the late Confederate states was nothing less than revolutionary; it would lead to more inter-sectional strife. The men who were organizing the Philadelphia convention, therefore, were patriots of the first order; they were coming together to perform one of the most glorious tasks in the history of the republic.

The call for this "National Union Convention" had gone out on June 25. Each Congressional district would elect two delegates, with representatives also from the District of Columbia and the territories. The essential ideas inspiring the movement were, first, that there was no right in the Constitution or in Congress "to separate states from the Union," and, second, that each state had the inherent right to determine the qualification of its electors, a denial, therefore, of the right of the central government to impose negro suffrage upon the South.

In Philadelphia there was no hall large enough to accommodate an assemblage of the size which this one promised to assume. A great frame structure called a "Wigwam" was erected on Girard Avenue at 20th Street in the northwestern part of the city. On the roof over the entrance was a flag-staff 100 feet in height. There were seats in the amphitheatre for 3000 people, in the galleries for 7000 more. From the speakers' stand rose an arch of 36 sections for the various states, each bearing its appropriate shield. These and the pillars and rafters were festooned with red, white and blue bunting and American flags.[2]

The trains and boats bore the delegates to the city in great numbers and with them came a host of retainers, spectators and newspaper correspondents. They packed the hotels. The lobby of the Continental on Chestnut Street was thronged

[1] Welles, vol. ii, pp. 555–7.
[2] Leslie's Illustrated Newspaper, Sept. 1, 1866; Phila. Ledger, Aug. 11 and 15, 1866.

with the visitors. In the crowd were hated "rebels" from the South and still more hated Copperheads, — Ben and Fernando Wood, William Bigler and, worse than all, Clement L. Vallandigham of Ohio, a sinner whom no one could believe had come for repentance. Alexander H. Stephens, the vice-president of the late Confederacy, had wisely remained at home. He wrote to Montgomery Blair saying that, while no man could more cordially approve and indorse the objects of the convention, he must doubt the propriety of his taking part in its deliberations.[1] But others had different views, and not only came to attend the meeting but presented credentials from constituencies which had duly elected them as delegates. The Radical press could not conceal its delight. This convention of brotherly love had been unmasked; these were "rebels" and "near rebels" who had gathered together to put the mark of their approval upon the policy of Andrew Johnson.[2] Ninety nine-one hundredths of them, said the New York Tribune, were men who had voted in 1864 for either Jefferson Davis or George B. McClellan.[3] The United States district attorney for western Pennsylvania threatened to resign his office. He wrote Johnson that he had expected the convention to "produce an abatement of an unreasoning Radical spirit." But it was filled with those who were "distinguished for little else than inveterate, malignant hostility to the war and the policy of Mr. Lincoln." The country would not "take counsel" of such as these.[4]

Clearly the managers of the meeting were disturbed. Everywhere, — in the corridors of the hotels, on the streets, — men asked one another — "With such delegates can the convention accomplish any good object?" "Will they turn out Vallandigham and the Woods?"[5] The tension was relieved in some degree when Fernando Wood withdrew from the New York

---

[1] N. Y. Tribune, July 30, 1866.
[2] Ibid., Aug. 14, 1866 — "A meeting of marvelous odds and ends, the reconstructed shreds and patches of rebeldom."
[3] Ibid., July 27, 1866.   [4] Johnson Papers.
[5] Phila. Ledger, Aug. 13, 1866.

delegation and Vallandigham was persuaded under pressure to give up his seat. But it was still for the Radicals the "Bread and Butter Convention," a gathering of some whose bread had been buttered by Johnson, such as Randall and Browning, and of others who hoped that in future it might be buttered for them by the giver of good at Washington.[1]

At midday, on August 14, the delegations filed into the great barn in the wood near Girard College though the roof was not yet in place, Governor Orr of South Carolina and General Couch of Massachusetts, arm in arm, leading the way. Here was the symbol of a reunited country. Men cheered and threw their hats into the air, ladies waved their handkerchiefs, the band played "Rally Round the Flag, Boys," then the "Star-Spangled Banner," and then "Dixie" amid renewed shouting. There were three cheers for the thirty-six states, three cheers for the Union, three cheers for the red, white and blue. Governor Randall called the meeting to order and installed General John A. Dix as temporary chairman. He in turn the next day resigned his place to the permanent chairman, Senator Doolittle, who directed the meeting with a gavel turned from a piece of live oak taken from the old ship of war *Constitution.* It was believed that there were 15,000 people in the hall while Doolittle was making his speech. A telegram from President Johnson, in which he said that "the people must be trusted and the country will be restored," caused a great demonstration of enthusiasm.[2]

But there was little more to be done except adopt a "Declaration of Principles," and issue an "Address to the People," which were brought forward by a committee standing under the chairmanship of Senator Edgar Cowan of Pennsylvania. The "Declaration," in the form of nine resolutions, restated the well-known policy of Andrew Johnson, and in the tenth hailed the President as a "chief magistrate worthy of the nation and equal to the great crisis upon which his lot is cast." He had proven himself "steadfast in his devotion to the Constitu-

---

[1] N. Y. Tribune, Aug. 17 and 20, 1866.
[2] Phila. Ledger, Aug. 16, 1866.

tion, the laws and interests of his country, unmoved by persecution and undeserved reproach." In the "Address" the convention called upon the people in every Congressional district in every state "to secure the election of members who, whatever other differences may characterize their political action, will unite in recognizing the right of every state of the Union to representation in Congress, and who will admit to seats in either branch every loyal representative from every state in allegiance to the government." Then upon the third day, the 16th of August, upon the motion of John Hogan, a Democratic congressman from Missouri, having performed "so gloriously" all its tasks, the convention adjourned *sine die*, and amid strains of "Home, Sweet Home" from the band, with cheers for Andrew Johnson and the presiding officer, Senator Doolittle, the "Bread and Butter" men dispersed to the hotels and railway stations.[1]

To the President and his friends this "great popular national mass meeting," as the New York Herald denominated it, seemed to be of enormous consequence. Now for the first time in five years representatives of all the states had met together in a political convention. Men from the North and the South sat side by side as if they "belonged to the same human family." The harmony and good feeling which had prevailed contrasted in the most striking way with the wrangling sessions and the bloodthirsty temper of the Radical Congress.[2] It was an unmistakable augury of the confusion and complete defeat of the "Jacobin faction" in the coming elections, which would determine whether the country was to have peace or a renewal of civil war.

Doolittle, Randall, Browning and the other managers of the convention frequently had written the President to tell him of the amity and good nature which everywhere prevailed.[3] General Dix declared it to be "the most able, harmonious and enthusiastic body of men of such a magnitude" he had ever met in his "long acquaintance with political affairs." It would

[1] Phila. Ledger, Aug. 17, 1866.
[2] N. Y. Herald, Aug. 15, 1866.   [3] Johnson Papers.

insure the success of Johnson's patriotic and unwavering
efforts to heal the breach between the two great sections of the
Union.[1] When the leaders reached Washington, they were
"overflowing with their success."[2]

The official proceedings were to be presented to the President by a committee appointed by the meeting for the purpose.
On the 18th, with Reverdy Johnson, Democratic senator
from Maryland, at their head, they were received in the East
Room of the White House. General Grant was induced to
stand beside the President.[3] Several members of the Cabinet
also were present. Reverdy Johnson spoke of "the spirit of
concord and brotherly affection" which had reigned in the
convention. Every heart was "full of joy," he said, "every
eye beamed with patriotic animation." Despondency gave place
to assurance that the late dreadful civil strife was ended, that a
blissful reign of peace, under the protection of the Constitution
and the laws, would have sway in all parts of the Union.[4]

The opportunity was at hand for the President to make
a speech, and he acquitted himself with more dignity than on
several previous and many later occasions. Language was
inadequate, he said, to express his emotions and to give voice
to his feelings. He was awed and overwhelmed by the sight of
those gathered before him. When his friends had telegraphed
him that the delegates from Massachusetts and South Carolina
had walked down the aisle arm in arm, he had been moved so
deeply that the tears filled his eyes; he could not complete
the reading of the despatch. The "Declaration of Principles"
made in Philadelphia was equal in importance, he continued,
to the Declaration of Independence of 1776. The convention
was the most notable which had ever met, barring possibly
the one of 1787 assembled to form the Federal Constitution.
The paper which the committee had placed in his hands was
a second proclamation of emancipation to the people of the
United States. His only sin, their only sin was in "daring

---

[1] Johnson Papers.   [2] Welles, vol. ii, p. 581.
[3] Cf. Adam Badeau, Grant in Peace, p. 38.
[4] Washington corr., N. Y. Tribune, Aug. 20, 1866.

to stand by the Constitution" of their fathers. He would go forward on his way. He could not be driven from it by the "taunts and jeers" of Congress, and of a "subsidized calumniating press."

Applause and cheers greeted the President as he was warmed to eloquence by his own words. There were cries of "That's so!" and "Glorious!" A brass band played "Hail to the Chief!" and the ceremonies were at an end.[1] The speeches, together with the proceedings, were printed in a pamphlet by the National Union Executive Committee and given general circulation. All of the returning delegates, Doolittle leading them, were full of the idea of persuading the President to dismiss Stanton.[2] Those who had come from Texas wrote that no event of which they could conceive would so sincerely gratify the people of that state as the removal of this "arbitrary and despotic man."[3] But difficulties stood in the way, and the days passed only with fruitless abuse of him and the rest of the "bloody Radicals."

In the midst of the celebration of good feeling which followed the Philadelphia convention the President, on August 20, 1866, issued a proclamation declaring at an end the insurrection in Texas. This state alone had remained under martial law. "Peace, order, tranquillity and civil authority now exist," said he, "in and throughout the whole of the United States of America." "Only saints," the New York Nation reminded its readers, were fit to exercise "such monstrous powers" as had been bestowed upon Lincoln and Johnson when the writ of habeas corpus was suspended, and saints in this world were few.[4] "The people may well rejoice," said the New York Herald, "at the glorious end we have at last reached."[5]

Meanwhile the "Jacobins" had no intention of letting the campaign proceed without a counterstroke. They had lost no opportunity to brand the members of the Philadelphia convention as traitors, and to banish them into outer darkness. There must be another convention — a convention of "South-

[1] Washington corr., N. Y. Tribune, Aug. 20, 1866.
[2] Welles, vol. ii, pp. 581-3.
[3] Johnson Papers, under date of Aug. 22.
[4] N. Y. Nation, Aug. 23, 1866.   [5] N. Y. Herald, Aug. 20, 1866.

ern Loyalists." It, too, would meet in Philadelphia. The call was issued from Washington on July 4. The number of "Loyalists" in the South was not large, nor did they come from classes of the population opulent enough to make it feasible for them to travel hundreds of miles to attend political meetings. To swell the proportions of the assemblage a hundred or more Radical members of Congress, a score of Republican governors and ex-governors and bodies of citizens of the old free states were induced to set off for Philadelphia in token of the North's sympathy, as the New York Tribune was pleased to say, with "the hunted, stricken" men who had suffered for their conscience' sake. The "eminent, fire-tried Southern Unionists," permitted to meet nowhere in the South because of "rebel" mobs, compelled in many instances to select their delegates secretly, would be welcomed now to the bosom of their friends.[1]

On the morning of September 3 the "Loyalists" and their attendant following began to gather in Independence Square. The Tennessee delegates, with Governor Brownlow at their head, were the first to appear upon the scene. They entered Independence Hall, where they were addressed by the late Secretary of the Interior, James Harlan. Others followed. Reception committees met the visitors, and they were paraded through the streets to the Union League Club house. At one o'clock they assembled in National Hall, which had been decorated appropriately for the use. In front of the speakers' stand were the lines:

> "Welcome, patriots of the South!
> Ye bore as Freedom's hope forlorn
> The private hate, the rebel scorn;
> Yet held through all the paths ye trod
> Your faith in man and trust in God."

Everywhere the eye met such mottoes as these:

"'The Union — it must and shall be preserved.' — Andrew Jackson";
"'There can be no neutrals — only patriots or traitors.' — S. A. Douglas";
"'When the wicked are in authority the people mourn.' — Isaiah,"

[1] N. Y. Tribune, Sept. 1, 1866.

together with extracts from the speeches of Andrew Johnson of two years ago. "Shall the traitors who brought this misery upon the state be permitted to control its destinies?" was followed by the word "No"; "Treason must be made odious, traitors must be punished and impoverished," by the comment — "And yet you pardon, honor and reward them." The stage was set for a political meeting, which, if not of such size as the Johnson rally in the "Wigwam" in August, was meant to awaken the nation. It went far to do so. The adversary was on his guard; he did not hesitate to condemn the men in attendance and to belittle their purposes. They were "self-appointed, representing nobody but themselves," said the New York World.[1] They were "ribald fanatics" and "mean whites." Day by day the World described their proceedings under the rubric — "The Bogus Southern Convention."

The Radicals, said the President's organ at Washington, the National Intelligencer, were in need of evidence from the mouths of Southern men that he had struck hands with the secessionists; that it was all a mistake about the negroes having been set free — they were still in slavery; that no Northerner could put his nose across Mason and Dixon's line without being knocked in the head by ferocious men with insatiable appetites for roasted Yankees, relics of the late rebellion, and so on.[2]

The Radical campaign managers had been unable to find enough delegates to fill the hall, said the New York Herald, and they had hired a lot of bootblacks, whitewashers and other negro "out-of-works" in Philadelphia. Daily they were presented to the readers of the Herald as "nigger worshippers" and "miscegens." It was a "black and tan convention," a "mongrel convention," a "miscegenation convention."[3] Nevertheless what was said and done at the meeting was carried far in the newspaper despatches, and had at least some of the influence which was desired by those who had organized the meeting.

[1] Sept. 4, 1866.   [2] Issue of Aug. 30, 1866.
[3] Issues of Sept. 4 to 8, 1866.

Such men as T. J. Durant and Henry C. Warmoth of Louisiana, Governor Brownlow and Horace Maynard of Tennessee, ex-Secretary James Speed of Kentucky, A. W. Tourgee of North Carolina, ex-Provisional Governor Hamilton of Texas, who had gone over to the Radicals "bag and baggage," [1] John Minor Botts of Virginia and J. A. J. Creswell of Maryland were numbered among the delegates. Durant was elected temporary, and Speed permanent chairman of the convention. Meantime the "honorary delegates," comprising a distinguished company of governors, ex-governors, and congressmen; Anna Dickinson the female orator; Fred Douglass, the fugitive slave, who had been used by the Abolitionists before the war; Theodore Tilton, and other persons of prominence in the North were holding meetings in another hall under the presidency of Governor Curtin of Pennsylvania. At night the streets were filled with torchlight processions. Radical speakers from many states made the welkin ring with accounts of the new treason in the South and of the numberless outrages upon the loyal men residing there. Denunciation of Johnson, bitter and coarse, was heard everywhere.

After five days the delegates concluded their sessions and, like the "Bread and Butter men" in August, they issued an address or appeal to the people, and adopted divers resolutions which were to be carried to the President. In Philadelphia, on the spot "where freedom was proffered and pledged by the Fathers of the republic," the representatives of eight millions of people asked their friends and brothers in the North for protection and justice. "Unexpected perfidy" had been discovered in the highest place of government, now "accidentally filled by one who adds cruelty to ingratitude and forgives the guilty, as he proscribes the innocent." Help was implored in combatting a reorganized enemy whose sole object it was to remit the control of the destinies of the Unionists of the South to "the contrivers of the rebellion." The border state and the old "rebel" state delegates split upon the rock of negro

[1] Gordon Granger to Pres. Johnson, June 12, 1866, in Johnson Papers.

suffrage. This policy the Maryland and Kentucky men refused to indorse, so the representatives of the "non-reconstructed" states issued a separate report urging the enfranchisement of the blacks by "national and appropriate legislation enforced by national authority."[1]

The soldiers returned from the war, now and for so long afterward a body to be used for political purposes, also arrayed themselves upon one side or the other of the controversy. The Johnson men met in a tent in Cleveland on September 17. They called their meeting a Soldiers' and Sailors' Convention and such generals as Wool, Custer, Rousseau, Ewing, Crittenden, Steedman and Gordon Granger played prominent parts in its deliberations. A number of ex-Confederates in Memphis, headed by General Forrest, the "butcher of Fort Pillow," whom the Radicals still wished to hang, had telegraphed their greetings which were doubtfully received. The speeches and resolutions followed the lines laid down by the "Bread and Butter men," in Philadelphia. Doolittle and eight or ten generals signed a request, which was forwarded to the President, that he dismiss Stanton whose presence at the head of the War Department, they said, greatly tended "to weaken" the administration.[2]

A week later the Radical soldiers convened in a shed called a "Wigwam" in Pittsburgh. Their number was large and their enthusiasm ardent. General Jacob D. Cox presided. In a lurid speech Ben Butler of Massachusetts advocated the hanging not only of Jeff Davis, but also of General Lee. Flags waved everywhere. The streets at night were ablaze with shouting men carrying kerosene lamps. Resolutions condemning Johnson and indorsing the whole Radical programme were adopted and given out to the press.[3]

The President's "swing around the circle" began on Tuesday morning, August 28. The members of his Cabinet had generally advised him to make the trip to Chicago, ostensibly

[1] Phila. Ledger, Sept. 3, 4, 5, 6, 7, 8, 9, 1866. See The Southern Loyalists' Convention (printed proceedings), Tribune Tracts, no. 2.
[2] Johnson Papers.   [3] N. Y. Herald, Sept. 27, 1866.

to attend the ceremonies which had been arranged in connection with the laying of the corner stone of a monument to Stephen A. Douglas, though really of course at such a time to meet the people and ask them for their votes.[1] But only two members, Seward and Welles, and the new Postmaster-General, Randall, bore him company. Seward was seized with the cholera on the way home, and his life for a time was believed to be near its end,[2] while Randall, who was bent upon business connected with his government office, was in attendance only a part of the time.[3] The heroes of the war on land and sea, General Grant and Admiral Farragut, who were persuaded to join the party, became the lions of the tour. It was particularly desired, by Seward, that they should accompany the President through Philadelphia, where it was suspected that, if their precious persons were not upon the train, it might be wrecked by wicked Radicals. As the mascots of the company they continued with it over the entire route.[4] Silently, while the President and Seward spoke, they seemed to lend their great military names and reputations in support of the Johnson cause.

The departure from Washington was quiet; the passage across Baltimore from one railway station to another was effected through a great crowd of huzzaing people. Governor Swann of Maryland accompanied the party to Havre-de-Grace, where a delegation of Delawareans appeared to welcome and escort the President through that state, to deliver him in turn at the Pennsylvania line to a committee from Philadelphia. The reception in that city was more enthusiastic than any could have anticipated in view of the known "black Republican" sympathies of so many of the people. The President reached his hotel in Chestnut Street, the Continental, under the escort of a procession of soldiers and fire companies. He remained overnight and before he left for New York the next day had made three speeches, one to the reception committee, another from the hotel balcony to a throng in the street and a

[1] Welles, vol. ii, p. 587.   [2] Ibid., pp. 594–5.
[3] Ibid., p. 589.   [4] Ibid., p. 584.

third from the same vantage point in the evening to a party of tailors, who came to establish a bond of feeling between themselves and one who was ready to own that he had risen from their ranks. Then a band serenaded him, and the German singing societies did him like honor in their way. The cheers and other signs of gratification by the great crowds were declared by so temperate a Philadelphia gazette as the Public Ledger to be of a kind which could leave no doubt as to their "sincerity and heartiness."

The route to New York led through Burlington, Bordentown, Trenton, New Brunswick and Newark. Committees with words of welcome, girls bearing bouquets, banners and flags, song and serenade, marked the party's progress. At several points the halts were long enough to admit of handshaking and the making of speeches. The Hudson was crossed at Jersey City, amid the booming of guns, through gaily decorated shipping. The President and his companions entered carriages at the Battery and were driven up Broadway to the City Hall, where they were welcomed by Mayor Hoffman. These ceremonies ended, four brigades, comprising more than twenty regiments of the National Guard of New York state, marched in review before the President. The streets were lent unusual animation by flags, banners and decorative devices of many kinds. "Thrice welcome, Andrew Johnson, the sword and buckler of the Constitution, the Union's hope and people's champion" stood out at one point along the line. "The Constitution — Washington established it, Lincoln defended it, Johnson preserved it" were the words inscribed upon another banner. Still another recalled a speech the President had made in March, 1866: "I feel that I can afford to do right and so feeling, God being willing, I intend to do right; and so far as in me lies I shall administer this government upon the principles that lie at the foundation of it."

But the principal event during the visit was an elaborate dinner at Delmonico's, where the President expounded his policies at length to a large number of the leading personages

of the city, who were his hosts. Then came a serenade by
brass bands in the street, and Mr. Johnson appeared upon the
balcony to speak to an immense crowd which pressed around
the hotel. On the following day the visitors were driven
through Central Park to the wharf where they were to board
a boat for Albany. The warmth of the President's reception
was undeniable. The Herald said that the men in attendance
at the dinner were on their feet constantly while he spoke.
The cheering was "tremendous." There had been no such outpouring of the people, said another witness, since the visit of
the Prince of Wales.[1]

The boat chosen to convey the presidential party up the
Hudson was the *River Queen* in whose cabin the commissioners
of the South had had their historic meeting with Lincoln and
Seward at Hampton Roads in February, 1865, to discuss the
terms of peace. The entire population of the towns upon the
way came out and lined the river shores. Cannon boomed,
handkerchiefs were waved, the President was cheered and at
points at which stops were made he spoke. The cadets were
drawn up for his inspection at West Point. As the boat neared
Albany the members of a reception, committee from that city
drew alongside to extend their hospitalities to the distinguished
travellers. Governor Fenton welcomed the President at the
capitol. From Albany the party proceeded to Seward's home
at Auburn,·with brief halts on the way at Schenectady, Utica,
Rome and Syracuse. At Niagara Falls, where Sunday was
spent, the President was tendered a ball. Then Buffalo, Erie
and Cleveland were visited in turn and the train proceeded
through northern Ohio towns to Detroit, whence progress was
continued across the state of Michigan to Chicago. Crowds,
both friendly and unfriendly, appeared at the railway stations.
The President spoke from the platform of his car, when the
arrangements of the managers of his tour did not admit of his
leaving it; Seward showed his face and expressed his sympathy
for the policies of his chief; Grant and Farragut were exhibited
to the populace.

[1] Phila. Ledger, Aug. 30, 1866.

At Chicago on September 6 the party soon performed its duty with reference to the Douglas monument. General Dix was the orator of the day. The President paid his tribute to Douglas from the same platform, attended a public reception arranged in his honor and hurried away to Lincoln's tomb at Springfield. At Alton he boarded a Mississippi River steamer called the *Andy Johnson* and escorted by a flotilla of 36 gaily decorated boats, symbolical of the whole number of federated states, made his way to St. Louis, where attentions similar to those which had been prepared for him in other cities were enjoyed, and the opportunity came for further repetitions of his views as to the correct course of the government with reference to the South. General Dix desired him to extend his tour over the completed parts of the Pacific Railroad "to the heart of the plains." [1] But the invitation had to be declined.

On the way east, through Indianapolis, he made many stops to talk to the crowds at the railway stations. At Louisville, he again embarked upon a steamer, to be taken up the Ohio to Cincinnati. At both these cities he was the recipient of notable public hospitalities intended in large part, as it seemed in many places, for the eminent men who accompanied him, and particularly for General Grant. More Ohio towns heard the President's voice before Pittsburgh was reached. In that city he met new crowds and then proceeded east over the mountains to Harrisburg for a reception at the capital of Pennsylvania. Great gloom was cast over the spirits of the party by reason of a disaster at Johnstown just before the President's train was ready to leave that place. Hundreds of persons standing upon a platform, swung across a dry canal, were precipitated in a mass when it gave way under their weight, and a score were killed or fatally injured, while upwards of 100 or 150 more were crushed, contused or otherwise wounded. The President passed on, sending back an expression of his sympathy and $500 for the use of the relief committee. From Harrisburg the train bore the travellers to Baltimore, where they en-

[1] Johnson Papers.

joyed a reception of which they had not had the time to avail themselves on the way out, and on Saturday evening, September 15, in good voice and unimpaired health after his extraordinary exertions, the President was again in the White House. Seward, who came by a separate train, because of his illness, must be removed from his coach in a litter and driven home in an ambulance.

The President in his "swing around the circle," if he had gained here and there a friend, had unmistakably increased the number and the ardor of his enemies. He was a square-built, broad-chested, compact, rugged man. The frost had touched his full head of deep black hair. He was "perfect in figure," said his private secretary, Benjamin C. Truman, and was always scrupulously dressed.[1] Small, sparkling, black eyes looked out from a smooth-shaven face in which many saw pertinacity and even obstinacy. His voice was resonant and far-reaching. His speech from the hotel balcony in New York was uttered so distinctly that a reporter at a distance of four blocks could correctly report it for his newspaper.[2] It was agreed by those who were not wholly unable to form fair judgments, because of their partisan feelings, that he was an orator of power. He was likely to be slow and uncertain when he began to speak but the words soon flowed from his lips, and then there were few who could honestly express a doubt of his earnestness and sincerity. It was plain to be seen by reading the report of any of his speeches that he was not a rhetorician; even his grammar was loose and faulty. But an address which read the next morning as if it were the out-giving of the most ignorant fellow, disconnected in thought and inelegant in expression, had glowed, when it was spoken, with a living fire.

So much may be granted. But there is little to urge in extenuation of the course of the argument used in the President's speeches as he proceeded from Washington to St. Louis and back again, of his rough abuse of those who did not think as

[1] Century Magazine, January, 1913.
[2] N. Y. World, Aug. 31, 1866.

he while he expounded his doctrines to the people, of his running colloquies with unfriendly persons in his audiences. He had a theory about the return of the states lately in rebellion which was simple, and he stated it over and over again. They had not been out of the Union — there never had been a time when the North was willing to recognize their breaking of the Federal bond. He had formulated a plan, indeed it had come down to him from Mr. Lincoln,[1] by which they could put off their "rebel" mantle — they one and all had laid it aside under his direction and their senators and representatives were again in Washington. Nothing remained to be done. There would be thirty-six states instead of twenty-five and the Union would be restored.

But what did we see? Radicals in control of Congress would not receive back the South's accredited delegates. They preached more bloodshed, new civil war. The penitent were not to be pardoned; they were to be reviled and kept under suspicion at arm's length while Mr. Johnson, and all who had wrought as he to extend them a kindly hand, were denounced as traitors. His policy was conformable to the traditions of the American government. He planted his feet upon the Constitution of the Union. The Radicals were centralizers and consolidators who, to gain their partisan purposes, would alter the entire character of the Federal commonwealth.

When, as he passed, he had not the time for more words, the President would say, "I leave in your hands the Constitution and the Union, and the glorious flag of your country not with 25 but with 36 stars." With this sentiment, too, he would conclude a longer speech. If Andrew Jackson in his grave could see the present plight of the land, the President declared with characteristic emphasis at Rome, N. Y., he would burst his coffin open, raise his bony arm, extend his long forefinger

[1] It is pointed out, of course, that Lincoln was acting under large and undefined war powers; that Johnson might not follow in this course now that the war was at an end. See, e.g., McCarthy, Lincoln's Plan of Reconstruction, p. 447. It is fruitless to speculate as to what Lincoln might have done had he lived to face the problems which arose after the war.

and say as of old: "By the Eternal! The Federal Union must and shall be preserved."[1] At the dedication ceremonies at Chicago he said that if Stephen A. Douglas could but know what was transpiring upon the earth, he would shake off the habiliments of the tomb and proclaim, "The Constitution and the Union, they must be preserved."[2]

Could the President have said so much patiently and in earnest, if not in well-selected words, as he proceeded on his way by railway train and steamboat, the public respect for him might have been increased by his trip. But his self-esteem was great. He never permitted his audience to forget that he had been a tailor, and that he had occupied every office in the gift of the people from a village alderman to the chief magistracy of the nation. And yet now there was a feeling that the thought of his lowly origins in some way nettled him. There was truth, perhaps, in the theory that as a "poor white" in the South he long had been ignored by the planter aristocracy, that now, as this aristocracy fawned upon him and nearly offered to take him into their hearts, he had been appreciably moved by their flattery.[3] The "'umble individual," as the Radical press would dub him, was proud indeed of his great eminence. If all his "I's" were suffused with tears, said a waggish paragrapher, salt water would flood the streets of Washington. One day the "Dead Duck" Forney in the Philadelphia Press headed the account of Johnson's progress from town to town with "I," the next day with "Me," again with "I, Me, My" or with "Myself."[4] His policy for the peaceful and immediate restoration of the Southern states came to be known everywhere as "My Policy," in the hope of ridiculing it out of countenance. It was "My Policy" in Philadelphia, "My Policy" in New York, "My Policy" in Albany, Auburn, Buffalo and Chicago.

In the speech which he had made from the balcony of the

[1] N. Y. Herald, Sept. 1, 1866.   [2] Ibid., Sept. 7, 1866.
[3] N. Y. Nation, Sept. 6, 1866; Blaine, Twenty Years of Congress, vol. ii, p. 69; Schurz, Reminiscences, vol. ii, p. 203.
[4] Phila. Press, Sept. 10, 11, 12, 13, 1866.

Continental Hotel in Philadelphia in response to serenaders,
he said, according to several reporters who were taking notes,
that "Our great Father in Heaven, the Lord of the world, was
a tailor by trade, and when you refer to the historical account
of this thing, you will find that my remarks are literally true."[1]
Some said that the President had been misunderstood. He had
likely alluded to Adam, who had made clothing of the leaves
of the fig. But others would not have it so. For was it not
written in Genesis, the third chapter and the twenty first
verse: "Unto Adam also, and to his wife, did the Lord God
make coats of skins, and clothed them."[2] Clearly this was
blasphemy, and for many days the press rang the changes on
the President's words to the tailors in Philadelphia.

From the hotel balcony in New York he as carelessly addressed another mob of people, who gathered under his window
and demanded a speech. There were men in high places in
the legislative department of the government who had "assailed, yes, denounced and traduced and outraged" him.
They had charged him with being "a usurper, a traitor and
everything that was inimical to the government."[3] "The
rebellion has been completely crushed in the South," said he
on this occasion. "I intend now to fight the enemies of the
Union in the North. God being willing, and with your help
I intend to fight out the battle with Northern traitors."

In Albany the President returned to the language of his
speech in Washington in April about "the foul whelps of sin,"
and the slander and calumny with which a "mercenary and
subsidized press" had been attempting to poison the public
mind. The American people, without calling him President,
knew that Andrew Johnson was a friend of the masses. Where
was the speech that he had ever made, or the vote that he had
ever given which was not for the advancement of the interests
of the masses of the people?[4] And so his tongue ran on from
day to day.

[1] Phila. Press, Aug. 29, 1866; cf. N. Y. Tribune, Aug. 29, 1866.
[2] Phila. Press, Sept. 1, 1866.
[3] N. Y. Herald, Aug. 30, 1866.   [4] Ibid., Aug. 3, 1866.

As the criticism of the press increased so did his exasperation. He was variously denominated a drunkard, though it appears from the most trustworthy accounts that such a charge was entirely unfounded,[1] a "renegade," a "traitor," the "great apostate," a "faithless demagogue,"[2] the "man made President by John Wilkes Booth," the "great accidental," the "great pardoner."

In an address to a crowd in Cleveland on the evening of September 3 the President fell completely from any grace which he may have gained as a citizen of Washington, and reverted to the slang-whanging, roistering methods of a village stump orator in Tennessee. Whenever he spoke his remarks were interrupted by such cries as "Hurrah for Andy Johnson!" "Go it, Andy!" "Bully for you, Andy!" "Give it to 'em, Andy!" "That's so!" "You're all right, Andy!" "Three cheers for Andy Johnson, President of the thirty-six states!" "Hang Thad Stevens!" On the other hand, unfriendly crowds would interject groans, hisses and uncomplimentary catchwords. As he travelled through the old Ohio Reserve, wedded to its Abolition idols, the accounts of his tactless and ill-tempered argument having preceded his coming, no warm welcome awaited him. At Oberlin, the seat of a well-known liberal seminary, the President seemed to have no friends. At Cleveland, however, the city authorities, though they held views antagonistic to his, made preparations for a polite reception of the party. It seemed unfitting, therefore, that he should use the opportunity for a particularly wild denunciation of his political enemies. As he proceeded with his harangue the lords of misrule took complete possession of the crowd. They hooted,

---

[1] See, for instance, Benjamin C. Truman's article in Century Magazine for January, 1913; McCulloch, Men and Measures, pp. 373-4.

[2] "Faithful among the faithless once we thought thee,
Faithless among the faithful now thou art;
To this sad depth has vain ambition brought thee,
Man of weak brain and cold, ungrateful heart.
Better for thee, our hope, once, and our pride,
If thou had'st fallen when great Lincoln died."
— Phila. Press, Aug. 28, 1866.

hurled at him questions about the New Orleans riot, shouted "Hang Jeff Davis!" "You be d—d!" "Shame!" "Don't get mad, Andy!" "Three cheers for Congress!" "Traitor, Traitor!" and other words and phrases invited by his manner. One thing led to another. When an interlocutor asked him why he did not hang Jeff Davis, he replied, "Why don't you hang him? I am not the Chief Justice. I am not the prosecuting attorney. I am not the jury." Some one cried, "Why not hang Thad Stevens and Wendell Phillips?" "Yes," said Johnson, "why not hang them?" He had fought traitors at the South; he would fight them at the North. The man who was opposed to the restoration of the Union, now that the war was ended, was as great a traitor as Jeff Davis or Wendell Phillips. As for him he was against them both.[1]

If the Cleveland meeting had been, up to this point, the most discreditable and damaging to the President, other demonstrations of a similar kind were to follow. The hanging out of black flags, as at Elyria, O.;[2] the exhibition of banners bearing such words as "No welcome to traitors," as at Chicago;[3] the playing of the "Dead March" by the bands did not indicate a strengthening of the bonds of sympathy between Mr. Johnson and the people of the West. He shouted his defiance at the crowds. He would do his duty, he said, and no power this side of the infernal regions could drive him from it.[4]

It was his practice to single out men who interrupted his speeches and deliver them rebukes, such as "Keep quiet till I have finished. Such fellows as you have kicked up all the rows in the last five years."[5] "I am not afraid to talk to the American people and all the little fellows they put into crowds to call out catchwords," he said in Detroit, after an uncivil interjection. "I care not for them. The whole kennel has been turned loose upon me long since; their little dogs, Blanche, Tray and Sweetheart, have been let loose yelping at my heels.

---

[1] Report in N. Y. Tribune, Sept. 5, 1866.
[2] N. Y. Herald, Sept. 5, 1866.   [3] Ibid., Sept. 7, 1866.
[4] Phila. Press, Sept. 9, 1866.
[5] As at Westfield, N. Y., N. Y. Herald, Sept. 4, 1866.

The whole pack of slanderers and calumniators had better get out of my way." The entire Congress, "this immaculate, this pure, this people-loving, this devoted Congress," might come down upon him. He would meet his enemies single-handed.

> "Come one, come all, this rock shall fly
> From its firm base as soon as I." [1]

At Norwalk, O., he said that it was time to stop "the sacrifice of blood and treasure." "Why don't you stop it at New Orleans?" a rowdy interjected. Johnson called for the fellow and denounced him. Could not an American citizen, said the President, express such a sentiment without being insulted? "That man does not know how to treat a fellow citizen with civility." [2] He cared not for dignity, he exclaimed at Cleveland, when an auditor complained that his speech ill became a President. "Traitor!" shouted another man in his audience. "I wish I could see that man," Johnson replied. "I would bet that if the light fell on your face cowardice and treachery would be seen in it." Such a one as had insulted him, he said again, had "ceased to be a man," and in ceasing to be this had "shrunk into the denomination of a reptile." Having "so shrunken as an honest man," he continued, "I tread upon him." [3]

At St. Louis he spoke from the portico of the Southern Hotel. Men in the crowd asked him about the New Orleans riot. Then he proceeded to talk at random. If you will consider the question of that riot, he said, you can trace it back to the Radical Congress. A plan was laid in Louisiana to give votes to negroes and to take votes away from white men. Another rebellion was commenced and it had originated in the national Congress. Every drop of blood which was shed in New Orleans rested upon their skirts; they alone were responsible. Going on, he let his shafts fly wildly at his detractors. They had called him Judas Iscariot. Once there had been a Judas — one

---

[1] N. Y. Herald, Sept. 5, 1866.   [2] Ibid., 1866.

[3] Report of Cleveland speech by a friend in Cleveland in a letter to Johnson, Sept. 14, 1866, in Johnson Papers.

of the twelve apostles. Oh, yes, the twelve apostles had had a Christ. Now if he were Judas, who had been his Christ? Was it Thad Stevens? Was it Wendell Phillips? Was it Charles Sumner? They asked him why he did not hang Jeff Davis and Thad Stevens and Wendell Phillips? He said again that a traitor at one end of the line was as bad as a traitor at the other.[1]

In Indianapolis, the next important city to be visited, the President was actually driven from the platform. The crowd groaned and shouted: "We want nothing to do with traitors!" "Shut up! We don't want to hear from you." There were cries on all sides for General Grant. Men were soon at work tearing down Johnson banners and transparencies. Fisticuffs led to a riot in which several were killed and injured.[2]

The position of Grant and Farragut had become increasingly embarrassing. The efforts of the Radicals to embroil both in the partisan acrimony of the hour were continuous, and here in the West success, but for their discretion, would have been at hand. The national hero on the sea occupied himself for the most part in kissing and patting the cheeks of the children which proud mothers brought forward for his admiration, while Grant was wont to steal away to the baggage car to smoke a cigar. They had been detailed, said the Radical press, by the commander-in-chief of the army and navy of the United States to make this journey with him, and as soldiers they had obeyed. Seward had brought them forward at the beginning of the tour and placed them on exhibition, it was complained, as though they were part and parcel of this body of itinerant harlequins. "Here is Grant," Seward would say. "He has done his duty. Here is Farragut, who has done his duty. Here is the President, who has done his duty, and now you men who vote — you are to do yours." The great soldier and the great sailor were being shown off, said the New York Tribune, as if they were "tame lions harnessed to the President's car."[3]

[1] N. Y. Herald, Sept. 10, 1876. [2] Ibid., Sept. 12, 1866.
[3] N. Y. Tribune, Sept. 8, 1866.

To prove how meanly they regarded Johnson, the crowds in the West systematically sought to honor Grant. They called for him in such tones that the President could not make himself heard from a speaker's stand or a car platform. They hailed him as the next President. It was noted and widely published that he and Johnson now were not often seen together. When a telegram was read in the Southern Loyalists' Convention in Philadelphia announcing that Grant and Farragut had left the party and were going on to Detroit alone, there was the wildest cheering amid strains from the "Star-Spangled Banner" from the band.[1] Some one had heard Grant remark that he was "disgusted with the trip" — he was "disgusted at hearing a man make speeches on the way to his own funeral."[2] For a part of the time his father was his travelling companion. It was believed by the Johnsonites that the General in this way was being carried over to the Radical ranks.[3] He resented the attendance upon the party of John Hogan, an Irish Democrat, a member of Congress from St. Louis, who was fond of using his stentorian voice to introduce the distinguished travellers at every stopping place. Grant called him a Copperhead.[4] In Cincinnati the General was obliged to issue a statement to a crowd which had attempted to call him out of a theatre. He was no politician he said. The President of the United States was his commander-in-chief. He was greatly annoyed by the demonstrations which were clearly "in opposition to the President." He would see those who sought thus to honor him on the following day in company with the President.[5]

In Louisville and Cincinnati Johnson repeated his speech about Judas Iscariot. In these cities, at the doorway of the South, he alluded more freely to the negro. He had done his part to strike the shackles from the slave, but now there were white men who needed emancipation. He knew some who seemed to forget that there were any but negroes in America.

---

[1] N. Y. World, Sept. 8, 1866.   [2] N. Y. Herald, Sept. 7, 1866.
[3] Welles, vol. ii, p. 592.   [4] Ibid.
[5] Cincinnati despatch in N. Y. Herald, Sept. 13, 1866.

Amid cries of "Bully boy, Andy, keep down the nigger!" and "Put down the nigger, Andy!" he would turn his harangue into this field. Reëntering Pennsylvania at Pittsburgh he was hooted from the platform. Indeed he was not allowed to begin his speech because of the demonstrations of a crowd more disrespectful and noisy than any which he had yet faced. It was a matter of congratulation among his friends when his trip was at its end.

Plainly "My Policy" had been set forward very little by the speeches in which the President had tried to expound it to the people. It was, said Welles, "essentially but one speech often repeated."[1] His words were always misquoted and burlesqued by the Radicals. Yet it is necessary to go no farther than the columns of administration newspapers to find proof of the tactlessness, when not actual ribaldry of his remarks. His well wishers aimed to impose silence upon him. Doolittle from Rochester urged that he more carefully weigh his words before uttering them.[2] Secretary Welles, Governor Tod and others used their influences to the same end, but without avail. The President in his egotism thought that they did not understand his power over the people as an orator.[3] It could be said, as at Cleveland, that the "Abolitionists" had hired ruffians to heckle him.[4] He could not hope to escape

---

[1] Welles, vol. ii, p. 647.

[2] The letter marked "confidential" is dated August 29. — "I am prompted to write you, and in the spirit of that true friendship which enables me to speak in all frankness, to say that I hope you will not allow the excitement of the moment to draw from you any extemporaneous speeches. You are followed by the reporters of a hundred presses who do nothing but misrepresent. I would say nothing which had not been most carefully prepared beyond a simple acknowledgment for their cordial reception. Our enemies, your enemies have never been able to get any advantage from anything you ever wrote. But what you have said extemporaneously in answer to some question or interruption has given them a handle to use against us. My sincere desire for your triumphant success in your great work emboldens me thus to write you as none but a sincere friend would do." — Johnson Papers; cf. Welles, vol. ii, p. 647.   [3] Welles, vol. ii, pp. 594, 648.

[4] Cleveland correspondents of the President, writing on Sept. 4 and 14 and other dates in Johnson Papers.

insult where Giddings and Wade had "preached treason" for thirty years. But no such excuses would serve the needs of so grave a case.

The country, said the New York Tribune, had watched "with a feeling of national shame the coarseness with which the President had turned a solemn journey to the tomb of a celebrated American into the stumping tour of an irritated demagogue." [1] The Radical Philadelphia Press declared that his speech in that city would be read "with black brows and fiery eyes by an insulted people." [2] To the New York Nation the President's utterances seemed "vulgar, egotistical and occasionally profane." They were "full of coarse abuse of his enemies and coarser glorification of himself." [3]

The Philadelphia Ledger spoke of his "indiscretion" in making remarks calculated to excite party feeling. In "bandying epithets" with brawlers he cheapened the first office in the land. The time would come, if this were to continue, when the President of the United States would command no more respect than "the commonest slangwhanger at a tavern meeting." [4] Mr. Johnson had "so singular a combination of defects for the office of a constitutional magistrate," said E. P. Whipple in the Atlantic Monthly, that he could have obtained his opportunity "to misrule the nation only by a visitation of Providence." [5]

The Cleveland speech, said the Leader of that city, was "a bitter political harangue, every word of which was an insult to his Radical hosts." It was "not even decent." [6] Loyal men, said the Indianapolis Journal and the Cincinnati Gazette, could not take part in the ceremonies arranged to welcome the President to those cities. He had basely betrayed those whose suffrages, aided by Lincoln's death, had raised him to his place. [7] "Every thoughtful man" who had heard the

[1] N. Y. Tribune, Sept. 8, 1866.   [2] Phila. Press, Aug. 29, 1866.
[3] N. Y. Nation, Sept. 6, 1866; cf. ibid., May 1, 1866, and North American Review for May, 1866.
[4] Phila. Ledger, Sept. 12, 1866.
[5] Atlantic Monthly, September, 1866.
[6] Quoted in N. Y. Tribune, Sept. 7, 1866.
[7] Quoted in National Intelligencer, Sept. 13, 1866.

President in Albany, said the Express of that city, did so with anger, but at the same time with "unfeigned sorrow." [1]

Administration gazettes were dumbfounded. Johnson's organ, the National Intelligencer, was silent. The New York World found an excuse for the President in "his straightforwardness and an irascible temper." Its response to his critics was a loud *tu quoque*. Who of all the Presidents, it asked, had been lower than Lincoln "in personal bearing"? What could be said of the nice manners of Andrew Jackson, another President from Tennessee? What was Chase's reputation for dignity as he dragged the mantle of the Chief Justice in the muddy ways of politics? Cromwell and Luther had been noted for the same "careless intrepidity" which the Radicals now complained of in President Johnson.[2] The New York Evening Post said that the speeches had "driven people's blood to their heads and aroused a storm of indignation throughout the country." His "petulant spirit" and "harsh temper" had awakened inevitably "a passionate feeling of hostility and opposition." [3] No matter what the people might think of his principles, said the President's friend, Henry J. Raymond, in the New York Times, they were "startled and bewildered" by the manner in which he advocated these principles. Americans could never see the dignity of the President forgotten or laid aside "without profound sorrow and solicitude." [4] The New York Herald had said in the President's behalf after the Cleveland speech — "When your house is on fire, when your property is being stolen, when the lives of those dear to you are imperilled, it is no time for dignity;" [5] but a few days later, seeing that much was awry, it proceeded to place the blame upon the shoulders of Mr. Seward. He was the Mephistopheles of the administration. It was plain that he had planned this unfortunate tour to damage the electoral prospects of "the earnest and honest President." [6] Color was given to this

---

[1] Quoted in N. Y. Nation, Sept. 6, 1866.
[2] N. Y. World, Sept. 4, 1866.
[3] N. Y. Evening Post, Sept. 1, 1866.   [4] N. Y. Times, Sept. 7, 1866.
[5] N. Y. Herald, Sept. 8, 1866.   [6] Ibid., Sept. 13, 1866.

theory by his retort to those members of the party who during the tour sought to induce him to restrain Johnson's wild tongue. The President, Seward said, was the best stump speaker in the United States.[1]

No voice was raised for Seward on either the one side or the other. Daily Johnson was taking refuge behind the folds of the old Republican cloak of his Secretary of State. This spare, wounded man, stricken by personal and domestic adversity to his naked soul, served his use no less than Grant and Farragut. If the President were a traitor, so was his Secretary of State. If the crowds could see in Johnson a false man, let them look at the hacks and scars of another one who had been placed, as it were, upon "a butcher's block" by the enemies of the government at Washington, and now stood on the platform beside him.[2] Together they were fighting this new fight for the preservation of the Union.

If Seward were distrusted by the Copperheads and their successors, the "Copperjohnsons," — the Radicals had a kindlier feeling for "rebels" than for these,[3] — who found in "My Policy" a statement of the dearest desires of their hearts, to his old friends, his present course seemed not short of incomprehensible. Marks of studied disrespect had been his portion repeatedly in his own state of New York.[4] The Nation said that he had "forgotten, or got rid of the prejudices and usages" of civilized society and seemed to "vie with the President in rant and indecency."[5]

Johnson's humor was in no way improved by the open neglect shown him by the state and municipal governments as he proceeded on his way. The Radical congressmen when he visited their districts gave him no welcome.[6] This deliberate omission of civility began in Wilmington, Del., when the mayor and councilmen would not receive the President. In Philadelphia he was ignored; the mayor pleading necessary absence

[1] Welles, vol. ii, p. 594.
[2] As at Cleveland, Phila. Press, Sept. 5, 1866.
[3] Welles, vol. ii, p. 590.   [4] Ibid., pp. 592–3.
[5] N. Y. Nation, Sept. 6, 1866.
[6] Welles, vol. ii, p. 589.

from the city because of the heat.[1] In New York, where the Copperheads and the "Copperjohnsons" abounded, the official reception, it was noted with unction by the Radical gazettes, was enthusiastic. In Pennsylvania, Illinois, Indiana, Michigan and Ohio, though the state capitals were visited, the governors did not appear. The receptions must be arranged by committees of private citizens, in which Democrats were the active leaders. In Cleveland the Republican government had evidenced a greater magnanimity, but the reward had been small, and the temper of the President not such as to encourage other communities to follow the city's example. In Baltimore, Indianapolis and Cincinnati the councils declined to act as hosts. In Chicago the Board of Trade room was sought for a reception, but when the organization, after an acrimonious discussion, forbade its use, if political speeches were to be delivered on the occasion, the committee transferred the ceremonies to the rotunda of a hotel. In Pittsburgh the mayor wrote the reception committee to say that since he had every reason to believe the President intended in that city to stigmatize as traitors those whose views on reconstruction coincided with his own, he must "from motives of self-respect" decline the invitation to be present.[2]

Following at the heels of the Presidential party came a body of campaigners from the Loyalists' Convention in Philadelphia. Johnson and Seward had journeyed to the tomb of Douglas; the Loyalists would make a pilgrimage over the same route to the grave of Lincoln, stopping by the way in the same manner to harangue the waiting crowds. Twenty or thirty started up through New Jersey soon after the convention closed, and went forward at the expense and risk of the Republican party committees of the various states. They had come, said Brownlow, as the stumping tour proceeded, "to try to wipe out the moccasin tracks of Andrew Johnson and William H. Seward," and of the "untamed and unmitigated Copperheads who are sliming and crawling along" in the wake of these two men.[3]

[1] Cf. Philadelphia North American and U. S. Gazette, Aug. 29, 1866.
[2] N. Y. Herald, Sept. 14, 1866.　　　　[3] Ibid., Sept. 12, 1866.

It was indeed a pestilent company, if it were intended to present to the people contrasting evidence of the gentility of the Radicals, to whom the manners of the President had seemed to give so much offence. General Butler, if he were not in the party, followed them closely. He had spoken from the same platform in Philadelphia. His gross and vindictive ribaldry, like Brownlow's, has found its equal in few men who have made their appearance in our public life. The two were well seconded by others, among the number "Jack" Hamilton, Andrew Jackson Hamilton, the provisional governor of Texas, a notable precursor of a type of "galvanized Yankee" who soon became the bane of the people of the old South. The administration organs, as he heaped his abuse upon Johnson and the plan of restoration proposed by the President, stripped his record bare. He was a drunkard and a thief, said they, a kidnapper of negroes, a whipper of slaves and a wife beater. He had headed a committee in Galveston which had commended Preston Brooks for thrashing Charles Sumner in the Senate chamber in 1856. He had been a secessionist in Texas long before other men had advocated the breaking up of the Union. Then he had left the state, and became a general in the Union army though he had never fought a battle, a governor of Texas though he had never governed it, because the people would not have such a governor. Now he was again in the North to misrepresent the Southern people.[1] One of the most eloquent members of the party was a negro clergyman from Louisiana named Randolph. After the meetings in New York some of the Southerners proceeded into New England, while others went up the Hudson. They were reunited; again divided to stump New York state, and again reunited in Erie, Pa.[2] Day by day these "travelling miscegens,"[3] this "black and tan litter" from the Philadelphia "kennel,"[4] these "bogus Southerners," these "torch and turpentine tourists," these "mean white, petticoated politicians and

---

[1] N. Y. World, Sept. 13, 1866, quoting Houston Journal; N. Y. World, Sept. 17, 1866.   [2] N. Y. Tribune, Sept. 10, 1866.
[3] N. Y. Herald, Sept. 11, 1866.   [4] Ibid., Sept. 21, 1866.

blaspheming parsons" were objects for the ribald wit of the Copperhead and Johnson sheets.

Not since 1860 had there been a campaign of so much acerbity, and clearly that one was out of the comparison, for beneath its flare were tense anxiety and solemn resolution to give restraint to men's passions. Now the nation, North and South, had gone the full length of the way. Every evil human sentiment had been called out by the war. Animosity, if it were not so active as when conflict actually raged upon the battle-field, only slumbered. New, rabid, relentless, vile men had risen to wealth and authority; they were making themselves an unscrupulous force in politics. The thrust and the parry of gentlemen seemed no longer to have any place in private or public disputation. Attack was made with the broad axe and the bludgeon. Such a desire to dominate, override and destroy whatever stood in the path of personal ambition, such scurrility in dealing with a man who might hold an opinion which differed from your own, such brutality in decrying him, had been seen never before in the history of the republic. While rowdy stump speakers held forth on the street corners and ruffians in the crowd interrupted them, while cannon roared, while bands blared, while red lights illuminated the night skies, while legions of men carried kerosene lamps or pine torches in long noisy processions, the fate of Andrew Johnson's policy as against that of Congress in reference to the restoration of the South was in the hands of the constitutional tribunal, the free American people.

The speeches on both sides were filled with recrimination, the Radicals with the more of it because of a knowledge of their power to play upon the infamous passions of men. The confiscation of Southern property, the general gibbeting of "rebels," government by standing army, punishment, retaliation, more blood and the proscription as traitors and Copperheads of all who thought as the President, with wild threats of his impeachment, filled the air by night and day.

Simon Cameron, in speaking at a hotel in Harrisburg, to soldiers home from the war, said that he had shared the view

of Stevens when Johnson had been nominated in 1864, and did
not think that "the low white of the South" was fit to be
President.   Educate him for a hundred years and you would not
lift him to a place of honor.   Why suffer him to remain if there
were a way to put him out?   A Radical orator in Tiffin, Ohio,
openly declared that Johnson had been a partner of Booth in
the assassination of Lincoln.   In a Radical parade in the streets
of Toledo a man, alluding to the President, shouted "We'll
hang the G—d—d traitor."   Depositions were taken and furnished the President to prove that clerks in the Treasury Department, and other government employees at Washington
were repeating the slander of the hustings.   They called him
a "sot," a "Copperhead," a "traitor," a "dirty dog" and a
"beast."   His likeness to a certain faithless man of Scripture
was remarked by many blaspheming tongues.   One who enjoyed his bounty in a Federal office did not scruple to say
that in all the 1800 years of the Christian era there had been
but two Judases — one Judas Iscariot who had betrayed the
Saviour of the world, the other Judas Andrew Johnson, the
President of the United States who had betrayed his party and
his country.[1]

The President and his friends were deeply agitated.   Many
feared attacks upon his body, and forcible outbreaks.   Stanton
must be removed.   "Push on!" said Samuel J. Randall.   "Relieve the people of their suspense."   Sherman should be
brought to Washington.[2]   Old Francis P. Blair offered the
same advice.   But he would put Grant in Stanton's place.[3]

A correspondent wrote to Johnson urging him to distribute
arms, and let all of them not be placed in Massachusetts and
"other crazy latitudes."   He should "fight the devil with
fire," pray to God, and "keep his powder dry."   The course
of Congress was revolutionary, said another.   "You are as much
bound to put it down as was Abraham Lincoln to wage the
war to suppress the late rebellion."   A man in Cincinnati
hoped that a call would be issued for 500,000 volunteers.   He

---

[1] Johnson Papers.   [2] Letter of Oct. 24 in Johnson Papers.
[3] Letter of Sept. 20 in Johnson Papers.

could raise 1000 in his Congressional district. Ohio would furnish the President 50,000 men inside of thirty days. Nothing less than this would prevent the destruction of the government.[1]

Careful inquiries were instituted as to the number of regular troops in Maryland that electoral disturbances might be prevented in that state. The situation early in November grew very threatening. General Grant himself visited Baltimore so to dispose armed forces that they could be made serviceable at need in maintaining the peace.

Secret agents made reports to the War Department or to the President concerning unlawful military organizations in Missouri, Tennessee and in other parts of the Union. But the wildest alarums were sounded in Ohio, Illinois and Indiana. A meeting of Radical governors had been held in St. Louis. The Union veterans were forming societies with no one knew what end in view. Sometimes they were called the Boys in Blue, and again they were parts of an organization which answered to the imposing name of the Grand Army of the Republic. The plans of those who stood at its head were being so rapidly advanced, particularly in Illinois, that it would hold its first national "encampment" at Indianapolis in November, 1866.[2] In the formation of its local posts Colonel James R. O'Beirne, who visited many towns and cities in the Mississippi Valley, saw the greatest peril for Johnson and the cause of constitutional liberty. He found muskets and ammunition in cars and railway stations. The Grand Army pretended to purposes purely social and charitable. They were in reality something else. At the first good day it would march on Washington to support Congress in a plan to seize the President. Secretly the members were introducing arms into their meeting rooms. O'Beirne had "forced" one of their lodges at night and had the most amazing accounts to render Mr. Johnson in "bulletins" as he passed from place to place in the pursuit of his investigations. This "G. A. R." had grips and pass-

[1] Johnson Papers.
[2] R. B. Beath, History of the Grand Army of the Republic, p. 79.

2 E

words, "solemn rituals" and oaths, ceremonies and mysteries. The men were drilled to the call of a bugle. In one post that O'Beirne had heard of the novitiate was blindfolded and placed in a kneeling position beside a coffin upon which the word "Andersonville" was written. There he must swear by the 300,000 graves of his comrades that he would be avenged. Soon it would be necessary to deal forcibly with these "rebels" of whose "power, danger and devilishness" he transmitted the fullest proof. They meant nothing less than "civil war." Indiana, O'Beirne said, was "a fit country for occupation." Once it had been necessary to use troops in this region to keep down the Copperheads; now the soldiery should be employed to keep down the Radicals.

A correspondent in Ohio whose letter came to the President gave alarming accounts of the activity of the "G. A. R." in that state. General George W. McCook said that everywhere they were buying and distributing arms. The President could have no conception of the magnitude of the danger. General Steedman was of opinion, so it was alleged, that military material should be ordered away from arsenals and forts in the jurisdiction of the Radical governors. It should be shipped to Washington for defence of the Federal government.[1]

The President took counsel of his fears as he was wont to do. Grant told him that there were only 2224 troops within easy reach of the national capital, and but 1550 of these were effectives. There was, Johnson found, "a revolutionary and turbulent disposition" in the country "which might at any moment assume insurrectionary proportions." The forces at hand in his judgment were not "adequate for the protection and security of the seat of government." He therefore asked Stanton to take such measures "at once" as will "insure its safety and thus discourage any attempt for its possession by insurgent or other illegal combinations."[2]

The outcome of a campaign conducted in such a manner at such a time was inevitable. First came the elections in Ver-

[1] Letters and bulletins in Johnson Papers during the campaign of 1866.
[2] Letter to Stanton, Nov. 1, 1866, in Johnson Papers.

mont on September 4, in Maine on September 10. In both states there were Radical Republican gains, those in Maine being particularly noteworthy. They were "startling and incomprehensible" to the Conservatives, said the New York Herald. They indicated "a popular ground swell wholly unexpected by the Radicals themselves."[1]

The returns from the "October states" were awaited with still greater interest. Pennsylvania, Ohio, Indiana and Iowa, after the most ardent canvasses on both sides, yielded decisive Republican majorities. The election of a Republican governor in Pennsylvania by a majority of 17,000 and the increase of a Radical congressman in the delegation from that state at Washington aroused much enthusiasm in the Radical camp.[2]

The same tendency marked the elections in November. The President had gained nothing by his appeal to the country. He had asked the Republicans to follow him; only Democrats did so. He had read himself out of his party. The 40th Congress was as Radical as the 39th had been, and encouraged by the popular indorsement the leaders prepared to conduct the nation's affairs with a high hand.

The lesson for the President, said the New York Times, was "to forego his own plans, and to aid Congress in giving effect to the plan which has secured the country's approval." For him to persist in the "iteration of his arguments and opinions

[1] N. Y. Herald, Sept. 12, 1866.

[2] "Hurrah for Pennsylvania! She's blazing up at last,
Like a red furnace molten with Freedom's rushing blast.
And the hunter scours his rifle and the boatman grinds his knife,
And the lover leaves his sweetheart and the husband leaves his wife,
And the women go out to harvest and gather the golden grain
While the bearded men are marching in the land of Anthony Wayne.

"Hurrah for Pennsylvania! Through every vale and glen,
Beating like resolute pulses she feels the tread of men.
She stands like an ocean breakwater in fierce rebellion's path
And shuns its angry surges and baffles its frantic wrath,
And the tide of slavery's treason shall dash on her in vain,
Rolling back from the ramparts of freedom, from the land of Anthony
    Wayne."
                                    — Lines in N. Y. Tribune, Oct. 11, 1866.

with not the remotest chance of success," would but render his opponents the more aggressive.[1] By "any further resistance to Congress," said the New York Herald, he could do nothing "but mischief to himself, the South and the Union." The constitutional amendment had superseded "his own favorite ideas of restoration." He could "tack ship and sail with the wind."[2] He had appealed to the country in vain, said the New York World. Why should he "sharpen acrimony by further opposition"? His views were well known. "No good purpose" would be served if he were to continue to engage in an "animated and aggressive presentation of them."[3]

On the other hand, it was pointed out that if the President had gained nothing for "My Policy," Congress, too, had worked itself into a deadlock with reference to its plan of restoration through the Fourteenth Amendment. The Southern states were not to be reorganized: they would not aid, therefore, in furnishing the Radicals with the necessary three-fourths majority which must ratify this amendment before it could take its place in the Constitution. And it was plain now, too, that Delaware, Maryland and Kentucky could not be relied upon to help Congress gain its end. The Radicals must go farther, if their designs upon the South were to succeed; they must adopt unconstitutional methods which sooner or later would meet with popular rebuke.[4]

Johnson on his side observed a discreet silence, though his friends were not unwilling to speak of the mistakes which the campaign had revealed. George Bancroft, after the news of the majorities in the "September states" had reached him, urged the President to "beware of the Copperheads." They were "dreadfully unpopular." The old nullification-secession party, he observed, never had received one-quarter of the votes of the people.[5] The pact made in Philadelphia had been broken, said General Dix. The Democrats were to follow the Con-

---

[1] N. Y. Times, Nov. 9, 1866.   [2] N. Y. Herald, Nov. 8, 1866.
[3] N. Y. World, Nov. 8, 1866.
[4] National Intelligencer, Dec. 3, 1866.
[5] Sept. 30, 1866, in Johnson Papers.

servative Republicans. Instead of this they must lead; they
must put themselves in places of prominence. The result was
due to the "utter selfishness and folly" of these men.[1]

The President declared to all with whom he did speak on
the subject that the result was not conclusive. The people had
been led away by excitement; they would yet reverse their
decision and adjudge him in the right.[2]

Some there were, it may be, who looked for an expression of
change in his views when Congress met. If it were so they were
doomed to disappointment. The President in his message indulged in no explosive words, no recriminating reflections. He
repeated a statement of his "policy." He noted the resumption
of Tennessee's relations with the Union. He deemed it, he
said, "a subject of profound regret," that Congress had "thus
far failed to admit to seats loyal senators and representatives"
of the other Southern states. To have received fifty members
of the House and twenty of the Senate would have done much
to renew and strengthen "our relations as one people." The
contention that the South was "conquered territory," he said,
was unsound, and he cited Congress' own course since the war
had begun to prove the untenability of such a theory. "The
interests of the nation," he said again, "are best to be promoted
by the revival of fraternal relations, the complete obliteration
of our past differences and the reinauguration of all the pursuits of peace." Finally he appealed for harmony between
himself and Congress to secure "the maintenance of the Constitution, the preservation of the Union and the perpetuity
of our free institutions."

It was noted that he had made no allusion to the Fourteenth
Amendment with which he from the first had had nothing
to do.

The Republican gazettes waved the message aside as of no
merit and of no guiding influence upon the course of the party.
The President, the New York Nation said, had been "reduced
to a cipher." Congress would deal with him in such a way

[1] Nov. 8, in Johnson Papers.
[2] National Intelligencer, Nov. 24, 1866.

that he would be made to realize "his defeat and future insignificance." The message was not worth any one's trouble of reading it.[1] It was as weak, said the New York Tribune, as one of Franklin Pierce; it was "a dreary, lifeless document." The duty devolving upon Congress at once became "more solemn and responsible." [2]

A plan to receive Congress when it should meet with mass parades and a general fanfare of Radicals, drawn not only from the city of Washington but from many other places, to show "how sternly loyalty could rebuke treason," had seemed to the Conservatives like the drum-beat of a revolutionary uprising.[3] But the demonstration degenerated into a small procession of negroes. The "Jacobins" were returned to the place of government and no one supposed that mercy of any kind would be extended to "rebel," Copperhead or Johnsonite. "I was a Conservative in the last session of this Congress," said Thad Stevens amid laughter, "but I mean to be a Radical henceforth." He had found upon his going home in the summer that the people were ahead of Congress on the Southern question. He did not intend that they should be ahead of him any longer.[4] The first days foretokened, as the New York World averred, "black and muttering skies and the forging of new thunderbolts to be hurled at the head of the President." [5] All kinds of requests and demands for information were forwarded to him and his heads of departments, often in the most uncivil terms.[6]

Steps were taken at once to restrict the President's powers in the granting of amnesty to the Southern people, and to hamper him in making removals from and new appointments to office. It was announced that, when the 39th Congress should end on March 4 next, the 40th would convene immediately, to watch the President and check his usurpations. Stevens began his attack upon the Johnson governments in

[1] N. Y. Nation, Dec. 6, 1866.   [2] N. Y. Tribune, Dec. 4, 1866.
[3] National Intelligencer, Nov. 10, 1866.
[4] Washington corr., N. Y. World, Dec. 3, 1866.
[5] Issue of Dec. 3, 1866.   [6] Welles, vol. ii, p. 634.

the South, in order to bring to a test vote his plan of treating the late Confederate states as "conquered provinces," [1] with a bill for organizing a new government "in the district comprising the former state of North Carolina." A convention of delegates to be chosen by both black and white voters should assemble in Raleigh on May 20, 1867. It was, said the National Intelligencer, an unconstitutional scheme which no sane man in the "better days of the republic would have thought within the range of possibility." [2] It was "a firebrand flung into the South to rekindle the old animosities," in the opinion of the New York World.[3]

Charles Sumner and other men were pressing the bill to enfranchise the negroes in the District of Columbia. This measure was brought forward in the Senate by Sumner before the session was an hour old, and he asked that it receive immediate consideration.[4] It was approved in less than a fortnight, on December 13, when only thirteen senators, two of them Republicans, Lafayette Foster of Connecticut and Van Winkle of West Virginia, voted against the bill.[5] The House acted promptly and decisively on the following day. There 46 members voted nay, nine of the number being accounted Republicans.[6]

That President Johnson would sign the bill no one believed. His veto message was received after the holiday recess. The good temper he evidenced in this paper and the cogency of the arguments against the enfranchisement of the negro, which he presented, should have won him a respectful hearing. But no Radical could be made to pause on his course by admonition from one who was swept aside as a betrayer of the party, if not a traitor to the commonwealth. The people of the District as recently as in 1865, said the President, in beginning

---

[1] For a statement of this theory as contrasted with the "state suicide" theory of Sumner see Dunning, Essays, pp. 105, 107–8; Fleming, Civil War and Reconstruction in Alabama, pp. 339–40.

[2] National Intelligencer, Dec. 1, 1866.

[3] N. Y. World, Dec. 14, 1866.

[4] Cong. Globe, 39th Cong., 2d sess., p. 2.   [5] Ibid., p. 109.

[6] Ibid., p. 138; cf. McPherson, History of Reconstruction, p. 160.

his statement, had voted upon the question as to whether they desired negro suffrage. Only 36 persons out of more than 7000 in Washington and Georgetown cities had expressed their approval of the plan. Congress, therefore, in passing such a bill had not had a suitable regard for the wishes of the people of the District. "Yesterday, as it were," the President continued, "four millions of persons were held in a condition of slavery that had existed for generations; to-day they are freemen." Could it be presumed that a class raised suddenly from such a state would be as well informed about affairs of government as intelligent white immigrants from European countries? Yet these latter must reside here for five years before they were introduced to the privileges of voting, and then were barred from the exercise unless they could furnish the state with evidence of their good moral character. Grave danger was to be apprehended from "an untimely extension of the elective franchise to any new class." Negro suffrage was an experiment which had not been tried, or even demanded by the people of the several states for themselves. In but few had such an "innovation" been introduced, and he could not bring himself to approve of it in the District of Columbia "as the beginning of an experiment on a larger scale." He regretted that he could not coöperate in this particular, as he would wish to do in all ways, to aid Congress in solving the questions dividing the country. But "no political truth is better established," said the President, "than that such indiscriminate and all-embracing extension of popular suffrage must end at last in its destruction." [1]

Immediately upon receipt of the message, on January 7, after various senators had spoken for an hour or two in further explanation of their views, the bill was passed over the veto [2] and on the following day, the 8th, the House approved the measure for the second time and it became a law amid the applause of negroes and white Abolitionists who crowded the galleries. A few days later both houses concurred in extending

[1] McPherson, History of Reconstruction, pp. 154-9.
[2] Ibid., p. 313.

the elective franchise to black men in the territories. The President, convinced of the futility of more words on the subject, made no response when this bill was sent to him for his signature, and it became a law without his approval.[1] The negro had been made the peer of the white man at the ballot box in all parts of the domain of the United States under direct Congressional control.

Other and more devious courses must be followed to achieve similar results in the Southern states. If ever there had been a time when Congress might have been content with the adoption of the Fourteenth Amendment as a condition upon which the Southern states might return to their Federal relationships, it had now passed. It is true that these terms had been held out to the South by the Committee on Reconstruction in its report in June, 1866. Many of the leaders on the Republican side in Congress were sincere in desiring that such an offer should be made, and if it were accepted, that it should be a bargain to be kept in good faith. But many more, judged by their acts and speeches, were without a wish to settle the great sectional controversy in such a manner. They regarded the proposal as a mere basis for a discussion during the approaching electoral campaign. When the waiting representatives of Tennessee were admitted to their seats, it was made entirely clear in the resolution of the Congress that the state's ratification of the amendment was but one of several acts denoting loyalty to the Union, and, therefore, but one of several reasons of nearly equal weight for reinstatement in the Union.[2] As for the other ten states, if they should ratify the measure, they might not come back until three-fourths of all the states had approved it and it became operative as a part of the Constitution. And this promise was a mere vague proposal contained in a Congressional committee report, and a bill which neither House went to the trouble to pass.

The ten states were justified in putting no certain trust in such assurances as reached them in regard to the sufficiency

[1] Cong. Globe, 39th Cong., 2d sess., Appendix, p. 181.
[2] McPherson, History of Reconstruction, p. 152.

of action on their part similar to Tennessee's. Texas rejected the amendment by an overwhelming vote in October, 1866, and within the next four months all the rest had followed the example. Simultaneously the three border states, Kentucky, Delaware and Maryland, rejected the amendment.[1] The proposed disfranchisement of the leading white men of the South was ground enough for the hostility of the people; there were other reasons for their opposition. "We will bear any ill," said a committee of the legislature in Florida, "before we will pronounce our own dishonor." The state was recognized as a state "for the highest purposes known to the Constitution, namely its amendment," but it was not recognized "for any of the benefits resulting" from the Federal relation. The people would not bring "as a peace offering the conclusive evidence" of their own "self-created degradation."[2]

It was held to be improper[3] for the President to have exerted his influence in one and perhaps more of the Southern states to prevent the ratification of the amendment.[4] But he had made no concealment of his antagonism to it from the beginning. It was not a greater offence when now he told Southern and Northern leaders who visited him at Washington that he disliked the measure. At the time Chase talked with him, just before the meeting of Congress in December, 1866, telling him that it would be "the part of patriotism and wisdom" to recommend the Southern states to ratify the amendment, he expressed "the most positive convictions" that his own policy was "soundest and ought to be adopted."[5] In the same sense he spoke to others, and it could have surprised

[1] McPherson, History of Reconstruction, p. 194.

[2] Annual Cyclopedia for 1866, p. 326; cf. Hollis, Early Period of Reconstruction in South Carolina, Johns Hopkins Studies, vol. xxiii, p. 66.

[3] Cf. Blaine, Twenty Years of Congress, vol. ii, p. 249.

[4] For Alabama, see Fleming, Civil War and Reconstruction in Alabama, pp. 396–7. For Virginia, see Schofield, Forty-six Years in the Army, p. 395. For Tennessee, see letter of Brownlow to Chase, Annual Report American Historical Association, 1902, vol. ii, p. 515.

[5] Letter to Wager Swayne, Chase MS. in Library of Historical Society of Pennsylvania.

few to learn that he had telegraphed ex-Governor Parsons of Alabama, while efforts were being made to reconsider the legislature's former adverse action in that state, that such a course would lead to no "possible good," and that there should be "no faltering on the part of those who are honest in their determination to sustain the several coördinate departments of the government in accordance with its original design." [1]

Senator John Sherman may have written to his brother, General Sherman, that if Johnson had fallen in with the plan of the 39th Congress concerning the Fourteenth Amendment, the "whole controversy" would have come to an end; that if the negro suffragist Radicals had opposed this policy with reference to reconstruction, they would have been beaten. [2] Other men then and since may have expressed opinions in a similar sense. [3] But to discuss what might have been in so highly hypothetical a case is a bootless exercise. This very Fourteenth Amendment looked to the future enfranchisement of the blacks. If the ballot were denied them, the states would have a reduced representation in Congress. [4] The amendment with its provisions in regard to civil rights, disfranchisement, the basis of representation in Congress and the Confederate debt was but one of a series of measures, in no instance necessarily final, aimed at the people lately in insurrection, both for punitive ends and by way of a guaranty for the future, and the Radical leaders, unless they were halted by some impressive electoral reverse, would not be turned aside.

Stevens had brought forward his plan for reorganizing the government of North Carolina amid the violent protests of

[1] Fleming, Documentary History of Reconstruction, vol. i, pp. 237-8.

[2] Sherman Letters, p. 299; cf. Chase's opinions in Warden, p. 651, and letter to Thomas Heaton, June 28, 1866, Chase MS., Library of Historical Society of Pennsylvania.

[3] Rhodes emphasizes this point and brings forward ample authorities, chaps. xxx and xxxi.

[4] The shadow of negro suffrage in the Fourteenth Amendment was influential in inducing Arkansas to withhold her ratification. See a resolution of the legislature cited in Fleming, Documentary History of Reconstruction, vol. i, pp. 236-7.

honest state rights' men, of whom the President was an example [1]
as well as those who, whether they lived above or below Mason
and Dixon's line, felt a sincere sympathy for the stricken
Southern people. Nothing came of this suggestion. The
select committee which had been appointed to investigate
the riots in New Orleans recommended a bill for the " reëstablishment of civil government in the state of Louisiana." It
called for the overthrow of the existing government, established
in this instance not by Johnson but by Lincoln, the incapacity
of which had been proven in the view of the committee by
recent events. In general the measure proposed the appointment by the President of a provisional governor and a council
of nine members, all Louisiana Loyalists, who were to exercise
full political power until a constitutional convention could be
assembled, and officers and a legislature might be chosen on a
basis of universal manhood suffrage "without distinction of
race or color." A brigadier-general with an ample force of
soldiers should be quartered within the state to maintain the
peace.[2]

The House passed the bill with astonishing rapidity by a
party vote on February 12.[3] Meanwhile Stevens was developing a measure of a more general scope, designed to bring
the entire South under military rule, and put an end, not only
in Louisiana but in nine other states as well, to the forms of
civil government established there with executive favor during
or since the war. On December 19 he advanced to the attack.
He would throw overboard completely the old plan of restoring
the states when they should adopt the Fourteenth Amendment.[4]
Those who ever had supposed that such a condition would
satisfy the requirements of the case had been "inconsiderate
and incautious." [5] His plan of restoration, which called for
nothing less than the complete enfranchisement of the blacks
in all parts of the South, was read in the House on January

---

[1] Even Boutwell has made a belated admission as to Johnson's
honesty, Reminiscences, vol. ii, p. 105.

[2] Cong. Globe, 39th Cong., 2d sess., p. 1129.

[3] Ibid., p. 1175.   [4] Ibid., p. 209.   [5] Ibid., p. 252.

3, 1867, immediately after the holidays.[1] This and other projects were referred to the Joint Committee on Reconstruction, from which they emerged on February 6,[2] in the form of a bill to abolish "the pretended state governments" of ten "so-called Confederate states," which had been "established without the authority of Congress and without the sanction of the people."[3] A system of Federal military government would be set up in their stead. "The necessity of it," said Kelley of Pennsylvania in the House, "arises from the perfidy of the President of the United States." The bill would abrogate "the results of executive usurpation by ignoring the existence of the illegal and anomalous governments" which he had established. They were "pretended states," "so-called states" which must be "declared void and set aside."[4] Again more letters and newspaper articles were read reciting outrages committed upon unoffending people in the late home of the rebellion. "In God's name, men of the Thirty-ninth Congress," said Kelley, as he came to the end of his speech, "do not interweave your names ignominiously" with Andrew Johnson's "by betraying the Union men of the South, and surrendering nearly one-half of the country to rebels whose power your army crushed."[5]

For two years, said Stevens, the South had been in "a state of anarchy." This bill was "for the purpose of putting under governments ten states now without governments."[6] Thousands of loyal white men, the old Radical continued, were "driven like partridges over the mountains — homeless, houseless, penniless." They now thronged the city of Washington asking the protection of the flag floating above the Speaker's chair.[7] "Generosity and benevolence" were "the noblest qualities of human nature," but, said he, "when you squander them upon vagabonds and thieves you do that which can

---

[1] Cong. Globe, 39th Cong., 2d sess., p. 250.   [2] Ibid., pp. 1036–7.
[3] "The most brutal proposition ever introduced into the Congress of the United States by a responsible committee," says Prof. J. W. Burgess in Reconstruction and the Constitution, p. 114.
[4] Cong. Globe, 39th Cong., 2d sess., p. 1177.   [5] Ibid., p. 1180.
[6] Ibid., p. 1076.   [7] Ibid., p. 1077.

command no respect from any quarter." He would not hug and caress "those whose hands are red and whose garments are dripping with the blood of our murdered kindred." Who would do this were "covering themselves with indelible stains which all the waters of the Nile " could not wash out.[1] The South had had no government for two years; the conqueror now would determine what kind of government should be established in the territory covered by his conquest.[2]

Eight millions or more of people occupying 630,000 square miles, said Mr. Boutwell, were "writhing under cruelties nameless in their character," all because, sitting enthroned in the executive department, there was one who guided "the destinies of the republic in the interest of rebels." [3] Amendments were proposed by influential Republican leaders, notably by Bingham and Blaine, for the purpose of putting a term to "bayonet rule," by the establishment of new state governments on the basis of universal suffrage. But Stevens who had been ready with a plan for reconstruction five weeks ago [4] was now obdurately committed to an unlimited period of military control.

The time allowed for debate was brief and the House, lashed forward by Stevens's tongue, passed the bill to put all of the ten states under the arbitrary command of five generals on February 13,[5] the day after the Louisiana bill had been approved, and both reached the Senate at about the same time.[6] The session was nearing its end and the leaders were intent upon the accomplishment of their full purpose. "Each is excellent," said Sumner, as Wade of Ohio called up one bill and Williams of Oregon the other. One was the beginning of a "true reconstruction"; the other the beginning of a "true protection." Both policies should go hand in hand as "the guardian angels of the republic." [7] Some sober words from

[1] Cong. Globe, 39th Cong., 2d sess., p. 1214.
[2] Ibid., p. 1076.   [3] Ibid., p. 1122.
[4] Ibid., p. 250.   [5] Ibid., p. 1213.
[6] An account of the framing and course of the bills is found in Fessenden's remarks in the Senate. — Ibid., pp. 1303–4.
[7] Ibid., p. 1303.

Fessenden in reference to the narrow application of the Louisiana bill, and the wider meaning of the other bill, which would bring all of the ten states under Federal management, were effective, and the consideration of the latter was proceeded with as rapidly as possible by the aid of night sessions.

In the form in which the bill had been received from the House it was purely a police measure. But many in the Senate, as in the House, as was evidenced by the support given the Bingham-Blaine amendment, would have nominated in the bond the conditions under which the South might come out from under the rule of the soldiery. The "true protection" and the "true reconstruction" of Sumner were now to be joined. So much was determined at a caucus of Republican senators on Saturday, February 16. A difference arose as to the need of requiring the conventions, after they were elected by white and black men voting side by side, to insert provisions in their constitutions guaranteeing suffrage to the negroes, since, as Fessenden alleged, these constitutions must be approved by Congress before they could come into force. But Sumner pursued this point relentlessly, won by a small majority and bound his fellow senators to his policy on the floor.[1]

The minority was tenacious. The leaders, Hendricks, Saulsbury, Garrett Davis, Cowan and McDougall for the Democrats, and Doolittle for the President, were close reasoners and able rhetoricians. As for Saulsbury he would not "touch, taste or handle the unclean thing." It sounded the death knell of civil and constitutional liberty. The Federal government was a mere agent created by the states. But here now was this agent reconstructing its creator.[2] "Your own Washington

---

[1] Letter of Sumner to Bright in Pierce, Memoir of Sumner, vol. iv, p. 320. Rhodes and Pierce support their accounts with the debate in the Senate of Feb. 10, 1870 (Cong. Globe, for the session, p. 1177 et seq.), Rhodes relying especially upon the recollections of Sherman and Seward. Cf. Welles, vol. iii, p. 47, who quotes Grimes to the effect that Sumner was far from pleased with what had been done, though he frequently in later life took credit to himself for the result. He at any rate was not present when the vote was taken in the Senate. (Pierce, vol. iv, p. 314.) [2] Cong. Globe, 39th Cong., 2d sess., p. 1375.

was called a rebel. You are descended from a race of rebels,"
said Saulsbury, pleading for the merciful treatment of the
South. "When they are successful your rebels become heroes."
Because he disapproved of other men he would not "come
in to usurp the seat of Almighty God," and cast the "thunderbolts of damnation" upon them and the land in which they
dwelt. The doctrine that there were no states, that they
had committed suicide, as Sumner averred, when they had
seceded from the Union, was "contradictory of the whole
theory" upon which the Republican party had carried on
the recent war.[1]

In forcibly imposing such a policy upon the South, said
McDougall, we are driving that section again into "a local
rebellion." Nobody could suppose that intelligent white
people would submit to being governed by a mass of negroes
just released from bondage,[2] "as ignorant as a horse in the stable
about all things that belong to government."[3]

"Is this what you call making peace?" asked Doolittle.[4]
It was "a declaration of war," said he, "against ten states of
this Union."[5] "Great God! has it come to this," he exclaimed
passionately, "that in this age, in this country, a republican
people and a pretended Republican party shall propose to establish such a dictatorship, such a despotism as this?" He
arraigned the Radical measures as "an open, shameless con-
fession before our country, and before the civilized world that
republican institutions are a failure." The idea of white
disfranchisement and negro domination was born of "unforgiving hate and lust for despotic power." It would produce
"such a horrible state of things as no language could describe,
and which it has never entered into the heart of man to conceive." The Louisiana bill was a bill, not "to reëstablish
civil government" there, as its name declared, but "to organize
hell" in that state. What now became of the "boasted Congressional policy"? For this was not reconstruction by

---

[1] Cong. Globe, 39th Cong., 2d sess., p. 1447.
[2] Ibid., p. 1377.
[3] Ibid., p. 1467.
[4] Ibid., p. 1375.
[5] Ibid., p. 1440.

Congress; it was reconstruction by the sword, reconstruction by the general of the army.[1]

But finally the last word had been said in opposition to the bill, and it was passed a few minutes after six o'clock on Sunday morning, February 17, by a vote of 29 to 10.[2] When it was returned to the House for the concurrence of that body, Thaddeus Stevens waxed wroth. "Heaven rules as yet and there are gods above," he had said, quoting "good old Laertes," in a flight of thanksgiving after the bill was passed by the House in its original form. But the changes it had undergone in the Senate aroused his passionate eloquence. This embittered, cynical, sarcastical old man was perhaps the worst possible leader in such a national emergency. His tongue dripped venom. Conscious of his power to create laughter by his sallies he was led to give even fuller play to his wit. The Senate, he said, instead of allowing to remain in the hands of the general of the army, *i.e.* of Grant, the power of appointment of the military officers who should command in the South, where the House had placed it, had preferred to intrust this duty to the President of the United States. How would the President execute this law? As he had executed "every law for the last two years, by the murder of Union men, and by despising Congress and flinging into our teeth all that we seek to have done." As for the Senate's proposal to unite with the House plan for restoring order in the South, a plan for reconstructing the states, it found its home only in the breasts of "chivalric gentlemen," concerned lest Southern representatives should not be in the House in time to vote for the next President of the United States. He would make no pledges as to the future to these "outlawed communities of robbers, traitors and murderers." He was not done with the hope that at least some of those who had murdered the brothers, fathers and children of the North would be imprisoned and hanged and their property confiscated.[3]

On the 20th, after further debate, the differences between

---

[1] Cong. Globe, 39th Cong., 2d sess., p. 1446.
[2] Ibid., p. 1469.   [3] Ibid., p. 1317.

the two chambers concerning the measure were adjusted. It was now known as the bill "to provide for the more efficient government of the rebel states." The House passed it by a vote of 126 to 46;[1] the Senate, by a vote of 35 to 7,[2] and it was sent to the President. That it would not be signed by him every one knew. It was specified that there should be five military districts. The first would cover Virginia; the second the Carolinas; the third Georgia, Alabama and Florida; the fourth Mississippi and Arkansas; the fifth Louisiana and Texas. The President must assign to each a force of soldiers sufficiently large to secure peace and good order, under the command of an officer not below the rank of a brigadier-general, until "loyal and republican state governments" could be "legally established." How Federal military law was to be administered was briefly recited in the act.

Section 5 which had originated in the Senate suggested a method by which the ten states might come out from under the military system. White and black men, voting together on equal terms in any state, might elect a convention to frame a constitution to be submitted to these white and black voters. If it should provide for negro suffrage; if it should be ratified by referendum by the white and black voters who had chosen the members of the convention, it must be sent to Congress. Then, if that body should approve of the instrument of government so formed, and the legislature of the state should adopt the Fourteenth Amendment to the Constitution of the United States, and a sufficient number of states to make up the required three-fourths majority should adopt this amendment that state should again be entitled to representation in Congress at Washington, and Federal troops would be withdrawn from its borders. Ex-"rebels" who had sworn to support the Constitution of the United States, and had afterward violated their oaths by joining their fortunes with those of the Confederacy, might not vote for members of, or occupy seats in the convention. Meantime such other governments as might exist in the ten Southern states would be held to be pro-

[1] Cong. Globe, 39th Cong., 2d sess., p. 1400.   [2] Ibid., p. 1645.

visional only, "subject to the paramount authority of the
United States."

The President gave himself the full constitutional period
in which to consider the bill and forward the statement of his
reasons for its disapproval. On the 2d of March his message,
which had been written for the most part by Jeremiah S. Black,
Buchanan's Attorney-General and Secretary of State, the
principal author now of many of his papers, acting as secretly
in the matter as had Bancroft in 1865,[1] reached Congress.
The President traversed much old ground concerning the
nature of the Constitution; the purposes for which the war
had been waged; the attitude of Congress, hitherto, concerning the seceding states in their relation to the Union. He
prayed and wept in turn with no unbecoming emphasis at the
bier of our free institutions. He disputed the facts upon which
Congress based the need for such a law affecting the South,
and reiterated his opinion that the governments existing there
were, on the whole, considering all the circumstances, capable
and effective.

Such a law as Congress proposed would establish an "absolute despotism." The brigadier in each district was made an
absolute monarch. Indeed such a power as would be his had
not been wielded "by any monarch in England for more than
500 years." The people of ten states would be reduced "to
the most abject and degrading slavery." The Constitution
of the United States prohibited bills of attainder. No
person could be convicted of and punished for a crime by mere
legislative proceeding. Yet here was such a bill directed
against the liberties of "nine millions of people at once." Not
one of these had been heard in his own defence, yet all were
adjudged guilty and consigned to the "most ignominious punishment ever inflicted on large masses of men." He wasted
few words upon the policy of "Africanizing" the Southern
states. But he paused in a discussion of more general ques-

[1] See Johnson Papers in the Library of Congress for Black's drafts
and revisions of drafts of the messages of 1866 and 1867 and of various
veto messages.

tions of constitutional law to condemn the plan "to force the right of suffrage out of the hands of the white people and into the hands of the negroes," as an "arbitrary violation" of guaranteed prerogatives of the states.

The message was received quietly in both houses. When the reading had ended in the popular branch of Congress, Thaddeus Stevens rose to move a passage of the bill over the President's veto. Certain minority leaders, while complaining of their impotency to resist the "purposes and numbers" of their opponents, yet found the occasion solemnly to protest "in the name of the Constitution, in the name of the republic, in the name of all we hold dear on earth," and denounced the measure as an "unholy design to destroy the republic," as a "monstrous scheme to subvert constitutional government in this country," as a "dissolution of the Union," as the "death knell of republican liberty." But in a few minutes, under a suspension of the rules, both majority and opposition proceeded to what Stevens ironically named "the funeral of the nation," and the bill was passed by a vote of 135 to 48.[1]   Great applause on the floor and in the galleries, which were packed with men in sympathy with the Congressional policies, greeted the Speaker's announcement. In the Senate the discussion was brief and progress was little less rapid. Here the vote was 38 to 10.[2]

The party press followed the party leaders in Congress in approving or condemning the measure. The National Intelligencer called it the "Destruction" instead of the Reconstruction bill; again it was the "Subversion bill." The establishment of these "military satrapies" was the "blackest record ever made by an assembly of the representatives of a free people." Never had one stamped itself "with greater ignominy."[3]   The New York World called the law "infamous and abominable." The Radicals had "abolished the Constitution."[4]

[1] Cong. Globe, 39th Cong., 2d sess., p. 1733.
[2] Ibid., p. 1976.
[3] National Intelligencer, Feb. 14, 1867.
[4] Issue of Feb. 28, 1867.

On the other hand the moderate gazettes pointed out, as Reverdy Johnson had done in the Senate, that both the Civil Rights and the Freedmen's Bureau bills already provided for a Federal exercise of military power in the South. This new plan to "bayonet" the late Confederate states back to their places in the Union was not more obnoxious than provisions of law already in force.[1] The people had spoken at the polls. The next Congress would be as pitiless as the last. No sensible man could think that in the Presidential election of 1868 the country would manifest a different sentiment. It is not what you want, but what you can get, said the Philadelphia Public Ledger. The dominant party had laid down a plan for the reconstruction of the Southern states. The sooner the distasteful work was begun by the Southern people the sooner it would be at an end, and they could return to the enjoyment of self-government.[2]

In the meantime bills to admit as states of the Union Colorado and Nebraska, which had failed in the last session, because of the President's objections, were again passed. His message vetoing the Colorado bill was received on January 29; the Nebraska bill on January 30. The former was not pressed in Congress, but the majority leaders at once took up the subject of Nebraska's claims to statehood, overrode the veto, and the territory, which was being rapidly filled with emigrants flocking in on the line of the new Pacific Railroad, and would furnish the Radicals with two senators, brought its star, the thirty-seventh, to the blue field of the nation's flag.

While his loose tongue rambled, on the "swing around the circle," Mr. Johnson had not failed to speak of the Federal office-holders. In Cleveland he called them a "common gang of cormorants and blood-suckers."[3] "God being willing," he said in St. Louis, "I will kick them out. I will kick them out just as fast as I can."[4]

[1] Cong. Globe, 39th Cong., 2d sess., p. 1973.
[2] Phila. Ledger, Feb. 22 and March 4, 1867.
[3] From the Cleveland Herald's (a Johnson paper's) version of the President's speech in that city in Fleming's Documentary History of Reconstruction, vol. i, p. 225.   [4] N. Y. Herald, Sept. 10, 1866.

This was empty braggadocio. As a matter of fact Johnson had been far from free and indiscriminate in the removal of office-holders, even when their antagonism to his course was carried to great and offensive lengths,[1] and his policy had undergone no material change in the past few months, since his return from his Western tour. It was near the end of October when McCulloch wrote to Samuel J. Tilden. "The President," said the Secretary of the Treasury, "desires to make as few changes as possible, and none on political grounds unless it is clear that the interests of the service, or the interests of the administration are to be certainly benefited by them."[2]

But Congress saw its opportunity, and a scheme to curb the President's power as to removals without the "advice and consent" of the Radical Senate was rapidly developed and passed. Mr. Johnson vetoed it on the same day he disapproved the Reconstruction bill. The measure expressed the complete distrust by Congress of the President. It was indeed an attack upon his personal integrity and patriotism. He was branded as one who had it in his mind to remove faithful friends of the Union and in their places to install ex-"rebels," Copperheads and other national enemies. The President's objections were based upon historical grounds with reference to the executive department of the government as it was created under the Constitution. But his message again fell upon deaf ears. The bill had been passed by a party vote in both Houses. Now it was repassed at once by practically the same majorities.[3]

Congress, in furtherance of its general policies, attached to the army appropriation bill provisions restricting the President in the exercise of his constitutional functions as commander-in-chief to the advantage of General Grant,[4] disbanded the

---

[1] McCulloch, Men and Measures, p. 377.

[2] John Bigelow, Letters and Memorials of S. J. Tilden, vol. i, p. 207.

[3] "This monstrous measure," J. W. Burgess calls it in his Reconstruction and the Constitution, p. 126.

[4] All military orders henceforward were to pass through Grant's hands as the general of the army, and his headquarters must remain in Washington. — "A gross usurpation" on the part of Congress, says J. W. Burgess, op. cit., p. 128.

militia forces in service in the Southern states, and prohibited the assembling and use of such bodies of state soldiery henceforth.   Mr. Johnson was constrained to approve these measures, or else veto the entire appropriation bill at the last hour of the session.   On March 2 he signed it under protest which he recorded in a brief message to the House.[1]

Congress now, as the New York Nation averred, was practically the entire government of the United States.   Debate was stifled everywhere.   In the House, with Stevens in control, in spite of his pharisaical expressions of desire to deal fairly by his foes, it had nearly ceased.   The good rule of arguing first and voting afterward had been reversed.   Now both houses voted without argument.   Such a plan, the Nation said with truth, would soon develop a temper among politicians which would render representative institutions " a sorry farce." [2]

Mr. Johnson's offending thus far had consisted in the making of speeches better befitting an alderman in a village in the Appalachian Mountains, which he was wont to boast that he had been, than a President of the United States addressing the inhabitants of the large Northern cities; and his lying bedfellow, by force of circumstances beyond his own control, with men who had been enemies, or at best cold friends of the Union during the war.   But malevolent accusation, born of party bitterness and ambition, was making him seem a character with as black a heart as any which had yet appeared in the course of American history.   Sumner's fanaticism now became something near to madness.   Always a mixture of the pedant and the schoolmaster, he was possessed as of a devil by humanitarian sentiments affecting the negro.   The irrationality of his mind on this subject, despite the learning called from every land and every age which he reflected in his speech, the power of his oratory and the honesty of his zeal, was obvious even to his excited contemporaries.   Sumner now likened the Presi-

[1] McPherson's History of Reconstruction, p. 178.   The passage of this bill seems to have been dictated directly by Stanton working behind the President's back through Boutwell and Thad Stevens. — Cf. Boutwell's Reminiscences, vol. ii, p. 108.

[2] N. Y. Nation, Nov. 29, 1866.

dent to Jefferson Davis, than whom, to the Radicals, none seemed so infamous.

"You have already conquered the chief of the rebellion," said the senator from Massachusetts. "I doubt not you will conquer his successor also." [1]

The air for months had been filled with hints of impeachment. The very children knew the name of Warren Hastings through a reading of the newspapers. History was raked and sieved for rules and precedents to justify a free people in ridding themselves of a faithless and contumacious civil servant. The Congressional campaign had bristled with threats of proceedings which might be directed against the President, and soon after the session began, on December 17, in the House, James M. Ashley of Ohio,[2] who for some time had sought the distinction of identifying his name with the measure, moved the appointment of a select committee of seven members "to inquire whether any acts have been done by any officer of the government of the United States which in contemplation of the Constitution are high crimes and misdemeanors, and whether said acts were designed or calculated to overthrow, subvert or corrupt the government of the United States." The resolution failed to receive a necessary two-thirds vote; 88 members voted for it and 49 against it, 15 Republicans acting with the Democrats.[3]

Three weeks later, on January 7, 1867, a Radical from Missouri named Loan offered a resolution for the impeachment of "the officer now exercising the functions pertaining to the office of President of the United States of America, and his removal from said office upon his conviction in due form of law of the high crimes and misdemeanors of which he is manifestly and notoriously guilty." The attempt to secure a vote

[1] Cong. Globe, 39th Cong., 2d sess., p. 1562.

[2] The reason for this man's peculiar antipathy, said the President, was based upon disappointment as to the bestowal of office. Soon after Johnson took the place of Lincoln, who had made a bargain to exchange a revenue collectorship for a Democratic vote for the constitutional amendment abolishing slavery, Ashley came in vain to ask that it be fulfilled. — N. Y. Tribune, July 30, 1867.

[3] McPherson's History of Reconstruction, p. 187; Cong. Globe, 39th Cong., 2d sess., p. 154.

failed. Another representative from Missouri, John R. Kelso, immediately submitted a similar resolution, and when the yeas and nays were taken the impeachment men mustered 104 votes against 40 on the other side.[1] Ashley now returned to the charge.

"I do impeach Andrew Johnson, Vice President and acting President of the United States, of high crimes and misdemeanors," said he.

"I charge him with a usurpation of power and violation of law:

"In that he has corruptly used the appointing power;

"In that he has corruptly used the pardoning power;

"In that he has corruptly used the veto power;

"In that he has corruptly disposed of public property of the United States;

"In that he has corruptly interfered in elections," etc.

He would have his accusations investigated by the Judiciary Committee of the House, and to that committee, amid commotion, the resolution was referred by a vote of 108 to 38.[2] The more influential Republican leaders were still unwilling to assume responsibility for a movement which would subject the nation at large, no less than its President, to unheard of disgrace. It was "not worth while," said Senator Grimes, "to establish an example which might result in making ours a sort of South American republic where the ruler is deposed the moment popular sentiment sets against him." [3]

A caucus of Republican congressmen which had met just prior to the presentation of the Loan, Kelso and Ashley resolutions had been sparsely attended. Only a few were ready to advocate so extraordinary a course.[4] Leading Radical newspapers, such as the New York Tribune, wildly anti-Johnson, counselled moderation on this point.[5] Wall Street and men everywhere, identified with the financial

---

[1] Cong. Globe, 39th Cong., 2d sess., p. 320.   [2] Ibid., pp. 320–1.

[3] Letter to his wife dated March 12, 1867, in Wm. Salter, Life of James W. Grimes, p. 323.

[4] Washington corr., N. Y. Tribune, Jan. 7, 1867.

[5] Ibid., Jan. 8, 1867.

interests of the country, feared the outcome of impeachment proceedings in the current state of the stock and gold markets.[1]

But desultory discussion of the subject proceeded in January and February. Loan of Missouri on January 14 dared to read from a carefully prepared manuscript charges connecting the President with the conspiracy to assassinate Lincoln. "Powerfully influenced by all the grosser animal instincts," said this man in his labored essay, "without moral culture or moral restraint, with a towering ambition," Andrew Johnson had lent himself to the "rebel cause." "His treachery" had made him President to serve the interests of the South. He who had created the universe had made a Heaven above and a hell below. Loan consigned the President and all the "apostates and renegades, rebel sympathizers and rebels, guerrillas, bushwhackers and cutthroats" in his train, to the lower regions straightway. Even Republicans, such as Robert S. Hale of New York, interrupted the coarse diatribe and aimed to have the Speaker call the offending member to order, but the reading proceeded to the end.[2]

Finally at three o'clock of the last day of the session, on a Sunday morning, the Judiciary Committee was ready with its report. No committee during the entire history of the government, said the eight men representing the Radical majority of the House, ever had been charged with so grave a duty. Witnesses had been called and heard, papers had been assembled, but the time at hand did not permit of a complete examination of the multitude of facts, wherefore, unable to arrive at definite conclusions, they would content themselves with a statement that "sufficient testimony" had not been brought to the committee's notice, "to justify and demand a further prosecution of the investigation." The matter was commended to the attention of the next Congress. Mr. Rogers of New Jersey made a minority report in which he declared that there was "not one particle of evidence to sustain any of the charges"

---

[1] National Intelligencer, Feb. 5, 1867.
[2] Cong. Globe, 39th Cong., 2d sess., pp. 443–6.

contained in Mr. Ashley's resolution. The case against the President was entirely "void of proof." [1]

Thus ended the life of the Thirty-ninth Congress, the "Rump Congress" of the New York World, the Congress which Mr. Johnson had declared was but a presumptive Congress "hanging upon the verge of the government"; [2] the Fortieth was at hand, full heir to all the acrid spirit of its predecessor.

Throughout these weeks of bitterness Mr. Johnson gave himself quietly to the performance of his official tasks. He had said little. He had attended a dinner on Jackson Day at the National Hotel in Washington when speeches were made by a number of leading Democrats. "The Federal Union — it must be preserved," was the keynote of the meeting. The President had spoken only briefly. He reiterated his creed. "No state of its own will," said he, "has the right under the Constitution to renounce its place in, or to withdraw from the Union. Nor has the Congress of the United States under the Constitution the power to degrade the people of any state by reducing them to the condition of a mere territorial dependency upon the Federal head. The one is a disruption and dissolution of the government; the other is consolidation and the exercise of despotic power. The advocates of either are alike enemies of the Union and of our Federal form of government." [3]

On March 5, 1867, he told General C. G. Halpine ("Miles O'Reilly"), in an interview in Washington, that, as to the "slights and indignities" which Congress had attempted to cast upon him for his devotion to his constitutional oath, he was unmoved, except as they affected the high office he held. A day of "wiser thought and sounder estimate" was near. He looked "with perfect confidence" for his vindication to the justice of that future which he was convinced could be not long delayed. [4]

When on his "swing around the circle" he had been inter-

[1] Cong. Globe, 39th Cong., 2d sess., pp. 1754–5.

[2] Words used by the President on Aug. 18, 1866, in his address to the delegation from the Phila. convention. — Phila. Ledger, Aug. 20, 1866.

[3] National Intelligencer, Jan. 9, 1897.

[4] McPherson's History of Reconstruction, p. 143.

rupted by men in the crowds to which he spoke with cries of "Hang Jeff Davis," as at Cleveland and St. Louis, he would retort, addressing the Radicals, "Why don't you hang him?" What meanwhile was the situation of the late President of the Confederate States? He had been removed from the wet, unhealthy casemates to another part of Fort Monroe, and had been put into an airy room in a building called Carroll Hall, which was used for officers' quarters. There were bars at his windows. An officer and ten sentinels guarded him. A light was burned in his room at night. Charles O'Conor, the eminent Democratic jurist of New York, whose Southern leanings had been ill-concealed during the war, and other lawyers tendered their services in his defence in the impending trial; but he could not reply to their friendly offers except through the War Department at Washington. Letters to and from his wife were subjected to censorship. A wealthy man in Baltimore said that bail money amounting to two millions of dollars could be procured in that city on five hours' notice.[1] As time passed the clamor to know why Davis was not tried and hanged, or else set at liberty, as his case deserved, grew louder. Both the House and the Senate interrogated the President, and he sent forward letters from Stanton and Speed.[2] The prisoner was held, said Secretary Stanton, on three accounts — for high treason in leading an insurrection against the government; for complicity in the assassination of Abraham Lincoln; and for the murder, by starvation and cruelty, of Union prisoners during the war.[3] The "bloody" Judge Advocate General, Holt, was eager for a military trial ere his authority should be curbed by the President's official declaration that the war was at an end. The punishment of "wretched hirelings," said he, was not sufficient to atone for the "monstrous crime against humanity"; the blood of Lincoln was "still calling to us from the ground," and Davis should follow Payne, Atzerodt and the others to the scaffold.[4]

---

[1] Phila. Ledger, June 14, 1866.
[2] Ibid., Jan. 11, 1866; House Ex. Doc., 39th Cong., 1st sess., no. 46.
[3] O. R., series ii, vol. viii, p. 843.   [4] Ibid., p. 855.

But Holt's views were not shared by men who played more important parts in the conduct of the government, and a regular trial in a court of law was promised the prisoner. Attorney-General Speed gave the opinion that, since the crimes with which Davis was charged had been committed in the Southern states, the Constitution required that he should be made to answer there for his iniquities.[1] The capital of the Confederacy had been located in Virginia; that state was convenient of access to Washington and to the prison house; the Chief Justice, Chase, himself elected to sit in this circuit. But, as no courts had been held in Virginia since the war, and no certain time, pending the restoration of the right to the writ of habeas corpus, was fixed for the resumption of regular sessions, "prisoner Davis" must await the reëstablishment of the judicial system in the territory whose political affairs he had done so much to disarrange.[2]

The country meanwhile became more and more restive. Davis was still in the custody of General Nelson A. Miles, whose guardianship was close. Thirty-six feet of knotted red tape which the prisoner said that he used to keep in place the mosquito netting over his bed was seized and sent to the War Office, on the ground that it was of sufficient length to reach from the ramparts to the moat to haul up a greater rope, whereby he might make his escape to a vessel arriving at night in the offing. His calling Miles a "miserable ass" for harboring such a suspicion made the relations no more cordial.[3] But the prisoner's pastor in Richmond began to make visits which, with the permission of the War Department, became as frequent as twice a month after January, 1866,[4] and he found a friend in the post surgeon, Dr. Cooper, whose reports of his condition from day to day, some of which were published, awakened widespread sympathy. The President of the Confederacy suffered from insomnolency, dyspepsia, neuralgia,

---

[1] O. R., series ii,vol. viii, pp. 844–5.

[2] For Chase's reasons for delay see Schuckers, Life of Chase, pp. 540–2.

[3] O. R., series ii, vol. viii, p. 841.   [4] Ibid., p. 872.

boils, carbuncles, erysipelas. Never during any night since his incarceration had he slept for two hours continuously. The creaking boots of the sentinels as they paced the floor, even after it was covered with straw matting, the noise as they hailed each other, the light in his room, his nervous and physical diseases, the lack of full opportunity for exercise were noted by the physician, who made so unfavorable a statement that many thought the distinguished culprit could not live for trial for his crimes.[1]

Mrs. Davis had been with her children in Canada. Her "prayer" to see her husband, written to the President, was offered, she said, "with tears enough to float it" to him, but he remained obdurate until April, 1866, when she came on from Montreal and was permitted, under parole, to go in and out of the fort daily for the comfort and health of the prisoner.[2] Repeatedly she addressed Mr. Johnson in her husband's behalf with all the warmth and passionate energy of a loving wife.[3] At length he was given the liberty of the grounds from sunrise to sunset. His condition somewhat improved, but in midsummer the surgeon, Cooper, reported further sufferings, and recommended a transfer, on account of the heat, to some garrison or fort in the Northern states. He suggested Newport on the sea-coast.[4] The advice was unheeded and Davis remained where he was. Enough about his condition escaped to arouse the Conservative press. The New York World spoke of the "wanton and wicked torture of an invalid." His keeper, General Miles, was likened to one of the grand inquisitors of Rome.[5] The Copperhead New York News said that "the martyr of Fortress Monroe" should be released on bail.[6] The Richmond Times, speaking for the South, declared that the breasts of all Americans must "swell with pity and indignation" upon reading Dr. Cooper's account of the "protracted

[1] O. R., series ii, vol. viii, p. 908.
[2] Ibid., pp. 900, 904.   [3] Johnson Papers.
[4] O. R., series ii, vol. viii, p. 947.
[5] N. Y. World, May 24, 1866.
[6] N. Y. News, May 24, 1866, quoted in O. R., series ii, vol. viii, p. 917.

torture" of "the illustrious statesman and pure, noble-hearted, Christian gentleman." President Johnson should "hunt down and punish" the guilty jailers.[1] General Miles deeply resented the attack upon his honor as a soldier. He declared that Dr. Cooper had originated the reports of Davis's distress with the purpose of arousing public sympathy in the "rebel chief's" behalf. The surgeon's wife was a "secessionist," and one of the "F. F. V's." He escorted Mrs. Davis in and out of the fort, and was noticeably attentive to her. A determined movement was on foot, since Davis "could not be a hero to make a martyr of him." [2] General Miles, contradicting Dr. Cooper's reports, found that Davis's condition was in no way worse than when he was received at the fort. Surgeon-General Barnes came to examine the prisoner and make a statement in the same sense.[3] Miles asked the War Department to permit him to admit newspaper writers so that they might find out and publish the truth about his administration, a request which was refused.

The criticism of the keeper of the prison, aided by Mrs. Davis's melting appeals, gradually sank into the conscience of Mr. Johnson, who issued orders for the General's removal. Letters from Miles to Stanton protesting against a step so injurious to his reputation, were without effect, and on September 1, 1866, he was mustered out of the service. The command was transferred to General Burton.[4] In October, 1866, the President again asked the Attorney-General for an opinion as to the legal aspects of the case. What further steps, if any, should be taken by the Executive to secure for Davis a speedy and impartial trial? Mr. Stanbery replied that nothing might be done. The prisoner must remain where he was until the court which had jurisdiction over him should be ready to act.[5] Finally the day came. After more than two years' confinement

---

[1] Richmond Times, May 24, 1866, quoted in O. R., series ii, vol. viii, pp. 917-8.   [2] O. R., series ii, vol. viii, p. 919.

[3] Ibid., p. 924; cf. Mrs. Davis, Memoirs of Her Husband, vol. ii, p. 759, where Cooper is more than corroborated.

[4] O. R., series ii, vol. viii, pp. 955-6.

[5] Johnson Papers, Oct. 6 and 12, 1866.

he was delivered up to the Circuit Court of the United States for the District of Virginia.[1] On Saturday, May 11, 1867, in company with Mrs. Davis, General Burton and several United States marshals, he was taken by steamer from the fort to Richmond, the old capital of the Confederacy.[2] Northern Radicals were certain that, by some rule of poetic justice, he would be thrown into Libby Prison to await the meeting of the court. Instead he was made comfortable at the Spottswood Hotel where he held an informal levee, shaking the hands of his friends and receiving bouquets.[3]

The court room on Monday, May 13, the day set for the proceedings, was crowded by notable personages. It was on the second floor of a Confederate Department building, full of memories of the war for the prisoner. The Chief Justice did not attend, and Judge Underwood presided. Davis arrived upon the arm of General Burton. His counsel, led by the distinguished Charles O'Conor, was faced on the other side by William M. Evarts of New York, special counsel detailed to the service by the Attorney-General. Bail was offered by O'Conor; pledges could be had in any amount from men representing all parties in every section of the country. The judge questioned whether the offence was bailable, but gave an opinion favorable to Mr. Davis, whereupon bondsmen to the number of fifteen or twenty, some from the North and others from the South, came forward to furnish the necessary assurances that he would answer for his offences in the court in the following November, when it was fairly certain, as the event proved, that the indictment, after further postponements, would be quashed.

One of the most remarked of the sights in the room was the gray head of Horace Greeley. The old editor of the New York Tribune who had been assailing slavery, secession and the whole spirit and body of the South, before, during and now since the war, who had not spared a phrase or syllable day by day in denunciation of the "rebels" from Davis down to the smallest

[1] O. R., series ii, vol. viii, pp. 983–6.
[2] N. Y. Herald, May 11, 1866.   [3] Ibid., May 13, 1867.

in the pack, had a very human side. His gazette contained articles hostile to capital punishment. He was preaching a doctrine described as "universal suffrage and universal amnesty" — *i.e.* that negroes should be allowed to vote and "rebels" should be forgiven. He was in attendance now at Richmond to sign his name at the head of the list of gentlemen who would coöperate to secure Davis's release, an act which threw his readers into consternation and almost stopped the sale of his books.[1] "The marshal will discharge the prisoner," the court announced after the bond had been executed. There was loud applause; men hurrahed and threw up their hats. Davis was congratulated on all sides.[2] As he returned to his hotel, blacks as well as whites cheered him, and he and his wife at once boarded a steamer for New York on their way to Canada. His arrival in that city was effected at midnight, and it received little notice. He was quietly taken to a hotel, frequented principally by Southern people, where he remained in seclusion for three or four days before proceeding secretly to join his children who were at school in Montreal.[3]

The result was hailed with mixed feelings. The New York Herald said that Davis's release would create "general satisfaction."[4] The Democratic Boston Post believed that it would meet with the "general approbation of the country."[5] The New York World rejoiced. That Davis had been held in prison so long was a "scandal of American justice."[6] The government had never wished to try the prisoner; only to load him with irons and torment his body and soul.[7] It was common remark among the journalists, gathered from all parts of the country at Richmond to report the proceedings, that the act of releasing Davis had done more for "real peace and reconstruction" than all the armies or statutes of the United States

[1] Recollections of a Busy Life, p. 424.
[2] N. Y. Herald, May 14, 1867.
[3] Ibid., May 20, 21, 22, 1867.   [4] Ibid., May 14, 1867.
[5] Quoted in N. Y. Herald, May 16, 1867.
[6] Issue of May 13, 1867.
[7] Issue of May 14, 1867.

government.[1] His liberation, said the New York Tribune, would be "hailed as a victory of common sense."[2] Jefferson Davis was "no longer a fact." He no longer represented "armed treason." The government had "dishonored" itself by holding him without trial for these many months.[3] Upon visiting Thiers in Paris that distinguished Frenchman told George Bancroft, now our minister to Prussia, that he highly commended the clemency which the nation had shown toward Davis. It had won Johnson "the esteem of all Europe."[4]

On the other hand, the New York Evening Post remarked that to release the President of the Confederacy without punishment was to serve notice to the world that the "crime of treason" was "as safe to commit" in the United States as peculation was in New York City.[5] The Philadelphia North American expressed its amazement that Davis, "the very pith and essence of the grand crime," could walk away "unscathed amid the bows of those whom he sought to destroy."[6] The Hartford Courant declared that the nation which could not hang "even one such traitor" did not "deserve the holy devotion of the dead 300,000."[7] The Philadelphia Press put the blame upon the shoulders of the President. The result was due to his "infirmity of purpose." The Confederate leader's punishment would be the detestation of a great people. He would live while he lived "a stranger in his own land — a man without a country."[8] Yet throughout the press, as with the people, there was a strong undercurrent of pleased relief that his imprison-

[1] Richmond corr., National Intelligencer, May 16, 1867.

[2] Issue of May 14, 1867.

[3] As for the "popular rage" excited by Greeley's action in becoming one of Davis's bondsmen it was "as the idle wind" which he heeded not. What was done he had done because he believed it to be right. — N. Y. Tribune, May 15, 1867; cf. Greeley's Recollections of a Busy Life, pp. 415, 424.

[4] Bancroft's letter to the President which was "not to be printed on any account" lest it be known that he was as much as a conveyor of such sentiments. — Johnson Papers for July, 1867.

[5] Quoted in Phila. Press, May 16, 1867.

[6] Phila. North American and Gazette, May 14, 1867.

[7] Quoted in N. Y. Herald, May 16, 1867.

[8] Phila. Press, May 14, 1867.

ment was at an end, and that the nation had foregone its boasted threat to hang him on a sour apple tree.

The scenes marking the last hours of the Thirty-ninth and the first hours of the Fortieth Congress [1] were, said the National Intelligencer, "utterly without precedent in the annals of the nation." [2] Not for a moment should any think that the conduct of the business of government had been remitted into the hands of the President. The rule of Congress must be uninterrupted and continuous, to which end the legislative day of Saturday, March 2, was prolonged into Sunday, and over Sunday night into Monday, when, at twelve o'clock noon, it could be said with truth "the king is dead, long live the king." There were recesses in the Senate and the House early in the mornings for sleep, and during Sunday at the period when men are commended to the duties of religious worship, but the members soon returned to their places. The minority leaders remarked that in addition to the ten Southern states which were still to be unrepresented, Tennessee, Kentucky, and five of the Northern states, including three in New England, had not yet held their elections, and therefore would have no delegates in the new Congress. Nearly one half the states of the Union would be without a voice in the determination of the important matters of government now before the country.[3]

But these facts excited no concern in the minds of the majority. In spite of a violent sleet storm all the available space at the session of Sunday night was occupied. New members appeared upon the floor, conversing with the old, until the House resembled a "political exchange." [4] A great crowd of persons filled the galleries, corridors and cloak rooms on Monday morning, pressing indeed into the area reserved for senators and representatives. The Senate in its last long "legislative day" had found the opportunity to elect as its presiding officer, to take the place of the urbane Mr. Foster, the bluff Benjamin

---

[1] Convened on March 4, 1867, in accordance with the terms of the act of January 22, 1867. [2] Issue of March 5, 1867.

[3] National Intelligencer, March 5, 1867; cf. Cong. Globe, 40th Cong., 1st sess., p. 3.

[4] Congressional report in Phila. Press, March 4, 1867.

F. Wade of Ohio.[1] It was very clear that such a man,[2] who was no parliamentarian, and who might not be able to control himself sufficiently to keep off the floor in a hot debate,[3] had not been chosen to the position with the thought that he should occupy it permanently. It was a sign, if not a threat, that more would follow; that when the Radicals had succeeded in removing Andrew Johnson from office by impeachment proceedings there was at hand one whom they would be glad to promote to the Presidency.

A joint committee of the two houses waited upon the President to ask if he had any further communications to make to them. He replied that he had not, and with truth as well as courtesy, "wished the senators and representatives a safe return to their families and homes," to which they, except in the cases of those who had not been reëlected for another term, were without present intention of returning. The hour of twelve having arrived, Wade declared the Senate of the Thirty-ninth Congress adjourned *sine die*, and without leaving his place proceeded to the work of organizing the body for a new session. In the House Speaker Colfax, when the clock marked noon, delivered a brief valedictory address in his most graceful phrases. As these parting words were said the gentlemen of another Congress, he observed, waited for their seats,[4] and, after the applause had subsided, Clerk McPherson appeared before the House. The roll was called; protests from the Democrats because of the exclusion of the Southern states, as at the opening of the Thirty-ninth Congress, were heard and Speaker Colfax was returned to the chair. In a few moments he was engaged in the delivery of salutatory remarks, as amiable as the farewell address with which he a few minutes before had fascinated his admirers on the floor and in the galleries.[5]

[1] Cong. Globe, 39th Cong., 2d sess., p. 2003.

[2] As uneducated a man as Horace Greeley, said the N. Y. Nation, July 4, 1867.

[3] N. Y. Nation, March 7, 1867; cf. N. Y. Tribune, Nov. 9, 1867, citing Cincinnati Commercial.

[4] Cong. Globe, 39th Cong., 2d sess., p. 1792.

[5] Ibid., 40th Cong., 1st sess., p. 4.

Very soon after the House was organized a petition was read from a number of "loyal men" in Virginia complaining of the conduct of the "rebel" authorities with reference to negroes who presented themselves as voters in a mayoralty election in Alexandria.[1] A resolution, introduced by Representative Kelley, directed the Judiciary Committee to prepare and present a bill to determine how men should be registered for voting, and how elections should be held in the South. On March 11 such a bill was reported to the House and passed.[2] On the 16th it received the approval of the Senate,[3] and soon, after the necessary conferences on the subject of amendments, it was ready to be sent to the President. This was an act supplementary to the act of March 2. The bill made it the duty of the commanding general in each district to register the voters black and white in such district; it prescribed an oath for these voters; it laid down rules for the election, under military oversight, of delegates to the conventions to form constitutions in the ten states; it made the commanding general in each district the judge of elections — he would certify and proclaim the result, he would notify the delegates when and where to assemble for their work; the constitutions framed in this way would then be submitted to the registered voters under the eye of the military.

The President as a matter of course disapproved this bill as he had that one which it was intended to supplement. "No consideration," he said, could induce him to sign it. "If ever the American citizen should be left to the free exercise of his own judgment," he continued, "it is when he is engaged in the work of forming the fundamental law under which he is to live." Congress declared that the governments in the Southern states must be "loyal and republican," and what was necessary to give them this character, as it appeared, was "universal negro suffrage," a question left to the determination of the states by the terms of the Federal Constitution. "Martial law, military coercion, political disfranchisement" were contrived solely to bring about this unconstitutional end. If this were re-

[1] Cong. Globe, 40th Cong., 1st sess., p. 17.
[2] Ibid., p. 67.   [3] Ibid., p. 171.

publicanism, the work of reconstruction could begin as well in Ohio and Pennsylvania, where blacks were not exercising the suffrage, as in Virginia and North Carolina. There was nothing for the South but "this fearful and untried experiment of complete negro enfranchisement," or indefinite submission to martial law. The condition of the Southern people seemed to him, said the President, "the most deplorable" to which any people could be "reduced." In contemplating the situation he was reminded of Daniel Webster's description of a South American state — "A military republic, a government formed on mock elections and supported daily by the sword." [1] The veto was received on the 23d day of March; on the same day both the House and the Senate repassed the bill, and it was declared to be a law. [2]

The way was now clear, said Samuel S. Marshall, a minority leader from Illinois, for fastening upon the country these "miserable mongrel governments." "Wandering vagabonds, calling themselves Southern loyalists," could go about among the negroes inciting them to set up black governments under black constitutions. [3] The future was shrouded in gloom.

Four weeks had not passed before the congressmen were ready to return to their law offices, their ploughed fields and their growing crops. The purpose, said the New York Nation, of the extraordinary session, extraordinary both because one Congress, in a hitherto unheard of way had convoked its successor, and because the two were merged so completely that when one ended and the other began was difficult to discern, had been subserved. [4] "Pocket vetoes" by the President of measures obnoxious to him were made useless, in view of the certain meeting of a new Congress as soon as the term of life of its predecessor had expired.

All the while the threat of impeachment was held over his head. The air still was full of dire muttering and promise.

[1] McPherson's History of Reconstruction, pp. 179–80.
[2] Cong. Globe, 40th Cong., 1st sess., pp. 303, 314.
[3] Ibid., p. 65.
[4] N. Y. Nation, April 4, 1867.

Ashley[1] but two or three days after the opening of the session brought forward a resolution and the House adopted it, passing on the work of the investigation into Mr. Johnson's misdemeanors, which the old Judiciary Committee had begun, to the new committee.[2] Such coarse abuse of the President as his the House yet had not heard. Johnson had come into office "through the door of assassination," said Ashley. He was guilty of "black and infamous crimes." He was a "loathing incubus" who had blotted the country's history "with its foulest blot." Such men were born into the world "to curse the human race but once in centuries."

The Speaker felt obliged to call Ashley to order. Randall, Democrat, asked amid amusement if there were an insane asylum near by; Wood and Boyer, other Democrats, expressed the hope that the gentleman might be permitted to proceed. The performance must react to the advantage of the President.[3] While such mad language could not have passed the lips of more than a few of the Radicals, the House was filled with men little less hostile, and now that they were about to leave the seat of government for a time they were not unmindful of their duty to themselves and to posterity with reference to one who stood "impeached before the nation." Various plans for the approaching recess were suggested by the leaders. Some would have had it continue until December; the country would be safe, they thought, in view of what had been done, for the ensuing eight months. But other men were not so confident. The House would have preferred to meet again in June. But the senators suggested the first Wednesday in July,[4] and so at the hour of noon on March 30, after a representative from Kansas named Clarke had got through a resolution requiring the Judiciary Committee to bring in its report on the impeachment question on the first meeting day after the recess,[5] the Congress adjourned to that date.

---

[1] Fittingly described by Dewitt as the "self-appointed scavenger to the Judiciary Committee" because of his activity in gathering material for its garbage can. — The Impeachment and Trial of Andrew Johnson, p. 154.   [2] Cong. Globe, 40th Cong., 1st sess., p. 25.
[3] Ibid., pp. 18–9.   [4] Ibid., p. 438.   [5] Ibid., pp. 452–5.

Meantime the President made it clear that he would place no obstructions in the path of Congress in the enforcement of the Reconstruction act.[1] Five generals who were to serve as military governors in the South were to be assigned to their commands. Rumor was busy with the name of Sherman to take the place of Sheridan who had been active on the Radical side during the riots in New Orleans. But "little Phil," as his friends were fond of calling him, was strongly entrenched in the popular fancy, and it would have been not easy to establish another in his stead in Louisiana and Texas. It was desired by the conservatives, too, that Hancock should be one of the appointees.[2] On March 11, 1867, Grant issued an order assigning Schofield to the first district, covering the state of Virginia with headquarters at Richmond; Sickles to the second district, comprising the Carolinas, with headquarters at Columbia; Thomas to the third district, resident at Montgomery, with command in Georgia, Florida and Alabama; Ord to the fourth district, with command of Mississippi and Arkansas; while Sheridan should remain at New Orleans. Thomas having asked for another field of service, Pope in a few days was given his place.[3] All had knowledge gained by experience in earlier commands in one or another part of the South, if not in the particular districts in which they were now to act.

For these appointments the credit, in the North, was generally given to Grant. They were received with satisfaction by the Radicals. Doubts were expressed only as to Schofield, whose conservative leanings were well known.[4] On the other hand, by the state rights' men near the President, such as Gideon Welles, what had been done was viewed with many misgivings,

[1] Cf. Stanbery in 4 Wallace, p. 492.
[2] Washington corr., N.Y. Herald, March 11, 1867; editorial in N. Y. Herald, March 13, 1867.
[3] McPherson's History of Reconstruction, p. 200.
[4] N. Y. Nation, March 21, 1867. A reason for such doubts may be found upon a reading of Schofield's Forty-six Years in the Army. "Only those who actually suffered the baneful effects of the unrestrained working of those laws" (the law of March 2, 1867 and its supplements), he wrote in that volume, "can ever realize their full enormity —" p. 396.

particularly as to Sheridan and Sickles. The "slime of the serpent," said he, was over them all.[1] The five generals assumed their commands and the work of reconstructing the South in accordance with the Congressional plan was begun.

Contentment, however, was not to be the portion of the Radicals for many days. When the "satraps," the "viceroys," the "little monarchs," as they came to be called by the state rights' men, grounded in the traditional principles of the Constitution, started to exercise their powers under the law, they encountered resistance which was reflected in intrigue and strife at Washington, and in the party press. Bold steps were taken by Sheridan immediately. Eight days after he had assumed office, on March 27, he removed Herron, the attorney-general of Louisiana, Mayor Monroe of New Orleans, and Judge Abell of a city district court for their parts in abetting the suffrage riots in the preceding year.[2] "Imported Yankees," meant to "irritate and insult" New Orleans, said one of the President's informants, were appointed to the vacant posts.[3] Early in June, J. Madison Wells, the civil governor of Louisiana, laboring under various charges, was removed. His conduct, Sheridan telegraphed to Stanton, had been "as sinuous as the mark left in the dust by the movement of a snake." He could boast not one friend who was an "honest man." He had made himself "an impediment to the faithful execution" of the military bill of March 2, and T. J. Durant was appointed in his stead. Durant declining, Benjamin F. Flanders was installed in the place.[4] Sheridan's bold acts, one rapidly following another, aroused widespread notice and criticism. Long denials of his charges and protests against his course were telegraphed and posted to the President.[5]

So much confusion arose, concerning the scope of the powers

[1] Welles, vol. iii, p. 65.

[2] Johnson Papers; Appleton's Cyclopedia for 1867, pp. 456-7; Sheridan's Memoirs, vol. ii, pp. 254-5.

[3] Johnson Papers, quoted in Fleming, Documentary History of Reconstruction, p. 442.

[4] Johnson Papers, June 3 to 6, 1867; Appleton's Cyclopedia for 1867, p. 459; Sheridan's Memoirs, vol. ii, pp. 267-8.   [5] Johnson Papers.

of the "viceroys," that the President requested an opinion of
his Attorney-General as to the meaning of the law. Stanbery
prepared his arguments, which were considered at length at
private conferences and in Cabinet meetings,[1] and the result
was two authorized statements overturning every Radical
calculation.[2] The military governor and his troops, said the
Attorney-General, were placed in the South in the interest of
peace and order; they must support the provisional governments, not destroy them. Governors and judges were not to
be removed, legislatures were not to be prohibited from assembling, laws made by these legislatures were not to be set aside in
favor of codes promulgated by military officers. Many classes
of ex-Confederates were to be registered and were to be allowed
to vote.[3] Under date of June 20, 1867, the President transmitted to the Southern commanders, through the Adjutant-
General's office, the result of his conferences with the Attorney-
General.[4]

Sickles in South Carolina said that he would not serve, if
his powers were to be curtailed in such a manner. He resigned
and demanded a court of inquiry.[5] Sheridan wrote to Grant
to protest against orders which he had received from the President. He said in effect that he proposed to follow his own
lights on the subject of the meaning of the law, toward which
the President was known to stand in "bitter antagonism."
His letter was declared to be insulting, impertinent, disrespectful, disobedient.[6] He himself was "arbitrary, tyrannical and
despotic."[7] But neither he nor Sickles was yet to be relieved
of command.

The situation did require the immediate attention of Congress which, in anticipation of such faithlessness, as they chose

[1] House Ex. Doc., 40th Cong., 1st sess., no. 34.

[2] The first issued under date of May 24 published in N. Y. Herald,
May 27; the second dated June 12 in N. Y. Herald, June 17, 1867;
Senate Ex. Doc., 40th Cong., 1st sess., no. 14.

[3] Welles, vol. iii, pp. 105, 107, 109–14.

[4] Richardson, Messages and Papers of the Presidents, vol. vi, pp.
552–6.   [5] Johnson Papers.

[6] Welles, vol. ii, pp. 117, 125.   [7] Ibid., p. 104.

to consider it, on the part of the President, had arranged to reassemble after a three months' recess on the third day of July. It was time that there should be further threatenings as to impeachment, and a strengthening of the lines on the question of reconstruction. If the President and Stanbery were of a mind to defy Congress in a paper opinion, Congress in another supplementary act would carry the subject well beyond the reach of the executive authority. Such a disposition of Johnson's provisional governments would be made that his further resistance would be impossible. Congress would not consent to have its will thwarted in this manner.[1] If the President should continue his obstinate and malicious opposition to the judgment and wishes of the people, said the Detroit Tribune, which was but one of many voices in the same sense, let him be removed from the office he was so unfit to occupy.[2]

The "perpetual session" would continue, said the Democratic Philadelphia Age, presenting the other side of the question. Congress "must watch over their stolen power with sleepless vigilance."[3] The South meanwhile looked on in utter hopelessness. "The cross is erected," said the Mobile Times, "and the lance is ready which will pierce her quivering flank."[4]

The leaders in Congress promptly attacked the work in hand. Sheridan was tendered a vote of thanks for the "able and faithful performance of his duties."[5] In both houses simultaneously the Stanbery opinions were brought under review, and plans were formulated to set them at naught. James Brooks, Fernando Wood and others, representing the minority, were afforded a brief opportunity by Thaddeus Stevens to record their continued opposition to the Radical course. This new reconstruction bill, said Mr. Mungen, a representative from Ohio, had for its purpose "only to more firmly rivet the chains of bondage upon the white men of the South."[6]

---

[1] Cincinnati Gazette and Detroit Post, quoted in Phila. Press, July 1, 1867.

[2] Quoted in Phila. Press, July 1, 1867.

[3] Ibid.

[4] Ibid.

[5] Cong. Globe, 40th Cong., 1st sess., p. 500.

[6] Ibid., p. 518.

But nothing which he, or others like him, might say would in any way avail. The majority, declared Brooks, were "above public opinion," not only of their own land but of the world. There was, however, an unwritten law, a law of God which would hold them responsible for the destruction of the institutions of their country.[1] It was an opportunity for Stevens again to explain his "conquered province" theory, to assert the absolute power of Congress over the people of the South and to advocate the further punishment of their persons and the confiscation of their property.[2]

The House and the Senate had divergent views, but on July 13, only ten days after they had reassembled, they were ready finally to pass their second supplementary reconstruction bill. The vote in the House was 112 to 22;[3] in the Senate, 31 to 6.[4] The provisional governments, if they should continue to exist in the Southern states, would do so, "subject in all respects to the military commanders of the respective districts and to the paramount authority of Congress." It was expressly stipulated that the commanders might at will remove civil officers, subject only to the disapproval of the general of the army of the United States, i.e. of Grant and never of Andrew Johnson. Removals already made were confirmed. Other provisions of the law assured the registration for voting of the negroes and the exclusion from the franchise of white men who had played their parts on the Southern side during the war.

The President's veto message came in less than a week, on July 19. It was a restatement of his case and, at points, from a somewhat new side. It was impossible to conceive, said he, of "any state of society more intolerable" than the condition to which the South was reduced by this series of laws. In ten states of the Union military government was declared to have "unlimited authority." Although American citizens living under the Constitution, the people were denied "every one of its sacred guarantees." Every civil officer of the state might

---

[1] Cong. Globe, 40th Cong., 1st sess., p. 539.
[2] Ibid., p. 545.   [3] Ibid., p. 638.   [4] Ibid.

be removed by a district commander. A power which, hitherto, all the departments of the Federal government, acting in concert or separately, had not dared to exercise was now to be conferred on a subordinate military officer. The President did not fail to note the attempt to relegate him to a minor place. It was a "great public wrong," he said, to confer powers intrusted to him alone by the Constitution "upon subordinate executive officers, and especially upon military officers." Yet he was still hopeful that in the end the "rod of despotism" would be broken, that the "armed heel of power" would be "lifted from the necks of the people," that "the principles of a violated Constitution " would be preserved.[1]

The only response to the reading of the message were clamorous demands in the House by Boutwell, Ben Butler, Thomas Williams, Schenck and other Radicals for the impeachment of the President, and the immediate passage of the bill over the veto by a large majority.[2] The Senate without debate repassed the bill in like manner.[3]

Congress was again ready to adjourn. The plans which had been laid for the consideration of the impeachment question had been frustrated by the firm stand of the chairman of the Committee on the Judiciary, James F. Wilson of Iowa. In June, during the recess, it had been announced that the vote was five to four against a trial of the President for his alleged crimes and misdemeanors, although a majority had agreed that his course was reprehensible, and, if they had been charged with making such a recommendation, that he should be censured.[4]

The committee had been directed to report at once upon the meeting of the House in July. On the 10th day of that month Chairman Wilson rose to explain that the examination of witnesses must be continued, that all the evidence was not at hand, wherefore a final judgment could not be reached. The committee would not be prepared to submit its report until the 16th day of the coming month of October.

---

[1] Cong. Globe, 40th Cong., 1st sess., pp. 741–3.
[2] Ibid., p. 747.　　　[3] Ibid., p. 732.　　　[4] Welles, vol. iii, p. 102.

The committeemen discussed their affairs with no little acrimony upon the floor of the House, Mr. Boutwell proclaiming the views of the minority, while Mr. Wilson firmly defended himself and those who held more moderate opinions. The question of the adjournment was closely bound up with the proposed impeachment. The openly expressed distrust of the President's purposes and the determination to remove the government from his faithless hands, marked every Radical speech. When a recess was again taken it should be only until October at the farthest, if the Judiciary Committee would be prepared with its report at that time.

But better counsels prevailed; the elections, it was agreed, should be held without interference by new schemes of Congress, and when adjournment came on July 20 it was until November 21, only a few days before the regular meeting day. By resolution the impeachment question was made the first to receive consideration at the hands of the House after it should reassemble. The recess ended and on November 25 it was announced that the judgment of the Judiciary Committee had been reversed. The members, who in June had stood five to four against the indictment and trial of the President, now stood five to four in favor of this course. John C. Churchill of New York had joined Boutwell, Thomas Williams, Francis Thomas and William Lawrence, while the chairman, Mr. Wilson, and Frederick E. Woodbridge of Vermont were left in the minority with the two Democratic members. Boutwell offered the report, which notwithstanding its length was ordered to be read by the clerk. It was said that five and perhaps ten hours would be required to go through with it, so the reading after a while was suspended and the concluding resolution was brought before the House — "That Andrew Johnson, President of the United States be impeached of high crimes and misdemeanors."

Expressions of approval, mingled with hisses, issued from the gallery, to meet with the reproof of Speaker Colfax. Mr. Wilson, for himself and Mr. Woodbridge, presented a minority report, and recommended "That the Committee on the Judiciary be discharged from the further consideration of the proposed impeachment of the President of the United States, and that the subject be laid upon the table."

Mr. Marshall and Mr. Eldridge, the Democratic members, presented a third report concurring in the main with the findings of Mr. Wilson and Mr. Woodbridge.[1]

Churchill for his change of heart was denounced by the friends of the President as a Judas. He had sold his honor for pieces of silver to be put into his hands later by the Radicals, and the opening lines in this dark chapter in the history of the country were written in irrevocable characters.[2] The various reports having been received, orders were given to print them and December 4, the third day of the "second session" of the Fortieth Congress into which the "first " (as the three short periods of life which Congress allowed itself in March, June and November, 1867, were called) imperceptibly passed was selected for the beginning of the discussion of this great matter in the House.[3]

The usurping Congress had overborne one of the "coördinate branches" of the government, of which the President and his friends so often spoke in their pleas for an adherence to the traditions of the Constitution. But they were not without hope that the third branch, the judicial, might come to their rescue. There was ground to believe that aid might be looked for in this direction, since several opinions handed down by the Supreme Court were decidedly unfavorable to the Radical view. Within a period of a few months six cases drew forth decisions from the nine justices on questions involving the nature of the government with reference to the great sectional controversy. In *ex parte* Milligan [4] in December, 1866, unanimously on several of the points involved in the dispute, by a vote of five to four on another point, the judges expressed an opinion adverse to military commissions, and the right to

---

[1] Cong. Globe, 40th Cong., 1st sess., pp. 791–2.

[2] National Intelligencer, Nov. 27, 1867 ; Cong. Globe, 40th Cong., 1st sess. ; cf. Welles, vol. iii, p. 238.

[3] Cong. Globe, 40th Cong., 1st sess., p. 792.   [4] 4 Wallace, p. 2.

arrest citizens and try them under suspension of the writ of habeas corpus when civil courts were open and remedy could be had through the regular agencies of justice. The effect of this decision was not only to ,free Milligan, who brought the action and who stood under sentence to be hanged, but to pronounce the government's execution of Wirz, Payne, Mrs. Surratt and others no more than common lynchings.[1] On January 14, 1867, the court by a vote of five to four took similar anti-Radical ground in the so-called "test oath" cases of Cummings [2] and Garland.[3] In the one the court dared to annul a provision of a state constitution, in the other a provision of an act of Congress, as ex post facto laws.

Two efforts, originating in Mississippi and Georgia, to secure a judgment restraining Congress from putting into effect the military reconstruction bills in the South, failed. Able counsel was employed but the Court discreetly on April 15 [4] and on May 15, 1867,[5] held that it was without jurisdiction in such a matter. The acts of Congress, the Court said, ·imposed duties which were "purely executive and political." The "impropriety" of "interference" by the judicial department of the government was obvious. The President and Congress were plainly informed that they might compose their quarrel as they best could. In the McCardle case, which again involved the question of the power of a military commission — this time with reference to an editor for alleged treasonable utterances in a newspaper in Vicksburg — the Court asserted its jurisdiction but reserved its decision.[6]

In the meanwhile Congress, well aroused, began to seek out methods of silencing the Supreme Court. In the view of the Radical leaders the "sovereign people," from whom the congressmen were drawn and to whom they must so frequently return for reëlection were as supreme and infallible as these:

[1] Horace White, Life of Lyman Trumbull, p. 289.
[2] Cummings vs. State of Missouri, 4 Wallace, p. 277.
[3] Ex parte Garland, 4 Wallace, p. 333.
[4] State of Mississippi vs. Johnson, 4 Wallace, p. 475.
[5] State of Georgia vs. Stanton, 6 Wallace, p. 50.
[6] Ex parte McCardle, 6 Wallace, p. 318.

same people had ever been in France during the period of the Convention. The checks and balances, the pride of our system of government, were obstacles in the pathway of popular rulership to be swept aside. When the Executive had stood in the way of the "people" he had been obliterated; the Supreme Court, if it should presume to assert an opposing authority, might count upon meeting a like fate. The National Anti-Slavery Standard read in the opinion in the Milligan case "an alliance, offensive and defensive," between the Supreme Court and the President. Wendell Phillips advocated the abolition of the Court. "The nation must be saved," said he, "no matter what or how venerable the foe whose existence goes down before that necessity." [1] The opinion, said Thaddeus Stevens, was "far more dangerous in its operation upon the lives and liberties" of loyal Americans than the Dred Scott decision. It placed "the knife of the rebel at the throat of every man who now or ever had declared himself a loyal Union man." [2]

Congress proposed to make it a rule that no judgment of the Supreme Court should be valid unless it be expressive of the views of all, or at least two-thirds of the justices. It was outrageous, said the Radical, Thomas Williams, in the House, that five men on the Supreme bench should be able to override the decision of perhaps 160 lawyers in the two houses of Congress. "The legislative power" which was the "true sovereign power of the nation" must be defended against the onslaughts of a small body of men in judicial office.[3] Bingham declared in the House that if the Court were "to defy a free people's will," it would only remain "for a people thus insulted and defied" to procure a constitutional amendment "annihilating the usurpers in the abolition of the tribunal itself." [4] Boutwell said that if there were not five judges on the bench with more respect for themselves than they had evidenced in the Garland case, it was high time for the legislative department of

[1] Quoted in A. B. Hart, Life of S. P. Chase, p. 346.
[2] Cong. Globe, 39th Cong., 2d sess., p. 251.
[3] Ibid., 40th Cong., 2d sess., p. 478.
[4] Ibid., 39th Cong., 2d sess., p. 502.

the government to step in and put such matters above the interference of such a body.[1] The New York Nation deprecated any weakening of the popular confidence in "this eminent Court," but it brought forward the precedent established in the Dred Scott case. That effort to fasten a certain political policy on the country had failed. If it were repeated, it must be met "not merely with contempt but with punishment." [2]

As the Radicals proceeded with their projects to hamper, if not to destroy, the Court, it seemed, said Representative Pruyn, that he stood "in the midst of a revolutionary tribunal." The Congress had killed the President and ten states; now the Supreme Court was to be robbed of the authority which had given it influence, dignity and strength from the first days of the government, and for no reason except that it might possibly render a decision which would come into conflict with the views and opinions of a majority of the members of the House.[3] Here was a "despotism," said Representative Marshall, not of one man, but of "a usurping Congress acting outside of and in defiance of the Constitution." [4]

Nothing came of the various projects to throttle the Court, although a bill, requiring two-thirds of the justices to concur before they could render a decision, was passed by the House on January 13, 1868, [5] to find a grave in a committee in the Senate. A law limiting the appellate jurisdiction of the Court was passed by both houses on March 12.[6] The President vetoed the measure on March 25 as legislation "not in harmony with the spirit and intention of the Constitution" and calculated to "affect injuriously the just equipoise of our system of government." [7] But it was promptly passed over the veto and the Speaker declared it to be a law.[8] An excuse being now at hand, the McCardle case was dismissed by the justices on the ground of no jurisdiction.[9]

---

[1] Cong. Globe, 39th Cong., 2d sess., p. 647.
[2] Issue of January 10, 1867.
[3] Cong. Globe, 40th Cong., 2d sess., p. 479.   [4] Ibid.
[5] Ibid., p. 489.   [6] Ibid., pp. 1847, 1859–61.
[7] Ibid., p. 2094.   [8] Ibid., pp. 2128, 2170.
[9] Ex parte McCardle, 7 Wallace, p. 506.

The threats of Congress had led to a distinct intimidation
of the Court which was reflected in its prudent refusal to be
drawn into the great political dispute. For it to have taken
the President's part would have resulted in its humiliation as
certainly as in his. Thus, with the acquiescence of the people
in a most remarkable manner, Congress had brought into submission the judicial, as it had subdued the executive department
of the government.

In the President's Cabinet the relations between the members
were strained to the last degree. The earlier desire for the
dismissal of the Secretary of War now became a demand on
the part of Mr. Johnson's friends. Stanton and the Judge
Advocate General, Holt, were suspected of having a part in every
Radical intrigue. They were in constant communication with
the leaders in Congress. They were more than ready at any
moment, it was believed, to betray the President. In them,
as advisers and coadjutors in the development of the President's
policy, no kind of confidence could be reposed. Both had been
members of the Buchanan Cabinet; both had been treacherous
in the view of the people of the South to the interests of that
section. Their sympathy which had been open before the war
had now turned, so it appeared, to deep hatred, to a vindictive
spirit of persecution, on the principle of human nature that
friends when they are estranged are wont to become one another's bitterest enemies; and nothing that the Southern element, acting in support of the President, could do to separate
Mr. Stanton and Mr. Holt from the administration would be
left undone.

The dismissal of the Radical military governors, Sheridan,
Sickles and Pope, also was loudly called for. Their orders
were now the law of the land in their respective districts by the
specific stipulation of Congress, and they went on week by
week with their "bayonet rule" quite pitilessly, as it seemed
to the people of the South. Sheridan in particular was marked
out for enmity and abuse. Eldridge, a Democratic leader in
the House, referring to the commanding general of the fifth
district's "insubordinate" letter to Grant, said that if he did

not apologize for his offence, he should be banished at once and forever from the military service of the United States.[1] Early in June he had removed Madison Wells, the civil governor of Louisiana; on July 30 he dismissed Governor Throckmorton of Texas,[2] and installed in the place Elisha M. Pease, who recently had been defeated in a popular election by Throckmorton by a vote of four to one.[3] A correspondent of the President in New Orleans wrote to say that he could convey no "adequate idea" of the feeling of the people there towards Sheridan. It was universally bitter. "All classes and everybody" would rejoice if he could be removed at once.[4] "God is on your side," wrote another correspondent. "Rout your enemies and save the country."[5] The President's advisers in Washington also warmly recommended the removal of "the little fellow."[6] But this was a feat not easily to be accomplished. Hugh McCulloch was right when he had said in a Cabinet meeting that action touching Sheridan at New Orleans would bring violent censure upon the head of the President.[7] He was one of the Northern idols of the war. A partisan press flattered him and caused the people to believe that he was above error, though it was necessary for even the most admiring of his advocates to admit that his despatches lacked a becoming reserve, and that his gifts in general did not well fit him for administrative office.

But Mr. Johnson was now ready to act, come what might. If Congress were willing to impeach him for removing "a turbulent and unfit man," said he to Secretary Welles, they might do so. However, it was not Sheridan, solely and alone, who was at fault; he was but a secondary personage. Others encouraged and supported him in opposing the President's

[1] Cong. Globe, 40th Cong., 2d sess., p. 544.

[2] For summaries of the orders of the various Southern military commanders for this period see McPherson's History of Reconstruction, pp. 316–25.

[3] Welles, vol. ii, p. 146; N. Y. Tribune Almanac for 1867, p. 68.

[4] July 25 in Johnson Papers.

[5] August 12 in Johnson Papers.

[6] Welles, vol. ii, p. 151.   [7] Ibid., p. 152.

views, and the most forward of these offenders was the Secretary of War. Stanton was now openly at variance with all the members of the Cabinet except the Secretary of State.[1] Seward's supple cunning as a politician often enabled him to seem to be upon both sides of a question. Stanton on the other hand was brusque and outspoken. He alone in the Cabinet had favored the bill to enfranchise the negroes in the District of Columbia.[2] No other had wished the President to sign the Colorado and Nebraska bills.[3] In February no member of the Cabinet, save Stanton, advised Johnson to withhold his veto from the Reconstruction bill. How long, asked Welles at that time, could the President go on "with such an opponent at his council board"?[4] Stanton was so violent in combatting Stanbery in the Cabinet meetings, at which the Attorney-General's opinion as to the meaning of the Reconstruction laws was being discussed, that Welles believed the Secretary of War the real author of the "plan of military despotic government to rule the South."[5]

As the weeks of the spring and early summer of 1867 passed, the relations of Stanton with his colleagues became less and less cordial, and important discussions were postponed until after the meetings were adjourned, and he had left the room. On the evening of February 11 the President's sage and mentor, old Mr. Blair, proposed a "*coup d'état*" — not less than a complete change of Cabinet officers. Stanton and all together should go, to make way for others likely to possess the confidence of the various groups and parties. All night, he wrote Johnson the next day, his head was athrob with the idea. John A. Andrew should be Secretary of State; George Peabody, Secretary of the Treasury; Horace Greeley, Postmaster-General; Governor Cox of Ohio, Secretary of the Interior; Senator Cowan of Pennsylvania, Attorney-General; Admiral Farragut, Secretary of the Navy; and General Grant, Secretary of War. "No patriot," Blair told the President, could refuse his aid in the great work of lifting the government above "revolutionary faction,"

[1] Welles, vol. iii, p. 66.   [2] Ibid., p. 4.
[3] Ibid., p. 22.   [4] Ibid., p. 49.   [5] Ibid., p. 110.

to save the Constitution and put into their places the dislocated members of the Union.[1] Two weeks later he was still urging the plan upon Johnson. There must be a "clean sweep." Such courses were adopted by all free governments in crises in their history like the present one.[2]

But nothing of this kind came to pass, though the time was drawing near when the President would be more than willing to part with one of the members of his Cabinet. He told Welles on June 30 that, since Stanton was laboring so manifestly to thwart him in the development of his policies, it was matter of surprise to him that the Secretary of War should persist in remaining in office.[3] While Sheridan might have been removed Johnson soon turned to the "fountain head of mischief," and on August 5 wrote to Stanton — "public considerations of a high character" constrained him to say that the Secretary's resignation would be accepted. Stanton at once replied that "public considerations of a high character" constrained him to decline to resign before the next meeting of Congress.[4] "It is impossible," said the President to Gideon Welles, "to get along with such a man in such a position, and I can stand it no longer."[5] It was supposed that one of the Blairs might now enter the Cabinet.[6] But an understanding was had with Grant, and on August 12 Stanton was suspended and ordered to transfer the office to the general of the army, who would discharge its duties *ad interim*.

Instantly there was a great pother. Stanton took refuge behind the Tenure of Office act. He could not be removed, he said, without the advice and consent of the Senate, though five months before he had been the warmest opponent of that measure, when its terms were under discussion in the Cabinet, and he and Seward together had drafted the message in which the President had vetoed it.[7] Many wrote and telegraphed to

[1] Letter of Feb. 12, 1867, in Johnson Papers.
[2] Letter of Feb. 24, 1867, in Johnson Papers.
[3] Welles, vol. iii, p. 123.
[4] Johnson Papers, vol. 117.
[5] Welles, vol. iii, p. 157.　　　　　　　　　　　　[6] Ibid., pp. 165–6.
[7] Ibid., pp. 54, 158–9; McCulloch, Men and Measures, p. 406.

him urging him on no account to relinquish his place. "The interests at stake," said Senator Morrill of Maine, "are not different nor less important now than when rebellion was flagrant."[1] But resistance promised to be unavailing, and, after Grant had written announcing his acceptance of the appointment, while commending Stanton's "zeal, patriotism, firmness and ability," the Secretary declared his intention of yielding "under protest to superior force."[2]

Holt had much reason to suppose that he, too, would be removed. For months he had been under attack for measures which many believed to have been vindictive concerning the trial and execution of the assassins of Lincoln, and for his part in seeking to establish Jefferson Davis's complicity in the crime. In September, 1866, he had asked for a court of inquiry that he might vindicate himself. But this was not granted him. He survived the storm which broke over Stanton's head and continued in his place, rendered by the course of affairs of diminishing influence.[3]

The way was now open for the attack upon Sheridan and the "arbitrary and violent" Southern "viceroys." The commander in the fifth district must be the first to be displaced. But the task of transferring Sheridan from New Orleans to some field of Indian warfare on the Western plains was still not simple. The President's calmness and deliberation in action often exasperated his friends. He had seemed greater than Jackson in 1866; now in 1867 it was believed on all sides that the hickory had gone out of him. He would have been above trouble at this hour, if he had not pursued the remarkable course of keeping his enemies in and his friends out of official place. He had "an unlimited amount of passive courage," said men in New York, "but none of the aggressive kind."[4] It was complained that he had no confidants, that he kept his own counsel and followed his own courses, when

[1] Stanton Papers in Library of Congress for August, 1867.
[2] McPherson's History of Reconstruction, pp. 261–2.
[3] Joseph Holt Papers in Library of Congress.
[4] Letter of Sept. 18, 1867, in Johnson Papers.

those around him who had his welfare at heart were ready with the most valuable advice.   He made up his mind, but was too slow to free himself of those who had become spies and traitors in his own household.   Stanton could and should have been removed months since; then he would have left office quietly. Other extreme men who were heaping up trouble for the administration should have been dealt with summarily in like manner in the beginning.   The President had tried to propitiate his enemies; they, while accepting his friendly advances, were plotting his confusion.[1]

Much of the advice which came to Johnson was selfish and was dismissed by him as such.   None could fairly say that he was less than firm in an adherence to his opinions when once he had formulated them, or less than obstinate in his determination to be rid of the man who defied his authority when that man's dismissal was finally resolved upon.   Grant used his persuasive powers in behalf of his friend when the President on August 17 ordered Sheridan to Kansas to relieve Hancock. It was "unmistakably the expressed wish of the country," Grant wrote, that Sheridan should not be removed.   He "earnestly urged in the name of a patriotic people," who had "sacrificed hundreds of thousands of loyal lives and thousands of millions of treasure, that this order be not insisted on." [2]   The people would not submit quietly to such treatment of Sheridan in view of his signal services during the war.[3]

But the President was unmoved by the appeal.   He was not aware that the question of Sheridan's staying or going had been submitted to the people so that their wishes could be known; his transfer to another post was imperative; "his rule" had been "one of absolute tyranny without reference to the principles of our government, or the nature of our free institutions." [4]   At one point, in the course of the dispute, Grant

[1] Welles, vol. iii, pp. 190–1; McCulloch, Men and Measures, pp. 369, 391; cf. Dunning, Reconstruction, Political and Economic, p. 92.

[2] House Ex. Doc., 40th Cong., 2d sess., no. 57, p. 4; Sheridan's Memoirs, vol. ii, p. 276.

[3] Letter of Aug. 1 in Johnson Papers.

[4] House Ex. Doc., 40th Cong., 2d sess., no. 57, p. 5.

seems even to have declined to carry out the President's instructions until Mr. Johnson in a Cabinet meeting said : "General Grant will understand it is my duty to see that the laws are executed, and also that when I assign officers to their duty that my orders must be obeyed." [1]

As a matter of course a great ado ensued in the Radical press. Sheridan, "the finest soldier of his time," said the New York Tribune, had been "sent out to haggle with the Indian chiefs and thieves of the Indian Bureau." [2] He had been "deposed, punished, disgraced." [3] The President was either "a lawbreaker or an imbecile." [4] To the Atlantic Monthly he was a "spiteful, inflated and unprincipled egotist." This exponent of the "New England conscience" declared boldly in favor of impeachment as a means of setting him out of the office he had been "too long allowed to dishonor." [5]

According to the President's original plan, General George H. Thomas, in command of the Army of the Cumberland, would have succeeded Sheridan at New Orleans, while Hancock would have followed Thomas at Louisville. But Thomas had an affection of the liver, the surgeons declared that his health would not permit him to proceed South, [6] and the fifth district, with headquarters at New Orleans, came under the command of Hancock. A week after Sheridan's transfer to the Kansas plains General Sickles was removed and General E. R. S. Canby took command in the Carolinas, [7] while Pope was allowed to remain in his place in Georgia, Alabama and Florida until the end of the year, when he was succeeded by Meade. [8]

[1] Johnson Papers; Welles's Diary, vol. iii, p. 187; cf. Grant's letters to the President of Aug. 1 and Aug. 17 in McPherson's History of Reconstruction, p. 307.

[2] N. Y. Tribune, Sept. 4, 1867.

[3] Ibid., Aug. 21, 1867.   [4] Ibid., Sept. 3, 1867.

[5] Issue for November, 1867.

[6] McPherson's History of Reconstruction, pp. 306–8.

[7] Report of Secretary of War for November, 1867; House Ex. Doc., 40th Cong., 2d sess., no. 46, pp. 7–8; Hollis, Early Period of Reconstruction in South Carolina, p. 71.

[8] Life and Letters of General Meade, vol. ii, p. 291.

Both Sheridan and Sickles were drafted by the Radical leaders to aid in the prosecution of the campaign for the election of the Republican ticket.[1] Sickles boarded a steamer at Charleston and was soon in New York. Wanting a leg, which he had lost on the field at Gettysburg, he had the figure for a popular hero.[2] But the attention bestowed upon him was small in comparison with that which awaited Sheridan, who first appeared in St. Louis. His progress from that place to Washington was little short of triumphal. In the national capital he received many testimonials of public affection,[3] and then passed north to Baltimore, Philadelphia, New York and the New England cities. Handshaking, feasts, processions, serenades, fireworks, complimentary speeches marked his course.[4] In the popular eye he seemed to be one of the greatest conquerors of history.

The events of this summer were very distasteful to Seward, whose position was becoming increasingly difficult.[5] On August 23 he quietly sent in his resignation to discover if it were the President's wish that he follow Stanton into private life.[6] The President as quietly declined to receive it. Nothing of the contemplated retirement of the Secretary of State was known even to his fellow members of the Cabinet, though he was under sharp attack constantly in the press and names of successors in the persons of David Dudley Field, Samuel J. Tilden and others were on the tongues of the politicians.[7] The Blairs, always hostile to Seward, again eagerly sought to compass his downfall. Old Francis P. Blair renewed his wish that the Cabinet be reorganized to bring into it "men of standing and enthusiasm." Now as earlier, Weed's hand was seen behind that

---

[1] Phila. Press, Oct. 10, 1867.

[2] N. Y. Tribune, Sept. 11, 1867.

[3] N. Y. Nation, Sept. 26, 1867.

[4] N. Y. Tribune, Sept. 13, 26, 30 et seq.

[5] F. W. Seward, Seward in Washington, vol. iii, p. 354.

[6] The letter concluded "with an earnest wish for the success of your arduous labors in conducting the public affairs of the country in this important crisis." — Johnson Papers.

[7] Welles, vol. iii, pp. 183–4.

of the "Premier," who to save his face could be appointed a plenipotentiary to some foreign power.[1]

Grant's position also was unpleasant and hard. He was being freely, indeed bitterly, criticised for permitting his great reputation to be used to forward the work of degrading Stanton and Sheridan,[2] until it was known how gallantly he had striven to turn the President aside. For Grant by this time had become a candidate for the Republican nomination for the Presidency, now only a few months away.[3] Indeed all matters in connection with impeachment, reconstruction and the general conduct of political affairs were under the influence of the approaching elections. Mr. Johnson may have been a candidate, though the wish that he might succeed himself must have been confined to his own breast.[4] Stanton, it was supposed, was acting with a view to his choice by the national nominating convention. Seward, deftly struggling to keep out of the controversy, though seeming to lean to the President's side, pointing to his purchase of Alaska and the plans he was revolving for the annexation of still more territory to the national domain, was clearly a candidate. Chief Justice Chase's claims and ambitions were widely known; thought of his advancement was never out of his own mind.

[1] Letter of Sept. 7, 1867. Montgomery Blair suggested the name of Dudley Field in Seward's place. — Letter of Aug. 26 in Johnson Papers.

[2] N. Y. Tribune, Aug. 21, 1867; N. Y. Nation, Aug. 22, 1867. Grant had hitherto successfully concealed his political views from both parties. It was not known that he had written to his friend E. B. Washburne, on March 4, 1867, calling Johnson's message concerning the Reconstruction bill "one of the most ridiculous veto messages that ever emanated from any President" (General Grant's Letters to a Friend, p. 52), or that a month later, on April 5, in a letter to the same friend, after alluding to the "administration and Copperhead influence" which was being used to defeat the objects of the bill, he had said that he felt the "same obligation" to remain at his post now as he had felt during the war. (Ibid., p. 55.)

[3] His taking Stanton's place, a correspondent wrote to Joseph Holt, would dispose of Grant completely as a Presidential candidate. By this act he had consigned himself "to the baffled career of General Scott and a hasty plate of soup." — Joseph Holt Papers, letter dated Aug. 13, 1867.

[4] Welles, vol. ii, p. 189.

But now Grant was rapidly distancing every rival and, at first, without conscious action on his part. Modestly he had held himself to be a soldier. He was without the smallest wish to embroil himself in politics, concerning which he frankly wanted knowledge. But, lest he be seized by the Conservatives, the Radicals brought him forward as their leader in the most boisterous manner. He was the principal hero of the war; by cajolery, adulation, violence or whatever means he must be persuaded to serve as the Congressional party's candidate for the Presidency in the elections of 1868. Now that he was acting Secretary of War, Radical counsellors of every degree of eagerness and sagacity pressed around him and filled him with advice which he ill knew how to follow. At once to serve a President and a Congress so widely apart in policy was an impossible undertaking. To pursue a middle course was scarcely less feasible in the excited state of the public mind on all political subjects. But his service to the Union was believed on every side to have been so very important, his own sympathy with the Congressional method of dealing with the South was known by his meddlesome friends to be so complete — it was real though he expressed his views only reluctantly and privately [1] — that mild protestations and silences, when he could not meet all the Radical expectations, were not taken amiss. He did not attend the Cabinet meetings with regularity, saying that he would prefer to remain at his desk in the performance of the duties of his department.[2] He gave certain evidence that his position was uncomfortable.

As soon as he quite understood he was likely to be the Radical nominee, the expression of his dissent in reference to the general question of the President's policies became more definite and open. Thus did he satisfy his sponsors and advocates. But thus, too, did he bring down upon his head the condemnation of the President's friends. Those of them who attempted to fathom his depths as a politician found him shallow. He was not a match for them in an argument on the subject of govern-

[1] Cf. General Grant's Letters to a Friend, pp. 52, 55.
[2] Welles, vol. iii, p. 188.

ment. He was, in truth, as Welles divined, a "political igno-
ramus." Neither his reading nor his associations had equipped
his mind for pondering any constitutional question, or reason-
ing it out. Andrew Johnson had not been tutored in college or
by books on the subject of polity, but he, like many who played
their parts in public life in the period before the war, had
mastered the rudiments of British and American constitutional history. In Grant, on the other hand, was seen a man —
and he was only one of a number coming forward to direct us
in matters of government — to whom our laws and institutions were little known. And now that he was "afflicted with
the Presidential disease," [1] and had fallen into the hands of
"Radical rogues," [2] as Mr. Welles averred, in describing the
process of change in his mind, it was difficult for him to state
his principles effectively, and to establish himself upon high
political ground.

On August 22 Welles found that he had been "tampered
with and flattered" by men who were intent upon using him
for partisan purposes.[3] Montgomery Blair who went to see
him to enlighten him on public matters "gave him up" on
August 24.[4] Welles was still hopeful that he could be saved
to the administration, but, on October 8, both he and the
President had reached the conclusion that he had "gone
entirely over to the Radicals, and was with Congress." [5]

The elections of 1867 were awaited with concern. Would
the people indorse Congress or the President? Would there
seem to be a drawing away from the Radicals in view of all
that they had said and done in the twelve months past with
reference to Southern reconstruction? Johnson did not err
again, as in 1866, to the extent of "swinging around the circle."
Early in June, however, he visited North Carolina to attend
the ceremonies which had been arranged in connection with
the erection of a monument in memory of his father in Raleigh,
and later in the month he proceeded to New England to be
present at the laying of the corner stone of a Masonic temple in

---

[1] Welles, vol. iii, p. 180. [2] Ibid., p. 185. [3] Ibid., p. 180.
[4] Ibid., p. 185. [5] Ibid., p. 232.

Boston. Even so much as this filled his friends with misgivings. His excellent old mentor, Thomas Ewing, reminded
him that there were "yet Antimasons as well as Masons."
The visit to Boston would prove to be "a disturbing element
in the coming elections," which now promised well. "Fifty
lying scamps dogging at your heels," said Ewing, would circu-
late more "fresh slander than could be corrected in six months."
He hoped that Johnson, if he were intent upon going out of
Washington, would "meddle not at all in politics even in
private conversation." He might say with Hotspur —

> "O! I am whipped with rods,
> Nettled and stung with pismires,"

but "he who is President must in his intercourse with the public
forget that he is a man." [1]

Yielding to the advice of his friends and his own better judgment, Johnson gave to his utterances a care which he might
well have exercised in the preceding year. Seward and Randall accompanied him on the journey South. Brief stops were
made at Richmond and other places. The exercises in the
cemetery at Raleigh touched him deeply, and the trip was accomplished without untoward incident.

Though he passed over unfriendly ground on his way to
Boston the President was the recipient of many agreeable
hospitalities. Again he was accompanied by Seward. Mayors
and governors welcomed him. Many more would have liked
to do so. Their invitations were framed in polite terms though
he generally declined them. His speeches aroused no marked
antipathy and after a week's absence he was again at his desk
in the White House. [2]

In addressing the constitutional convention of Maryland
in session at Annapolis, on June 29, he spoke of his recent trips.
"A short time since sectional hatred was so intense," he said,
"that it would have been unsafe for the chief magistrate of
the Union to have proceeded as far South as the capital of
North Carolina." But "reviewing the incidents connected with

[1] May 24, 1867, in Johnson Papers.   [2] Johnson Papers.

my journey to that state and with my visit to the North," he continued, "I am inclined to believe that the days of bitterness are passing away." He asked for a "closer intimacy" between the sections. Their feelings one for the other then would tend to become of a "kindlier nature." The "attrition of companionship would gradually but surely wear away the sharp angles of asperity" which had produced "such woeful consequences." [1]

The elections drew on apace. The October states spoke in no uncertain voice. The results were a surprise to the conservatives who had never hoped for such a change of popular feeling. To Welles the news was "hardly credible." He thought that the Pennsylvania and Ohio returns indicated the "downfall" of the Radical party.[2] Geary, the Republican candidate for governor in Pennsylvania, in 1866, had received a majority of 17,000; the Democratic supreme court judge standing at the head of the ticket in 1867 was elected by a majority of about 1000. The Republican majority of 43,000 in Ohio in 1866 was reduced to 3000 in 1867. Connecticut elected a Democratic governor. A Republican majority of 14,000 in New York in 1866 was now converted into a Democratic majority of nearly 50,000. Governor Bullock in Massachusetts had had a majority of 65,000 in 1866; now it was 28,000. Governor Chamberlain in Maine whose majority in 1866 was 28,000 a year later had but 11,000.

The North itself would not have negro suffrage. Several states had refused to amend their constitutions in this regard in 1865. More followed in 1867, the old Abolition state of Ohio by a majority of 40,000. Similar proposals were defeated in Kansas and Minnesota.[3] It was, said one of the President's friends, "a gigantic rebuke" to his foes.[4] Men carrying torches and muslin transparencies, bearing such legends as "Washington, the Founder; Lincoln, the Defender; Johnson, the Saviour of the Union," and again, as always and as a matter of course, "The Federal Union — it must and shall be preserved," paraded

[1] Johnson Papers.   [2] Welles, vol. iii, p. 232.
[3] N. Y. Tribune Almanac for 1868.   [4] Johnson Papers.

the streets of Washington. Artillery salutes were heard on all sides. The President was serenaded in honor of the victory. He made a speech in which he again expressed his confidence in the people. They would come to his defence and the republic would yet be saved.[1] It was impossible for the President and his friends to understand, said the Abolitionist New York Nation, that the Radical excitement over the work of making the negro from Africa, lately in slavery, the white man's equal was more than an "outburst of revolutionary madness which would pass away as did that of the Long Parliament and the Convention in France."[2]

The result might have given pause to the Radicals. But it was taken to mark only a temporary reaction of feeling, such as is frequently seen in a democracy in the course of the ebb and flow of its mind. No plan of the leaders underwent material alteration, though it is likely that the voice of the people a little cooled the "Radical mania" for impeachment,[3] while it also may have strengthened the resolution of the President to convert the suspension of Stanton into a dismissal, and to name another permanently in his stead. General Sherman was called to Washington where he remained for several weeks. Because of his known dislike for Stanton it was believed that he would exert a salutary influence upon Grant. It was considered possible that he himself could be induced to accept the place,[4] though he soon disabused the mind of any who may have cherished such an expectation. The President, he complained, was "constantly" sending for him.[5] But he would live in Washington on no account; it was "full of spies and slanderers."[6] He would not permit himself "to be used" against Grant who had acted "so fairly and generously" by him "on all occasions."[7] Stanton should resign, said Sher-

---

[1] N. Y. Tribune, Nov. 14, 1867.

[2] N. Y. Nation, April 11, 1867. As a matter of fact it was just this. But the madness did not pass in one or three years; it would rage for thirty years.

[3] Welles, vol. iii, p. 239.

[4] Ibid., pp. 221–2; Sherman's Home Letters, p. 369.

[5] Sherman's Home Letters, p. 368.   [6] Ibid., p. 370.   [7] Ibid., p. 372.

man, but both he and the President were "strong, stubborn, wilful men" who would "embroil the world rather than yield their point." [1] The whole matter, in Sherman's view, had resolved itself into "a war between parties"; and neither one cared "a damn for the service [*i.e.* the military service] or the country." [2] He "felt" for Johnson in such a situation. The President's first efforts to reconstruct the South were right; but now he was "like Lear roaring at the wild storm, bareheaded and helpless." He was attempting to govern after he had "lost the means to govern," and he wanted Sherman "to go with him into the wilderness." [3] This could not be, for the hero of the "march to the sea" wished for nothing so much as the privilege of returning to his headquarters in the West whence he had reluctantly come.[4] The effort to drag this fine soldier into the imbroglio having failed, Governor Jacob D. Cox of Ohio, Frank Blair and others were spoken of by the President and his advisers as suitable men to relieve Grant of the temporary duties assigned to him at the head of the War Department.[5] The Radicals on their side went so far as to suggest the arrest of the President, even before their proposed impeachment of him for his misdemeanors, in order to gain control of his office and install Wade or another in the White House.[6]

The "first session" of the Fortieth Congress having come to an end, after three adjournments, on Monday, December 2, 1867, the "second" or regular session immediately convened. The President maintained a high tone in his message. He reasserted that the ten Southern states were "still members of the national Union." He recommended the repeal of the acts of Congress which had placed those states "under the domination of military masters." He could not approve of the enfranchisement of the blacks. He would do much to aid the negroes to improve their positions and fortunes, but their incapacity for government was manifest; he would not be willing to give them the suffrage with which to destroy them-

---

[1] Sherman's Home Letters, p. 365.   [2] Ibid., p. 366.
[3] Ibid., p. 373.   [4] The Sherman Letters, pp. 300–2.
[5] Welles, vol. iii, pp. 231–2.   [6] Ibid., pp. 234–5.

selves as well as the white race. The present time was "peculiarly unpropitious" for conferring such a privilege upon them, now that the foundations of society were broken up at the end of a great civil war. He believed that the people would be equal to the arduous task confronting them, but it would be "worse than madness" to expect that the negro would perform it for them. Of all the dangers we had been called to face none was so great as those which were certain to result from the success of the present effort "to Africanize" one-half of the country. If the negro governments of Congress could be established in the South, it would cost a standing army and probably two hundred millions per annum to maintain them. Such an expenditure would gravely imperil the public credit.

The Tenure of Office act, the President said, was disorganizing the public service rapidly. Officers which he appointed no longer felt themselves accountable to him. So long as such an act remained upon the statute books he could not perform his constitutional duty of seeing that the laws were faithfully executed. Reflection must convince all, said he, that "our best course is to take the Constitution for our guide, walk in the path marked out by the founders of the republic and obey the rules made sacred by the observance of our great predecessors." He found satisfaction, which he did not neglect to express, in the result of the late elections. He restated his confidence in the "wisdom and virtue" of the people. In "due time" they could be relied upon to "come to the rescue of their own institutions."

The message was received with scant respect in either branch of Congress. In the House Schenck complained that, although it was addressed to Congress, it had been printed first in the newspapers. Covode had a theory that it had been sold for money to the gazettes by some one in the White House. Logan found a passage in it about "executive resistance" which might lead to "violent collision" between the President and Congress, and was for dismissing the pages lest they be mistaken for a "military force," to avoid the impending "civil conflict." [1]

[1] Cong. Globe, 40th Cong., 2d sess., pp. 11–12.

In the Senate Mr. Drake of Missouri offered a resolution denouncing as reprehensible the President's statement of his opinion in his message that the reconstruction acts of Congress were "plainly unconstitutional." [1]

When the day set for taking up the impeachment question in the House, December 4, arrived, that body was busily engaged with a bill to repeal the cotton tax; on the following day, the 5th, the discussion was begun. The Speaker admonished the spectators in the galleries beforehand that order must be preserved, or he would clear them. The members, too, upon the floor of the House were informed of his determination to prevent their outbursts, whether of sympathy or disapprobation. [2] Boutwell, for himself and his colleagues of the Judiciary Committee, opened the cause to the House. He put to rest theories that the President, when he was impeached, might be suspended from duty immediately. Even this Radical must recognize that Mr. Johnson would be entitled to his office until he should be convicted of his alleged crimes by the Senate. Various acts since May, 1865, were recited in proof of the "evil character of the President." Taken together they constituted nothing less than a conspiracy to bring about "the restoration of the rebels to power under and in the government of the country." In the light of these facts there could be no doubt, said Boutwell, as to the "criminality" of the President's "purpose." It was his duty to take care that the laws be faithfully executed. He had not done so. He had disregarded this injunction of the Constitution. His impeachment was the "only means" by which Congress could secure the execution of the laws. [3]

The case was weak. Boutwell himself seemed conscious of the difficulty of bringing an impressive array of facts to bear upon the man whom he was seriously asking the House to indict for trial for some great state crime. It was one thing to deliver a stump speech denouncing a political opponent; another to present in a rational form with judicial gravity the

---

[1] Cong. Globe, 40th Cong., 2d sess., p. 19.   [2] Ibid., p. 61.
[3] Appendix, Cong. Globe, 40th Cong., 2d sess., pp. 54–62.

reasons for a legal proceeding hitherto unheard of in the constitutional history of the country.[1] The forensic effort fell rather flat. It was followed by a much shorter speech by Mr. Wilson, the chairman of the committee, in behalf of the minority. He had been "astonished at the line of argument" of Mr. Boutwell. The President could not be impeached except for some crime "known to the law." The House must be guided by law and not "by that indefinite thing called its conscience." Mr. Boutwell had said that if Mr. Johnson were not put out of his office, he might interfere with the course of the elections in the Southern states next year. "Are we," asked Wilson, "to impeach the President for what he may do in the future? Do our fears constitute in the President high crimes and misdemeanors?" He moved that the subject be laid upon the table.[2] The vote was not long delayed. On the 7th the Boutwell resolution to impeach the President was disagreed to, 57 members voting for it and 108 against it.[3]

But the wrangling of the factions continued; the warmth of the struggle daily increased. The people were not permitted to forget by such a paper as the New York Tribune that Andrew Johnson had "reeled" into the Vice-President's office. His "beastly intoxication" while taking the oath; his maudlin speeches since that time; his political usurpations; his sale of pardons; his studied part in "fomenting the rebel spirit" furnished themes for the eloquence of Sumner in the Senate. The President, said this chief Radical, was "a terror to the good and a support to the wicked." [4]

Amid all this unseemly personal combat it was difficult to believe that the struggle was still one for humanity, as the old Abolition element averred. Just as the war had not been waged to free the negro from bondage, a purpose which it was necessary for President Lincoln to conceal when he did not positively disavow it, so now after the war the strife, except to a few minds, had little enough to do with the improvement of

[1] N. Y. Nation, Dec. 12, 1867.
[2] Appendix, Cong. Globe, 40th Cong., 2d sess., pp. 62–5.
[3] Cong. Globe, 40th Cong., 2d sess., p. 68.   [4] Ibid., p. 542.

the lot of the black man. Outrages upon the ex-slaves in the South there were in plenty. Their sufferings were many. But white men, too, were victims of lawless violence, and in all portions of the North as well as in the late "rebel" states. Not a political campaign passed without the exchange of bullets, the breaking of skulls with sticks and stones, the firing of rival club-houses. Republican clubs marched the streets of Philadelphia, amid revolver shots and brickbats, to save the negroes from the "rebel" savages in Alabama.[1] The "very spirit of Cain," the New York Nation said in the summer of 1866, seemed to stalk over the land.[2] Noble motives which earlier had governed men were swept aside and were lost in the general saturnalia of malignity. The troops serving in the South were there not so much to protect the negroes as to punish their old masters; not so much to guard the imperilled interests of the Southern "loyalists," of whom a deal had been said, as to exasperate the President and the members of his party in the North. The project to make voters out of black men was not so much for their social elevation as for the further punishment of the Southern white people — for the capture of offices for Radical scamps and the intrenchment of the Radical party in power for a long time to come in the South and in the country at large. One Northern state had followed another in refusing to give the ballot to its own negroes. In Northern cities like Philadelphia and New York white men had but very lately begun to sit beside Africans in omnibuses and street cars.[3] It seemed like a voice out of the past when the New York Tribune complained that the President was one to whom a negro had been for fifty years not more than "a skilled mule." [4]

It was assumed that Thaddeus Stevens's Committee on Reconstruction was dead, but the ghost was seen when its chairman on December 7 moved to refer so much of the Presi-

[1] Compare for instance Phila. Ledger, Oct. 6 and 8, 1866.
[2] N. Y. Nation, June 26, 1866.
[3] Phila. Ledger, Feb. 8, April 27, May 18, 1865.
[4] N. Y. Tribune, Dec. 9, 1867.

dent's message as referred to reconstruction to that arbitrary
and proscriptive body of men. It had been no Committee on
Reconstruction, said Representative Ross of Illinois; it had
been a committee "to prevent reconstruction." But for this
committee the South would have been reconstructed long since.[1]
The Speaker of the House at length was authorized to appoint
a new committee of nine members under the chairmanship of
Mr. Stevens, constituted in the main as the old had been.[2]
Into its hands the subject of impeachment soon was given.

The dispute of the President and Mr. Stanton, — with
General Grant, the *ad interim* appointee, standing between the
two adversaries, — and their respective followings, advanced
rapidly. The matter reached the Senate without delay. The
President gave his reasons for ousting Stanton under date of
December 12, 1867,[3] and a month later, on January 13, 1868,
it was resolved by a vote of 35 to 6 that these were insufficient.
The President under the terms of the Tenure of Office act was
without right in such a case except with the concurrence of
the Senate, which now non-concurred.[4] The next day, January
14, General Grant bolted one door of the Secretary's room at
the War Department on the inside, locked the other door on
the outside, delivered the key to the Adjutant-General and
proceeded to the headquarters of the army where he wrote a
letter to the President relinquishing his office. The key found
its way to the waiting Mr. Stanton who returned to his old
desk and resumed the discharge of his duties, but, as he wrote
to Speaker Colfax, "without any personal or written communication with the President." [5]

Meanwhile the General of the Army when he visited the
President, on Sunday, January 19, was instructed verbally

[1] Cong. Globe, 40th Cong., 2d sess., pp. 71–2.

[2] Ibid., p. 95.

[3] Richardson, Messages and Papers, vol. vi, pp. 583–94; Welles,
vol. iii, p. 240; Phila. Press, Dec. 13, 1867.

[4] Phila. Press, Jan. 4, 1868. "Common sense and common de-
cency required in such a case the retirement of the subordinate." —
J. W. Burgess, Reconstruction and the Constitution, p. 163.

[5] Letter of Feb. 4, 1868.

"to disregard the orders of the Honorable E. M. Stanton as Secretary of War" until he (Grant) should be assured that they were the orders of the President.[1] Grant waited four days for a definite reply to a letter asking that these instructions should be furnished him in writing, when he renewed his request. The written order in the same sense was then issued by the President and at once Grant answered in effect that he would decline to obey it. He now, as earlier, would honor the commands of Stanton, since that officer was in receipt of no instructions from the President impairing or limiting his authority as the head of the War Department.[2]

A great political case was being prepared and staged for the public delectation. Day by day the leaders fairly roared their anger and defiance, the Radical press bristled with rancorous phrase and abusive epithet till worse treasons, it seemed, than Andrew Johnson's never had been known. What Grant had said to the President, what the President had said to Grant, engaged the mind and tongue of every man. To make their positions clear to the public they wrote more letters and called witnesses to testify as to the truth of their words and the purity of their motives.

The President had taken early occasion to discuss with Grant the question of a possible non-concurrence on the part of the Senate. He himself had called at the War Department to make certain of the General's sentiments on this point. Grant had promised, so Mr. Johnson alleged, after stating his disinclination to be a party to a political controversy, in case the Senate seemed likely to decide against the President, to give the latter timely notice of his intended action, so that another might be designated for the succession. Indeed several conversations of the same tenor, so the President said, were held; but Grant, instead of following the course which had been agreed upon, instead of "returning the office" to the President "prior to a decision of the Senate," waited until the vote had been taken, then vacated his desk and allowed

---

[1] Letter of Grant to the President, Jan. 24, 1868.
[2] McPherson's History of Reconstruction, p. 284.

Stanton to move into the place. He had been asked, and promised to see Stanton with a view to securing a resignation "for the good of the service." Of such conferences, if any were held, no account reached the President. As to Grant's version of what had occurred at a certain Cabinet meeting, given out to the press, Mr. Johnson's recollection of the words spoken and promises made was "diametrically the reverse." In a word Mr. Johnson charged Grant with bad faith and a complete perversion of the truth.

Grant replied temperately in his own defence under ample Radical advice, never withheld from him, and now offered with increasing freedom. In his concluding sentences he referred with sincere feeling to the violent assaults upon his "honor as a soldier and integrity as a man." He could not but regard "the whole matter from the beginning to the end," said he, as an attempt to involve him "in the resistance of law," for which the President himself had "hesitated to assume the responsibility in orders," as was evidenced by the instructions lately issued to him from the Executive Mansion to disobey the Secretary of War, although that officer's authority had not been countermanded.

A week later the President again addressed the General alluding once more to the "extraordinary character" of his letter, and the manner in which it had been furnished to the press. Grant's attitude now was declared to be "insubordinate." He had stated his intention of disobeying the orders of the President who was made by the Constitution the commander-in-chief of the army and navy. It was clear by this time, said Mr. Johnson, that Grant had accepted the office of Secretary of War "not in the interest of the President but of Mr. Stanton." The President had had a certain definitely understood object in view. He believed the Tenure of Office act, which was guiding the Senate's course, in conflict with the Constitution of the United States, and he desired to bring the subject into the courts. But Grant, so the President alleged, had held the place for the very purpose of preventing an appeal to judicial process, until such time as Stanton's reinstatement could be effected. Confidence had been reposed in the General; he had not deserved it. By trickery he had defeated the President's plans; whilst professing friendliness he had made himself a partner of the enemy.

The question of fact between Mr. Johnson and General Grant was referred to the five Cabinet members who were present at the time the conversation was held. All wrote letters giving their accounts of what had been said. Welles and McCulloch unqualifiedly supported the President; Randall and Browning by circumlocution reached essentially the same conclusions, while Seward, with his accustomed talent, succeeded in a long statement in escaping the responsibility of favoring either adversary.[1]

The Radicals' delight because of Grant's firm stand against the President was great. When Thaddeus Stevens was asked for his opinion of the General he said: "He is a bolder man than I thought him; now we will let him into the church."[2] Grant campaign clubs were formed. Everywhere in the North and West men organized committees to advance his claims upon the country as a Presidential candidate.[3]

Ten days passed. Then on February 21 Johnson addressed a letter to Stanton notifying him of his removal. His functions would "terminate upon receipt of this communication." He would transfer to the custody of General Lorenzo Thomas all records, papers, etc. in his official charge. Thomas now was a man nearly sixty-four years of age. He was a native of Delaware who had fought in the Florida, Mexican and Civil wars. Earlier under Lincoln he had held the office of Adjutant-General. He had just been ordered to resume his old position with a view to his further advancement, since he was held by the President to be a "right-minded" man.[4] He was instructed to enter at once upon the discharge of his duties.

[1] Richardson, Messages and Papers, vol. vi, pp. 603–20; McPherson's History of Reconstruction, pp. 286–91; Welles, vol. iii, pp. 259–64, 267–74, 276.

[2] Phila. Ledger, Feb. 10, 1868.   [3] N. Y. Nation, Jan. 2, 1868.

[4] Welles, vol. iii, p. 279; cf. Dewitt, The Impeachment and Trial of Andrew Johnson, p. 343.

The President informed the Senate of what he had done; General Thomas accepted the appointment "with gratitude" for the confidence reposed in him and attempted to take possession of the office.

The excitement in Washington reached a height unknown since the assassination of Lincoln. Crowds filled the lobbies and bar-rooms of the hotels and surged through the streets.[1] Thomas ordered Stanton out, Stanton in turn ordered Thomas as a subordinate to return to his duties as Adjutant-General. Writs were issued in order to test the rights of the contending parties in the courts. The wildest rumors were afloat — that the troops were coming; that Stanton would be set out of his place by the application of military force; that the President was about to declare himself dictator and begin a new civil war.[2] Stanton slept throughout the night on a lounge; his meals were sent to him in his office lest Thomas steal in while he should be away; sentinels were posted inside and outside of his door to ward off possible stealthy attacks. Senators, representatives and sympathizers in all parts of the country telegraphed, wrote, visited him urging him to follow Sumner's laconic advice, which was to "stick."[3] For days he did not budge out of his office. Roscoe Conkling was in the midst of a speech when the news of Stanton's removal reached the Senate. At once other business in that body came to a standstill and the members went into executive session behind closed doors. A fierce and protracted debate ensued.[4] After seven hours it was resolved by a vote of 28 to 6 that "under the Constitution and laws of the United States the President has no power to remove the Secretary of War and designate any other officer to perform the duties of that office *ad interim*."[5] Mr. Johnson instantly responded in vindication of his course and "earnestly" protested against the Senate's action in charging him with "a violation of the Constitution and the laws of the

---

[1] Washington corr., N. Y. Tribune, Feb. 22, 1868.
[2] Ibid., Phila. Press and Phila. Ledger, Feb. 22, 1868.
[3] Phila. Press, Feb. 24, 1868.   [4] Welles, vol. iii, p. 285.
[5] McPherson's History of Reconstruction, p. 263.

United States" in the removal of a member of his Cabinet.[1] The paper was again written in a temperate spirit; it carefully set forth the history and nature of the American government.

Though the President retained his composure he was obstinately determined that his rights should be defined by the Supreme Court. His authority by the use of the veto was at an end; he had been stripped of the appointive power by a law enacted vindictively, and, as he and his advisers believed, unconstitutionally. The army was performing a service in the South which he loathed. It was coercing the white population, enfranchising the ignorant ex-slaves, and endeavoring to set up negro governments directed by political renegades from the old states of the North. The officers of the army, though he was its commander-in-chief, from Grant downward, — with Stanton as Secretary of War, become faithless in his own house, inspiring them to disloyalty, — had ceased to do him honor or to heed his orders. He looked about him for support which it seemed impossible to obtain anywhere, unless it should come perchance from the people to whom appeal would be made in the national elections near at hand. Sherman's repose was again disturbed. He was offered a brevet generalship and was invited to take a command at Washington equal to Grant's, in the hope, as the National Intelligencer said, of better assuring the safety of the republic.[2] If civil revolution were not out of the minds of the Radicals, it was also reckoned within the range of possible things by the President's friends.[3]

Instantly there was a renewal and a very great increase of the offers of military aid to the President. A correspondent in Cleveland would have him surround his person "with a human wall — a living wall of patriots ready for the worst."[4] Delawareans said that they would stand by him "to the death." If Congress should seize and confine him, they would set him at liberty.[5] A colonel of cavalry in New Jersey said that New

[1] Richardson, Messages and Papers, vol. vi, pp. 622–7.
[2] N. Y. Tribune, citing National Intelligencer, Feb. 20, 1868.
[3] Welles, vol. iii, pp. 287–9.
[4] Feb. 15, in Johnson Papers.   [5] Ibid.

Jersey only awaited the order to "fall in." Thousands of old
soldiers there would enlist "to sustain the constitutional authority." Tens of thousands in New York would march to
the President's defence. He could have 2000 Pennsylvanians
"that were never whipped." "To crush a viper one should
set his heel upon its head." Thirty thousand true men in
Virginia would shoulder arms to "preserve the Union and the
Constitution." The new town of Omaha begged to be allowed
to send the President "a personal body guard." A man in
Charlestown, Mass., in the shadow of Bunker Hill, had raised
a regiment for President Polk to go to Mexico; he could raise
ten for Andrew Johnson. The "Jackson Guards" of Worcester,
Mass., offered him their services. A correspondent in Indiana
had 5000 men for the President's immediate use. "Be firm,"
said another correspondent in that state, and, "By the Eternal!
never surrender." If troops were needed, they would be sent
without delay. The "Radical hell-hounds," the "vultures
gathered around the dying remains of liberty" must be driven
out of Washington. Kentucky would give the President
50,000 soldiers at once and 100,000 at need to gain the great
end. Tennesseeans would "spill" for him "the last drop of
blood that flows through their veins." General McClernand
and General Harney were ready for the new war.[1] Temptation
was at his hand, and if the President had wished to appeal to
force, as Jackson might have done in a like case, so that man's
friends presumed to think, there were those who seemed to
be ready to go with him the full length of the way.

Grant had failed the Conservatives; what would Sherman
do at this critical hour? He did not positively decline the new
service to which he was assigned, but every word in his letter to
the President was eloquent with his disgust. If he knew how
otherwise to maintain his family, he would resign his commission
in the army at once to engage in some business undertaking, so
that he might free himself from "the unhappy complications"
that seemed to be closing about him in spite of his "earnest
efforts" to avoid them. He would resign anyhow rather than

[1] Johnson Papers, Feb. 15 to March 3, 1868.

face possibility of difficulty between himself and Grant. If the President should insist upon his coming East, he must ask to be allowed to make his headquarters in New York instead of in Washington. This "simple concession," said he, would "much soften the blow which right or wrong I construe as one of the hardest I have sustained in a life somewhat checkered with adversity." He telegraphed his brother John to oppose the confirmation of his name in the Senate.

Johnson could make but one reply. "As your assignment to a new military division seems so objectionable," he wrote, "you will retain your present command," thereby promptly winning the warmest expressions of gratitude. Sherman said that he had always been opposed to brevets, though they were now lavished on all, even on non-combatants. Lawyers better than soldiers could discover the methods of determining constitutional questions. His feeling about politics "in their ordinary meaning," he continued, amounted to a "prejudice." The coming elections he hoped would quietly settle the grave national dispute. But "any decision," he concluded sagely, "even if wrong in principle, if submitted to, will be far better than a renewal of strife." [1]

Johnson now turned to General George H. Thomas, who also declined an honor which, if it were accepted, might seem to place him in open rivalry with, if not in actual hostility to, Grant. "I earnestly request you to recall the nomination," Thomas telegraphed to the President. "I have done no service since the war to deserve so high a compliment, and it is now too late to be regarded as a compliment, if conferred for services during the war." [2] The Senate had refused to confirm the appointment of Lorenzo Thomas as Secretary of War; Johnson thereupon sent in the name of Thomas Ewing, Sr., of Ohio, General Sherman's foster father and father-in-law, who in the emergency had been giving the General as well as the President sage counsel. Charles Francis Adams had re-

---

[1] Letters of Feb. 14, 19 and 20, in Johnson Papers; cf. The Sherman Letters, pp. 303–4; Sherman's Home Letters, pp. 371–2.

[2] Feb. 22, in Johnson Papers.

signed as Minister to England. To win Democratic support for his failing cause the President nominated General George B. McClellan to the vacant post.

Nothing availed. The New York Tribune and the New York Herald called the removal of Stanton a "*coup d'état.*" The Philadelphia Press said that "Andrew Johnson, by the wrath of God, President of the United States" had by this act "culminated his career of shame, disgrace and crime." [1] He was "the head and front of a new conspiracy to destroy the government as dangerous as that" which the people of the North had just suppressed.[2] He had assumed the powers of a dictator, said the Boston Journal; he was subverting the government.[3] The Reading, Pa., Despatch called him a tyrant, a despot, a usurper.[4] The New York Tribune, which had taken credit to itself for its forbearance hitherto, now declared that "this most infamous chief magistrate should be swept out of office." [5] "Impeach the scoundrel and do it instantly!" exclaimed the Harrisburg, Pa., Telegraph.[6]

The leaders in the House needed no goad to their energies. Every detail of the plot to place the President in a position in which he could not extricate himself from the accumulating enmities of the Radical portion of the country had been arranged. Stanton had played his part bluffly and arrogantly. Grant, reticent, trained to obedience as a soldier, honestly desiring to escape intrigue, yet yielding, had become an instrument to serve the common end. All was in readiness for the Presidential campaign of 1868, and he who had been the "hero of Appomattox" was now to stand forth in sock and buskin as the hero of the grand political melodrama which was to make Mr. Johnson into one of the greatest of state criminals and to bury him, if possible, for all time beneath a people's scorn.

[1] Phila. Press, Feb. 22, 1868.   [2] Ibid., Feb. 24, 1868.
[3] Cited in N. Y. Tribune, Feb. 25, 1868.
[4] Cited in Phila. Press, Feb. 24, 1868.
[5] N. Y. Tribune, Feb. 24, 1868.
[6] Cited in N. Y. Tribune, Feb. 25, 1868.

CHAPTER VIII

MEXICO, IRELAND AND ALASKA

THE neighbors living to the south of us at the coming into power of the new Republican party were in the midst of what Secretary Seward described as a "chronic reign of disorder." [1] In the past forty years, said Thomas Corwin, whom President Lincoln had charged with the Mexican mission, the country had tried thirty-six different forms of government. In this period of time the Mexican republic had had no less than 73 presidents. The national resources were spent and the population was exhausted by warfare waged uninterruptedly for four decades. [2] The destinies of the country now had come into the hands of Benito Juarez, a full-blooded Indian of ability, held in esteem by the faction not subject to the clerical and reactionary influences, so long the bane of Mexican political life. Indeed he had decreed the final separation of church and state. [3] For three years he had defended his place by arms, and only lately, in January, 1861, had he succeeded in overcoming opposition to the extent of gaining possession of the capital.

Secretary Seward, upon entering the State Department, found the archives full of complaints as to the spoliation of the property of Americans, and the cruel and dastardly murder of our citizens, resident in Mexico, throughout a long term of years. Travellers at this moment were not safe on the high roads. Ways so well travelled as those leading from the capital down to the sea at Vera Cruz were infested with banditti. No kind of public obligation was being honored. There was not a dollar in the Treasury. Interest on the national debt could not be paid.

[1] House Ex. Doc., 37th Cong., 2d sess., no. 100, p. 5.
[2] Ibid., p. 12.   [3] J. M. Taylor, Maximilian and Carlotta, p. 27.

One forced loan followed another to keep in the field enough troops to save Mexico City itself from pillage.

But internal conditions in the United States had been such as to make intervention on our part in behalf of our citizens far from feasible. The situation was improved in no wise, now that we had advanced from mutual distrust of North and South to actual civil strife, and Secretary Seward found it convenient to say that Juarez, having but lately fought his way into the capital, should be allowed to establish his government. The world should wait to see if, under his administration, peace and order might not be restored. Of much greater present interest was it to make certain that J. T. Pickett, who had been our consul at Vera Cruz, and other Confederate emissaries, should not effect some alliance with the Mexicans for the advantage of the seceding Southern states.[1] For this reason President Lincoln considered Mr. Corwin's task in Mexico "the most important one within the whole circle of our international relations." [2]

As between a possible union of Mexico with the Southern Confederacy and the arrival of the troops of a European power upon Mexican soil the President, in the first months of the war, was disposed to regard the activity of a foreign government in that quarter as the smaller of the two dangers. In any case the plans for intervention in Europe were proceeded with, and the United States, when it was not fully preoccupied with larger matters, surveyed the developing scene.

In some particulars the cause of the uneasiness and resentment of the countries of Europe having interests in Mexico was greater than our own. Not one which was not groaning under a weight too heavy to be patiently borne. Foreign bondholders loudly complained. The British legation in Mexico City had been broken into and money to pay the interest on Mexican bonds, awaiting transshipment, had been stolen. Murder followed murder. In July, 1861, an old and respected British resident of Mexico named Beale was called out of his house

[1] House Ex. Doc., 37th Cong., 2d sess., no. 100, pp. 8, 16, 20.
[2] Ibid., p. 6.

by a party of men on horseback, who set upon him with guns, swords and knives amid cries of "Death to foreigners!" [1]

The French were not more fortunate. It may or may not have been true that they laid too much stress upon a bullet which was found in the column of the gallery of their legation and which, so they supposed, had been fired in August, 1861, at the French minister during the celebration of a "Juarist" victory over the "rebels" in one of the provinces.[2] There were outrages in plenty upon the persons and property of Frenchmen in Mexico.[3] Spain nursed similar grievances, covering many years, which now cried for reparation. That this or that ex-president, or other political adventurer of Mexico, had fared forth to bear tales, and gain support in European courts for his particular claims little influenced the governments of England, Spain and France when they signed a convention at London on the last day of October, 1861, for combined naval and military operations in which the United States would be invited to join. They were "compelled" to this course, said the three contracting parties, "by the arbitrary and vexatious conduct" of the Mexican authorities, with a view to securing "more efficacious protection for the persons and properties of their subjects." Each and all agreed not to seek for themselves "any acquisition of territory," or, indeed, "any special advantage," and, furthermore, "not to exercise in the internal affairs of Mexico any influence of a nature to prejudice the right of the Mexican nation to choose and to constitute freely the form of its government." [4]

No time was lost by any one of the Allies, but Spain, by reason of her proximity to the scene, soon put to sea from Cuba with 6000 men of all arms on 14 transports and 12 warships,[5] and was at Vera Cruz landing her men early in December. The British squadron of nine or ten ships did not arrive until the 6th of January, while the French squadron, commanded by the Admiral de la Gravière, and bearing Lieutenant-General Prim, the Spanish commander-in-chief, made port three days

---

[1] House Ex. Doc., 37th Cong., 2d sess., no. 100, pp. 273, 319.
[2] Ibid., pp. 122–3.   [3] Ibid., pp. 319–20.
[4] Ibid., pp. 136–7.   [5] Ibid., p. 417.

later, on the 9th day of the month.   Already the city was completely occupied by the troops of Spain.   Hundreds down with
disease were in hospital.   An old convent set aside for the
British marines they were displeased to find too filthy for their
use.[1]   The disproportionate strength of the Spanish contingent
of the expedition, and its haste in setting out for the scene, at
once created a breach in the relations of the Allies, which
subsequent events tended rapidly to increase.   But, differences
temporarily composed, the European commanders were soon
collecting the customs to indemnify foreign creditors, their
troops advanced without resistance to camping places a few
miles in the interior and they issued a proclamation to the people.
The expedition, they said, was "necessary and indispensable."
Those who alleged that the foreign fleets and soldiers had come
with "hidden plans of conquest," intending to interfere with
the policy and administration of the country, studied only to
deceive.   The Allies would be an "anchor of salvation."
They would "stretch a friendly hand to the people on whom
Providence has showered all his gifts, and whom they see with
grief, wasting their strength and destroying their vitality under
the violent action of civil war and perpetual convulsions." [2]

In the meantime Corwin in the American legation in Mexico
City, and Secretary Seward, were using their offices to prevent
any undue encroachment of the European powers.   The
Chargé of the Juarez government at Washington, Matias
Romero, neglected no opportunity to stimulate our State Department to action in behalf of the interests which he represented.
One statement followed another.   Protest followed protest.
Already on September 24, 1861, Mr. Seward had desired Minister Adams in London to inform the government of Great Britain
that the United States must look with "deep concern" upon the
proposed armed movement against Mexico.[3]   All three of the

---

[1] House Ex. Doc., 37th Cong., 3d sess., no. 54.

[2] Proclamation of Jan. 10, 1862, ibid., p. 602.   The "real enemy"
in Mexico, said the French Admiral de la Gravière, was anarchy, and
this was "an enemy with which it was useless to treat." — House Ex.
Doc., 37th Cong., 2d sess., no. 100, p. 176.

[3] House Ex. Doc., 37th Cong., 2d sess., no. 100, p. 192.

Allies were informed in due time that we would not be a party
to the Convention of London of October 31.[1] While they
might seek a redress of their grievances it must be understood
that they were to bring about no political change "in opposition
to the will of the Mexican people." Least of all would a monarchical government find favor upon this continent and win the
admiration of the United States.[2]

Corwin at Mexico City complained that he was outweighed
in the scale. All Europe had its diplomatic representatives
there, while, for America, he stood alone, barring an agent from
Ecuador.[3] Romero did not hesitate to appeal to all our
traditional sympathies for a republican form of government.
The institutions prevailing in Mexico, he would tell Mr. Seward,
were identical with those in the United States. The subversion
of these institutions in that country would give them "a rude
shock that would cause them to totter throughout the other
republics of this continent."[4] If the Allies had come to collect
a debt, money must be lent to Mexico so that she could pay
her creditors. With this end in view, Corwin asked for five or
ten millions of dollars,[5] but the demands of the war against the
South were so great, said Secretary Seward, that to make such
an advance would be impossible, even if it should seem to be
expedient.[6] At President Lincoln's desire, however, Corwin
began the negotiation of a treaty, wherein we would pledge a
sum large enough to pay the interest at the rate of three per
cent for a term of five years upon some $63,000,000 due foreign
bondholders of Mexico, to be secured by public lands and mineral
rights in the states of Lower California, Chihuahua, Sonora and
Sinaloa.[7] The articles were signed and the Mexican government began to draw upon the United States, only to have the
paper protested when it reached Washington,[8] for the Senate
did not ratify the arrangement,[9] and this attempt to buy off
the invaders and send them home came to a futile end.

[1] House Ex. Doc., 37th Cong., 2d sess., no. 100, pp. 188–9.
[2] Ibid., pp. 208, 217, 221.   [3] Ibid., p. 39.
[4] Ibid., p. 134.   [5] Ibid., p. 23.   [6] Ibid., p. 30.
[7] Ibid., p. 22 — Seward to Corwin, Sept. 2, 1861.
[8] Ibid., 3d sess., no. 54, p. 546.   [9] Ibid., p. 645.

All the while there were rumors that one or another of the Allies intended to overstep the limits defined by the terms of the Convention of London. It would be seen at length, men said, that some one had not been open and honest. This intervention to secure the payment of a debt was nothing less than a scheme slyly to evade, if not directly to violate, the principles of the Monroe Doctrine with reference to European aggressions upon the American continent. Before long the Mexican republic would disappear, and some monarchy would rise in its place under the protection of a European flag. The Allies, having withdrawn a little way to high ground back from the coast, desired to advance still farther upon the tableland lying between Vera Cruz and Mexico City to escape the sickly climate. Preliminaries to this end were signed on February 19, at La Soledad, in conference with representatives of the Juarez government,[1] who were pleased to suppose that they were shrewdly playing one ally against another, with a view to bringing them soon into such hostility, that they would again go their separate ways. Rumors that the Archduke Ferdinand Maximilian, brother of the Emperor of Austria, was to be provided with a throne reached the ears of Lord John Russell in England; various ex-dictators of Mexico and their mischievous retainers were making the circuit of the European courts; clerical and other discredited factions were under arms threatening the "Juarist" government at home and confirming the impression that there was still insecurity, if not great domestic discontent in Mexico; the French without the knowledge or consent of their allies were increasing the size of their expeditionary force. The breach widened apace.

An infamous man who earlier had been President and upon whose head rested the responsibility for some of the blackest of massacres, General Miramon, had arrived at Vera Cruz on an English mail steamer. Armed partisans on horseback awaited him to carry him into the mountains, to join his sympathizers for the purpose of engaging in guerilla warfare.[2] He was sent back to Havana whence he had come. But France, on her side,

---

[1] House Ex. Doc., 37th Cong., 3d sess., no. 54, pp. 42, 46.
[2] Ibid., pp. 617, 627.

received and protected General Juan N. Almonte and a party of refugees who had been rusticating in exile in Europe, who had visited the Emperor Napoleon at Paris, and who came openly intent upon establishing communication with Marquez and other odious leaders of bands in the interior. English and Spanish protests ensued at once without moving the French plenipotentiary in his resolution to sustain the refugees.

The pecuniary claims of France took on preposterous proportions. Lord John Russell observed that the demands were not supported by vouchers, or proof of any kind of indebtedness for injuries suffered in Mexico. There was the monstrous Jecker loan of $750,000 to the falling government of Miramon a few years earlier for which a party of Swiss usurers were to receive $15,000,000. This claim was now lodged against the Juarez government. France presumed to say that she would collect this sum also.[1] The end of the coalition was at hand. In the middle of April the English and Spanish forces withdrew to Vera Cruz, and made their departure from the country. The English plenipotentiary, Sir C. Lennox Wyke, embarked for New York; the Spanish representative, General Prim, for Havana.[2] Almonte issued an address to the people asking them to flock to his standard; Juarez declared hostilities against the French. In September, 1862, General Forey came at the head of important reinforcements, superseding General Lorencez in command of the French expeditionary army, and the way was prepared for an active military campaign.

Whatever had been France's earlier designs they were little masked after General Forey's arrival in Mexico. Louis Napoleon's instructions to that officer, bearing the date of July 3, 1862, left no room for misunderstanding. "It is to our interest," said the Emperor, speaking for the French nation, "that the republic of the United States shall be powerful and prosperous, but it is not at all to our interest that she should grasp the whole Gulf of Mexico and rule thence the Antilles as well as South America." If a "stable government" can be established in Mexico by French aid, he continued, "we shall have restored

[1] House Ex. Doc., 37th Cong., 3d sess., no. 54, pp. 607, 715–6.
[2] Ibid., p. 743.

to the Latin race on the other side of the ocean its force and its prestige; we shall have guaranteed the safety of our own and the Spanish colonies in the Antilles; we shall have established our benign influence in the centre of America." National honor and policy and the commercial welfare of France imposed upon her "the duty of marching upon Mexico, there boldly planting our flag and establishing perhaps a monarchy, if not incompatible with the national sentiment of the country." [1]

Not much more was needed, especially when it was known that the Mexican refugees in Napoleon's confidence in Paris, such as Almonte, were now on the ground to forward his ends by inciting the people to a new civil revolution. But the game still called for deceit. In an address to the Mexicans upon his arrival in Vera Cruz, General Forey announced that he had come not to make war upon the people but upon "a handful of men without scruples and without conscience who have trampled upon the rights of men."

As soon as they should be liberated by French arms, he said, "they will freely elect the government which they please." Wherever, in Europe or America, the French flag was seen it stood for "the cause of the people and of civilization." [2] Again, on February 15, 1863, Forey said that the soldiers of France had come upon "no other mission, be it well understood, after they have dragged by force from him who pretends to be the expression of the national will [Juarez] the just reparation of our wrongs . . . but that of consulting the national wish as to the form of government that the people desire." [3] On their side the United States would insist, said Secretary Seward at Washington, on June 21, 1862, that France should not "improve the war she makes to raise up in Mexico an anti-republican or anti-American government, or to maintain such a government there." [4] In this spirit each diplomatic communication was framed, while France always responded that her purpose was a

---

[1] Senate Ex. Doc., 38th Cong., 2d sess., no. 11, p. 272.
[2] House Ex. Doc., 37th Cong., 3d sess., no. 54, p. 354.
[3] Senate Ex. Doc., 38th Cong., 2d sess., no. 11, p. 114.
[4] House Ex. Doc., 37th Cong., 3d sess., no. 54, p. 530.

war only to right her wrongs, not to establish a government in
defiance of the popular will.

But the advances of the French army on Mexican soil met
with unexpected obstructions. Almonte's power over the
people had been overstated to Napoleon. The uprising which
the returned exile expected to lead added little strength to the
expeditionary movement. The fear of openly antagonizing
the United States was never quite out of the minds of the Emperor, his foreign minister, M. Thouvenel, and their advisers in
Paris. But finally in May, 1863, Puebla fell after a long siege,
and two or three weeks later, on June 10, Juarez and his tatter-
demalions having withdrawn into the mountains, Forey made
a practically unresisted entry into the capital. He wrote home
that he had been received by "the entire population" of the
city with "an enthusiasm approaching to delirium." His soldiers were "literally overwhelmed with bouquets and wreaths."
With the officers of his staff he attended a Te Deum in "the
magnificent cathedral filled with an immense multitude," afterward conducting a review of the troops amid cries of "Vive
l'empereur" and "Vive l'imperatrice." He had not the words
to express the feelings of his heart: such an experience must
remain "a sweet remembrance" until the end of his life. The
Emperor wished Mexico to be "regenerated to a new life."
With the aid of "all true Mexicans," under "Divine protection,"
General Forey would strive to make so much come to pass.[1]

General Almonte was now put at the head of a regency of three
members chosen by a Superior Junta of 35 men, whom General
Forey and the French plenipotentiary in Mexico, de Saligny,
had named for the task. Robbers under the name of guerrillas,
it was complained, infested all the roads, stopped public conveyances at the very gates of Mexico City, plundered farm-
houses and spread terror on every side. Trade was paralyzed.
Instantly steps were taken to clear the neighborhood of the
capital of these outlaws, and to prepare the way for "the establishment of a regular government and the pacification of the
country." [2] The duty of determining what form this regular

[1] House Ex. Doc., 39th Cong., 1st sess., no. 73, part i, pp. 217-8.
[2] Ibid., pp. 219-20.

government should assume was confided to a so-called Assembly of Notables, composed of the 35 members of the Superior Junta and 215 other men.[1] It was only a few days before this Assembly made it known that the Mexican nation had adopted as its government "a limited hereditary monarchy, with a Catholic prince as sovereign," serving under the title of the Emperor of Mexico. The crown would be offered to the Archduke Ferdinand Maximilian of Austria; if he should decline the nation would look to his Majesty, Napoleon III, Emperor of the French, "to indicate for it another Catholic prince."[2]

Immediately a delegation of Mexican monarchists proceeded to Europe, with the new crown in their hands, to proffer it to the Emperor-elect. The Archduke Ferdinand Maximilian, yet but thirty, the handsome, fair-haired younger brother of the Emperor Francis Joseph of Austria, was one of the most admired royal figures of Europe. Brilliant nuptial ceremonies had united him but lately with a beautiful princess, Carlotta, daughter of Leopold I, King of the Belgians, and granddaughter of Louis Philippe. He had tried a governorship of crown lands; he had gone to sea in the navy; he had led a scientific expedition to Brazil. There were accounts of a dispute with his brother and he had retired among his books to the pleasant castle of Miramar, near Trieste, overlooking the blue surfaces of the Adriatic. There the Mexican party appeared on October 3, 1863, and there with glib and unctuous tongues they delivered their invitation on behalf of the Assembly of Notables. "Without you, prince," said the Most Excellent Don José Maria Gutierrez de Estrada, a former Mexican foreign minister, the spokesman of the deputation, "believe it from these lips, which have never served the purposes of flattery, without you all our efforts to save the country will be vain." The people will "require only to see" you and your "noble consort" in order to "love" you. "May we be enabled," the speaker continued, "to carry the joyous tidings to a country awaiting them in longing anxiety, — joyous tidings not only for us Mexicans but also for France?"[3]

---

[1] Senate Ex. Doc., 38th Cong., 2d sess., no. 11, pp. 254–5.
[2] Ibid., p. 260.   [3] Ibid., pp. 261–2.

The prince was "profoundly grateful." He reminded his
visitors that he was a descendant of Charles V, and expressed
his favor for the project. But Napoleon, who so ostentatiously
mixed Divine right with the plebiscite, had concerned himself
about the popular will, and Maximilian sent the deputies home.
His final answer would depend upon "a vote of the whole
country." "If substantial guarantees for the future can be
obtained, and if the universal suffrage of the noble Mexican
people select me as its choice," he would be ready, he averred,
with the consent of his brother, under Almighty protection
"to accept the throne." [1]

So the vote was to be taken, though it was pertinently observed that seven-eighths of the population of Mexico and
twenty nine-thirtieths of its territory lay beyond the military
lines held by the French troops; and the small area under their
protection, extending mainly from Mexico City down to the sea,
was overrun by 72 hostile guerrilla bands, each containing from
70 to 300 men. [2] Drouyn de Lhuys succeeded Thouvenel as
Napoleon's Minister of Foreign Relations, and his orders to
General Bazaine, who would take the place of Forey when that
commander had returned to France, on the subject of a plebiscite had been plain, even before Maximilian's answer had been
secured. It was manifestly impossible to consult the people
directly. Any collection of their suffrages would be a farce.
But such a ratification, for use in the diplomatic controversy
with the United States, the French Foreign Office must have,
and armed with a statement that an election had been held,
and that the archduke was the choice of a vast majority of the
nation, a Mexican deputation in April, 1864, again visited him
in his castle of Miramar.

In flattering phrases the Señor Estrada, who had come in
October, again addressed the prince. The drawing-room of the
palace was filled with nobles, aides-de-camp and chamberlains
in brilliant uniforms. The archduke himself wore the dress of a
vice-admiral of the Austrian navy. He made a speech in which
he said that, inasmuch as the conditions he had named in Octo-

[1] Senate Ex. Doc., 38th Cong., 2d sess., no. 11, p. 262.   [2] Ibid., p. 276.

ber had been fulfilled, he was willing to heed the call to the new throne beyond the sea. Thereupon the Mexicans who were present acclaimed their sovereign, shouting "God save the Emperor Maximilian I" and "God save the Empress Carlotta." Salutes fired from the bastions of the castle were followed by the reports of artillery in the harbor and town of Trieste. It was "a sure pledge of the salvation of Mexico," said Estrada. "Every year on this day our children will offer up their thanksgivings to Heaven in gratitude for our miraculous deliverance." The Mexicans bent their knees before Maximilian and kissed his hand, and then were ready to visit the Princess Carlotta, surrounded by her ladies in her apartments, and do homage in like manner before her. The next day the Emperor and Empress set out for their new dominions by way of Rome, whither they would wend their steps to receive the blessings of the Pope.[1]

At the same time a treaty was signed between "the government of the Emperor of the French and that of the Emperor of Mexico." In this convention it was specified that the French army in Mexico should be reduced, as soon as a sufficient number of native soldiers could be enlisted in the service, to a corps of 20,000 men, including the foreign legion of 8000 men who were to remain in the country for six years after all the other French troops had been withdrawn. France should frequently send her naval vessels into Mexican ports. Other articles prescribed how the cost of the service should be met, and the indemnities which were to be paid to France out of the Mexican revenues for the wrongs she had suffered in the past, and for her present sacrifices in the interest of a stable system of government.[2] Belgium would send a small body of troops as a guard of honor for the Empress, a princess of her royal line; Austria, a similar guard for the Emperor. The principal powers of Europe at once recognized the new government and accredited representatives to it at Mexico City.

Meantime an imposing squadron of Austrian war-ships dropped anchor in the harbor of Vera Cruz and the young royal

---

[1] House Ex. Doc., 39th Cong., 1st sess., no. 73, part i, pp. 127-32; ibid., part ii, pp. 371-3.   [2] Ibid., part i, p. 124.

pair, accompanied by a retinue befitting persons of their rank, out of which to constitute a court, disembarked amid salvos of artillery and other suitable demonstrations, ready for their progress to the capital. The French army had prepared the welcome, assisted by eager Mexicans, whose fawning they devoutly hoped would bring them preferment at the hands of the new Emperor. In a proclamation he told the people what he would aim to do for their advancement under "the civilizing flag of France." On June 12, 1864, he made a triumphal entry into the capital. A brilliant military pageant passed through the streets, the troops being followed by a crowd of Indians in their strange native dress. The Emperor and the Empress amid "vivas" rode under arches festooned with flowers. Flags and banners were seen on every hand. The bells of the cathedral and of the churches clanged. Ladies on the balconies clapped their hands, waved their handkerchiefs and scattered gold and silver leaf and the petals of roses upon Maximilian and his princess. He began to confer orders upon his flatterers, and thus the ill-starred Mexican empire was established, while Grant fought his bloody battles in the Wilderness, McClellan threatened to wrest the Presidency from Lincoln and men at the North spoke of peace with the South at whatever price.

As soon as the new plenipotentiaries from Europe began to arrive, our Minister Corwin started home by way of Havana. It was impracticable for the legation to accompany President Juarez on his wanderings in the interior, though at Washington Romero continued to represent the republican government, and with great vigor. Public sentiment was deeply stirred by the course of events.

Suggestions through diplomatic channels that the United States should recognize and lend its support to the Empire were repelled. On the 4th day of April, by a unanimous vote the House of Representatives at Washington passed a resolution, sponsored by Henry Winter Davis, of Maryland, declaring that it did not accord with the policy of the United States to acknowledge any monarchical government erected on the ruins of any republican government in America under the auspices of any European power. It must be understood that the American people were not indifferent spectators of the deplorable events in Mexico. The Archduke Maximilian was the "Archdupe" of Louis Napoleon, said the Democratic leader, S. S. Cox, in supporting this Republican measure, and it was only with great difficulty that the most serious complications with France were averted.[1] "Do you bring us peace or bring us war?" asked Drouyn de Lhuys of Minister Dayton at Paris, when the latter visited the French Foreign Office. It was necessary for the minister to explain that the resolution required the concurrence of the Senate and the signature of the President before it could become an official expression of the national sense. While, as Mr. Seward observed, it might "truly interpret the unanimous sentiment of the United States in regard to Mexico," while as Mr. Dayton said it might contain "nothing more than had been constantly held out to the French government from the beginning," it is undeniable that but for the cool head of the President and his Secretary of State,[2] and the sagacity of Sumner[3] and some other members of the Senate we should have drifted rapidly into a foreign war.[4]

The first months of Maximilian's reign revealed a policy which was wholly in the interest of good order. The French army pressed into the interior and garrisoned many of the towns. Five railroads were projected and work proceeded actively upon one designed to connect the capital with the coast at Vera Cruz. As the finances, which were put in charge of an expert from Europe, would permit, wagon roads were constructed; steamer and telegraph lines were established; schools were founded; the parks and pavements in Mexico City were improved; the erection of a fine theatre in the capital was begun. Juarez was reduced to the rank of an outlaw chieftain with a few men at his heels. He was driven from pillar to post, and at

---

[1] Cong. Globe, 38th Cong., 1st sess., p. 1408.

[2] "Why," Seward wrote to Bigelow, under date of May 21, 1864, "should we gasconade about Mexico when we are in a struggle for our own life?" — F. Bancroft, Life of Seward, vol. ii, p. 430.

[3] Pierce, Memoir and Letters of Sumner, vol. iv, pp. 117–8.

[4] House Ex. Doc., 38th Cong., 1st sess., no. 92, pp. 2–4.

length orders were issued to shoot his followers on sight that the country at the earliest possible day might be restored to peace.

The republican cause never seemed so nearly lost. The order for the extermination of the guerrillas in Juarez's train was made to seem very black in Washington. Romero wrote notes to Seward condemning in unmeasured language the outrages of the European "usurper," the French "mannikin" and his "pretended government," which was supported by a "wicked war" waged by the "tyrant of France."[1] The night had fallen upon liberty in Mexico. The American government awaited the propitious hour, and, once the rebellion in the South was at an end, the State Department in its communications with France spoke in plainer tones. The public mind, long intent upon one object, which now had been achieved, was free to seek new interests and tasks. The victorious armies were released to right other wrongs, and none seemed so grave as this one which had been committed here at our very doors during our preoccupation with the gravest domestic concerns.

A great body of sentiment in France as in England had been unfavorable to the North in its contest with the Confederacy. The hope had been felt and expressed that the rupture between the Northern and the Southern states might be made complete and permanent. No man was dull enough not to know that this was the dearest desire of Louis Napoleon. The Rio Grande had been kept open to the Confederates for the import and export trade during the war; up and across this river arms had been shipped to them. "Rebels" had fled over the border with munitions to escape surrender, and they had been protected, so it was alleged, by the imperial Mexican government. Maximilian had been receiving prominent Confederate leaders; he loaded them with honors and offices. He offered lands to colonists and strove, it was charged and believed, to make Mexico a haven for the enemies of the United States until, growing strong again, they could launch a new assault against

[1] See for example House Ex. Doc., 39th Cong., 2d sess., no. 76, pp. 21 and 42.

free government. Thus the public mind travelled rapidly; it found dangers which did not exist and magnified others which in reality were small.

No man was more eager for armed intervention than General Grant. The attempt to establish a monarchical government on this continent by foreign bayonets, he told President Johnson in June, 1865, was "an act of hostility against the government of the United States."[1] He attended a Cabinet meeting and pressed his views upon the administration.[2] There was "but one opinion as to the duty of the United States toward Mexico, or rather the usurper in that country," he said again in September. He wished the President to adopt such measures as would send home the French troops and secure "the supremacy of the republican government."[3] Once he recommended the delivery to a Mexican agent in New York of a supply of Springfield rifles and other military equipment on the man's simple note of hand. Twice he urged the sale of war material to the Mexican Liberals on the Texas border. The President and the Cabinet, to whom the requests came, completely disapproved such suggestions[4] without turning Grant away from his ill-considered plans. He went so far as to complete the arrangements for General Schofield to visit Mexico, and to take command of an army of Juarez's adherents to operate against the French. That general, who was then in Raleigh, N. C., came to Washington. He was granted a leave of absence for a year with the power to go beyond the limits of the United States. The cost of the expedition would be met by the sale of a Mexican republican loan, — thirty millions of bonds secured by some agricultural and mineral lands, to bear interest at the rate of seven per cent a year in gold. Beautifully engraved pieces of paper exhibited vignettes of Juarez and Lincoln, a pole surmounted by the liberty cap and a figure of Liberty leaning upon a globe with a scroll bearing the words "Monroe Doctrine."[5] The Mexican Fiscal Agency in

[1] O. R., series i, vol. xlviii, part ii, p. 923.
[2] Diary of Gideon Welles, vol. ii, p. 317.
[3] O. R., series i, vol. xlviii, part 2, p. 1221.
[4] Stanton Papers in Library of Congress, Jan. 9, April 25, and July 17, 1866.   [5] N. Y. Herald, Oct. 27, 1865.

Broadway, the windows of which were adorned with the Mexican and American flags, was formally opened on November 2, 1865, with speeches by Minister Romero, "Sunset" Cox, General Lew Wallace, Robert Dale Owen and others, and ten of the proposed thirty millions sought purchasers at sixty cents on the dollar.[1] The issue was extensively advertised. It was pointed out that at the sale price the yield in interest would be nearly twelve per cent in gold or seventeen per cent in currency annually. "Every lover of republican institutions" was asked to buy "at least one bond." The loan was commended as "the most desirable investment ever offered."[2]

Sheridan in command on the border was ordered to hold ordnance and stores in readiness in Texas for Schofield's use, and to place at his disposal troops who might be willing to volunteer for this service.[3] But the sale of the loan proceeded very slowly and Seward advocated a different policy. To him Mexico offered no new problems; he, as Welles observed, acted from intelligence while Grant was obeying an impulse. The Empire in Mexico was perishing, Seward believed, and Maximilian, if let alone, would depart the country in six months, perhaps in sixty days.[4] Before setting about his quixotic duties Schofield visited Cape May, where he met the Secretary of State, who advocated a trip to France instead of a military expedition. The Emperor of the French should be urged to withdraw peacefully. "I want you to get your legs under Napoleon's mahogany," said Seward to Schofield, "and tell him that he must get out of Mexico."[5] The way was prepared for the mission by diplomatic correspondence and, with two officers of staff, the general sailed for England on November 15, 1865. Early in December he appeared in Paris to begin the performance of his tasks.

Whatever may have resulted from Schofield's conversations in France little enough value seems to have attached to another

---

[1] N. Y. Herald, Nov. 3, 1865.   [2] N. Y. Tribune, Jan. 5, 1866.

[3] Schofield, Forty-six Years in the Army, pp. 380–2; cf. A. Badeau, Grant in Peace, pp. 99–100.

[4] Welles, vol. ii, p. 317.

[5] Schofield, Forty-six Years in the Army, p. 385.

embassy which Mr. Seward organized. Now that Corwin was no longer able to exercise his functions in Mexico City as the representative of the United States without a recognition of the Empire, which we on no account would give, it was proposed to appoint a new minister and accredit him to the Juarez government. No man knew the precise whereabouts of the republican capital. It passed from place to place, following the movements of the president. But the industrious Romero said so much in praise of the government, and it seemed to most people in the United States so excellent, merely because it was a republic rather than a monarchy, that it was a duty to bring it into relationship with Washington.

The first plan, announced late in 1865, was to make General John A. Logan the plenipotentiary of the United States. He had publicly expressed his opinions, which were very warlike, and the suggestion to name a man so outspoken and so little accustomed to diplomatic usages to such a post made a "disagreeable impression" in France.[1] At length Lewis D. Campbell of Ohio was designated for the service. For a number of years he had been a member of Congress and since the beginning of Johnson's administration had been constant in his offers of advice and his expressions of friendship. He intimated that he could much better serve the President in a larger way, possibly in the Cabinet, but his name was sent to the Senate as minister to Mexico long to lie there without confirmation. He had wiped the blood out of Sumner's eyes and restored that statesman to consciousness at the time of the Preston Brooks assault before the war, and now he wondered whether what he had done was worth the trouble.[2] But the Radicals after a while approved his name, and he was ready to wend his way toward the "Halls of the Montezumas." Grant was to have accompanied the new minister, but he, surmising that there was perhaps a wish

---

[1] House Ex. Doc., 39th Cong., 1st sess., no. 73, part i, p. 283; John Bigelow, Retrospections of an Active Life, vol. iii, p. 298; H. M. Flint, Mexico under Maximilian, pp. 169–71.

[2] Johnson Papers.

to be rid of him at Washington, refused to go.   It was a "diplomatic service," he said, for which he was not fitted "either by education or taste." [1]   Therefore General Sherman, who liked the assignment little better, was sent instead.   The *Susquehanna*, which had just been fitted out for service in the North Atlantic squadron, was detailed to convey the two men southward. [2]   They received their instructions.   "In no event," said Seward to Campbell, "will you officially recognize the Prince Maximilian, who claims to be Emperor, or any other person, chief or combination as exercising the executive authority of Mexico," than President Juarez. [3]

The *Susquehanna* left New York on November 10, 1866, and proceeded to Havana, going thence to Vera Cruz.   But she was unable to land the ambassadors, since that port was in the hands of Maximilian, and Juarez could not be reached by that road.   He was said to be, at the time, at or near San Luis Potosi.   Therefore the ship weighed anchor and steamed away to Tampico, where it arrived on December 4.   This place was in possession of the republican troops.   Here it was learned that Juarez was still at Chihuahua, and after sending him a message General Sherman and Minister Campbell continued north to Brazos Santiago in Texas.   They visited Matamoras.   But both men were now heartily tired of the wild goose chase upon which they had come.   "I have not the remotest idea," Sherman wrote to his brother, "of riding on muleback a thousand miles in Mexico to find its chief magistrate." [4]   Campbell determined to remain after Sherman had returned home, with a view to establishing communication with Juarez through Monterey, but he found that the Liberal chiefs now were at war with one another.   "I am somewhat in the situation of Japhet in search of his father," he wrote the President from Port Isabel. [5]   He was "wandering by sea and by land on the inhospitable border of Mexico," he told Seward, and the service was not more

[1] Johnson Papers, Oct. 21, 1866 ; Adam Badeau, Grant in Peace, p. 54.
[2] Welles, vol. ii, p. 621.
[3] F. W. Seward, Seward at Washington, vol. iii, p. 362.
[4] Sherman Letters, p. 282.   [5] Johnson Papers.

pleasant for him than it was profitable to the government.[1] He concluded that his presence on the frontier must be "unimportant, if not harmful, until the residence of the republican government under Juarez shall have been definitely ascertained," [2] and before Christmas time the new envoy extraordinary and minister plenipotentiary was in New Orleans, while General Sherman had resumed his command in St. Louis.

It was all "a miserable bungling piece of business" in the opinion of Welles, who ordered the *Susquehanna* back to New York,[3] and the Secretary of the Navy correctly voiced the feelings of many other men.

Service more effective in shaping the course of affairs was boldly performed, as the opportunity offered, by General Sheridan. Grant abated none of his faith because of the changing of his plan to despatch Schofield to Mexico. "The Secretary of State, I fear," Grant wrote to Sheridan, "is working against the Liberal cause in Mexico." [4] He believed that the French invasion was a part of the Southern rebellion and that the task of restoring peace would not be completed until the foreign army, and the Emperor, whom it had set upon a throne, were expelled.[5] Nine and a half-tenths of the Mexican people, Sheridan said, were opposed to Maximilian and wished him out of the country.[6] With Grant's secret favor Sheridan made feints upon the border. He despatched scouts across the Rio Grande to obtain information and opened communication with Juarez. He conducted inquiries as to forage and let go undenied reports that he meant to enter Mexico with a considerable body of troops. He required ex-Confederate émigrés to procure military permits before crossing the international boundary. He even supplied the republican leaders with arms, despite the protests of the State Department at Washington, and by his activity in a number of ways so alarmed the Impe-

[1] House Ex. Doc., 40th Cong., 1st sess., no. 30, p. 31.

[2] Ibid., p. 23.

[3] Diary, vol. ii, p. 649.

[4] O. R., series i, vol. xlviii, part ii, p. 1242.

[5] Personal Memoirs of P. H. Sheridan, p. 210.

[6] O. R., series i, vol. xlviii, part ii, p. 1252.

rialists and put heart into the "Juarists" that Maximilian's power in northern Mexico was in no long time brought to an end.[1]

Meanwhile, though he must frown upon the more direct methods of the military commanders, Seward was pressing Maximilian by every diplomatic agency at his hand. He protested to France through John Bigelow, now our minister in Paris, against the order to treat the "Juarists" as "gangs of criminals and robbers" to be shot whenever they could be captured. This rule he declared to be in violation of the "rights which the law of nations invariably accords to prisoners of war." It was "repugnant to the sentiments of modern civilization and the instincts of humanity." [2] It was no matter that Juarez's term as president had come to an end in the midst of the country's troubles. Most arbitrarily and irregularly he had declared himself reëlected in spite of the protests of a rival for the place, a fact which failed to unsettle the complete faith reposed in him in the United States.[3]

The French were enlisting troops in Egypt, since it was held that colored men could better withstand the inroads of the Mexican climate. These, Seward said, were servile; he protested against their use in the campaign in defence of Maximilian's throne.[4] He was informed that the Emperor would attempt to introduce in Mexico a kind of peonage not easily distinguishable from slavery. The Southern planter with his blacks might cross the border and perpetuate an abominable social system, which by a long war the United States had just put under foot. Seward was heard from also on this subject.[5] Austria was said to be recruiting volunteers for the Mexican service. She must cease, Seward wrote to Minister Motley at Vienna.[6] The war of France against Mexico, now in progress

[1] Personal Memoirs of P. H. Sheridan, pp. 217, 218, 224.
[2] Senate Ex. Doc., 39th Cong., 1st sess., no. 5, pp. 19–20.
[3] House Ex. Doc., 39th Cong., 1st sess., no. 73, part i, p. 523; Dip. corr., 1866–7, vol. iii, pp. 17–23.
[4] Senate Ex. Doc., 39th Cong., 1st sess., no. 6, p. 69.
[5] House Ex. Doc., 39th Cong., 1st sess., no. 13, p. 12.
[6] Senate Ex. Doc., 39th Cong., 1st sess., no. 54, pp. 3, 4.

for several years, had begun "with a disclaimer of all political and dynastic designs." But that war, Seward continued, has "subsequently taken upon itself and now distinctly wears the character of an European intervention to overthrow that domestic republican government, and to erect in its stead a European imperial military despotism by military force." [1]

The French must get out of Mexico. What would follow this movement need not be anticipated. Bismarck had opened his series of Prussian wars. He would soon strike at Austria. The fate of France also impended, in dynastic weakness and a tottering financial structure. The opposition in the French Chambers, while not numerically strong, under leaders like Jules Favre, pitilessly assailed the government for its Mexican policy. The expedition had been undertaken to collect a few paltry claims, this orator said; the nation had expended upon it already in June, 1865, 400 millions of francs.[2] A year later, said La Liberté, though the debt to be recovered was insignificant, Mexico owed France 250 millions of francs.[3]

The Foreign Office in Paris would have it understood that the French nation did not carry "monarchical traditions in the folds of its flag," [4] that France did not have "the habit of marching except to her own tune," [5] and that her troops would retire, when they did retire, "because it suited her convenience and interests to retire, and for no other reason." [6] But the Emperor was heartily weary of the whole subject; with "that wretched miserable Mexico," Drouyn de Lhuys told Bigelow, he would be glad to be done.[7] "Our occupation," the Minister of Foreign Affairs wrote to the Minister of France in Mexico in January, 1866, "must be brought to an end," and Baron Saillard was sent out to prepare the way for that result.[8]

As a beginning of the unwelcome business, Napoleon in a

[1] Senate Ex. Doc., 39th Cong., 1st sess., no. 54, p. 9.
[2] House Ex. Doc., 39th Cong., 1st sess., no. 20, p. 214.
[3] Ibid., 2d sess., no. 76, p. 137.
[4] Ibid., 1st sess., no. 73, part i, p. 287.   [5] Ibid., part ii, p. 544.
[6] Senate Ex. Doc., 39th Cong., 1st sess., no. 56.
[7] John Bigelow, Retrospections, vol. iii, p. 461.
[8] House Ex. Doc., 39th Cong., 2d sess., no. 76, p. 57.

speech opening the legislative chambers announced that the
expedition to Mexico "approached its close." [1] In due time
it was determined that the troops should be withdrawn in three
parts, the first in November, 1866, the second in March, 1867,
and the remainder in November, 1867.[2] The republican forces
in Mexico were returning to areas which for a time had been
cleared of them, and Maximilian's doom seemed near at hand.
He was urged to abdicate and return to his beloved Miramar.
Napoleon sent General Castelnau upon a special mission to
Mexico to say that not another man, not another cent of money
could be given to the failing cause.[3] Carlotta, the Emperor's
brave and amiable princess, in the heat of summer, embarked
for Europe. Every argument which love of her husband could
suggest, every female grace which could be called upon to move
Napoleon and others whom she had crossed the sea to visit,
she fully employed. Her health broke down; soon her reason
was quite dethroned.

Maximilian's impulse was to go to her and leave his new
realm behind him forever. On a patriotic national anniver-
sary in September, 1865, he had told the people that now every
drop of his blood was Mexican.[4] No Hapsburg, he proudly
said, had ever deserted an arduous post. But torn between
duty to the country whose affairs he had come to direct, and
love for his wife, his home and even his own personal safety,
in October, 1866, he left Mexico City for Orizaba. The Austrian frigate, *Elizabeth*, stood in the roadstead at Vera Cruz
ready to carry him back to Europe. It was confidently supposed that he would board the ship and depart. But by the
first day of December he had resolved to remain to meet whatever fate the future might hold for him.

The French government had not kept its faith on the subject
of the departure of the first detachment of the expeditionary
army in the autumn of 1866, and Minister Bigelow at once

[1] House Ex. Doc., 39th Cong., 1st sess., no. 73, part ii, p. 560.
[2] John Bigelow, Retrospections of an Active Life, vol. ii, pp. 414,
428; Dip. corr., 1866-7, vol. i, pp. 306, 378.
[3] House Ex. Doc., 40th Cong., 1st sess., no. 30, p. 14.
[4] Ibid., 39th Cong., 1st sess., no. 73, part i, p. 233.

pressed the Marquis de Moustier, who had taken Drouyn de Lhuys's place at the Foreign Office. Even the Emperor himself was visited and made to explain his course.[1] Seward's exertions were redoubled, through every agency of the State Department, though outwardly his attitude was calm. To questioners he replied as Lincoln had done by relating a story. He likened Maximilian to a rat looking for a hole to crawl out of. We could afford to indulge him a little; his end was not far away.[2] "The moral influence wielded by the government of the United States has destroyed this Empire," said Marshal Bazaine to General Magruder in Mexico City. He informally proposed to open negotiations with the United States with a view to the establishment of some new form of government in order to protect the interests of French subjects in Mexico.[3] The Marquis de Moustier and a group of men in Paris stood behind this plan. Let a president be chosen, any one acceptable to the people and to the United States, always excepting Juarez with whom France so long had been at war.[4] Maximilian and the French in Paris were no longer friends. He would hold no communication with them.[5] Minister Bigelow informed Seward that there were two governments in Mexico, besides that which was recognized by the United States; of one of these Maximilian was the head, of the other Marshal Bazaine.[6]

For Napoleon there was no alternative. "Circumstances stronger than my will," he wrote to Bazaine, must influence him in the choice of his course,[7] and he was better than his promise. The whole army retired in the spring of 1867. It evacuated Mexico City on February 5, Bazaine still declaring for the government which had sent him out, "that our mission has never had other object, and that it has never entered within

[1] House Ex. Doc., 40th Cong., 1st sess., no. 30, p. 14; Dip. corr., 1866-7, vol. i, pp. 364, 366.

[2] Phila. Ledger, Aug. 30, 1866.

[3] House Ex. Doc., 40th Cong., 1st sess., no. 30, p. 11.

[4] John Bigelow, Retrospections, vol. iii, pp. 498, 618-9, 625; Dip. corr., 1867-8, vol. i, pp. 218, 290.

[5] Bigelow, Retrospections, vol. iii, p. 624.

[6] Ibid., pp. 418, 499.   [7] Ibid., p. 498.

the intention of France to impose upon you [the Mexican people] any form whatever of government contrary to your sentiments." [1] The interior was cleared of foreign troops; the rear guard on February 22 had reached Puebla. Eight thousand were already in Vera Cruz embarking upon transports and ironclads for the journey back to France.[2] Only about 1500 men who volunteered to continue in the service were left to Maximilian, in addition to the Mexican troops who were fighting for the Empire under native chiefs.[3]

All foreign interests took alarm. What remained of Maximilian's government was discredited on every hand. Great disappointment was felt because of the failure of his attempts to secure the recognition of the United States. He had come as a close friend, if not as an agent of the church, but by the liberality of his rule he had estranged the Mexican clergy. Indeed the entire Papal influence seemed now to be hostile to him.[4] He was surrounded by some of the most infamous men whom the history of the country had disclosed. The representatives in Mexico of Great Britain, Prussia, France, Spain, Belgium and Italy united in denouncing the president of the cabinet, Lares, for robbing the national treasury while he had been a member of Santa Anna's ministry in 1855. The odious careers of Marquez and Miramon who were defending the imperial cause in the field were known to all men. The Emperor was asked not "to prolong a fruitless resistance." [5] But

---

[1] House Ex. Doc., 39th Cong., 1st sess., no. 73, part ii, p. 233. The Emperor in explaining his course to the Chambers in 1867 said: "The idea which had presided over the expedition to Mexico was a grand one: to regenerate a people; to implant amongst them ideas of order and of progress; to open to our commerce vast outlets; and to leave as the trace of our passage the memory of services rendered to civilization. Such was my desire as well as yours. But in the day when the extent of our sacrifices appeared to me to go beyond the interests which had called to us from the other side of the Atlantic I spontaneously decided on the recall of our army." — Dip. corr., 1867–8, vol. i, p. 232.

[2] Senate Ex. Doc., 40th Cong., 1st sess., no. 20, pp. 141–2.

[3] Ibid., p. 233.

[4] John Bigelow, Retrospections, vol. ii, pp. 459–60.

[5] House Ex. Doc., 40th Cong., 1st sess., no. 30, p. 50.

he could not heed such appeals. On February 16 he moved
out of Mexico City at the head of a small body of men to join
his forces at Queretaro, under the command of Miramon.[1]
The Liberals, led by General Escobedo, pressed that place
closely, and on the morning of May 14, 1867, through the
treachery of a member of his staff, who for a sum of money
introduced the republican advance guard into the Emperor's
camp at night, it fell. Maximilian, Miramon, Tomas Mejia
and many other officers of the imperial forces were made
prisoners of war. In a really noble spirit the Emperor begged
that his attendants be well treated. In loyalty they had followed him "through dangers and vicissitudes." Let the punishment be visited upon his person, if his captors thought a victim
necessary. From his temporary capital in San Luis Potosi
Juarez ordered Maximilian, Miramon and Mejia before a court
martial. A slight delay was granted in order that time might
be had for defending counsel to pass the lines and arrive from
Mexico City, which, commanded by Marquez, was under siege
by the Liberal General, Porfirio Diaz.

Long before the end Maximilian's kindred and friends in
Europe had begun their intercessions with the hope of saving
his life. Secretary Seward in response to their addresses and
in answer to the humane impulses of the American people,
urged, through every avenue, the lenient treatment of the royal
prisoner. As early as in April, the Emperor of Austria had
asked for some guaranty of his brother's safety. The United
States should intervene "to spare the world a bloody drama,
and the imperial family in Vienna a terrible grief." [2] Belgium
made a similar request.[3] In a like sense the Queen of England
and the Emperor of France [4] made their influences felt at
Washington as well as in Mexico.

Our Minister Campbell, after he had returned to New Orleans
from his futile trip with Sherman along the coast of Mexico,

[1] House Ex. Doc., 40th Cong., 1st sess., no. 30, p. 45.
[2] Senate Ex. Doc., 40th Cong., 1st sess., no. 20, pp. 57–9; Dip.
corr., 1867–8, vol. i, pp. 564–7.
[3] Dip. corr., 1867–8, vol. i, pp. 636–7.   [4] Ibid., pp. 242, 252.

maintained his make-believe legation on American soil. He was urged by Seward to communicate to Juarez the desire of the United States that Maximilian and his supporters should be accorded the consideration due to prisoners of war under the laws of civilized nations. A special messenger, John White, was procured for the service. The United States despatch boat, *Blackbird*, put at his disposal by General Sheridan, was to proceed in haste to Tampico. But when White came to Brazos Santiago he received information which led him to go the rest of the way overland. It was a rough country, beset with brigands and guerrillas, and the distance to be traversed was not less than 1700 miles, yet he accomplished the journey to San Luis Potosi and back to New Orleans in 13 days.[1]

Even this service, though it was performed promptly, promised to be fruitless, and Campbell chafed under the restraints of his situation. He quarrelled with his secretary, a man named Plumb, with whom he complained it was a "punishment" to be associated. Plumb in turn wrote to the State Department that he was "ashamed" to be seen with Campbell.[2] The minister would return home for a time to solace a sick daughter and to adjust his private affairs. But he was desired to remain where he was. Against his protests he and the members of his suite were paid in paper money instead of specie, since they continued in residence in the United States. He had been pressed, without result, to depart for Juarez's capital, wherever it might be. Now while Maximilian's life was in peril and American interests imperatively demanded that we have a representative on the ground, Seward ordered the minister to his post at once by way of Havana. But there the yellow fever raged, said Mr. Campbell, and, disgusted with the treatment which he had received from first to last at the hands of the State Department on the subject of his impossible mission, he resigned while the crisis was at its height. American interests in Mexico City were confided to the care of Consul Otterbourg, who continued to serve as

---

[1] House Ex. Doc., 40th Cong., 1st sess., no. 30, pp. 58–66.
[2] Johnson Papers.

chargé, until in a little while General Rosecrans went thither as our minister.

The council of war to try the prisoners for their lives met in the Theatre Iturbide in Queretaro. The court sat on the stage, while curious crowds filled the auditory. The proceedings were soon ended. Maximilian and his two generals, adjudged guilty, were condemned to be shot at three o'clock on the afternoon of the 16th day of June. Baron Magnus, the Prussian minister, said that his sovereign, as well as Maximilian's brother, the Emperor of Austria; his cousin, the Queen of England; his brother-in-law, the King of the Belgians; his cousin, the Queen of Spain, and the Kings of Italy and Sweden would jointly and severally guarantee that no one of the three prisoners ever again would set foot upon the soil of Mexico. Seward told Romero that the Prince Maximilian would renounce forever all projects in his late realm; the Emperor of Austria would reëstablish him at once in his rights of succession as archduke. The despatch was forwarded by telegraph to New Orleans in time to catch a steamer to Matamoras.[1]

But Juarez was not to be moved to mercy. No pardon could be given, he said. "The weightiest reasons of justice and the necessity of securing the peace of the nation" opposed the exercise of executive clemency.[2] Our expression of a desire for the safety of Maximilian, so it was said, but increased the peril of the unfortunate prince's situation. Juarez could not afford to let it be thought that he had acted in this matter at the dictation of the government of the United States.[3]

The most that was gained for the prisoners was a reprieve of three days in which to adjust their affairs. Then at seven o'clock on the morning of the 19th of June they were taken from the convent which had been their prison house to the Hill of the Bells and, surrounded by a hollow square of troops, were shot to death. The execution of Maximilian, said the New York Tribune, was "an insult to America." We had asked only "the poor boon" of this man's life and it was refused,

---

[1] Senate Ex. Doc., 40th Cong., 1st sess., no. 20, pp. 17–22.
[2] Ibid., pp. 44, 47.   [3] Ibid., p. 247.

though we had made possible Mexico's triumph over France. Here was but one witness among many ready to attest to the archduke's "progressive statesmanship." He was "an accomplished gentleman." At the end he had proved that he was also "a brave and a self-denying soldier." [1] The sight of him driving through the country behind his team of cream-colored mules, his polite and simple ways as he went in and out among the people, the kindliness and sympathy which he and his Empress had exhibited in their daily lives, were not forgotten by any who now came forward to appraise his character. Offensive orders which had seemed to be his were issued at the dictation of Marshal Bazaine. In killing him, said the London Times, the Mexican republican government had committed "a cruel and dastardly act." He was but a French pawn; not the author, but the victim of dire events — to be plain a victim of Napoleon who, said the Pall Mall Gazette, had deserted and betrayed a friend at the cost of that friend's life.[2]

The day following Maximilian's death, Marquez surrendered Mexico City to General Diaz, who had been besieging the place for upwards of 70 days. In less than a week Vera Cruz also fell, and the "Empire" definitely came to its end. On July 15th, Benito Juarez returned to the capital, after an absence of four years. Seward put a United States revenue cutter at the disposal of Madame Juarez, who had been an exile in New York. She and her seven children, and the members of her suite, repaired to New Orleans, from which place they were duly conveyed by the government of the United States to Vera Cruz.[3] Maximilian's kindred in Europe, after a few months' delay, enjoyed the consolation of receiving his remains for burial in Austria. "The republic of Mexico having been relieved from foreign intervention," said President Johnson to Congress when it assembled in December, was "earnestly engaged in efforts to reëstablish her constitutional system of government."

[1] New York Tribune, July 1, 1867.
[2] Quoted in N. Y. Tribune, July 18, 1867.
[3] Senate Ex. Doc., 40th Cong., 1st sess., no. 20, pp. 284–6.

The "Irish republic," while it led a more shadowy existence than the republic of Mexico, made similar demands upon American sympathy. The Fenian Brotherhood, and Sisterhood, for there were auxiliary bodies of women to prepare lint and bandages for the wounded in the coming war for independence, and to organize fairs and festivals for the pecuniary benefit of the movement, directed a new Irish conspiracy. At its head stood James Stephens, who by travel on foot over every part of Ireland had intimately acquainted himself with the character of the people, and gained their confidence. In a peasants' rising in 1848 he had been wounded in the thigh. Subsequently he escaped to France, where for several years he followed his studious inclinations, all the while nourishing a desire to strike a blow for Irish freedom. In 1857 he returned to England and formed his secret political Fenian society. Soon he had brought into the organization 30,000 men, who were drilled and otherwise prepared for military service. In each town the system called, in the first place, for a leader who was to be known as a "Centre," and was to exercise the duties of a colonel. This "Centre" formed "Circles," each comprising from 50 to 150 men standing under the direction of "A," "B," "C," etc., in the order of their creation, "A," "B," "C," etc., having the rank and authority of captains in a regiment. There was dire need of money to promote the scheme, and in 1858 Stephens visited America, which had become a haven for large numbers of his countrymen. He was met in New York by John O'Mahony and Michael Doheny, old comrades in revolution in 1848, and efforts were made to consolidate the Irish in the United States. Societies were established in many places. But money came slowly in, and Stephens after a few months of travel and observation returned home.[1]

The Civil War in the United States made the work of liberating Ireland through American aid even more difficult than it

[1] For these and other facts see a book entitled James Stephens, Chief Organizer of the Irish Republic, Embracing an Account of the Origin and Progress of the Fenian Brotherhood, published anonymously by Carleton, New York, 1866.

otherwise might have been. Up to this time Stephens had been the acknowledged head of the Fenian organization, both in Europe and America, but in the winter of 1863–4 a convention, to be followed by a large fair, was called to meet in Chicago. Delegates came to it from many states and, after prolonged debate, they determined to establish a separate national organization under the presidency of O'Mahony with the purpose of giving orders to, rather than receiving them from, the leaders in Ireland. Stephens, with a view to finding out what his new position might be in reference to American aid for his war for Irish freedom, which was still never begun, again visited America. He issued further appeals, but he received, so he alleged, but a paltry $15,000.[1] Another convention assembled in Cincinnati in January, 1865, but the sinews of war were still denied him, though he wrote to the body restating his urgent needs. Instead of money delegates were sent to Ireland with papers which the British authorities seized. Stephens was arrested, as were many other leaders, and a series of state trials and penal sentences produced a panic among the conspirators.

The Irish in America now were more than ever disposed to follow their own lights. Many had seen service in the Union armies during the war and came out of it doughty soldiers, ready for the most daring undertakings. The hour to strike in Ireland seemed farther than ever away; the Fenians in America would advance upon and seize Canada. The way was clear. The American nation would not be allowed to forget what useful services the Irish had performed in its recent struggle to put down rebellion in the South, nor the enmity which England had shown for the Union during the progress of the conflict. The people of the United States had gained their independence from England by revolution, and had founded a republic. Could it be supposed that they would raise a hand to prevent the Irish from coming to enjoy so excellent a boon by exactly similar means? The English government during the late war with the South had recognized the belligerent rights of the Southern states. Could the American government

[1] Op. cit., p. 62.

do less for Ireland when she should be at war with Great Britain? Stephens's attack on English power through Ireland might be well enough; much better would it be to gain a base in America for the manufacture of munitions and the fitting out of fleets which, sailing down the St. Lawrence, might bring British tyranny to an end.

In October, 1865, Fenians from many parts of the country gathered in Philadelphia. For days the secret and public meetings continued. All the militant Irish of America were organized into a "Republic," with a "Congress," a "Secretary of War," a "Secretary of the Treasury," and so forth. Each state would have its "Senators," and there would be a complete independent Irish government, patterned after the government of the United States, making laws, declaring wars and exercising the powers of sovereignty within the boundaries of the United States. O'Mahony was reëlected President. The costly mansion of a man named Moffatt, a manufacturer and vender of pills, in Union Square in New York, was hired for the uses of the conspirators. Bonds began to be printed. Pieces of paper adorned with pictures of the goddess of liberty, harps, shamrocks and sunbursts, promising to pay the holders the sums of money named upon their face, "ninety days after the establishment of the Irish Republic," were sold. Poor scullion girls, the Pats and Mikes who were digging ditches and building railroad embankments over all the United States, were besought to give their savings to the pure patriots about to strike the fetters from Ireland.[1] Such fantastic designs upon a well-founded government scarcely ever had been cherished by any body of fools in the history of nations. Such fraud and downright stealing of money from the ignorant and the poor in the name of country, it may be hoped, will be seen not soon again.

Quarrels not only about policies, but also for the possession of the funds, were promptly developed within the organization. "The" O'Mahony, "Head Centre," or President, as he might be called, was an impractical idealist. In person he was near-

[1] Fac-simile of bond in Frank Leslie's Newspaper, Dec. 2, 1865.

sighted; his hair was long — he had vowed that he would not cut it until Ireland should be free. But he had the love of a faction in the party, and he was possessed of enough common sense to see the futility of conquering England by way of Canada. Such old-fogyish methods were not for another group of leaders, who seceded from the organization to march under the banners of William R. Roberts, Vice-President of the "Republic," and General Thomas W. Sweeny, "Secretary of War." These men would capture Canada at once.

Roberts was a master hand in the general occupation of "twisting the British lion's tail." He would begin a speech with praise of the spirit of the American colonies, which had enabled them to rise against "his imbecile Majesty, the royal brute, George III" and proceed to denounce the "Saxon cutthroats," the "Norman robbers," the "human butchers and the brutal and unrelenting tyrants" who were treading out the life of Ireland to-day. The Irish people were made strong by the "concentrated hate of seven centuries of insult and wrongs, burning and seething" in their hearts; the Fenian Brotherhood wrought for the triumph of "the holiest cause that tongue or sword of mortal ever lost or gained."[1] "Terrific cheering" and cries of "God bless him" from men and women with wet eyes attested to his oratorical power and their emotionalism.

Sweeny, born in Cork in 1822, had lost an arm at Cherubusco in our Mexican War and bore the wounds of service in the Union army during the Civil War. He and his following felt themselves deeply outraged when he was dismissed from the United States service because of his activity in the Fenian organization. They said it was but one more proof of Seward's obsequious allegiance to Great Britain.[2]

The Brotherhood in America was now definitely divided into the O'Mahonyites and the followers of Roberts, and the war for the freedom of Ireland had degenerated into little more than a fight for the possession of the money contributed by a horde of unhappy dupes.

[1] Address at Cooper Institute, N. Y., Sept. 27, 1865, a pamphlet.
[2] Phila. Ledger, Jan. 10, 1866; New York Nation, Jan. 18, 1866.

As preposterous as their antics were, there was real fear from time to time that these international adventurers might mar our pleasant diplomatic relations with Great Britain. The habeas corpus act had been suspended in Ireland. Men were arrested upon mere suspicion. Some Oulahan, Casey or O'Boyle, an American citizen, a gallant soldier, it now and again appeared, in the late war for the Union, was arrested for high crimes and misdemeanors. How monstrous did it seem when one who had fought in forty battles against the "rebels" in the South and carried a dozen "honorable wounds" became a victim of "British tyranny"! On April 20, 1866, there were in Irish jails no less than 54 men who asserted that they were American citizens.[1] Letters from their friends, memorials from private associations, resolutions of boards of aldermen in cities and of state legislatures came to American Consul West at Dublin, Minister Adams in London, the Secretary of State and the President at Washington. All the agencies of the United States government must be employed to secure the release of this Oulahan, Casey or O'Boyle from vile imprisonment. They had perpetrated deeds for which, said the London Times, they would have been hanged in America.[2] Lord Clarendon expressed the hope that Minister Adams would not attempt "to hold over them the shelter of his diplomatic mantle."[3] But the State Department evaded no duty and took the pains repeatedly to inquire about the fate of Irish American prisoners in Ireland, and to protest, when grounds for intervention were at hand. On the other side, not unnaturally, pressure was brought to bear upon the British Cabinet to remonstrate with the United States for permitting soldiers to be drilled and money to be collected within its territory for the purpose of conducting a war against a friendly power.[4]

Meanwhile James Stephens, C.O.I.R., cabalistic letters which meant simply that he was the Chief Organizer of the Irish Republic, with the assistance of friends, had escaped by

---

[1] House Ex. Doc., 40th Cong., 2d sess., no. 157, p. 219.
[2] Dip. corr. for 1867–8, vol. i, pp. 171–3.
[3] Ibid. for 1866–7, vol. i, p. 76.   [4] Ibid., p. 103.

a rope ladder from Richmond prison near Dublin and was besought to come to America to harmonize the contending Fenian factions. The O'Mahony men in particular urged him to cross the sea, since he, as they, desired that the war might begin in Ireland rather than on the St. Lawrence. The C.O.I.R. went to France, embarked on the French steamer, *Napoleon III*, and arrived in New York in May, 1866. He was a small, thick-set, wiry man. He now wore a full beard and was quite bald. In no way did he seem to be the great leader of a national revolution. But he met a warm welcome. He was serenaded by a band, cheered by the crowds and his hand was wrung by all sorts and conditions of men at his hotel. No attempt was made to conceal the fact that there had been extravagance and theft. The dinners and suppers, the cigars and champagnes, the Turkey carpets, the stuffed furniture and the gilt mirrors at the Moffatt mansion on Union Square were denounced without stint. It was computed that the American branch of the Brotherhood had received nearly $2,000,000 a year.[1] Stephens said that there had come to him less than $150,000 in eight years. Indeed these $150,000 were all that had reached him from America at any time for the fitting out of the Irish revolution.[2]

The C.O.I.R. sought the resignations of all the American leaders. "The" O'Mahony promptly sent in his; Roberts at first evidenced a disposition to follow the example, but under the advice of the "Senate" he thought better of the plan and determined to hold fast to his place. The peace movement, therefore, came to nothing, and the adherents of the two factions continued to call one another thieves and to exchange like opprobrious names. Stephens succeeded in closing the Moffatt mansion, the lease was offered for sale at $1000 a month and the fine furniture was put under the hammer at an auction house. The officers installed there were dismissed — he ought to have hanged them, he was told by men in his audiences as he later toured the country to make fresh appeals for money to

[1] Phila. Ledger, Dec. 18, 1865.
[2] Ibid., May 19, 1866; Life of Stephens, p. 115.

overthrow the British government by means of his Irish troops. He had held out his hands to the leaders in America, he said; he had received only insults in return.[1]

Meantime his advice was flouted in yet graver ways. O'Mahony, though he had opposed a Canadian expedition, had so far yielded as to favor the projects of B. Doran Killian. Killian had been "Secretary of the Treasury" of the "Republic" in the Moffatt house, and assuring himself of the Roberts faction's purpose to invade Canada, rather than let them gain all the glory of the feat, he prepared to strike a blow from the borders of the state of Maine. At the time there were signs of dissatisfaction in New Brunswick with reference to the union of that province with Canada, and Killian, with sagacity, would launch his assault upon Great Britain at a weak point. He and his confederates moved with secrecy, as befitted men directing so important a military expedition. In April, 1866, an iron steamer was purchased in New York. It was to be filled with arms and sent to Eastport, whence descent would be made upon the island of Campobello on the other side of the British line. Killian who was on the ground gave out the word that he came to attend a Fenian convention. Irishmen arrived on the boats and trains until several hundred were at hand ready for the expected raid. But the sailing of the vessel containing the arms was stopped; the provincial authorities, highly excited by the prospect of an invasion, which might assume no one knew what magnitude, called out troops and sent them to the frontier; British war-ships appeared upon the scene; General Meade hurried north with several companies of artillery; and the undertaking ended in complete failure and ridicule.[2] A few hundred stand of arms, which had come from Portland in a schooner, were seized by order of the United States government on complaint of the British consul,[3] and the "soldiers," deceived and disgusted with such leadership, made their way back as best they could to their various homes.

---

[1] Phila. Ledger, June 1, 1866.

[2] Life and Letters of General Meade, vol. ii, p. 285.

[3] Cf. Diary of Gideon Welles, vol. ii, p. 486.

News of the fiasco had awaited Stephens upon his arrival in New York harbor. It was, he said, "suicidal"; [1] again he denounced it as "wild and criminal." [2] But in his despite the Roberts invasion soon followed. Mysterious accounts of the mobilization of groups of men in the West were circulated in May. Other bodies of men, it was announced, were in motion in the East. The alarm created by the movement was out of all proportion to the actual peril which it spelled for Canada. On May 30th several hundred Fenians were assembled secretly at Buffalo, at Rouse Point, N. Y., and at St. Albans, Vt. Possibly 1500 men crossed the Niagara River in canal boats drawn by tugs on June 1st and with wild cheers raised the green flag over Fort Erie, an old and now abandoned redoubt opposite Buffalo, thrown up by the British during the War of 1812. [3] Companies of regulars and volunteers, assembled from all parts of Canada, moved down and, on the 2d day of June, there was a collision which in Fenian military history came to be known as "the battle of Limestone Ridge." Several were killed and wounded on each side. A considerable number of Irishmen were captured by the Canadian forces and those who remained, without food or artillery, were glad to return to the United States. Farther north, at the head of Lake Champlain, where simultaneously another invading force was active, the Fenians had no better success, though a thousand or more crossed the boundaries of Vermont, and ravaged the country around St. Armand for forty-eight hours until they could be made to recross the line.

Meanwhile our government was not idle. Meade was soon upon the scene. [4] Arms intended for the campaign were seized. Fenians who were returning and some who had not yet crossed the Niagara River were arrested for violating the neutrality laws. Fifteen hundred and sixty-six men were paroled at Buffalo and commanded to go to their homes. Several carloads of the "soldiers" were captured and turned back in

[1] Phila. Ledger, May 12, 1866.   [2] Ibid., June 26, 1866.
[3] N. Y. Tribune, June 2, 1865.
[4] Life and Letters of General Meade, vol. ii, pp. 286–7.

Vermont. The leaders, including Roberts and Sweeny, were arrested and held for trial for their crimes.

The two elements in the Cabinet, Johnson and anti-Johnson, had feared to make any movement which would alienate the Irish vote, and each party aimed to put the blame for action upon the shoulders of the other.[1] But when the right time came, the President issued a proclamation reminding the filibusters of the unlawfulness of their operations and commanding them to disperse.[2] The United States authorities were exhorted to make arrests and bring transgressors to justice at once.[3] Seward informed Great Britain of the steps which the government had taken to bring the border buffoonery to an end. But so much threat and promise from so many noisy fighters prevented an immediate return of public assurance. The Canadian government, it was said, expended two and a half millions of dollars to repel the Irish invasion.[4] The anti-English newspapers, led by Greeley's New York Tribune, which in and out of season in the past had condemned all Irishmen as Democrats, but now pretended to think that they were about to perform the praiseworthy service of dismembering the British Empire, assailed the administration for interfering in the case. Politicians, eagerly seeking the Irish vote, espoused the Fenian cause and proposed in Congress to change the neutrality laws. The men who had been caught must be released.[5] A war of words was waged, Stephens and his party blacking the names of Roberts and Sweeny, who responded in kind with the fervor of their race, while all together heaped abuse upon England and Englishmen, and those who expressed sympathy or even toleration for the British nation.

Stephens, on his side, called Sweeny a coward. He might

---

[1] Diary of Gideon Welles, vol. ii, p. 520. A party of Irish leaders in September, 1866, wrote to Johnson telling him that they would stump the country against him, if he did not secure the release of their friends in prison in England. — Johnson Papers.

[2] Welles, vol. ii, p. 524.   [3] Dip. corr. for 1866–7, vol. i, p. 135.

[4] Phila. Ledger, June 19, 1866.

[5] Resolution of House of Representatives of July 23; see House Ex. Doc., 39th Cong., 1st sess., no. 154.

have led his soldiers to victory; but while they went forward he did not move a foot off American soil.[1] Any who would even talk about a Canadian invasion was "a mortal enemy to his country and his race." As for Stephens he would attack England at her vital point in, Ireland. He would unfurl the green flag at the head of 50,000 men before the end of the year 1866.[2] He knew the armies of Europe, he said in Philadelphia, and there had never been such an army as that which he had organized to fight for Irish liberty.[3]

Men on the other side stood ready to prove that Stephens was really a British spy in disguise. He had got out of Richmond prison; how had he escaped, if not by purchase of his freedom in promises to betray his trust and engagement to serve the enemy?[4] At any rate, said the New York Nation, voicing an intelligent, unpartisan view, he was "the most impudent of all the famous blatterers and swindlers" who had ever crossed the water "to ply their vocation on American soil."[5]

Sweeny, in the custody of the United States authorities in St. Albans, Vt., issued an address to his brother Fenians. The fault lay with the United States government, not with him, he said. But for its unaccountable interference "no power which England could have brought to bear" would have impeded "the triumphant advance of our brave boys" until "the green flag of our fathers" should have been made to float from the dome of Canada's capitol.[6] The president of the Fenian "Senate" also issued an address in which he denounced the "treachery" of Seward. It was with amazement and disgust that he noted how "the name of American republicanism" had been "sullied by such truckling to the necessities of foreign despotism."[7]

But these futile attempts to effect the conquest of Great Britain by means of a Canadian invasion did not deter the

[1] N. Y. Tribune, Aug. 29, 1866. [2] Ibid., Oct. 29, 1866.
[3] Phila. Ledger, June 1, 1866. [4] Ibid., June 27, 1868.
[5] N. Y. Nation, Jan. 3, 1867.
[6] N. Y. Tribune, July 6, 1866. [7] Ibid., July 2, 1866.

leaders from planning new ones. They awaited only the propitious moment, so they loudly alleged, and they kept the United States, as well as the British authorities, in a state of tension for several months. At a Fenian picnic near Buffalo in August, attended by thousands, the "battles" of June were fought over again by sham armies for the sake of the spectacle, but no attempt was made to cross the river. At a Fenian congress in Troy, N. Y., early in September, Roberts received a vote of confidence by a reëlection to the presidency of the Brotherhood, and plans were laid for another grand movement toward the north.[1]

The fact that the Canadian government had seized and held for trial a number of men who had crossed the border in June provoked continual agitation, especially as their cases were now being argued and sentence was being passed upon their crimes. Soon two were condemned to death. One of these, McMahon by name, was an Irish priest who had gone with the army, so it was alleged, to administer spiritual consolation to the wounded; while the other, Lynch, was declared to have been a newspaper correspondent.[2] That they should be hanged was preposterous, and the Fenians in the United States again loudly defied Great Britain. Roberts counselled the Irish everywhere to form themselves into military companies ready for call to service at any moment. The United States neutrality laws would be amended, British influence would soon cease to rule the government at Washington "to your injury and America's shame."[3] The Fenians in Philadelphia passed long resolutions reciting how the Irish had never done England an injury. They had "educated her ignorant kings when her people were buried in Saxon barbarism." Yet did she repay them in this manner. By every means in her power she had sought during the Civil War to help the "rebels" accomplish the dissolution of the Union. Strange it was, therefore, that the United States now should aid her and not the Irish

---

[1] N. Y. Tribune, Sept. 8, 1866.
[2] Phila. Ledger, Nov. 1, 1866; Dip. corr. for 1867–8, vol. i, pp. 182, 193–5. [3] N. Y. Tribune, Nov. 3, 1866.

who had fought that this Union might live. Come what might they would meet the issue as befitted a race which had never "accepted the yoke of the Norman robber." [1] The "Brothers," in Buffalo, pledged themselves to wage war against the "hereditary enemy" as long as Almighty God should permit them to exist; [2] and in Indianapolis they warned Canada that the execution of the Irish prisoners condemned to death would be a "bugle note" for the gathering of an army which would drive the last vestige of British power from the continent of America. [3] Fenians in New York dared Canada to fulfil her threat to hang these men. "The outrage" would be avenged "in the blood of the British oligarchy." [4] Indeed indignation meetings were held on every hand. Rumors of shipments of arms and movements of Irish recruits filled every newspaper. Men on the plains, when they met a coach with news from the East, anxiously inquired whether the Fenians had yet taken Montreal. Out of so much sound it seemed that there must come some military achievement worthy of the name.

The Irish Americans who were under sentence in Canada, like those in the jails of Ireland, sought the protection of the United States government. Seward, who had been so pro-British at the time of the raid, must now, as a matter of course, intercede for the lives of these border warriors. On October 27 he wrote the British minister in their behalf. Their offences were "eminently political." "Sound policy," he said, "coincided with the best impulses of a benevolent nature in recommending tenderness, amnesty and forgiveness." [5] Lynch and McMahon did not stand alone. At the assizes in Toronto in November, 1866, and in January, 1867, nineteen more of the raiders were convicted. [6] But as the day of execution for those who were to be capitally punished approached the prisoners

[1] N. Y. Tribune, Oct. 31, 1866.　　　　[2] Ibid., Nov. 6, 1866.
[3] Phila. Ledger, Nov. 6, 1866.
[4] N. Y. Tribune, Oct. 29, 1866.
[5] Dip. corr. for 1866–7, vol. i, p. 260.
[6] House Ex. Doc., 40th Cong., 1st sess., no. 9; Dip. corr. for 1867–8, vol. i, p. 189.

were granted a respite, which was followed by a commutation of their sentences.[1]

The feeling between the factions did not grow more cordial. The tide against Stephens set in strongly, as the year ended without his promised rising in Ireland. He was compelled to hide himself in New York. The Roberts men accused him of having collected $250,000 in America within a few months.[2] He was "a self-convicted scoundrel and cheat," said a writer in one of their gazettes.[3] A call was issued for a public meeting by "the duped and plundered Irishmen of New York to denounce James Stephens and his infamous colleagues in robbery." [4] At length he secretly made his way to Paris and his enemies were in undisputed control of the field.

At a congress in Cleveland in September, 1867, there was much discussion of plans for renewed attacks upon Canada, but the bonds of the Irish Republic at this time were selling for only twenty cents on the dollar,[5] and to rational men the prospect of any repetition of a raid over the border seemed very remote.

Local disturbances and riots in Ireland by detachments of Stephens's army were followed with interest and sympathy in the United States. Thousands of Irishmen in New York, Philadelphia and other cities proceeded through the streets behind sable hearses, the green flag draped in black, the bands playing dirges and dead marches in honor of the "Manchester Martyrs," as they called three men who were executed for attacking a van containing Fenian prisoners, and shooting a police officer in the streets of that city in England.[6] The municipal governments favored and assisted these and other Fenian demonstrations, and there was ground for fear that a spirit of truculence in the face of this foreign influence would have unhappy results in larger political fields. Though Minister Adams had saved the lives of two men sentenced to death for

[1] Dip. corr. for 1867–8, vol. i, p. 181; Phila. Ledger, Dec. 8, 1866.
[2] Phila. Ledger, Jan. 11, 1867.
[3] Ibid., Jan. 9, 1867.   [4] Ibid., Jan. 12, 1867.
[5] N. Y. Tribune, Sept. 4, 1867.
[6] Ibid., Nov. 29 and Dec. 5, 1867, and Jan. 9, 1868; Phila. Ledger, Jan. 9, 1868.

the shares they had taken in the riot in Manchester, it was proposed in the House of Representatives at Washington to prefer charges against him and to impeach him for his failure to do more in Ireland's behalf.[1] The Irish in America were now more than a party, said the New York Nation ; they formed "a separate political community" which, by flattery, every aspiring faction sought to entice into its particular fold.[2] And the cajolery and cozening of this element proceeded, though it was clear to every intelligent mind that independent nationality for the Irish, as Canning had said, was as unattainable as the restoration of the Heptarchy. Ireland as a nation was as dead as Naples or Hanover.[3]

At the very moment when the officers of the telegraph company which was extending its lines north from California to Behring Strait, for a connection with Europe via Siberia, were making excuses for the abandonment of their project, and Mr. Seward was forwarding them his condolences,[4] the Secretary of State and Baron Edward de Stoeckl, the Czar's minister at Washington, were discussing the terms of a treaty for the transfer of all the Russian colonies in America to the United States. The territory in question formed the extreme northwestern arm of the continent of North America. It extended north on the coast from the old line of 54 degrees and 40 minutes, so famous in history, 200 miles below a harbor and little town called New Archangel, on the island of Sitka in the Alexander Archipelago, to the polar regions, and west to the narrow channel over which, by a few hours' navigation, a voyager might be brought to the coast of Asia. The country embraced in the proposed cession then ran south in a broad peninsula which terminated in a long chain of isles and islets called the Aleutian Islands, enclosing Behring Sea. Upwards of 500,000 square miles of land were comprised in the Russian colonies in America. The country had 4000 statute miles of coast indented by capacious bays and good harbors. It was piled high with mountains, one of them, the peak of St. Elias, at the time believed

---

[1] N. Y. Nation, Nov. 28, 1867.   [2] Ibid., June 27, 1867.
[3] Ibid., Dec. 27, 1866.   [4] N. Y. Tribune, April 2, 1867.

to be the loftiest on the continent.   It was penetrated by great
navigable rivers.   The adjoining waters were studded with
islands — archipelago was added to archipelago.   A careful
measurement of all their shores, it was said, would increase the
coast line to 11,270 miles.

The land had been Russia's by right of discovery.   Peter the
Great, the shipbuilder, a lover of exploration, desired to know
whether Asia and America were joined in one continent or were
separated by an arm of the sea.   He died before his design to
send an expedition to the region could be realized, and his
Empress, Catherine, was left to carry forward his plans.   Vitus
Behring, a Dane, was engaged to make the voyage into these
strange waters.   In 1728 he set out in a small packet boat from
the Asiatic coast and entered the sea and the strait which came
afterward, appropriately, to bear his name.   The Russian title
was confirmed by later navigators.   To reap the advantages of
the trade in peltry in this district a company was formed in St.
Petersburg, in 1799, on the lines of the Hudson's Bay Company, which under British charter operated in the Arctic latitudes farther east in America.   Posts were established to engage in the same business in a like manner.   Under the name
of the Russian American Company it was granted and exercised
patriarchal powers over the country, politically as well as com-
mercially.   When its charter expired its rights were extended
for another period of years, and now the time was near at hand
when they again would need to be extended.   Recently it had
underlet some part of its franchises to the Hudson's Bay Company, and ambitious men in California were desirous that an
American company should be created to take over these interests.
Vague suggestions that the entire country might be ceded to
the United States had been heard in Washington before the
Civil War, but now at its end, with the public finances in disorder, in a time of unparalleled political disturbance, it would
have seemed impossible to most men, if they had pondered the
question at all, that the project could be revived.[1]

[1] These facts are gleaned mainly from Sumner's speech in the
United States Senate, House Ex. Doc., 40th Cong., 2d sess., no. 177,

Necessary it may have been under all the circumstances to act quickly and stealthily. At any rate such was the course adopted by the Secretary of State. He was a recognized disciple of national expansion. Standing at St. Paul in 1860, Seward had said to the Russian people: "Go on and build up your outposts all along the coast, up even to the Arctic Ocean; they will yet become the outposts of my own country — monuments of the civilization of the United States in the northwest." [1] Enthusiasm and destiny working to one end now brought his prophecy to realization. With an informal tender of the country at a price of $10,000,000 it was as informally stated that $5,000,000 might be paid for it. Bargaining led to an agreement in a provisional way to fix the sum at $7,000,000, to which it was conceived that $200,000 might be added to effect the extinguishment of certain franchises held by the Russian trading company.

Seward wrote confidentially to Stanton on March 14 requesting the Secretary of War to ask Halleck in San Francisco by telegraph for his opinion of the value of the Russian colonies "supposing that at some future period it might be in contemplation to buy these possessions for the United States." [2] Five days later, on March 19, the proposed treaty appeared in a Cabinet meeting and met the favor of the President and of every one present.[3] But certain negotiations were yet to be concluded before the papers could be signed. It was on the evening of the 29th day of March, near the end of the first of the series of short sessions of a new Congress, at loggerheads with the President and with all who, like Mr. Seward, gave their adhesion to Johnson's policies, that the Secretary of State was interrupted at a game of whist by the Russian minister. Informed that the minister had just received advices from St. Petersburg, conferring upon him full authority to proceed, Mr.

p. 124; cf. K. Coman, Economic Beginnings of the Far West, vol. i, pp. 193–221.

[1] F. W. Seward, Seward at Washington, vol. iii, p. 346.
[2] Stanton Papers in Library of Congress.
[3] Welles, vol. iii, p. 68.

Seward summoned his clerks and secretaries to the State Department, while Baron de Stoeckl assembled his forces at the Russian legation. Charles Sumner, the chairman of the Senate Committee on Foreign Relations, was sent for also, and before the clock had struck four on the morning of the 30th the papers were ready, the signatures were attached and the work was at an end.[1]

In a few hours more "the treaty between the United States of America and the Emperor of all the Russias, for the cession to the United States of all the territory and dominion now possessed by his Majesty on the continent of America and in the adjacent islands," made its appearance in the Senate for the "advice and consent" of that body. It was read for the first time and on Mr. Sumner's motion was referred to his Committee on Foreign Relations.[2]

The news of what had been done now went to the country to fill men with amazement. The most that even well-read persons knew about Russian America was the fact that it was being crossed by a telegraph line bound dubiously for Europe through Siberia; that its waters contained whales which New Bedford men each season tried to catch, their boats having been sunk, burned and scattered at a recent time by the "rebel pirate," *Shenandoah;* that it was the home of the fur seal and of an animal with tusks of ivory called the walrus. There was a general turning to the encyclopædias and the gazetteers, whence little light was shed upon the subject. A few had read the lines in Campbell's "Pleasures of Hope," which now came forward to plague the annexationists, for here the pilot's bark, careering "o'er unfathomed fields," swept on

> "where scarce a summer smiles
> On Behring's rocks or Greenland's naked isles.
> Cold on his midnight watch the breezes blow
> From wastes that slumber in eternal snow,
> And waft across the waves' tumultuous roar
> The wolf's long howl from Ounalaska's shore."

[1] F. W. Seward, Seward at Washington, vol. iii, pp. 347–9; E. L. Pierce, Memoirs and Letters of Sumner, vol. iv, pp. 324–5.

[2] Executive Journal of the Senate, vol. xv, pp. 588–9.

Only a rare scientist, and the engineers who had been planting telegraph poles in the country, had more particular knowledge about it. No one had wished for such an annexation of land, barring the people on the Pacific coast who promptly came forward with nearly unanimous voice in support of the treaty. Already, so it was said, we were burdened with territory which we had no population to fill. The Indians within the present boundaries of the republic strained our power to govern aboriginal peoples. Could it be that we would now, with open eyes, seek to add to our difficulties by increasing the number of such peoples under our national care? The purchase price was large; the annual charges for administration, civil and military, would be yet greater, and continuing. The territory included in the proposed cession was not contiguous to the national domain. It lay away at an inconvenient and a dangerous distance. The treaty had been secretly prepared, and signed and foisted upon the country at four o'clock in the morning. It was a dark deed done in the night.

These considerations were entirely apart from others having to do with the character of the territory which it was proposed that we should buy. The New York World said that it was a "sucked orange." It contained nothing of value but fur-bearing animals, and these had been hunted until they were nearly extinct. Except for the Aleutian Islands and a narrow strip of land extending along the southern coast the country would be not worth taking as a gift.[1] If the truth were known, the treaty would be found to conceal a plot against the life of that obstreperous man, General Ben Butler, who could now be got rid of by appointing him governor of the new territory.[2] Unless gold were found in the country much time would elapse before it would be blessed with Hoe printing presses, Methodist chapels and a metropolitan police.[3]

It was "a frozen wilderness," said the New York Tribune.[4]

[1] N. Y. World, April 1, 1867.
[2] Ibid., quoted in Phila. Ledger, April 3, 1867.
[3] Ibid., April 2, 1867.
[4] Washington corr. of the Tribune, April 9, 1867.

No one knew what we wanted of it unless it were "to take a solitude and call it Seward, by erecting it into a territory," said the New York Nation.[1] The expense of supporting one soldier in Washington was $1100 a year, said the New York Tribune; it would be twice as much in "Seward's desert." On the Nebraska plains it was costing the government $115,000 to kill one Indian; it would cost $300,000 a head to kill Seward's Indians. Not in the history of diplomacy had been seen "such insensate folly as this treaty." There should be appropriate punishment for a Secretary of State who "secretly and unadvisedly, and of his own reckless folly and wastefulness" had put the country in such a position that for the Senate to reject the treaty would appear to be a violation of the public faith.[2]

In truth now it did seem that to ratify the action of the State Department was almost a national duty. The powerful adhesion of Sumner, which Seward had shrewdly enough obtained beforehand, was decisive for many senators, who otherwise would have opposed this measure as they had arrayed themselves against other policies of the administration. The press was quickly enlisted in the work of making sentiment favorable to the treaty. The country to be ceded to us was ten times as large as New York state. It was larger than the original thirteen states of the Union, larger than the empires of France and Austria, taken together.[3] It had a climate temperate and cold by turns, according as it was desired to prove a point concerning a valuable resource. It should be annexed for its wheat and its whales, its barley and its walrus, its turnips and its icebergs, its gold and its white bears. Everywhere winter slept in the lap of May.[4] To aid his journalists Seward was dining the "conscript fathers," the "Esquimaux senators," as they were called, to increase their enthusiasm for the project, and to bring more into the "Ring." The Secretary's dinner table was covered first with a map of Russian America,

[1] April 4, 1867.

[2] Washington corr., N. Y. Tribune, April 9, 1867.

[3] N. Y. Herald, April 2, 1867.   [4] N. Y. Tribune, April 9, 1867.

and this cloth was spread with "roast treaty, boiled treaty, treaty in bottles, treaty in decanters, treaty garnished with appointments to office," until little remained to be done.[1]

But considerations more potent than these were the facts that Russia had shown herself to be a friend of the North in its late war with the Southern Confederacy, and that England at this same time had been a nearly open enemy. On the one side Russia might not be rebuffed by declining her hand when she had extended it, offering her territory on this continent for a paltry $7,200,000; on the other side England was to be discomfited. It was known, said the newspapers, that Sir Frederick Bruce, the British Minister at Washington, upon the receipt of the news of the signing of the treaty, had telegraphed home to ask what he should do in the grave case.[2] Russian America on the Pacific Coast in our hands, it would be not long before the British possessions there would come to us also. The cession, said the New York Herald, might be taken to be a "hint" from the Czar to England and France that they had "no business on this continent." "It was in short a flank movement" upon Canada. Soon the world would see in the northwest "a hostile cockney with a watchful Yankee on each side of him," and John Bull would be led to understand that his only course was a sale of his interests there to Brother Jonathan.[3]

In one way or another, for this reason or that, the senators were soon aligned under Sumner's leadership on the side of the treaty. The few days at his disposal were busily occupied in digesting the material in Washington on the subject of the country which it was proposed to purchase. Printed accounts in other languages were brought to his hand through the services of translators attached to the legations. On April 8 the treaty was reported out of the Committee on Foreign Relations without amendment with a recommendation that it be ratified,[4]

---

[1] N. Y. Herald, April 9, 1867; N. Y. Tribune, April 9, 1867.
[2] Washington corr., N. Y. Tribune, April 1, 1867.
[3] N. Y. Tribune, April 1, 1867.
[4] Executive Journal, vol. xv, p. 662.

and the next day Sumner delivered an address of three or more hours in length, which remains to this time an unusually fair and informing statement as to the history, the climate, the natural configuration, the population, the resources — the forests, mines, furs, fisheries — of this particular part of the earth's surface. He appealed to the testimony of geographers and navigators — Humboldt, Billings, Lisiansky, Luetke, Kotzebue, Portlock, Cook, Meares, von Wrangel. When he had finished, he observed that he had "done little more than hold the scales." If these had inclined on either side, he continued, it was "because reason or testimony on that side was the weightier."

But he had not hesitated to use some of the rhetoric of the advocate. Soon, said he, if the land were annexed to the United States "a practical race of intrepid navigators will swarm the coast ready for any enterprise of business or patriotism. Commerce will find new arms; the country new defenders; the national flag new hands to bear it aloft." Bestow the republican form of government upon the territory, he urged, "and you will bestow what is better than all you can receive, whether quintals of fish, sands of gold, choicest fur or most beautiful ivory." Cato had said that kings were "carnivorous animals." Therefore the Roman Senate had decreed that none should be allowed within the gates of the city. "Our city," exclaimed Sumner, "can be nothing less than the North American continent with the gates on all the surrounding seas." He found the treaty to be "a visible step" in this direction. By its terms we should "dismiss one more monarch from this continent." One by one they had retired — "first France; then Spain; then France again, and now Russia, all giving way to that absorbing unity which is declared in the national motto — *E pluribus unum*." [1]

Some Senators were still unconvinced, Fessenden of Maine leading the number. He vainly urged a postponement of final action until the following day, but the motion failed by a vote

[1] From Sumner's speech printed in House Ex. Doc., 40th Cong., 2d sess., no. 177, pp. 124–89; Sumner's Works, vol. xi, pp. 183 et seq.

of 29 to 12. Standing with him in opposition were Anthony of Rhode Island, Chandler of Michigan, Conkling of New York, Cragin of New Hampshire, Ferry of Connecticut, Henderson of Missouri, Howe of Wisconsin, Lot Morrill of Maine, Justin Morrill of Vermont, Patterson of New Hampshire and Tipton of Nebraska. But all abandoned him in the final division except Morrill of Vermont, though two Senators, Ferry and Howe, abstained from taking part in the ballot, and on April 9 the treaty was ratified.[1]

While the purchase money was yet to be paid to Russia, and this sum could not be appropriated for the purpose without the assent of the House of Representatives, and muttering loud and general was heard, indicating that such action might not be had without angry scenes, it was assumed that the new country was now a part of the United States. Stump orators and torchlight processions, said the Philadelphia Ledger,[2] would soon be seen in this "dreary waste of glaciers, icebergs, white bears and walrus, fit only as it was for the Esquimaux and drinkers of train oil."[3] As Sumner had declared, no region of equal extent upon the globe was so little known with the exception of the centre of Africa, or possibly Greenland. The interior was in every respect *terra incognita*. A coast survey party under command of Captain W. A. Howard was embarked upon the revenue cutter *Lincoln* at San Francisco, and sent forward at once. George Davidson was in charge of the observations. Sites were to be chosen for custom houses, available coaling stations were to be found, routes were to be laid down for navigators. Scientists acting under the direction of the Smithsonian Institution accompanied the party. A botanist would study the vegetable life, a geologist would note the mineral formations, a meteorologist would make records concerning the climate.[4] Ceremonies were arranged to signalize

[1] Executive Journal, vol. xv, p. 675.   [2] April 11, 1867.
[3] House Ex. Doc., 40th Cong., 2d sess., no. 177, p. 28.
[4] The valuable report of Mr. Davidson and his associates is to be found in House Ex. Doc., 40th Cong., 2d sess., no. 177, pp. 190–361. The results of the trip are summarized in Lippincott's Magazine for November, 1868.

the transfer of the country from the Russian to the American flag. Steamer communication between San Francisco and New Archangel was opened at once.[1] Secretary of the Treasury McCulloch instructed the collector of the port at San Francisco to despatch an agent to the new territory to see that duties were levied and paid on imports from foreign countries.[2]

Travellers bound north for speculation or adventure and the members of the government expedition learned much concerning the ceded territory during the ensuing months. It contained "inexhaustible" coal supplies.[3] The fisheries were even more valuable than had been foreseen. Not less than 100,000 square miles of water were available for the catching of cod. What the Grand Banks of Newfoundland were in the North Atlantic these new banks would be for the fishermen of future years in the North Pacific. The salmon were more numerous here than in Oregon and Washington; 2000 might be taken in a seine at a single haul. The ivory which came from the walrus tusk was worth 70 cents a pound in gold, and this animal abounded everywhere. As for the whale he found at once his retreat and his playground in these waters. No less than 70 American whalers came hither and returned to New Bedford and other ports, at the end of voyages lasting sometimes for two or three years, heavily laden with oil and bone.[4] It was not true that the fur-bearing animals were growing scarce, except in the case of the sea otter in whose peltry there once had been a lucrative trade. The animal was still hunted singly in the skin canoe and was taken with darts nimbly thrown by the aborigines. The number obtained annually was not above 1100, though 70 years before in the Alexander Archipelago alone it had been 8000. So rare now was this "incomparable fur," as Sumner had called it in his speech in the Senate, that each skin was worth not less than from $40 to $70.[5] In respect

[1] Phila. Ledger, May 15, 1867; House Ex. Doc., 40th Cong., 2d sess., no. 177, p. 14.   [2] Phila. Ledger, June 1, 1867.

[3] Correspondence Baltimore Sun, cited in Phila. Ledger, Aug. 18, 1868; cf. Phila. Ledger, Feb. 6, 1868.

[4] Mr. Davidson in Lippincott's Magazine, November, 1868.

[5] House Ex. Doc., 40th Cong., 2d sess., no. 177, pp. 213, 254.

of the red and white fox, the fur seal, the beaver, lynx, sable, muskrat and mink the supply was not diminishing. The Russian trading company had restricted the catch, had restocked the country to prevent the destruction of species, had forbidden the discharge of firearms except under definite conditions, and had made wise regulations of other kinds.

More important than all the rest of the country, so it seemed to many men, was a little island, made up of mossy hills, called St. Paul, in the Pribilof group, set out several hundred miles from the mainland in Behring Sea. This was the home of the fur seal.[1] Here could be seen "a numberless congregation of living animals," varying in size from small pups of 50 pounds to old sea lions of two tons in weight. The animals of about 200 pounds were selected for their skins, after they had been driven inland, where natives armed with clubs struck them upon their snouts until the ground was covered with the dead carcasses. The Russian export of skins in recent years was variously estimated at from 75,000 to 180,000 annually.[2]

True the country was not contiguous to the United States, but it was not so far away from Washington and the civilization of the Atlantic seaboard as California had been up to a very recent time. Everyone could remember when San Francisco might be reached only after six weeks' travel from New York by way of the Isthmus of Panama. Sitka over the Pacific Railroad from Omaha was now but 23 days from New York.[3] Literally on such an empire as Uncle Sam's had become, in summer days at least, the sun never set. A traveller told of reading until midnight in the long evenings by natural light, though it grew dark at two on winter afternoons.[4] As the tide of settlement had come east bringing with it the corrected time of Russia the day in Sitka was earlier by 24 hours than in the United States. The Sitka Sunday was the American Saturday.

[1] House Ex. Doc., 40th Cong., 2d sess., no. 131, p. 5.
[2] See for instance House Ex. Doc., 40th Cong., 2d sess., no. 177, p. 213; House Misc. Doc., 40th Cong., 2d sess., no. 131, p. 5; Senate Ex. Doc., 40th Cong., 2d sess., no. 50.
[3] Davidson's article in Lippincott's Magazine, November, 1868.
[4] Corr. Baltimore Sun quoted in Phila. Ledger, Aug. 18, 1868.

The people were reckoning their time also in accordance with the unreformed Julian calendar, and their Christmas was not celebrated until Twelfth Night in January.

The climate, on the coast at least, was modified by the warm currents of the sea so that, as had been said in incredulous ears, Sitka even in midwinter was not colder than Philadelphia or Washington. Proof of this was found in the fact that the company which here had built ponds, whereon to freeze and collect ice for shipment to San Francisco and China, had been obliged to give up its design. The blocks were neither hard nor thick enough for transportation, and the business must be transferred some 500 miles west, across the gulf, to Kodiak Island which furnished lower temperatures.

It was agreed that the climate was detestable. Heavy rain and dense mist made life unpleasant, and fruitage, because of an absence of sunshine, slow. There were 21 inches of rain in August, 1867, when the government expedition visited the country, 16 in September and 15 in October, a total precipitation of 52 inches in the three months. The forests around Sitka were so wet that they would not burn.[1] The ground was covered to the depth of one or two feet with a damp moss, called sphagnum.[2]

Mr. Sumner in the Senate had said that the whole country did not contain more than 2500 white Russians and half-breeds, and 8000 aborigines, in all about 10,000 persons under the direct government of the fur company, and possibly 50,000 natives of various ethnological groups living outside its jurisdiction. Later estimates did not materially differ from these. The whites were settled at 23 trading posts, placed conveniently on the islands and coasts. At some not more than four or five men were stationed, to trap animals on their own account, and to collect peltry from the Indians for storage and shipment when the company's boats should arrive to take it away. None of the posts except two merited particular attention. New Archangel, or Sitka, as it was now coming to be called, had been

[1] House Ex. Doc., 40th Cong., 2d sess., no. 177, p. 163.
[2] Lippincott's Magazine, November, 1868.

established in 1804 to care for the valuable trade in the skins of the sea otter which then abounded in the Alexander Archipelago. But it still contained only 116 buildings and these were low cabins constructed of hewn logs. In 1833 the place had had 847 inhabitants; only 968 lived here on January 1, 1867. Outside the palisades which surrounded the town was a village of 1000 bold and treacherous Indians. The second most important post was St. Paul on Kodiak Island to which the ice company had gone when it found the winters too warm at Sitka. This town contained about 100 houses, similar to those in New Archangel, and the population was said to number 283 souls.[1]

Not a little excitement followed the purchase of the country by the United States. Speculation began; prices rose. The country on all sides of Sitka was "mapped, bounded and described by stakes," in confident expectation of a land boom.[2] Pioneers had invaded even the garden surrounding the governor's house and the church property.[3] The place would follow the example of San Francisco. In ten years it would be a city of 50,000 people.[4] This far northwestern territory, said General Halleck, in command of the Military Division of the Pacific with his headquarters at San Francisco, whose enthusiasm for the purchase was constant, would soon become what Nature had intended it to be, "the New England of the Pacific."[5]

Throughout the summer the arrangements for the transfer of the country from Russia to the United States proceeded. There was immediate need of a name by which it might be designated. Russian America it had been; it was this no longer. It was the home of the walrus; it had come from Russia and the wags in Congress and the gazettes had not been slow to christen it "Walrussia." But this name, which every one soon

---

[1] Lippincott's Magazine, November, 1868.

[2] Sitka corr., N. Y. Tribune, Oct. 26, 1867.

[3] House Ex. Doc., 40th Cong., 2d sess., no. 177, p. 197; cf. Alfred Holman, article in Century Magazine, February, 1913.

[4] Corr. of Boston Journal reprinted in Phila. Ledger, Dec. 25, 1867.

[5] House Ex. Doc., 40th Cong., 2d sess., no. 177, p. 102.

came to know, was for the convenience of the headline writer
in the newspaper or to add point to the wit of an unfriendly
orator.   Already in his speech in the Senate on April 9 Sumner
pleaded for an "indigenous" name, for "one of the autoch-
thons of the soil."   Alaska was this; it was euphonious.   What
then could be better?   Long ago Captain Cook, the first Eng-
lishman to visit the region, had found it in use among the natives.   It was applied now to the promontory extending south
to the Aleutian Islands.   It was the word earlier used by the
Aleuts when they pointed to the "great land" which lay beyond their island, the continent of America.[1]   General Halleck
wrote to the Adjutant-General's office in Washington on May
22, 1867, urging the choice of this name.[2]   Seward put his
weight in the scales also [3] and soon it was adopted by the government, the newspapers and the public generally.[4]

The military district of Alaska was created.   At first attached
to the Military Department of Washington Territory,[5] because
of greater convenience of administration, since connections
by ship were with San Francisco, the new district was soon
transferred to the Department of California.[6]   General Jefferson C. Davis was put in command, and on September 25, 1867,
he, with two companies of troops, embarked for the north.
He reached Sitka on October 10, and, going ashore, paid his
respects to Prince Maksoutoff, the Russian governor.   Meantime President Johnson had appointed General Lovell H.
Rousseau commissioner on the part of the United States, formally to receive the country from the hands of a Russian commissioner, designated by the Czar.   This officer, Captain Alexis
Pestchouroff, accompanied by a representative of the Russian
American Company, met General Rousseau in New York, and
together they set sail for San Francisco by way of the Isthmus
of Panama.   They were received at the Golden Gate with

[1] House Ex. Doc., 40th Cong., 2d sess., no. 177, p. 189.
[2] Ibid., pp. 56–8.
[3] F. W. Seward, Seward at Washington, vol. iii, p. 369.
[4] Sumner's Works, vol. xi, pp. 347–8, note.
[5] Phila. Ledger, July 24, 1867.
[6] Ibid., Sept. 21, 1867.

salutes from the batteries, and proceeded to Alaska on the U. S. man-of-war, *Ossipee*, on September 27. The ceremonies of the transfer were celebrated in Sitka on October 18. Russian and American soldiers paraded in front of the governor's house, the Russian colors were lowered and the stars and stripes hoisted in their stead amid peals of artillery. The salutes at an end, Captain Pestchouroff said, "General Rousseau, by authority from His Majesty, the Emperor of Russia, I transfer to the United States the territory of Alaska." General Rousseau replied in similarly formal terms as he accepted the ceded territory. A number of forts, blockhouses and timber buildings were made over to the Americans. The troops occupied the barracks; General Davis established his residence in the governor's house, and Russia's proprietorship of her Arctic empire was at an end.

The money which we had bound ourselves to pay in the treaty was still to be provided by Congress, and the House had yet to say whether it would give its assent to what had been going forward in the State Department with the favor of the Senate. When the members convened in December, 1867, the rumbling was grave. General N. P. Banks of Massachusetts, chairman of the House Committee on Foreign Affairs, ably led the struggle for the passage of the bill. He, like Sumner in the Senate, gave the strength of his person and his place on the side of annexation. The purchase was "necessary," said he, "for the defence of this country, for the preservation of its institutions and its power." Such an acquisition of territory carried the jurisdiction of the United States within 500 miles of the coast of Asia. Men might say that Alaska was valueless. They could study the history of the United States. Other men had said as much of Louisiana and California when the national boundaries were extended to bring them to us.[1]

But the sober and eloquent arguments of this man, and of others like him, did not prevent many from attacking the treaty in violent terms. General Cadwallader C. Washburn of Wisconsin spoke with the most virulence in opposition to the pur-

[1] Cong. Globe, 40th Cong., 2d sess., Appendix, p. 386.

chase. This "Walrussia," he said, should not be taken over by the United States "in the present financial condition of the country." The Secretary of State, with the privity of the Senate, had negotiated a treaty for which no man had asked, which no newspaper had advocated; we were to pay $7,000,000 for what we did not need, for what nobody wanted and for what, as far as it appeared, was utterly worthless.[1] The skies rained upon the country 300 days in a year. In it domestic animals were unknown; men found there no food but fish. "None but malefactors" would ever live in such a place.[2]

Even Sumner had not hesitated to suggest that the course of the Secretary of State in signing the treaty had been summary,[3] and he expressed a hope that the action of the President and the State Department in so important a matter, without consultation with the Senate, which fairly shared this power, might not become a precedent for future practice.[4] Speakers in the House were yet more jealous of the prerogatives which they supposed adhered to their branch of the Congress. Without their favor nothing might be done in such a case, but here their authority had been flouted, their very existence had been ignored by both the President and the Senate until now, months later, a demand was made upon them for an appropriation of money.[5] And they were not asked to do this; they were told that they must do it.

Since the United States already had taken formal possession of Alaska, to refuse to ratify the State Department's arrangements for the purchase would discredit the nation. Seward, said General Washburn, could "get out of the scrape" as best he could.[6] With as much right, said another member, could the President have directed the troops to occupy Canada or Mexico. The act was "as unauthorized as it was unnecessary," and it was "deserving of the severest condemnation."[7]

[1] Cong. Globe, 40th Cong., 2d sess., p. 135.   [2] Ibid., p. 138.
[3] House Ex. Doc., 40th Cong., 2d sess., no. 177, p. 134.
[4] Ibid., p. 143.
[5] J. G. Blaine, Twenty Years in Congress, vol. ii, pp. 337-9. ;
[6] Cong. Globe, 40th Cong., 2d sess., p. 139.
[7] Ibid., p. 3623.

Speech followed speech to state and prove what were the constitutional powers of the House on the subject of treaties with foreign governments.

Other members in voicing their objections to the bill uttered the opinion, which had been heard before on many sides, that the country was large enough without further acquisitions of territory. Texas, if that state were as densely populated as Massachusetts, would contain all the inhabitants of the republic. Hundreds of millions could find happy homes within our old boundaries. Alaska in the west would be just as useful to us as Greenland in the east, and not a whit more so. Gentlemen in Congress had $10,000,000 in currency to give to Russia for a country containing from 50,000 to 70,000 Indians and creoles of a debatable character, but nothing to remove the obstructions in the Ohio and the Mississippi rivers, so that millions of "intelligent, industrious, enterprising, thoroughgoing, reliable, loyal people" could navigate 2000 miles of water on the borders of twelve states of the Union.[1] If we wanted territory detached from the body of the national domain, said Ben Butler, why did we not buy Crete and free that suffering island from the yoke of the Turks? We could get it for one-half the price which Seward had promised to give the Czar for Russian America, and it was nearer our own doors.[2]

Equally as much exaggeration marked the debate on the other side. Old Thaddeus Stevens, in bringing the Radicals to the defence of the measure, said that the climate was warmed not only by the breezes of the Pacific Ocean, but also by a thousand springs whose waters here boiled up from the earth.[3] Twelve times as large as Virginia the people were invited to believe that it would one day be as valuable a part of the republic. Gentlemen were very economical, said William Mungen of Ohio, replying to an argument as to the great cost of the new territory, on all subjects except negro bureaus and military despotisms in the Southern states. Congress could build a college to educate "the colored cuss" from Africa;

[1] Cong. Globe, 40th Cong., 2d sess., Appendix, p. 380.
[2] Ibid., p. 402.   [3] Cong. Globe, 40th Cong., 2d sess., p. 3661.

it could not give a few dollars for a country containing gigantic forests, rich mines, inexhaustible fisheries which would furnish occupation, money and homes for millions of people for ages to come.[1] The purchase, said Ignatius Donnelly, of Minnesota, was but one step in the inevitable movement to extend our nationality over the entire continent of North America. Our form of government was adapted to the needs of men wherever they might be; he would extend its beneficent influences from the Isthmus of Panama "to the extremest limits of human habitation under the frozen constellations of the north." [2]

Horace Maynard, the orator who during the war with lion heart had stood for the Union in Tennessee, looked forward to a day when the civilization of the world should be transferred from the shores of the Atlantic to those of the Pacific Ocean, and when all that was "excellent and exalted in human affairs" should be found upon the coast of "that benign sea." Like England the United States would "replenish the earth and subdue it, and have dominion over it." Terminus, our god, was "an advancing not a retreating divinity," and such a national spirit would at length make us the mistress of the world.[3]

When all was said and done, the conviction grew here, as it had in the Senate, that, while we were dealing with a friend when we made this purchase from Russia, we were at the same time in some way spitefully serving England. Western British America, now that Alaska was ours, would soon be added to the Union. Men believed with Ignatius Donnelly that this part of the British Empire would be pressed out, set as it soon would be between our upper and nether millstones. "These jaws of the nation" would swallow it up.[4] By accepting the treaty, said Mr. Mungen, "we cage the British lion on the Pacific coast; we cripple that great and grasping monopoly, the Hudson's Bay Company." [5]

Finally the discussion came to an end, and on July 14, 1868, the bill was passed by a vote of 113 to 43.[6] In a preamble

---

[1] Cong. Globe, 40th Cong., 2d sess., p. 3659.　　[2] Ibid., p. 3660.
[3] Ibid., Appendix, p. 403.　　[5] Ibid., p. 3659.
[4] Cong. Globe, 40th Cong., 2d sess., p. 3660.　　[6] Ibid., p. 4055.

the House had asserted its right to be consulted in regard to future purchases of territory. It was known that for months past Mr. Seward had been laying plans to transfer St. Thomas, and likely other West Indian islands, to the American flag. That Greenland and Iceland had become a part of the American republic, men said, might be in any morning's news. But the Senate struck out this attack upon one of its constitutional prerogatives, action which the New York Tribune denominated "the height of arrogance." [1] The conferees met, and while Mr. Loughridge, one of the House managers, declared that in signing the treaty the President had been "guilty of a high-handed usurpation," [2] on July 23 the last vote was taken and the State Department happily was enabled to make good its pledges to the Czar.

The tongue of scandal now began to wag. It was said, mostly by newspaper correspondents in Washington and the gazettes in various parts of the country which they served, that those who were in charge of the Alaska bill had distributed money with a free hand to secure its approval by Congress. Various reports were in the air, but the most definite was one which found publication in the Worcester Spy to the effect that of the entire sum of $7,200,000 voted to pay for Russia's colonies in America only $5,000,000 had reached that government. The rest fell into the hands of a ring of lobbyists and newspaper men, the chief of whom was the old Secretary of the Treasury, Robert J. Walker, resident in Washington and practising law there, who had been retained by the Russian Legation for the purpose of influencing legislation. Seward credited the reports and carried them to President Johnson. In the rancor of the hour Thaddeus Stevens and General Banks were not spared, and they, among other men, were accused of having taken money in exchange for their support of the bill. [3]

A very little of the whole charge proved to be true, after an investigation conducted by the Committee on Public Expendi-

[1] N. Y. Tribune, July 21, 1868.
[2] Cong. Globe, 40th Cong., 2d sess., p. 4394.
[3] Johnson Papers. See W. A. Dunning, Political Science Quarterly, September, 1912.

tures of the House. The newspaper correspondents, who filled Washington at the end of the war and formed a kind of third branch of Congress, to be reckoned with in any matter of legislation involving the payment of money or the granting of privileges, were brought up to the bar for examination. One and then another testified to what they surmised and what they had heard in the form of surmises from the mouths of their fellows in newsmongery. Secretary Seward, Riggs, the Washington banker, through whom the money passed on its way to the Russian legation; Spinner, the Treasurer of the United States; Walker and others appeared to state what they knew about the affair. It was made clear that the reports had originated in the heads of a few newspaper men who, with effrontery, had asked for money to guide their pens, who upon being told that none was being given out "to get Alaska through" disbelieved their informants, and then in pique circulated the story about a corrupt lobby. It did appear, however, that Mr. Walker had received $26,000 in gold and that he had given $5000 in greenbacks, taken from this sum, to counsel associated with him in the case, while $3000 in gold had been offered to Colonel John W. Forney of the Daily Chronicle of Washington, for having "rendered valuable service by opening its columns" to articles favorable to the purchase, including some which had been written by Walker personally. Colonel Forney declining to receive the sum, it had found its way into the pockets of that man's brother, D. C. Forney.

The committee made two reports. Four members contented themselves by denouncing "the loose morality" of several Washington journalists who sent to their papers "nebulous gossip" instead of facts, while four other members censured Mr. Walker who had secretly sold his "extraordinary influence" to a foreign government in connection with a matter which concerned the course and fortunes of his own.[1]

[1] House Reports, 40th Cong., 3d sess., no. 35.

INDEX

40th Congress, 452; admonishes members of House, 483.

Collins, Perry McDonough, his plans for Russian American telegraph line, 196, 200–3; work on his line ceases, 213, 537.

Colorado, negro suffrage in, 140; Johnson vetoes statehood bill, 180; becomes a territory, 280, 288; emigration to, 280–3; miners buy from Mormons, 287; enabling act for, 289; freights over plains to, 305; women needed in, 319; Indians isolate, 339–40; Sand Creek, 340–4; statehood bill again passed and vetoed, 437; Stanton in favor of statehood for, 469.

Colorado River, navigation of, 290.

Columbia, proposed territory of, 337.

Columbia River, steamboats on, 289; salmon in, 294; navigation of, 294–5, 297, 303, 309.

Columbia, S. C., plundered, 66.

Comanches, 348, 358.

Comstock Ledge, 288.

Coney Island, 271.

Confederacy in the South, collapse of, 1, 9–10, 49–50; rewards for capture of heads of, 8–9; capture of leaders of, 10–4; gathering up ends of the, 14–6; prison system of, 20; population of, 50–2; bonds and currency of, 107.

Conkling, Roscoe, 160, 490, 545.

Connecticut, free schools in, 55; negro suffrage defeated in, 140; elects Democratic governor, 479; ratifies 14th Amendment, 377.

Conness, Senator of California, 220.

Connor, General, 288, 347, 350, 360, 362.

"Conquered provinces," Stevens's theory in regard to, 155, 423, 430, 460.

"Contrabands," 25, 88.

Contract and Finance Company, 329.

Conway, officer of Freedmen's Bureau, 182.

Cooke, Jay, loan agent, 26, 27–8; sale of "seven-thirties," 267; new mansion of, 270; asked to finance Northern Pacific Railroad, 332.

Cooke, General P. St. George, 361, 363.

Cooper, Dr., Jefferson Davis's physician, 445–7.

Cooper, Peter, 196, 197.

Copperheads, praise Johnson, 170–1; in Philadelphia convention, 387; feeling against, 412–3; defeat Johnson in 1866, 420–1.

Corn, trade in, in Chicago, 233–4.

"Corners" in grain in Chicago, 234.

Corse, General, 185.

Corwin, Thomas, minister to Mexico, 467; protests against occupation of Mexico by European troops, 498–9; seeks loan for Mexico, 499; starts home, 507, 512.

Cotton crop in 1865, 112–3.

Couch, General, of Massachusetts, 388.

Covode, John, 157, 185, 482.

Cowan, Edgar, Senator from Pennsylvania, 153; supports Johnson, 166; in Philadelphia convention, 388; opposes reconstruction bill, 431; suggested for Attorney-General, 469.

Cox, General Jacob D., 395, 469, 481.

Cox, S. S., 167, 511.

Cragin, Senator, of New Hampshire, 545.

Crawford, Governor, of Kansas, 365, 367.

Crédit Mobilier, formation of, 324; dispute regarding, 325; mentioned, 329.

Creeks, 340, 354.

Creswell, J. A. J., 394.

Crittenden, General, 395.

Cromwell, Oliver, 171, 411.

Crook, General, 363.

Cuba, cable to, 213–4.

Culver, Charles V., rise and fall of, 261–2, 274.

Cummings test oath case, 464.

Cunard, Sir Samuel, his steamer line, 215–6.

Currency, inflation of, 189, 265–6.

Curtin, Governor, of Pennsylvania, 394.

Curtis, General S. R., 342, 349, 351.

Custer, General George A., 186, 364, 367–8, 378, 395.

Cutler, R. King, 131.

DABNEY, THOMAS, 116.

Dakota, territory of, formed, 280, 284; Wyoming formed and taken from, 336–8.

"Darien Route," 221.

Davidson, George, 545.

Davis, Admiral C. H., 220, 221.

Davis, Garrett, Senator, from Kentucky, attacks Freedmen's Bureau bill, 163; on vagabond negroes, 178; opposes military reconstruction, 431.

Davis, George, 131.

Davis, Henry Winter, 39, 41, 507.

Davis, Jefferson, told of collapse of Lee's lines, 1; expected capture of,

settlement of, 283–5; miners buy
from Mormons, 287; territory
formed, 289; route to, by way of
Missouri, 297; roads to, 300; trade
to, over Missouri River, 301–3; route
to, by way of Columbia River, 303;
stage line to, 308–9, 317; vigilantes
in, 335; buffaloes in, 352; defence
of Powder River Road to, 360–2.
Montezuma, proposed territory of, 337.
Moore, Governor, 13.
Morgan, Senator, of New York, sup-
ports President, 166; opposes Presi-
dent, 177–8.
Mormons at Salt Lake, 279, 285;
Holladay trades with, 307; dis-
loyalty of, 316; limiting authority
of, 337; accused of fomenting In-
dian troubles, 356.
Morrill, Justin S., 160, 545.
Morrill, Lot M., 202, 471, 545.
Morse, S. F. B., Prof., 196.
Motley, J. L., minister to Austria, 515.
Moustier, Marquis de, 518.
Mumford, New York defaulter, 273.
Mungen, William, favors purchase of
Alaska, 553, 554.
Murphy, Governor, of Arkansas, 100,
132.
"My Policy," 402–3, 409, 420.

NAPIER, LORD, 199.
Napoleon III, Emperor of France,
telegraphs to Maximilian, 211;
instructs General Forey, 501–2;
fears United States as he invades
Mexico, 503; pledges aid to new
empire, 504; plebiscite, 505; enters
into treaty with Mexico, 506; near
war with United States, 508; hears
from Seward after war, 509; sympathy for the South, 509–10;
prepares to leave Mexico, 516–7;
Carlotta visits, 517; asked to explain delay in withdrawing troops,
518; finally withdraws, 518–9;
Maximilian a victim of, 523.
Nasby, Petroleum V., 172.
National Banks in South, 107; in
United States in 1865, 189.
Nebraska, Johnson's pocket veto of
bill to admit, 180; settlement of,
276; territory divided, 280; enabling act for, 289; bill to admit
again passed and vetoed, 437;
passed over veto, 437; Stanton
favors statehood, 469.
Negroes, their place in reorganized
governments of the South, 35–6;
friends of, aroused, 37; enfranchise-

ment demanded, 38–40, 139–42;
Greeley advocates suffrage for,
42–3; education of, forbidden, 54;
leaving plantations, 63–4; prejudices against them in freedom, 70,
73–5; plans to colonize, 75–80;
their faithfulness to masters, 81;
contracts with, for work in freedom,
82; advice for, 83; occupy confiscated lands, 84–5; credulity of,
85–6; ordered to remain on plantations, 86–7; education of, after war,
89–91; as troops in South, 94–5,
102–3, 148; schools ridiculed, 99;
white soldiers persecute, 101; disputes between them and their ex-
masters, 104–6; Northern fears for
their future in South, 125–6; com-
petency as witnesses in court,
126–8; laws regarding, in Mississippi, 128; in South Carolina,
129; in Louisiana, 131; in Tennessee, 132; Southern codes concerning, 136–7; meet and ask for
suffrage, 142; Johnson promises to
be Moses of, 158; suffrage for, in
District of Columbia, 160–1, 423–4;
bill to protect civil rights of, 175–8;
demoralized by Freedmen's Bureau,
182; civil rights of, in 14th Amendment, 183–4; attacked in Memphis,
379–80; riots in New Orleans, 381–
4; enfranchised in territories, 424–
5; general enfranchisement the
end in view in 14th Amendment,
427; Johnson opposes suffrage for,
482; insincerity of movement to
enfranchise, 485.
Nevada, territory formed, 288;
admitted as state, 289.
New Brunswick, Fenian raid on, 530.
Newfoundland, grants concessions to
Cyrus Field, 196–7.
New Granada, negro colony in, 77.
New Hampshire, ratifies 14th Amendment, 377.
New Jersey, "redeemed," 139.
New Mexico, territory divided, 289–
90; Indian depredations in, 346.
New Orleans, population of, 51; condition of, after war, 59; riots in, 381–4,
406, 428.
Newport, fashionable summer life in,
271.
New York City, centre of speculation
and luxury, 269–70.
New York Central Railroad, 239.
New York State, ratifies 13th Amend-
ment, 117; Republicans carry, in
1865, 138–9; foreign population

VERMONT COLLEGE
MONTPELIER, VERMONT